CHAS. F. BROWNE
(ARTEMUS WARD)

HENRY W. SHAW
(JOSH BILLINGS)

SAML. L. CLEMENS
(MARK TWAIN)

MELVILLE D. LANDON
(ELI PERKINS)

KINGS

OF THE

PLATFORM AND PULPIT

BY

MELVILLE D. LANDON
(ELI PERKINS)

BIOGRAPHIES, REMINISCENCES AND LECTURES OF

ARTEMUS WARD, SAM COX, BILL ARP, MARK TWAIN, ROBERT BURDETTE,
GEORGE W. PECK, NASBY, MRS. PARTINGTON, DOESTICKS, JOSH
BILLINGS, DANBURY NEWS MAN, BILL NYE, BRET
HARTE, GEO. W. CABLE, FAT CON-
TRIBUTOR, ELI PERKINS

AND THE MASTER LECTURES OF

T. DEWITT TALMAGE, DWIGHT L. MOODY, SAM JONES, CHAUNCEY M. DEPEW,
ROBERT G. INGERSOLL, JOHN B. GOUGH, WENDELL PHILLIPS,
CHAS. H. SPURGEON, BEN BUTLER, JOS. COOK, EUGENE
FIELD, HORACE GREELEY, MAX O'RELL,
JOSEPH PARKER, ROBT. COLLYER

AND

PERSONAL REMINISCENCES AND ANECDOTES
OF NOTED AMERICANS

PROFUSELY ILLUSTRATED

CHICAGO

NEW YORK   LONDON   BERLIN   PARIS

THE WERNER COMPANY

1896

ANNOUNCEMENT.

Many of the great lectures in "Kings of the Platform and Pulpit" are published from the manuscripts of the distinguished authors.

The illustrations which appear, with the literary accompaniment of pen pictures, serve to make the personality of these noted characters distinct and life-like.

"Kings of the Platform and Pulpit" contains the most comprehensive *resumé* of the humor, wisdom, philosophy and religion of the century. The book also abounds in anecdotes, epigrams, lectures and reminiscences—both personal and political—of a vast number of famous Americans.

The following list of *noms de plume* of noted men of letters, many of whom have contributed to these pages, will be of interest to the reader.

DISTINGUISHED LECTURERS, HUMORISTS AND WRITERS.

" Josh Billings "—Henry W. Shaw.

" Andrew Jack Downing "—Seba R. Smith.

" Artemus Ward "—Charles Farrar Browne.

" Bill Arp "—Charles H. Smith.

" Gath "—George Alfred Townsend.

" Fat Contributor "—A. Miner Griswold.

" Hawkeye Man "—Robert J. Burdette.

" Howadjii "—George William Curtis.

" Ik Marvel "—Donald Grant Mitchell.

" James Yellowplush "—Wm. H. Thackeray.

" John Paul "—Charles H. Webb.

" John Phœnix "—Capt. George H. Derby.

" Mark Twain "—Samuel L. Clemens.

" Max Adler "—Charles H. Clark.

" Eli Perkins "—Melville D. Landon.

" Petroleum V. Nasby "—David Locke.

" Bill Nye "—Edgar W. Nye.

" Danbury News Man "—Jas. M. Bailey.

" Old Si "—Samuel W. Small.

" Orpheus C. Kerr "—Robert H. Newell.

" Peleg Wales "—Wm. A. Croffut.

" Peter Plymley "—Sidney Smith.

" Miles O'Reilly "—Charles G. Halpin.

" Peter Parley "—H. C. Goodrich.

" Ned Buntline "—Col. Judson.

" Brick Pomeroy "—M. M. Pomeroy.

" Josiah Allen's Wife "—Marietta Holley.

" Doesticks "—Mortimer M. Thompson.

" Mrs. Partington "—Benj. P. Shillaber.

" Spoopendyke "—Stanley Huntley.

" Uncle Remus "—Joel Chandler Harris.

" Hosea Bigelow "—James Russell Lowell.

" Fanny Fern "—Sara Payson Willis.

" Grand Father Lickshingle " — Robert W. Criswell.

" M. Quad "—Charles B. Lewis.

KINGS OF THE PLATFORM AND PULPIT.

CONTENTS.

ILLUSTRATIONS.

PORTRAITS.

FAC-SIMILES OF HANDWRITING.

ILLUSTRATIONS OF ARTEMUS WARD'S PANORAMIC LECTURE.

MISCELLANEOUS ILLUSTRATIONS.

"ARTEMUS WARD."

BIOGRAPHY AND REMINISCENCES.

Charles Farrar Browne, better known to the world as "Artemus Ward," was born at Waterford, Oxford county, Maine, on the 26th of April, 1834, and died of consumption at Southampton, England, on Wednesday, the 6th of March, 1867. Artemus Ward's grandfather (Thaddeus) raised five sons in Waterford — Daniel, Malbory, Jabez, Levi and Thaddeus. His father was Levi Browne, who died in 1847, after being justice of the peace for many years. His mother, Caroline E. Browne, died in 1878. She was a woman of strong character, and came from good Puritanic stock.

I once asked Artemus about his Puritanic origin, when he replied:

"I think we came from Jerusalem, for my father's name was Levi, and we had a Moses and a Nathan in the family; but my poor brother's name was Cyrus; so, perhaps, that makes us Persians."

The humorist was full of happy wit even when a boy. His mother, from whom the writer received several letters, told me that Artemus was out very late one night at a spelling bee, and came home in a driving snow-storm.

"We had all retired," said Mrs. Browne, "and Artemus went around the house and threw snow-balls at his brother Cyrus' window, shouting for him to come down quickly. Cyrus appeared in haste, and stood shivering in his night-clothes.

"'Why don't you come in, Charles? The door is open.'

"'Oh,' replied Artemus, 'I could have gotten in all right, Cyrus; but I called you down because I wanted to ask you if you really thought it was wrong to keep slaves.'"

Charles received his education at the Waterford school, until family circumstances induced his parents to apprentice him to learn the rudiments of printing in the office of the Skowhegan *Clarion*, published some miles to the north of his native village. Here he passed through the dreadful ordeal to which a printer's "devil" is

2   19

generally subjected. He always kept his temper; and his amusing jokes are even now related by the residents of Skowhegan.

In the spring after his fifteenth birthday, Charles Browne bade farewell to the Skowhegan *Clarion;* and we next hear of him in the office of the *Carpet-Bag,* edited by B. P. Shillaber (" Mrs. Partington"). In these early years young Browne used to "set up" articles from the pens of Charles G. Halpine (" Miles O'Reilly") and John G. Saxe, the poet. Here he wrote his first contribution in a dis-

ARTEMUS WARD'S FIRST CONTRIBUTION TO THE PRESS.

guised hand, slyly put it into the editorial box, and the next day enjoyed the pleasure of setting it up himself. The article was a description of a Fourth-of-July celebration in Skowhegan. The spectacle of the day was a representation of the Battle of Yorktown, with George Washington and Gen. Cornwallis in character. The article pleased Mr. Shillaber, and Mr. Browne, afterward speaking of it, said: " I went to the theater that evening, had a good time of it, and thought I was the greatest man in Boston."

While engaged on the *Carpet-Bag,* the subject of our sketch closely studied the theater and courted the society of actors and actresses. It was in this way that he gained that correct and valuable knowledge of the texts and characters of the drama which enabled him in after years to burlesque them so successfully. The humorous writings of Seba Smith were his models, and the oddities of "John Phœnix" were his especial admiration.

Being fond of roving, Charles Browne soon left Boston, and, after traveling as a journeyman printer over much of New York and Massachusetts, he turned up in the town of Tiffin, Seneca county, Ohio, where he became reporter and compositor, at four dollars per week. After making many friends among the good citizens of Tiffin, by whom he is remembered as a patron of side-shows and traveling circuses, our hero suddenly set out for Toledo, Ohio, where he immediately made a reputation as a writer of sarcastic paragraphs in the columns of the Toledo *Commercial.* He waged a vigorous newspaper war with the reporters of the Toledo *Blade,* but, while the *Blade* indulged in violent vituperation, "Artemus" was good-natured and full of humor. His column soon gained a local fame, and every body read it. His fame even traveled as far as Cleveland, where, in 1858, when Mr. Browne was twenty-four years of age, Mr. J. W. Gray, of the Cleveland *Plaindealer,* secured him as local reporter, at a salary of twelve dollars per week. Here his reputation first began to assume a national character, and it was here that they called him a "fool" when he mentioned the idea of taking the field as a lecturer. Speaking of this circumstance, while traveling down the Mississippi with the writer, in 1865, Mr. Browne musingly repeated this colloquy:

WISE MAN—"Ah! you poor, foolish little girl—here is a dollar for you."

FOOLISH LITTLE GIRL—"Thank you, sir; but I have a sister at home as foolish as I am; can't you give me a dollar for her?"

Charles Browne was not successful as a news reporter, lacking enterprise and energy, but his success lay in writing up, in a burlesque manner, well-known public affairs like prize-fights, races, spiritual meetings, and political gatherings. His department became wonderfully humorous, and was always a favorite with readers whether there was any news in it or not. Sometimes he would have a whole column of letters from young ladies in reply to a fancied matrimonial advertisement, and then he would have a column of answers to general correspondents like this:

VERITAS—Many make the same error. Mr. Key, who wrote the "Star Spangled Banner," is not the author of Hamlet, a tragedy. He wrote the banner business, and assisted in "The Female Pirate," *but did not write Hamlet.* Hamlet was written by a talented but unscrupulous man named Macbeth, afterwards tried and executed for "murdering sleep."

YOUNG CLERGYMAN—Two pints of rum, two quarts of hot water, tea-cup of sugar, and a lemon; grate in nutmeg, stir thoroughly and drink while hot.

It was during his engagement on the *Plaindealer* that he wrote,
dating from Indiana, his first communication—the first published
letter following this sketch, signed "Artemus Ward," a *sobriquet*
purely incidental, but borne with the "u" changed to an "a" by
an American revolutionary general. It was here that Mr. Browne
first became, in words, the possessor of a moral show, "consisting
of three moral bares, a kangaroo (a amoozing little rascal; 'twould
make you larf yourself to death to see the little kuss jump and
squeal), wax figures of G. Washington, &c., &c." Hundreds of
newspapers copied this letter, and Charles Browne awoke one
morning to find himself famous.

In the *Plaindealer* office, his companion, George Hoyt, writes:
"His desk was a rickety table which had been whittled and gashed
until it looked as if it had been the victim of lightning. His chair
was a fit companion thereto—a wabbling, unsteady affair, sometimes with four and sometimes with three legs. But Browne saw
neither the table, nor the chair, nor any person who might be near
—nothing, in fact, but the funny pictures which were tumbling out
of his brain. When writing, his gaunt form looked ridiculous
enough. One leg hung over the arm of his chair like a great hook,
while he would write away, sometimes laughing to himself, and
then slapping the table in the excess of his mirth."

While in the office of the *Plaindealer*, Mr. Browne first conceived the idea of becoming a lecturer. In attending the various
minstrel shows and circuses which came to the city, he would frequently hear repeated some story of his own which the audience
would receive with hilarity. His best witticisms came back to him
from the lips of another, who made a living by quoting a stolen
jest. Then the thought came to him to enter the lecture field himself, and become the utterer of his own witticisms, the mouthpiece
of his own jests.

On the 10th of November, 1860, Charles Browne, whose fame,
traveling in his letters from Boston to San Francisco, had now
become national, grasped the hands of his hundreds of New York
admirers. Cleveland had throned him the monarch of mirth, and
a thousand hearts paid him tributes of adulation as he closed his
connection with the Cleveland press.

Arriving in the Empire City, Mr. Browne soon opened an engagement with *Vanity Fair*, a humorous paper after the manner of

London *Punch*, and ere long he succeeded Mr. Charles G. Leland as editor. Mr. Charles Dawson Shanly says: "After Artemus Ward became sole editor, a position which he held for a brief period, many of his best contributions were given to the public; and, whatever there was of merit in the columns of *Vanity Fair* from the time he assumed the editorial charge, emanated from his pen." Mr. Browne himself wrote to a friend: "Comic copy is what they wanted for *Vanity Fair.* I wrote some and it killed it. The poor paper got to be a conundrum, and so I gave it up."

The idea of entering the field as a lecturer now seized Mr. Browne stronger than ever. Tired of the pen, he resolved on trying the platform. His Bohemian friends agreed that his fame and fortune would be made before intelligent audiences. He resolved to try it. What should be the subject of my lecture? How shall I treat the subject? These questions caused Mr. Browne grave speculations. Among other schemes, he thought of a string of jests combined with a stream of satire, the whole being unconnected—a burlesque upon a lecture. The subject—that was a hard question. First he thought of calling it "My Seven Grandmothers," but he finally adopted the name of "Babes in the Woods," and with this subject, Charles Browne was introduced to a metropolitan audience, on the evening of December 23, 1861. The place was Clinton Hall, which stood on the site of the old Astor Place Opera House, where, years ago, occurred the Macready riot, and where now is the Mercantile Library. Previous to this introduction, Mr. Frank Wood accompanied him to the suburban town of Norwich, Connecticut, where he first delivered his lecture and watched the result. The audience was delighted, and Mr. Browne received an ovation. Previous to his Clinton Hall appearance, the city was flooded with funny placards reading:

ARTEMUS WARD
WILL
SPEAK A PIECE.

Owing to a great storm, only a small audience braved the elements, and the Clinton Hall lecture was not a financial success. It consisted of a wandering batch of comicalities, touching upon every thing except "The Babes." Indeed it was better described by the lecturer in London, when he said, "One of the features of my entertainment is, that it contains so many things that don't have any thing to do with it."

In the middle of his lecture, the speaker would hesitate, stop, and say: "Owing to a slight indisposition, we will now have an intermission of fifteen minutes." The audience looked in utter dismay at the idea of staring at vacancy for a quarter of an hour, when, rubbing his hands, the lecturer would continue: "But, ah—during the intermission I will go on with my lecture!"

Mr. Browne's first volume, entitled "Artemus Ward; His Book," was published in New York, May 17, 1862. The volume was everywhere hailed with enthusiasm, and over forty thousand copies were sold. Great success also attended the sale of his three other volumes published in '65, '67 and '69.

Mr. Browne's next lecture was entitled "Sixty Minutes in Africa," and was delivered in Musical Fund Hall, Philadelphia. Behind him hung a large map of Africa, "which region," said Artemus, "abounds in various natural productions, such as reptiles and flowers. It produces the red rose, the white rose and the neg-roes. In the middle of the continent is what is called a 'howling wilderness,' but, for my part, I have never heard it howl, nor met with any one who has."

After Mr. Browne had created immense enthusiasm for his lectures and books in the Eastern States, which filled his pockets with plenty of money, he started, October 3, 1863, for California. Previous to starting, he received a telegram from Thomas Maguire, of the San Francisco Opera House, inquiring "what he would take for forty nights in California." Mr. Browne immediately telegraphed back:

> Brandy and water,
> A. WARD.

and, though Maguire was sorely puzzled at the contents of the dispatch, the press got hold of it, and it went through California as a capital joke.

Mr. Browne first lectured in San Francisco on "The Babes in the Wood," November 13, 1863, at Pratt's Hall. T. Starr King took a deep interest in him, occupying the rostrum, and his general reception in San Francisco was warm.

Mr. Browne returned overland from San Francisco, stopping at Salt Lake City. He took a deep interest in Brigham Young and the

Mormons. The Prophet attended his lecture. When the writer
lectured in the Mormon theater twenty years afterward, Brigham
Young was present. The next day my wife and I were entertained
at the Lion House, the home of the Prophet, when he and Hiram
Clausen gave me many reminiscences of the humorist's visit.

Mr. Browne wrote many sketches for the newspaper about the
Mormons and the rude scenes he encountered on the overland stage,
which afterward appeared in his Mormon lecture. Delving through
a trunk full of Artemus Ward's papers and MSS. to-day, I found this
sketch. I give it in his own handwriting. Any journalist will see,
by his correct punctuation, that he was a man of culture. This lith-
ographed sketch shows his character. It proves that he was once a
type-setter. It is the best index to the culture and technical knowledge of the humorist that could be given:

THE MISSOURIAN IN UTAH.

The Missourian, from Pike
County, is the hero of a good
many stories out here.
The following ~~essay~~ is old
on the plains, but it
is probably new in the
States:

Traveler ~~————~~ comes across an
~~immigrant~~ wagon, on the pole of

which sits a dirty boy
with a sick baby in his
arms.

"What's the matter, Sonny?"
says the traveler.

"Matter 'nuff! This old
wagin is clean broke, dad
an' marm ar' dead
drunk; brother Jim's playin'
poker with a gin-u-wine
gambler; Sister Sal's
down in the woods
courtin' with a in-tire
stranger; this baby's got
the diaree, an' I don't
care a ____ whether I
ever reach Califorrny or not!"

Returning overland, through Salt Lake to the States, in the fall of 1864, Mr. Browne lectured again in New York, this time on the "Mormons," to immense audiences, and in the spring of 1865 he commenced his tour through the country, everywhere drawing enthusiastic audiences both North and South.

It was while on this tour that the writer of this sketch again spent some time with him. We met at Memphis and traveled down the Mississippi together. At Lake Providence the "Indiana" rounded up to our landing, and Mr. Browne accompanied the writer to his plantation, where he spent several days, mingling in seeming infinite delight with the negroes. For them he showed great fondness, and they used to stand around him in crowds, listening to his seemingly serious advice. We could not prevail upon him to hunt or to join in any of the equestrian amusements with the neighboring planters, but a quiet fascination drew him to the negroes. Strolling through the "quarters," his grave words, too deep with humor for darky comprehension, gained their entire confidence. One day he called up Uncle Jeff., an Uncle-Tom-like patriarch, and commenced in his usual vein: "Now, Uncle Jefferson," he said, "why do you thus pursue the habits of industry? This course of life is wrong—all wrong—all a base habit, Uncle Jefferson. Now try and break it off. Look at me,—look at Mr. Landon, the chivalric young Southern plantist from New York, he toils not, neither does he spin; he pursues a career of contented idleness. If you only thought so, Jefferson, you could live for months without performing any kind of labor, and at the expiration of that time feel fresh and vigorous enough to commence it again. Idleness refreshes the physical organization—it is a sweet boon! Strike at the roots of the destroying habit to-day, Jefferson. It tires you out; resolve to be idle; no one should labor; he should hire others to do it for him;" and then he would fix his mournful eyes on Jeff. and hand him a dollar, while the eyes of the wonder-struck darky would gaze in mute admiration upon the good and wise originator of the only theory which the darky mind could appreciate. As Jeff. went away to tell the wonderful story to his companions, and backed it with the dollar as material proof, Artemus would cover his eyes, and bend forward on his elbows in a chuckling laugh.

"Among the Mormons" was delivered through the States, everywhere drawing immense crowds. His manner of delivering his discourse was grotesque and comical beyond description. His quaint and sad style contributed more than any thing else to render his entertainment exquisitely funny. The programme was exceedingly droll, and the tickets of admission presented the most ludicrous of ideas. The writer presents a fac-simile of an admission ticket which was presented to him in Natchez by Mr. Browne:

ADMIT THE BEARER

AND ONE WIFE.

Yours Trooly,

A. WARD.

In the spring of 1866, Charles Browne first timidly thought of going to Europe. Turning to Mr. Hingston one day, he asked: "What sort of a man is Albert Smith? Do you think the Mormons would be as good a subject to the Londoners as Mont Blanc was?" Then he said: "I should like to go to London and give my lecture in the same place. Can't it be done?"

Mr. Browne sailed for England soon after, taking with him his Panorama. The success that awaited him could scarcely have been anticipated by his most intimate friends. Scholars, wits, poets and novelists came to him with extended hands, and his stay in London was one ovation to the genius of American wit. Charles Reade, the novelist, was his warm friend and enthusiastic admirer; and Mr. Andrew Haliday introduced him to the "Literary Club," where he became a great favorite. Mark Lemon came to him and asked him to become a contributor to *Punch*, which he did. His *Punch* letters were more remarked in literary circles than any other current matter. There was hardly a club-meeting or a dinner at which they were not discussed. "There was something so grotesque in the idea," said a correspondent, "of this ruthless Yankee poking among the revered antiquities of Britain, that the beef-eating British themselves could not restrain their laughter." The story of his

Uncle William who "followed commercial pursuits, glorious commerce—and sold soap!" and his letters on the Tower and "Chowser," were palpable hits, and it was admitted that *Punch* had contained nothing better since the days of "Yellowplush." This opinion was shared by the *Times*, the literary reviews, and the gayest leaders of society. The publishers of *Punch* posted up his name in large letters over their shop in Fleet street, and Artemus delighted to point it out to his friends. About this time Mr. Browne wrote to his friend, Jack Rider, of Cleveland :

This is the proudest moment of my life. To have been as well appreciated here as at home, to have written for the oldest comic journal in the English language, received mention with Hood, with Jerrold and Hook, and to have my picture and my *pseudonym* as common in London as New York, is enough for

Yours truly,

A. WARD.

England was now thoroughly aroused to the merits of Artemus Ward, and he set out to deliver his first lecture in Egyptian Hall. His subject was "The Mormons." It was the great lecture of his life, and was made up from all of his lectures. It has in it snatches from "Babes in the Wood" and "Sixty Minutes in Africa." This lecture appears in this book precisely as delivered, and prepared by myself, after hearing him deliver it many times. His first London lecture occurred Tuesday evening, November 13, 1866. Within a week immense crowds were turned away every night, and at every lecture his fame increased, until sickness brought his brilliant success to an end, and a nation mourned his retirement.

On the evening of Friday, the seventh week of his engagement at Egyptian Hall, Artemus became seriously ill, an apology was made to a disappointed audience, and from that time the light of one of the greatest wits of the centuries commenced fading into darkness. The press mourned his retirement, and a funeral pall fell over London. The laughing, applauding crowds were soon to see his consumptive form moving toward its narrow resting place in the cemetery at Kensal Green.

By medical advice, Charles Browne went for a short time to the Island of Jersey—but the breezes of Jersey were powerless. He wrote to London to his nearest and dearest friends—the members of a literary club of which he was a member—to complain that his "loneliness weighed on him." He was brought back, but could not sustain the journey farther than Southampton. There the members of the club traveled from London to see him—two at a time—that he might be less lonely.

His remains were followed to the grave from the rooms of his friend, Arthur Sketchley, by a large number of friends and admirers, the *literati* and press of London paying the last tribute of respect to their dead brother. The funeral services were conducted by the Rev. M. D. Conway, formerly of Cincinnati, and the coffin was temporarily placed in a vault, from which it was removed by his American friends, and his body now sleeps by the side of his father, Levi Browne, in the quiet cemetery at Waterford, Maine. Upon the coffin is the simple inscription :

> "CHARLES F. BROWNE,
> *AGED 32 YEARS,*
> BETTER KNOWN TO THE WORLD AS 'ARTEMUS WARD.'"

His English executors were T. W. Robertson, the playwright, and his friend and companion, E. P. Hingston. His literary executors were Horace Greeley and Richard H. Stoddard. The humorist left a will which is now in the vault of the Oxford County Probate Court at Paris Hill, Maine. The writer paid a special trip to Paris Hill to see this will. It is inscribed on two sheets of heavy parchment about two feet square in the most elaborate style of the scrivener's art. The will was made in England, and was sent over in a tin box, about the shape of a cigar box, on which is stamped the British coat-of-arms and the letters, " V. R."

The will begins thus : " This is the will of me, Charles Farrar Browne Ward, known as ' Artemus Ward.' " The testator directs that his body shall be buried in Waterford Upper Village, but in a codicil changes the place of his entombment to Waterford Lower Village. He bequeaths his library to the best scholar in the schools at Waterford Upper Village, and his manuscripts to R. H. Stoddard and Charles Dawson Stanley. After making several bequests to his mother and relatives, he gives the balance of his property to found " an asylum for worn-out printers." Horace Greeley to be the sole trustee, and his receipt to be the only security to be demanded of him.

An Oxford county man, referring to the will, said:

" Either Artemus intended that his will should be a post-mortem joke or he was robbed ; for upon his death a very small property was found—hardly enough to pay the minor bequests, let alone founding a printers' hospital."

R. H. Stoddard and Charles Dawson Stanley never asked for the humorist's manuscripts. George W. Carleton, his publisher, had them, and finally turned them over to the writer, who has them now in his possession. T. W. Robertson, the playwright, and his friend and companion, E. P. Hingston, were his English executors. It seems sad, that, after such careful provisions on the part of the humorist, on the writer of this memoir should devolve the loving work of transmitting many of the humorists' best creations to posterity.

Besides other bequests, Artemus gave a large sum of money to his little valet, a bright little fellow ; though subsequent *denouments* revealed the fact that he left only a six-thousand-dollar house in Yonkers. There is still some, mystery about his finances, which may one day be revealed. It is known that he withdrew $10,000 from the Pacific Bank to deposit it with a friend before going to England ; besides this, his London *Punch* letters paid a handsome profit. Among his personal friends were George Hoyt, the late Daniel Setchell, Charles W. Coe, and Mr. Mullen, the artist, all of whom he used to style " my friends all the year round."

Personally, Charles Farrar Browne was one of the kindest and most affectionate of men, and history does not name a man who was so universally beloved by all who knew him. It was remarked, and truly, that the death of no literary character since Washington Irving caused such general and widespread regret.

In stature he was tall and slender. His nose was prominent— outlined like that of Sir Charles Napier, or Mr. Seward; his eyes brilliant, small, and close together; his mouth large, teeth white and pearly; fingers long and slender; hair soft, straight and blonde; complexion florid ; mustache large, and his voice soft and clear. In bearing, he moved like a natural-born gentleman. In his lectures he never smiled—not even while he was giving utterance to the most delicious absurdities; but all the while the jokes fell from his lips as if he were unconscious of their meaning. While writing his lectures, he would laugh and chuckle to himself continually.

There was one peculiarity about Charles Browne—he never made an enemy. Other wits in other times have been famous, but a satirical thrust now and then has killed a friend. Diogenes was the wit of Greece, but when, after holding up an old dried fish to draw away the eyes of Anaximenes' audience, he exclaimed " See how an old fish is more interesting than Anaximenes," he said a funny thing, but he stabbed a friend. When Charles Lamb, in answer to the doting mother's question as to how he liked babies, replied, " b–b–boiled, madam, boiled !" that mother loved him no more ; and when John Randolph said " thank you !" to his constituent who kindly remarked that he had the pleasure of " passing " his house, it was wit at the expense of friendship. The whole English school of wits—with Douglas Jerrold, Hood, Sheridan, and Sidney Smith, indulged in repartee. They were parasitic wits. And so with the Irish, except that an Irishman is generally so ridiculously absurd in his replies as to excite only ridicule. " Artemus Ward " made you laugh and love him too.

The wit of " Artemus Ward " and " Josh Billings " is distinctively American. Lord Kames, in his " Elements of Criticism," makes no mention of this species of wit, a lack which the future rhetorician should look to. We look in vain for it in the English language of past ages, and in other languages of modern time. It is the genus American. When Artemus says, in that serious manner, looking admiringly at his atrocious pictures, " I love pictures— and I have many of them—beautiful photographs—of myself," you smile, and when he continues, " These pictures were painted by the old masters : they painted these pictures and then they—they expired," you hardly know what it is that makes you laugh outright, and when Josh Billings says in his Proverbs, wiser than Solomon's, " You'd better not know so much, than know so many things that ain't so," the same vein is struck, but the text-books fail to explain scientifically the cause of our mirth.

The wit of Charles Browne is of the most exalted kind. It is only scholars and those thoroughly acquainted with the subtlety of our language who fully appreciate it. His wit is generally about historical personages like Cromwell, Garrick or Shakespeare, or a burlesque on different styles of writing, like his French novel, when " hifalutin " phrases of tragedy come from the clodhopper who— " sells soap and thrice—refuses a ducal coronet."

Mr. Browne mingled the eccentric even in his business letters. Once he wrote to his publisher, Mr. G. W. Carleton, who had made some alterations in his MSS.: " The next book I write I'm going to get you to write." Again he wrote in 1863 :

DEAR CARL:—You and I will get out a book next spring, which will knock spots out of all comic books in ancient or modern history. And the fact that you are going to take hold of it convinces me that you have one of the most massive intellects of this or any other epoch. Yours, my pretty gazelle,

A. WARD.

When Charles F. Browne died he did not belong to America, for, as with Irving and Dickens, the English language claimed him. Greece alone did not suffer when the current of Diogenes' wit flowed on to death. Spain alone did not mourn when Cervantes, dying, left Don Quixote the " knight of la Mancha." When Charles Lamb ceased to tune the great heart of humanity to joy and gladness, his funeral was in every English and American household, and when Charles Browne took up his silent resting place in the somber shades of Kensal Green, jesting ceased, and one great Anglo-American heart,

Like a muffled drum went beating
Funeral marches to his grave.

ARTEMUS WARD'S PANORAMA.

(ILLUSTRATED AS DELIVERED AT EGYPTIAN HALL, LONDON.)

PREFATORY NOTE.

BY MELVILLE D. LANDON ("ELI PERKINS").

The fame of Artemus Ward culminated in his last lectures at Egyptian Hall, Piccadilly, the final one breaking off abruptly on the evening of the 23d of January, 1867. That night the great humorist bade farewell to the public, and retired from the stage to die! His Mormon lectures were immensely successful in England. His fame became the talk of journalists, savants and statesmen. Every one seemed to be affected differently, but every one felt and acknowledged his power! " The Honorable Robert Lowe," says Mr. E. P. Hingston, Artemus Ward's bosom friend, "attended the Mormon lecture one evening, and laughed as hilariously as any one in the room. The next evening Mr. John Bright happened to be present. With the exception of one or two occasional smiles, he listened with grave attention."

The *London Standard*, in describing his first lecture in London, aptly said, "Artemus dropped his jokes faster than the meteors of last night succeeded each other in the sky. And there was this resemblance between the flashes of his humor and the flights of the meteors, that in each case one looked for jokes or meteors, but they always came just in the place that one least expected to find them. Half the enjoyment of the evening lay, to some of those present, in listening to the hearty cachinnation of the people, who only found out the jokes some two or three minutes after they were made, and who laughed apparently at some grave statements of fact. Reduced to paper, the showman's jokes are certainly not brilliant; almost their whole effect lies in their seeming impromptu character. They are carefully led up to, of course; but they are uttered as if they are mere afterthoughts of which the speaker is hardly sure."

His humor was so entirely fresh and unconventional, that it took his hearers by surprise, and charmed them. His failing health compelled him to abandon the lecture after about eight or ten weeks. Indeed, during that brief period, he was once or twice compelled to dismiss his audience. Frequently he sank into a chair and nearly fainted from the exertion of dressing. He exhibited the greatest anxiety to be at his post at the appointed time, and scrupulously exerted himself to the utmost to entertain his auditors. It was not because he was sick that the public was to be disappointed, or that their enjoyment was to be diminished. During the last few weeks of his lecture-giving, he steadily abstained from accepting any of the numerous invitations he received. Had he lived through the following London fashionable season, there is little doubt that the room at Egyptian Hall would have been thronged nightly. The English aristocracy have a fine, delicate sense of humor, and the success, artistic and pecuniary, of "Artemus Ward," would have rivaled that of the famous "Lord Dundreary." There were many stupid people who did not understand the "fun" of Artemus Ward's books. There were many stupid people who did not understand the fun of Artemus Ward's lecture on the Mormons. Highly respectable people—the pride of their parish—when they heard of a lecture "upon the Mormons," expected to see a solemn person, full of old saws and new statistics, who would denounce the sin of polygamy—and rave without limit against Mormons. These uncomfortable Christians do not like humor. They dread it as a certain personage is said to dread holy water, and for the same reason that thieves fear policemen — it finds them out. When these good idiots heard Artemus offer, if they did not like the lecture in Piccadilly, to give them free tickets for the same lecture in California, when he next visited that country, they turned to each other indignantly, and said, "What use are tickets for California to us? We are not going to California. No! we are too good, too respectable to go so far from home. The man is a fool!" One of these vestrymen complained to the doorkeeper, and denounced the lecturer as an imposter — "and," said the wealthy parishioner, "as for the panorama, it is the worse painted thing I ever saw."

During the lecture, Artemus was always as solemn as the grave. Sometimes he would seem to forget his audience, and stand for several seconds gazing intently at his panorama. Then he would start up and remark apologetically, "I am very fond of looking at my pictures." His dress was always the same—evening toilet. His manners were polished and his voice gentle and hesitating. Many who had read of the man who spelled joke with a "g" looked for a smart old man with a shrewd cock eye, dressed in vulgar velvet and gold, and they were hardly prepared to see the accomplished gentleman with slim physique and delicate white hands.

The letters of Artemus Ward in *Punch*, from the tomb of Shakespeare and the London Tower, had made him famous in England, and in his audience were the nobility of the realm. His first lecture in London was delivered at Egyptian Hall,

Tuesday, November 13, 1866. The room used was that which had been occupied by Mr. Arthur Sketchley, adjoining the one in which Mr. Arthur Smith formerly made his appearences.

Punctually at eight o'clock he would step, hesitatingly, before the audience, and, rubbing his hands bashfully, commence the lecture.

LIFE SKETCH OF ARTEMUS WARD WHILE LECTURING.

THE LECTURE.

You are entirely welcome, ladies and gentlemen, to my little picture-shop.

I couldn't give you a very clear idea of the Mormons—and Utah—and the plains — and the Rocky Mountains — without opening a picture-shop —— and therefore I open one.

I don't expect to do great things here — but I have thought that if I could make money enough to buy me a passage to New Zealand I should feel that I had not lived in vain.

3

I don't want to live in vain.   I'd rather live in Margate — or here.   But I wish when the Egyptians built this hall they had given it a little more ventilation.

If you should be dissatisfied with any thing here to-night — I will admit you all free in New Zealand — if you will come to me there for the orders.   Any respectable cannibal will tell you where I live.   This shows that I have a forgiving spirit.

I really don't care for money.   I only travel round to see the world and to exhibit my clothes.   These clothes I have on were a great success in America.

How often do large fortunes ruin young men!   I should like to be ruined, but I can get on very well as I am.

I am not an artist.   I don't paint myself ——though perhaps if I were a middle-aged single lady I should —— yet I have a passion for pictures. I have had a great many pictures — photographs — taken of myself. Some of them are very pretty — rather sweet to look at for a short time — and as I said before, I like them.   I've always loved pictures.

I could draw on wood at a very tender age.   When a mere child I once drew a small cart-load of raw turnips over a wooden bridge. —— The people of the village noticed me.   I drew their attention.   They said I had a future before me.   Up to that time I had an idea it was behind me.

Time passed on.   It always does, by the way.   You may possibly have noticed that Time passes on.   It is a kind of way Time has.

I became a man.   I haven't distinguished myself at all as an artist — but I have always been more or less mixed up with art.   I have an uncle who takes photographs — and I have a servant who —— takes any thing he can get his hands on.

When I was in Rome —— Rome in New York State I mean —— a distinguished sculpist wanted to sculp me.   But I said "No."   I saw through the designing man.   My model once in his hands — he would have flooded the market with my busts —— and I couldn't stand it to see every body going round with a bust of me.   Every body would want one of course — and wherever I should go I should meet the educated classes with my bust, taking it home to their families.   This would be more than my modesty could stand —— and I should have to return to America —— where my creditors are.

I like art.   I admire dramatic art — although I failed as an actor.

It was in my schoolboy days that I failed as an actor. —— The play was "the Ruins of Pompeii." —— I played the ruins.   It was not a very successful performance — but it was better than the "Burning Mountain." He was not good. He was a bad Vesuvius.

The remembrance often makes me ask — "Where are the boys of my youth?" I assure you this is not a conundrum. Some are amongst you here —— some in America —— some are in jail.

Hence arises a most touching question — "Where are the girls of my youth?" Some are married —— some would like to be.

Oh my Maria! Alas! she married another. They frequently do. I hope she is happy — because I am.* Some people are not happy. I have noticed that.

A gentleman friend of mine came to me one day with tears in his eyes. I said, "Why these weeps?" He said he had a mortgage on his farm—and wanted to borrow £200. I lent him the money—and he went away. Some time after he returned with more tears. He said he must leave me forever. I ventured to remind him of the £200 he borrowed. He was much cut up. I thought I would not be hard upon him—so told him I would throw off one hundred pounds. He brightened—shook my hand — and said — "Old friend — I won't allow you to outdo me in liberality —— I'll throw off the other hundred."

As a manager I was always rather more successful than as an actor.

Some years ago I engaged a celebrated Living American Skeleton for a tour through Australia. He was the thinnest man I ever saw. He was a splendid skeleton. He didn't weigh any thing scarcely —— and I said to myself — the people of Australia will flock to see this tremendous curiosity. It is a long voyage — as you know — from New York to Melbourne — and to my utter surprise the skeleton had no sooner got out to sea than he commenced eating in the most horrible manner. He had never been on the ocean before — and he said it agreed with him —— I thought so! —— I never saw a man eat so much in my life. Beef — mutton — pork —— he swallowed them all like a shark —— and between meals he was often discovered behind barrels eating hard-boiled eggs. The result was that, when we reached Melbourne, this infamous skeleton weighed 64 pounds more than I did!

I thought I was ruined —— but I wasn't. I took him on to California —— another very long sea voyage —— and when I got him to San Francisco I exhibited him as a fat man.

---

* "*Because I am!*" — (Spoken with a sigh.) It was a joke which always told. Artemus never failed to use it in his "Babes in the Wood" lecture, and the "Sixty Minutes in Africa," as well as in the Mormon story.

This story hasn't any thing to do with my entertainment, I know —— but one of the principal features of my entertainment is that it contains so many things that don't have any thing to do with it.

My orchestra is small —— but I am sure it is very good — so far as it goes. I give my pianist ten pounds a night — and his washing.

I like music. I can't sing. As a singest I am not a success. I am saddest when I sing. So are those who hear me. They are sadder even than I am.

The other night some silver-voiced young men came under my window and sang — " Come where my love lies dreaming." —— I didn't go. I didn't think it would be correct.

I found music very soothing when I lay ill with fever in Utah —— and I was very ill —— I was fearfully wasted. My face was hewn down to nothing — and my nose was so sharp I didn't dare to stick it into other people's business — for fear it would stay there — and I should never get it again. And on those dismal days a Mormon lady —— she was married — tho' not so much so as her husband — he had fifteen other wives —— she used to sing a ballad commencing " Sweet bird — do not fly away! " —— and I told her I wouldn't. She played the accordion divinely — accordingly I praised her.

I met a man in Oregon who hadn't any teeth — not a tooth in his head —— yet that man could play on the bass drum better than any man I ever met. He kept a hotel. They have queer hotels in Oregon. I remember one where they gave me a bag of oats for a pillow —— I had night mares of course. In the morning the landlord said — How do you feel — old hoss — hay? —— I told him I felt my oats.

Permit me now to quietly state that altho' I am here with my cap and bells, I am also here with some serious descriptions of the Mormons — their manners — their customs —— and while the pictures I shall present to your notice are by no means works of art — they are painted from photographs actually taken on the spot — and I am sure I need not inform any person present who was ever in the Territory of Utah that they are as faithful as they could possibly be.

I went to Great Salt Lake City by way of California.

I went to California on the steamer " Ariel."

Oblige me by calmly gazing on the steamer "Ariel"——and when you go to California be sure and go on some other steamer——because the "Ariel" isn't a very good one.

When I reached the "Ariel"—at pier No. 4—New York—I found the passengers in a state of great confusion about their things—which

STEAMER ARIEL.

were being thrown around by the ship's porters in a manner at once damaging and idiotic. So great was the excitement—my fragile form was smashed this way—and jammed that way—till finally I was shoved into a state-room which was occupied by two middle-aged females—who said, "Base man—leave us—O, leave us!"——I left them——O h—I left them!

We reached Acapulco on the coast of Mexico in due time. Nothing of special interest occurred at Acapulco——only some of the Mexican ladies are very beautiful. They all have brilliant black hair——hair "black as starless night"——if I may quote from the "Family Herald." It don't curl.—— A Mexican lady's hair never curls —— it is straight as an Indian's. Some people's hair won't curl under any circumstances.—— My hair won't curl under two shillings.*

The Chinese form a large element in the population of San Francisco —and I went to the Chinese Theatre.

THE GREAT THOROUGHFARE OF THE IMPERIAL CITY
OF THE PACIFIC COAST.

A Chinese play often lasts two months. Commencing at the hero's birth, it is cheerfully conducted from week to week till he is either killed or married.

---

* "Under Two Shillings." Artemus always wore his hair straight until after his severe illness in Salt Lake City. So much of it dropped off during his recovery that he became dissatisfied with the long meager appearance his countenance presented when he surveyed it in the looking-glass. After his lecture at the Salt Lake City Theatre he did not lecture again until we had crossed the Rocky Mountains and arrived at Denver City, the capital of Colorado. On the afternoon he was to lecture there, I met him coming out of an ironmonger's store with a small parcel in his hand. "I want you, old fellow," he said; "I have been all round the city for them, and I've got them at last." "Got what?" I asked. "A pair of curling-tongs. I am going to have my hair curled to lecture in to-night. I mean to cross the plains in curls. Come home with me and try to curl it for me. I don't want to go to any idiot of a barber to be laughed at." I played the part of *friseur*. Subsequently he became his own "curlist," as he phrased it. From that day forth Artemus was a curly-haired man.

The night I was there a Chinese comic vocalist sang a Chinese comic song. It took him six weeks to finish it — but as my time was limited I went away at the expiration of 215 verses. There were 11,000 verses to this song — the chorus being "Tural lural dural, ri fol day " —— which was repeated twice at the end of each verse —— making — as you will at once see — the appalling number of 22,000 "tural lural dural, ri fol days" ——and the man still lives.

Virginia City — in the bright new State of Nevada.

A wonderful little city — right in the heart of the famous Washoe silver regions —— the mines of which annually produce over twenty-five millions of solid silver. This silver is melted into solid bricks — of about the size of ordinary house-bricks — and carted off to San Francisco with mules. The roads often swarm with these silver wagons.

One hundred and seventy-five miles to the east of this place are the Reese River silver mines — which are supposed to be the richest in the world.

The great American Desert in winter-time —— the desert which is so frightfully gloomy always. No trees —— no houses —— no people —

save the miserable beings who live in wretched huts and have charge of the horses and mules of the Overland Mail Company.

Plains Between Virginia City and Salt Lake.—This picture is a great work of art.——It is an oil painting—d o n e i n p e t r o l e u m. It is by the old masters. It was the last thing they did before dying. T h e y d i d t h i s a n d t h e n t h e y e x p i r e d.

PLAINS BETWEEN VIRGINIA CITY AND SALT LAKE.

The most celebrated artists of London are so delighted with this picture that they come to the hall every day to gaze at it. I wish you were nearer to it—so you could see it better. I wish I could take it to your residences and let you see it by daylight. Some of the greatest artists in London come here every morning before daylight with lanterns to look at it. T h e y s a y t h e y n e v e r s a w a n y t h i n g l i k e i t b e f o r e —— and they hope they never shall again.

When I first showed this picture in New York, the audiences were so enthusiastic in their admiration of this picture that t h e y c a l l e d f o r t h e a r t i s t —— and when he appeared they threw brick-bats at him.

A bird's-eye view of Great Salt Lake City —— the strange city in the desert about which so much has been heard —— the city of the people who call themselves Saints.

I know there is much interest taken in these remarkable people — ladies and gentlemen —— and I have thought it better to make the purely descriptive part of my entertainment entirely serious. —— I will not — then — for the next ten minutes — confine myself to my subject.

BIRD'S EYE VIEW OF SALT LAKE CITY.

Some seventeen years ago a small band of Mormons — headed by Brigham Young — commenced in the present thrifty metropolis of Utah. The population of the Territory of Utah is over 100,000 — chiefly Mormons —— and they are increasing at the rate of from five to ten thousand annually. The converts to Mormonism now are almost exclusively confined to English and Germans. Wales and Cornwall have contributed largely to the population of Utah during the last few years. The population of Great Salt Lake City is 20,000. The streets are eight rods wide and are neither flagged nor paved. A stream of pure mountain spring water courses through each street and is conducted into the gardens of the Mormons. The houses are mostly of adobe, or sun-dried brick, and present a neat and comfortable appearance. They are usually a story and a half high. Now and then you see a fine modern house in Salt Lake City, but no house that is dirty, shabby and dilapidated; because there are no absolutely poor people in Utah. Every Mormon has a nice garden, and every Mormon has a tidy dooryard. Neatness is a great characteristic of the Mormons.

The Mormons profess to believe that they are the chosen people of God —— they call themselves Latter-day Saints —— and they call us people of the outer world Gentiles. They say that Mr. Brigham Young is a prophet — the legitimate successor of Joseph Smith — who founded the Mormon religion. They also say they are authorized — by special revelation from heaven — to marry as many wives as they can comfortably support.

This wife-system they call plurality. The world calls it polygamy. That at its best it is an accursed thing, I need not of course inform you —— but you will bear in mind that I am here as a rather cheerful reporter of what I saw in Utah —— and I fancy it isn't at all necessary for me to grow virtuously indignant over something we all know is hideously wrong.

You will be surprised to hear — I was amazed to see — that among the Mormon women there are some few persons of education — of positive cultivation. As a class, the Mormons are not an educated people, but they are by no means the community of ignoramuses so many writers have told us they were.

The valley in which they live is splendidly favored. They raise immense crops. They have mills of all kinds. They have coal, lead and silver mines. All they eat, all they drink, all they wear they can produce themselves, and still have a great abundance to sell to the gold regions of Idaho on the one hand and the silver regions of Nevada on the other.

The president of this remarkable community —— the head of the Mormon church —— is Brigham Young. He is called President Young — and Brother Brigham. He is about 54 years old, altho' he doesn't look to be over 45. He has sandy hair and whiskers, is of medium height, and is a little inclined to corpulency. He was born in the State of Vermont. His power is more absolute than that of any living sovereign. Yet he uses it with such consummate discretion that his people are almost madly devoted to him, and that they would cheerfully die for him if they thought the sacrifice were demanded, I can not doubt.

He is a man of enormous wealth. One-tenth of every thing sold in the Territory of Utah goes to the church —— and Mr. Brigham Young is the church. It is supposed that he speculates with these funds —— at all events, he is one of the wealthiest men now living —— worth several millions, without doubt. He is a bold — bad man —— but that he is also a man of extraordinary administrative ability, no one can doubt who has watched his astounding career for the past ten years. It is only fair for me to add that he treated me with marked kindness during my sojourn in Utah.

The <i>West Side of Main Street — Salt Lake City</i> — including a view of the Salt Lake Hotel. It is a temperance hotel.* I prefer temperance hotels—altho' they sell worse liquor than other kind of

* "<i>Temperance Hotel.</i>" At the date of our visit, there was only one place in Salt Lake City where strong drink was allowed to be sold. Brigham Young himself owned the property, and vended the liquor by wholesale, not permitting any of it to be drunk on the premises. It was a coarse, inferior kind of whisky, known in Salt Lake as "Valley Tan." Throughout the city there was no drinking-bar nor billiard room, so far as I am aware. But a drink on the sly could always be had at one of the hard-goods stores, in the back office behind the pile of metal saucepans, or at one of the dry-goods stores, in the little parlor in the rear of the bales of calico. At the present time I believe that there are two or three open bars in Salt Lake, Brigham Young having recognized the right of the "Saints" to "liquor up" occasionally. But whatever other failings they may have, intemperance can not be laid to their charge. Among the Mormons there are no paupers, no gamblers and no drunkards

hotels.   But the Salt Lake Hotel sells none ———— nor is there a bar
in all Salt Lake City ———— but I found when I was thirsty — and I generally am — that I could get some very good brandy of one of the elders
— on the sly — and I never on any account allow my business to interfere with my drinking.

There is the *Overland Mail Coach* —— that is, the den on wheels in
which we have been crammed for the past ten days — and ten nights.
—— Those of you who have been in Newgate*—— —— —— ——
—— —— —— ——and stayed there any length of time
—— as visitors —— can realize how I felt.

The American Overland Mail Route commences at Sacramento, California, and ends at Atchison, Kansas.   The distance is two thousand two
hundred miles —— but you go part of the way by rail.   The Pacific
Railway is now completed from Sacramento, California, to Fulsom,

---

* "*Been in Newgate.*"   The manner in which Artemus uttered this joke was peculiarly
characteristic of his style of lecturing.   The commencement of the sentence was spoken as if
unpremeditated; then, when he got as far as the word "Newgate," he paused, as if wishing to
call back that which he had said.   The applause was unfailingly uproarious.

California,——which only leaves two thousand two hundred and eleven miles to go by coach. This breaks the monotony——it came very near breaking my back.

The Mormon Theatre.—This edifice is the exclusive property of Brigham Young. It will comfortably hold 3,000 persons—and I beg you will believe me when I inform you that its interior is quite as brilliant as that of any theater in London.

The actors are all Mormon amateurs, who charge nothing for their services.

You must know that very little money is taken at the doors of this theater. The Mormons mostly pay in grain—and all sorts of articles.

The night I gave my little lecture there, among my receipts were corn—flour—pork—cheese—chickens——on foot and in the shell.

One family went in on a live pig——and a man attempted to pass a "yaller dog" at the box office—but my agent repulsed him. One offered me a doll for admission——another infant's clothing. I refused to take that——as a general rule I do refuse.

In the middle of the parquet—in a rocking chair—with his hat on—sits Brigham Young. When the play drags—he either goes out or falls into a tranquil sleep.

A portion of the dress-circle is set apart for the wives of Brigham Young.   From ten to twenty of them are usually present.   His children fill the entire gallery—and more too.

The East Side of Main Street — Salt Lake City — with a view of the Council Building.   The Legislature of Utah meets there.   It is like all legislative bodies.   They meet this winter to repeal the laws which they met and made last winter——and they will meet next winter to repeal the laws which they met and made this winter.

I dislike to speak about it——but it was in Utah that I made the great speech of my life.   I wish you could have heard it.   I have a fine education.   You may have noticed it.   I speak six different languages——London—Chatham—and Dover——Margate—Brighton—and Hastings.   My parents sold a cow and sent me to college when I was quite young.   During the vacation I used to teach a school of whales—and there's where I learned to spout.——I don't expect applause for a little thing like that.   I wish you could have heard that speech, however.   If Cicero——he's dead now——he has gone from us—— but if old Ciss* could have heard that effort it would

---

* "Old Ciss." Here again no description can adequately inform the reader of the drollery which characterized the lecturer. His reference to Cicero was made in the most lugubrious manner, as if he really deplored his death and valued him as a schoolfellow loved and lost.

have given him the rinderpest. I'll tell you how it was. There are sta-
tioned in Utah two regiments of U. S. troops —— the 21st from California and the 37th from Nevada. The 20-onesters asked me to present a
stand of colors to the 37-sters, and I did it in a speech so abounding in
eloquence of a bold and brilliant character —— and also some sweet talk
—— real pretty shop-keeping talk —— that I w o r k e d t h e e n t h u-
s i a s m o f t h o s e s o l d i e r s u p t o s u c h a p i t c h — that they came
very near shooting me on the spot.

Brigham Young's Harem. These are the houses of Brigham Young.
The first one on the right is the Lion House — so called because a crouch-
ing stone lion adorns the central front window. The adjoining small
building is Brigham Young's office — and where he receives his visitors.
The large house in the center of the picture — which displays a huge
bee-hive — is called the Bee House. The bee-hive is supposed to be sym-
bolical of the industry of the Mormons. Mrs. Brigham Young the first
— now quite an old lady — lives here with her children. None of the
other wives of the Prophet live here. In the rear are the school-houses
where Brigham Young's children are educated.

Brigham Young has two hundred wives. J u s t t h i n k o f t h a t !
Oblige me by thinking of that. That is — he has eighty actual wives
and he is spiritually married to one hundred and twenty more. These

spiritual marriages ——as the Mormons call them —— are contracted with aged widows — who think it a great honor to be sealed —— the Mormons call it being sealed —— to the Prophet.

So we may say he has two hundred wives. He loves not wisely —but two hundred well. He is dreadfully married. He's the most married man I ever saw in my life.

I saw his mother-in-law while I was there. I can't exactly tell you how many there is of her—but it's a good deal. It strikes me that one mother-in-law is about enough to have in a family — unless you're very fond of excitement.

A few days before my arrival in Utah, Brigham was married again to a young and really pretty girl —— but he says he shall stop now. He told me confidentially that he shouldn't get married any more. He says that all he wants now is to live in peace for the remainder of his days — and have his dying pillow soothed by the loving hands of his family. Well — that's all right —— that's all right — I suppose —— but if *all* his family soothe his dying pillow—he'll have to go out-doors to die.

By the way — Shakespeare indorses polygamy. He speaks of the Merry Wives of Windsor. How many wives did Mr. Windsor have ?—— But we will let this pass.

Some of these Mormons have terrific families. I lectured one night by invitation in the Mormon village of Provost —— but during the day I rashly gave a leading Mormon an order admitting himself and family. It was before I knew that he was much married—— and they filled the room to overflowing. It was a great success —— but I didn't get any money.

Heber C. Kimball's Harem. Mr H. C. Kimball is the first vice-president of the Mormon church, and would, consequently, succeed to the full presidency on Brigham Young's death.

Brother Kimball is a gay and festive cuss, of some seventy summers —— or some'ers thereabout. He has one thousand head of cattle and a hundred head of wives. He says they are awful eaters.

H. C. KIMBALL'S HAREM.

Mr. Kimball had a son —— a lovely young man —— who was married to ten interesting wives. But one day —— while he was absent from home —— these ten wives went out walking with a handsome young man — which so enraged Mr. Kimball's son — which made Mr. Kimball's son so jealous — that he shot himself with a horse pistol.

The doctor who attended him —— a very scientific man —— informed me that the bullet entered the inner parallelogram of his diaphragmatic

4

thorax, superinducing membraneous hemorrhage in the outer cuticle of his basiliconthamaturgist. It killed him. I should have thought it would.   (Soft music.)*

I hope his sad end will be a warning to all young wives who go out walking with handsome young men.   Mr. Kimball's son is now no more. He sleeps beneath the cypress, the myrtle and the willow.   This music is a dirge by the eminent pianist for Mr. Kimball's son.   He died by request.

I regret to say that efforts were made to make a Mormon of me while I was in Utah.

It was leap-year when I was there—and seventeen young widows—— the wives of a deceased Mormon——offered me their hearts and hands. I called on them one day—and, taking their soft white hands in mine—— which made eighteen hands altogether——I found them in tears. .

And I said——" Why is this thus?   What is the reason of this thus-ness?"

They hove a sigh——seventeen sighs of different size.   They said:

" Oh—soon thou wilt be gonested away!"

I told them that when I got ready to leave a place I wentested.

They said, " Doth not like us?"

I said, "I doth, I doth!"

I also said: " I hope your intentions are honorable—as I am a lone child——my parents being far—far away."

They then said, " Wilt not marry us?"

I said, "Oh — no —— it can not was."

Again they asked me to marry them — and again I declined.   When they cried:

" Oh — cruel man!   This is too much —— oh! too much?"

I told them that it was on account of the muchness that I declined.

---

* "Soft Music." Here Artemus Ward's pianist (following instructions) sometimes played the Dead March from " *Saul*." At other times, the Welsh air of " Poor Mary Ann ;" or any thing else replete with sadness which might chance to strike his fancy. The effect was irresistibly comic.

This *Mormon Temple* is built of adobe, and wili hold five thousand persons quite comfortably. A full brass and string band often assists the choir of this church ——— and the choir, I may add, is a remarkably good one.

MORMON TEMPLE.

Brigham Young seldom preaches now. The younger elders, unless on some special occasion, conduct the services. I only heard Mr. Young once. He is not an educated man, but speaks with considerable force and clearness. The day I was there there was nothing coarse in his remarks.

These are the *Foundations of the Magnificent Temple* the Mormons are building. It is to be built of hewn stone—and will cover several

FOUNDATIONS OF THE TEMPLE.

acres of ground. They say it shall eclipse in splendor all other temples in the world. They also say it shall be paved with solid gold.

It is perhaps worthy of remark that the architect of this contemplated gorgeous affair repudiated Mormonism—and is now living in London.

The Temple as It Is to Be.—This pretty little picture is from the architect's design, and can not, therefore, I suppose, be called a fancy sketch.

THE TEMPLE AS IT IS TO BE.

Should the Mormons continue unmolested, I think they will complete this rather remarkable edifice.

Great Salt Lake.———The great salt dead sea of the desert.

I know of no greater curiosity than this inland sea of thick brine. It is eighty miles wide and one hundred and thirty miles long. Solid masses of salt are daily washed ashore in immense heaps, and the Mormon in want of salt has only to go to the shore of this lake and fill his cart. Only—the salt for table use has to be subjected to a boiling process.

GREAT SALT LAKE.

These are facts—susceptible of the clearest possible proof. They tell one story about this lake, however, that I have my doubts about. They say a Mormon farmer drove forty head of cattle in there once, and they came out first-rate pickled beef.———

*   *   *   *   *
*   *   *   *   *
*   *   *   *   *
*   *   *   *   *
*   *   *   *   *

I sincerely hope you will excuse my absence —————— I am a man short — and have to work the moon myself.*

I shall be most happy to pay a good salary to any respectable boy of good parentage and education who is a good moonist.

The Endowment House.—In this building the Mormon is initiated into the mysteries of the faith.

Strange stories are told of the proceedings which are held in this building —— but I have no possible means of knowing how true they may be.

---

* "*The Moon Myself.*" Here Artemus would leave the rostrum for a few moments, and pretend to be engaged behind. The picture was painted for a night-scene, and the effect intended to be produced was that of the moon rising over the lake and rippling on the waters. It was produced in the usual dioramic way, by making the track of the moon transparent, and throwing the moon on from the bull's eye of a lantern. When Artemus went behind, the moon would become nervous and flickering, dancing up and down in the most inartistic and undecided manner. The result was that, coupled with the lecturer's oddly expressed apology, the "moon" became one of the best laughed-at parts of the entertainment.

Salt Lake City is fifty-five miles behind us—and this is *Echo Cañon,* in reaching which we are supposed to have crossed the summit of the Wahsatch mountains. These ochre-colored bluffs ———— formed of conglomerate sandstone, and full of fossils———— signal the entrance to the cañon. At its base lies Weber Station.

Echo Cañon is about twenty-five miles long. It is really the sublimest thing between the Missouri and the Sierra Nevada. The red wall to

ECHO CAÑON.

the left develops farther up the cañon into pyramids, buttresses and castles——honeycombed and fretted in nature's own massive magnificence of architecture.

In 1856 Echo Cañon was the place selected by Brigham Young for the Mormon General Wells to fortify and make impregnable against the advance of the American army, led by General Albert Sidney Johnston. It was to have been the Thermopylæ of Mormondom——but it wasn't. General Wells was to have done Leonidas——but he didn't.

A More Cheerful View of the Desert.—The wild snow-storms have left us—and we have thrown our wolf-skin overcoats aside. Certain tribes of far-western Indians bury their distinguished dead by placing them high in air and covering them with valuable furs————that is a

A MORE CHEERFUL VIEW OF THE DESERT.

very fair representation of these mid-air tombs. Those animals **are** horses————I know they are—because my artist says so. I had the picture two years before I discovered the fact. The artist came to me about six months ago, and said: "It is useless to disguise it from you any longer————t h e y a r e h o r s e s."

It was while crossing this desert that I was surrounded by a band of
Ute Indians. They were splendidly mounted. They were dressed in
beaver-skins, and they were armed with rifles, knives and pistols.

What could I do?—— What could a poor, old orphan do? I'm a
brave man. The day before the battle of Bull's Run I stood in the highway while the bullets —— those dreadful messengers of death —— w e r e

OUR ENCOUNTER WITH THE INDIANS.

passing all around me thickly —— in wagons —— on their
way to the battlefield.* But there were too many of these Injuns.
There were forty of them — and only one of me —— and so I said:

"Great Chief, I surrender." His name was Wocky-bocky.

---

*"Their Way to the Battlefield." This was the great joke of Artemus Ward's first lecture,
"The Babes in the Wood." He never omitted it in any of his lectures, nor did it lose its
power to create laughter by repetition. The audiences at the Egyptian Hall, London, laughed
as immoderately at it as did those of Irving Hall, New York, or of the Tremont Temple, in
Boston.

He dismounted and approached me. I saw his tomahawk glisten in the morning sunlight. Fire was in his eye. Wocky-bocky came very close to me and seized me by the hair of my head. He mingled his swarthy fingers with my golden tresses, and he rubbed his dreadful Thomashawk across my lily-white face. He said:

"Torsha arrah darrah mishky bookshean!"

I told him he was right.

Wocky-bocky again rubbed his tomahawk across my face, and said: "Wink-ho — loo-boo!"

Says I: "Mr. Wocky-bocky," says I, "Wocky — I have thought so for years — and so's all our family."

He told me I must go to the tent of the Strong-Heart and eat raw dog.† It don't agree with me. I prefer simple food. I prefer pork-pie, because then I know what I'm eating. But as raw dog was all they proposed to give to me, I had to eat it or starve. So at the expiration of two days I seized a tin plate and went to the chief's daughter, and I said to her in a silvery voice——in a kind of German-silvery voice——I said:

"Sweet child of the forest, the pale-face wants his dog."

There was nothing but his paws! I had paused too long! Which reminds me that time passes. A way which Time has.

I was told in my youth to seize opportunity. I once tried to seize one. He was rich. He had diamonds on. As I seized him — he knocked me down. Since then I have learned that he who seizes opportunity sees the penitentiary.

---

† "Raw Dog." While sojourning for a day in a camp of Sioux Indians, we were informed that the warriors of the tribe were accustomed to eat raw dog to give them courage previous to going to battle. Artemus was greatly amused with the information. When, in after years, he became weak and languid, and was called upon to go to lecture, it was a favorite joke with him to inquire, "Hingston, have you got any raw dog?"

The Rocky Mountains.—I take it for granted you have heard of these popular mountains. In America they are regarded as a great success, and we all love dearly to talk about them. It is a kind of weakness with us. I never knew but one American who hadn't something — some time — to say about the Rocky Mountains, and he was a deaf and dumb man who couldn't say any thing about nothing.

THE ROCKY MOUNTAINS.

But these mountains, whose summits are snow-covered and icy all the year round, are too grand to make fun of. I crossed them in the winter of '64 — in a rough sleigh drawn by four mules.

This sparkling waterfall is the Laughing-Water alluded to by Mr. Longfellow in his Indian poem — "Higher-Water." The water is higher up there.

The Plains of Nebraska.—These are the dreary plains over which we rode for so many weary days. An affecting incident occurred on these plains some time since, and I am sure you will pardon me for mentioning it.

THE PLAINS OF NEBRASKA.

On a beautiful June morning — some sixteen years ago ——
(Music, very loud till the scene is off.)

<pre>
   *   *   *   *   *
   *   *   *   *   *
   *   *   *   *   *
   *   *   *   *   *
   *   *   *   *   *
   *   *   *   *   *
</pre>

———— and she fainted on Reginald's breast !*

—————————————————————————————————————

* " On Reginald's Breast." At this part of the lecture Artemus pretended to tell a story —the piano playing loudly all the time. He continued his narration in excited dumb-show —his lips moving as though he were speaking. For some minutes the audience indulged in unrestrained laughter.

The Prairie on Fire.—A prairie on fire is one of the wildest and grandest sights that can be possibly imagined.

These fires occur — of course — in the summer — when the grass is dry as tinder ——— and the flames rush and roar over the prairie in a

THE PRAIRIE ON FIRE.

manner frightful to behold. They usually burn better than mine is burning to-night. I try to make my prairie burn regularly —and not disappoint the public——but it is not as high-principled as I am.

Brigham Young at Home.—The last picture I have to show you repre-
sents Mr. Brigham Young in the bosom of his family. His family is
large—and the olive branches around his table are in a very tangled
condition. He is more a father than any man I know. When

BRIGHAM YOUNG AT HOME.

at home——as you here see him——he ought to be very happy
with sixty wives to minister to his comforts—and twice
sixty children to soothe his distracted mind. Ah! my
friends——what is home without a family?

What will become of Mormonism?   We all know and admit it to be a hideous wrong —— a great immoral stain upon the 'scutcheon of the United States.   My belief is that its existence is dependent upon the life of Brigham Young.   His administrative ability holds the system together —— his power of will maintains it as the faith of a community. When he dies, Mormonism will die too.   The men who are around him have neither his talent nor his energy.   By means of his strength, it is held together.   When he falls, Mormonism will also fall to pieces.

That lion — you perceive — has a tail.*   It is a long one already. Like mine— it is to be continued in our next.

The Curtain Fell for the last time on Wednesday, the 23d of January, 1867.   Artemus Ward had to break off the lecture abruptly.   He never lectured again.

---

* " The Lion has a Tail."   The lion on a pedestal as painted in the panorama—its long tail outstretched until it exceeded the length of the lion was a pure piece of frolic on the part of Artemus.   The Bee Hive and the Lion suggesting strength and industry are the emblems chosen by Brigham Young to represent the Mormons.

PROGRAMME USED AT

EGYPTIAN HALL,

PICCADILLY.

Every Night (except Saturday) at 8,

SATURDAY MORNINGS AT 3.

ᴀ̀RTEMUS ᴡARD

AMONG THE MORMONS.

*During the Vacation the Hall has been carefully Swept out, and a new Door-Knob
has been added to the Door.*

MR. ARTEMUS WARD *will call on the Citizens of London, at their residences, and
explain any jokes in his narrative which they may
not understand.*

A person of long-established integrity will take excellent care of Bonnets, Cloaks, etc.,
during the Entertainment; the Audience better leave their money, however, with MR. WARD;
he will return it to them in a day or two, or invest it for them in America as they may
think best.

☞ Nobody must say that he likes the Lecture unless he wishes to be thought
eccentric; and nobody must say that he doesn't like it unless he really *is* eccentric. (This
requires thinking over, but it will amply repay perusal.)

*The Panorama used to Illustrate Mr. Ward's Narrative is rather worse than
Panoramas usually are.*

MR. WARD will not be responsible for any debts of his own contracting.

5

PROGRAMME.

———o———

I.

APPEARANCE OF ARTEMUS WARD,

Who will be greeted with applause. ☞ The Stall-keeper is particularly requested to attend to this. ☜ When quiet has been restored, the Lecturer will present a rather frisky prologue, of about ten minutes in length, and of nearly the same width. It perhaps isn't necessary to speak of the depth.

II.

THE PICTURES COMMENCE HERE, the first one being a view of the California Steamship. Large crowd of citizens on the wharf, who appear to be entirely willing that ARTEMUS WARD shall go. "Bless you, Sir!" they say. "Don't hurry about coming back. Stay away for years, if you want to!" It was very touching. Disgraceful treatment of the passengers, who are obliged to go forward to smoke pipes, while the steamer herself is allowed 2 Smoke Pipes amidships. At Panama. A glance at Mexico.

III.

THE LAND OF GOLD.

Montgomery Street, San Francisco. The Gold Bricks Street Scenes. "The Orphan Cabman, or the Mule Driver's Step-Father." The Chinese Theatre. Sixteen square yards of a Chinese Comic Song.

IV.

THE LAND OF SILVER.

Virginia City, the wild young metropolis of the new Silver State. Fortunes are made there in a day. There are instances on record of young men going to this place without a shilling—poor and friendless—yet by energy, intelligence, and a careful disregard to business, they have been enabled to leave there, owing hundreds of pounds.

V.

THE GREAT DESERT AT NIGHT.

A dreary waste of Sand. The Sand isn't worth saving, however. Indians occupy yonder mountains. Little Injuns seen in the distance trundling their war-hoops.

VI.

A BIRD'S-EYE VIEW OF GREAT SALT LAKE CITY.

With some entirely descriptive talk.

VII.

MAIN STREET, EAST SIDE.

The Salt Lake Hotel, which is conducted on Temperance principles. The land-lord sells nothing stronger than salt butter.

VIII.

THE MORMON THEATRE.

The Lady of Lyons was produced here a short time since, but failed to satisfy a Mormon audience, on account of there being only one Pauline in it. The play was revised at once. It was presented the next night, with fifteen Paulines in the cast, and was a perfect success. ☞ All these statements may be regarded as strictly true. Mr. WARD would not deceive an infant.

IX.

MAIN STREET, WEST SIDE.

This being a view of Main Street, West side, it is naturally a view of the West side of Main Street.

X.

BRIGHAM YOUNG'S HAREM.

Mr. Young is an indulgent father, and a numerous husband. For further particulars call on Mr. WARD, at Egyptian Hall, any Evening this Week. This paragraph is intended to blend business with amusement.

XI.

HEBER C. KIMBALL'S HAREM.

We have only to repeat here the pleasant remarks above in regard to Brigham.

INTERMISSION OF FIVE MINUTES.

XII.

THE TABERNACLE.

XIII.

THE TEMPLE AS IT IS.

XIV.

THE TEMPLE AS IT IS TO BE.

XV.

THE GREAT SALT LAKE.

XVI.

THE ENDOWMENT HOUSE.

The Mormon is initiated into the mysteries of his faith here. The Mormon's religion is singular and his wives are plural.

XVII.

ECHO CAÑON.

XVIII.

THE DESERT, AGAIN.

A more cheerful view. The Plains of Colorado. The Colorado Mountains "might have been seen" in the distance, if the Artist had painted 'em. But he is prejudiced against mountains, because his uncle once got lost on one.

XIX.

BRIGHAM YOUNG AND HIS WIVES.

The pretty girls of Utah mostly marry Young.

XX.

THE ROCKY MOUNTAINS.

XXI.

THE PLAINS OF NEBRASKA.

XXII.

THE PRAIRIE ON FIRE.

RECOMMENDATIONS.

TOTNES, *Oct. 20th, 1866.*

MR. ARTEMUS WARD: My dear Sir—My wife was dangerously unwell for over sixteen years. She was so weak that she could not lift a teaspoon to her mouth. But in a fortunate moment she commenced reading one of your lectures. She got better at once. She gained strength so rapidly that she lifted the cottage piano quite a distance from the floor, and then tipped it over on to her mother-in-law, with whom she had had some little trouble. We like your lectures very much. Please send me a barrel of them. If you should require any more recommendations, you can get any number of them in this place, at two shillings each, the price I charge for this one, and I trust you may be ever happy.

I am, Sir,

Yours truly, and so is my wife,   R. SPRINGERS.

An American correspondent of a distinguished journal in Yorkshire thus speaks of Mr. WARD's power as an Orator:

It was a grand scene, Mr. ARTEMUS WARD standing on the platform, talking: many of the audience sleeping tranquilly in their seats; others leaving the room and not returning; others crying like a child at some of the jokes—all, all formed a most impressive scene, and showed the powers of this remarkable orator. And when he announced that he should never lecture in that town again, the applause was absolutely deafening.

Doors open at Half-past Seven, commence at Eight.

Conclude at Half-past Nine.

EVERY EVENING EXCEPT SATURDAY.

SATURDAY AFTERNOONS AT 3 P. M.

ARTEMUS WARD,

𝕳𝖎𝖘 𝕻𝖗𝖔𝖌𝖗𝖆𝖒𝖒𝖊.

DODWORTH HALL, 806 BROADWAY, NEW YORK.

OPEN EVERY EVENING.

1.—Introductory.
2.—The Steamer Ariel, *en route.*
3.—San Francisco.
4.—The Washoe Silver Region.
5.—The Plains.
6.—The City of Saints.
7.—A Mormon Hotel.
8.—Brigham Young's Theatre.
9.—The Council-House.
10.—The Home of Brigham Young.
11.—Heber C. Kimball's Seraglio.
12.—The Mormon House of Worship.
13.—Foundations of the New Temple.
14.—Architect's View of the Temple when finished.
15.—The Great Dead Sea of the Desert.
16.—The House of Mystery.
17.—The Cañon.
18.—Mid-Air Sepulture.
19.—A Nice Family Party at Brigham Young's.

It requires a large number of Artists to produce this Entertainment. The casual observer can form no idea of the quantity of unfettered genius that is soaring, like a healthy Eagle, round this Hall in connection with this Entertainment. In fact, the following gifted persons compose the

Official Bureau.

Secretary of the Exterior	Mr. E. P. Hingston.
Secretary of the Treasury	Herr Max Field,
	(Pupil of Signor Thomaso Jacksoni.)
Mechanical Director and Professor of Carpentry	Signor G. Wilsoni.
Crankist	Mons. Aleck.
Assistant Crankist,	Boy (orphan).
Artists	Messrs. Hilliard & Maeder.
Reserved Chairists	Messrs. Persee & Jerome.
Moppist	Signorina O'Flaherty.
Broomist	Mlle. Topsia de St. Moke.
Hired Man	John.
Fighting Editor	Chevalier McArone.
Dutchman	By a Polish Refugee, named McFinnigin.
Doortendist	Mons. Jacques Ridera.
Gas Man	Artemus Ward.

This Entertainment will open with music. The Soldiers' Chorus from " Faust."
☞ First time in this city. ✦

Next comes a jocund and discursive preamble, calculated to show what a good education the Lecturer has.

*

* *

View the first is a sea-view.—Ariel navigation.—Normal school of whales in the distance.—Isthmus of Panama.—Interesting interview with Old Panama himself, who makes all the hats.   Old Pan is a likely sort of man.

*

* *

San Francisco.—City with a vigilant government.—Miners allowed to vote. Old inhabitants so rich that they have legs with golden calves to them.

*

* *

Town in the Silver region.—Good quarters to be found there.—Playful population, fond of high-low-jack and homicide.—Silver lying around loose.—Thefts of it termed silver-guilt.

*

* *

The plains in Winter.—A wild Moor, like Othello.—Mountains in the distance forty thousand miles above the level of the highest sea (Musiani's chest C included.) —If you don't believe this you can go there and measure them for yourself.

*

* *

Mormondom, sometimes called the City of the Plain, but wrongly ; the women are quite pretty.—View of Old Poly Gamy's house, etc.

*

* *

The Salt Lake Hotel.—Stage just come in from its overland route and retreat from the Indians.—Temperance house.—No bar nearer than Salt Lake sand-bars.— Miners in shirts like Artemus Ward his Programme—they are read and will wash.

*

* *

Mormon Theatre, where Artemus Ward lectured.—Mormons like theatricals, and had rather go to the Play-house than to the Work-house, any time.—Private boxes reserved for the ears of Brother Brigham's wives.

*

* *

INTERMISSION OF FIVE MINUTES.

Territorial State House.—Seat of the Legislature.—About as fair a collection as that at Albany—and "we can't say no fairer than that."

*

*   *

Residence of Brigham Young and his wives.—Two hundred souls with but a single thought, Two hundred hearts that beat as one.

*

*   *

Seraglio of Heber C. Kimball.—Home of the Queens of Heber.—No relatives of the Queen of Sheba.—They are a nice gang of darlings.

*

*   *

Mormon Tabernacle, where the men espouse Mormonism and the women espouse Brother Brigham and his Elders as spiritual Physicians, convicted of bad doct'rin.

*

*   *

Foundations of the Temple.—Beginning of a healthy little job.—Temple to enclose all out-doors, and be paved with gold at a premium.

*

*   *

The Temple when finished.—Mormon idea of a meeting-house.—N. B.   It will be bigger, probably, than Dodworth Hall.—One of the figures in the foreground is intended for Heber C. Kimball.—You can see, by the expression of his back, that he is thinking what a great man Joseph Smith was.

*

*   *

The Great Salt Lake.—Water actually thick with salt—too saline to sail in.— Mariners rocked on the bosom of this deep with rock salt.—The water isn't very good to drink.

*

*   *

House where Mormons are initiated.—Very secret and mysterious ceremonies.— Anybody can easily find out all about them though, by going out there and becoming a Mormon.

*

*   *

Echo Cañon.—A rough bluff sort of affair.—Great Echo.—When Artemus Ward went through, he heard the echoes of some things the Indians said there about four years and a half ago.

The Plains again, with some noble savages, both in the live and dead state.—The dead one on the high shelf was killed in a Fratricidal Struggle.—They are always having Fratricidal Struggles out in that line of country.—It would be a good place for an enterprising Coroner to locate.

*

* *

Brigham Young surrounded by his wives.—These ladies are simply too numerous to mention.

*

* *

☞ Those of the Audience who do not feel offended with Artemus Ward are cordially invited to call upon him, often, at his fine new house in Brooklyn. His house is on the right hand side as you cross the Ferry, and may be easily distinguished from the other houses by its having a Cupola and a Mortgage on it.

*

* *

☞ Soldiers on the battle-field will be admitted to this Entertainment gratis.

*

* *

☞ The Indians on the Overland Route live on Route an Herbs. They are an intemperate people. They drink with impunity, or any body who invites them.

*

* *

☞ Artemus Ward delivered Lectures before
ALL THE CROWNED HEADS OF EUROPE

ever thought of delivering lectures.

TICKETS 50 CTS.	RESERVED CHAIRS $1.
Doors open at 7.30 P. M.	Entertainment to commence at 8.

JOSH BILLINGS STRUGLING WITH HIS GREAT COMIC LECTURE.

"JOSH BILLINGS."

BIOGRAPHY AND REMINISCENCES.

Henry W. Shaw, the well-known wit and satirist, better known as "Josh Billings," was born at Lanesborough, Mass., in 1818, of a family of politicians, his father and grandfather having both been in Congress. He went early in life to the West, where for twenty-five years he was a farmer and auctioneer. He did not begin to write for publication till he was forty-five years old. He has been one of the most popular of popular lecturers. Mr. Shaw died at Monterey, Cal., October 14, 1885. He is the author of several books which have been collected into one large volume by Mr. Dillingham, successor to Geo. W. Carleton, and which is still having an immense sale. Mr. Shaw left an accomplished wife and a beautiful daughter to mourn his loss. He died wealthy, but his greatest legacy to his family was his literary reputation. His fame spread through England as well as America.

The last time I saw Josh Billings was on a Madison avenue street car in New York City. I think of him as I saw him then, sitting in the corner of the car, with his spectacles on his nose, and in a brown study. His mind was always on his work, and his work was to think out dry epigrams so full of truth and human nature that they set the whole world laughing. That morning, when the old man espied me, he was so busy with his thoughts that he did not even say good morning. He simply raised one hand, looked over his glasses and said, quickly, as if he had made a great discovery:

"I've got it, Eli!"

"Got what?"

"Got a good one—lem me read it," and then he read from a crumpled envelope this epigram that he had just jotted down:

"*When a man tries to make himself look beautiful, he steals — he steals a woman's patent right —*—how's that?"

"Splendid," I said. "How long have you been at work on it?"

"Three hours," he said, "to get it just right."

Mr. Shaw always worked long and patiently over these little paragraphs, but every one contains a sermon. When he got five or six written, he stuck them into his hat and went down and read them to G. W. Carleton, his publisher and friend, who was an excellent judge of wit, and he and Josh would laugh over them.

One day I told Josh that I would love him forever and go and put flowers on his grave if he would give me some of his paragraphs in his own handwriting. He did it, and when he died I hung a wreath of *immortelles* on his tombstone at Poughkeepsie. These are the sparks from his splendid brain just as he gave them to me:

ONST

The man who kan wear a paper collar, a whole week, and keep it klean.—aint good for enny thing else.= Jess so. Josh Billings.

TWIST

Thare iz only one thing that kan be sed in favour ov tite Boots.—they make a man forgit all his other Sorrows.= Josh Billings.

Three Times

Mules are like summen, very cornupt at harte,—I hav known them to be good mules for 6 months, just to git a good chance to kik sumboddy= Josh Billings=

IV and last
Thare iz 2 things in this world
for which we are never fully
prepared, and that iz,—twins.
Jess so, Jess so, Josh Billings.

The next day after Josh gave me the above epigrams, he came and dined with me, and together we smoked and laughed and fixed the following interview :

" Mr. Billings, where were you educated ? "

" Pordunk, Pennsylvania."

" How old are you ? "

" I was born 150 years old—and have been growing young ever since."

" Are you married ? "

" Once."

" How many children have you ? "

" Doublets."

" What other vices have you ? "

" None."

" Have you any virtues ? "

" Several."

" What are they ? "

" I left them up at Poughkeepsie."

" Do you gamble ? "

" When I feel good."

" What is your profession ? "

" Agriculture and alminaxing."

" How do you account for your deficient knowledge in spelling ? "

" Bad spells during infancy, and poor memory."

" What things are you the most liable to forget ? "

" Sermons and debts."

" What professions do you like best ? "

" Auctioneering, base-ball and theology."

" Do you smoke ? "

" Thank you, I'll take a Partaga first."

" What is your worst habit?"

" The coat I got last in Poughkeepsie."

" What are your favorite books?"

" My alminack and Commodore Vanderbilt's pocketbook."

" What is your favorite piece of sculpture?"

" The mile stone nearest home."

" What is your favorite animal?"

" The mule."

" Why?"

" Because he never blunders with his heels."

" What was the best thing said by our old friend Artemus Ward?"

" All the pretty girls in Utah marry *Young*."

" Do you believe in the final salvation of all men?"

" I do—let me pick the men!"

In the evening Josh and I reviewed the interview, and pronounced it faithfully rendered. He wished to add only that Mr. Carleton, who published his alminack, had the most *immense* intellect of this or any other age.

Josh Billings' Lecture.

WIT, PHILOSOPHY AND WISDOM.

This is Josh Billings' last Lecture Programme :

SYNOPSIS OF THE LECTURE BY JOSH.

1—Remarks on Lecturing — General Overture.

2—The Best Thing on Milk.

3—The Summer Resort.

4—Josh on Marriage.

5—Josh on the Mule.

6—The Handsome Man, a Failure.

7—The Dude a Failure.

8—What I know about Hotels.

9—The Bumble-bee.

10—The Hornet.

11—The Quire Singer.

12—Josh on Flirting.

13—Courtin'.

Josh Billings' lecture was unique. It was an hour of short paragraphs, every one worth its weight in gold. The great philosopher always wore long hair (to cover a wart on the back of his neck), and always sat down when he lectured. He delivered his quaint philosophy with his bright eyes looking over his glasses. His lecture was too deep to be popular. It was really the college professor or reflecting judge who fully appreciated him. Think of such paragraphs as these tumbling out once in a minute:

Ladies and Gentlemen:—

I hope you are all well. [Looking over his glasses.]

Thare is lots ov folks who eat well and drink well, and yet are sick all the time. Theze are the folks who alwuz " enjoy poor health."

Then I kno lots ov people whoze only reckomendashun iz, that they are helthy——so iz an onion. [Laughter.]

The subject of my lecture is Milk—plain M-i-l-k.

The best thing I've ever seen on milk is cream. [Laughter.]

That's right [joining]. " People of good sense" are thoze whoze opinyuns agree with ours. [Laughter].

People who agree with you never bore you. The shortest way to a woman's harte iz to praze her baby and her bonnet, and to a man's harte to praze hiz watch, hiz horse and hiz lectur.

Eliar Perkins sez a man iz a bore when he talks so much about himself that you kant talk about yourself. [Laughter.]

Still I shall go on talking.

Comik lekturing iz an unkommon posky thing to do.

It iz more unsarting than the rat ketching bizzness az a means ov grace, or az a means ov livelyhood.

Most enny boddy thinks they kan do it, and this iz jist what makes it so bothersum tew do.

When it iz did jist enuff, it iz a terifick success, but when it iz over-did, it iz like a burnt slapjax, very impertinent.

Thare aint but phew good judges ov humor, and they all differ about it.

If a lekturer trys tew be phunny, he iz like a hoss trying to trot backwards, pretty apt tew trod on himself. [Laughter.]

Humor must fall out ov a man's mouth, like musik out ov a bobalink, or like a yung bird out ov its nest, when it iz feathered enuff to fly.

Whenever a man haz made up hiz mind that he iz a wit, then he iz mistaken without remedy, but whenever the publick haz made up their mind that he haz got the disease, then he haz got it sure.

Individuals never git this thing right, the publik never git it wrong.

Humor iz wit with a rooster's tail feathers stuck in its cap, and wit iz wisdom in tight harness.

If a man is a genuine humorist, he iz superior to the bulk ov hiz audience, and will often hev tew take hiz pay for hiz services in thinking so.

Altho fun iz designed for the millyun, and ethiks for the few, it iz az true az molasses, that most all aujiences hav their bell wethers, people who show the others the crack whare the joke cums laffing in. (Where are they to-night?) [Laughter.]

I hav known popular aujences deprived ov all plezzure during the recital ov a comik lektur, just bekauze the right man, or the right woman, want thare tew point out the mellow places.

The man who iz anxious tew git before an aujience, with what he calls a comik lektur, ought tew be put immediately in the stocks, so that he kant do it, for he iz a dangerous person tew git loose, and will do sum damage.

It iz a very pleazant bizzness tew make people laff, but thare iz much odds whether they laff *at you,* or laff at *what yu say.*

When a man laffs at *yu,* he duz it because it makes him feel superior to you, but when yu pleaze him with what yu have uttered, he admits that yu are superior tew him. [Applause.]

The only reazon whi a monkey alwus kreates a sensashun whareever he goes, is simply bekauze—he is a monkey.

Everyboddy feels az tho they had a right tew criticize a comik lectur, and most ov them do it jist az a mule criticizes things, by shutting up both eyes and letting drive with hiz two behind leggs. [Laughter.]

One ov the meanest things in the comik lektring employment that a man haz to do, iz tew try and make that large class ov hiz aujience laff whom the Lord never intended should laff.

Thare iz sum who laff az eazy and az natral az the birds do, but most ov mankind laff like a hand organ—if yu expect tew git a lively tune out ov it yu hav got tew grind for it.

In delivering a comik lektur it iz a good general rule to stop sudden, sometime before yu git through.

This brings me to Long branch.

Long branch iz a work ov natur, and iz a good job. It iz a summer spot for men, wimmin and children, espeshily the latter. Children are az plenty here, and az sweet az flowers, in an out door gardin. I put up at the Oshun Hotel the last time i was thare, and I put up more than I ought to. Mi wife puts up a good deal with me at the same hotel, it iz an old-fashioned way we have ov doing things. She allways goes with me, to fashionable resorts, whare young widows are enny ways plenty, to put me on mi guard, for i am one ov the easyest creatures on reckord to be impozed upon, espeshily bi yung widders. She is an ornament to her sex, mi wife iz. I would like to see a young widder, or even an old one, git the start ov me, when mi wife iz around. [Laughter.] If I just step out sudden, to get a weak lemonade, to cool mi akeing brow, mi wife goes to the end ov the verandy with me, and waits for me, and if i go down onto the beach to astronomize just a little, all alone, bi moon-lite, she stands on the bluff, like a beakon lite, to warn me ov the breakers.

The biggest thing they hav got at Long branch, for the present, iz the pool ov water, in front ov the hotels. This pool iz sed bi good judges to be 3,000 miles in length, and in sum places 5 miles thick. Into this pool, every day at ten o'klock, the folks all retire, males, females, and widders, promiskuss. The scenery here iz grand, especially the pool, and the air iz az bracing az a milk puntch. Drinks are reasonable here, espeshily out ov the pool, and the last touch ov civilizashun haz reached here also, sum enterprising mishionary haz just opened a klub house, whare all kind ov gambling iz taught.

Long branch iz a healthy place.

Men and women here, if they ain't too lazy, liv sumtimes till they are eighty, and destroy the time a good deal as follows: The fust thirty years they spend in throwing stuns at a mark, the seckond thirty they spend in examining the mark tew see whare the stuns hit, and the remainder is divided in cussing the stun-throwing bizziness, and nussing the rumatizz.

A man never gits to be a fust klass phool until he haz reached seventy years, and falls in luv with a bar maid of 19, and marrys her, and then,— * * * * * Here he took out his Waterbury watch, and remarked, as he wound it up, "You kant do two things to wonst." [Great laughter.]

I luv a Rooster for two things. One iz the crow that iz in him, and the other iz, the spurs that are on him, to bak up the crow with.

There was a little disturbance in the gallery now, and Uncle Josh looked over his glasses and remarked:

"Yung man, please set down, and keep still, yu will hav plenty ov chances yet to make a phool ov yureself before yu die." [Laughter.]

The man or mule who can't do any hurt in this world kan't do any good. [Laughter.]

This brings me to the Mule — the pashunt mule. The mule is pashunt because he is ashamed of hisself. [Laughter.] The mule is haf hoss and haf jackass, and then kums tu a full stop, natur diskovering her mistake. Tha weigh more accordin tu their heft than enny other creeter, except a crowbar. Tha kant heer enny quicker nor further than the hoss, yet their ears are big enuff fur snowshoes. You kan trust them with enny one whose life aint worth more than the mule's. The only way tu keep them into a paster is tu turn them into a medder jineing and let them jump out. [Laughter.] Tha are reddy for use jest as soon as tha will do tu abuse. Tha aint got enny friends, and will live on huckleberry bush, with an akasional chance at Kanada thissels. Tha are a modern invention. Tha sell fur more money than enny other domestic animal. You kant tell their age by looking into their mouth enny more than you could a Mexican cannon. Tha never have no disease that a good club won't heal. If tha ever die tha must come right to life agin, fur I never herd nobody say "ded mule." I never owned one, nor never mean to, unless there is a United States law passed requiring it. I have seen educated mules in a sircuss. Tha could kick and bite tremenjis. . . . Enny man who is willing to drive a mule ought to be exempt by law from running for the legislatur. Tha are the strongest creeters on arth, and heaviest according tu their size. I herd of one who fell oph from the tow-path of the Eri canawl, and sunk as soon as he touched bottom, but he kept on towing the boat tu the next stashun, breathing through his ears, which was out of the water about two feet six inches. I didn't see this did, but Bill Harding told me of it, and I never knew Bill Harding tu lie unless he could make something out of it. There is but one other animal that kan do more kicking than a mule, and that is a Quire Singer. [Laughter.] A quire singer giggles during the sermon and kicks the rest of the week. My advice to quire singers is as follows:

Put your hair in cirl papers every Friday nite soze to have it in good shape Sunday morning. If your daddy is rich you can buy some store hair. If he is very rich buy some more and build it up high onto your head; then get a high-priced bunnit that runs up very high at the high part of it, and get the milliner to plant some high-grown artificials onto the highest part of it. This will help you sing high, as soprano is the highest part.

When the tune is giv out, don't pay attention to it, and then giggle. Giggle a good eel.

Whisper to the girl next you that Em Jones, which sets on the 2nd seet from the front on the left-hand side, has her bunnit with the same color exact she had last year, and then put your book to your face and giggle.

Object to every tune unless there is a solow into it for the soprano. Coff and hem a good eel before you begin to sing.

When you sing a solow shake the artificials off your bunnit, and when you come to a high tone brace yourself back a little, twist your head to one side and open your mouth the widest on that side, shet the eyes on the same side jest a trivhle, and then put in for dear life.

6

When the preacher gets under hed way with his preachin, write a note on the blank leaf into the fourth part of your note book. That's what the blank leaf was made for. Git sumbody to pass the note to sumbody else, and you watch them while they read it, and then giggle. [Laughter.]

If anybody talks or laffs in the congregashun, and the preacher takes notis of it, that's a good chants for you to giggle, and you ought to giggle a great eel. The preacher darsent say any thing to you bekaus you are in the quire, and he can't run the meetin' house at both ends without the quire. If you had a bow before you went into the quire, give him the mitten—you ought to have somebody better now.

Don't forget to giggle.

The quire singer suggests the bumble-bee.

The bumble-bee iz more artistic than the mule and as busy as a quire singer. The bumble-bee iz a kind ov big fly who goes muttering and swearing around the lots during the summer looking after little boys to sting them, and stealing hunny out ov the dandylions and thissells. Like the mule, he iz mad all the time about sumthing, and don't seem to kare a kuss what people think ov him.

A skool boy will studdy harder enny time to find a bumble-bee's nest than he will to get hiz lesson in arithmetik, and when he haz found it, and got the hunny out ov it, and got badly stung into the bargin, he finds thare aint mutch margin in it. Next to poor molassis, bumble-bee hunny iz the poorest kind ov sweetmeats in market. Bumble-bees have allwuss been in fashion, and probably allwuss will be, but whare the fun or proffit lays in them, i never could cypher out. The proffit don't seem to be in the hunny, nor in the bumble-bee neither. They bild their nest in the ground, or enny whare else they take a noshun too, and ain't afrade to fite a whole distrikt skool, if they meddle with them. I don't blame the bumble-bee, nor enny other fellow, for defending hiz sugar: it iz the fust, and last law of natur, and i hope the law won't never run out. The smartest thing about the bumble-bee iz their stinger. [Laughter.]

Speaking of smart things brings me to the hornet:

The hornet is an inflamibel buzzer, sudden in hiz impreshuns and hasty in his conclusion, or end.

Hiz natral disposishen iz a warm cross between red pepper in the pod and fusil oil, and hiz moral bias iz, " git out ov mi way."

They have a long, black boddy, divided in the middle by a waist spot, but their phisikal importance lays at the terminus of their subburb, in the shape ov a javelin.

This javelin iz alwuz loaded, and stands reddy to unload at a minuit's warning, and enters a man az still az thought, az spry az litening, and az full ov melankolly az the toothake.

Hornets never argy a case ; they settle awl ov their differences ov opinyon by letting their javelin fly, and are az certain to hit az a mule iz.

This testy kritter lives in congregations numbering about 100 souls, but whether they are mail or female, or conservative, or matched in bonds ov wedlock, or whether they are Mormons, and a good many ov them kling together and keep one husband to save expense, I don't kno nor don't kare.

I never have examined their habits much, I never konsidered it healthy.

Hornets build their nests wherever they take a noshun to, and seldom are disturbed, for what would it profit a man tew kill 99 hornets and hav the 100th one hit him with hiz javelin? [Laughter.]

They bild their nests ov paper, without enny windows to them or back doors. They have but one place ov admission, and the nest iz the shape ov an overgrown pineapple, and is cut up into just as many bed-rooms as there iz hornets.

It iz very simple to make a hornets' nest if yu kan [Laughter] but i will wager enny man 300 dollars he kant bild one that he could sell to a hornet for half price.

Hornets are as bizzy as their second couzins, the bee, but what they are about the Lord only knows; they don't lay up enny honey, nor enny moncy; they seem to be bizzy only jist for the sake ov working all the time; they are alwus in as mutch ov a hurry as tho they waz going for a dokter.

I suppose this uneasy world would grind around on its axle-tree onst in 24 hours, even ef thare want enny hornets, but hornets must be good for sumthing, but I kant think now what it iz.

Thare haint been a bug made yet in vain, nor one that want a good job; there is ever lots of human men loafing around blacksmith shops, and cider mills, all over the country, that don't seem to be necessary for anything but to beg plug tobacco and swear, and steal water melons, but yu let the cholera break out once, and then yu will see the wisdom of having jist sich men laying around; they help count. [Laughter.]

Next tew the cockroach, who stands tew the head, the hornet haz got the most waste stummuk, in reference tew the rest of hiz boddy, than any of the insek populashun, and here iz another mystery; what on 'arth duz a hornet want so much reserved corps for?

I hav jist thought — tew carry his javelin in; thus yu see, the more we diskover about things the more we are apt to know.

It iz always a good purchase tew pay out our last surviving dollar for wisdum, and wisdum iz like the misterious hen's egg; it ain't laid in yure hand, but iz laid away under the barn, and yu have got to sarch for it.

The hornet iz an unsoshall kuss, he iz more haughty than he is proud, he is a thorough-bred bug, but his breeding and refinement has made him like sum other folks I know ov, dissatisfied with himself and every boddy else, too much good breeding ackts this way sometimes.

Hornets are long-lived — I kant state jist how long their lives are, but I know from instinkt and observashen that enny krittur, be he bug or be he devil, who iz mad all the time, and stings every good chance he kan git, generally outlives all his nabers.

The only good way tew git at the exact fiteing weight of the hornet is tew tutch him, let him hit you once with his javelin, and you will be willing to testify in court that somebody run a one-tined pitchfork into yer; and as for grit, i will state for the informashun of thoze who haven't had a chance tew lay in their vermin wisdum az freely az I hav, that one single hornet, who feels well, will brake up a large camp-meeting. [Laughter.]

What the hornets do for amuzement is another question i kant answer, but sum ov the best read and heavyest thinkers among the naturalists say they have target excursions, and heave their javelins at a mark ; but I don't imbide this assershun raw, for i never knu enny body so bitter at heart as the hornets are, to waste a blow.

Thare iz one thing that a hornet duz that i will give him credit for on my books—he alwuz attends tew his own bizziness, and won't allow any boddy else tew attend tew it, and what he duz iz alwuz a good job; you never see them altering enny thing; if they make enny mistakes, it is after dark, and aint seen.

If the hornets made half az menny blunders az the men do, even with their javelins, every boddy would laff at them.

Hornets are clear in another way, they hav found out, by trieing it, that all they can git in this world, and brag on, is their vittles and clothes, and yu never see one standing on the corner ov a street, with a twenty-six inch face on, bekause sum bank had run oph and took their money with him.

In ending oph this essa, I will cum tew a stop by concluding, that if hornets was a little more pensive, and not so darned peremptory with their javelins, they might be guilty of less wisdom, but more charity.

This brings me to Flirts.

Flirts are like hornets, only men like to be stung by them.

Some old bachelors git after a flirt, and don't travel as fast as she doz, and then concludes awl the female group are hard to ketch, and good for nothing when they are ketched.

A flirt is a rough thing to overhaul unless the right dog gets after her, and then they make the very best of wives.

When a flirt really is in love, she is as powerless as a mown daisy. [Laughter.]

Her impudence then changes into modesty, her cunning into fears, her spurs into a halter, and her pruning-hook into a cradle.

The best way to ketch a flirt is tew travel the other way from which they are going, or sit down on the ground and whistle some lively tune till the flirt comes round. [Laughter.]

Old bachelors make the flirts and then the flirts get more than even, by making the old bachelors.

A majority of flirts get married finally, for they hev a great quantity of the most dainty tidbits of woman's nature, and alwus have shrewdness to back up their sweetness.

Flirts don't deal in po'try and water grewel; they have got to hev brains, or else somebody would trade them out of their capital at the first sweep.

Disappointed luv must uv course be oll on one side ; this ain't any more excuse fur being an old bachelor than it iz fur a man to quit all kinds of manual labor, jist out uv spite, and jine a poor-house bekase he kant lift a tun at one pop.

An old bachelor will brag about his freedom to you, his relief from anxiety, hiz indipendence. This iz a dead beat, past resurrection, for everybody knows there ain't a more anxious dupe than he iz. All his dreams are charcoal sketches of boarding-school misses ; he dresses, greases hiz hair, paints his grizzly mustache, cultivates bunyons and corns, to please his captains, the wimmen, and only gets laffed at fur hiz pains.

I tried being an old bachelor till I wuz about twenty years old, and came very near dieing a dozen times. I had more sharp pain in one year than I hev had since, put it all in a heap. I was in a lively fever all the time.

I have preached to you about flirts (phemale), and now I will tell you about Dandies.

The first dandy was made by Dame Nature, out of the refuse matter left from making Adam and Eve. He was concocted with a bouquet in one hand and a looking-glass in the other. His heart was dissected in the thirteenth century, and found to be a pincushion full of butterflies and sawdust. He never falls in love, for to love requires both brains and a soul, and the dandy has neither. He is a long-lived bird ; he has no courage, never marries, has no virtues, and is never guilty of first-class vices.

What about Marriage?

They say love iz blind, but a good many fellows see more in their sweethearts than I can.

Marriage is a fair transaction on the face ov it.

But thare iz quite too often put-up jobs in it.

It is an old institushun—older than the Pyramids, and az phull ov hyrogliphics that nobody can parse.

History holds its tongue who the pair waz who fust put on the silken harness, and promised to work kind in it, thru thick and thin, up hill and down, and on the level, rain or shine, survive of perish, sink or swim, drown or flote.

But whoever they waz, they must hev made a good thing out of it, or so menny ov their posterity would not hev harnessed up since and drove out.

Thare iz a grate moral grip to marriage; it iz the mortar that holds the sooshul bricks together.

But thare ain't but darn few pholks who put their money in matrimony who could set down and give a good written opinyun whi on airth they come to did it.

This iz a grate proof that it iz one ov them natral kind ov acksidents that must happen, jist az birdz fly out ov the nest, when they hev featherz enuff, without being able tew tell why.

Sum marry for buty, and never diskover their mistake: this is lucky.

Sum marry for money, and don't see it.

Sum marry for pedigree, and feel big for six months; and then very sensibly cum tew the conclusion that pedigree ain't no better than skim-milk.

Sum marry bekawze they hev been highsted sum whare else; this iz a cross match, a bay and a sorrel: pride may make it endurable.

Sum marry for luv, without a cent in their pockets, nor a friend in the world, nor a drop ov pedigree. This looks desperate, *but it iz the strength of the game.*

If marrying for luv aint a success, then matrimony is a ded beet.

Sum marry because they think wimmen will be scarce next year, and live tew wonder how the crop holdz out.

Sum marry tew get rid ov themselves, and discover that the game waz one that two could play at, and neither win.

Sum marry the second time tew get even, and find it a gambling game—the more they put down the less they take up.

Sum marry, tew be happy, and, not finding it, wonder where all the happiness goes to when it dies.

Sum marry, they can't tell why, and live they can't tell how.

Almost every boddy gets married, and it is a good joke.

Sum marry in haste, and then sit down and think it carefully over.

Sum think it over careful fust, and then set down and marry.

Both ways are right, if they hit the mark.

Sum marry rakes tew convert them. This iz a little risky, and takes a smart missionary to do it.

Sum marry coquetts. This iz like buying a poor farm heavily mortgaged, and working the balance of your days to clear oph the mortgages.

Married life haz its chances, and this iz just what gives it its flavor. Every boddy luvs tew phool with the chances, bekawze every boddy expekts tew win. But I am authorized tew state that every boddy don't win.

But, after all, married life iz full az certain az the dry goods bizness.

Kno man kan tell jist what calico haz made up its mind tew do next.

Calico don't kno even herself.

Dry goods ov all kinds iz the child ov circumstansis.

Sum never marry, but this iz jist ez risky; the diseaze iz the same, with another name to.

The man who stands on the banks shivering, and dassent, iz more apt tew ketch cold than him who pitches hiz head fust into the river.

Thare iz but few who never marry bekawze they *won't*—they all hanker, and most ov them starve with bread before them (spread on both sides), jist for the lack ov grit.

Marry young! iz mi motto.

I hev tried it, and I know what I am talking about.

If enny boddy asks you whi you got married (if it needs be), tell him *"yu don't recollekt."*

Marriage iz a safe way to gamble—if yu win, yu win a pile, and if yu loze, yu don't loze enny thing, only the privilege of living dismally alone and soaking your own feet.

I repeat it, in italics, *marry young!*

Thare iz but one good excuse for a marriage late in life, and that is —*a second marriage.*

When you are married, don't swap with your mother-in-law, unless yu kin afford to give her the big end of the trade. Say "how are you" to every boddy. Kultivate modesty, but mind and keep a good stock of impudence on hand. Be charitable—three-cent pieces were made on purpose. It costs more to borry than it does to buy. Ef a man flatters yu, yu can kalkerlate he is a roge, or yu are a fule. Be more auxus about the pedigree yur going to leave than yu are about the wun somebody's going to leave you. Sin is like weeds—self-sone and sure to cum. Two lovers, like two armies, generally get along quietly until they are engaged.

I will now give young men my advice about getting married.

Find a girl that iz 19 years old last May, about the right hight, with a blue eye, and dark-brown hair and white teeth.

Let the girl be good to look at, not too phond of musik, a firm disbeleaver in ghosts, and one ov six children in the same family.

Look well tew the karakter ov her father ; see that he is not the member ov enny klub, don't bet on elekshuns, and gits shaved at least 3 times a week.

Find out all about her mother, see if she haz got a heap ov good common sense, studdy well her likes and dislikes, eat sum ov her hum-made bread and apple dumplins, notiss whether she abuzes all ov her nabors, and don't fail tew observe whether her dresses are last year's ones fixt over.

If you are satisfied that the mother would make the right kind ov a mother-in-law, yu kan safely konklude that the dauter would make the right kind of a wife. [Applause.]

What about courtin'?

Courting is a luxury, it is sallad, it is ise water, it is a beveridge, it is the pla spell ov the soul.

The man who has never courted haz lived in vain; he haz bin a blind man amung landskapes and waterskapes ; he has bin a deff man in the land ov hand orgins, and by the side ov murmuring canals. [Laughter.]

Courting iz like 2 little springs ov soft water that steal out from under a rock at the fut ov a mountain and run down the hill side by side singing and dansing and spatering each uther, eddying and frothing and kaskading, now hiding under bank, now full ov sun and now full of shadder, till bime by tha jine and then tha go slow. [Laughter.]

I am in favor ov long courting ; it gives the parties a chance to find out each uther's trump kards; it iz good exercise, and is jist as innersent as 2 merino lambs.

Courting iz like strawberries and cream, wants tew be did slow, then yu git the flavor.

Az a ginral thing i wouldn't brag on uther gals mutch when i waz courting, it mite look az tho yu knu tew mutch.

If yu will court 3 years in this wa, awl the time on the square, if yu don't sa it iz a leettle the slikest time in yure life, yu kan git measured for a hat at my expense, and pa for it.

Don't court for munny, nor buty, nor relashuns, theze things are jist about az onsartin as the kerosene ile refining bissness, libel tew git out ov repair and bust at enny minnit.

Court a gal for fun, for the luv yu bear her, for the vartue and bissness thare is in her; court her for a wife and for a mother; court her as yu wud court a farm — for the strength ov the sile and the parfeckshun ov the title; court her as tho' she want a fule, and yu a nuther; court her in the kitchen, in the parlor, over the wash tub, and at the pianner; court this wa, yung man, and if yu don't git a good wife and she don't git a good hustband, the falt won't be in the courting.

Yung man, yu kan rely upon Josh Billings, and if yu kant make these rules wurk, jist send for him, and he will sho yu how the thing is did, and it shant kost you a cent.

I will now give the following Advice to Lecture Committees outside of this town:

1. Don't hire enny man tew lectur for yu (never mind how moral he iz) unless yu kan make munny on him.

2. Selekt 10 ov yure best lookin and most talking members tew meet the lekturer at the depot.

3. Don't fail tew tell the lekturer at least 14 times on yure way from the depot tew the hotel that yu hav got the smartest town in kreashun, and sevral men in it that are wuth over a millyun.

4. When yu reach the hotel introduce the lekturer immejiately to at least 25 ov yure fust-klass citizens, if you hav tew send out for them.

5. When the lekturer's room iz reddy go with him in masse to hiz room and remind him 4 or 5 more times that yu had over 3 thousand people in yure city at the last censuss, and are a talking about having an opera house.

6. Don't leave the lekturer alone in his room over 15 minits at once; he might take a drink out ov his flask on the sli if yu did.

7. When yu introjuce the lekturer tew the aujience don't fail tew make a speech ten or twelve feet long, occupying a haff an hour, and if yu kan ring in sumthing about the growth ov yure butiful sitty, so mutch the better. [Laughter.]

8. Always seat 9 or 10 ov the kommitty on the stage, and then if it iz a kommik lektur, and the kommitty don't laff a good deal, the aujience will konklude that the lektur iz a failure; and if they do laff a good deal, the aujience will konklude they are stool-pigeons. [Laughter.]

9. Jist az soon az the lectur is thru bring 75 or 80 ov the richest ov yure populashun up onto the stage and let them squeeze the hand and exchange talk with the lekturer.

10. Go with the lekturer from the hall tew hiz room in a bunch, and remind him once or twice more on the way that yure sitty iz a growing very rapidly, and ask him if he don't think so.

11. If the lekturer should inquire how the comik lekturers had succeeded who had preceded him, don't forget tew tell him that they were all failures. This will enable him tew guess what they will say about him just az soon az he gits out ov town. [Laughter.]

12. If the lekturer's fee should be a hundred dollars or more, don't hesitate tew pay him next morning, about 5 minnits before the train leaves, in old, lop-eared one-dollar bills, with a liberal sandwitching ov tobbakko-stained shinplasters.

13. I forgot tew say that the fust thing yu should tell a lekturer, after yu had sufficiently informed him ov the immense growth ov yure citty, iz that yure people are not edukated up tew lekturs yet, but are grate on nigger-minstrels.

14. Never fail tew ask the lekturer whare he finds the most appreshiated aujiences, and he won't fail tew tell yu (if he iz an honest man) that thare ain't no state in the Union that begins tew kompare with yures.

15. Let 15 or 20 ov yure kommitty go with the lekturer, next morning, tew the kars, and az each one shakes hands with him with a kind ov deth grip, don't forget tew state that yure citty iz growing very mutch in people.

16. If the night iz wet, and the inkum ov the house won't pay expenses, don't hesitate tew make it pay by taking a chunk out ov the lekturer's fee. The lekturers all like this, but they are too modest, as a klass, tew say so.

17. I know ov several other good rules tew follow, but the abuv will do tew begin with.

Your Schoolmaster will tell you the rest.

Thare iz one man in this world to whom i alwus take oph mi hat, and remain uncovered untill he gits safely by, and that iz the distrikt skoolmaster.

When I meet him, I look upon him az a martyr just returning from the stake, or on hiz way thare tew be cooked.

He leads a more lonesum and single life than an old bachelor, and a more anxious one than an old maid.

He iz remembered jist about az long and affektionately az a gide board iz by a traveling pack pedlar.

If he undertakes tew make his skollars luv him, the chances are he will neglekt their larning; and if he don't lick them now and then pretty often, they will soon lick him. [Laughter.]

The distrikt skoolmaster hain't got a friend on the flat side ov earth. The boys snow-ball him during recess; the girls put water in hiz hair die; and the skool committee make him work for haff the money a bartender gits, and board him around the naberhood, whare they giv him rhy coffee, sweetened with mollassis, tew drink, and kodfish bawls 3 times a day for vittles. [Laughter.]

And, with all this abuse, I never heard ov a distrikt skoolmaster swareing enny thing louder than — *Condem it.*

Don't talk tew me about the pashunce ov anshunt Job.

Job had pretty plenty ov biles all over him, no doubt, but they were all ov one breed.

Every yung one in a distrikt skool iz a bile ov a diffrent breed, and each one needs a diffrent kind ov poultiss tew git a good head on them.

A distrikt skoolmaster, who duz a square job and takes hiz codfish bawls reverently, iz a better man to-day tew hav lieing around loose than Solomon would be arrayed in all ov hiz glory.

Soloman waz better at writing proverbs and manageing a large family, than he would be tew navigate a distrikt skool hous.

Enny man who haz kept a distrikt skool for ten years, and boarded around the naberhood, ought tew be made a mager gineral, and hav a penshun for the rest ov his natral days, and a hoss and waggin tew do hiz going around in.

But, az a genral consequence, a distrikt skoolmaster hain't got any more warm friends than an old blind fox houn haz.

He iz jist about az welkum az a tax gatherer iz.

He iz respekted a good deal az a man iz whom we owe a debt ov 50 dollars to and don't mean tew pay.

He goes through life on a back road, az poor az a wood sled, and finally iz missed — but what ever bekums ov hiz remains, i kant tell.

Fortunately he iz not often a sensitive man; if he waz, he couldn't enny more keep a distrikt skool than he could file a kross kut saw. [Laughter.]

Whi iz it that theze men and wimmen, who pashuntly and with crazed brain teach our remorseless brats the tejus meaning ov the alphabet, who take the fust welding heat on their destinys, who lay the stepping stones and enkurrage them tew mount upwards, who hav dun more hard and mean work than enny klass on the futstool, who have prayed over the reprobate, strengthened the timid, restrained the outrageous, and flattered the imbecile, who hav lived on kodfish and vile coffee, and hain't been heard to sware — whi iz it that they are treated like a vagrant fiddler, danced to for a night, paid oph in the morning, and eagerly forgotten.

I had rather burn a coal pit, or keep the flys out ov a butcher's shop in the month ov August, than meddle with the distrikt skool bizzness. [Applause.]

I propose now to close by making Twelve Square Remarks, to-wit:

1. A broken reputashun iz like a broken vase; it may be mended, but allways shows where the krak was.

2. If you kant trust a man for the full amount, let him skip.   This trying to git an average on honesty haz allways bin a failure.

3. Thare iz no treachery in silence; silence is a hard argument to beat.

4. Don't mistake habits for karacter.   The men ov the most karacter hav the fewest habits.

5. Thare iz cheats in all things; even pizen is adulterated.

6. The man who iz thoroughly polite iz 2-thirds ov a Christian, enny how.

7. Kindness iz an instinkt, politeness only an art.

8. Thare iz a great deal ov learning in this world, which iz nothing more than trying to prove what we don't understand.

9. Mi dear boy, thare are but few who kan kommence at the middle ov the ladder and reach the top; and probably you and I don't belong to that number.

10. One ov the biggest mistakes made yet iz made by the man who thinks he iz temperate, just becauze he puts more water in his whiskey than his nabor does.

11. The best medicine I know ov for the rumatism iz to thank the Lord—that it aint the gout. [Laughter.]

12. Remember the poor.   It costs nothing. [Laughter.]

JOSH BILLINGS' AULMINAX.

Mr. Shaw had a wonderful success with his burlesque **almanac.** He sold hundreds of thousands of copies, and it was always reproduced in England. He generally dedicated the almanac to some business house for $500 in cash, and got his money for it. Below are Uncle Josh's weather predictions for March:

March begins on Saturday, and hangs out for 31 days.

Saturday, 1st.—Sum wind; look out for squalls, and pack peddlers; munny iz tight, so are briks. Ben Jonson had his boots tapped 1574; eggs a dollar a piece, hens on a strike; mercury 45 degrees above zero; snow, mixed with wind.

Sunday, 2nd.—Horace Greeley preaches in Grace church; text, "the gentleman in black;" wind northwest, with simptoms of dust; hen strike continues; the ringleaders are finally arrested and sent to pot; eggs eazier.

Monday, 3rd.—Big wind; omnibus, with 17 passengers inside, blown over in Broadway; sow lettuce, and sow on buttons; about these days look out for wind; Augustus Ceazer sighns the tempranse pledge 1286; strong simptoms ov spring; blue birds and organ grinders make their appearance; sun sets in wind.

Tuesday, 4th.—Augustus Ceazer breaks the pledge 1286; "put not you trust in kings and princes;" much wind with rain; a whole lot ov naughty children destroyed in Mercer street by wind; several gusts ov wind; buckwheat slapjacks invented 1745; Andy Johnson commits suicide; grate failure in Wall street; the Bulls fail tew inflate Erie; windy.

Wenesday, 5th.—A good day tew set a hen; mutch wind; "he that spareth the child, hateth the rod;" wind raises awnings, and hoop skirts; William Seward resigns in favor ov Fernando Would; Thad Stevens jines the Mormons.

Thursday, 6th.—Wind generally, accompanied with wind from the east; the Black Crook still rages; more wind; whisky hots still in favor ov the seller; sow peas and punkin pies, for arly sass; babes in the woods born 1600; wind threatens.

Friday, 7th.—Fred Douglass nominated for president by the demokrats; black clouds in the west; wind brewing; grate scare in Nassau street; a man runs over a horce; Docktors Pug and Bug in immediate attendance; horce not expekted tew live. Rain and snow and wind and mud, about equally mixt.

Saturday, 8th.—Horce more easier this morning; mint julips offered, but no takers. About these days expect wind; wind from the northwest; a good day for wind mills. Half-past 5 o'clock, P. M., the following notis appears on all the bulletin boards: "Doctor Pug thinks the horce, with the most skillful treatment at the hands ov the attendant physicians, may possibly be rendered suitable for a clam wagon, and Doctor Bug corroborates Pug, *provided*, the oleaginous dipthong that connects the parodial glysses with the nervaqular episode is not displaced; if so, the most consumit skill ov the profeshion will be requisite to restore a secondary unity." Later—"The horce has been turned out tew grass."

Sunday, 9th.—This is the Sabbath, a day that our fathers thought a good deal ov. Mutch wind (in some ov the churches); streets lively, bissiness good; prize fight on the palisades; police reach the ground after the fight is aul over, and arrest the ropes and the ring. Wind sutherly; a lager-beer spring discovered just out ov the limits ov the city; millions are flocking out to see it.

Monday, 10th.—A gale, mile stuns are torn up bi the rutes; fight for 700 dollars and the belt, at Red Bank, Nu Jersey, between two well known roosters; oysters fust eaten on the half shell 1342, by Don Bivalvo, an Irish Duke; sun sets in the west.

Tuesday, 11th.—Roosters still fighting; indications ov wind; counterfeit Tens in circulashun on the Faro Bank; look out for them; milk only 15 cents a quart; thank the Lord, "the good time" has finally come; Don Quixot fights his first wind mill, 1510, at short range, and got whipped the second round; time, 14 minnits.

9:30 P. M.—Torch-lite procession at Red Bank, in honor ov the winning rooster.

Wednesday, 12th.—Sum wind, with wet showers; showers smell strong ov dandy-lions and grass; gold, 132 17-16; exchange on Brooklin and Williamsburgh, one cent (by the ferry boats).

Thursday, 13th.—Bad day for the aulminak bissiness; no nuze; no wind; no cards; no nothing.

Friday, 14th.—Wendal Phillips tares up the constitushun ov the United States; "alas! poor Yorick;" rain from abuv; strawberries, watermillions and peaches git-ting skase; rain continners, accompanied with thunder and slight moister; mercury abuv zero.

Saturday, 15th.—Grate fraud diskovered in the custom house—3 dollars missing; fifty subordinates suspended; a wet rain sets in; robbins cum, and immediately begin tew enquire for sum cherrys.

Sunday, 16th.—Henry W. Beecher preaches in Brooklyn by partickular request; dandylions in market, only 15 cents a head.

Monday, 17th.—Plant sum beans; plant them deep; if yu don't they will be sure tew cum up. Robinson Cruso born 1515, all alone, on a destitute iland. Warm rain, mixt with wind; woodchucks cum out ov their holes and begin tew chuck a little.

Tuesday, 18th.—Look out for rain and yu will be apt tew see it; wind sow by sow west; ice discovered in our Rushion purchiss; miners rushing that way; geese are seen marching in single phile, a sure indicashun ov the cholera; musketose invented by George Tucker, Esq., 1491; patent applied for, but refused, on the ground that they might bight sumboddy.

Wenesday, 19th.—A mare's nest discovered in Ontary county; a warm and slightly liquid rain; thousands ov people hav visited the nest; windy; the old mare is dredful cross and kickful; hens average an egg a day, beside several cackels.

Thursday, 20th.—Appearance ov rain; plant corn for early whiskey; frogs hold their fust concert—Ole Bullfrog musical direcktor—matinee every afternoon; snakes are caught wriggling (an old trick ov theirs); a warm and muggy night; yu can hear the bullheads bark; United States buys the iland ov Great Britain.

NIGGERS DON'T KNOW ENOUGH TO VOTE.

See page 69.

"PETROLEUM V. NASBY."

BIOGRAPHY AND REMINISCENCES.

David Ross Locke was born in Vestal, Broome county, N. Y., in 1833, and died in New York City in 1888. He is sometimes called a humorist, but he always pre ferred to be called a satirist. He was the Cervantes of America. His mission was to exaggerate error, and make it odious.

Mr. Nasby's political influence was so great that National Committees waited upon him for advice, and Presidential candidates were glad to listen to his words of counsel.

The satirist published several books, all of which had an immense sale. He died leaving an estate in Toledo worth more than a million of dollars, besides his great newspaper, *The Toledo Blade*, now edited by his son. He left an accomplished wife and a family of gifted children, who well do honor to the man whom President Lincoln envied.

One day, speaking of satire, the gifted man said to me:

"I can kill more error by exaggerating vice than by abusing it. In all my writings I have not said one unkind word about any people or party. I have simply exaggerated errors in politics, love and religion, until the people saw these errors, and rose up against them. The humorist would describe 'Deeken Pogram' and 'Joe Bigler,' of the 'Confedrit X Roads,' just as they are. That would have caused laughter; but I exaggerated these characters, as Cervantes exaggerated Don Quixote, and made them ridiculous."

Charles Sumner, in his introduction to Nasby's great book, said: "President Lincoln read every letter from Nasby's pen."

Mr. Nasby's satires have always been directed against such evils as slavery, intemperance and partisan suffrage. He has always maintained the true democracy, that one man is as good as another if he is as clean and as well educated.

"One day," said Nasby, "a poor ignorant white man came to the polls in Kentucky to vote.

" 'I wish you would oblige me by voting this ticket,' said a light-colored mulatto, who was standing near the polls.

" 'What kind of ticket is it?' asked the poor white man.

" 'Why,' said the mulatto ' you can see for yourself.'

" ' But I can't read.'

" 'What! can't you read the ballot you have there in your hand, which you are about to vote?' exclaimed the colored man.

" ' No,' said he ' I can't read at all.'

" 'Well,' said the colored man, ' this ballot means that you are in favor of the fifteenth amendment giving equal franchise to both white and colored citizens.'

" ' It means to let the nigger vote, does it?'

" ' Yes sir.'

" 'Then I don't want it. *Niggers don't know enough to vote!*' "

Of late years Mr. Nasby did all of his writing on a type-writer which he took with him on the cars. While the train was going forty miles an hour he would write those cross-road letters which have made him famous. One day I wrote to him for his autograph, for Sam Cox, who wanted it to sell at a fair. Mr. Cox screamed with laughter when the autograph came written by a type-writer!

Our engraver reproduces it in *fac simile.*

The Toledo Blade.

TOLEDO, O.29,____NOV. 29,_____1883,

DEAR LANDON:—

ENCLOSED FIND MY AUTOGRAPH.

I WAS MINDED TO WRITE IT WITH MY MACHINE.

SOME THOUSANDS OF YEARS HENCE IT WILL HAVE A VALUE,

WISHING YOU SUCCESS, I AM

TRULY,

D. R. LOCKE,

Mr. Locke meant this as a joke, for in a day or two came his real autograph, the one attached to his picture, and this note:

Dear Eli: My father's *nom de plume* I hardly think has any particular significance The word " Nasby" was coined probably from a remembrance of the battle of Naseby. About the time the Nasby letters were commenced in the *Toledo Blade,* the petroleum excitement was raging in Pennsylvania, and Vesuvius was used for euphony. Father never gave any other explanation of this pseudonym than the above.

ROBINSON LOCKE.

The best monument that Mr. Locke's sons can rear to their distinguished father is to foster the great newspaper which he established, and they are doing it.

When asked about Lincoln's love for Nasby, the senator said:

"I once called on the President late in the evening of March 17, 1865. We had a long talk in his private office, at the White House, which lasted till midnight. As I rose to go he said:

"'Come to me when I open shop in the morning; I will have the order written, and you shall see it.'

"'When do you open shop?' I asked.

"'At nine o'clock,' he replied.

"At the hour named I was in the same room that I had so recently left. Very soon the President entered, stepping quickly with the promised order in his hands, which he at once read to me. It was to disapprove and annul the judgment and sentence of a court martial in a case that had excited much feeling. While I was making an abstract of the order for communication by telegraph to the anxious parties, he broke into quotation from Nasby. Finding me less at home than himself with his favorite humorist, he said pleasantly.

"'I must initiate you,' and then repeated with enthusiasm the message he had sent to Mr. Nasby: 'For the genius to write these things I would gladly give up my office.'

"A few weeks after this, April 14th," said Mr. Sumner, "the bullet from the pistol of J. Wilkes Booth took the great President's life."

NASBY'S LECTURE
ON
THE WOMAN QUESTION.

Ladies and Gentlemen:—I adore woman. I recognize the importance of the sex, and lay at its feet my humble tribute. But for woman, where would we have been? Who in our infancy washed our faces, fed us soothing syrup and taught us "How doth the little busy bee?"

Woman!

To whom did we give red apples in our boyhood? For whom did we part our hair behind, and wear No. 7 boots when No. 10's would have been more comfortable? [Laughter.] And with whom did we sit up nights, in the hair-oil period of our existence? And, finally, whom did we marry? But for woman what would the novelists have done? What would have become of Sylvanus Cobb, Jr., if he had had no women to make heroines of? And without Sylvanus Cobb, Bonner could not have made *The Ledger* a success; Everett would be remembered not as the man who wrote for *The Ledger*, but merely as an orator and statesman; Beecher never would have written " Norwood," and Dexter might to-day have been chafing under the collar in a dray! But for woman George Washington would not have been the father of his country; the Sunday-school teachers would have been short the affecting story of the little hatchet and the cherry tree, and half the babies in the country would have been named after some one else. Possibly they might have all been Smiths. But for woman Andrew Johnson never would have been, and future generations would have lost the most awful example of depravity the world has ever seen. I adore woman, but I want her to keep her place. I don't want woman to be the coming man. [Laughter.]

In considering this woman question, I occupy the conservative stand-point. I find that, from the most gray-headed times, one-half of the human race have lived and moved by the grace and favor of the other half. From the beginning woman has occupied a dependent position, and has been only what man has made her. The Turks, logical fellows, denied her a soul, and made of her an object of barter and sale; the American Indians made of her a beast of burden. In America, since we extended the area of civilization by butchering the Indians, we have copied both. [Laughter.] In the higher walks of life she is a toy to be played with, and is bought and sold; in the lower strata she bears the burdens and does the drudgery of servants, without the ameliorating conditions that make other servitude tolerable and possible to be borne. But I am sure that her present condition is her proper condition, for it always has been so.

Adam subjugated Eve at the beginning, and, following precedent, Cain subjugated his wife. Mrs. Cain, not being an original thinker, imitated her mother-in-law, who probably lived with them, and made it warm for her, [Laughter] as is the custom of mothers-in-law, and the precedent being established, it has been so ever since. I reject with scorn the idea advanced by a schoolmistress, that Eve was an inferior woman, and therefore submitted; and that Eve's being an inferior woman was no reason for classing all her daughters with her.

"Had I been Eve," she remarked, "I would have made a different precedent!" and I rather think she would.

The first record we have of man and woman is in the first chapter of Genesis. "So God created man in his own image. And he made man of the dust of the earth." In the second chapter we have a record of the making of woman by taking a rib from man. Man, it will be observed, was created first, showing conclusively that he was intended to take precedence of woman. This woman, to whom I referred a moment since, denied the correctness of the conclusion. Man was made first, woman afterward — isn't it reasonable to suppose that the last creation was the best? "If there is any thing in being first," she continued, "man must acknowledge the supremacy of the goose, for the fowl is first mentioned." [Laughter.] And she argued further: "Man was made of the dust of the earth, the lowest form of matter; woman was made of man, the highest and most perfect form. It is clear that woman must be the better, for she was made of better material!" [Laughter.] But, of course, I look upon this as mere sophistry.

I attempted to trace the relative condition of the sexes from the creation down to the fall of man, but the Bible is silent upon the subject, and the files of the newspapers of the period were doubtless all destroyed in the flood. I have not been able to find that any have been preserved in the public libraries of the country. But it is to be presumed that they lived upon precisely the terms that they do now. I shall assume that Eve was merely the domestic servant of Adam — that she rose in the morning, careful not to disturb his slumbers — that she cooked his breakfast, called him affectionately when it was quite ready, waited upon him at table, arranged his shaving implements ready to his hand, saw him properly dressed — after which she washed the dishes, and amused herself darning his torn fig leaves till the time arrived to prepare dinner, and so on till nightfall, after which time she improved her mind, and, before Master Cain was born, slept. She did not even keep a kitchen girl; at least I find no record of any thing of the kind. Probably at that time the emigration from Ireland was setting in other directions, and help was hard to get. That she was a good wife, and a contented one, I do not doubt. I find no record in the Scriptures of her throwing tea-pots, or chairs, or brooms, or any thing of the sort at Adam's head, nor is it put down that at any time she intimated a desire for a divorce, which proves conclusively that the Garden of Eden was not located in the State of Indiana. But I judge that Adam was a good, kind husband. He did not go to his club at night, for, as near as I can learn, he had no club. His son Cain had one, however, [Laughter] as his other son, Abel, discovered.

I am certain that he did not insist on smoking cigars in the back parlor, making the curtains smell. I do not know that these things are so; but as mankind does to-day what mankind did centuries ago, it is reasonable to assume, when we don't know any thing about it, that what is done to-day was done centuries ago. The bulk of mankind have learned nothing since Adam's time. Eve's duties were not as trying as those piled upon her daughters. As compared with the fashionable women of to-day, her lot was less perplexing. Society was not so exacting in her time. She had no calls to make, or parties to give and attend. Her toilet was much simpler, and did not require the entire resources of her intellect. If her situation is compared with that of the wives of poorer men, it will be found to be better. They had no meat to dress, flour to knead, or bread to bake. The trees bore fruit, which were to be had for the picking; and as they were strict vegetarians, it sufficed. I have wished that her taste in fruit had been more easily satisfied, for her unfortunate craving after one particular variety brought me into trouble. But I have forgiven her. I shall never reproach her for this. She is dead, alas! and let her one fault lie undisturbed in the grave with her. It is well that Eve died when she did. It would have broken her heart had she lived to see how the most of her family turned out. [Laughter.]

I insist, however, that what labor of a domestic nature was done, she did. She picked the fruit, pared it and stewed it, like a dutiful wife. She was no strong-minded female, and never got out of her legitimate sphere. I have searched the book of Genesis faithfully, and I defy any one to find it recorded therein that Eve ever made a public speech, or expressed any desire to preach, practice law or medicine, or sit in the legislature of her native State. What a crushing, withering, scathing, blasting rebuke to the Dickinsons, Stantons, Blackwells and Anthonys of this degenerate day.

I find in the Bible many arguments against the equality of woman with man in point of intellectual power. The serpent tempted Eve, not Adam. Why did he select Eve? Ah, why, indeed! Whatever else may be said of Satan, no one will, I think, question his ability! I do not stand here as his champion or even apologist; in fact, I am willing to admit that in many instances his behavior has been ungentlemanly, but no one will deny that he is a most consummate judge of character, and that he has never failed to select for his work the most fitting instruments. When America was to be betrayed the first time, Satan selected Arnold; and when the second betrayal of the Republic was determined upon, he knew where Jefferson Davis, Floyd and Buchanan lived. When there is a fearful piece of jobbery to get through Congress or the New York legislature, he never fails to select precisely the right persons for the villainy. Possibly he is not entitled to credit for discrimination in these last-mentioned bodies, for he could not very well go wrong. He could find instruments in either, with both hands tied and blindfolded. But this is a digression. Why did Satan select Eve? Because he knew that Eve, the woman, was weaker than Adam the man, and therefore best for his purpose. This reckless female insisted that Satan approached

Eve first, because he knew that woman was not afraid of the devil; [Laughter] but I reject this explanation as irrelevant.

At this point, however, we must stop. Should we go on, we would find that Eve, the weak woman, tempted Adam, the strong man, with distinguished success, which would leave us in this predicament: Satan, stronger than Eve, tempted her to indulge in fruit. Eve's weakness was demonstrated by her falling a victim to temptation. Eve tempted Adam; Adam yielded to Eve; therefore, if Eve was weak in yielding to Satan, how much weaker was Adam in yielding to Eve ? If Satan had been considerate of the feelings of the conservatives, his best friends, by the way, in all ages, he would have tempted Adam first and caused Adam to tempt Eve. This would have afforded us the edifying spectacle of the strong man leading the weak woman, which would be in accordance with our idea of the eternal fitness of things. But now that I look at it again, this wouldn't do ; for it is necessary to our argument that the woman should be tempted first, to prove that she was the weaker of the two. I shall dismiss Adam and Eve with the remark, that, notwithstanding the respect one ought always to feel for his ancestors, those whose blood is the same as that running in his veins, I can not but say that Adam's conduct in this transaction was weak. If Adam's spirit is listening to me to-night, I can't help it. I presume he will feel badly to hear me say it, but truth is truth. Instead of saying boldly, " I ate ! " he attempted to clear his skirts by skulking behind those of his wife. " The woman thou gavest me tempted me and I did eat," he said, which was paltry. Had Adam been stronger minded, he would have refused the tempting bite, and then only woman would have been amenable to the death penalty that followed. This would have killed the legal profession in Chicago, for what man who was to live forever would get a divorce from his wife who could live but eighty or ninety years at best ?

As a conservative, I must say that woman is the inferior of man. This fact is recognized in all civilized countries and in most heathen nations. The Hindoos, it is true, in one of their practices, acknowledge a superiority of woman. In Hindostan, when a man dies, his widow is immediately burned, that she may follow him—an acknowledgment that woman is as necessary to him in the next world as in this. [Laughter.] As men are never burned when their wives die, it may be taken as admitting that women are abundantly able to get along alone. [Laughter.] Or, perchance, it may be because men in that country, as in this, can get new wives easier than women can get new husbands. The exit from this world by fire was probably chosen, that the wife might in some measure be fitted for the climate in which she might expect to find her husband.

The inferiority of the sex is easy of demonstration. It has been said that the mother forms the character of the man so long, that the proposition has become axiomatic. If this be true, we can crush those who prate of the equality of women, by holding up to the gaze of the world the inferior men she has formed. Look at the Congress of the United States. Look at Garret Davis. By their works ye shall know them. It won't do to cite me to the mothers of the good and great men whose names adorn American history. The number is too small. There's George Washington, Wendell Phillips, Abraham Lincoln, and one other whose name all the tortures of the Inquisition could not make me reveal. Modesty forbids me. [Laughter.]

Those who clamor for the extension of the sphere of woman, point to the names of women illustrious in history, sacred and profane. I find, to my discomfiture, that some of the sex really excelled the sterner. There was Mrs. Jezebel Ahab, for instance. Ahab wanted the vineyard of Naboth, which Naboth refused to sell, owing to a prejudice he had against disposing of real estate which he had inherited. Ahab, who was not an ornament to his sex, went home sick and took to his bed like a girl, and turned away his face, and would eat no bread. Mrs. Ahab was made of sterner stuff.

"Arise," said Mrs. A.; "be merry. I will give thee the vineyard of Naboth the Jezreelite."

And she did it. She trapped him as neatly as David did Uriah. She suborned two sons of Belial (by the way Belial has had a large family, and the stock has not run out yet) to bear false witness against him, saying that he had blasphemed God and the king, and they took him out and stoned him. Ahab got the vineyard. It is true this lady came to a miserable end, but she acomplished what she desired.

Miss Pocahontas has been held up as a sample of female strength of mind. I don't deny that she displayed some decision of character, but it was fearfully unwomanly. When her father raised his club over the head of the astonished Smith, instead of rushing in so recklessly, she should have said, "Please pa, don't." Her recklessness was immense. Suppose Pocahontas had been unable to stay the blow, where would our Miss have been then?—she never would have married Rolfe; what would the first families of Virginia have done for somebody to descend from? When we remember that all the people of that proud State claim this woman as their mother, we shudder, or ought to, when we contemplate the possible consequences of her rashness.

Delilah, whose other name is not recorded, overcame Samson the first and most successful conundrum maker of his age, and Jael, it will be remembered, silenced Sisera forever.   Joan of Arc conquered the English after the French leaders failed, and Elizabeth of England was the greatest of English rulers.   I acknowledge all this, but then these women had opportunities beyond those of women in general.   They had as many opportunities as the men of their respective periods had, and consequently, if they were mentally as great as men—no, that isn't what I mean to say—if the men of the period were no greater, mentally, than they —no—if the circumstances which surrounded them gave them opportunities, which being mentally as great as men—I have this thing mixed up somehow, and it don't result as it ought to—but this is true; Delilah, Elizabeth, Joan of Arc—all and singular, unsexed themselves, and did things unbecoming ladies of refinement and cultivation.   Joan's place was spinning flax in her father's hut, and not at the head of armies.   Had she followed the natural mode of feminine life, she would not have been burned at the stake, and the English would not have been interrupted in their work of reducing France to the condition of an English province. Had I lived in France, I should have said, "Down with her!   Let us perish under a man rather than be saved by a woman!"   Joan should have been ashamed of herself — I blush for her.   Had Elizabeth been content to entrust her kingdom to the hands of her cabinet, she would have left it in the happy condition of the United States at the close of Buchanan's administration, but she would have been true to our idea of the womanly life.

There is, in the feminine character, a decisive promptness which we must admire.   Eve ate the apple without a moment's hesitation, and the characteristic is more beautifully illustrated in the touching and well reported account of the courtship and marriage of Rebekah with Isaac. Abraham's servant was sent, it will be remembered, by such of you as have read the Bible, and I presume there are those here who have [Laughter], to negotiate for a wife for young Isaac among his kindred, as he had as intense a prejudice against the Canaanites as have the democracy of the present day.   This servant, whom we will call Smith, as his name, unfortunately, has not been preserved, and Laban, the brother of Rebekah, had almost arranged the matter.   The servant desired to return with the young lady at once, but the mother and brother desired her to remain some days, contrary to modern practice, in that the parents now desire the young lady to get settled in her own house and off their hands as soon as possible.   The servant insisted, whereupon the mother remarked, "We will call the damsel and inquire at her mouth." They called Rebekah and asked, "Wilt thou go with this man?"

It is related of a damsel in Pike county, Missouri, who was being wedded to the man whose choice she was, when the minister officiating asked the usual question, "Wilt thou have this man to be thy wedded husband?" that, dropping her long eyelashes, she promptly answered, "You bet!" Even so with Rebekah. She neither fainted, simpered nor blushed. She did not say that she hadn't a thing fit to put on—that her clothes weren't home from the dressmaker's. No! Using the Hebrew equivalent for " you bet!"—for Rebekah was a smart girl, and young as she was, had learned to speak Hebrew—when the question was put to her, " Wilt thou go with this man?" she answered, "I will, "—and she went. I don't know that this proves any thing, unless it be that women of that day took as great risks for husbands as they do now. Miss Rebekah had scarcely been introduced to her future husband. It might be interesting to trace the history of this woman, but I have hardly the time. I will say, however, that she was a mistress of duplicity. To get the blessing of her husband for her pet son Jacob, she put false hair upon him to deceive the old gentleman, and did it. From that day to this, women in every place but this, have deceived men, young as well as old, with false hair.

The feminine habit of thought is not such as to entitle them to privileges beyond those they now enjoy. No woman was ever a drayman; no woman ever carried a hod; no woman ever drove horses on the canals of the country; and what is more to the point, no woman ever shoveled a single wheel-barrow of earth on the public works. I triumphantly ask, Did any woman assist in preparing the road bed of the Pacific Railway? did any woman drive a spike in that magnificent structure? No woman is employed in the forging department of any shop in which is made the locomotives that climb the Sierra Nevada, whose head-lights beam on the valleys of the Pacific coast—the suns of our commercial system.

Just as I had this arranged in my mind, this disturbing female, of whom I have spoken once or twice, asked me whether carrying hods, driving horses on canals, or shoveling dirt on railways, had been, in the past, considered the best training for intelligent participation in political privileges? She remarked, that, judging from the character of most of the legislation of which she had knowledge, these had been the schools in which legislators had been trained, but she hardly believed that I would acknowledge it. "Make these the qualifications," said she, "and where would you be, my friend, who have neither driven a spike, driven a horse, or shoveled dirt? It would cut out all of my class (she was a teacher)—indeed I know of but two women in America who would be admitted. The two women I refer to fought a prize fight in Connecticut recently, observing all the rules of the English ring, and they displayed as much gameness as was ever shown by that muscular lawmaker, the Hon. John Morrissey. These women ought to vote, and if, in the good time coming, women distribute honors as men have done, they may go to Congress."

I answered, that these classes had always voted, and therefore it was right that they should always vote.

" Certainly they have," returned she, " and, as I have heard them addressed a score of times as the embodied virtue, honesty and intelligence of the country, I have come to the conclusion that there must be something in the labor they do which fits them peculiarly for the duties of law-making."

My friend is learned. She has a tolerable knowledge of Greek, is an excellent Latin scholar, and, as she has read the Constitution of the United States, she excels in political lore the great majority of our representatives in Congress. But, nevertheless, I protest against her voting for several reasons.

1. She can not sing bass ! Her voice, as Dr. Bushnell justly observes in his blessed book, is pitched higher than the male voice, which indicates feminine weakness of mind.

2. Her form is graceful rather than strong.

3. She delights in millinery goods.

4. She can't grow whiskers.

In all of these points nature has made a distinction between the sexes which can not be overlooked.

To all of these she pleaded guilty. She confessed that she had not the strength necessary to the splitting of rails; she confessed that she could neither grow a beard nor sing bass. She wished she could grow a beard, as she knew so many men whose only title to intellect was their whiskers. But she said she took courage when she observed that the same disparity was noticeable in men. Within the range of her acquaintance she knew men who had struggled with mustaches with a perseverance worthy of a better cause, and whose existence had been blighted by the consciousness that they could not. Life was to them, in consequence, a failure. Others she knew who had no more strength than a girl, and others whose voices were pitched in a childish treble. If beards, heavy voices and physical strength were the qualifications for the ballot, she would at once betake herself to razors, hair invigorators, and gymnasiums. She went on thus:

" In many respects," she said, " the sexes are alike. Both are encumbered with stomachs and heads, and both have bodies to clothe.

So far as physical existence is concerned they are very like. Both are affected by laws made and enacted, and both are popularly supposed to have minds capable of weighing the effect of laws. How, thrust into the world as I am, with a stomach to fill and limbs to clothe, with both hands tied, am I to live, to say nothing of fulfilling any other end?"

"Woman," I replied, "is man's angel."

"Stuff and nonsense," was her impolite reply. "I am no angel. I am a woman. Angels, according to our idea of angels, have no use for clothing. Either their wings are enough to cover their bodies, or they are so constituted as not to be affected by heat or cold. Neither do they require food. I can not imagine a feminine angel with hoop skirts, Grecian bend, gaiters and bonnet; or a masculine angel in tight pantaloons, with a cane and silk hat. Angels do not cook dinners, but women do. Why do you say angels to us? It creates angel tastes, without the possibility of their ever satisfying those tastes. The bird was made to soar in the upper air, and was, therefore, provided with hollow bones, wings, etc. Imagine an elephant or a rhinoceros possessed with a longing to soar into the infinite ethereal. Could an elephant, with his physical structure, be possessed with such a longing, the elephant would be miserable, because he could not. He would be as miserable as Jay Gould is, with an ungobbled railroad; as Bonner would be if Dexter were the property of another man; and as James G. Blaine is with the presidency before him. It would be well enough to make angels of us, if you could keep us in a semi-angelic state; but the few thus kept only make the misery of those not so fortunate the more intense. No; treat us rather as human beings, with all the appetites, wants and necessities of human beings, for we are forced to provide for those wants, necessities and appetites."

I acknowledge the correctness of her position. They must live; not that they are of very much account in and of themselves, but that the nobler sex may be perpetuated to adorn and bless the earth. Without woman it would take less than a century to wind up man, and then what would the world do? This difficulty is obviated by marriage. All that we have to do is to marry each man to one woman, and demand of each man that he care for and cherish one woman, and the difficulty is got along with. And got along with, too, leaving things as we desire them, namely, with the woman dependent upon the man. We proceed upon the proposition that there are just as many men as there are women in the world; that all men will do their duty in this particular, and at the right time; that every Jack will get precisely the right Jill, and that every Jill will be not only willing, but anxious, to take the Jack the Lord sends her, asking no questions.

If there be one woman more than there are men, it's bad for that woman. I don't know what she can do, unless she makes shirts for the odd man, at twelve and a half cents each, and lives gorgeously on the proceeds of her toil. If one man concludes that he won't marry at all, it's bad for another woman, unless some man's wife dies and he marries again. That might equalize it, but for two reasons: It compels the woman to wait for a husband until she possibly concludes it isn't worth while ; and furthermore, husbands die as fast as wives, which brings a new element into the field—widows; and pray what chance has an inexperienced man against a widow determined upon a second husband?

I admit, that if there were as many men as women, and if they should all marry, and the matter be all properly fixed up at the start, that our present system is still bad for some of them. She, whose husband gets to inventing flying machines, or running for office, or any of those foolish or discreditable employments, would be in a bad situation. Or, when the husband neglects his duty, and refuses to care for his wife at all; or, to state a case which no one ever witnessed, suppose one not only refuses to care for his wife, but refuses to care for himself! Or, suppose he contracts the injudicious habit of returning to his home at night in a state of inebriation, and of breaking chairs and crockery and his wife's head and other trifles—in such a case I must admit that her position would be, to say the least, unpleasant, particularly as she couldn't help herself. She can't very well take care of herself; for to make woman purely a domestic creature, to ornament our homes, we have never permitted them to think for themselves, act for themselves, or do for themselves. We insist upon her being a tender ivy clinging to the rugged oak; if the oak she clings to happens to be bass-wood, and rotten at that, it's not our fault. In these cases it's her duty to keep on clinging, and to finally go down with it in pious resignation. The fault is in the system, and as those who made the system are dead, and as six thousand brief summers have passed over their tombs, it would be sacrilege in us to disturb it. Customs, like cheese, grow mitey as they grow old.

Let every woman marry, and marry as soon as possible. Then she is provided for. Then the ivy has her oak. Then if her husband is a good man, a kind man, an honest man, a sober man, a truthful man, a liberal man, an industrious man, a managing man, and if he has a good business and drives it, and meets with no misfortunes, and never yields to temptations, why, then the maid promoted to be his wife will be tolerably certain to, at least, have all that she can eat, and all that she can wear, as long as he continues so.

This disturbing woman, of whom I have spoken once or twice, remarked that she did not care for those who were married happily, but she wanted something done for those who were not married at all, and those who were married unfortunately. She liked the ivy and the oak-tree idea, but she wanted the ivy—woman—to have a stiffening of intelligence and opportunity, that she might stand alone in case the oak was not competent to sustain it. She demanded, in short, employment at any thing she was capable of doing, and pay precisely the same that men receive for the same labor, provided she does it as well.

This is a clear flying in the face of Providence. It is utterably impossible that any woman can do any work as well as men. Nature decreed it otherwise. Nature did not give them the strength. Ask the clerks at Washington, whose muscular frames, whose hardened sinews, are employed at from twelve hundred to three thousand dollars per annum, in the arduous and exhausting labor of writing in books, and counting money, and cutting out extracts from newspapers, and endorsing papers and filing them, what they think of that? Ask the brawny young men whose manly forms are wasted away in the wearing occupation of measuring tape and exhibiting silks, what they think of it? Are women, frail as they are, to fill positions in the government offices? I ask her sternly: "Are you willing to go to war? Did you shoulder a musket in the late unpleasantness?"

This did not settle her. She merely asked me if I carried a musket in the late war. Certainly I did not. I had too much presence of mind to volunteer. Nor did the majority of those holding official position. Like Job's charger, they snuffed the battle afar off — some hundreds of miles — and slew the haughty Southron on the stump, or by substitute. But there is this difference: we could have gone, while women could not. And it is better that it is so. In the event of another bloody war, one so desperate as to require all the patriotism of the country to show itself, I do not want my wife to go to the tented field, even though she have the requisite physical strength. No, indeed! I want her to stay at home — with me! [Laughter.]

In the matter of wages, I do not see how it is to be helped. The woman who teaches a school, receives, if she has thoroughly mastered the requirements of the position, say six hundred dollars per year, while a man occupying the same position, filling it with equal ability, receives twice that amount, and possibly three times. But what is this to me? As a man of business, my duty to myself is to get my children educated at the least possible expense. As there are but very few things women are permitted to do, and as for every vacant place there are a hundred women eager for it, as a matter of course, their pay is brought down to a very fine point.   As I said some minutes ago, if the men born into the world would marry at twenty-one, each a maiden of eighteen, and take care of her properly, and never get drunk or sick, or any thing of that inconvenient sort, and both would be taken at precisely the same time with consumption, yellow fever, cholera, or any one of those cheerful ailments, and employ the same physician, that they might go out of the world at the same moment, and become angels with wings and long white robes, it would be well enough.   The men would then take care of the women, except those who marry milliners, in which case the women take care of the men, which amounts to the same thing, as the one dependent upon somebody else is taken care of.   But it don't so happen.   Men do not marry as they ought at twenty-one; they put it off to twenty-five, thirty or forty, and many of them are wicked enough not to marry at all, and of those who do marry there will always be a certain per cent. who will be dissipated or worthless.   What then?   I can't deny that there will be women left out in the cold.   There are those who don't marry, and those who can not.   Possibly the number thus situated would be lessened if we permitted women to rush in and seize men, and marry them, *nolens volens,* but the superior animal will not brook that familiarity.   He must do the wooing — he must ask the woman in his lordly way.   Compelled to wait to be asked, and forced to marry that they may have the wherewithal to eat and be clothed, very many of them take fearful chances.   They dare not, as a rule, refuse to marry.   Man must, as the superior being, have the choice of occupations, and it is a singular fact that, superior as he is by virtue of his strength, he rushes invariably to the occupations that least require strength, and which women might fill to advantage.   They monopolize all the occupations — the married man has his family to take care of — the single man has his back hair to support; what is to become of these unfortunate single women — maids and widows?   Live they must.   They have all the necessities of life to supply, and nothing to supply them with.   What shall they do?   Why, work of course.   But they say, "We are willing to work, but we must have wages."   Granted.   But how shall we get at the wages?   What shall be the standard?   I must get my work done as cheaply as possible.   Now, if three women — a widow, we will say, with five children to support; a girl who has to work or do worse, and a wife with an invalid husband to feed, clothe and find medicine for — if these three come to my door, clamoring for the love of God for something to do, what shall I, as a prudent man, do in the matter?   There are immutable laws governing all these things — the law of supply and demand.   Christ, whose mission was with the poor, made other laws, but Christ is not allowed to have any thing to do with business. Selfishness is older than Christ, and we conservatives stick close to the oldest. What do I do? Why, as a man of business, I naturally ascertain which of the three is burdened with the most crushing responsibilities and necessities. I ascertain to a mouthful the amount of food necessary to keep each, and then the one who will do my work for the price nearest starvation rates gets it to do. If the poor girl prefers the pittance I offer her to a life of shame, she gets it. If the wife is willing to work her fingers nearer the bone than the others, rather than abandon her husband, she gets it, and, speculating on the love the mother bears her children, I see how much of her life the widow will give to save theirs, and decide accordingly. I know very well that these poor creatures can not saw wood, wield the hammer, or roll barrels on the docks. I know that custom bars them out of many employments, and that the more manly vocations of handling ribbons, manipulating telegraphic instruments, etc., are monopolized by men. Confined as they are to a few vocations, and there being so many hundreds of thousands of men who will not each provide for one, there are necessarily ten applicants for every vacancy, and there being more virtue in the sex than the world has ever given them credit for, of course they accept, not what their labor is worth to me and the world, but what I and the world choose to give for it. It is bad, I grant, but it is the fault of the system. It is a misfortune, we think, that there are so many women, and we weep over it. I am willing to shed any amount of tears over this mistake of nature.

But women are themselves to blame for a great part of the distress they experience. There is work for more of them, if they would only do it. The kitchens of the country are not half supplied with intelligent labor, and therein is a refuge for all women in distress.

I assert that nothing but foolish pride keeps the daughters of insolvent wealth out of kitchens, where they may have happy underground homes and three dollars per week, by merely doing six hours per day more labor than hod-carriers average.

This is what they would do were it not for pride, which is sinful. They should strip the jewels off their fingers, the laces off their shoulders; they should make a holocaust of their music and drawings, and, accepting the inevitable, sink with dignity to the washing of dishes, the scrubbing of floors, and the wash-tub. This their brothers do, and why haven't they their strength of mind? Young men delicately nurtured and reared in the lap of luxury, never refuse the sacrifice when their papas fail in business. They always throw to the winds their cigars;

8

they abjure canes and gloves, and mount drays, and shoulder saw-bucks
—any thing for an honest living. I never saw one of these degenerate
into a sponge upon society rather than labor with his hands! Did you?
I never saw one of this class get to be a faro dealer, a billiard marker, a
borrower of small sums of money, a lunch-fiend, a confidence-man, or
any thing of the sort. Not they! Giving the go-by to every thing in
the shape of luxuries, they invariably descend to the lowest grades of
manual labor rather than degenerate into vicious and immoral courses.
Failing the kitchen, women may canvass for books, though that occupation, like a few others equally profitable, and which also brings them
into continual contact with the lords of creation, has a drawback in the
fact that some men leer into the face of every woman who strives to do
business for herself, as though she were a moral leper; and failing all
these, she may at least take to the needle. At this last occupation she
is certain of meeting no competition, save from her own sex. In all my
experience, and it has been extensive, I never yet saw a man making
pantaloons at twelve and one-half cents per pair. But they will not all
submit. Refusing to acknowledge the position in life nature fixed for
them, they rebel, and unpleasantnesses take place. An incident which
fell under my observation recently, illustrates this beautifully. A young
lady, named Jane Evans, I believe, had sustained the loss of both her
parents. The elder Evanses had been convinced by typhoid fever that
this was a cold world, and, piloted by two doctors, had sailed out in
search of a better one. Jane had a brother, a manly lad of twenty, who,
rather than disgrace the ancient lineage of the Evanses by manual labor,
took up the profession of bar-tender. Jane was less proud, and as her
brother did nothing for her, she purchased some needles, and renting a
room in the uppermost part of a building in a secluded part of the city
of New York, commenced a playful effort to live by making shirts at
eighteen cents each, for a gentleman named Isaacs. She was situated,
I need not say, pleasantly for one of her class. Her room was not large,
it is true, but as she had no cooking-stove or bedstead, what did she want
of a large room? She had a window which didn't open, but as there
was no glass in it, she had no occasion to open it. This building commanded a beautiful view of the back parts of other buildings similar in
appearance, and the sash kept out a portion of the smell. Had that sash
not been in that window-frame, I do not suppose that she could have
staid on account of the smell; at least I heard her say that she got just
as much of it as she could endure. And in this delightful retreat she
sat and sat, and sewed and sewed. Sometimes in her zeal she would sew
till late in the night, and she always was at her work very early in the

morning. She paid rent promptly, for the genial old gentleman of whom she leased her room had a sportive habit of kicking girls into the street who did not pay promptly, and she managed every now and then, did this economical girl, to purchase a loaf of bread, which she ate.

One Saturday night she took her bundle of work to the delightful Mr. Isaacs. Jane had labored sixteen hours per day on them, and she had determined, as Sunday was close at hand, to have for her breakfast, in addition to her bread, a small piece of mutton. Mutton! Luxurious living destroyed ancient Rome! But Mr. Isaacs found fault with the making of these shirts. "They were not properly sewed," he said, and he could not, in consequence, pay her the eighteen cents each for making, which was the regular price. Jane then injudiciously cried about it. Now, Mr. Isaacs was, and is, possessed of a tender heart. He has a great regard for his feelings, and, as he could not bear to see a woman cry, he forthwith kicked her out of his store into the snow.

What did this wicked girl do? Did she go back and ask pardon of the good, kind, tender-hearted Mr. Isaacs? Not she! On the contrary, she clenched her hands, and, passing by a baker's shop, stole a loaf of bread, and, brazen thing that she was, in pure bravado, she ate it in front of the shop. She said she was hungry, when it was subsequently proven that she had eaten within forty hours. Justice was swift upon the heels of the desperate wretch—it always is, by the way, close behind the friendless. She was arrested by a policeman, who was opportunely there, as there was a riot in progress in the next street at the time, which was providential, for had there been no riot in the next street, the policeman would have been in that street, and Jane Evans might have got away with her plunder. She was conveyed to the city prison; was herded in a cell in which were other women who had progressed farther than she had; was afterward arraigned for petty larceny and sent to prison for sixty days. Now, see how surely evildoers come to bad ends. The wretched Jane—this fearfully depraved Jane—unable after such a manifestation of depravity to hold up her head, fell into bad ways. Remorse for the stealing of that loaf of bread so preyed upon her that she wandered about the streets of the city five days, asking for work, and finally threw herself off a wharf. Oh, how her brother, the bartender, was shocked at this act! Had she continued working cheerily for Mr. Isaacs, accepting the situation like a Christian, taking life as she found it, would she have thrown herself off a dock? Never! So you see women who do not want to steal bread, and be arrested, and go off wharves, must take Mr. Isaacs' pay as he offers it, and must work cheerily sixteen hours a day, whether they get any thing to eat or not.   Had this wretched girl gone back contentedly to her room, and starved to death cheerfully, she would not have stolen bread, she would not have lacerated the feelings of her brother, the bartender, and would have saved the city of New York the expense and trouble of fishing her out of the dock.   Such women always make trouble.

The women who fancy they are oppressed, demand, first, the ballot, that they may have power to better themselves; and, second, the change of custom and education, that they may have free access to whatever employment they have the strength and capacity to fill, and to which their inclination leads them.

Most emphatically I object to the giving of them the ballot.   It would overturn the whole social fabric.   The social fabric has been overturned a great many times, it is true—so many times, indeed, that it seems rather to like it; but I doubt whether it would be strong enough to endure this.   I have too great, too high, too exalted an opinion of woman.   I insist that she shall not dabble in the dirty pool of politics; that she shall keep herself sacred to her family, whether she has one or not; and under no consideration shall she go beyond the domestic circle of which she is the center and ornament.   There are those who have an insane yearning to do something beyond the drudgery necessary to supply the commonest wants of life, and others who have all of these, who would like to round up their lives with something beyond dress and the unsatisfactory trifles of fashionable life.   There may be women turning night into day over the needle, for bread that keeps them just this side of potter's field, who are unreasonable enough to repine at the system that compels them to this; and they may, possibly, in secret wish that they had the power in their hands that would make men court their influence, as the hod-carrier's is courted, for the vote he casts.   The seamstress toiling for a pittance that would starve a dog, no doubt prays for the power that would compel lawmakers to be as careful of her interests as they are of the interests of the well-paid male laborers in the dock-yards, who, finding ten hours a day too much for them, were permitted by act of Congress to draw ten hours' pay for eight hours' work. The starved colorer of lithographs, the pale, emaciated tailoress, balancing death and virtue; drawing stitches with the picture of the luxurious brothel held up by the devil before her, where there is light, and warmth, and food, and clothing, and where death is, at least, farther off ; no doubt this girl wishes at times that she could have that potent bit of paper between her fingers that would compel blatant demagogues to talk of the rights of workingwomen as well as of workingmen.

But won.... would lose her self-respect if she mixed with politicians. Most men do; and how could woman hope to escape. Think you that any pure woman could be a member of the New York, New Jersey or Pennsylvania legislatures, and remain pure? For the sake of the generations to come, I desire that one sex, at least, shall remain uncontaminated. Imagine your wife or your sister accepting a bribe from a lobby member! Imagine your wife or your sister working a corrupt measure through the legislature, and becoming gloriously elevated upon champagne in exultation over the result! No! I insist that these things shall be confined to man, and man alone.

The mixing of women in politics, as all the writers on the subject have justly remarked, would lower the character of the woman without elevating that of the man. Imagine, oh my hearers, a woman aspiring for office, as men do! Imagine her button-holing voters, as men do! **Imagine her lying glibly and without scruple, as men do! Imagine her** drinking with the lower classes, as men do! of succeeding by the grossest fraud, as men do! of stealing public money when elected, as men do! and finally of sinking into the lowest habits, the vilest practices, as Dr. Bushnell, in several places in his blessed book on the subject, asserts that men do! You see, to make the argument good that women would immediately fall to a very deep depth of degradation the moment they vote, we must show that the act of voting compels men to this evil; at least that is what Dr. Bushnell proves, if he proves any thing. We must show that the holding of an office by man is proof positive that he has committed crime enough to entitle him to a cell in a penitentiary, and that he who votes is in a fair way thereto. Before reading the doctor's book, I was weak enough to suppose that there were in the United States some hundreds of thousands of very excellent men, whose long service in church and state was sufficient guarantee of their excellence; whose characters were above suspicion, and who had lived, and would die, honest, reputable citizens. But as all male citizens above the age of twenty-one vote, and as voting necessarily produces these results, why, then we are all drunkards, tricksters, thieves and plunderers. This disturbing woman, to whom I read Dr. Bushnell's book, remarked that if voting tended to so demoralize men, and as they had always voted, it would be well enough for all the women to vote just once, that they might all go to perdition together. I am compelled to the opinion that the doctor is mistaken. I know of quite a number of men who go to the polls unmolested, who vote their principles quietly, and go home the better for having exercised the right. I believe that, before and since Johnson's administration, there have been honest men in office.

But no woman could do these things in this way. It would unsex her, just as it does when a woman labors for herself alone.

Again, I object to giving the ballot to woman, because we want peace. We don't want divided opinion in our families. As it is, we must have a most delightful unanimity. An individual can not possibly quarrel with himself. As it is now arranged, man and wife are one, and the man is the one. [Laughter.] In all matters outside the house the wife has no voice, and consequently there can be no differences. Oh, what a blessed thing it would be if the same rule could obtain among men! Had the radicals had no votes or voices, there would have been no war, for the democracy, having it all their own way, there would have been nothing to quarrel about. It was opposition that forced Jefferson Davis to appeal to arms. True, the following of this idea would dwarf the Republicans into pygmies, and exalt the democracy into giants. My misguided friend, Wendell Phillips, would shrink into a commonplace man, possibly he would lose all manhood, had he been compelled to agree with Franklin Pierce or hold his tongue. It would be bad for Wendell, but there would have been a calm as profound as stagnation itself. Our present system may be bad for women, but we, the men, have our own way—and peace. Our wives and daughters are, I know, driven, from sheer lack of something greater, to take refuge in disjointed gabble of bonnets, cloaks and dresses, and things of that nature, their souls are dwarfed as well as their bodies, their minds are diluted—but we have peace.

Once more. It would unbalance society. Starting upon the assumption that women have no minds of their own, and would always be controlled by men, we can show wherein the privilege would work incalculable mischief. Imagine Brigham Young marching to the polls at the head of a procession of wives one hundred and seventy-three in number, all of them with such ballots in their hands as he selects for them! Put Brigham and his family in a close congressional district, and he would swamp it. Then, again, if they should think for themselves, and vote as they pleased, they would overthrow Brigham. In either case the effect would be terrible.

What shall we do with the woman question? It is upon us, and must be met. I have tried for an hour to be a conservative, but it won't do. Like poor calico, it won't wash. There are in the United States some millions of women who desire something better than the lives they and their mothers have been living. There are millions of women who have minds and souls, and who yearn for something to develop their minds and souls. There are millions of women who desire to have something to think about, to assume responsibilities, that they may strengthen their moral natures, as the gymnast lifts weights to strengthen his physical nature. There are hundreds of thousands of women who have suffered, in silence, worse evils by far than the slaves of the South, who, like the slaves of the South, have no power to redress their wrongs, no voice so potent that the public must hear. In the parlor, inanity and frivolity; in the cottage, hopeless servitude, unceasing toil; a dark life, with a darker ending. This is the condition of women in the world to-day. Thousands starving physically for want of something to do, with a world calling for labor ; thousands starving mentally, with an unexplored world before them. One-half of humanity is a burden on the other half.

I know, Oh, ye daughters of luxury, that you do not desire a change ! There is no need of it for you. Your silks could not be more costly, your jewels could not flash more brightly, nor your surroundings be more luxurious. Your life is pleasant enough. But I would compel you to think, and thinking, act. I would put upon your shoulders responsibilities that would make rational beings of you. I would make you useful to humanity and to yourselves. I would give the daughters of the poor, as I have helped to give the sons of the poor, the power in their hands to right their own wrongs. [Applause.]

There is nothing unreasonable in this demand. The change is not so great as those the world has endured time and again without damage. To give the ballot to the women of America to-day, would not be so fearful a thing as it was ten years ago to give it to the negro, or as it was a hundred years ago to give it to the people. [Applause.]

I would give it, and take the chances. [Applause.] The theory of Republicanism is, that the governing power must rest in the hands of the governed. There is no danger in truth. If the woman is governed, she has a right to a voice in the making of laws. To withhold it is to dwarf her, and to dwarf woman is to dwarf the race.

I would give the ballot to woman for her own sake, for I would enlarge the borders of her mind. I would give it to her for the sake of humanity. I would make her of more use to humanity by making her more fit to mold humanity. I would strengthen her, and through her the race. The ballot of itself would be of direct use to but few, but indirectly its effects would reach through all eternity. It would compel a different life. It would compel woman to an interest in life, would fit her to struggle successfully against its mischances, and prepare her for a keener, higher, brighter appreciation of its blessings. Humanity is now one-sided. There is strength on the one side and weakness on the other. I would have both sides strong. I would have the two sides equal in strength, equally symmetrical; differing only as nature made them, not as man and custom have distorted them. In this do we outrage custom? Why, we have been overturning customs six thousand years, and there are yet enough hideous enormities encumbering the earth to take six thousand years more to kill. In the beginning, when force was the law, there were kings. The world tired of kings. There were false religions. Jesus of Nazareth overturned them. Luther wrecked a venerable system when he struck the church of Rome with his iron hand; your fathers and mine stabbed a hoary iniquity when they overturned kingcraft on this continent, and Lovejoy, Garrison and Phillips struck an institution which ages had sanctioned when they assaulted slavery. The old is not always the best.

I would have your daughters fitted to grapple with life alone, for no matter how you may leave them, you know not what fate may have in store for them. I would make them none the less women, but stronger women, better women. Let us take this one step for the sake of humanity. Let us do this much toward making humanity what the Creator intended it to be—like Himself. [Applause.]

NASBY'S BEST STORY.

One of Nasby's best satires was his description how the colored people were kept out of the white school of the Confedrit Cross Roads. Says the Satirist:

Our teacher was a young lady from New Hampshire. She had abolition blood in her yankee veins. When the niggers came to her school, what do you think she did? Send them away? No, she received 'em, gave 'em seats and put 'em into classes—think on that—with white children! I tell you there wuz trouble in our town. I, as a leading Democrat, wuz sent for to wunst, and gladly I come. I wuz never so gratified in my life. Had smallpox broken out in that skool, there woodent hev bin half the eggscitement in the township. It wuz the subjick uv yooniversal talk everywhere, and the Democrisy wuz a bilin like a pot. I met the trustees uv the town, and demanded ef they intended tamely to submit to this outrage? I askt em whether they intended to hev their children set side by side with the decendants uv Ham, who wuz comdemned to a posishen uv inferiority forever? Kin you, I asked, so degrade yourselves, and so blast the self-respeck uv yoor children?

And bilin up with indignashen, they answered "never!" and yoonanimously requested me to accompany 'em to the skoolhouse, that they mite peremptory expel these disgustin beins who hed obtrooded themselves among those uv a sooperior race.

On the way to the skoolhouse, wich wuz perhaps a mile distant, I askt the Board ef they knowed those girls by site. No, they replied, they hed never seed 'em. "I hev bin told," sed I, "that they are nearly white."

"They are," sed one uv 'em, "quite white." "It matters not," sed I, feelin that there wuz a good opportoonity for improvin the occashen, "it matters not. There is suthin in the nigger at wich the instink uv the white man absolootly rebels, and from wich it instinktively recoils. So much experience hev I had with 'em, that put me in a dark room with one uv 'em, no matter how little nigger there is in 'em, and that unerrin instink wood betray 'em to me, wich, by the way, goes to prove that the dislike we hev to 'em is not the result uv prejudis, but is a part uv our very nacher, and one uv its highest and holiest attriboots."

Thus communin, we entered the skoolhouse. The skoolmarm wuz there, ez brite and ez crisp ez a Janooary mornin; the skolers wuz ranged on the seets a studyin ez rapidly ez possible.

"Miss," sed I, "we are informed that three nigger wenches, daughters of one LETT, a nigger, is in this skool, a minglin with our daughters ez a ekal. Is it so?"

"The Misses LETT are in this skool," sed she, ruther mischeeviously, "and I am happy to state that they are among my best pupils."

"Miss," sed I sternly, "pint 'em out to us!"

"Wherefore?" sed she.

"That we may bundle 'em out!" sed I.

"Bless me!" sed she, "I reely coodent do that. Why expel 'em?"

"Becoz," sed I, "no nigger shel contaminate the white children uv this deestrick. No sech disgrace shel be put on to 'em."

"Well," sed this aggravatin skoolmarm, wich wuz from Noo Hamshire, "yoo put 'em out."

"But show me wich they are."

"Can't you detect 'em, sir? Don't their color betray 'em? Ef they are so neer white that you can't select 'em at a glance, it strikes me that it can't hurt very much to let 'em stay."

I wuz sorely puzzled. There wuzn't a girl in the room who looked at all niggery. But my reputashun wuz at stake. Noticin three girls settin together who wuz somewhat dark complectid, and whose black hair waved, I went for 'em and shoved out, the cussid skoolmarm almost bustin with lafter.

Here the tragedy okkerred.   At the door I met a man who rode four miles in his zeal to assist us.   He hed alluz hed an itchin to pitch into a nigger, and ez he cood do it now safely, he proposed not to lose the chance.   I wuz a puttin on 'em out, and hed jist dragged 'em to the door, when I met him enterin it.

"Wat is this?" sed he, with a surprised look.

"We're puttin out these cussid wenches, who is contaminatin yoor children and mine," sed I.   "Ketch hold uv that pekoolyerly disgustin one yonder," sed I.

"Wenches!   You d—d skoundrel, them girls are my girls."

And without waitin for an explanashen, the infooriated monster sailed into me, the skoolmarm layin over on one uv the benches explodin in peels uv lafter.   The three girls, indignant at bein mistook for nigger wenches, assisted their parent, and between 'em, in about four minutes I wuz insensible.   One uv the trustees, pityin my woes, took me to the neerest railroad stashen, and somehow, how I know not, I got home, where I am at present recooperatin.

I hev only to say that when I go on sich a trip again, I shel require as condishen precedent that the Afrikins to be put out shel hev enuff Afrikin into 'em to prevent sich mistakes.   But, good Lord, wat hev'ent I suffered in this cause?

PETROLEUM V. NASBY, P. M.
(wich is Postmaster.)

JOHN B. GOUGH
ROBT. J. INGERSOLL

HENRY WARD BEECHER
CHAUNCEY M. DEPEW

HENRY WARD BEECHER.

PREACHER, ORATOR, PATRIOT AND WIT.

BIOGRAPHY AND REMINISCENCES.

This book abounds in sunshine from living men, but the great Beecher, dead, still lives in the American heart. His sunshine is in every household. He was the purest type of the robust, free American.

Henry Ward Beecher was born in Litchfield, Conn., in 1813, and died in Brooklyn in 1887. He was educated in New England, studied theology in Ohio, and at the age of twenty-four commenced preaching in Lawrenceburg, Ind. He preached in the West for ten years. It was in the wild West that he got his boundless experience in human nature and freedom in the expression of his thoughts. He inherited muscle and an impulsive nature from his Litchfield ancestor. He was too great to be a polished scholar. His intellect was too fertile for established creeds. Creeds and dogmas stand still; Beecher was always growing. His fertility of intellect was amazing. "For full fifty years," says Edward Pierpont, "he talked to the public, and no man ever said so much and repeated so little. His humor was immense, as any one could see by looking into his great, broad, laughing face. His heart was warm with love and his personal magnetism wonderful. He did not reflect; *he felt*, and put his feelings into burning words. His imagination was large and his hope as boundless as his love. Talmage and Moody are great, but they stood still, walled in with creeds and dogmas, while Beecher, like Swing, traveled on and on, and the theology of Calvin and Wesley and Jonathan Edwards grew mean and small. He taught the church to think. He put his arms around the slave. He stood with Garrison and Wendell Phillips, yes, led them on till victory was won. A constitution with slavery in was naught to him. His conscience told him slavery was wrong, and he fought it whole-hearted to the end. He loved our young republic—loved free speech, and, when division came, he stood for unity and law."

Oliver Wendell Holmes says: "Beecher was a mighty power in the land, and his work was a living work, and its results can never be known until the books of heaven are balanced."

Mr. Beecher never cared to be called a humorist, but his wit and humor were as keen as his logic. He never strayed away from his train of thought to gather in a witty idea to illustrate his sermons. Neither did he avoid wit. When a witty idea stood before him, he grasped it and bent it to illustrate his thought. His conception of wit was as quick as lightning. It came like a flash (often in a parenthesis), and it often instantly changed the tears of his hearers to laughter.

When Dr. Collyer asked the great preacher why the newspapers were always referring to the Plymouth brethren, but never spoke of the Plymouth sisters, he could not help saying:

"Why, of course, the brethren embrace the sisters!"

Mr. William M. Evarts was once talking with General Grant about the great Brooklyn divine, when suddenly the distinguished lawyer musingly asked:

"Why is it, General, that a little fault in a clergyman attracts more notice than a great fault in an ordinary man?"

"Perhaps," said the General, thoughtfully, "it is for the same reason that a slight shadow passing over the pure snow is more readily seen than a river of dirt on the black earth."

In all of his humor, Mr. Beecher never harmed a human soul. His mirth was innocent, and his wit was for a grand purpose.

I was talking with Mr. Beecher one day about humor. He was always ready to talk to any man who had a good idea or a good story, but he wanted the story to be as pure as a parable. He wanted it to prove or illustrate some idea.

"Humor," said Beecher, "is everywhere. Humor is truth. Even John Bunyan was a humorist. It was humor when Bunyan made Christian meet one 'Atheist' trudging along with his back to the Celestial City.

"'Where are you going?' asked the Atheist, laughing at Christian.

"'To the Celestial City,' replied Christian, his face all aglow with the heavenly light.

"'You fool!' said Atheist, laughing, as he trudged on into the darkness. 'I've been hunting for that place for twenty years and have seen nothing of it yet. Plainly it does not exist.'

"Heaven was behind him," said Beecher, seriously.

There was one kind of men, however, that Beecher disliked to talk to—cranks, and they were always calling on him.

"What did he do with them?" you ask.

Well, he always turned them over to Mrs. Beecher with the remark, "Mother, you take care of this interesting man."

Beecher liked to talk of his early poverty. He always treated poverty in a humorous vein. "Once," he said, "I was the poorest man in Lawrenceburg, Ind., where I supplied my first church, away back in 1836. I was so poor that I couldn't buy firewood to keep us warm, without going without books. I remember one Sunday morning there came a big flood in the Ohio. I was preaching at the time, and I looked out of the window and saw the flood-wood go sailing by my house. It seemed wrong for me to see so much good wood going by and I not able to catch it."

"What did you do?" I asked.

"Why, I rushed that sermon through, hurried home, and that afternoon, with the aid of Deacon Anderson, I got out enough driftwood to keep Mrs. Beecher in firewood for three months, and all the while," he said, looking up and smiling at his wife, "Mother stood in the doorway and cheered us on." Then, looking quizzically at Mrs. Beecher, he said, "Didn't you, Mother?"

"No, Henry, you never did any such thing," said Mrs. Beecher, who never could see through any of the great preacher's jokes.

"In 1838," said Mr. Beecher, "I was so poor that I rode clear to Fort Wayne from Indianapolis on horseback, and delivered a sermon dedicating the Fort Wayne Presbyterian church, and only got $25 for it. Then I went to New York to attend the Congregational convention. While in New York I went to Dr Prime, of the *Observer*, and offered to write weekly letters from the West at a dollar a piece."

"Did Prime take you up?" I asked.

"Yes, and paid me $5 in advance."

"And you actually wrote letters for a dollar a column?"

"No," said Mr. Beecher, laughing, "the next day Prime thought it over, repented of his haste and profligacy, and wrote me that he did not think my letters would be worth it."

"But oh," he groaned, turning to Mrs. Beecher, "it was a bitter disappointment to us—wasn't it, Mother?"

One day, speaking of puns, Mr. Beecher said Mrs. Beecher received one on his name that was very complete. Then Mrs. Beecher went and got an old scrap book and read:

Said a great Congregational preacher
To a hen: "You're a beautiful creature;"
The hen, just for that, laid three eggs in his hat,
And thus did the Henry Ward Beecher.

"From Lawrenceburg," said Mr. Beecher, in a serious conversation one day, " we went to Indianapolis. I was quite proud of the change, but it was hard work—this missionary work in the new West. I remember the first revival I had in my Indianapolis church. I had been laboring at Terre Haute in a revival—the first that I ever worked in—and I came home full of fire and zeal, praying all the way. There was a prayer that began in Terre Haute and ended in Indianapolis, eighty miles apart. I recollect that, when I got home and preached, I gave an account of what I had seen in Terre Haute. The next night I began a series of protracted meetings. The room was not more than two-thirds full, and the people were apparently dead to spiritual things. On the second night, I called for persons who would like to talk with me to remain. I made a strong appeal, but only one person—a poor German servant-girl—stopped. All the children of my friends, the young people that I knew very well, got up and went out ; all went out except this one servant-girl, who answered to my sermon call. I remember that there shot through me a spasm of rebellion. I had a sort of feeling, ' For what was all this precious ointment spilled ? Such a sermon as I had preached, such an appeal as I had made, with no result but this!'

"In a second, however, almost quicker than a flash," continued Mr. Beecher, " there opened to me a profound sense of the value of any child of the Lord Jesus Christ. This was Christ's child, and I was so impressed with the thought that any thing of his was unspeakably precious beyond any conception which I could form, that tears came into my eyes and ran down my cheeks, and I had the feeling to the very marrow that I would be willing to work all my days among God's people if I could do any good to the lowest and the least creature. My pride was all gone, my vanity was all gone, and I was caught up into a blessed sense of the love of God to men, and of my relation to Christ; and I thought it to be an unspeakable privilege to unloose the shoe-latchets from the poorest of Christ's disciples. And out of that spirit came the natural consequences."

"During that revival," continued Mr. Beecher, "I remember how I was called to see a sick girl who was perhaps seventeen or eighteen years of age. A gentleman informed me that she had been sick for twelve months, and that she had become quite disconsolate.

I WAS SO POOR THAT I RODE ALL THE WAY TO FORT WAYNE
AND DELIVERED A SERMON FOR $25.

"'Go and see her,' said another, 'for if any body ought to be comforted, she ought to be. She has the sweetest disposition, and she is the most patient creature imaginable; and you ought to hear her talk. One can hardly tell whether she talks or prays. It is heaven to go into her room.'

"'I wanted a little more of the spirit of heaven, so I went to see her.

"'I hear of what you are doing in your revival,' she said, 'and of what my companions are doing, and I long to go out and labor for Christ; and it seems very strange to me that God keeps me here on this sick-bed.'

"'My dear child,' I said, 'don't you know that you are preaching Christ to this whole household, and to every one that knows you? Your gentleness and patience and Christian example are known and read by them all. You are laboring for Christ more effectually than you could anywhere else.' Her face brightened, she looked up without a word and gave thanks to God."

On one occasion, I asked Mr. J. B. Pond, who traveled with the great divine for 100,000 miles, while he lectured 1,200 times and took in $250,000, what kind of a companion Beecher was.

"He was," said Mr. Pond, "an all-round, jovial, companionable and good-natured man. He had no eccentricities. Wherever he went, he was like an electric light, reflecting brightness and commanding respect. I have been with him when the mob hooted at his heels and spat upon him; when crowds jeered and hurled all sorts of epithets at him, and when it looked as if he were going to be stoned and trampled to death. He never betrayed fear, never grew angry, but, turning to me, he would say:

"'I do not blame them, for they know not what they do.'

"When we arrived in a town, as a rule, a crowd was at the depot to see Mr. Beecher. At Clinton, Iowa, the greatest insults were offered to him. The train arrived late, and we managed to get to the hotel without being overrun by the usual mob at the depot. After a hasty supper, we concluded to walk to the hall where the lecture was to be delivered. Great throngs lined the streets, eager to see Mr. Beecher. We walked side by side through a wall of human beings, a large crowd following at our heels, hooting and jeering. I happened to turn, and saw three or four men spitting upon Mr. Beecher's back. He never said a word, but manfully

9

walked along. When we arrived at the hall, we found the members of the committee who were to introduce the lecturer and sit upon the platform grouped around laughing and guying each other about appearing in public with Mr. Beecher. Even the chairman was disposed to be reticent and surly toward us. Women in the audience tittered, and it looked as if an outbreak of rudeness could not be avoided. Every body seemed ready to cast the first stone.

"Before that audience, inimical and prepared to hiss, Mr. Beecher won one of the greatest triumphs of his life. I shall never forget the scene. He pulled off his overcoat, and, without even a look of anger, threw it aside. Throwing back his long, snow-white locks, revealing a high forehead and a frank, determined face, he walked upon the platform. The chairman coldly said: "Mr. Beecher, ladies and gentlemen." The orator stepped to the front of the platform and began his speech in a clear, ringing voice that instantly hushed the suppressed murmur and jeers. From that time until he closed the great audience was with him. Such flights of oratory, bursts of eloquence and keen, irresistible humor I never heard from his lips before. Tears, laughter and round after round of applause greeted him, and when he ceased the audience remained, as if it could not depart. The peroration that the great orator delivered brought the people to their feet. He walked behind the scene and picked up his overcoat. The audience would not go, but lingered to catch a glimpse of him. Throwing down his overcoat, he stepped into the auditorium. Women and men shook him by the hand; some wanted to touch his garments, if nothing else, and for an hour he talked to them socially, and they reluctantly parted fr m him.

"We went to our hotel," continued Major Pond, "and had a lunch of crackers and cheese, which he was in the habit of taking in the evening after a lecture. He remarked:

"'Well, Pond, I never had greater reason to talk than to-night. I feel that what I said will do some good and convince my hearers of errors they labored under.'

"One day, after an experience with a mob, he happened to pick up a Chicago paper and glance over it. Holding it in his hand, pointing to headlines of slang and vituperation, he said:

"'No wonder the people are so rough and vulgar when daily fed upon such sensational nastiness.'

"At that time the Chicago papers were not refined, I must confess. Now the Windy City has a Browning Club, and the citizens have discussions about Sappho, all of which indicates progress.

"Going from Davenport, Iowa, to Muscatine, on the cars, a little incident occurred that showed Mr. Beecher's politeness and genial disposition. Two ladies, refined and well dressed, sat behind him in the cars. He was leaning back, reading a novel and oblivious to his surroundings. I sat opposite to him and could see the ladies. They discovered on his overcoat a few gray hairs and began to quietly pick them off to keep as souvenirs. He felt and knew evidently what was going on, for he said:

"'Conductor, are there are any flies in this car?'

Then turning, he saw what the ladies were doing. They begged his pardon and said they saw a gray hair or two on his overcoat, which they brushed away. With a twinkle in his eyes he replied that his wife was never so careful about taking away his hair.

Mr. Beecher had a deep sympathy for every one in trouble, and poor people in trouble were always coming to him.

"Personal sympathy," said the great preacher one day, "is what we all want. I remember the first time any one ever sympathized with me."

"When was it?" I asked.

"Well, one evening, when on the farm up in Litchfield, my father said to me (I was a little boy then): 'Henry, take these letters and go down to the postoffice with them.'

"I was a brave boy, and yet I had imagination. And thousands of people are not so cowardly as you think. Persons with quick imaginations and quick sensibility people the heavens and the earth, so that there are a thousand things in them that harder men do not think of and understand. I saw behind every thicket some shadowy form; and I heard trees say strange and weird things; and in the dark concave above I could hear flitting spirits. All the heaven was populous to me, and the earth was full of I know not what strange sights. These things wrought my system to a wonderful tension. When I went pit-a-pat along the road in the dark, I was brave enough; and if it had been anything that I could have seen; if it had been any thing that I could have fought, it would have given me great relief, but it was not. It was only a vague, outlying fear. I knew not what it was. When father said to me,

'Go,' I went, for I was obedient. I took my old felt hat and stepped out of the door; and Charles Smith (a great, thick-lipped black man who worked on the farm, and who was always doing kind things) said to me: 'Look here, I will go with you.' Oh, sweeter music never came out of any instrument than that. The heaven was just as full, and the earth was just as full, as before; but now I had somebody to go with me. It was not that I thought he was going to fight for me. I did not think there was going to be any need of fighting, but I had somebody to lean on; somebody to care for me; somebody to help and succor me. Let any thing be done by direction, let any thing be done by thought or rule, and how different it is from its being done by personal inspiration!"

"Speaking of the mystery of conversion," one day said Mr. Beecher, "I can best illustrate conversion by a story. When I was about four years old, my father married, and I had a second mother. It was a great event, this second mother coming to us children. I remember Charles and Harriet and I all slept in the same room. We were expecting that father would come home with our 'new mother' that night. Just as we had all got into our trundle-beds up-stairs, and were about falling asleep, we heard a racket down-stairs, and every mother's son and daughter of us began to halloo, 'Mother! *mother!* MOTHER!' And presently we heard a rustling on the stairs, and in the twilight we saw a dim shadow pass into the room, and somebody leaned over the bed and kissed me, and kissed Charles and said: 'Be good children, and I will see you to-morrow.'

"I remember very well how happy I was. I felt that I had a mother. I felt her kiss and I heard her voice. I could not distinguish her features, but I knew that she was my mother. That word mother had begun to contain a great deal in my estimation.

"It seems to me it is very much in that way that God comes to human souls—as a shadow, so to speak; without any great definiteness, and yet with an attitude and a love-producing action; without any clear, distinct, reportable sensations, but producing some great joy, conferring some great pleasures, as though some great blessing had come to us. Was not my mother's presence real to us when, in the twilight of the evening, she for a moment hovered over us and kissed us 'How do you do?' and 'Good-by?' And is it not a reality when the greater Mother and Father does the same to the souls of men in their twilight?"

INTERIOR OF MR. BEECHER'S STUDY.

"But is conversion in religion absolutely necessary?" I asked.

"Yes, some time in life it becomes necessary. It is the balm of Gilead. It will heal a broken heart. It will fill a void in life that nothing else will fill. I knew a man who had no companion but his little child. The child filled his whole heart. He and his wife lived apart, and by-and-by she died, but she left the dear little babe. The babe was his sun and heaven and God—everything to him. She was his morning star, for he waked to think of her before any other one, and to frolic with her, and chat and prattle with her. And his last thought, as he left the house, was of her. And now and then she gleamed into his thoughts all day long in his business. And when the evening came she was his bright evening star. And when he went home at night, and she greeted him at the door, he caught her in his arms and inwardly thanked God. She sickened; and he said to God: 'Kill me, but spare the child.' And God took the child. And he said: 'I have nothing left.' He lay before God as the flax lies before the flail, and said: 'Strike! strike! I am dead. I am cut up from the roots. Strike!' He would have died if he could, but he could not. Nobody can die that wants to. It is folks who want to live that die, apparently. And finding that he could not die, by-and-by he got up and crept into life again, and said: 'What do I care whether I make or lose?' He had no longer any motive for laying up property. And so he said: 'If there is anything in religion, I am going to try to get it. I shall die if I do not have something.' Then religion came to him. It filled the great void and vacuum of his soul. Religion can take the place of wife, mother and the dear baby, too. Nothing else will do it."

"But is it not enough to be a moral man?" I asked.

"No, Christianity goes beyond morality. A Christian is always a moral man, but a moral man is not always a Christian. The Christian and the moralist are alike in many things, but by-and-by the Christian will be admitted to a sphere which the moralist can not enter.

"A barren and a fruitful vine are growing side by side in the garden, and the barren vine says to the fruitful one: 'Is not my root as good as yours?'

"'Yes,' replies the vine, 'as good as mine.'

" ' And are not my bower-leaves as broad and spreading, and is not my stem as large and my bark as shaggy ?'

" ' Yes,' says the vine.

" ' And are not my leaves as green, and am I not taller than you ?'

" ' Yes,' meekly replies the vine, ' but I have blossoms.'

" ' Oh! blossoms are of no use.'

" ' But I bear fruit.'

" ' What! those clusters ? Those are only a trouble to a vine.'

" But what thinks the vintner ? He passes by the barren vine; but the other, filling the air with its odor in spring, and drooping with purple clusters in autumn, is his pride and joy; and he lingers near it and prunes it, that it may become yet more luxuriant and fruitful. So the moralist and the Christian may grow together for a while; but by-and-by, when the moralist's life is barren, the Christian's will come to flower and fruitage in the Garden of the Lord. ' Herein is my Father glorified, that ye bear much fruit.' "

" What do you actually know about God and a hereafter, after all these years of preaching and study ?" I asked.

Mr. Beecher thought a moment, looked puzzled, and finally said : " I know no more than the wise Dr. Alexander did. I have been a teacher of theology all my life, like the Doctor, and I only know that I am a sinner and that Jesus Christ is my Savior."

Every foreigner who came to America always wanted to meet Beecher. Canon Farrar once wrote: " I went over to Brooklyn to hear Beecher. It would have been impossible for any one to hear him without being struck with his wonderful power."

Mr. Andrew Carnegie took Matthew Arnold over to Plymouth Church. " After the service," said Mr. Carnegie, " Mr. Beecher came direct to us, and as I introduced him, he extended both arms, grasped the hands of the apostle of sweetness and light, and said, ' I am very glad to see you, Mr. Arnold. I have read, I think, every word you have ever written, and much of it more than once, and always with profit.'

Mr. Arnold returned Mr. Beecher's warmth—as who could ever fail to respond to it?—and said, ' I fear, then, you found some words about yourself which should not have been written !'

" ' Not at all, not at all !' was the prompt response, and another hearty shake of both hands, for he still grasped those of his critic. ' Those were the most profitable of all.' "

"Upon another occasion," said Mr. Carnegie, "I had gone with a well-known English divine, the Rev. Joseph Parker, to Plymouth Church, and in the party was Miss Ingersoll, whom I introduced to Mr. Beecher, saying: 'This is ∖he daughter of Colonel Ingersoll; she has just heard her first sermon, and been in a church for the first time.'

"As with Mr. Arnold, Beecher's arms were outstretched at once; and grasping hers, he said, as he peered into her fair face, 'Well, you are the most beautiful heathen I ever saw. How is your father? He and I have spoken from the same platform for a good cause, and wasn't it lucky for me I was on the same side with him! Remember me to him.'"

Dr. Parker said of Beecher, afterward: "Take him in theology, botany, agriculture, medicine, physiology and modern philosophy, and it might be thought, from the range of his reading and the accuracy of his information, that he had made a specialty of each."

There were two great epochs in Beecher's life—his fight against human slavery from 1850 to 1860, and his fight for the Republic in England in 1861. In the anti-slavery times, Mr. Beecher flung himself, with all the ardor of his soul, and with all his splendid eloquence, into the task of rousing the moral sentiment of the Christian people of the North against slavery. Says Washington Gladden: "He was clear, positive and uncompromising. I remember the day when from Beecher's lips flashed these words: 'I would die myself, cheerfully and easily, before a man should be taken out of my hands when I had the power to give him liberty and the hound was after him for his blood. I would stand as an altar of expiation between slavery and liberty, knowing that through my example a million men would live. A heroic deed in which one yields up his life for others is his Calvary. It was the hanging of Christ on that hill-top that made it the highest mountain on the globe. Let a man do a right thing with such earnestness that he counts his life of little value, and his example becomes omnipotent. Therefore it is said that the blood of the martyrs is the seed of the Church. There is no such seed planted in this world as good blood!'"

Mr. Beecher took immense delight in his Peekskill farm, though it was an expensive luxury. He had a thousand flowers and a thousand shrubs, and he knew every one of them. They were his pets. Sometimes he would get up at four o'clock in the morning, and when Mrs. Beecher asked him where he was going, he would say :

"I'm going to talk with my flowers, Mother."

If any one asked him about the revenue of his farm, he would say : "O, I get that in health and joy and in texts for my books and sermons!"

"If you want to know how much I make off of my farm," he said, "go to Mark Twain: he knows, and he's put it on paper."

The great preacher never tired reading Mark Twain's description of his Peekskill farm, and he would laughingly show his friends an old newspaper with Twain's article marked with blue pencil.

This is the article:

Mr. Beecher's farm at Poughkeepsie consists of thirty-six acres, and is carried on on strictly scientific principles. He never puts in any part of a crop without consulting his book. He plows and reaps and digs and sows according to the best authorities—and the authorities cost more than the other farming implements do. As soon as the library is complete, the farm will begin to be a profitable investment. But book-farming has its drawbacks. Upon one occasion, when it seemed morally certain that the hay ought to be cut, the hay book could not be found, and before it was found it was too late, and the hay was all spoiled. Mr. Beecher raises some of the finest crops of wheat in the country, but the unfavorable difference between the cost of producing it and its market value after it is produced has interfered considerably with its success as a commercial enterprise. His special weakness is hogs, however. He considers hogs the best game a farm produces. He buys the original pig for a dollar and a half, and feeds him forty dollars' worth of corn, and then sells him for about nine dollars. This is the only crop he ever makes any money on. He loses on the corn, but he makes seven dollars and a half on the hog. He does not mind this, because he never expects to make any thing on corn any way. And any way it turns out, he has the excitement of raising the hog any how, whether he gets the worth of him or not. His strawberries would be a comfortable success if the robins would eat turnips, but they won't, and hence the difficulty.

One of Mr. Beecher's most harassing difficulties in his farming operations comes of the close resemblance of different sorts of seeds and plants to each other. Two years ago his far-sightedness warned him that there was going to be a great scarcity of watermelons, and therefore he put in a crop of seven acres of that fruit. But when they came up they turned out to be pumpkins, and a dead loss was the consequence. Sometimes a portion of his crop goes into the ground the most promising sweet potatoes, and comes up the most execrable carrots. When he bought his farm he found one egg in every hen's nest on the place. He said that that was just the reason that so many farmers failed—they scattered their forces too much—concentration was the idea. So he gathered those eggs together, and put them all under one experienced hen. That hen roosted over the contract night and day for many weeks, under Mr. Beecher's personal supervision, but she could not "phase" them eggs. Why? Because they were those shameful porcelain things which are used by modern farmers as "nest-eggs."

Mr. Beecher's farm is not a triumph. It would be easier if he worked it on shares with some one; but he can not find any body who is willing to stand half the expense, and not many that are able. Still, persistence in any cause is bound to succeed. He was a very inferior farmer when he first began, but a prolonged and unflinching assault upon his agricultural difficulties has had its effect at last, and he is now fast rising from affluence to poverty.

Mr. Beecher was very fond of his brother, Thomas K. Beecher, of Elmira. "The people don't understand Tom," he said. "Why, one of his Elmira deacons actually left the church because Tom wrote that ' Brother Watkins—Ah.' They didn't know that it was all innocent fun. This is the article; read it, but you want to put on the Methodist prayer-meeting tone, you know," and Mr. Beecher handed me this copy of his brother's funny travesty (to be read through the nose):

My beloved brethren, before I take my text I must tell you about parting from my old congregation. On the morning of the last Sabbath, I went into the meeting-house to preach my farewell discourse. Just in front of me sot the old fathers and mothers in Israel; the tears coursed down their furrowed cheeks, their tottering forms and quivering lips breathed out a sad farewell, Brother Watkins—ah! Just back of them sot the middle-aged men, brethren; health and vigor beamed from every countenance and stood in every eye, and as I looked down upon them they seemed to say, farewell, Brother Watkins—ah! On the next seat back of them sot the boys and girls that I had baptized and gathered into the Sabbath school; many times had they been rude and boisterous, but now their merry laugh was hushed, and in the silence I could hear there, too, farewell, Brother Watkins—ah! Around on the back seats and in the isles stood and sot the colored brethren, and as I looked down upon them I could see there in their dreamy eyes, farewell, Brother Watkins—ah!

When I had finished my discourse and shaken hands with the brethren, I went out to take a last look at the old church; the broken steps, the flopping blinds and the moss-covered roof breathed a sad farewell, Brother Watkins—ah! Then I mounted my old gray mare, with all my earthly possessions in my saddle-bags, and as I rode down the streets the servant-girls stood in the doors, and waved with their brooms a farewell, Brother Watkins—ah! And as I passed out of the village the low wind blew softly through the trees, farewell, Brother Watkins—ah! And I came down to the brook-ah, and the old mare stopped to drink-ah; the water rippled over the pebbles, farewell, Brother Watkins—ah! And even the little fishes seemed to say, as they gathered around, farewell, Brother Watkins—ah! And I was slowly passing up the hill, meditating upon the sad vicissitudes and mutations of life, when suddenly out bounded a big hog from a fence corner, and it scared my old mare-ah, and I came to the ground with my saddle-bags by my side-ah, and as I lay there in the dust of the road, the old mare ran up the hill-ah, and as she turned the top she waved her tail back at me, seemingly to say-ah, farewell, Brother Watkins—ah!

Mr. Beecher had but one life-long enemy, and that was the gifted Charles A. Dana, who pursued him, even beyond his grave.

Still the great divine always had a kind word for Mr. Dana. He admired his talents. One day, speaking of Dana, he said:

" Dana said a smart thing to-day."

" What was it ? " I asked.

" When they were discussing at the editorial convention what was proper to put in a newspaper, Dana said: 'Well, gentlemen, I don't know what you think, but I'm willing to permit a report of any thing in my paper that the Lord permits to happen.' But in my case," said Beecher, laughing, " Dana goes away beyond Providence."

BEECHER'S LECTURE THOUGHTS.

MISFORTUNE.—The steel that has suffered most is the best steel. It has been in the furnace again and again; it has been on the anvil; it has been tight in the jaws of the vice; it has felt the teeth of the rasp; it has been ground by emery; it has been heated and hammered and filed until it does not know itself, and it comes out a splendid knife. And if men only knew it, what are called their "misfortunes" are God's best blessings, for they are the moulding influences which give them shapeliness and edge, and durability and power.

REFORMATION.—When I was a boy, and I would go over to Aunt Bull's, who had several ugly dogs about her premises, I used to go barefooted, and make as little noise as possible, and climb over fences, and go a round-about way, so as, if possible, to get into the house before the dogs knew that I was coming. If I had acted as many reformers do, I should have gone with my pockets full of stones, and fired handful after handful at the dogs, and in the universal barking and hullabaloo should have said: "See what a condition of things this is! What a reformation is needed here!"

AGNOSTICISM AND FAITH.—Whatever men may scientifically agree to believe in, there is in men of noble nature something which science can neither illumine nor darken. When Tyndall was walking among the clouds during a sunset upon the Alps, his companion said to him, "Can you behold such a sublime scene as this and not feel that there is a God?" "Oh," said he, "I feel it. I feel it as much as any man can feel it; and I rejoice in it, if you do not tell me I can prove it." The moment you undertake to bring the evidence with which he dealt with matter to the ineffable and the hereafter, then, he says, "I am agnostic. I don't know. It isn't true;" but the moment you leave the mind under the gracious influence of such a scene, it rises above the sphere of doubt or proof, and he says, "I accept it."

THE LOST CHILD.

THE LITCHFIELD SABBATH.—That Sunday of my childhood, the marvelous stillness of that day over all Litchfield town hill; that wondrous ringing of the bell; the strange interpretation that my young imagination gave to the crowing of the cock and to the singing of the birds; that wondering look which I used to have into things; that strange lifting half-way up into inspiration, as it were; that sense of the joyful influence that sometimes brooded down like a stormy day, and sometimes opened up like a gala day in summer on me, made Sunday a more effectually marked day than any other of all my youthful life, and it stands out as clear as crystal until this hour. It might have been made happier and better if there had been a little more adaptation to my disposition and my wants; but, with all its limitations, I would rather have the other six days of the week weeded out of my memory than the Sabbath of my childhood. And this is right. Every child ought to be so brought up in the family, that when he thinks of home the first spot on which his thought rests shall be Sunday, as the culminating joy of the household.

LOST CHILD.—In Indiana, on the verge of civilization, there was a poor family—it was in pioneer life. There were two children—one too small to get out of the house and the other five years old. The father was gone. The oldest child ran to the woods; the mother went to find it; spent and tired, she gave the alarm. Men were summoned· they started about the middle of the day, went out with torches at night, and the next day, and the night following. The third day one of the pioneers came across the little fellow in a thicket, spent and weary. In triumph he seized the child, and took a bee-line for home. He shouted; the mother heard the shout. I never knew what happened when the mother got her child. He stammered as he told it. The human heart is yet a human heart. When you bring back God's child, lost in the world's wilderness, there's joy in heaven.

COMMUNION WITH GOD.—When I walked one day on the top of Mount Washington (glorious day of memory! such another day, I think, I shall not experience till I stand on the battlements of the New Jerusalem), how I was discharged of all imperfection! The wide, far-spreading country which lay beneath me in beauteous light—how heavenly it looked! And I communed with God. I had sweet tokens that He loved me. My very being rose right up into His nature. I walked with Him. And the cities far and near—New York, and all the cities and villages that lay between it and me—with their thunder; the wrangling of human passions below me, were to me as if they were not. Standing, as I did, high above them, it seemed to me as though they did not exist. There were the attritions, and cruel grindings, and cries, and tears, and shocks, of the human life below, but I was lifted up so high that they were nothing to me. The sounds died out, and I was lost with God. And the mountain-top was never so populous to me as when I was absolutely alone. So it is with the soul that goes up into the bosom of Christ. There is a reach where the arrows of envy cannot strike you.

KINDNESS.—No man has any right to make that which he believes to be the truth of God, any less exacting, less sharp or clear, because he thinks his fellow-men will not accept it if he states it in his blankest and baldest form. I read an incident in a newspaper the other day, that seems to me to illustrate this point. A tired and dusty traveler was leaning against a lamp-post in the city of Rochester, and he turned and looked on a boy in the crowd around him, and said:

" How far is it to Farmington? "

" Eight miles," said the boy.

" Do you think it is so far as that?" said the poor, tired traveler.

" Well, seeing that you are so tired, I will call it seven miles."

The boy, with his heart overflowing with the milk of human kindness, pitied the exhausted traveler and chose to call it seven miles. I know that I have seen statements of the truth that have dictated the same answer. Never make the road from Rochester to Farmington seven miles when you know it is eight. Do not do a wrong to truth out of regard for men.

PERFECTION.—The perfection of the schools is a kind of mandarin, perfection. Suppose a Chinese mandarin, whose garden was filled with dwarfed plants and trees, should show me an oak tree, two feet high, growing in a pot of earth, and should say to me, " A perfect tree must be sound at the root—must it not? And it must have all its branches complete and its leaves green. Look here....It is a perfect tree; why do you not admire it ?" Miserable two-foot oak ! I turn from it to think of God's oak in the open pasture, a hundred feet high, wide-boughed and braving the storm. Now when a man comes to me talking of perfection, and says, " A perfect man must have such-and-such qualities—must he not? He must control his passions and appetites. He must not sin in this thing or in that thing. Such am I. I do not commit this fault, or fall into that error. I have trained and schooled myself. Behold me ; I am perfect," I can but exclaim, " Miserable two-foot Christian !" I have no patience with this low standard, these earthly comparisons, this relative goodness. I must outgrow this pot of earth. God's eternity is in my soul, and I shall need it all to grow up to the measure of the stature of the fulness of Christ.

SPIRIT.—Before any daisy or violet, before any blossom is seen in the field, the sun lies with its bosom to the ground, crying to the flower, and saying, "Why tarriest thou so long?" and day after day the sun comes, and pours its maternal warmth upon the earth, and coaxes the plant to grow and bloom. And when days and weeks have passed, the root obeys the call and sends out its germ, from which comes the flower. Had it not been for the sun's warmth and light, the flower could never have come to itself. So the Eternal Spirit of God rests on the human soul, warming it, quickening it, calling it and saying, "O my son! where art thou?" And at last it is this Divine sympathy and brooding influence that brings men to God, and leads them to say, "Am I not sinful?" and to yearn for something higher and purer and holier. It was God's work. He long ago was working in you, to will and to do of His own good pleasure.

RICHES.—I asked, in New Hampshire, how much it took to make a farmer rich there, and I was told that if a man was worth five thousand dollars he was considered rich. If a man had a good farm, and had ten thousand dollars out at interest, oh! he was very rich—"passing" rich. I dropped a little farther down, into Concord, where some magnates of railroads live (they are the aristocrats just now), and I found that the idea of riches was quite different there. A man there was not considered rich unless he had a hundred or a hundred and fifty thousand dollars, in pretty clear stuff. I go to New York, and ask men how much it takes to make one rich, and they say, "There never was a greater mistake made than that of supposing that five or six hundred thousand dollars make a man rich. What does that sum amount to?" I go into the upper circles of New York, where millionaires, or men worth a million dollars or over, used to be considered rich, and there, if a man is worth five or ten millions it is thought that he is "coming on." It is said, "He will be rich one of these days." When a man's wealth amounts to fifty or a hundred millions he is very rich. Now if such is the idea of riches in material things, what must riches be when you rise above the highest men to angels, and above angels to God! What must be the circuit which makes riches when it reaches Him? And when you apply this term, increscent, to the Divine nature, as it respects the qualities of love and mercy, what must riches be in God, the Infinite, whose experiences are never less wide than infinity! What must be love and mercy, and their stores, when it is said that God is rich in them.

FRUITS, MEN KNOWN AND JUDGED BY.—At a horticultural show there is a table running through a long hall for the exhibition of fruit; and this table is divided up into about twenty-five compartments, which are assigned to as many exhibitors for the display of their productions. I go along the table and discuss the merits of the various articles. Here is a man who has pears and apples and peaches and cherries and plums. They are not very good ; they are fair ; they are about as good as the average of the fruit on the table; but they do not beat any body else's. I see fruit that is just as good all the way down the table. But the man to whom it belongs says, " Mine ought to take the premium." " Why? " I say. " Because it was raised on ground whose title goes back to the flood. No man has a right to claim the premium unless he can show that the title of his land goes clear down to the flood. I can prove that my title is clear, and I insist upon it that I ought to have the premium. That other fruit may have some ground for pretense, but it is uncovenanted." I go to the next compartment, and I say to the man there, " Your fruit looks fair. It is about on an average with the rest." " On an average with the rest ! There is nothing like it on the table." " Why so ? " " Because it was raised under glass. Those other fellows raised theirs in the open air. This is church-fruit. It was all raised in definite enclosures, according to prescriptions which have come down from generation to generation. In judging of my fruit you must take into consideration that it was raised according to the ordinances. It is pattern-fruit." He insists that his fruit is better than any of the rest on account of the way in which he raised it. I go to the next compartment. There I see some magnificent fruit, and I say to the man:

" Where did you raise this fruit ? "

" It came from the highway near my house," he says.

" From the highway ? "

" Yes. It grew on a wilding that I found growing there. I cleared away the brush that was choking it, and trimmed it a little, and it produced this fruit."

" Well," I say, " I think that is the best fruit on the table."

From the whole length of the table, on both sides, there arises the acclamation, " What ! are you going to give that man the premium, who has no title for his land, no greenhouse, and nothing but the highway to raise his fruit in ? What sort of encouragement is that to regular fruit-growers ? " The whole commotion is stopped by the man who has the awarding of the premium saying—

" The order of this show is : ' By their fruits shall ye know them.' "

EVOLUTION AND IMMORTALITY.—Then there is beyond that an element in evolution which endears it to me and to every man ; I think it throws bright gleams on the question of immortality. I see that the unfolding series in this world are all the time from lower to higher, that the ideal is not reached at any point, that the leaf works toward the bud, and the bud toward the blossom, and the blossom toward the tree, and that in the whole experience of human nature, and in the whole economy of the providence of God in regard to the physical world, every thing is on the march upward and onward. And one thing is very certain, that neither in the individual nor in the collective mass has the intimation of God in the human consciousness verified and fulfilled itself. The imperfection shows that we are not much further than the bud; somewhere we have a right to a prescience of the blossom, and the last we can see of men and of the horizon is when their faces are turned as if they were bound for the New Jerusalem, upward and onward. I think there is no other point of doctrine that is so vital to the heart of mankind as this—we shall live again; we shall live a better and a higher and a nobler life. Paul says: "If in this life only we have hope, we are, of all men, most miserable;" and ten thousand weary spirits in every community are saying: "Oh, this life has been a stormy one to me; full of disappointments, full of pains and sorrows and shames and poverty and suffering, and now comes this vagabond philosophy, and dashes out of my hand the consolation of believing that I am to live again." And it is the cry of the soul: "Lord let me live again." The accumulated experience of this life ought to have a sphere in which it can develop itself and prove itself. Now, I have this feeling—I thank God that the belief in a future and in an immortal state is in the world; I thank God that it is the interest of every man to keep it in the world; I thank God that there is no power of proof in science that we shall not live. Science may say: "You can not demonstrate it;" but I believe it; then it is my joy. Can you go to the body of the companion of your love, the lamp of your life, and bid it farewell at the grave? One of the most extraordinary passages in the Gospels is that where the disciples John and Peter ran to the grave of Jesus and saw the angels sitting, and they said to them: "I know whom ye seek; He is not here; He is risen." But what a woe if one bore mother or father, wife or child, to the open grave, and there was no angel in it; if you said farewell forever as the body was let down to its kindred earth. It is the hope of a joyful meeting by-and-by that sustains grief and bereavement in these bitter losses in life. Science can not destroy belief such as this of immortality after resurrection; it can not take it away; it can not destroy it, and it is the most precious boon we have in life—the faith that, through Jesus Christ, we shall live again, and live forever.

JAS. WHITCOMB RILEY   CHAS. B. LEWIS
ROBT. T. BURDETTE   (M QUAD)
(THE HAWKEYE MAN)   BENJ. P. SHILLABER
                                  (MRS. PARTINGTON)

THE "HAWKEYE MAN."

BIOGRAPHY AND REMINISCENCES.

This sweetest and loveliest character of American literature, Robert J. Burdette, resides, at present, in a beautiful home in Bryn Mawr, Pa. Mark Twain, in his "Library of Wit and Humor," says:

Robert J. Burdette was born at Greensburgh, Pa., July 30, 1844. His family removed to Illinois when Robert was a boy. He was educated in the Peoria public schools. He enlisted in the army in 1862. On his return from the war, he engaged in railroad work, and afterward became associate editor of the Burlington *Hawkeye*, in the columns of which he did the first literary work which made him famous. Mr. Burdette, besides publishing a volume of sketches, has been a contributor to numerous magazines and periodicals. He is at present a licentiate, and often preaches from the pulpits of the Methodist Church.

Previous to going on the *Hawkeye*, Mr. Burdette established a newspaper in Peoria. One day I met the humorist, and asked him how his Peoria paper succeeded.

" Did you make much money ? "

" Money ? " repeated Burdette. " M-o-n-e-y ! Did you ever start a paper ? "

" No, I believe not," I said.

" Well, you ought to try it. I started one once. Yes, I started one. We called it the Peoria *Review*, and it was started ' to fill a long-felt want.' "

" Did you have any partners ? " I asked.

" Yes, Jerry Cochrane was my partner. There were several very comforting things on that paper. For instance, Jerry and I always knew on Monday that we would not have money enough to pay the hands off on Saturday, and we never had. The hands knew it, too, so their nerves were never shocked by a disappointment. We ran that way for a while, getting more deeply in debt all the time. At last, one morning, I entered the office and found Jerry looking rather solemn.

"'Jerry,' said I, 'you want another partner.'

"'Yes, we need a new one,' he rejoined.

"'A business man,' said I.

"'One with executive ability,' said he.

"'A financier,' I observed.

"'A man who can take hold of things and turn them into money,' he concluded.

"'Then I have got the man you want,' said I, and I introduced Frank Hitchcock, the sheriff. Jerry said Frank was the man he had been thinking of, so we installed him at once."

"Was Hitchcock a good business man?" I asked.

"O, yes, everything he touched turned into money. He proved to be all we anticipated, and he ran the paper with the greatest success until he had turned that too into money."

"What was the final result?"

"Well, when we wound up the concern, there was nothing left but two passes — one to Cincinnati and one to Burlington. We divided them and went in different directions."

Robert Burdette's wit generally borders on satire. That is, he takes some foible of fashion, or some foolish domestic custom, and exaggerates it. To illustrate, the humorist thus satirized the irritable wife:

Mrs. Jones was at a party the other night smiling so serenely to every one, when the handsome Captain Hamilton, who reads poetry oh, so divinely, and is oh, so nice, stepped on her dress as she was hurrying across the room.

K-r-r-rt! R'p! R'p! how it tore and jerked, and how the captain looked as though he would die as he said:

"My dear Mrs. Jones, I was so clumsy!"

"O dear, no, Captain," she sweetly said, smiling till she looked like a seraph who had got down here by mistake, "it's of no consequence, I assure you, it doesn't make a particle of difference, at all."

Just twenty-five minutes later her husband, helping her into the street car, mussed her ruffle.

"Goodness gracious me!" she snapped out, "go way and let me alone; you'll tear me to pieces if you keep on."

Then she flopped down on the seat so hard that everything rattled, and the frightened driver ejaculated, "There goes that brake chain again," and crawled under the car with his lantern to see how badly it had given way!

When I asked the humorist what was the best joke he ever saw, he said:

"It occurred in our Peoria Bible class. Our dear, good old clergyman, one hot summer afternoon, was telling us boys, how we should never get excited.

" 'Boys,' he said, 'you should never lose your tempers—never let your angry passions rise. You should never swear or get angry, or excited. I never do. Now, to illustrate,' said the clergyman, pointing toward his face, 'you all see that little fly on my nose. A good many wicked, **worldly** men would get angry at that fly, but I don't !'

" 'What do I do?

" 'Why, my children, I simply say go away fly——go away—— and——*gosh blast it! it's a* WASP!'"

Robert J. Burdette is beloved by every one. He never had an enemy. One day when I made this remark to Petroleum V. Nasby, he said:

" Yes, Burdette is a lovely character, but a woe was pronounced against him in the Bible."

" How was that?" I asked.

" Why the Bible says 'woe unto you when all men speak well of you.'"

BURDETTE'S RISE AND FALL OF THE MUSTACHE.

Ladies and Gentlemen:—Adam raised Cain, but he did not raise a mustache. He was born a man, a full grown man, and with a mustache already raised.

If Adam wore a mustache, he never raised it. It raised itself. It evolved itself out of its own inner consciousness, like a primordial germ. It grew, like the weeds on his farm, in spite of him, and to torment him. For Adam had hardly got his farm reduced to a kind of turbulent, weed-producing, granger-fighting, regular order of things— had scarcely settled down to the quiet, happy, care-free, independent life of a jocund farmer, with nothing under the canopy to molest or make him afraid, with every thing on the plantation going on smoothly and lovely, with a little rust in the oats; army worm in the corn; Colorado beetles swarming up and down the potato patch; cutworms laying waste the cucumbers; curculio in the plums and borers in the apple trees; a new kind of bug that he didn't know the name of desolating the wheat fields; dry weather burning up the wheat; wet weather blighting the corn; too cold for the melons, too dreadfully hot for the strawberries; chickens dying with the pip; hogs being gathered to their fathers with the cholera; sheep fading away with a complication of things that no man could remember; horses getting along as well as could be expected, with a little spavin, ring-bone, wolf-teeth, distemper, heaves, blind staggers, collar chafes, saddle galls, colic now and then, founder occasionally, epizootic when there was nothing else; cattle going wild with the horn ail; moth in the bee-hives; snakes in the milk house; moles in the kitchen garden—Adam had just about got through breaking wild land with a crooked stick, and settled down comfortably, when the sound of the boy was heard in the land.

Did it ever occur to you that Adam was probably the most troubled and worried man that ever lived?

We have always pictured Adam as a careworn looking man; a puzzled looking granger who would sigh fifty times a day, and sit down on a log and run his irresolute fingers through his hair while he wondered what under the canopy he was going to do with those boys, and whatever was going to become of them. We have thought, too, that as often as our esteemed parent asked himself this conundrum, he gave it up. They must have been a source of constant trouble and mystification to him. For you see they were the first boys that humanity ever had any experience with. And there was no one else in the neighborhood who had any boy, with whom Adam, in his moments of perplexity, could consult. There wasn't a boy in the country with whom Adam's boys were on speaking terms, and with whom they could play and fight.

Adam, you see, labored under the most distressing disadvantages that ever opposed a married man, and the father of a family. He had never been a boy himself, and what could he know about boy nature or boy troubles and pleasure? His perplexity began at an early date.

Imagine, if you can, the celerity with which he kicked off the leaves, and paced up and down in the moonlight the first time little Cain made the welkin ring when he had the colic. How did Adam know what ailed him? He couldn't tell Eve that she had been sticking the baby full of pins. He didn't even know enough to turn the vociferous infant over on his face and jolt him into serenity. If the fence corners on his farm had been overgrown with catnip, never an idea would Adam have had what to do with it. It is probable that after he got down on his knees and felt for thorns or snakes or rats in the bed, and thoroughly examined young Cain for bites or scratches, he passed him over to Eve with the usual remark:

"There, take him and hush him up, for heaven's sake," and then went off and sat down under a distant tree with his fingers in his ears, and perplexity in his brain.

And young Cain just split the night with the most hideous howls the little world had ever listened to. It must have stirred the animals up to a degree that no menagerie has ever since attained. There was no sleep in the vicinity of Eden that night for any body, baby, beasts or Adam. And it is more than probable that the weeds got a long start of Adam the next day, while he lay around in shady places and slept in troubled dozes, disturbed, perhaps, by awful visions of possible twins and more colic. [Laughter.]

And when the other boy came along, and the boys got old enough to sleep in a bed by themselves, they had no pillows to fight with, and it is a moral impossibility for two brothers to go to bed without a fracas. And what comfort could two boys get out of pelting each other with fragments of moss or bundles of brush? What dismal views of future humanity Adam must have received from the glimpses of original sin which began to develop itself in his boys. How he must have wondered what put into their heads the thousand and one questions with which they plied their parents day after day. We wonder what he thought when they first began to string buckeyes on the cat's tail. And when night came, there was no hired girl to keep the boys quiet by telling them ghost stories, and Adam didn't even know so much as an anecdote.

Cain, when he made his appearance, was the first and only boy in the fair young world. And all his education depended on his inexperienced parents, who had never in their lives seen a boy until they saw Cain. And there wasn't an educational help in the market. There wasn't an alphabet block in the county; not even a Centennial illustrated handkerchief. There were no other boys in the republic, to teach young Cain to lie, and swear, and smoke, and drink, fight and steal, and thus develop the boy's dormant statesmanship, and prepare him for the sterner political duties of his maturer years. There wasn't a pocket knife in the universe that he could borrow—and lose, and when he wanted to cut his finger, as all boys must do, now and then, he had to cut it with a clam shell. There were no country relations upon whom little Cain could be inflicted for two or three weeks at a time, when his wearied parents wanted a little rest. There was nothing for him to play with. Adam couldn't show him how to make a kite. He had a much better idea of angels' wings than he had of a kite. And if little Cain had even asked for such a simple bit of mechanism as a shinny club, Adam would have gone out into the depths of the primeval forest and wept in sheer mortification and helpless, confessed ignorance.

I don't wonder that Cain turned out bad. I always said he would. For his entire education depended upon a most ignorant man, a man in the very palmiest days of his ignorance, who couldn't have known less if he had tried all his life on a high salary and had a man to help him. And the boy's education had to be conducted entirely upon the catechetical system; only, in this instance, the boy pupil asked the questions, and his parent teachers, heaven help them, tried to answer them. And they had to answer at them. For they could not take refuge from the steady stream of questions that poured in upon them day after day, by interpolating a fairy story, as you do when your boy asks you questions about something of which you never heard. For how could Adam begin, "Once upon a time," when with one quick, incisive question, Cain could pin him right back against the dead wall of creation, and make him either specify exactly what time, or acknowledge the fraud? How could Eve tell him about "Jack and the bean stalk," when Cain, fairly crazy for some one to play with, knew perfectly well there was not, and never had been, another boy on the plantation? And as day by day Cain brought home things in his hands about which to ask questions that no mortal could answer, how grateful his bewildered parents must have been that he had no pockets in which to transport his collections. For many generations came into the fair young world, got into no end of trouble, and died out of it, before a boy's pocket solved the problem how to make the thing contained seven times greater than the container.

The only thing that saved Adam and Eve from interrogational insanity was the paucity of language. If little Cain had possessed the verbal abundance of the language in which men are to-day talked to death, his father's bald head would have gone down in shining flight to the ends of the earth to escape him, leaving Eve to look after the stock, save the crop, and raise her boy as best she could. Which would have been 6,000 years ago, as to-day, just like a man.

Because, it was no off-hand, absent-minded work answering questions about things in those spacious old days, when there was crowds of room, and every thing grew by the acre. When a placid but exceedingly unanimous looking animal went rolling by, producing the general effect of an eclipse, and Cain would shout,

"Oh, lookee, lookee Pa! what's that?"

Then the patient Adam, trying to saw enough kitchen wood to last over Sunday, with a piece of flint, would have to pause and gather up words enough to say:

"That, my son? That is only a mastodon giganteus; he has a bad look, but a Christian temper."

And then presently:

"Oh, pa! pa! What's that over yon?"

" Oh, bother," Adam would reply; " it's only a paleotherium, mammalia pachydermata." [Laughter.]

" Oh, yes; theliocomeafterus. Oh! lookee, lookee at this 'un! "

" Where, Cainny? Oh, that in the mud? That's only an acephala lamelli branchiata. It won't bite you, but you mustn't eat it. It's poison as politics."

" Whee! See there! see, see, see! What's him? "

" Oh, that? Looks like a plesiosaurus; keep out of his way; he has a jaw like your mother."

" Oh, yes; a plenosserus. And what's that fellow, poppy? "

" That's a silurus malaptorus. Don't you go near him, for he has the disposition of a Georgia mule."

" Oh, yes; a slapterus. And what's this little one? "

" Oh, it's nothing but an aristolochioid. Where did you get it? There, now, quit throwing stones at that acanthopterygian; do you want to be kicked? And keep away from the nothodenatrichomanoides. My stars, Eve! where did he get that anonaceo-hydrocharideo-nymphæoid? Do you never look after him at all? Here, you Cain, get right away down from there, and chase that megalosaurius out of the melon patch, or I'll set the monopleuro branchian on you." [Laughter.]

Just think of it, Christian man with a family to support, with last year's stock on your shelves, and a draft as long as a clothes-line to pay to-morrow! Think of it, woman with all a woman's love and constancy, and a mother's sympathetic nature, with three meals a day 365 times a year to think of, and the flies to chase out of the sitting-room; think, if your cherub boy was the only boy in the wide, wide world, and all his questions which now radiate in a thousand directions among other boys, who tell him lies and help him to cut his eye-teeth, were focused upon you! Adam had only one consolation that has been denied his more remote descendants. His boy never belonged to a base ball club, never smoked cigarettes, and never teased his father from the first of November till the last of March for a pair of roller skates.

Well, you have no time to pity Adam. You have your own boy to look after. Or, your neighbor has a boy, whom you can look after much more closely than his mother does, and much more to your own satisfaction than to the boy's comfort.

Your boy is, as Adam's boy was, an animal that asks questions. If there were any truth in the old theory of the transmigration of souls, when a boy died he would pass into an interrogation point. And he'd stay there. He'd never get out of it; for he never gets through asking questions. The older he grows the more he asks, and the more

perplexing his questions are, and the more unreasonable he is about wanting them answered to suit himself.   Why, the oldest boy I ever knew —
he was fifty-seven years old, and I went to school to him — could and did
ask the longest, hardest, crookedest questions [Laughter], that no fellow,
who used to trade off all his books for a pair of skates and a knife with
a corkscrew in it, could answer.   And when his questions were not
answered to suit him, it was his custom — a custom more honored in
the breeches, we used to think, than in the observance — to take up a
long, slender, but exceedingly tenacious rod, which lay ever near the
big dictionary, and smite with it the boy whose naturally derived Adamic
ignorance was made manifest.

Ah, me, if the boy could only do as he is done by, and ferule the man
or the woman who fails to reply to his inquiries, as he is himself corrected for similar shortcomings, what a valley of tears, what a literally
howling wilderness he could and would make of this world. [Laughter.]

Your boy, asking to-day pretty much the same questions, with heaven
knows how many additional ones, that Adam's boy did, ist old, every
time he asks one that you don't know any thing about, just as Adam
told Cain fifty times a day, that he will know all about it when he is a
man.   And so from the days of Cain down to the present wickeder generation of boys, the boy ever looks forward to the time when he will be a
man and know every thing.

And now, not entirely ceasing to ask questions, your boy begins to
answer them, until you stand amazed at the breadth and depth of his
knowledge.   He asks questions and gets answers of teachers that you and
the school board know not of.   Day by day, great unprinted books, upon
the broad pages of which the hand of nature has traced characters that
only a boy can read, are spread out before him.   He knows now where
the first snow-drop lifts its tiny head, a pearl on the bosom of the barren
earth, in the spring; he knows where the last Indian pink lingers, a
flame in the brown and rustling woods, in the autumn days.   His pockets
are cabinets, from which he drags curious fossils that he does not know
the names of; monstrous and hideous beetles and bugs and things that
you never saw before, and for which he has appropriate names of his own.
He knows where there are three oriole's nests, and so far back as you can
remember, you never saw an oriole's nest in your life.   He can tell you
how to distinguish the good mushrooms from the poisonous ones, and
poison grapes from good ones, and how he ever found out, except by eating both kinds, is a mystery to his mother.   Every root, bud, leaf, berry
or bark, that will make any bitter, horrible, semi-poisonous tea, reputed
to have marvelous medicinal virtues, he knows where to find, and in the

season he does find, and brings home, and all but sends the entire family to the cemetery by making practical tests of his teas.

And as his knowledge broadens, his human superstition develops itself. He has a formula, repeating which nine times a day, while pointing his finger fixedly toward the sun, will cause warts to disappear from the hand, or, to use his own expression, will "knock warts." [Laughter.] If the eight-day clock at home tells him it is two o'clock, and the flying leaves of the dandelion declare it is half-past five, he will stand or fall with the dandelion.

He has a formula, by which any thing that has been lost may be found. He has, above all things, a natural, infallible instinct for the woods, and can no more be lost in them than a squirrel. If the cow does not come home — and if she is a town cow, like a town man, she does not come home, three nights in the week — you lose half a day of valuable time looking for her. Then you pay a man three dollars to look for her two days longer, or so long as the appropriation holds out. Finally, a quarter sends a boy to the woods; he comes back at milking time, whistling the tune that no man ever imitated, and the cow ambles contentedly along before him.

He has one particular marble which he regards with about the same superstitious reverence that a pagan does his idol, and his Sunday-school teacher can't drive it out of him, either. Carnelian, crystal, bull's eye, china, pottery, boly, blood alley, or commie, whatever he may call it, there is "luck in it." When he loses this marble, he sees panic and bankruptcy ahead of him, and retires from business prudently, before the crash comes, failing, in true centennial style, with both pockets and a cigar box full of winnings, and a creditors' meeting in the back room.

A boy's world is open to no one but a boy. You never really revisit the glimpses of your boyhood, much as you may dream of it. After you get into a tail coat, and tight boots, you never again set foot in boy world. You lose this marvelous instinct for the woods, you can't tell a pig-nut tree from a pecan; you can't make friends with strange dogs; you can't make the terrific noises with your mouth, you can't invent the inimitable signals or the characteristic catchwords of boyhood.

He is getting on, is your boy. He reaches the dime-novel age. He wants to be a missionary. Or a pirate. So far as he expresses any preference, he would rather be a pirate, an occupation in which there are more chances for making money, and fewer opportunities for being devoured. He develops a yearning love for school and study about this time, also, and every time he dreams of being a pirate he dreams of hanging his dear teacher at the yard arm in the presence of the delighted scholars. His voice develops, even more rapidly and thoroughly than his morals. In the yard, on the house top, down the street, around the corner; wherever there is a patch of ice big enough for him to break his neck on, or a pond of water deep enough to drown in, the voice of your boy is heard. He whispers in a shout, and converses, in ordinary, confidential moments, in a shriek. He exchanges bits of back-fence gossip about his father's domestic matters, with the boy living in the adjacent township, to which interesting revelations of home-life the intermediate neighborhood listens with intense satisfaction, and the two home circles in helpless dismay. He has an unconquerable hatred for company, and an aversion for walking down stairs. For a year or two his feet never touch the stairway in his descent, and his habit of polishing the stair rail by using it as a passenger tramway, soon breaks the other members of the family of the careless habit of setting the hall lamp or the water pitcher on the baluster post. He wears the same size boot as his father; and on the dryest, dustiest days in the year, always manages to convey some mud on the carpets. He carefully steps over the door mat, and until he is about seventeen years old, he actually never knew there was a scraper at the front porch.

About this time, bold but inartistic pencil sketches break out mysteriously on the alluring background of the wall paper. He asks, with great regularity, alarming frequency and growing diffidence, for a new hat. You might as well buy him a new disposition. He wears his hat in the air and on the ground far more than he does on his head, and he never hangs it up that he doesn't pull the hook through the crown; unless the hook breaks off or the hat rack pulls over.

He is a perfect Robinson Crusoe in inventive genius. He can make a kite that will fly higher and pull harder than a balloon. He can, and, on occasion, will, take out a couple of the pantry shelves and make a sled that is amazement itself. The mouse-trap he builds out of the water pitcher and the family Bible is a marvel of mechanical ingenuity. So is the excuse he gives for such a selection of raw material. When suddenly, some Monday morning, the clothes line, without any just or apparent cause or provocation, shrinks sixteen feet, philosophy cannot make you believe that Professor Tice did it with his little barometer. Because, far down the dusty street, you can see Tom in the dim distance, driving a prancing team, six-in-hand, with the missing link.

You send your boy on an errand. There are three ladies in the parlor. You have waited as long as you can, in all courtesy, for them to go. They have developed alarming symptoms of staying to tea. And you know there aren't half enough strawberries to go around. It is only a three minutes' walk to the grocery, however, and Tom sets off like a rocket, and you are so pleased with his celerity and ready good nature that you want to run after him and kiss him. He is gone a long time, however. Ten minutes become fifteen, fifteen grow into twenty; the twenty swell into the half hour, and your guests exchange very significant glances as the half becomes three-quarters. Your boy returns at last. Apprehension in his downcast eyes, humility in his laggard step, penitence in the appealing slouch of his battered hat, and a pound and a half of shingle nails in his hands.

"Mother," he says, "what else was it you told me to get besides the nails?" [Laughter.] And while you are counting your scanty store of berries to make them go round without a fraction, you hear Tom out in the back yard whistling and hammering away, building a dog house with the nails you never told him to get.

Poor Tom, he loves at this age quite as ardently as he makes mistakes and mischief. And he is repulsed quite as ardently as he makes love. If he hugs his sister, he musses her ruffle, and gets cuffed for it. Two hours later, another boy, not more than twenty-two or twenty-three years older than Tom, some neighbor's Tom, will come in, and will just make the most hopeless, terrible, chaotic wreck of that ruffle that lace or footing can be distorted into. And the only reproof he gets is the reproachful murmur, "Must he go so soon?" [Laughter] when he doesn't make a movement to go until he hears the alarm clock go off upstairs and the old gentleman in the adjoining room banging around building the morning fires, and loudly wondering if young Mr. Bostwick is going to stay to breakfast?

Tom is at this age set in deadly enmity against company, which he soon learns to regard as his mortal foe. He regards company as a mysterious and eminently respectable delegation that always stays to dinner, invariably crowds him to the second table, never leaves him any of the pie, and generally makes him late for school. Naturally, he learns to love refined society, but in a conservative, non-committal sort of a way, dissembling his love so effectually that even his parents never dream of its existence until it is gone.

Poor Tom, his life is not all comedy at this period. Go up to your boy's room some night, and his sleeping face will preach you a sermon on the griefs and troubles that sometimes weigh his little heart down almost to breaking, more eloquently than the lips of a Spurgeon could picture them. The curtain has fallen on one day's act in the drama of his active little life. The restless feet that all day long have pattered so far—down dusty streets, over scorching pavements, through long

stretches of quiet wooded lanes, along the winding cattle paths in the
deep, silent woods; that have dabbled in the cool brook where it
wrangles and scolds over the shining pebbles, that have filled your
house with noise and dust and racket, are still. The stained hand outside the sheet is soiled and rough, and the cut finger with the rude
bandage of the boy's own surgery, pleads with a mute, effective pathos
of its own, for the mischievous hand that is never idle. On the brown
cheek the trace of a tear marks the piteous close of the day's troubles,
the closing scene in a troubled little drama; trouble at school with
books that were too many for him; trouble with temptations to
have unlawful fun that were too strong for him, as they are frequently
too strong for his father; trouble in the street with boys that were
too big for him; and at last, in his home, in his castle, his refuge,
trouble has pursued him, until, feeling utterly friendless and in every
body's way, he has crawled off to the dismantled den, dignified usually
by the title of "the boy's room," and his overcharged heart has welled
up into his eyes, and his last waking breath has broken into a sob, and
just as he begins to think that after all, life is only one broad sea of
troubles, whose restless billows, in never-ending succession, break and
beat and double and dash upon the short shore line of a boy's life,
he has drifted away into the wonderland of a boy's sleep, where fairy
fingers picture his dreams. [Applause.]

How soundly, deeply, peacefully he sleeps. No mother, who has
never dragged a sleepy boy off the lounge at 9 o'clock, and hauled him
off upstairs to bed, can know with what a herculean grip a square
sleep takes hold of a boy's senses, nor how fearfully and wonderfully
limp and nerveless it makes him; nor how, in direct antagonism to all
established laws of anatomy, it develops joints that work both ways, all
the way up and down that boy.

And what pen can portray the wonderful enchantments of a boy's
dreamland ! No marvelous visions wrought by the weird, strange power
of hasheesh, no dreams that come to the sleep of jaded woman or tired
man, no ghastly specters that dance attendance upon cold mince pie,
but shrink into tiresome, stale, and trifling commonplaces compared
with the marvelous, the grotesque, the wonderful, the terrible, the
beautiful and the enchanting scenes and people of a boy's dreamland.
This may be owing, in a great measure, to the fact that the boy never
relates his dream until all the other members of the family have related
theirs; and then he comes in, like a back county, with the necessary
majority; like the directory of a western city, following the census of a
rival town.

Tom is a miniature Ishmaelite at this period of his career. His hand is against every man, and about every man's hand, and nearly every woman's hand, is against him, off and on. Often, and then the iron enters his soul, the hand that is against him holds the slipper. He wears his mother's slipper on his jacket quite as often as she wears it on her foot. And this is all wrong, unchristian and impolitic. It spreads the slipper and discourages the boy. When he reads in his Sunday-school lesson that the wicked stand in slippery places, he takes it as a direct personal reference, and he is affronted, and may be the seeds of atheism are implanted in his breast. Moreover, this repeated application of the slipper not only sours his temper, and gives a bias to his moral ideas, but it sharpens his wits. How many a Christian mother, her soft eyes swimming in tears of real pain that plashed up from the depths of a loving heart, as she bent over her wayward boy until his heart-rending wails and piteous shrieks drowned her own choking, sympathetic sobs, has been wasting her strength, and wearing out a good slipper, and pouring out all that priceless flood of mother love and duty and pity and tender sympathy upon a concealed atlas back, or a Saginaw shingle. [Laughter.]

It is a historical fact that no boy is ever whipped twice for precisely the same offense. He varies and improves a little on every repetition of the prank, until at last he reaches a point where detection is almost impossible. He is a big boy then, and glides almost imperceptibly from the discipline of his father, under the surveillance of the police.

By easy stages he passes into the uncomfortable period of boyhood. His jacket develops into a tail-coat. The boy of to-day, who is slipped into a hollow, abbreviated mockery of a tail-coat, when he is taken out of long dresses, has no idea—not the faintest conception of the grandeur, the momentous importance of the epoch in a boy's life, that was marked by the transition from the old-fashioned cadet roundabout to the tail-coat. It is an experience that heaven, ever chary of its choicest blessings, and mindful of the decadence of the race of boys, has not vouchsafed to the untoward, forsaken boys of this wicked generation. When the roundabout went out of fashion, the heroic race of boys passed away from earth, and weeping nature sobbed and broke the moulds. The fashion that started a boy of six years on his pilgrimage of life in a miniature edition of his father's coat, marked a period of retrogression in the affairs of men, and stamped a decaying and degenerate race. There are no boys now, or very few, at least, such as peopled the grand old earth when the men of our age were boys. And that it is so, society is to be congratulated. The step from the roundabout to the tail-coat was a leap in life. It was the boy Iulus, doffing the *prætexta* and flinging upon his shoulders the *toga virilis* of Julius; Patroclus, donning the armor of Achilles, in which to go forth and be Hectored to death.

Tom is slow to realize the grandeur of that tail-coat, however, on its trial trip. How differently it feels from his good, snug-fitting, comfortable old jacket. It fits him too much in every direction, he knows. Every now and then he stops with a gasp of terror, feeling positive, from the awful sensation of nothingness about the neck, that the entire collar has fallen off in the street. The tails are prairies, the pockets are caverns, and the back is one vast, illimitable, stretching waste. How Tom sidles along as close to the fence as he can scrape, and what a wary eye he keeps in every direction for other boys. When he forgets the school, he is half tempted to feel proud of his toga; but when he thinks of the boys, and the reception that awaits him, his heart sinks, and he is tempted to go back home, sneak up stairs, and rescue his worn, old jacket from the rag-bag. He glances in terror at his distorted shadow on the fence, and, confident that it is a faithful outline of his figure, he knows that he has worn his father's coat off by mistake.

He tries various methods of bottoning his coat to make it conform more harmoniously to his figure and his ideas of the eternal fitness of things. He buttons just the lower button, and immediately it flies all abroad at the shoulders, and he beholds himself an exaggerated mannikin of "Cap'n Cuttle." Then he fastens just the upper button, and the frantic tails flap and flutter like a clothes-line in a cyclone. Then he buttons it all up, *a la militaire,* and tries to look soldierly, but the effect is so theological-studently that it frightens him until his heart stops beating. As he reaches the last friendly corner that shields him from the pitiless gaze of the boys he can hear howling and shrieking not fifty yards away, he pauses to give the final ajustment to the manly and unmanageable raiment. It is bigger and looser, flappier and wrinklier than ever. New and startling folds, and unexpected wrinkles, and uncontemplated bulges develop themselves, like masked batteries, just when and where the effect will be most demoralizing. And a new horror discloses itself at this trying and awful juncture. He wants to lie down on the side walk and try to die. For the first time he notices the color of his coat. Hideous! He has been duped, swindled, betrayed— made a monstrous idiot by that silver-tongued salesman, who has palmed off upon him a coat 2,000 years old; a coat that the most sweetly enthusiastic and terribly misinformed women's missionary society would hesitate to offer a wild Hottentot; and which the most benighted, old-fashioned Hottentot that ever disdained clothes, would certainly blush to wear in the dark, and would probably decline with thanks. Oh, madness! The color is no color. It is all colors. It is a brindle—a veritable, undeniable brindle. There must have been a fabulous amount of brindle cloth made up into boys' first coats, sixteen or eighteen or nineteen years ago, because out of 894—I like to be exact in the use of figures, because nothing else in the world lends such an air of profound truthfulness to a discourse—out of 894 boys I knew in the first tail-coat period, 893 came to school in brindle coats. And the other one—the 894th boy—made his wretched debut in a bottle-green toga, with dreadful, glaring brass buttons. He left school very suddenly, and we always believed that the angels saw him in that coat, and ran away with him. But Tom, shivering with apprehension, and faint with mortification over the discovery of this new horror, gives one last despairing scrooch of his shoulders, to make the coat look shorter, and, with a final frantic tug at the tails, to make it appear longer, steps out from the protecting ægis of the corner, is stunned with a vocal hurricane of—

" Oh, what a coat!" and his cup of misery is as full as a rag-bag in three minutes.

Passing into the tail-coat period, Tom awakens to a knowledge of the broad physical truth, that he has hands. He is not very positive in his own mind how many. At times he is ready to swear to an even two, one pair; good hand. Again, when cruel fate and the non-appearance of some one's else brother has compelled him to accompany his sister to a church sociable, he can see eleven; and as he sits bolt upright in the grimmest of straight-back chairs, plastered right up against the wall, as the "sociable" custom is, or used to be, trying to find enough unoccupied pockets in which to sequester all his hands, he is dimly conscious that hands should come in pairs, and vaguely wonders, if he has only five pair of regularly ordained hands, where this odd hand came from. And hitherto, Tom has been content to encase his feet in any thing that would stay on them. Now, however, he has an eye for a glove-fitting boot, and learns to wreath his face in smiles, hollow, heartless, deceitful smiles, while his boots are as full of agony as a broken heart, and his tortured feet cry out for vengeance upon the shoemaker, and make Tom feel that life is a hollow mockery, and there is nothing real but soft corns and bunions.

And: His mother never cuts his hair again. Never. When Tom assumes the manly gown, she has looked her last upon his head, with trimming ideas. His hair will be trimmed and clipped, barberously it may be, but she will not be accessory before the fact. She may sometimes long to have her boy kneel down before her, while she gnaws

11

around his terrified locks with a pair of scissors that were sharpened
when they were made; and have since then cut acres of calico, and miles
and miles of paper, and great stretches of cloth, and snarls and coils of
string, and furlongs of lamp wick; and have snuffed candles; and dug
refractory corks out of the family ink bottle; and punched holes in
skate-straps; and trimmed the family nails; and have even done their
level best, at the annual struggle, to cut stove-pipe lengths in two; and
have successfully opened oyster and fruit cans; and pried up carpet
tacks; and have many a time and oft gone snarlingly and toilsomely
around Tom's head, and made him an object of terror to the children in
the street, and made him look so much like a yearling colt with the run
of a bur pasture, that people have been afraid to approach him too suddenly, lest he should jump through his collar and run away. [Applause.]

He feels, too, the dawning consciousness of another grand truth in
the human economy. It dawns upon his deepening intelligence with
the inherent strength and the unquestioned truth of a new revelation,
that man's upper lip was designed by nature for a mustache pasture.
How tenderly reserved he is when he is brooding over this momentous
discovery. With what exquisite caution and delicacy are his primal
investigations conducted. In his microscopical researches it appears to
him that the down on his upper lip is certainly more determined down,
more positive, more pronounced, more individual fuzz than that which
vegetates in neglected tenderness upon his cheeks. He makes cautious
explorations along the land of promise with the tip of his tenderest
finger, delicately backing up the grade the wrong way, going always
against the grain, that he may the more readily detect the slightest
symptom of an uprising by the first feeling of velvety resistance. And
day by day he is more and more firmly convinced that there is in his lip
the primordial germs, the protoplasm of a glory that will, in its full
development, eclipse even the majesty and grandeur of his first tail-coat.
And in the first dawning consciousness that the mustache is there, like
the vote, and only needs to be brought out, how often Tom walks down
to the barber shop, gazes longingly in at the window, and walks past.
And how often, when he musters up sufficient courage to go in, and
climbs into the chair, and is just on the point of huskily whispering to
the barber that he would like a shave, the entrance of a man with a
beard like Frederick Barbarossa, frightens away his resolution, and he
has his hair cut again. The third time that week, and it is so short
that the barber has to hold it with his teeth while he files it off, and
parts it with a straight edge and a scratch awl. Naturally, driven
from the barber chair, Tom casts longing eyes upon the ancestral shaving machinery at home. And who shall say by what means he at length

obtains possession of the paternal razor? No one. Nobody knows. Nobody ever did know. Even the searching investigation that always follows the paternal demand for the immediate extradition of whoever opened a fruit can with that razor, which always follows Tom's first shave, is always, and ever will be, barren of results.

All that we know about it is, that Tom holds the razor in his hand about a minute, wondering what to do with it, before the blade falls across his fingers and cuts every one of them. First blood claimed and allowed, for the razor. Then he straps the razor furiously. Or, rather, he razors the strap. He slashes and cuts that passive instrument in as many directions as he can make motions with the razor. He would cut it oftener if the strap lasted longer. Then he nicks the razor against the side of the mug. Then he drops it on the floor and steps on it and nicks it again. They are small nicks, not so large by half as a saw tooth, and he flatters himself his father will never see them. Then he soaks the razor in hot water, as he has seen his father do. Then he takes it out, at a temperature anywhere under 980° Fahrenheit, and lays it against his cheek, and raises a blister there the size of the razor, as he never saw his father do, but as his father most assuredly did, many, many years before Tom met him. Then he makes a variety of indescribable grimaces and labial contortions in a frenzied effort to get his upper lip into approachable shape, and, at last, the first offer he makes at his embryo mustache he slashes his nose with a vicious upper cut. He gashes the corners of his mouth; wherever those nicks touch his cheek they leave a scratch apiece, and he learns what a good nick in a razor is for, and at last when he lays the blood-stained weapon down, his gory lip looks as though it had just come out of a long, stubborn, exciting contest with a straw-cutter.

But he learns to shave, after a while—just before he cuts his lip clear off. He has to take quite a course of instruction, however, in that great school of experience about which the old philosopher had a remark to make. It is a grand old school; the only school at which men will study and learn, each for himself. One man's experience never does another man any good; never did and never will teach another man any thing. If the philosopher had said that it was a hard school, but that some men would learn at no other than this grand old school of experience, we might have inferred that all women, and most boys, and a few men were exempt from its hard teachings. But he used the more comprehensive term, if you remember what that is, and took us all in. We have all been there. There is no other school, in fact. Poor little Cain; dear, lonesome, wicked little Cain—I know it isn't fashionable to pet him; I know it is popular to speak harshly and savagely about our eldest brother, when the fact is we resemble him more closely in disposition than any other member of the family — poor little Cain never knew the difference between his father's sunburned nose and a glowing coal, until he had pulled the one and picked up the other. And Abel had to find out the difference in the same way, although he was told five hundred times, by his brother's experience, that the coal would burn him and the nose wouldn't. And Cain's boy wouldn't believe that fire was any hotter than an icicle, until he had made a digital experiment, and understood why they called it fire. And so Enoch and Methusaleh, and Moses, and Daniel, and Solomon, and Cæsar, and Napoleon, and Washington, and the President, and the governor, and the mayor, and you and I have all of us, at one time or another, in one way or another, burned our fingers at the same old fires that have scorched human fingers in the same monotonous old ways, at the same reliable old stands, for the past 6,000 years, and all the verbal instruction between here and the silent grave couldn't teach us so much, or teach it so thoroughly, as one well-directed singe. And a million of years from now — if this weary old world may endure so long — when human knowledge shall fall a little short of the infinite, and all the lore and erudition of this wonderful age will be but the primer of that day of light — the baby that is born into that world of knowledge and wisdom and progress, rich with all the years of human experience, will cry for the lamp, and, the very first time that opportunity favors it, will try to pull the flame up by the roots, and will know just as much as ignorant, untaught, stupid little Cain knew on the same subject. Year after year, century after unfolding century, how true it is that the lion on the fence is always bigger, fiercer and more given to majestic attitudes and dramatic situations than the lion in the tent. And yet it costs us, often as the circus comes around, fifty cents to find that out.

But while we have been moralizing, Tom's mustache has taken a start. It has attained the physical density, though not the color, by any means, of the Egyptian darkness—it can be felt; and it is felt; very soft felt. The world begins to take notice of the new-comer; and Tom, as generations of Toms before him have done, patiently endures dark hints from other members of the family about his face being dirty. He loftily ignores his experienced father's suggestions that he should perform his tonsorial toilet with a spoonful of cream and the family cat. When his sisters, in meekly dissembled ignorance, inquire, "Tom, what *have* you on your lip?" he is austere, as becomes a man annoyed by the frivolous small talk of women. And when his younger brother takes advantage of the presence of a numerous company in the house, to shriek over the baluster up stairs, apparently to any boy any where this side of China, "Tom's a raisin' mustachers!" Tom smiles, a wan, neglected-orphan smile ; a smile that looks as though it had come up on his face to weep over the barrenness of the land ; a perfect ghost of a smile, as compared with the rugged, 7x9 smiles that play like animated crescents over the countenances of the company. But the mustache grows. It comes on apace; very short in the middle, very no longer at the ends, and very blonde all round. Whenever you see such a mustache, do not laugh at it ; do not point at it the slow, unmoving finger of scorn. Encourage it; speak kindly of it; affect admiration for it; coax it along. Pray for it—for it is a first. They always come that way. And when, in the fullness of time, it has developed so far that it can be pulled, there is all the agony of making it take color. It is worse, and more obstinate, and more deliberate than a meershaum. The sun, that tans Tom's cheeks and blisters his nose, only bleaches his mustache. Nothing ever hastens its color ; nothing does it any permanent good ; nothing but patience, and faith, and persistent pulling.

With all the comedy there is about it, however, this is the grand period of a boy's life. You look at them, with their careless, easy, natural manners and movements in the streets and on the base ball ground, and their marvelous, systematic, indescribable, inimitable and complex awkwardness in your parlors, and do you never dream, looking at these young fellows, of the overshadowing destinies awaiting them, the mighty struggles mapped out in the earnest future of their lives, the thrilling conquests in the world of arms, the grander triumphs in the realm of philosophy, the fadeless laurels in the empire of letters, and the imperishable crowns that He who giveth them the victory binds about their brows, that wait for the courage and ambition of these boys? [Applause.]

Why, the world is at a boy's feet; and power and conquest and leadership slumber in his rugged arms and care-free heart. A boy sets his ambition at whatever mark he will—lofty or groveling, as he may elect— and the boy who resolutely sets his heart on fame, on wealth, on power, on what he will; who consecrates himself to a life of noble endeavor, and lofty effort; who consentrates every faculty of his mind and body on the attainment of his one darling point; who brings to support his ambition, courage and industry and patience, can trample on genius; for these are better and grander than genius; and he will begin to rise above his fellows as steadily and as surely as the sun climbs above the mountains.

Hannibal, standing before the Punic altar fires and in the lisping accents of childhood swearing eternal hatred to Rome, was the Hannibal at twenty-four years commanding the army that swept down upon Italy like a mountain torrent, and shook the power of the mistress of the world, bid her defiance at her own gates, while affrighted Rome huddled and cowered under the protecting shadows of her walls.   [Applause.]

Napoleon, building snow forts at school and planning mimic battles with his playfellows, was the lieutenant of artillery at sixteen years, general of artillery and the victor of Toulon at twenty-four, and at last Emperor—not by the paltry accident of birth which might happen to any man, however unworthy, but by the manhood and grace of his own right arm, and his own brain, and his own courage and dauntless ambition—Emperor, with his foot on the throat of prostrate Europe.   [Applause.]

Alexander, daring more in his boyhood than his warlike father could teach him, and entering upon his all conquering career at twenty-four, was the boy whose vaulting ambition only paused in its dazzling flight when the world lay at his feet.

And the fair-faced soldiers of the Empire, they who rode down upon the bayonets of the English squares at Waterloo, when the earth rocked beneath their feet, and the incense smoke from the altars of the battle god shut out the sun and sky above their heads, who, with their young lives streaming from their gaping wounds, opened their pallid lips to cry, "Vive L'Empereur," as they died for honor and France, were boys —schoolboys—the boy conscripts of France, torn from their homes and their schools to stay the failing fortunes of the last grand army, and the Empire that was tottering to its fall.   You don't know how soon these happy-go-lucky young fellows, making summer hideous with base ball slang, or gliding around a skating rink on their back, may hold the State and its destinies in their grasp; you don't know how soon these boys may make and write the history of the hour; how soon, they alone, may shape events and guide the current of public action; how soon one of them may run away with your daughter or borrow money of you. [Laughter.]

Certain it is, there is one thing Tom will do, just about this period of his existence.   He will fall in love with somebody before his mustache is long enough to wax.

Perhaps one of the earliest indications of this event, for it does not always break out in the same manner, is a sudden and alarming increase in the number and variety of Tom's neckties.   In his boxes and on his dressing case, his mother is constantly startled by the changing and increasing assortment of the display. Monday he encircles his tender throat with a lilac knot, fearfully and wonderfully tied; a lavender tie succeeds, the following day; Wednesday is graced with a sweet little tangle of pale, pale blue, that fades at a breath; Thursday is ushered in with a scarf of delicate pea green, of wonderful convolutions and sufficiently expansive, by the aid of a clean collar, to conceal any little irregularity in Tom's wash day; Friday smiles on a sailor's knot of dark blue, with a tangle of dainty forget-me-nots embroidered over it; Saturday tones itself down to a quiet, unobtrusive, neutral tint or shade, scarlet or yellow, and Sunday is deeply, darkly, piously black. It is difficult to tell whether Tom is trying to express the state of his distracted feelings by his neckties, of trying to find a color that will harmonize with his mustache, or match Laura's dress.

And during the variegated necktie period of man's existence how tenderly that mustache is coaxed and petted and caressed. How it is brushed to make it lie down and waxed to make it stand out, and how he notes its slow growth, and weeps and mourns and prays and swears over it day after weary day. And now, if ever, and generally now, he buys things to make it take color. But he never repeats this offense against nature. He buys a wonderful dye, warranted to "produce a beautiful, glossy black or brown at one application, without stain or injury to the skin." Buys it at a little shabby, round the corner, obscure drug store, because he is not known there. And he tells the assassin who sells it him, that he is buying it for a sick sister. And the assassin knows that he lies. And in the guilty silence and solitude of his own room, with the curtains drawn, and the door locked, Tom tries the virtues of that magic dye. It gets on his fingers, and turns them black to the elbow. It burns holes in his handkerchief when he tries to rub the malignant poison off his ebony fingers. He applies it to his silky mustache, real camel's hair, very cautiously and very tenderly, and with some misgivings. It turns his lip so black it makes the room dark. And out of all the clouds and the darkness and the sable splotches that pall every thing else in Plutonian gloom, that mustache smiles out, grinning like some ghastly hirsute specter, gleaming like the moon through a rifted storm cloud, unstained, untainted, unshaded; a natural, incorruptible blonde. That is the last time any body fools Tom on hair dye.

The eye he has for immaculate linen and faultless collars. How it amazes his mother and sisters to learn that there isn't a shirt in the house fit for a pig to wear, and that he wouldn't wear the best collar in his room to be hanged in.

And the boots he crowds his feet into ! A Sunday-school room, the Sunday before the picnic or the Christmas tree, with its sudden influx of new scholars, with irreproachable morals and ambitious appetites, doesn't compare with the overcrowded condition of those boots. Too tight in the instep; too narrow at the toes ; too short at both ends ; the only things about those boots that don't hurt him, that don't fill his very soul with agony, are the straps. When Tom is pulling them on, he feels that if somebody would kindly run over him three or four times with a freight train, the sensation would be pleasant and reassuring and tranquilizing. The air turns black before his starting eyes, there is a roaring like the rush of many waters in his ears; he tugs at the straps that are cutting his fingers in two and pulling his arms out by the roots, and just before his bloodshot eyes shoot clear out of his head, the boot comes on—or the straps pull of. Then when he stands up, the earth rocks beneath his feet, and he thinks he can faintly hear the angels calling him home. And when he walks across the floor the first time, his standing in the church and the Christian community is ruined forever. Or would be if any one could hear what he says. He never, never, never gets to be so old that he can not remember those boots, and if it is seventy years afterward, his feet curl up in agony at the recollection. The first time he wears them, he is vaguely aware, as he leaves his room that there is a kind of "fixy" look about him, and his sisters' tittering is not needed to confirm this impression.

He has a certain half-defined impression that every thing he has on is a size too small for any other man of his size. That his boots are a trifle snug, like a house with four rooms for a family of thirty-seven. That the hat which sits so lightly on the crown of his head is jaunty but limited, like a junior clerk's salary; that his gloves are a neat fit, and can't be buttoned with a stump machine. Tom doesn't know all this: he has only a general, vague impression that it may be so. And he doesn't know that his sisters know every line of it. For he has lived many years longer, and got in ever so much more trouble, before he learns that one bright, good, sensible girl—and I believe they are all that—will see and notice more in a glance, remember it more accurately, and talk more about it, than twenty men can see in a week. Tom does not know, for his crying feet will not let him, how he gets from his room to the earthly paradise where Laura lives. Nor does he know, after he gets there, that Laura sees him trying to rest one foot by setting it up on the heel. And she sees him sneak it back under his chair, and tilt it up on the toe for a change. She sees him ease the other foot a little by tugging the heel of the boot at the leg of the chair—a hazardous, reckless, presumptuous experiment. Tom tries it so far one night, and slides his heel so far up the leg of his boot, that his foot actually feels comfortable, and he thinks the angels must be rubbing it. He walks out of the parlor sideways that night, trying to hide the cause of the sudden elongation of one leg, and he hobbles all the way home in the same disjointed condition. But Laura sees that too. She sees all the little knobs and lumps on his foot, and sees him fidget and fuss, she sees the look of anguish flitting across his face under the heartless, deceitful, veneering of smiles, and she makes the mental remark that master Tom would feel much happier, and much more comfortable, and more like staying longer, if he had worn his father's boots.

But on his way to the house, despite the distraction of his crying feet, how many pleasant, really beautiful, romantic things Tom thinks up and recollects and compiles and composes to say to Laura, to impress her with his originality and wisdom and genius and bright, exuberant fancy and general superiority over all the rest of Tom kind. Real earnest things, you know; no hollow, conventional compliments, or nonsense, but such things, Tom flatters himself, as none of the other fellows can or will say. And he has them all in beautiful order when he gets at the foot of the hill. The remark about the weather, to begin with; not the stereotyped old phrase, but a quaint, droll, humorous conceit that no one in the world but Tom could think of. Then, after the opening overture about the weather, something about music and Beethoven's sonata in B flat, and Haydn's symphonies, and of course something about Beethoven's grand old Fifth symphony, somebody's else mass, in heaven knows how many flats; and then something about art, and a profound thought or two on science and philosophy, and so on to poetry, and from poetry to "business."

But alas, when Tom reaches the gate, all these well ordered ideas display evident symptoms of breaking up; as he crosses the yard, he is dismayed to know that they are in the convulsions of a panic, and when he touches the bell knob, every, each, all and several of the ideas, original and compiled, that he has had on any subject during the past ten years, forsake him and return no more that evening.

When Laura opened the door, he had intended to say something real splendid about the imprisoned sunlight of something beaming out a welcome upon the what-you-may-call-it of the night or something. Instead of which he says, or rather gasps:

"Oh, yes, to be sure; to be sure; ho."

And then, conscious that he has not said anything particularly brilliant or original, or that most any of the other fellows could not say with a little practice, he makes one more effort to redeem himself before he steps into the hall, and adds:

" Oh, good morning; good morning."

Feeling that even this is only a partial success, he collects his scattered faculties for one united effort, and inquires:

" How is your mother? "

And then it strikes him that he has about exhausted the subject, and he goes into the parlor, and sits down, and just as soon as he has placed his reproachful feet in the least agonizing position, he proceeds to wholly, completely and successfully forget every thing he ever knew in his life. He returns to consciousness to find himself, to his own amazement and equally to Laura's bewilderment, conducting a conversation about the crops, and a new method of funding the national debt, subjects upon which he is about as well informed as the town clock. He rallies, and makes a successful effort to turn the conversation into literary channels by asking her if she has read " Daniel Deronda," and wasn't it odd that George Washington Eliot should name her heroine " Grenadine," after a dress pattern? And in a burst of confidence he assures her that he would not be amazed if it should rain before morning (and he hopes it will, and that it may be a flood, and that he may get caught in it, without an ark nearer than Cape Horn). And so, at last, the first evening passes away, and, after mature deliberation and many unsuccessful efforts, he rises to go. But he does not go. He wants to; but he doesn't know how. He says good evening. Then he repeats it in a marginal reference. Then he puts it in a foot-note. Then he adds the remarks in an appendix and shakes hands. By this time he gets as far as the parlor door, and catches hold of the knob and' holds on to it as tightly as though some one on the other side were trying to pull it through the door and run away with it. And he stands there a fidgety statue of the door holder. He mentions, for not more than the twentieth time that evening, that he is passionately fond of music, but he can't sing. Which is a lie; he can. Did she go to the centennial? " No." " Such a pity—" he begins, but stops in terror, lest she may consider his condolence a reflection upon her financial standing. Did he go? Oh, yes; yes; he says, absently, he went. Or, that is to say, no, not exactly. He did not exactly go to the Centennial; he staid at home. In fact, he had not been out of town this summer. Then he looks at the tender little face; he looks at the brown eyes, sparkling with suppressed merriment; he looks at the white hands, dimpled and soft, twin daughters of the snow; and the fairy picture **grows** more lovely as he looks at it, until his heart outruns his fears; he must speak, he must say something impressive and ripe with meaning, for how can he go away with this suspense in his breast? His heart trembles as does his hand; his quivering lips part, and—Laura deftly hides a vagrant yawn behind her fan. Good-night, and Tom is gone.

There is a dejected droop to the mustache that night, when in the solitude of his own room Tom releases his hands from the despotic gloves, and tenderly soothes two of the reddest, puffiest feet that ever crept out of boots not half their own size, and swore in mute but eloquent anatomical profanity at the whole race of boot-makers. And his heart is nearly as full of sorrow and bitterness as his boots. It appears to him that he showed off to the worst possible advantage; he is dimly conscious that he acted very like a donkey, and he has the not entirely unnatural impression that she will never want to see him again. And so he philosophically and manfully makes up his mind never, never, never, to think of her again. And then he immediately proceeds, in the manliest and most natural way in the world, to think of nothing and nobody else under the sun for the next ten hours. How the tender little face does haunt him. He pitches himself into bed with an aimless recklessness that tumbles pillows, bolster and sheets into one shapeless, wild, chaotic mass, and he goes through the motions of going to sleep, like a man who would go to sleep by steam. He stands his pillow up on one end, and pounds it into a wad, and he props his head upon it as though it were the guillotine block. He lays it down and smooths it out level, and pats all the wrinkles out of it, and there is more sleeplessness in it to the square inch than there is in the hungriest mosquito that ever sampled a martyr's blood. He gets up and smokes like a patent stove, although not three hours ago he told Laura that he de - tes - ted tobacco.

This is the only time Tom will ever go through this, in exactly this way. It is the one rare, golden experience, the one bright, rosy dream of his life. He may live to be as old as an army overcoat, and he may marry as many wives as Brigham Young, singly, or in a cluster, but this will come to him but once. Let him enjoy all the delightful misery, all the ecstatic wretchedness, all the heavenly forlornness of it as best he can. And he does take good, solid, edifying misery out of it. How he does torture himself and hate Smith, the empty-headed donkey, who can talk faster than poor Tom can think, and whose mustache is black as Tom's boots, and so long that he can pull one end of it with both hands. And how he does detest that idiot Brown, who plays and sings, and goes up there every time Tom does, and claws over a few old, forgotten five-finger exercises and calls it music; who comes up there, some night when Tom thinks he has the evening and Laura all to himself, and brings up an old, tuneless, voiceless, cracked guitar, and goes crawling around in the wet grass under the windows, and makes night perfectly hideous with what he calls a serenade. And he speaks French, too, the beast. Poor Tom; when Brown's lingual accomplishments in the language of Charlemagne are confined to— "aw — aw — er ah — vooly voo?" and, on state occasions, to the additional grandeur of "avy voo mong shapo?" But poor Tom, who once covered himself with confusion by telling Laura that his favorite in "Robert le Diable" was the beautiful aria, "Robert toy que jam," considers Brown a very prodigal in linguistic attainments; another Cardinal Mezzofanti; and hates him for it accordingly. And he hates Daubs, the artist, too, who was up there one evening and made an off-hand crayon sketch of her in an album. The picture looked much more like Daubs' mother, and Tom knew it, but Laura said it was oh, just delightfully, perfectly splendid, and Tom has hated Daubs most cordially ever since. In fact, Tom hates every man who has the temerity to speak to her, or whom she may treat with ladylike courtesy.

Until there comes one night when the boots of the inquisition pattern sit more lightl yon their suffering victims; when Providence has been on Tom's side and has kept Smith and Daubs and Brown away, and has frightened Tom nearly to death by showing him no one in the little parlor with its old-fashioned furniture but himself and Laura and the furniture; when, almost without knowing how or why, they talk about life and its realities instead of the last concert or the next lecture; when they talk of their plans, and their day dreams and aspirations, and their ideals of real men and women; when they talk about the heroes and heroines of days long gone by, grey and dim in the ages that are ever made young and new by the lives of noble men and noble women who lived, and never died in those grand old days, but lived and live on, as imperishable and fadeless in their glory as the glittering stars that sang at creation's dawn; when the room seems strangely silent, when their voices hush; when the flush of earnestness upon her face gives it a tinge of sadness that makes it more beautiful than ever; when the dream and picture of a home Eden, and home life, and home love, grows every moment more lovely, more entrancing to him, until at last poor blundering, stupid Tom, speaks without knowing what he is going to say, speaks without preparation or rehearsal, speaks, and his honest, natural, manly heart touches his faltering lips with eloquence and tenderness and earnestness, that all the rhetoric in the world never did and never will inspire; and——. That is all we know about it. Nobody knows what is said or how it is done. Nobody. Only the silent stars or the whispering leaves, or the cat, or maybe Laura's younger brother, or the hired girl, who generally bulges in just as Tom reaches the climax. All the rest of us know about it is, that Tom doesn't come away so early that night, and that when he reaches the door he holds a pair of dimpled hands instead of the insensate door knob. He never clings to that door knob again; never. Unless Ma, dear Ma, has been so kind as to bring in her sewing and spend the evening with them. And Tom doesn't hate any body, nor want to kill any body in the wide, wide world, and he feels just as good as though he had just come out of a six months' revival; and is happy enough to borrow money of his worst enemy.

But, there is no rose without a thorn. Although, I suppose on an inside computation, there is, in this weary old world as much as, say a peck, or a peck and a half possibly, of thorns without their attendant roses. Just the raw, bare thorns. In the highest heaven of his newly found bliss, Tom is suddenly recalled to earth and its miseries by a question from Laura which falls like a plummet into the unrippled sea of the young man's happiness, and fathoms its depths in the shallowest place. "Has her own Tom"—as distinguished from countless other Toms, nobody's Toms, unclaimed Toms, to all intents and purposes swamp lands on the public matrimonial domain—"Has her own Tom said any thing to pa?"

"Oh, yes! pa;" Tom says. "To be sure; yes."

Grim, heavy-browed, austere pa. The living embodiment of business. Wiry, shrewd, the life and mainspring of the house of Tare & Tret. "'M. Well. N' no," Tom had not exactly, as you might say, poured out his heart to pa. Somehow or other he had a rose-colored idea that the thing was going to go right along in this way forever. Tom had an idea that the programme was all arranged, printed and distributed, rose-colored, gilt-edged and perfumed. He was going to sit and hold Laura's hands, pa was to stay down at the office, and ma was to make her visits to the parlor as much like angels', for their rarity and brevity, as possible. But he sees, now that the matter has been referred to, that it is a grim necessity. And Laura doesn't like to see such a spasm of terror pass over Tom's face; and her coral lips quiver a little as she hides her flushed face out of sight on Tom's shoulder, and tells him how kind and tender pa has always been with her, until Tom feels positively jealous of pa. And she tells him that he must not dread going to see him, for pa will be, oh, so glad to know how happy, happy, happy he can make his little girl. And as she talks of him, the hard working, old-fashioned tender-hearted old man, who loves his girls as though he were yet only a big boy, her heart grows tenderer, and she speaks so earnestly and eloquently that Tom, at first savagely jealous of him, is persuaded to fall in love with the old gentleman—he calls him "pa," too, now—himself.

But oy the following afternoon this feeling is very faint.   And when he enters the counting room of Tare & Tret, and stands before pa—Oh, land of love, how could Laura ever talk so about such a man ! Stubbly little pa ; with a fringe of the most obstinate and wiry gray hair stand- ing all around his bald, bald head ; the wiriest, grizzliest mustache bristling under his nose ; a tuft of tangled beard under the sharp chin, and a raspy undergrowth of a week's run on the thin jaws ; business, business, business, in every line of the hard, seamed face, and profit and loss, barter and trade, dicker and bargain, in every movement of the nervous hands.   Pa ; old business ! He puts down the newspaper a little way, and looks over the top of it as Tom announces himself, glanc- ing at the young man with a pair of blue eyes that peer through old- fashioned iron-bowed spectacles, that look as though they had known these eyes and done business with them ever since they wept over their A B C's or peeked into the tall stone jar Sunday afternoon to look for the doughnuts.

Tom, who had felt all along there could be no inspiration on his part in this scene, has come prepared.   At least he had his last true statement at his tongue's end when he entered the counting-room.   But now, it seems to him that if he had been brought up in a circus, and cradled inside of a sawdust ring, and all his life trained to twirl his hat, he couldn't do it better, nor faster, nor be more utterly incapable of doing any thing else.   At last he swallows a lump in his throat as big as a ballot box, and faintly gasps :

"Good morning."

Mr. Tret hastens to recognize him.   "Eh ? oh ; yes ; yes ; yes ; I see ; young Bostwick, from Dope & Middlerib's.   Oh yes.   Well—?"

"I have come, sir," gasps Tom, thinking all around the world from Cook's explorations to "Captain Riley's Narrative," for the first line of that speech that Tare & Tret have just scared out of him so completely that he dosen't believe he ever knew a word of it.   "I have come—" and he thinks if his lips didn't get so dry and hot they make his teeth ache, that he could get along with it : "I have sir,—come, Mr. Tret ; Mr. Tret, sir—I have come—I am come—"

"Yes, ye-es," says Mr. Tret, in the wildest bewilderment, but in no very encouraging tones, thinking the young man probably wants to bor- row money ; " Ye-es ; I see you've come.   Well ; that's all right ; glad to see you. [Laughter.] Yes, you've come ?"

Tom's hat is now making about nine hundred and eighty revolutions per minute, and apparently not running up to half its full capacity.

"Sir ; Mr. Tret," he resumes, "I have come, sir ; Mr. Tret—I am here to—to sue—to sue, Mr. Tret—I am here to sue—"

"Sue, eh ?" the old man echoes sharply, with a belligerent rustle of the newspaper; "sue Tare & Tret, eh? Well, that's right, young man; that's right. Sue, and get damages. We'll give you all the law you want."

Tom's head is so hot, and his heart is so cold, that he thinks they must be about a thousand miles apart.

"Sir," he explains, "that isn't it. It isn't that. I only want to ask—I have long known—Sir," he adds, as the opening lines of his speech come to him like a message from heaven, "Sir, you have a flower, a tender, lovely blossom ; chaste as the snow that crowns the mountain's brow; fresh as the breath of morn; lovelier than the rosy-fingered hours that fly before Aurora's car; pure as the lily kissed by dew. This precious blossom, watched by your paternal eyes, the object of your tender care and solicitude, I ask of you. I would wear it in my heart, and guard and cherish it—and in the—"

"Oh-h, ye-es, yes, yes," the old man says, soothingly, beginning to see that Tom is only drunk. " Oh, yes, yes; I don't know much about them myself ; my wife and the girls generally keep half the windows in the house littered up with them, winter and summer, every window so full of house plants the sun can't shine in. Come up to the house, they'll give you all you can carry away, give you a hat full of 'em."

"No, no, no ; you don't understand," says poor Tom, and old Mr. Tret now observes that Tom is very drunk indeed. " It isn't that, sir. Sir, that isn't it. I—I—I want to marry your daughter !"

And there it is at last, as bluntly as though Tom had wadded it into a gun and shot it at the old man. Mr. Tret does not say anything for twenty seconds. Tom tells Laura that evening that it was two hours and a half before her father opened his head. Then he says, " Oh, yes, yes, yes, yes ; to be sure ; to—be—sure." And then the long pause is dreadful. "Yes, yes. Well, I don't know. I don't know about that, young man. Said any thing to Jennie about it?"

"It isn't Jennie," Tom gasps, seeing a new Rubicon to cross; "its——"

"Oh, Julie, eh ? well, I don't——"

"No, sir," interjects the despairing Tom, "it isn't Julie, its——"

"Sophie, eh ? Oh, well, Sophie——"

"Sir," says Tom, "if you please, sir, it isn't Sophie, its——"

"Not Minnie, surely? Why Minnie is hardly—well, I don't know. Young folks get along faster than——"

"Dear Mr. Tret," breaks in the distracted lover, "it's Laura."

As they sit and stand there, looking at each other, the dingy old counting-room, with the heavy shadows lurking in every corner, with its time-worn, heavy brown furnishings, with the scanty dash of sunlight breaking in through the dusty window, looks like an old Rubens painting ; the beginning and finishing of a race: the old man, nearly ready to lay his armor off, glad to be so nearly and so safely through with the race and the fight that Tom, in all his inexperience and with all the rash enthusiasm and conceit of a young man, is just getting ready to run and fight, or fight and run, you never can tell which until he is through with it. And the old man, looking at Tom, and through him, and past him, feels his old heart throb almost as quickly as does that of the young man before him. For looking down a long vista of happy, eventful years bordered with roseate hopes and bright dreams and anticipations, he sees a tender face, radiant with smiles and kindled with blushes; he feels a soft hand drop into his own with its timid pressure; he sees the vision open, under the glittering summer stars, down mossy hillsides, where the restless breezes, sighing through the rustling leaves, whispered their tender secret to the noisy katydids; strolling along the winding paths, deep in the bending wild grass, down in the star-lit aisles of the dim old woods; loitering where the meadow brook sparkles over the white pebbles or murmurs around the great flat stepping-stones; lingering on the rustic foot-bridge, while he gazes into eyes eloquent and tender in their silent love-light; up through the long pathway of years, flecked and checkered with sunshine and cloud, with storm and calm, through years of struggle, trial, sorrow, disappointment, out at last into the grand, glorious, crowning beauty and benison of hard-won and well-deserved success, until he sees now this second Laura, re-imaging her mother as she was in the dear old days. And he rouses from his dream with a start, and he tells Tom he'll "talk it over with Mrs. Tret and see him again in the morning."

And so they are duly and formally engaged ; and the very first thing they do, they make the very sensible, though very uncommon, resolution to so conduct themselves that no one will ever suspect it. And they succeed admirably. No one ever does suspect it. They come into church in time to hear the benediction—every time they come together. They shun all other people when church is dismissed, and are seen to go home alone the longest way. At picnics they are missed not more than fifty times a day, and are discovered sitting under a tree, holding each other's hands, gazing into each other's eyes and saying—nothing. When he throws her shawl over her shoulders, he never looks at what he is doing, but looks straight into her starry eyes, throws the shawl right over her natural curls, and drags them out by the hairpins. If, at sociable or festival, they are left alone in a dressing-room a second and a half, Laura emerges with her ruffle standing around like a railroad accident; [laughter] and Tom has enough complexion on his shoulder to go around a young ladies' seminary. When they drive out, they sit in a buggy with a seat eighteen inches wide, and there is two feet of unoccupied room at either end of it. Long years afterward, when they drive, a street-car isn't too wide for them; and when they walk, you could drive four loads of hay between them.

And yet, as carefully as they guard their precious, little secret, and as cautious and circumspect as they are in their walk and behavior, it gets talked around that they are engaged. People are so prying and suspicious.

And so the months of their engagement run on; never before or since, time flies so swiftly—unless, it may be, some time when Tom has an acceptance in bank to meet in two days, that he can't lift one end of—and the wedding day dawns, fades, and the wedding is over. Over, with its little circle of delighted friends, with its ripples of pleasure and excitement, with its touches of home love and home life, that leave their lasting impress upon Laura's heart, although Tom, with man-like blindness, never sees one of them. Over, with ma, with the thousand and one anxieties attendant on the grand event in her daughter's life hidden away under her dear old smiling face, down, away down under the tender, glistening eyes, deep in the loving heart; ma, hurrying here and fluttering there, in the intense excitement of something strangely made up of happiness and grief, of apprehension and hope; ma, with her sudden disappearances and flushed reappearances, indicating struggles and triumphs in the turbulent world down stairs; ma, with the new fangled belt with the dinner-plate buckles, fastened on wrong side foremost, and the flowers dangling down the wrong side of her head, to Sophie's intense horror and pantomimic telegraphy; ma, flying here and there, seeing that every thing is going right, from kitchen to dressing-rooms; looking after every thing and every body, with her hands and heart just as full as they will hold, and more voices calling, "ma," from every room in the house than you would think one hundred mas could answer.

But she answers them all, and she sees after every thing, and just in the nick of time prevents Mr. Tret from going down stairs and attending the ceremony in a loud-figured dressing-gown and green slippers; ma, who, with the quivering lip and glistening eyes, has to be cheerful, and lively, and smiling; because, if, as she thinks of the dearest and

best of her flock going away from her fold, to put her life and her happiness into another's keeping, she gives way for one moment, a dozen
reproachful voices cry out, "Oh-h ma!" How it all comes back to
Laura, like the tender shadows of a dream, long years after the dear,
dear face, furrowed with marks of patient suffering and loving care,
rests under the snow and the daisies; when the mother love that
glistened in the tender eyes has closed in darkness on the dear old home;
and the nerveless hands, crossed in dreamless sleep upon the pulseless
breast, can never again touch the children's heads with caressing
gesture; how the sweet vision comes to Laura, as it shone on her wedding morn, rising in tenderer beauty through the blinding tears her
own excess of happiness calls up, as the rainbow spans the cloud only
through the mingling of the golden sunshine and the falling rain.
[Applause.]

   And Pa, dear, old, shabby Pa, whose clothes will not fit him as they
fit other men; who always dresses just a year and a half behind the
style; Pa, wandering up and down through the house, as though he
were lost in his own home, pacing through the hall like a sentinel,
blundering aimlessly and listlessly into rooms where he has no business,
and being repelled therefrom by a chorus of piercing shrieks and
hysterical giggling; Pa, getting off his well-worn jokes with an assumption of merriment that seems positively real; Pa, who creeps away by
himself once in a while, and leans his face against the window, and
sighs, in direct violation of all strict household regulations, right against
the glass, as he thinks of his little girl going away to-day from the
home whose love and tenderness and patience she has known so well.
Only yesterday, it seems to him, the little baby girl, bringing the first
music of baby prattle into his home; then a little girl in short dresses,
with school-girl troubles and school-girl pleasures; then an older little
girl, out of school and into society, but a little girl to Pa still. And
then ——. But somehow, this is as far as Pa can get; for he sees, in
the flight of this, the first, the following flight of the other fledglings;
and he thinks how silent and desolate the old nest will be when they
have all mated and flown away. He thinks, when their flight shall have
made other homes bright, and cheery, and sparkling with music and
prattle and laughter, how it will leave the old home hushed, and quiet
and still. How, in the long, lonesome afternoons, mother will sit by
the empty cradle that rocked them all, murmuring the sweet old cradle-
songs that brooded over all their sleep, until the rising tears check
the swaying cradle and choke the song — and back, over river, and
prairie and mountain, that roll, and stretch and rise between the

old home and the new ones, comes back the prattle of her little ones, the rippling music of their laughter, the tender cadences of their songs, until the hushed old home is haunted by memories of its children—gray and old they may be, with other children clustering about their knees; but to the dear old home they are "the children" still. And dreaming thus, when Pa for a moment finds his little girl alone—his little girl who is going away out of the home whose love she knows, into a home whose tenderness and patience are all untried—he holds her in his arms and whispers the most fervent blessing that ever throbbed from a father's heart; and Laura's wedding day would be incomplete and unfeeling without her tears. So is the pattern of our life made up of smiles and tears, shadow and sunshine. Tom sees none of these background pictures of the wedding day. He sees none of its real, heartfelt earnestness. He sees only the bright, sunny tints and happy figures that the tearful, shaded background throws out in golden relief; but never stops to think that, without the shadows, the clouds, and the somber tints of the background, the picture would be flat, pale and lusterless.

And then, the presents. The assortment of brackets, serviceable, ornamental and—cheap. The French clock, that never went, that does not go, that never will go. And the nine potato mashers. The eight mustard spoons. The three cigar stands. Eleven match safes; assorted patterns. A dozen tidies, charity fair styles, blue dog on a yellow background, barking at a green boy climbing over a red fence, after seal brown apples. The two churns, old pattern, straight handle and dasher, and they have as much thought of keeping a cow as they have of keeping a section of artillery. Five things they didn't know the names of, and never could find anybody who could tell what they were for. And a nickel plated, pocket corkscrew, that Tom, in a fine burst of indignation, throws out of the window, which Laura says is just like her own, impulsive Tom. And not long after, her own, impulsive Tom catches his death of cold and ruins the knees of his best trowsers crawling around in the wet grass hunting for that same corkscrew. Which is also just like her own, impulsive Tom.

And then, the young people go to work and buy e-v-e-r-y thing they need, the day they go to housekeeping. Every thing. Just as well, Tom says, to get every thing at once and have it delivered right up at the house, as to spend five or six or ten or twenty years in stocking up a house, as his father did. And Laura thinks so, too, and she wonders that Tom should know so much more than his father. This worries Tom himself, when he thinks of it, and he never rightly understands how it is, until he is forty-five or fifty years old, and has a Tom of his own to direct and advise him. So they make out a list, and revise it, and rewrite it, until they have every thing down, complete, and it isn't until supper is ready, the first day, that they discover there isn't a knife, a fork, or a plate or a spoon in the new house. And the first day the washerwoman comes, and the water is hot, and the clothes are all ready, it is discovered that there isn't a wash-tub nearer than the grocery. And further along in the day the discovery is made that while Tom has bought a clothes line that will reach to the north pole and back, and then has to be coiled up a mile or two in the back yard, there isn't a clothes pin in the settlement. And, in the course of a week or two, Tom slowly awakens to the realization of the fact that he has only begun to get. And if he should live two thousand years, which he rarely does, and possibly may not, he would think, just before he died, of something they had wanted the worst way for five centuries, and had either been too poor to get, or Tom had always forgotten to bring up. So long as he lives, Tom goes on bringing home things that they need—absolute, simple necessities, that were never so much as hinted at in that exhaustive list.

And old Time comes along, and knowing that the man in that new house will never get through bringing things up to it, helps him out, and comes around and brings things, too. Brings a gray hair now and then, to stick in Tom's mustache, which has grown too big to be ornamental, and too wayward and unmanageable to be comfortable. He brings little cares and little troubles, and little trials and little butcher bills, and little grocery bills, and little tailor bills, and nice, large millinery bills, that pluck at Tom's mustache and stroke it the wrong way and make it look more and more as pa's did the first time Tom saw it. He brings, by and by, the prints of baby fingers, and pats them around on the dainty wall paper. Brings, some times, a voiceless messenger that lays its icy fingers on the baby lips, and hushes their dainty prattle, and in the baptism of its first sorrow, the darkened little home has its dearest and tenderest tie to the upper fold. Brings, by and by, the tracks of a boy's muddy boots, and scatters them all up and down the clean porch. Brings a messenger, one day, to take the younger Tom away to college. And the quiet the boy leaves behind him, is so much harder to endure than his racket, that old Tom is tempted to keep a brass band in the house until the boy comes back. But old Time brings him home at last, and it does make life seem terribly real and earnest to Tom, and how the old laugh rings out and ripples all over Laura's face, when they see old Tom's first mustache, budding and struggling into second life, on young Tom's face.

And still old Time comes round, bringing each year whiter frosts to scatter on the whitening mustache, and brighter gleams of silver to glint the brown of Laura's hair. Bringing the blessings of peaceful old age and a lovelocked home to crown these noble, earnest, real, human lives bristling with human faults, marred with human mistakes, scarred and seamed and rifted with human troubles, and crowned with the compassion that only perfection can send upon imperfection. Comes, with happy memories of the past, and quiet confidence for the future. Comes, with the changing scenes of day and night; with winter's storm and summer's calm; comes, with the sunny peace and the backward dreams of age; comes, until one day, the eye of the relentless, old reaper rests upon old Tom, standing right in the swath, amid the golden corn. The sweep of the noiseless scythe, that never turns its edge, Time passes on, old Tom steps out of young Tom's way, and the cycle of a life is complete. [Applause.]

BURDETTE'S ROMANCE OF THE CARPET.

Basking in peace, in the warm Spring sun,
South Hill smiled upon Burlington.

The breath of May! and the day was fair,
And the bright motes danced in the balmy air,

And the sunlight gleamed where the restless breeze
Kissed the fragrant blooms on the apple trees.

His beardless cheek with a smile was spanned
As he stood with a carriage-whip in his hand.

And he laughed as he doffed his bob-tailed coat,
And the echoing folds of the carpet smote.

And she smiled as she leaned on her busy mop,
And said she would tell him when to stop.

So he pounded away till the dinner bell
Gave him a little breathing spell.

But he sighed when the kitchen clock struck one;
And she said the carpet wasn't done.

But he lovingly put in his biggest licks,
And pounded, like mad, till the clock struck six.

And she said, in a dubious kind of way,
That she guessed he could finish it up next day.

Then all that day, and the next day too,
The fuzz from the dustless carpet flew.

And she'd give it a look at eventide,
And say, " Now beat on the other side."

And the new days came, as the old days went,
And the landlord came for his regular rent.

And the neighbors laughed at the tireless boom,
And his face was shadowed with clouds of gloom;

Till, at last, one cheerless Winter day,
He kicked at the carpet and slid away,

Over the fence and down the street,
Speeding away with footsteps fleet;

And never again the morning sun
Smiled at him beating his carpet drum;

And South Hill often said, with a yawn,
" Where has the carpet martyr gone? "

     *   *   *   *   *   *

Years twice twenty had come and passed,
And the carpet swayed in the autumn blast,

For never yet, since that bright spring time,
Had it ever been taken down from the line

Over the fence a gray-haired man
Cautiously clim, clome, clem, clum, clam;

He found him a stick in the old woodpile,
And he gathered it up with a sad, grim smile

A flush passed over his face forlorn
As he gazed at the carpet, tattered and torn;

And he hit it a most resounding thwack,
Till the startled air gave its echoes back.

And out of the window a white face leaned,
And a palsied hand the sad eyes screened.

She knew his face—she gasped, she sighed:
" A little more on the under side."

Right down on the ground his stick he throwed,
And he shivered and muttered, "Well, I am blowed!"

And he turned away, with a heart full sore,
And he never was seen, not none no more.

BURDETTE'S MASTER-PIECE.

On the road once more, with Lebanon fading away in the distance, the fat passenger drumming idly on the window-pane, the cross passenger sound asleep, and the tall, thin passenger reading "Gen. Grant's Tour Around the World," and wondering why "Green's August Flower" should be printed above the doors of "A Buddhist Temple at Benares." To me comes the brakeman, and, seating himself on the arm of the seat, says:

"I went to church yesterday."

"Yes?" I said, with that interested inflection that asks for more. "And what church did you attend?"

"Which do you guess?" he asked.

"Some union mission church," I hazarded.

"No," he said, "I don't like to run on these branch roads very much. I don't often go to church, and when I do I want to run on the main line, where your run is regular and you go on schedule time and don't have to wait on connections. I don't like to run on a branch. Good enough, but I don't like it."

"Episcopal?" I guessed.

"Limited express," he said, "all palace cars and $2 extra for seat, fast time and only stop at big stations. Nice line, but too exhaustive for a brakeman. All train men in uniform, conductor's punch and lantern silver-plated, and no train boys allowed. Then the passengers are allowed to talk back at the conductor, and it makes them too free and easy. No, I couldn't stand the palace cars. Rich road, though. Don't often hear of a receiver being appointed for that line. Some mighty nice people travel on it, too."

"Universalist?" I suggested.

"Broad gauge," said the brakeman; "does too much complimentary business. Every body travels on a pass. Conductor doesn't get a fare once in fifty miles. Stops at flag stations, and won't run into any thing but a union depot. No smoking-car on the train. Train orders are rather vague, though, and the trainmen don't get along well with the passengers. No, I don't go to the Universalist, but I know some good men who run on that road."

"Presbyterian?" I asked.

"Narrow gauge, eh?" said the brakeman. "Pretty track, straight as a rule; tunnel right through a mountain rather than go around it; spirit-level grade; passengers have to show their tickets before they get on the train. Mighty strict road, but the cars are a little narrow; have to sit one in a seat, and no room in the aisle to dance. Then there are no stop-over tickets allowed; got to go straight through to the station you're ticketed for, or you can't get on at all. When the car is full, no extra coaches; cars built at the shop to hold just so many, and nobody else allowed on. But you don't often hear of an accident on that road. It's run right up to the rules."

"Maybe you joined the Free-Thinkers?" I said.

"Scrub road," said the brakeman; "dirt roadbed and no ballast; no time card and no train dispatcher. All trains run wild, and every engineer makes his own time, just as he pleases. Smoke if you want to; kind of go-as-you-please road. Too many side-tracks, and every switch wide open all the time, with the switchman sound asleep and the target lamp dead out. Get on as you please and get off when you want to. Don't have to show your tickets, and the conductor isn't expected to do any thing but amuse the passengers. No, sir. I was offered a pass, but I don't like the line. I don't like to travel on a road that has no terminus. Do you know, sir, I asked a division superintendent where that road run to, and he said he hoped to die if he knew. I asked him if the general superintendent could tell me, and he said he didn't believe they had a general superintendent, and if they had, he didn't know any thing more about the road than the passengers. I asked him whom he reported to, and he said 'Nobody.' I asked a conductor whom he got his orders from, and he said he didn't take orders from any living man or dead ghost. And when I asked the engineer whom he got his orders from, he said he'd like to see any body give him orders; he'd run the train to suit himself, or he'd run it into the ditch. Now, you see, sir, I'm a railroad man, and I don't care to run on a road that has no time, makes no connections, runs nowhere, and has no superintendent. It may be all right, but I've railroaded too long to understand it."

"Maybe you went to the Congregational church?"

"Popular road," said the brakeman; "an old road, too—one of the very oldest in this country. Good roadbed and comfortable cars. Well managed road, too; directors don't interfere with division superintendents and train orders. Road's mighty popular, but it's pretty independent, too. Yes, didn't one of the division superintendents down East discontinue one of the oldest stations on this line two or three years ago? But it's a mighty pleasant road to travel on. Always has such a pleasant class of passengers."

"Did you try the Methodist?" I said.

"Now you're shouting!" he said, with some enthusiasm. "Nice road, eh? Fast time and plenty of passengers. Engines carry a power of steam, and don't you forget it; steam-gauge shows a hundred and enough all the time. Lively road; when the conductor shouts 'All aboard,' you can hear him at the next station. Every train-light shines like a headlight. Stop-over checks are given on all through tickets; passenger can drop off the train as often as he likes, do the station two or three days, and hop on the next revival train that comes thundering along. Good, whole-souled, companionable conductors; ain't a road in the country where the passengers feel more at home. No passes; every passenger pays full traffic rates for his ticket. Wesleyanhouse air brakes on all trains, too; pretty safe road, but I didn't ride over it yesterday."

"Perhaps you tried the Baptist?" I guessed once more.

"Ah, ha!" said the brakeman; "she's a daisy, isn't she? River road; beautiful curves; sweep around any thing to keep close to the river, but it's all steel rail and rock ballast, single track all the way, and not a side-track from the roundhouse to the terminus. Takes a heap of water to run it through; double tanks at every station, and there isn't an engine in the shops that can pull a pound or run a mile with less than two gauges. But it runs through a lovely country, those river roads always do; river on one side and hills on the other, and it's a steady climb up the grade all the way till the run ends where the fountain-head of the river begins. Yes, sir; I'll take the river road every time for a lovely trip, sure connections and a good time, and no prairie dust blowing in at the windows. And yesterday, when the conductor came around for the tickets with a little basket punch, I didn't ask him to pass me, but I paid my fare like a little man—twenty-five cents for an hour's run and a little concert by the passengers throwed in. I tell you, pilgrim, you take the river road when your want——"

But just here the long whistle from the engine announced a station, and the brakeman hurried to the door, shouting:

"Zionsville! The train makes no stops between here and Indian-apolis!"

BURDETTE'S COUNTRY PARSON.

The parson of a country church was lying in his bed; three months' arrears of salary was pillowing his head; his couch was strewn with tradesmen's bills that pricked his sides like thorns, and nearly all life's common ills were goading him with thorns. The deacon sat beside him, as the moments ticked away, and bent his head to catch the words his pastor had to say:

"If I never shall arise from this hard bed on which I lie, if my warfare is accomplished and it's time for me to die, take a message to the sexton, before I pass away; tell him fires are for December and open doors for May.   Tell him when he lays the notice upon the pulpit's height to shove them 'neath the cushion, far out of reach and sight. And when he hears the preacher's voice in whispers soft expire, that is the time to slam the doors and rattle at the fire.   And tell the other deacons, too, all through the busy week, to hang their boots up in the sun to hatch a Sunday squeak; with steel-shod canes to prod the man who comes to sleep and snore; and use the boys who laugh in church to mop the vestry floor.   There's another, too, the woman who talks the sermon through; tell her I will not mind her buzz—my hearing hours are few; tell her to hang her mouth up some Sunday for a minute, and listen to a text, at least, without a whisper in it.   And tell the board of trustees not to weep with bitter tears, for I can't be any deader now than they have been for years.   And tell half my congregation I'm glad salvation's free, for that's the only chance for them—between the desk and me.   And a farewell to the choir—how the name my memory racks! If they could get up their voices as they do their backs—why the stars would hear their music and the welkin would rejoice, while the happy congregation could not hear a single voice.   But tell them I forgive them, and oh, tell them I said I wanted them to sing for me— when you're sure that I am dead."

His voice was faint and hoarser, but it gave a laughing break, a kind of gurgling chuckle, like a minister might make.   And the deacon he rose slowly, and sternly he looked down upon the parson's twinkling eyes with a portentous frown, and he stiffly said " good morning," as he went off in his ire, for the deacon was the leader of that amiable choir.

"ENGAGED."

"ELI PERKINS."

Melville D. Landon (Eli Perkins) was born in Eaton, Madison County, N. Y. September 7, 1839. He graduated at Union College, Schenectady, N. Y., in 1861. His father was John Landon from Litchfield County, Conn. Mr. Landon entered the service in the Clay Battalion in Washington, in April, 1861; was in the United States Treasury, and afterward became a planter in Louisiana. In 1867, the humorist visited Europe, and was selected by Cassius M. Clay, as Secretary of Legation at St. Petersburgh. Since then he has been engaged in literature. He has published four books: "The History of the Franco-Prussian War," G. W. Carleton & Co.; "Saratoga in 1901," Sheldon & Co.; "Eli Perkins at Large," Ford and Hurlbert, and "Wit and Humor of the Age," The Western Publishing House, Chicago. He has delivered thous-ands of humorous and philosophical lectures throughout the Union; is a member of the American Association for the Advancement of Science, and lives with an accomplished wife and interesting family, in a beautiful, brown stone residence, 44 East Seventy-sixth street, New York.

Melville D. Landon's wit and humor has been widely copied, and he has done much towards a philosophical analysis of wit. Like all wits he deals a good deal in the imagination. He believes, and proves in his lectures, that all wit is imagination, while all humor is the absolute truth itself. His exaggerations have been so much on the Baron Munchausen order, that the press of the country are always referring humorously to his veracity.

One day a reporter of the New York *World* asked Mr. Perkins how his veracity first came to be questioned.

"Who questioned it first?"

"Well," said Eli, "I don't mind telling you the truth about this. The name Eli ran easily into alie, olie and uli, and the paragraphers have used it as a lay figure to hang their jokes on. Lewis, of the Detroit *Free Press*, got to calling me Eliar Perkins, and Josh Billings said, 'truth is stranger than fiction—to Eli Perkins.'

"One day Nasby wrote this paragraph: 'While Eli Perkins was .ı Toledo, Congressman Frank Hurd questioned his veracity. This made Eli very indignant, and he immediately challenged Hurd to a deadly duel. On the morning of the duel Frank Hurd was in San Francisco, and Eli was in Halifax.'"

"What was the funniest paragraph the boys ever wrote about you?"

"It was this way: I wrote up the Ohio gas wells for the New York *Sun*. Of course I described them glowingly and truthfully. Well, the Chicago *Times* copied the article with this editorial paragraph:

"Our readers will notice that in another column Eli Perkins has written up the Ohio gas wells. He speaks very favorably of them, which is very magnanimous on the part of Mr. Perkins, when we come to consider that these gas wells are the only real rivals that he has."

"One day," continued Eli, "I was riding in the Pullman car with Wm. M. Evarts, our distinguished lawyer. I had been reading an article on sleep, in a health paper, and, turning to Mr. Evarts, I said:

"'Mr. Evarts, to sleep well, is it the best to lie on the right side or on the left side?'

"'If you are on the right side, Eli,' said the great lawyer, 'it isn't usually necessary to lie at all.'"

Mr. Perkins always looks on the funny side of all questions, and he will tell a joke as quick at his own expense, as at the expense of his brother humorist.

"One day," says the humorist, "a young gentleman came to me on the Boston and Maine train, and, smiling and bowing, politely asked me if I was the gentleman who delivered the lecture before the Portsmouth Y. M. C. A. the night before.

"I am," said Mr. Perkins, with some pride.

"Well, I want to thank you for it. I don't know when I ever enjoyed myself more than when you were talking."

"You are very complimentary," said Eli, blushing to his ears— "very complimentary. I am glad my humble effort was worthy of your praise," and the complimented humorist took the young man warmly by the hand.

"Yes," continued the young man, "it gave me immense pleasure. You see I am engaged to a Portsmouth girl, and her three sisters all went, and I had my girl in the parlor all to myself. Oh, it was a happy night!—the night you lectured in Portsmouth! When are you going to lecture there again?"

At another time the Yale football team, after beating Princeton, came back to the hotel tired and exhausted.

"Landlord," said the tired captain, as the rest of the team were yawning in the office, after supper—"I say, landlord, is there any thing quiet in the amusement line going on in Princeton to-night?"

"Well, there's Eli Perkins' lecture at the Y. M. C. A. and——"

"O, that's too active. He'll keep us laughing and thinking. We want something restful. We want sleep—quiet sleep."

"O well, then," said the landlord, catching at a new idea, "try Joseph Cook, on Evolution, at the Methodist Church. That comes the nearest to bed-time of any thing in Princeton to-night."

Speaking of short courtship, Eli Perkins says: "The quickest courtship I ever heard of, was when my Uncle, Consider Perkins, courted the widow Jenkins up in Connecticut."

"How sudden was the courtship?"

"Well, my Uncle Consider cantered his horse over to the widow's farm before breakfast one morning, hustled into the house and gasped:

"Widder Jenkins, I'm a man of business. I am worth $10,800, and want you for a wife. I give you just three minutes to answer.'

"'I don't want ten seconds, old man,' she replied as she shook out the dish cloth. 'I'm a woman of business, worth $16,000, and I wouldn't marry you if you were the last man on earth! I give you four seconds to git!'"

Mr. Perkins has told a good many stories on Ben Butler. In a political speech, Eli said: "There was an old Deacon Butler, of Lowell, who had one son, Ben. This Ben was very smart at every thing, but the deacon could not tell what profession to give him. So one day he put the boy in a room with a Bible, an apple and a dollar bill."

"'If I find Ben reading the Bible when I return,' said the deacon, 'I shall make him a clergyman; if eating the apple, a farmer; and if interested in the dollar bill, a banker.'

"What was the result?" you ask.

"Well," said Eli, "when the deacon returned he found his son sitting on the Bible, with the dollar bill in his pocket, and the apple almost devoured."

"What did he do with him ? "

"Why, he made him a politician, and is still running for Governor of Massachusetts. Ben is still devouring that apple."

On another occasion the humorist said : " General Butler went into a hospital in Washington not long since, to express sympathy with the patients.

" ' What is the matter with you, my man ? ' asked the General, as he gazed at a man with a sore leg.

" ' Oh, I've got gangrene, General.'

" ' Gangrene ! why, that's a very dangerous disease, my man — v-e-r-y d-a-n-g-e-r-o-u-s,' said General Butler. ' I never knew a man to have gangrene and recover. It always kills the patient or leaves him demented. I've had it myself.' "

To pay the humorist back for his many banterings, Butler arose at a dinner, at which the humorist was present, and said :

"Gentlemen, I have the honor of knowing three of the greatest liars — the greatest living liars in America."

"Who are they ? " asked the venerable Sam Ward, as he dropped a chicken partridge to listen to the General.

"Well, sir," said the General, as he scratched his head thoughtfully, "Mark Twain is one, and Eli Perkins is the other two!"

One day I asked Mr. Perkins to tell me the most disagreeable position he was ever placed in.

"Well," said Eli, "it was when I was a witness — when Lawyer Johnson had me as a witness in a wood case. In my direct testimony I had sworn truthfully that John Hall had cut ten cords of wood in three days. Then Johnson sharpened his pencil and commenced examining me.

'Now, Mr. Perkins,' he began, 'how much wood do you say was cut by Mr. Hall ? '

'Just ten cords, sir,' I answered, boldly. 'I measured it.'

'That's your impression ? '

'Yes, sir.'

'Well, we don't want impressions, sir. What we want is facts, before this jury — f a-c t-s, sir, facts ! '

'The witness will please state facts hereafter,' said the Judge, while the crimson came to my face.

'Now, sir,' continued Johnson, pointing his finger at me, 'will you swear that it was more than nine cords ? '

'Yes, sir. It was ten cords — just—'

'There! never mind,' interrupted Johnson. 'Now, how much less than twelve cords were there?'

'Two cords, sir.'

'How do you know there were just two cords less, sir? Did you measure these two cords, sir?' asked Johnson, savagely.

'No, sir, I —'

'There, that will do! You did not measure it. Just as I expected. All guess work. Now didn't you swear a moment ago that you measured this wood?'

'Yes, sir, but——'

'Stop, sir! The jury will note this discrepancy.'

'Now, sir,' continued Johnson, slowly, as he pointed his finger almost down my throat, 'Now, sir, on your oath, will you swear that there were not ten cords and a half?'

'Yes, sir,' I answered meekly.

'Well now, Mr. Perkins, I demand a straight answer—a truthful answer, sir.' 'Now, on your solemn oath, how many cords were there?'

'T—T—Ten c-c-cords,' I answered, hesitatingly.

'You swear it?'

'I—I—d—d—do.'

'Now,' continued Johnson, as he smiled satirically, 'do you know the penalty of perjury, sir?'

'Yes, sir, I think——'

'Never mind what you think, sir. Thoughts and opinions are not facts. Now I say, on your oath, on your s-o-l-e-m-n oath, with no evasion, are you willing to perjure yourself by solemnly swearing that there were more than nine cords of wood?'

'Yes, sir, I——'

'Aha! Yes, sir. You are willing to perjure yourself then? Just as I thought (turning to the Judge); you see, your Honor, that this witness is prevaricating. He is not willing to swear that there were more than nine cords of wood. It is infamous, gentlemen of the jury, such testimony as this." The jury nodded assent and smiled sarcastically at me.

'Now,' said Johnson, 'I will ask this perjured witness just one more question.'

'I ask you, sir—do you know—do you realize, sir, what an awful—a-w-f-u-l thing it is to tell a lie?'

'Yes, sir,' I said, my voice trembling.

'And, knowing this, you swear on your solemn oath that there were about nine cords of wood?'

'No, sir, I don't do any thing of——'

'Hold on, sir! Now how do you know there were just nine cords?'

'I don't know any such thing, sir! I——'

'Aha! you don't know then? Just as I expected. And yet you swore you did know. Swore you measured it. Infamous! Gentlemen of the jury, what shall we do with this perjurer?'

'But I——'

'Not a word, sir—hush! This jury shall not be insulted by a perjurer!

'Call the next witness!'

"'This is why,' said the humorist, 'that I am now unfit to keep the books in a lunatic asylum.'"

When I asked the humorist how it happened that he became a writer and lecturer, he said, gravely:

"I studied law once in the Washington Law School. In fact, I was admitted to the bar. I shall never forget my first case. Neither will my client. I was called upon to defend a young man for passing counterfeit money. I knew the young man was innocent, because I lent him the money that caused him to be arrested. Well, there was a hard feeling against the young man in the county, and I pleaded for a change of venue. I made a great plea for it. I can remember, even now, how fine it was. It was filled with choice rhetoric and passionate oratory. I quoted Kent and Blackstone and Littleton, and cited precedent after precedent from the Digest of State Reports. I wound up with a tremendous argument, amid the applause of all the younger members of the bar. Then, sanguine of success, I stood and awaited the Judge's decision. It soon came. The Judge looked me full in the face and said:

"Your argument is good, Mr. Perkins, very good, and I've been deeply interested in it, and when a case comes up that your argument fits, I shall give your remarks all the consideration that they merit. Sit down!'

"This is why I gave up law and resorted to lecturing and writing for the newspapers."

Eli Perkins' witty and humorous articles would fill volumes, and his name will go down to posterity and become brighter and brighter as the people find out what a vast amount of good literary work be has done.

ELI PERKINS' LECTURE.

THE PHILOSOPHY OF WIT AND HUMOR.

The aim of Mr. Landon in his lectures has always been to convey truth as well as to produce laughter. His sharp distinction between wit and humor is consistently and strongly carried through his lectures and writings. Heretofore, humor has usually been placed over wit. Mr. Landon proves that wit is more intellectual than humor. He separates satire and ridicule, showing that satire is to kill error, while ridicule is to kill truth.

In representing a live lecture, bristling with gesture, genuine eloquence, or mock oratory, the cold dead types can convey but a vague idea. Much is left to the lively Imagination of the reader.

Ladies and Gentlemen:—Before making any remark on the subject of "Wit and Humor," we will first ask the simple, natural questions, What are "Wit and Humor?" What is it that produces laughter? Here we all laugh a hundred times a day; now, I say, what is it that produces this laughter?

I know the old rhetoricians, Lord Kames and Whateley and Blair and Wayland, all tell us that "wit is a short-lived surprise"—that laughter is always produced by a "short-lived surprise;" and there they stop. But that is a false definition. False? Prove it! If wit were a "short-lived surprise," as they say, that is, if laughter were caused by a "short-lived surprise," then those railroad passengers who pitched over Ashtabula bridge must have screamed with laughter—for it was a "short-lived surprise." [Laughter.]

Again: Suppose you were walking along and a serpent should dart out in front of you. It would be a "short-lived surprise," but it would not produce any laughter—would it? But if you were walking along and you should see a double-headed rooster—running both ways to get away from itself—[laughter] you all would burst out laughing.

So you see, my friends, that laughter is not always produced by a "short-lived surprise," but laughter is always caused by some deformity, some eccentricity in art or nature. But that deformed thing which makes us laugh is something which we neither love nor hate; for laughter is an emotion and not a passion. You wouldn't laugh at your own deformed child, because you love it. But you would laugh at something which you neither love nor hate—like deformed music—you neither love it nor hate it—deformed grammar, deformed rhetoric, deformed spelling, deformed oratory, deformed gesture and deformed truth itself. You would not laugh at a chariot wheel rolling grandly down the street, and nothing, says Hogarth, is more beautiful than a rolling wheel; but dish that wheel, pull the spokes over and let it come along lop-sided and you would all burst out laughing.

Now, as we never laugh at a perfect thing, we never laugh at the climax in rhetoric. The climax is a perfect sentence; but we do all laugh at the anti-climax, which is a deformed sentence—a case where that same perfect sentence runs right against a post and breaks off.

As good an example of the anti-climax as I know of occurred over in New Jersey the other day. A good old colored clergyman was describing a storm, and he pictured it something like this:

"The winds howled like the roaring of Niagara; the thunder rumbled and grumbled and pealed like Vesuvius laboring with an earthquake; the lurid lightnings flashed through the sky like—like—sixty!" [Laughter.]

Now, if that comparison had been complete, there would have been no laughter. What did we laugh at? We laughed at deformed rhetoric. The deformity causes both the surprise and laughter. Without it there could be neither.

Suppose your physician should give you as lame a definition as the rhetoricians have been giving you for a thousand years? Suppose, when you asked him what killed his patients, he should say, "My patients died from want of breath!"

"But what caused the want of breath?"

"Oh, the *genus*, disease—*species*, small-pox!" [Laughter.]

What we want is the cause of the cause, so to-night I give you the genus and species of all deformities which will cause laughter. No, not all of the deformities—we haven't time to talk about deformed music; but you know if some one were playing a beautiful symphony on an organ here, and a key should get caught and s-q-u-e-a-k! should go through the audience [laughter], how you would all burst out laughing.

We haven't time to talk about deformed spelling, but you all know that two-thirds of dear old Josh Billings' wit was caused by deformed spelling; half of Nasby's wit was deformed spelling, and the funniest thing in Thackeray's "Yellow Plush Papers" was when he spelled gentlemen "gen'lemen."

13

All the dialects, too — the Dutch dialect, Irish dialect and negro dialect — are funny; and why? Because they are a language deformed. I could tell you a simple story in plain English, and you wouldn't smile at all, and then I could tell that same story in an Irish, Scotch, Dutch or negro dialect, and you would all burst out laughing. So, if you ever have a story that isn't funny enough to suit you, put it into any dialect that you can command, and you'll double the fun of it. To illustrate the fun of dialect:

One frosty morning I met a German, shivering with the cold, and remarked:

"Hans, you have frozen your nose."

"Nein, he froze hisself, Mr. Berkins."

"How did it happen, Hans?"

"I no understand dis ting. I haf carry dot nose dese fordy year, unt he nefer freeze hisself before." [Laughter.]

A good instance of Irish brogue, or dialect, is instanced in Mrs. Colonel Kelly's cross-examination in the O"Toolihan suit for damages.

"You claim, Mrs. Colonel Kelly," said the Judge, "that Mrs. O'Toolihan gave you that bruised and blackened face?"

"She did, yer Honor — indade she did, or I'm not Irish born."

"And what you want in damages, Mrs. Kelly?"

"It is damages yez says, yer Honor? Damages! No, bad luck ter the O'Toolihan, I have dam–ages enough. I wants sat-is-fac-shun, begorry!" [Laughter.]

Another case. John Quinn, our Irish waiter, jerked his finger out of a box of turtles, and held it up in great pain.

"What are you doing there, John?" I asked.

"I wor investigating."

"Investigating what?"

"I wor trying to see which was the head and which was the tail ov that baste over there in the corner ov the box."

"What do you want to know that for?"

"I've a curiosity to know whether I've been bit or stung." [Laughter.]

Again, an Irish judge, who had been over from the old sod but two years, was examining a Corkonian who had just arrived in New York.

"Phat's yer name, yez spalpeen?" he asked.

"Patrick McGoolihan, yer Honor."

"Is it an Irishman yez are? Begorra, yez shows it by yer sthrong wakeness for the Oirish accint."

"Yis, yer Honor; I was born abroad."

"That's what oi thought, sorr. Yer accint is froightful. Yer not in Oirland, mon, and yez should spake our Unighted Shtates toong more dacently and not be givin' uz yer furren brogue."

Nothing is more amusing than to hear that rich, Irish brogue:

"Phat is this I see, Moike?" asked Mr. O'Kelly. "And is it dhrinkin whiskey yez are? Sure it was only yestherday ye towld me ye was a taytotler."

"Well, your right, Mister O'Kelly," said Mike, "it's quoite right ye are—I am a taytotler, it's true, but begorra I'd have ye understhand I—I—I'm not a bigoted taytotler."

Scotch dialect is always dry and funny:

"Dae ye ken," said a member of the Newark Caledonian Club, as he walked homeward from church with a fellow-countryman, "dae ye ken, I think oor minister's in the habit o' gemblin'?"

"What gars ye think that?"

"I'll tell ye, Sandy. Ae Sunday no lang ago in his prayer instead o' saying, O, Thou who hast the hearts of kings in Thy hands, he prayed, 'O, Thou, who has the king of hearts in Thy hands.' What dae ye think o' that?"

"It dis'na look richt," commented the other, shaking his head sadly.

The simplest incident, if told with a dialect, will produce laughter. For instance:

Two Germans met in San Francisco. After affectionate greeting, the following dialogue ensued:

"Fen you said you hev arrived?"

"Yesterday."

"You came dot Horn around?"

"No."

"Oh! I see; you came dot isthmus across?"

"No."

"Oh! den you come dot land over?"

"No."

"Den you hef not arrived?"

"Oh! yes, I hef arrived. I come dot Mexico throught." [Laughter.]

The Hebrew dialect is funny because it is simple, and every one can understand it. Yet many Hebrew stories would be ruined if told in good English. For instance:

One day I met my friend Jacob from Chatham street. He looked very sad, and I said:

"Why so gloomy this morning, Jacob?"

"Ah, my poor leetle Penjamin Levi—he is tead!"

"Dead? You surprise me. How did that happen?"

"Vell, you see, my leetle Penjamin he vas at der synagogue to say his brayers, and a boy put his het at der door and gries, 'Job Lot!' and leetle Penjamin—he vas gilt in der grush." [Laughter.]

The Chinese dialect, or pigeon English, is always funny.

Mrs. Van Auken, of Fifth avenue, recently employed a Chinese cook—Ah Sin Foo. When the smiling Chinaman came to take his place, Mrs. Van Auken asked him his name.

"What is your name, John?" commenced the lady.

"Oh! my namee, Ah Sin Foo."

"But I can't remember all that lingo, my man. I'll call you Jimmy."

"Velly wellee. Now what chee namee I callee you?" asked Ah Sin, looking up in sweet simplicity.

"Well, my name is Mrs. Van Auken; call me that."

"Oh! me can no 'member Missee Vannee Auken. Too big piecee namee. I callee you Tommy—Missee Tommy." [Laughter.]

The Italian dialect is sweet and laughter-provoking. A New York policeman thus accosted an Italian organ-grinder:

"Have you a permit to grind this organ in the street?"

"No. Me no habbe de permit."

"Then, sir, it becomes my duty to request you to accompany me—"

"Alla righta. Vatta you sing?" [Laughter.]

The dialect of the dude is very modern, but we recognize it as a deformed language.

"Going widing to-day, Awthaw?" asked one dude of another.

"Naw. Got to work, demmit."

"So sawy, deah boy. What is the—aw—blawsted job, eh?"

"Maw's written me a lettaw, and I've—aw—got to wead it befaw I can make another dwaft on haw. Did you evaw heah of such a boah?"

"Nevaw, deah boy, nevaw." [Laughter.]

Dialect itself is funny, but when you clothe a witty idea in dialect it doubles the fun. For instance: I lectured in a good old Quaker town up in Pennsylvania a few weeks ago, and after the lecture, the lecture committee came to me with my fee in his hand, and said, as he counted the roll of bills:

"Eli, my friend, does thee believe in the maxims of Benjamin Franklin?"

"Yea," I said.

"Well, friend Eli, Benjamin Franklin, in his Poor Richard maxims, says that 'Time is money.'"

"Yea, verily, I have read it," I said.

"Well, Eli, if 'Time is money,' as thy friend, Poor Richard, says, and thee believe so, then verily I will keep the money and let thee take it out in time." [Laughter.]

The deformed language of the colored preacher always produces laughter among the whites, while the colored auditors, who do not see the deformity, never dream of smiling.

So I always love to hear the good old orthodox colored preacher. He may trip in his grammar and pronounce his words wrong, but the child-like faith of the true Christian is always there. I heard a sermon once from a dear, good old clergyman, who had once been a slave in Maryland, and who had converted many souls. The words were often wrong but the true spirit was there. I remember the old man started off with these words:

"I takes my tex' dis maunin', bredrin', from dat po'tion ob de scripter whar de Postol Paul p'ints his pistol to de Fenians." [Laughter.]

Do not laugh my friends, for the old man grew very eloquent over the text. He implored the thoughtless young men to be kind to their fathers and mothers. "Don't wed yerself to strange godeses," he said, "an' leave yer ol' fadder an' mudder to starve." [Laughter.]

"Why, bress yer soul, young men," he continued, "I'ze got an' ol' mudder, an' I hab to do fo' her, ye see, an' ef I don't buy her shoes an' stockin's she don't get none. Now, ef I war to get married, young men, I'd hab to buy des fings for my wife, an' dat would be taking de shoes and stockin's *right out o' my mudder's mouf*." [Laughter.]

In the evening, said Mr. Perkins, the good old preacher, in announcing his text, said:

"Dis ebenin', brederin', de Lord willin', I will preach from de tex', "An St. Paul planted and Apollinaris watered." [Laughter.]

Deformed words will always produce laughter. All the wit in Mrs. Malaprop's and in Mrs. Partington's sayings was caused by using deformed words. See how funny is a paragraph from that dignified man, Benjamin P. Shellabar.

"Diseases is very various," said Mrs. Partington. "Now they say old Mrs. Haze has got two buckles on her lungs. Deacon Sempson has got tonsors of the throat. Aunt Mary Smith is dying of hermitage of the lungs, and now "Josh Billings" finds himself in a jocular vein. New names and new nostrils every where!"

"They say Mrs. Putnam, who has such a lovely husband, can't bear children," I remarked.

"Perhaps if she could she would like them better," replied the old lady, disdainfully.   Then she wiped her glasses and looked over them to read the close type in the advertisements.

When her eye wandered down the amusement column she read that at the Academy of Music the "Prayer of Moses was being executed on one string."

"The Prayer of Moses executed on one string," she repeated.   "Well, I declare!   Praying to be cut down I suppose.   Poor Moses!" she sighed, "executed on one string! [Laughter.] Well, I don't know as I ever heard of any body being executed on two strings, unless the rope broke." [Laughter.]

Again: A deformed quotation will produce laughter.   This is why the parody, which is the original poem deformed, always amuses people. Jo Mills, the brother of D. O. Mills, used to open oysters, but becoming rich he joined the stock exchange, and while on Wall street, he kept all the bankers laughing at his deformed quotations.   Once, on returning from Havana to Key West, he telegraphed August Belmont, to tell the brokers that after a stormy sail he had at last landed on Terre Cotta. [Laughter.]   When Mr. Mills arrived in New York, Russell Sage asked him, how he felt.   "I felt very bad before the trip," said Jo, "but now, slapping his leg with his hand, I feel *new plus ulster.*"   [Laughter.]

Stammering stories are a species of dialect, and are funny on account of the deformity of the language.   To illustrate a stammering story:

I was lecturing up at Ballston Spa, and the chairman of the lecture committee, Major Stevens, who is a great stammerer, was rather late in calling on me at the hotel.   When he finally came, I said:

"Major, where've you been?   Where've you been?"

"I've b—b—been down to, been d—d—down t—t—to—to———"

"Where did you say?"   [Laughter.]

"I've been d—d—down to A—A—Albany, the c—c—c—capital."

"What have you been down to Albany for?"

"I've b—b—been there to see the m—m—members of the leg—leg—legislature."

"What did you want to see the members of the legislature for?"

"Well, I wanted to get 'em to c—c—change the state con—consti—constitution."

"Why, what did you want to change the New York State constitution for?"

"Because the st—st—state constitution g—g—guarantees to ev—ev—every m—m—man f—f—free s—s—speech, and I w—w—want it or I w—w—want the d—d—darned thing changed!"   [Loud laughter.]

There is another deformity that I will refer to, very prolific of laughter—deformed grammar. To illustrate: I saw a little girl learning to read the other day.

Said I: "Little girl, didn't you have a hard time learning to read?"

"Yes," she said, "I did have a hard time—a very hard time learning to read, but I kept on learning to read—kept on learning to read and bime-by I rode." [Laughter.]

Another instance of deformed grammar: Two little girls were playing in their play-house. They had a mock kitchen and one of them was passing the pickles, tomatoes and potatoes to the other, when finally one took a potato on a fork and said:

"Shall I skin this potatoe for you Jenny?"

"No," replied Jenny, "you needn't skin that potato for me; I have one already 'skun.'" [Laughter.]

Another instance of deformed grammar—well it occurred at the hotel where I'm staying, not ten minutes ago: I heard a couple of chambermaids talking in the hall. They were talking about "banging" their hair. One of them asked the other if she banged her hair.

"Yes," she said, "I ba-ba-bang my hair—I keep banging my hair, but it don't stay b-b-bung! [Great laughter.]

One Sunday morning I attended Dr. Potter's service in Grace Church, New York. After waiting a while I dropped into one of the back pews. The owner soon came in, and seeing me sitting in her pew nervously approached Sexton Brown and said:

"Mr. Brown why do you permit a stranger to occupew my pie?" [Laughter.]

Listen to the deformed grammar in the stanza about the cautious burglar:

> A cautious look around he stole,
>   His bags of chink he chunk;
> And many a wicked smile he smole,
>   And many a wink he wunk.

You would hardly think that a deformed quotation will always produce laughter. Now, how often have you heard the quotation "I have other fish to fry?" When you used the expression you did not really mean that you were really going out to cook any fish. You simply said it to indicate haste, but while in Boston, General Butler said that one day he was returning home from—prayer meeting [laughter] when he overheard a young Harvard student saying good-bye to his Boston sweetheart. He was just saying good-bye, had just kissed her ear (left ear over the gate) the last, last time, when he said, "There! Good-bye,

Mariah, I must go now. I've got to go and cook another fish!" [Laughter.]

There is one other deformity which is a great source of laughter, and that is deformed logic, and where do we find deformed logic?

Why, every single pun or conundrum that was ever made in the English language is simply the deformed logic of Aristotle and Plato in another form, and those old Greeks used to laugh at the very same puns and conundrums that we do, and they laughed at them in the form of a syllogism, while we laugh at them in the modern form of the pun and conundrum. To prove this I will make a conundrum and then change it to a false syllogism.

Now, why are conundrums funny?

It is because in every conundrum you prove something to be true which you really know to be false. It is the false logic that you are laughing at. To prove this I will make a conundrum and change it to the syllogistic form of the Greeks.

I will make a conundrum about that distinguished colored statesman — that learned colored man — Fred Douglass — proving something to be true about him that you know to be false:

Conundrum: Why is Fred Douglass a very wicked man?

Answer: Because he is supported by black legs.

Now, the syllogist would put this conundrum into a syllogism like this:

First premise: Any one supported by black legs must be very wicked.

Second premise: Frederick Douglass is supported by black legs.

Conclusion: Therefore, Frederick Douglass must be very wicked.

In both cases an untruth has been proven by false logic.

Now, the syllogism, or deformed logic, was the common form of all wit among the Greeks. For instance, Aristippus came into Athens one day, and saw Diogenes, and instead of giving him a conundrum, he gave him this syllogism:

" All words, O Diogenes," said Aristippus, " come out of your mouth, do they not?"

" Yes, granted. All words do come out of my mouth."

" Well, snakes and toads are words, aren't they? Then they come out of your mouth." [Laughter.]

We have changed a conundrum to a syllogism, and now we will change a syllogism to a conundrum. We will prove a hen to be immortal by both.

Syllogism: (Major) — Any one whose sun never sets is immortal.

             (Minor) — A hen's son never sets.

             (Conclusion) — Therefore, a hen is immortal.

[Laughter.]

The conundrum would be: "Why is a hen immortal? Because her son never sets."

Now, up to this time we have spoken of the ordinary, regular conundrum; but we can have a deformed conundrum. A deformed conundrum is a case where the conundrum kicks back, or where the answer is different from what you expect. It is a kind of conundrum that a smart, shrewd boy generally gives to his poor old father, when he comes home from college. [Laughter.] I remember I got one on to my father when I returned home from college [laughter], and he turned round to a neighbor, the tears streaming down his cheeks, and said, "Brother Jones, that conundrum cost me seven hundred dollars." [Laughter.]

To illustrate one of these deformed conundrums: Henry Bergh gave me one just before he died, and I've been trying for six months to find out what he meant by it. He died without giving me the answer. [Laughter.] Perhaps you can help me out. He came to me and said he had a deformed conundrum.

"What is it, Mr. Bergh?"

"Well, what is the difference between your mother-in-law and a tree?"

"I don't know," I said; "I don't think there is much difference. [Laughter.] But what is the difference?"

"Well, the difference is this: A tree leaves every spring—and—and —." [Loud laughter interrupted the lecturer.]

"Well, I see you've all brought your mothers-in-law with you. [Laughter.] That's right, every man should bring his mother-in-law to a humorous lecture; it's the only way you can get even with her." [Laughter.]

There is a species of deformed logic where the effect follows the cause suddenly, without any logical reasoning. In the following case the boy's funeral takes place before his death is announced:

> 'Tis only an infant pippin,
>   Growing on a limb;
> 'Tis only a typical small boy,
>   Who devours it with a vim.

> 'Tis only a doctor's carriage,
>   Which stopped before the door;
> But why go into details—
>   The services begin at four. [Laughter.]

"Now where else do you find deformed logic ?   The paradox is deformed logic.   The paradox is a case where a sentence deforms its
own thought.   The thought is deformed.   With the anti-climax, the
sentence, the framework around the thought, is deformed, but with the
paradox the thought itself is deformed.   A very good instance of the
paradox—deformed logic—happened over in Omaha a few years ago.
William M. Evarts, our ex-secretary of State, was over there, and was
asked to deliver a speech—a dinner speech.   In this speech Mr. Evarts
complimented the West, in the following paradox:

"I like the West—I like her self-made men—and the more I travel
west, the more I meet with her public men, the more I am satisfied of
the truthfulness of the Bible statement, that the " wise man came from
the east !" [Loud laughter.]

Another case of the paradox, was when the man was trying on a new
pair of boots.   He pulled away—pulled away—pulled the straps off, and
his friend said to him, "Why, George, you'll never get those boots on till
you've worn 'em a spell!"   [Laughter.]

Again: A judge in Dublin asked an Irish policeman, "When did
you last see your sister ?"

"The last time I saw her, my lord, was about eight months ago,
when she called at my house, and I was out."   [Laughter.]

"Then you did not see her on that occasion?"

"No, my lord; I wasn't there."   [Laughter.]

Again: At a crowded concert to hear Patti the other night, a
young lady was looking for a seat.

"It is a seat you want, Miss?" asked the Irish usher.

"Yes, a seat, please."

"Indade, Miss," said Pat, "I should be glad to give you a sate, but
the empty ones are all full."   [Laughter.]

Again: An Irishman describing the trading powers of the genuine
Yankee, said :

"Bedad, if he was cast away on a desolate island, he'd get up the next
mornin' and go round selling maps to the inhabitants."   [Laughter.]

Again: An Irishman boasted that he had often skated sixty miles a
day.

"Sixty miles!" exclaimed an auditor, "that is a great distance; it
must have been accomplished when the days were the longest."

"To be sure it was; I admit that," said the ingenious Hibernian,
"but whoile ye're standin', sit down, an' oi'll tell ye all about it."

Again: An Irish lover said, "It is a great comfort to be alone,
especially when yer swateheart is wid ye."   [Laughter.]

WOULD YOU TAKE ANYTHING, BRIDGET?

See page 205.

Again: You all remember the triumphant appeal of an Irishman, a lover of antiquity, who, in arguing the superiority of old architecture over the new, said:

" Where will you find any modern building that has lasted so long as the ancient?"

Again: An Irishman got out of his carriage at a railway station for refreshments, but the bell rang and the train left before he had finished his repast.

"Hould on!" cried Pat, as he ran like a mad man after the car, "hould on, ye murthen ould stame injin—ye've got a passenger on board that's left behind." [Laughter.]

Again: My wife's cook was sick. She was sure she was going to die. It was the colic.

" Would you take any thing, Bridget?" asked my wife, pouring out some bitter cordial.

" Indade," said Bridget, " I would take any thing to make me well, if I knew it would kill me." [Laughter.]

Again: "A man who'd maliciously set fire to a barn," said Elder Podson, " and burn up a stable full of horses and cows, ought to be kicked to death by a jackass, and I'd like to be the one to do it." [Laughter.]

Again: Two deacons once disputing about a proposed new grave yard, one remarked, " I'll never be buried in that ground as long as I live!" "What an obstinate man!" said the other. "If my life is spared I will." [Laughter.]

Said Congressman Ben Eggleston, of Ohio, to Sam Cox, of New York, who was trying to tell him something about hogs: " You can't tell me any thing about hogs. I know more about hogs than you ever dreamt of. I was brought up in Cincinnati right among 'em." [Laughter in Louisville, but tears in Cincinnati.]

Another instance of deformed logic, or the paradox, was the case of the two farmers who were talking about the sun and the moon. One was trying to prove that the moon was of more account than the sun.

" How do you make that out?" asked his friend.

" Why," said he, " the moon shines at night when it's dark, and the sun shines in the daytime when it's light enough without it." [Laughter.]

* * * * * * * * * * *

There is one other deformity that I will speak of, and that is deformed truth, [laughter] hyperbole, extravagant statement, or, in plain English, lying. [Laughter.]

Now, I don't say that to be witty, you must always be telling lies. If that were the case, the editors would be the funniest men in the world; [laughter] but I do say that a great, big, innocent Baron Munchausen exaggeration—a deformed truth—is just as funny as any other deformity and for the same philosophical reason.   But O, my friends, it must be an innocent exaggeration.   It must be an exaggeration to make your fellow-men happy and to harm no man—and for this reason the humorists—no not the humorists; and right here I am going to draw a line between wit and humor that has never been drawn.   Why not the humorists?   Because the humorist always tells the absolute truth.   This is the difference between wit and humor.   Humor is always the absolute truth, close to life, dialect and all, while wit is always a "magnification" or a "minification."   Humor, I say, is the actual incident photographed, while wit is simply imagination which when expressed in words is exaggeration.

Dickens was the king of the humorists, but those stories that Dickens wrote, the story of "Sam Weller," "Little Nell," and "Smike," and "Oliver Twist," as you know, were all absolutely true.*   Bret Harte's "Luck of Roaring Camp" is another charming piece of humor—absolute truth.   But the wits all deal in the imagination; they are all great truth deformers, all great liars!   Mark Twain is a fearful—liar. [Laughter.]   But Mark Twain is both a humorist and a wit.   Whenever he tells the absolute truth, close to life, like Dickens, he is a humorist; but just the moment he lets his imagination play—just the moment he begins to exaggerate—stretch it a little—then that humor blossoms into wit.

To show you the fine dividing line between wit and humor—the invisible line—and how humor can gradually creep into wit through exaggeration, Mark Twain, in one of his books, has a chapter on building tunnels out in Nevada.   He goes on for five pages with pure humor—pure truth.   He describes those miners just as they are—describes their dialects, describes their bad grammar, describes the tunnel; but Mark can't stick to the truth very long before he begins to stretch it a little.   He soon comes to a miner who thinks a good deal of his tunnel. They all tell him he'd better stop his tunnel when he gets it through the

---

* The London *Literary World* says: Smike is still living in Bury, St. Edmund's, where he keeps a toy shop.   He is a tall, hatchet-faced old gentleman, proud of his romantic eminence. Carker was connected, through his father, with an eminent engineering firm, and lived in Oxford road, where he prowled about, a nuisance to all the servant girls in the neighborhood. Carker, Major Bagstock, Mrs. Skewton, whose real name was Campbell, and her daughter, were well-known characters in Leamington.   Fifty years ago the Shannon coach, running between Ipswich and London, was driven by a big, burly old fellow named Cole, who was the veritable elder Weller.

hill, but he says he "guesses not — it's his tunnel," so he runs his tunnel right on over the valley into the next hill. [Loud laughter.] You who can picture to yourselves this hole in the sky, held up by trestle work, will see where the humor leaves off and the wit begins—where the truth leaves off and the exaggeration commences. [Applause.]

We see humor all around us every day. Any one can write humor who will sit down and write the honest truth. There is no imagination in humor, while wit is all imagination—like the tunnel. Humor is what has been; wit is what might be. I saw as good a piece of humor to-day as I ever saw in my life. I wish I had photographed it. I would if I had thought that it could be so good. A dear, good old lady and her daughter came into the depot at Poughkeepsie. She wasn't used to traveling, and was very nervous. Her eyes wandered about the depot a moment, and then she walked nervously up to the station window and tremblingly asked:

"When does the next train go to New York?"

"The next train, madam," said the agent, looking at his watch, "goes to New York at exactly 3.30."

"Will that be the first train?" [Laughter.]

"Yes, madam, the first train."

"Isn't there any freights?"

"None."

"Isn't there a special?"

"No, no special."

"Now if there was a special would you know it?" [Laughter.]

"Yes."

"And there isn't any—ain't they?"

"None."

"Well I'm awful glad—awful glad," said the old lady, "Now Mariah you and I can cross the track." [Loud laughter.]

There is not a day but what every one in my audience sees something funnier than that. All you have to do is to describe it truthfully to make humor of it.

Take the simple scene of two married women taking leave of each other at the gate on a mild evening and describe it truthfully and it will be humor. To illustrate, two women shake hands and kiss each other over the gate and then commences the conversation:

"Good-bye!"

"Good-bye. Come down and see us soon."

"I will. Good-bye."

"Good-bye. [Laughter.] Don't forget to come soon."

"No, I won't. Don't *you* forget to come up."

"I won't. Be sure and bring Sarah Jane with you next time."

"I will. I'd have brought her this time, but she wasn't very well. She wanted to come awfully."

"Did she now? That was too bad! Be sure and bring her next time." [Laughter.]

"I will. And you be sure and bring baby."

"I will. I forgot to tell you that he's cut another tooth." [Laughter.]

"You don't say so! How many has he now?"

"Five. It makes him awfully cross."

"I dare say it does this hot weather."

"Well, good-bye! Don't forget to come down." [Louder.]

"No I won't. Don't you forget to come up. Good-by!" [Still louder.]

"Good-bye!" [Screaming.]

"Good-bye!" [Yelling.]

Now this is a very shallow conversation but the humorist who can render such scenes close to life has his fortune in his hands. But there is a humor where imagination is added to the truth, that almost leaves the domain of humor and blossoms into wit.

There is a kind of half-sad humor where two earnest people misconstrue each other's thoughts. I once heard a dialogue between a sweet, dear old clergyman of Arkansaw and an illiterate parishioner, which with a little of my own imagination added illustrates this idea:

"Your children here all turned out well, I reckon," said the clergyman as he sat down to dinner with the parishioner he had not seen in church for several years.

"Well, yes, all but Bill, pore feller."

"Drunk licker, I reckon," said the clergyman, sorrowfully."

"Oh, no, never drunk no licker, but he hain't amounted to nothin'. Bill was deceived, an' it ruint him."

"Love affair? Married out of the church maybe?"

"Yes, an' a mighty bad love affair."

"She deceived him, eh?"

"Terribly, terribly."

"Ruined his spiritual life and he married a scoffer?"

"Oh no, she married him; married him? I guess she did!" [Laughter]

"But confidentially, what was the cause of your son's grief and ruin?"

"Well you see, brother Munson, she was a widder an' let on she wuz well off, but she wan't. W'y she wan't able to get Bill a decent suit o' clothes the week airter they wuz married. Poor Bill has gone ragged ever since the weddin'. Poor boy, he's lost all confidence in wimmen, Bill has." [Laughter.]

To illustrate how humor can run into the imagination and become wit:

A young lady came into Alexander Weed's drug store, and asked him if it were possible to disguise castor oil.

"It's horrid stuff to take, you know. Ugh!" said the young lady, with a shudder.

"Why, certainly," said Mr. Weed, and just then, as another young lady was taking some soda water, Mr. Weed asked her if she wouldn't have some, too. After drinking it the young lady lingered a moment, and finally observed:

"Now, tell me, Mr. Weed, how you would disguise castor oil?"

"Why, madam, I just gave you some—"

"My gracious me!" exclaimed the young lady. "Why, I wanted it for my sister!" [Loud laughter.]

This is wit, because it ends up with a snap of the imagination. So I say wit is pure Baron-Munchausen exaggeration or minification. The story teller exaggerates, the actor exaggerates, the writer exaggerates, and the witty artist exaggerates.

Gil Blas, Gulliver's Travels, Don Quixote and the Tale of a Tub are instances of pure imagination, pure fancy. There is no special genius displayed in reporting a scene close to life. Dickens ceases to be a humorist when he lets his imagination play in the speech of Buzfuz, and Mark Twain is irresistibly witty when he comes to the bust of Columbus and the tomb of Adam. Herein differs the Wit from the Humorist. The Humorist is a faithful photographer. He tells just what he hears and sees, while the Wit lets his imagination and fancy play. I believe the Wit is as far beyond the Humorist as the ideal picture is beyond the humdrum portrait. A witty sketch is as much beyond a humorous sketch as Raphæl's ideal Sistine Madonna is beyond Rubens' actual portrait of his fat wife. One is ideal, the other is real. Any patient toiler can write humor, while it is only the man with brain and imagination who can write wit. [Applause.]

As perfect a piece of humor as was ever written is Mark Twain's description of Tom Sawyer whitewashing the fence. Human nature bristles all through it. The Detroit *Free Press* man is a humorist. All of his stories are based on the truth. Old "Bijah" was an actual character; and Mr. Lewis simply described his acts close to life. Brother Gardner was once a real character and The Lime Kiln Club existed.

14

Mr. Lewis described the meetings of the club so true to life that he once received a letter from a member of the Indiana State legislature who wanted to come to Detroit and join the club. [Laughter.] Mr. Lewis always takes real characters and makes them act in the newspaper just as they act in nature.

How many times we have all seen the little quarrels of loving brides and grooms. Picture to yourselves a young married couple fixing up their first home:

"How glad I am, dearie, that our tastes are so very similar," said young Mrs. Honeylip to her husband when they had returned from their bridal tour and were furnishing the flat in which they were to be "so perfectly happy."

"We agree about every thing, don't we, darling?" she continued. "We both wanted cardinal and gray to be the prevailing tones in the parlor, we agreed exactly about the blue room, and both wanted oak for the dining room and hall. We like the same kind of chairs. Oh, we agree exactly, don't we, and how nice it is. I'd feel dreadful if we didn't agree, particularly about any important thing."

"So would I, darling," he said. "It's lovely to live in such perfect harmony. Now, I guess I'll hang this lovely little water color your aunt gave us right over this cabinet, shan't I?"

"I don't hardly know, my dear. Wouldn't it look better over that bracket on the opposite wall?"

"I hardly think so, love; the light is so much better here."

"Do you think so, George? Really, now, I don't like it in that light."

"You don't? Why, it's just the light for it. It's entirely too dark for a water color on the other wall."

"I don't think so at all. Water colors don't want a great deal of light."

"They certainly don't want to be in the shade."

"They certainly don't want to hang in a perfect glare of light."

"I guess I've hung pictures before to-day, and——"

"Oh, George, how cross you are!" [Laughter.]

"I'm no crosser than you, and——"

"You are, too, and I—I—oh, how can you be so cruel?"

"Pshaw, Helen, I only said——"

"Oh, I know, and it has broken my heart."

"There, there, dear——"

"Oh, it has! I—I—George do you really want me to go back to mamma and papa?"

"Why, darling, you know——"

"Be—be—cause, boo, hoo! if you d—d—o, boo, hoo! I will. It would be better, boo, hoo! than for us to quarrel so over every thing, and——"

"There, there, my dear, I——"

"Mamma was afraid we were too unlike in disposition to get along well, but I—I—oh, George this is too perfectly dreadful!" [Laughter.]

.:   *   *   *   *   *   *   *   *   *

Now I will show you how the wit and humorist do their work. I'll lift the veil right here. The humorist takes any ordinary scene, like the old lady in the depot, and describes it true to life. That's all. Dickens used to go down into the slums of London and get hold of such quaint characters as Bill Sykes and Nancy. Then he used to watch them, hear every word they uttered—hear their bad grammar and dialect—see every act they performed. Then he used to come into his room, sit down and write a photograph of what he saw and heard. And that was humor—truth in letter and in spirit.

The humorist is truer than the historian. [Sensation] The historian is only true in spirit, while the humorist is true in spirit and in letter. Sir Walter Scott, when he wrote true humor was truer than Macaulay. [Sensation.] Take King James of Scotland. He had never stepped upon English soil. He could not speak the English language. He spoke a sweet Scotch dialect. But when Macaulay makes King James speak, he puts in his mouth the pure English of Addison and Dr. Johnson. He deceives us to add dignity to his history. [Applause.] Not so with Sir Walter Scott. When he describes King James in Ivanhoe he puts nature's dialect in his mouth — that sweet Scotch dialect— and Sir Walter Scott is truer than Macaulay. [Applause.]

Humor is what has been; wit is what might be. Humor is the absolute truth, dialect and all, and wit is that same truth exaggerated by the imagination — carried farther than nature, like Mark Twain's tunnel. [Applause.]

The most humorous thing "The Danbury News Man" ever wrote, was that account of putting up a stovepipe, and that actually occurred. The Danbury News Man and his wife were going to church one day, and the stovepipe fell down. He called his wife back to help him put it up; but she was a very religious woman, and went on to church and left him to put up that stovepipe alone. He put up that stovepipe. [Laughter.] That stovepipe did every thing that any stovepipe could do. [Laughter.] It didn't go out of the room. [Laughter.] I had a stovepipe once that got out the back door, went clear around the block twice, and came back and got onto the wrong stove. [Loud laughter.] Well, after he got the stovepipe put up, he sat down and wrote a faith-ful account of it, and you enjoy reading it. You say "that is so true!" That man put up a stovepipe—he's been there! [Laughter].

Now, if the writer had wanted to add wit to his humor, he would only have had to add imagination. In his mind's eye he could have put two joints on the stovepipe, and the soot could have poured right out of one joint down his shirt collar, and he could have shaken it out of the bottom of his trousers; [Laughter] and the other joint could have slipped right over his head and taken off one of his ears. [Laughter.] But that would have been a lie, for the stovepipe was No. 6, and his head was No. 7. [Laughter.]

The most humorous creations of the Danbury News man are his description of cording the bedstead and Mrs. Munson "shooing" the hen. We can see Mrs. Munson now. Her husband, the old farmer, had been at work all the morning with two hired men and three dogs trying to drive the hens into the coop. Mrs. Munson looked up from her churning, saw the situation and screamed:

"John! I'll 'shoo' those hens!"

Then she goes out — gets her eyes on the hens — holds up her dress from both sides — then drops her whole body as she says "Sh———!" [Laughter.] That settles it! [Loud laughter.]

*   *   *   *   *   *   *   *   *   *   *   *

We have shown what wit and humor are, and now we come to satire. And what is satire?

Satire is a species of wit. Satire is to exaggerate an error and make it odious. Nasby was a satirist. He always called himself a satirist—not a humorist. He never tried to produce laughter. His aim was to convince people of error, by exaggerating that error so that they could see it. His mission was to exaggerate error, or overstate it and make it hideous. So Nasby never told a truth in his life—in the newspapers. Of course he has told private truths at home—to his wife. [Laughter.] Even the date of every letter Nasby ever wrote was an exaggeration. There is no such place as the "Confederate Cross-Roads" in Kentucky, no "Deacon Pogram"—all an exaggeration! The mission of the satirist, I say, is to exaggerate an error. Why, you can kill more error with exaggeration in a week than you can kill with truth in a thousand years.

How long had they been trying to break up that awful error of knight-errantry in Spain? They couldn't do it. They flung arguments at it; the arguments fell to the ground, and the error of knight-errantry went on. One day Cervantes, that great Spanish satirist, wrote Don Quixote—a pure exaggeration—no Don Quixote ever existed, no Sancho Panza. It was knight-errantry exaggerated, and the people saw the crime and ground it under their feet. Juvenal changed the political history of Rome with satire, as Thackeray ran snobbery out of England by exaggerating it in satire.

Nasby created red-nosed Deacon Pogram, placed him in the Cross-Road, Bourbon county, saloon, filled him with rum, riot and rebellion, made him abuse the "nigger" and the Republican party, and defend slavery. He made the secessionist odious, and did more with his satire to kill slavery and rebellion than Wendell Phillips did with his denunciation. [Applause.]

Satire is used all through the Bible to kill error. Job used it—Elijah and our Savior—what cutting satire did our Savior use to call the attention of the Jews to their crimes. Don't you remember, when the Jews were washing their hands before and after every meal—little one-cent observances, while great crimes went creeping into Judea—Christ wanted to call their attention to their crimes. He used satire. With what dreadful satire He exclaimed:

" Ye are blind leaders of the blind. Ye strain at a gnat and swallow a camel!"

Our Savior didn't mean to say these Jews could literally swallow a camel—He knew they'd try—   [Laughter interrupted this sentence.]

If I want to satirize the humbuggery of our jury system, I exaggerate a juryman's ignorance, and then the people see it. For example: A Chicago lawyer was visiting New York for the first time. Meeting a man on the crowded street, he said:

" Here, my friend, I want you to tell me something about this city."

" I don't know any thing about it," said the hurrying business man, with a far-away look.

" What street is this?"

"I don't know," said the busy man, with his mind occupied, and staring at vacancy.

" What city is it?"

" Can't tell; I am busy."

" Is it London or New York?"

"Don't know any thing about it."

" You don't?"

" No."

" Well, by Heavens, sir, you are the very man I'm looking for. I've been looking for you for years."

"What do you want me for?"

"I want you to sit on a jury in Chicago." [Loud laughter.]

Satire intensifies an absurdity. Now if I were going to expose the error of evolution, which is a direct assault upon the Bible, I would not deny evolution, I would satirize it.

I would say with Darwin and Huxley, that before we can adopt evolution and modern reason we must do away with the Bible. Yes, destroy the old Bible !

The old theory of creation is all wrong. Nothing was created. Every thing grew. In the old Bible we read: "In the beginning God created heaven and earth."

"Now this is all wrong," says Darwin and I. "Our new Bible is to commence like this:

GENESIS. CHAP. I.

(1) There never was a beginning. The Eternal, without us that maketh for righteousness, took no notice whatever of any thing.

(2) And Cosmos was homogeneous and undifferentiated and somehow or an other evolution began, and molecules appeared. [Laughter.]

(3) And molecule evolved protoplasm, and rhythmic thrills arose and then there was light.

(4) And a spirit of energy was developed and formed the plastic cell, whence arose the primordial germ.

(5) And the primordial germ became protogene, and protogene somehow shaped eocene—then was the dawn of life. [Laughter.]

(6) And the herb yielding seed, and the fruit-tree yielding fruit after its own kind, whose seed is in itself, developed according to its own fancy. And the Eternal, without us that maketh for righteousness, neither knew nor cared any thing about it. [Laughter.]

(7) The cattle after his kind, the beast of the earth after his kind, and every creeping thing became evolved by heterogeneous segregation and concomitant dissipation of motion.

(8) So that by survival of the fittest there evolved the simiads from the jelly fish, and the simiads differentiated themselves into the anthropomorphic primordial types.

(9) And in due time one lost his tail. This was Adam and he became a man. [Laughter.] And behold he was the most cunning of all animals; and lo! the fast men killed the slow men, and it was ordained to be in every age that the fittest should survive!

(10) And in process of time, Moses and Christ died, and by natural selection and survival of the fittest, Matthew Arnold, Herbert Spencer, and Charles Darwin appeared, and behold it was very good. [Applause.]

*   *   *   *   *   *   *   *   *   *   *   *

Now we come to the hardest of all things to explain, and that is ridicule
—and what is ridicule?

Ridicule bears the same relation to the truth that wit does to humor—it
is the truth exaggerated. Satire is to exaggerate an error till you see it
and stamp it out; while ridicule is to exaggerate a truth, deform it and
you laugh it out. With satire the error goes with a kick, while with ridicule the truth goes with a laugh. [Applause.] Ridicule is an awful
weapon, because with it you can harm the truth. In fact the only way
to harm truth is to ridicule it. Deny truth? That don't hurt truth any.
You will simply impeach your own veracity—kill yourself. But you can
ridicule truth and, as the lawyer's say, "laugh it out of court." This is the
reason why lawyers always use ridicule—in all law cases only one side is
right; the other must be wrong; and the man who is on the wrong side,
if he is a good lawyer, will not say a word about his side, but he will walk
over to the right side, exaggerate it and "laugh it out of court."

To show you how lawyers ridicule the truth, to kill it: I attended a
murder case a while ago in Akron, Ohio. It was a homicide case—a
case where a man had accidentally killed his friend. This lawyer wanted
to win the sympathy of the jury, and he told the jury, in a very pathetic
and truthful manner, how bad his client felt.

"O! My client felt so bad," he began in weeping tones—"felt so
bad when he killed his friend; the tears rolled down his cheeks; he
knelt down by that fallen form!"

Well, the jury knew that his touching pathos was true, and so did
the other lawyer. Still he could not let it stand because it had touched
the jury. What did he do? Why, he took that true pathos right over
on the other side, exaggerated it, and turned it into ridicule, and
laughed it out of court.

"Yes," he said with exaggerated pathos, "he did feel bad when he
killed his friend. The tears *did* roll down his cheeks. He took off one
boot, and emptied it [laughter]; then he cried some more; then he
emptied his other boot [laughter]; then he tied his handkerchief around
his trousers—cried 'em full, boo—hoo!" [Laughter.]

In a moment he had that jury laughing at exaggerated truth and
pathos.

The truth was gone!

A good lawyer never denies a true statement before the jury; it is
much easier to exaggerate that statement, and make the jury "laugh it
out of court."

Ingersoll in his discussions with Talmage, never denied a true state
ment of Talmage. He exaggerated them, and made them ridiculous.

For instance, Talmage made a statement about Jonah. He said, "Perhaps the whale didn't swallow Jonah. Perhaps the whale simply took Jonah in his mouth, carried him round a day or two, and then vomited him up." That was enough for Bob. He didn't deny it. He went across the platform, and exaggerated Talmage's statement.

"Yes," said Ingersoll. "I can see Jonah in the whale's mouth—he ties himself up to a tooth and when the whale chews, Jonah, he crouches down—crouches down, [laughter, while Bob crouches down, keeping time with the whale's jaw,] and, by-and-by, when the whale isn't looking, Jonah, he jumps over into a hollow tooth, builds a fire, reaches out and catches a few fish and fries 'em; peek-a-boo!" [Great laughter.] And so he laughs Talmage's statement out of court; but has he denied it? Not at all.

Now, again, when Ingersoll wants to ridicule the church, he doesn't take the church of to-day. He couldn't ridicule that. So what does he do? Why he goes back four hundred years for that church. He goes back to the barbarous inquisition, when every man was a savage, with a spear in one hand and a hatchet in the other, trying to kill his fellow-man. [Applause.] He goes back to bloody Spain, where the State had seized the church, and they were burning Protestants at the stake, pulling their arms out on the rack, or boring their eyes out with augurs; or he goes to England in the time of Bloody Mary, when the State had seized the church, and the church was not [applause] where they were toasting John Huss, and Cranmer and Lattimer in the fires of the Inquisition—where they were burning the saints' eyes out—I say he finds the church in the hands of Bloody Mary, and he takes that church and puts it down before our young men of to-day. Then he sets Deacon Thompson to boring Deacon Monson's eyes out with an augur, and then asks our young if they want to belong to any such wicked old church as that? [Laughter.]

Now, that isn't the church they are asked to belong to. [Applause.]

Ridicule is to harm truth, not error. Our clergymen have no occasion to use ridicule, for the business of the clergyman is not to harm truth but to harm error. So he can use satire all day long, because our Savior used it. Our Savior never used ridicule. [Applause.] In fact, when any man uses ridicule in speech or editorial he is trying to stab the truth, for that is what the weapon is for.

Still, our clergymen should understand ridicule, so as not to deny it. There is your trouble. You have been denying ridicule all these days, when you should have explained it. If you want to answer Ingersoll, don't deny his ridicule, but explain it.

I heard Ingersoll deliver his great lecture on the "Mistakes of Moses," in Indianapolis. Splendid speech! I wouldn't take one plume from the hat of that eloquent infidel! But what did that speech consist of? Like all of his speeches, it was made up of nine magnificent truths about human liberty, and human love, and wife's love, and then he took one little religious truth, multiplied it by five, turned it into ridicule and "laughed it out of court." And the result? Why, the next day, as usual, all our clergymen came out and denied the whole lecture—denied ridicule! That is the mistake our clergymen have been making for ten years. I meet young men every day trembling in the balance, because you clergymen have denied too much, and not explained at all. You have not met the infidel logically. If I had followed the great agnostic, I should have said:

" Why, Ingersoll, you have just found out that Moses and the Jews, the anti-Christ, made mistakes! We Christians knew that Moses made mistakes two thousand years ago. It is written there in the Bible as plain as day how Moses murdered an Egyptian, hid him in the sand and lied about it. Why, Bob, if Moses and the Jews hadn't made mistakes there wouldn't have been any New Testament, there wouldn't have been any Christianity, there wouldn't have been any need of Christ. Christ came to correct the mistakes of Moses. [Applause.] Why, Bob, where did you get your news? You must have just got your Jerusalem Herald — delayed in a storm!" [Laughter.]

Then I would have said to those Ingersollized Christians, "Why, my dear, trembling brothers and sisters, we haven't got to defend Moses, the Jew, because he made mistakes, because he murdered and lied; [sensation] we Christians haven't got to defend the faltering Noah when he got drunk; we Christians haven't got to defend David when he became a Nero and slayed and debauched his people; and we Christians haven't got to defend that miserable king of the Jews, Solomon, when he had four hundred more wives than Brigham Young. [Sensation.] But all we Christians have got to do, and it is so easy, is to stand by the Bible account—that the Bible is true, just as it is written in black and white! They did make mistakes, those Jews did, and they made such grievous mistakes that God threw the whole Jewish dispensation overboard as a failure — God did nothing in vain—and started a new dispensation, the Christian dispensation, and sent His only beloved Son, Christ, to sit on the throne at the head of it. [Applause.] What! you defending the unbelieving Jew — the anti-Christ? God never defended them. They did just the best they could, those poor Jews did, without Christ. [Applause.] There could be no perfection without Christ. [Applause.]

"Now, Christians, wait till some one shall assault Christianity, not Judaism; wait till some one shall assault Christ, not Moses. But no one has assaulted Christ. Renan? Never. Ingersoll? Never. When they come to Christ they stand with heads uncovered. [Loud applause.]

"I would say more on this theological subject—I would kill the devil—I hate him, and I would kill him, but I see there are several clergymen present and they—have—their — families—to—support!" [Loud laughter drowned the speaker's voice.]

The fact is, a great many people who never think of reading the Scriptures, but who keep a dusty Bible to press flowers in and as a receptacle for receipts for making biscuits, often cavil about some theology that they hear about in the corner grocery. A grocery theologian said to me one day, "You don't believe in Noah and the flood, do you?" "Yes," I said, "and in the Johnstown flood too, when 18,000 were eating and drinking and 'that flood came and took them off.' Christ said that 'when He should come again it would be as in the days of Noah.'"

"And the whale story, too. Do you believe that?"

"Now there is your corner grocery theology again. The Bible don't say any thing about a whale. It says, 'And God prepared a great fish,' and if God could make the universe—if He could say, 'let there be light,' He could say, 'let there be a big fish.' The world is a miracle, the violet is a miracle, man is a miracle, the fish is a miracle."

"And that story of Balaam. Do you believe that?" says the grocery theologian. "Why, scientists have examined the mouth of an ass, and they say it is physically impossible for him to speak."

To this I answer with all the sarcasm of Moody: "If you will make an ass I will make him speak!" It's all a miracle, life, joy, laughter, tears and death, and he who can create man can resurrect his soul and waft it away to eternal joy! [Loud applause.]

*　*　*　*　*　*　*　*　*　*　*　*

What is pathos?

Pathos is the absolute truth about a solemn subject; but when pathos is rendered true to nature, it is just as entertaining as humor. How many times you have seen a sentimental young lady reading a sorrowful love story. She would read and cry, read and cry—the villain still pursued her! [Loud laughter.] She enjoyed that pathos. If she hadn't she would have thrown that book away.

I saw an old slave woman die on a Louisiana plantation during the war. The scene was humorous and pathetic:

"Doctor, is I got to go?" asked the venerable Christian, her eyes filled with tears of joy.

"Aunt 'Liza, there is no hope for you."

"Bress the Great Master for His goodness. Ise ready."

The doctor gave a few directions to those colored women who sat around 'Liza's bed, and started to leave, when he was recalled by the old woman, who was drifting out with the tide:

"Marse John, stay wid me till it's ober. I wants to talk ob de old times. I knowed you when a boy, long 'fore you went and been a doctor. I called you Marse John den; I call you de same now. Take yo' ole mammy's hand, honey, and hold it. Ise lived a long, long time. Ole marster and ole missus hab gone before, and de chillun from de old place is scattered ober de world. I'd like to see 'em 'fore I starts on de journey to-night. [Sensation.] My ole man's gone, and all de chillun I nussed at dis breast has gone too. Dey's waitin' for dere mudder on de golden shore. I bress de Lord, Marse John, for takin' me to meet 'em dar. Ise fought de good fight, and Ise not afraid to meet de Savior. No mo' wo'k for poor, ole mammy, no mo' trials and tribulations—hold my hand tighter, Marse John—fadder, mudder—marster—missus—chillun—Ise gwine home. [Tears in the audience.]

The soul, while pluming its wings for its flight to the Great Beyond, rested on the dusky face of the sleeper, and the watchers, with bowed heads, wept silently. She was dead! [Sensation.]

Is exaggeration wit?

You have no idea how much of our innocent laughter is caused by innocent exaggeration. We see it all around us. If a person imagines a thing and expresses it, that is exaggeration. You can't imagine a thing that is. You must imagine something that is not. It is only the brightest people who have vivid imaginations, and it is only the brightest people who have wit.

The charm of the Poet is caused by his imagination or exaggeration. When the divine Psalmist says "the morning stars sang together," it is imagination. Don't hold the Psalmist to strict account. Joaquin Miller in a late poem speaks of the "clinking stars."

"Why, Joaquin," I said, when I met him, "did you ever hear the stars clink?" "No," he said laughing, "but the old poetical exaggeration about the stars singing got to be a 'chestnut' and I thought I'd make my stars clink" [Laughter.]

Dear old Longfellow was a sweet Christian, and still he tunes his liar [laughter] and sings:

"The sun kissed the dew drops and they were pearls."

This is the sweet wit of the imagination—from Apollo's lyre. [Laughter.]

Our clergymen are about the brightest wits we have, because they have the brightest imaginations. I met a clergyman on the cars to-day.

I'm sorry I talked to him, for I found afterward, from the brakeman, that he used to be a chaplain in the army — and sometimes these old chaplains are loaded [laughter] — and I think he had several charges in him that hadn't been shot off since Gettysburg. [Laughter.] Well, we were talking about cannons, and he asked me if I had seen the cannon they had just cast for West Point.

I told him I hadn't. "How does it work?"

"Well, it carries the biggest ball—"

"How does it work?"

"They shot that cannon off the other day, but the ball was so large that it stood right still, and the cannon — went twelve miles! ' [Laughter.]

I found out afterward that he was really a clergyman — in good standing — in Chicago. [Laughter drowned the sentence.]

Now, this was from an innocent clergyman. [Laughter.] But exaggeration is just as likely to come from a simple farmer. One day, out in Sioux county, the extreme northwestern county of Nebraska, I met the professional homesteader. He stood by a prairie schooner, out of which came a stove-pipe. Behind was a cow and calf and two dogs.

"Where is your home?" I asked.

"H'nt got no house," he said, as he kicked one of the dogs and took a chew of tobacco.

"Where do you live?"

"Where'd I live!" he exclaimed, indignantly. "I don't have to live any where. I'm marchin' ahed of civ'lization, sir. I'm homesteadin'."

"Well, where do you sleep?"

"Sleep? I sleep over on the Government land, drink out of the North Platte, eat jack rabbits and raw wolf. But it's gettin' too thickly settled round here, for me. I saw a land agent up at Buffalo Gap to-day, and they say a whole family is comin' up the North Platte fifty miles below here. It's gettin' too crowded for me here, stranger. I leave for the Powder river country to-morrow. I can't stand the rush!" [Laughter.]

But if you want to see gigantic, innocent exaggeration, you must go West. There, among the mountain peaks and broad prairies, the imagination has something to feed upon. Their imaginations are brighter in the West than ours in the East, and then they are not troubled with these compunctions of conscience. In the East here many of us are so good — so good! that if we get hold of a good joke we go right out back side of the orchard, get right down in the corner of the fence and giggle

— all to ourselves. [Laughter.] That's the meanest kind of close commun-
ionism. [Laughter.] But while you are going West, you must go to the
prairie or the mountains to find imagination. Go to Kansas — that's
where exaggeration lives — that's where it stays. Let exaggeration get
away from Kansas, and, if there isn't a string tied to it, it will go right
back there again — so natural! [Laughter.]

Now I was out in Kansas City after that great cyclone they had there
three years ago. Terrible cyclone! A third of Kansas City blown away
— three splendid churches went up with the rest. But they were all perfectly happy. You can't make those Kansas people feel bad, since they've
got prohibition. [Applause.] If they have grasshoppers out there now,
they telegraph right over to New England, "Got grasshoppers! Got grasshoppers!!" [Laughter] And then they claim that their land is so rich
that they raise two crops, grasshoppers and corn. [Loud laughter.]

Well, the next day after I got to Kansas City, I went up on the bluffs
with Colonel Coates. He was going to show me where his house had stood
the day before. Not one brick left on another — trees blown out by the
roots!

Said I, "Colonel, you had a terrible cyclone here yesterday, didn't
you?"

"Well, there was a little d–r–a–f–t—" [Laughter interrupting the
sentence.]

So you see you can "minify" truth as well as magnify it, and it will
produce just as much laughter.

"Well," said I, "Colonel, how hard did it blow here in Kansas City?
Don't deceive me now; how hard did it blow?"

"Blow," he said, "why, it blew—it blew my cook stove—blew it
away over—blew it seventeen miles, and the next day came back and got
the griddles!" [Laughter.]

"Did it hurt anybody?"

"Hurt anybody! Why, there were some members of the legislature
over here looking around with their mouths open. We told 'em they'd
better keep their mouths closed during the hurricane, [laughter] but
they were careless—left their mouths open, and the wind caught 'em in
the mouth and turned 'em inside out!" [Great laughter.]

"Did it kill them?" I asked eagerly.

"No," said the colonel, wiping his eyes, "it didn't kill 'em, but they
were a good deal discouraged." [Laughter.]

"Why," he continued enthusiastically, "it blew some of those legislators—blew 'em right up against a stone wall and flattened 'em out as
flat as pan cakes—and—"

"Why, what did you do with them?" I asked.

"Do with them! why, we went out the next day—scraped them legislators off—scraped off several barrels full of 'em—[laughter] and sent them over to New England and sold them for liver pads!" [Loud laughter.]

Out in Dakota they have imaginations as elastic as their climate: "One day," said Elder Russell, "it is a blizzard from Winnipeg, and the next day it is a hot simoon from Texas. Sometimes the weather changes in a second. Now, one morning last spring, to illustrate, Governor Pierce, of Bismarck, and I were snow-balling each other in the court-yard of the capitol. Losing my temper, for the Governor had hit me pretty hard, I picked up a solid chunk of ice and threw it with all my might at his Excellency, who was standing fifty feet away."

"Did it hurt him?" I asked.

"Yes," said the clergyman, regretfully, "it did hurt him, and I'm sorry I did it now, but it was unintentional. You see, as the chunk of ice left my hand, there came one of those wonderful climatic changes incident to Dakota, the mercury took an upward turn, the ice melted in transit and the hot water scalded poor Governor Pierce all over the back of his neck." [Laughter.]

A good instance of exaggeration was the case of Deacon Munson, of Central New York. They said he was so mean that he used to stop his clock nights—to keep the gearing from wearing out. [Laughter.]

I did't see this, but the neighbors said the Deacon kept a dairy, and after skimming his milk on top, he used to walk up and down the street, and if no one was looking, he would turn it over and skim it on the bottom. [Laughter.] But that wasn't dishonest. It was only frugal. He had a perfect right to skim it on the sides—on the end—[Laughter interrupted the sentence.]

But there was one very queer thing the Deacon used to do. He used to come down to the butcher-shop every Saturday night, take off his old slouch hat, full of something or other, and ask the butcher if he wouldn't please restuff——them——sausage skins?" [Great laughter.]

One day I asked the Deacon if there were any potato bugs this year?

"Potato bugs!" he repeated almost contemptuously, "why I counted 462 potato bugs this morning on one stalk, in one field, and in the other field they had eaten up the potatoes, vines, fences and trees, and were sitting around on the clouds, waiting for me to plant the second crop." [Laughter.]

"Why," he continued, as he gesticulated wildly, "I had potato-bugs this morning march right into my kitchen—march right up to a red-hot stove—yank red-hot potatoes right out of the oven! [Great laughter.] I wasn't surprised at all! But I was surprised when I went down to Townsend's store after dinner to see potato-bugs crawling all over Townsend's books to see who'd bought seed potatoes for next year." [Loud laughter.]

If you want to see gigantic, innocent exaggeration, you must go down South—go down to Kentucky or Tennessee. Let a Kentuckian get hold of a new joke, and he just leaps onto a thoroughbred horse and flies for his neighbor's. Half of the horses around Lexington are lame—caused by getting there early with jokes. [Laughter.]

And no mean man does that. O, the man that rides up in front of your house a cold, stormy day, beckons to you, and you come shivering down to the gate, and he tells you a joke that makes you laugh ha! ha!! and you go back into the house and put your arms around your wife's neck and kiss her—no mean man does that! [Applause.]

Now, I was down in Kentucky last spring, during the overflow on the Ohio, and I went across the Ohio to Cairo—Cairo on the Ohio river—and sometimes under it. [Laughter.] It was a great deluge. But the women were all perfectly happy. If there is anything that a woman loves—utterly loves—it is to have plenty of nice, wet water [laughter] to wash, and as the water had been pouring down the chimneys for the last week, faster than it could run out of the front door, they were perfectly happy. But the next day after I got there, the river went down and the streets were very muddy. I met a Kentucky clergyman there who told me about the mud.

"You ought to see the mud over in Levy street," he said, "mud! mud! mud! Why, I was riding over there in my carriage this morning, and I jumped off and went into the mud clear to my ankles."

"Why," said I, "that wasn't very deep."

"Well," he said, "I jumped head first." [Laughter.]

"But you ought to go over on Water street, there's mud for you! Why, I was walking along on Water street—walking along carefully (they all walk carefully in Cairo—buck-shot land), walking along carefully right in the middle of the street, when I saw a stove-pipe hat. I ran up to it and kicked it, and hit a man right in the ear." [Laughter.]

"What are you doing here?" I asked, "what are you doing here?"

"Keep still! keep still! keep still!" he said, "I'm sitting in a load of hay." [Loud laughter.]

[Mr. Perkins now gave laughter-provoking illustrations of deformed oratory and deformed gesture which made the audience roar with laughter, but which can not be reported. In fact the funniest passages in the lectures of Bill Nye, Artemus Ward, Griswold and Burdette, can not be reproduced in cold type. They must be heard.]

The deformity of an interruption by the audience often causes laughter. It causes a deformity of a chain of thought. For instance, when President Garfield was running for Congress, in war times, he made a war speech in Ashtabula. "Gentlemen," he said, "we have taken Atlanta, we have taken Savannah, Columbus and Charleston, and now at last we have captured Petersburg and occupy Richmond, and what remains for us to take?"

"Take a drink !" shouted an Irishman. [Laughter.]

"What we want," said Sam Cox, in a great low tariff speech in Tammany Hall, "what we want is plain common sense—plain common sense——"

"That's just what you do want, Sam!" interrupted a wicked Republican. [Laughter.]

An anti-temperance man arose in the temperance convention at Des Moines. He looked so good and benevolent that every one took him for a reformer, but they soon found out their mistake.

"Speaking of temperance, gentlemen of the convention," he said, "speaking of temperance, I wish that there was but one saloon in the United States, and——"

"And what then?" interrupted the President.

"And that I owned it !" But the wicked man's voice was drowned amid hisses and laughter.

Speaking of witty oratory, I've heard Fred Douglass convulse an audience. At the reception of O'Connell, in Masonic Hall, Philadelphia, Douglass' wit and eloquence had a wonderful effect on the audience. Remember it was a black man among Irishmen.

Mr. Douglass told about a conversation that was overheard in a crowd between two Irishmen after he had made a speech in Ohio.

Said one Irishman: " That's a mighty phoine speech fer to be made by a nayger."

" Ah, yes, it was quoite phoine; but he is only half a nayger."

" Well, if half a nayger can make a speech like that, phwat the divil kind of a magnificent speech would a whole nayger make? " [Great laughter.]

Douglass only consented to address the Irishmen in order to give a little color to the meeting. [Laughter.]

But the great point of Douglass' speech was reached when he said, slowly and solemnly: "Fifty years ago I stood on the same platform with Daniel O'Connell, the Irish liberator, on the banks of the Liffey, and before the vast throng he turned to me and said: 'I rejoice to grasp by the hand the black O'Connell of America.'" [Great applause.]

Speaking of paradoxes for the eye as well as the brain. For instance, three snakes grab each other by the tail and commence swallowing each other, and they keep it up till they all disappear. [Laughter.]

A printer would laugh to see a verse of poetry deformed by setting it up from right to left, instead of the regular way.

> em ot smees tI
> eb ot thguo erehT
> gnitirw fo elyts laiceps A
> esoht fo esu roF
> 'esorp ni kniht ohW
> .gnitidni rieht ni emyhr dnA

All the fun in Humpty Dumpty is caused by sensuous deformities, not intellectual. [Applause.]

 *   *   *   *   *   *   *   *   *   *   *

Now with our new theory of the deformities we can produce laughter talking on any subject. We could produce laughter describing a battle—a bloody battle. Take the battle of Bull Run. Now, what could be more dreadful than that bloody battle of Bull Run—with its gore and carnage, and a nation's life at stake. But to make people laugh, you would have to describe that battle as my Uncle William would. He was there, Uncle William was, boldly fighting for three days—sometimes on one side and then on the other. [Laughter.]

I can see my Uncle in my mind's eye fighting at Bull Run, even as I saw him with my real eye fighting at the battle of Gettysburg—for, I, too, was there, fighting for my country, [applause] and while that bloody conflict was at its height, and while the bloody messengers of death flew thick and fast around me—— I—I left! [Loud laughter.]

At one time I saw a brigade of rebels coming up on the right flank and another coming up on the left flank, and I just stepped aside and —let them come up! [Laughter.]

Why, my Uncle William, for distinguished services at the battle of Bull Run, thrice refused a—a German silver watch—stem winder. [Laughter.] When General Butler urged it upon him he said:

"No, your Honor, I am not guilty, [laughter] give it to General Butler. He ought to be watched. [Laughter.]

Alas! my uncle afterwards fell in the battle of the Wilderness—but —he got up again! [Laughter.]
15

He said he didn't want to stand there and—and interfere with the bullets. [Loud laughter.]

When I asked Uncle William what was the worst battle he was ever in—where the balls were the thickest—he said:

"Gettysburg was the spot. The balls flew around us like hail-stones, cannister hissed through the air and——"

"Why didn't you get behind a tree?"

"Get behind a tree!" said he, "Why, there weren't trees enough for the officers." [Laughter.]

Yes, my uncle was a patriotic man. He loved the glorious stars and stripes—loved to rally around the dear old flag, and he said he was willing to leave right in the thickest of the fight any time, just to go to the rear and rally around it. [Loud laughter.]

Again, suppose you should ask a wit like Artemus Ward to produce laughter talking about temperance. He could do it by using deformed oratory, rhetoric, grammar and the other deformities which I have mentioned. He would have to talk a good deal, as my Uncle Consider would.

My Uncle Consider says, if he had his way, he would make every man temperate, if he had to hang him to do it. [Laughter.]

One day he came to me, and said he, "Eli, if you drink wine, you will walk in winding ways; if you carry too much beer, the bier will soon carry you; if you drink brandy punches, you will get handy punches, and if you get the best of whisky, whisky will get the best of you." [Laughter.]

Now my Uncle William is not temperate like my Uncle Consider. Far different.

You could see by his features, if you could see them, that he used to indulge in the flowing bowl. He used to drink every once in a while with people who invited him, and then he used to slide out and drink between drinks by himself. [Laughter.]

He used to drink with impunity—or with anybody else who invited him. [Laughter.]

One day he asked Uncle Consider to drink with him. The good old man took umbrage—but Uncle William he took whisky. [Laughter.]

Uncle William used to do a great many queer things when he had taken too much whisky with his water. One day he insisted against his wife's wishes—against his wife's advice—(O, gentlemen, you should never go against your wife's advice! Our wives know more than we—they know more than we—and they are willing to admit it) [loud laughter]—I say my Uncle William insisted against his wife's wishes on smoking on a load of hay—coming home shortly afterward without any whiskers or eyebrows, and the iron work of his wagon in a gunny-bag. [Laughter.]

Why, drinking so hard made my Uncle William so absent-minded that one night he came home from the lodge, got up and washed the face of the clock and then deliberately got down and wound up the baby and set it forward fifteen minutes. [Loud laughter.]

* * * * * * * * * * * *

What is caricature?

Caricature is wit with the brush. But there never was a caricaturist who ever produced laughter without deforming something—either magnifying or minifying it, and whenever Tom Nast or Cruikshanks or John Leech or Hogarth, those splendid caricaturists, have produced laughter, they have had to deform something—that is add imagination to fact.

When Nast wanted to make us all laugh at Carl Schurz, in the Blaine campaign, he had to exaggerate him. You wouldn't have laughed at Carl Schurz if Nast had painted him truthfully; you never laugh at the truth in art. Instead of that, Nast, you remember, exaggerated Carl Schurz. He painted him with a lean, lank, long neck. Then he put some great green goggles on him. Then he stuck some little pipe-stem legs into him. [Laughter.] Now, Carl Schurz' legs are bigger than slate pencils. [Laughter.]

You all noticed that Tom Nast didn't make any fun of Carl Schurz at the last election—and do you know why? It was because they were brother mugwumps, [laughter] and one mugwump never makes fun of another mugwump. In order to make fun of a mugwump you've got to exaggerate him, and —— you can't do it. [Loud laughter.] Nature has finished him. [Continued laughter]

Suppose a witty artist, a caricaturist, wanted to make you laugh at Ben Butler. How would he go to work? Just like the writer. First he would paint Ben Butler just as he is. No laughter now. Then he would look for some salient feature about Butler that he could exaggerate. He would take his wife with him. Our wives are very observing. She would look at Butler's eyes and say:

"Why husband, Butler's eyes are cut on a bias!"

"So they are—and then he cuts them more on the bias—this way [pulling down the outside corners of his eyes, amid great laughter].

"And he's got a little bald spot on the top of his head!"

"So he has—and he makes a great big bald spot all over his head" [moving the palm of his hand all over his head].

"And he's got little short hair sticking out from under that bald spot?"

" So he has, and the artist makes long hair sticking down this way [the speaker still putting down his eye-lids and rolling his eye-balls up, amid great laughter], and when the artist gets through with this picture, he's got a better likeness of Butler than a photograph — and you recognize it quicker than a photograph, because the caricaturist has multiplied the points of likeness, carried them farther than nature.

BEN BUTLER, CARICATURED BY NAST.

One day, after I had made these remarks on caricature, **Tom Nast,** that great caricaturist, took up this old piece of wrapping paper [holding it up to the audience] and a boot brush, and the great caricaturist made ten lightning strokes of the brush, but they were the strokes of a master— and the result was this wonderful picture of Butler—beautiful Butler! [Great laughter in the audience as the humorist displayed the Caricature.]

Now, again, suppose a true artist should paint a mule—a patient mule. A mule is patient because he is ashamed of himself. [Laughter.] If he should paint that mule truthfully, you wouldn't laugh. Why, I saw a mule painted in St. Petersburg, Russia, by that great animal painter, Shreyer, that sold for fifteen thousand dollars—a simple mule eating a lock of hay—while the original mule from which he painted it you could buy for a dollar and thirty cents. [Laughter.] No one laughed at that mule. They stood by it in mute admiration. They said, "what a master is this who can paint a mule like that." They stood before that mule as solemnly and religiously as I saw the tourists standing before Raphael's Sistine Madonna, in Dresden. But another artist, a witty artist, painted that mule and everybody was laughing at it. First he painted the mule truthfully. No laughter now. Then he looked for some salient feature of the mule that he could exaggerate. He didn't take his wife with him—O, no, a man can see the main features of the mule! [Laughter.] Smart man! [Laughter.] Well he took that main feature of the mule — that mule's ear, [laughter] and ran it on up through the trees, and the chickens were roosting on it. [Laughter.] Then he took the other main feature and spread it around on the ground and the boys were skating on it. [Laughter.]

Now, when Shreyer painted that mule eating a lock of hay and sold it for fifteen thousand dollars—and that is no uncommon thing in art. Why, one day Knaus, that great German artist, painted a dirty, sooty chimney-sweep—a colored chimney-sweep at that. You wouldn't have that chimney-sweep in your door-yard. But just the moment he got it done, so truthfully was it painted that A. T. Stewart paid him forty thousand dollars for it. That is what art will do.

And Dickens used to go down into the slums of London, get hold of such strange characters as Bill Sykes and Nancy—murderers and murderesses. You wouldn't speak to Nancy Sykes. "Go away, don't come near me!" But Dickens describes them so truthfully in his book, that by-and-by you read about them on Sunday morning in your parlor. [Applause.] And Meissonier, that great French master, once painted a miserable Dutch Spy. You wouldn't have that spy on your door-step. But when he got it done, so truthfully was it painted that Vanderbilt gave him fifty thousand dollars for it, and, to-day, that spy hangs in that beautiful, brown stone, palace on Fifth avenue. That is what art will do. So I say when Shreyer painted that mule and sold the picture for fifteen thousand dollars, what did he sell? He didn't sell the mule; you could buy the mule for five. *He sold the truth.* [Applause.] The truth on canvas. O, he who can paint the truth on canvas like Shreyer and Meissonier or Knaus—or he who can write it on paper like Dickens and Washington Irving—money can't buy it. [Applause.]

So, I say, that all good humor, in art or literature, is the truth itself; and all good wit in art or literature is based upon the truth. It is the truth improved upon by the human imagination—carried farther than nature and made truer than it was before, like the picture of Butler [Applause.] But O, what a gift it is to follow nature! Suppose Nast, in caricaturing Bulter, had not followed nature! Suppose, instead of painting Butler's eyes "more on the bias," he had lifted them up straight?

He would have looked like a Chinaman. His work would have been a wretched botch.

Now, again, suppose a caricaturist wanted to exaggerate a pug nose, how would he do it? Why, he'd make it pugger and pugger till it finally dwindled down to a wart. [Laughter.] Again, when it comes to human character, what a task it is to improve upon nature! To do that, the writer should not only be a philosopher, but he should be a moral man, and it were better were he a Christian. The world is full of wicked books where the writers have not improved upon human character. They have not exaggerated it upward toward Heaven and virtue, but downward, away from truth, toward vice and hell! [Applause.] That is what is the matter with Peck's "Bad Boy." Peck wasn't a philosopher when he wrote that book, and instead of exaggerating that sweet boy up toward Heaven, he exaggerated him downward toward vice, and the book is gone, condemned by morality. You will see it in no school library. Was it based upon the truth? Many of you have read it as the brakeman dropped it, and now, tell me frankly, could there be a father in real life so ignorant, so stupid and low, that he would let his boy take him by the ear, lead him out into the garden, tell him to kneel down, and let a buck—buck—buck him? [Laughter.]

Why a boy mean enough to treat his father so—revere thy father!— and a father silly enough to allow himself to be treated so; why they both ought to be taken by the seats of their trousers and dropped down a well! [Applause.] And they have been dropped down a well. Human nature, refined hum n nature, couldn't stand it.

But Mrs. Burnett has come with that same boy again. She is a master of her art. She takes that same sweet boy, calls him Lord Fauntleroy, and exaggerates him upward toward Heaven and virtue. Sweet boy! And when our good mothers see him in the play, so pure and gentle, so true to nature, they want to hug him to their bosoms. [Applause.]

Mothers, if your boy's soul has been blackened by Peck's bad boy, buy him Lord Fauntleroy and whiten it out again! [Applause.]

Now Baron Munchausen will live a thousand years. We see him in every school library, bound in calf. He never debased human character. I'd as soon think of having a library without "Don Quixote," without Dean Swift's "Tale of a Tub," without "Gulliver's Travels" or without that splendid humor of John Bunyan, as to have a library without Baron Munchausen. [Applause.]

John Bunyan a humorist! I should say so! You white-haired Christians who have been in the Slough of Despond with the load of sin upon your back—who have come up through the Wilderness of Doubt and who now stand on the shores of the beautiful River of Life, looking at the pearly gates of Paradise beyond—Christians, you know John Bunyan has described your case close to life a thousand times. [Applause.] John Bunyan, we take off our hats to you, the King of humorists and the King of Truth! [Loud applause.]

To illustrate one of Baron Munchausen's exaggerations, I change one of his stories into modern language. One day the Baron was riding along in his cutter hunting for wolves near St. Petersburgh, when he was attacked by a fierce pack of wolves from behind. Oh, they were savage fellows, these wolves were, with ponderous, open jaws! Pretty soon a wolf made a leap for him. The Baron laid right down in his cutter, the wolf went right over the cutter, mouth open, bit a hole right into the horse, when the Baron jumped up, kicked the wolf clear in—the wolf went on eating—eating—ate his way right to the bit, and the Baron drove that wolf right into St. Petersburgh! [Uproarious laughter.]

In conclusion I will say that the brightest wit will not produce laughter unless you can get your audience to thinking. They talk about the five senses, seeing, hearing, smelling, tasting and feeling ; the sixth sense is the brain, the very dome of a man's head, and that is for wit.

It is only the virtuous man who has a clear head, who can see through the most subtle wit. The wicked man, sordid with vice, and with mind blunted with intemperance, cannot appreciate a fine joke. Such jokes we should keep for the clear-eyed moral man. He appreciates them, and that is his reward for being virtuous. Be virtuous and you will be happy —see more joy and jokes in life. I know this from my own experience. [Laughter.]

The clear-eyed moral man is a millionaire—at heart. God gives him a thousand dollars' worth of enjoyment out of common things every day.   Never discourage the happy story-teller.   I have listened many a time to the recital of a long story out of my own book!   I didn't ring the chestnut bell on the dear good soul who tried to make me happy.   One of the greatest blessings ever given to man is that of laughter.   I have seen many men who could create laughter, and who could enjoy laughter, but I have never yet heard any one thank God for the blessing of laughter.   The chestnutphobia is the thing we should avoid.   The glorious sunshine is a chestnut, the sparkling water is a chestnut, the mother love is a chestnut, aye, happiness itself is a chestnut.   The man who is afflicted with chestnutphobia would become tired of the harps of heaven after a thousand years, and long for another instrument.   The new song would become old to him—he would yearn for a change of programme.

"O, rippling river of laughter, thou art the blessed boundary line betwixt the beast, and men, and every wayward wave of thine doth drown some fretful fiend of care !   O, laughter, rosy-dipped laughter of joy! there are dimples enough in thy cheeks to catch and hold and glorify all the tears of grief!"

"But the source of that river must be in the fountain of purity." [Applause.]

ELI PERKINS' CHILDREN STORIES.

For years Eli Perkins has been writing children stories, inspired mostly by his little girl Ethel.   A few of them are appended:

A SWEET COMPLIMENT.—That was a delicate compliment given by a ragged, little Irish newsboy, to the pretty girl who bought a paper of him.   "Poor little fellow," said she, "ain't you very cold?"

"I was, ma'am, before you passed," he replied.

IS GOD DEAD?—"Papa," asked a little girl whose father had become quite worldly, and had given up family prayers—"I say, papa, is God dead?"

"No, my child, why do you ask that?"

"Why, Pa, you never talk to him now as you used to do."

These words haunted him until he was reclaimed.

ETHEL'S CARES.—"Oh, dear! " said little Ethel, "I have so many cares.   Nothing but trouble all the time."

"What has happened now, Ethel?" asked her sympathetic play-fellow.

"Why, yesterday a little baby sister arrived, and papa is on a journey. Mamma came very near being gone, too.   I don't know what I should have done if mamma hadn't been home to take care of it!"

Exact Obedience.—"Ethel, I'd like just awfully to kiss you, but I expect it wouldn't do. You know your mamma said you mustn't never kiss the boys," said Willie, regretfully, as he looked in Ethel's beautiful eyes.

"Yes, that's just what she said, Willie. That is, it's about what she said. I 'member just as well! She says to me, she says, 'Ethel don't you ever let me see you kiss the boys.' Mamma she's gone over to Mrs. Woodsess."

Ethel's Grandmother.—When Ethel tumbled down and broke a basket of eggs, the children all cried:

"Oh, Ethel, won't you catch it when your mother sees those broken eggs. Won't you, though!"

"No, I won't tach it, either," said Ethel. "I won't tach it at all. I'z dot a dranmother!"

Ethel's Bible Explanation.—"What is it to bear false witness against thy neighbor?" asked Ethel's benevolent old clergyman to the infant class of Sabbath-school scholars.

"It's telling falsehoods about them," said little Emma.

"Partly right, and partly wrong," said the clergyman.

"I know," said Ethel, holding her little hand high up in the air. "It's when nobody did anything and somebody went and told of it."

Children's Innocent Love.—"It was a sweet love saying, and worthy of Him who took little children up."

Little Philip fell down stairs one day and injured his face so seriously that for a long time he could not speak. When he did open his lips, however, it was not to complain of pain. Looking up at his mother, he whispered, trying to smile through his tears:

"I'm pretty glad 'twasn't my little sister!"

Ethel's Excuse.—Ethel used to play a good deal in the Sabbath-school class. One day she had been very quiet. She sat up prim and behaved herself so nicely, that, after the recitation was over, the teacher remarked:

"Ethel, my dear, you were a very good little girl to-day."

"Yes'm. I couldn't help being good. I dot a tiff neck."

Ethel's Wisdom.—When Ethel's mother came back from the opera she stooped over to kiss her. As her big eyes opened, her mother said: "My darling, did you say your prayers to-night?"

"Yes, mamma, I said 'em all alone."

"But who did you say them to, Ethel, when the maid was out with me?"

"Well, mamma, when I went to bed I looked around the house for somebody to say my prayers to, and there wasn't nobody in the house to say 'em to, and so I said 'em to God."

HIS LIP SLIPPED.—Ethel went to Dodworth's dancing class, and one day, when the little boys and girls were dancing, they say Freddy Vanderbilt kissed her.

When she got home she rushed up to her mother with tears in her eyes, and exclaimed, "O, mamma, a boy kissed me!"

"O, Ethel," said her mother, with mock grief. "I'm so ashamed to think you should let a little boy kiss you!"

"Well, mamma," said Ethel, after a little reflection, "I couldn't help it."

"You couldn't help it?" exclaimed her mother.

"No, mamma. You see Freddy and I were dancing the polka, Freddy had to stand up close to me, and all at once his lip slipped and the kiss happened."

ETHEL'S QUEER ANSWER.—When Ethel was five years old she caught a cold that made her very hoarse, and right in the middle of it she went to pay a visit to Mrs. James Shindler, her grandmother. During the day she recited her various successes at school, and ended by declaring that she could read a good deal better than Sabrina, who was eight years old.

"But wouldn't it sound better if some one else said it?" asked Mrs. Shindler.

"Yes," answered Ethel with a sober countenance, "I think it would; I have such a bad cold I tant say it very well."

WITTY BLUNDER.—In Portland, where I lectured for the Y. M. C. A., I was asked to say something to the Sabbath-school scholars on Sunday evening. Now my talks are "keyed up" to college audiences or church audiences, which are about as keen of appreciation as college audiences. I could not think of any thing to talk about, so I looked at the children and said:

"Now, children, about what shall I talk to-night?"

"About three minutes," said a little girl.

The witty answer convulsed the church with laughter, and the ice once broken, I had no trouble afterwards."

THOSE WICKED UNCLES.—In my Sunday-school class when I was in college, was a dear, sweet little boy. He was beloved by every one, and especially by his Uncle William. Still his uncle used to tease him a good deal, and teach him all kinds of nonsense rhymes, just to plague his mother. One day I was telling the children about satan. I told them that satan was a wicked tempter, and that is why our Savior said, "Get thee behind me, Satan!"

"Now," said I, "can any of you children tell me any thing about Satan."

"Alfred can," spoke up one little fellow.

"Well, Alfred," I said, "you can stand up and tell us what you know about Satan."

Then Alfred arose proudly, and repeated in a boyish key:

> "Now I lay me down to sleep,
> I pray the Lord my soul to keep;
> If I die before I wake,
> It'll puzzle Satan to pull me straight."

"Why, Alfred," I said, in amazement, "did your mother teach you that?"

"No, but my Uncle William did!"

CHILDREN'S DREADFUL QUESTIONS. — One day I sat on the New York Central train, behind a pale, care-worn lady, who was taking a little boy from Albany to Rochester. As the little boy was of a very inquiring mind, and every thing seemed to attract his attention, I could not help listening to some of his questions.

"What is that, Auntie?" the little boy commenced, pointing to a stack of hay on the marsh.

"Oh, that's hay, dearest," answered the care-worn lady.

"What is hay, Auntie?"

"Why, hay is hay, dear."

"But what is hay made of?"

"Why, hay is made of dirt and water and air."

"Who makes it?"

"God makes it, dear."

"Does he make it in the day time or in the night?"

"In both, dear."

"And Sundays?"

"Yes, all the time."

"Ain't it wicked to make hay on Sunday, Auntie?"

"Oh, I don't know. I'd keep still, Willie, that's a dear. Auntie is tired."

After remaining quiet a moment, little Willie broke out:

"Where do stars come from, Auntie?"

"I don't know; nobody knows."

"Did the moon lay 'em?"

"Yes, I guess so," replied the wicked lady.

"Can the moon lay eggs, too?"

"I suppose so. Don't bother me."

A short silence, when Willie broke out again:

"Bennie says oxins is a owl, Auntie; is they?"

"Oh, perhaps so!"

"I think a whale could lay eggs—don't you, Auntie?"

"Oh, yes; I guess so," said the shameless woman.

"Did you ever see a whale on his nest?"

"Oh, I guess so."

"Where?"

"I mean no. Willie, you must be quiet; I'm getting crazy!"

"What makes you crazy, Auntie?"

"Oh, dear, you ask so many questions!"

"Did you ever see a little fly eat sugar?"

"Yes, dear."

"Where?"

"Willie, sit down on the seat, and be still, or I'll have to shake you! Now, not another word!"

And the lady pointed her finger sharply at the little boy, as if she were going to stick a pin through him. If she had, what a wicked woman she would have been!

And still there are 8,946,217 sweet, innocent little boys, just like Willie, in the United States, who, though innocent themselves, cause a good deal of mental profanity.

ELI PERKINS' LECTURE TICKET.

Eli Perkins often used, for college lectures, a burlesque admission ticket. We copy one used at Union College, Schenectady, his *alma mater*.

SEASON TICKET

GOOD ANYWHERE ON EARTH FOR 962 YEARS.

ELI PERKINS

AT LARGE.

ADMIT THE BEARER to Eli Perkins' Lecture, anywhere in the world, for years and years.

The Lecturer will commence at 8 o'clock sharp, and continue till somebody request him to stop.

In case of an accident to the lecturer, or if he should die or be hung before the evening of the disturbance, this ticket will admit the bearer to a front seat at the funeral, where he can sit and enjoy himself the same as at the lecture.

The highest priced seats, those nearest the door, are reserved for the particular friends of the speaker.

[Please don't turn over.

On the reverse side of the card were the following burlesque press testimonials:

OPINIONS OF THE PRESS.

Mr. Perkins refers with pride to the following high testimonials:

When Eli Perkins delivered his lecture in the Illinois House of Reprehensibles, there was a great rush—hundreds of people left the building, and they said if he had repeated it the next night they would have left the city.—*Chicago Times.*

Mr. Beecher, an author quite well known in Brooklyn, thus writes to the London *Times* in regard to Mr. Perkins' eloquence:

Words cannot describe the impressive sight. How sublime! to see Mr. Perkins standing perfectly erect, with one hand on his broad, massive, thick skull, talking to the educated classes—to see the great orator declaiming perfectly unmoved, while streams of people got up and went out! How grand a spectacle, as joke after joke fell from the eloquent lips of this Cicero of orators, to watch the enthusiastic crowds arising, majestically, as one man and waving their hands as they clamorously demanded their—money back at the box office.

Says the genial editor of the *Congressional Globe:*

We never, but once, experienced more real genuine pleasure than when this eloquent man (Mr. Perkins) closed his remarks. That occasion was when we won the affections of a beautiful young lady, and gained a mother-in-law—and then saw that mother-in-law sweetly and serenely pass away.

P. S.—Eli Perkins distributes a six-dollar Chromo to all who remain to the end of the lecture. Parties of six who sit the lecture out, will be given a House and Lot.

DR. ROBT. COLLYER   REV. DEWITT TALMADGE

REV: D. M. MOODY   REV. SAM. JONES

THE "DANBURY NEWS MAN."

BIOGRAPHY AND REMINISCENCES.

James Montgomery Bailey, who has made himself famous as the "Danbury News Man," was born in Albany, New York, September 25, 1841. On completing his education, he gave his services to his country, and fought through the late war in a Connecticut regiment. After the war he settled in Danbury and established the *News*. His articles were widely copied wherever the English language went, and his fame will go down with the foremost humorous writers of the country. Mr. Bailey has written several books, and his "Life in Danbury" is now having a large sale.

Mr. Bailey's wit has a delicious mental flavor. In fact, it is always the shrewd, thoughtful man who enjoys it. It is not in long, inane dialogues, but a flash of thought. The humorist says a poor man came to him with tears in his eyes one day, asking for help for his destitute and starving children.

"What do you need most?" asked Mr. Bailey.

"Well, we need bread, but if I can't have that I'll take tobacco."

One day a solemn and religious Danbury man hailed a charcoal peddler with the query :

"Have you got charcoal in your wagon?"

"Yes, sir," said the expectant driver, stopping his horses.

"That's right," observed the religious man with an approving nod, "always tell the truth and people will respect you."

And then he closed the door just in time to escape a brick hurled by the wicked peddler.

"Speaking of lazy men," said Mr. Bailey, "we have a man in Danbury so lazy that instead of shoveling a path to the front gate he pinches the baby's ear with the nippers till the neighbors come rushing in to tread down the snow."

A Danbury man was bargaining for a house of old McMasters, and asked him if the house was cold.

"Cold," said the old man, cautiously, "I can't say as to that, it stands out doors."

Speaking of the Indian raids, says Bailey: "The Modocs have made another raid on our people, and murdered them. If ever our government gets hold of these savages, gets them right where they can not escape, gets them wholly into its clutches—some contractor will make money."

Mr. Bailey's humor also consists in truthful descriptions of domestic life. His descriptions are so true that they are absolutely photographed on the mind of the reader. He can close his eyes and see with his mind's eye the very scenes depicted.

In this paragraph on the wheelbarrow you can see the wheelbarrow as plainly as if it were painted on canvas.

Says Mr. Bailey:

If you have occasion to use a wheelbarrow, leave it, when you are through with it, in front of the house with the handles towards the door. A wheelbarrow is the most complicated thing to fall over on the face of the earth. A man will fall over one when he would never think of falling over any thing else. He never knows when he has got through falling over it, either; for it will tangle his legs and his arms, turn over with him and rear up in front of him, and just as he pauses in his profanity to congratulate himself, it takes a new turn, and scoops more skin off of him, and he commences to evolute anew, and bump himself on fresh places. A man never ceases to fall over a wheelbarrow until it turns completely on its back, or brings up against something it can not upset. It is the most inoffensive looking object there is, but it is more dangerous than a locomotive, and no man is secure with one unless he has a tight hold of its handles and is sitting down on something. A wheelbarrow has its uses, without doubt, but in its leisure moments it is the great blighting curse on true dignity.

When I asked Mr. Bailey what was the funniest incident he ever saw, he said:

I was on the train the other day going to New York. As the train stopped at Stamford, an antique-looking dame thrust her head out of the window opposite the refreshment room door, and shouted,

"Sonny!"

A bright-looking boy came up to the window.

"Little boy," said she, "have you a mother?"

"Yes, ma'am."

"Do you love her?"

"Yes, ma'am."

"Do you go to school?"

"Yes, ma'am."

"And are you faithful to your studies?"

"Yes, ma'am."

CAN I TRUST YOU TO DO AN ERRAND FOR ME?

See page 241.

"Do you say your prayers every night?"

"Yes, ma'am."

"Can I trust you to do an errand for me?"

"Yes, ma'am."

"I think I can too," said the lady, looking steadily down on the manly face. "Here is five cents to get me an apple. Remember God sees you."

"Speaking of good stories, what is the best thing that ever really occurred in Danbury?" I asked.

"It was this way: One of our school committee-men, Eben Tower, was to visit the Danbury school. That he might make a good appearance, his wife, the day before, mended his trousers and accidently left the needle in the seat of the garment.

"When Eben arrived at the school, he stiffly returned the salutation of the polite teacher, and majestically settled into the 'company chair.' It didn't seem to the most acute observer that he had but just touched the chair, when he at once began to ascend. A wave of perplexed pain passed over his face, as his hand soothingly parted his coat tails.

"'Perhaps you prefer an arm chair,' said the teacher, blandly.

"'Yes, I never could sit in a cane seat.'

"A wooden chair was at once offered him, into which he dropped almost as swiftly as he got out of it again.

"'Any thing the matter?' asked the teacher, as the old man stood on his feet with a red face and an unnatural fire in his eye.

"'Any thing the matter!' he shouted, as he shook his fist angrily at vacancy. 'Any thing the matter! Yes, there is. Gimme my hat;' and as he danced toward the door he shouted back, 'school or no school, I kin whip the pewserlanermus boy what stuck the pin in them cheers.'

"'Lor, Eben!' exclaimed his wife, as he tore into the house, 'what's the matter with you?'

"'Matter!' shouted the infuriated man, as he snatched off his coat and flung it out of the window, 'I have been made the fool of the entire district by that sneakin' teacher,' and his Sunday hat flew through another window. 'Pins stuck into my cheer as I was a-settin' down as onsuspishus like as I am a-settin' down now in my own—

"'Lucretia!' he ominously howled, as he sprung out of *that* chair, and spasmodically went for the wounded part with both hands, 'you're foolin' with your best friend now, and he ain't in the humor to stand the triflin'.'

"In an instant it flashed into the good lady's mind what the trouble really was. In the next instant Eben's nether garment was over her arm, and there—there in the midst of the repairs glistened the source of all the annoyance.

"The unfortunate man gave one brief stare at the evil thing, and falteringly remarked, as he thought of the future, 'I'd agi'n twenty dollars, Lucretia, if you hadn't found it'."

DANBURY NEWS MAN'S LECTURE.

Mr. Bailey sent the following letter with the MSS. of his lecture. "England from a Back Window:"

J. M. BAILEY
Proprietor.

Danbury, Conn. Aug 27 1889.

Ladies and Gentlemen:—Being of a confiding nature and brought up amid the simple influences of a country village, my friends have feared that in this lecture experiment I might become too communicative, and say things that had better be left unsaid. There is such a thing as being too communicative, you know. I have an illustration in view. There is no object so capable of inundating the human system with the two extremes of joy and anguish as a shingle. Balance a shingle on a brick; put a lump of mud on one end and violently strike the other with a rock, and the mud immediately begins to climb up the infinitude of space. Split a shingle a part of its length, get the dog next door to back into the opening, and an effect is produced which will arouse an entire community to a clearer conception of the realities of life.

Of the agony a shingle can impart, it is not my purpose to speak. There are some things too sacred to drag before a public assembly.

Now there is not a shingle in all England. An American with one bunch of shingles and a change of clothing might travel all over Britain without a penny expense. As there are no shingles, so, also, there is not a wooden dwelling in England. This fact placed a Manchester gentlemen in a rather embarrassing position. He had sojourned in the States several years, and returned to his native land fully primed with valuable information. [Laughter.] Several nights after, while entertaining a few friends in the private bar-parlor of the White Horse Tavern, he ventured on the astounding assertion that, while in America, he had seen a building moved, and, being made desperate by the horrified expression on the faces of his companions and the utter impossibility of backing safely out, followed up the sensation by recklessly claiming that he had seen a three-story tenement going down the middle of a street. Immediately an impressive and ominous silence fell upon the auditors, and presently they arose, one by one, and, with glances of significant pity on the hardened narrator, moodily retired from the room, leaving him entirely alone with his seared conscience. The last one to leave overhauled his predecessor in the entry, and in a gloomy whisper observed that "*that* was the bloodiest lie he had ever heard." And to this day that returned Englishman is eyed with suspicion.

So much for being too communicative.

We are all more or less conceited until we travel. Our own institutions and customs are considered the best until we have had opportunity to compare them with others. And yet, travel does not always remove or even modify prejudice. People who run through a foreign country under the impression that their own land is immeasurably superior in every respect—a notion they express on all occasions—can not hope to get a very clear idea of that country or of those who inhabit it. Consequently, we have travelers' stories which go to show that England is principally smoke and fog, and its people close-mouthed, surly and selfish. I feel safe in saying that of every one hundred Americans who go to Europe, ninety-five stay less than three weeks in England, while they cheerfully spend months on the continent.

And yet, England, with the wonderful beauty of its scenery, the glory of its charities, the whirl of its dissipation, the value of its history, and the hospitality of its people, outranks any nation on the globe.

A newly arrived American is readily recognized in England. There is so much of him [laughter] that he can easily be seen on the darkest night. He feels that the eyes of an effete monarchy—properly shaded—are upon him; that his coming is the opportunity of a lifetime for a down-trodden people, to refresh their sight with a free-born citizen.

While I am upon this subject, I might mention that the English enjoy a few mistaken ideas in regard to us. There are a great many things they do not understand, although I think I detected an improvement after my arrival. I have said that all the English are not burly, self-containing and exclusive. And I tried to show those with whom I came in contact that all Americans are neither boors nor assassins—the only two classes many of the British seem to recognize among us. It is the style of American journalism to exaggerate, I am pained to say. Another sad feature is jesting on tragic subjects. These excesses are readily seized upon by the English press, and the incidents sown broadcast among their people as illustrative of our character. It is the misfortune of the English not to understand an American joke. I had a painful evidence of that while conversing with a fellow-countryman in the coffee room of a London hotel. He spoke to me of the great number of bow-legged people he had met in England, and asked what was, in my opinion, the cause. I told him it must have resulted from their standing too long at a time, contemplating their national debt. Whereupon an English gentleman sitting near said:

"And aren't there many bow-legged people in your country?"

"No, sir."

"Perhaps your national debt is so large your people don't have to stand up to see it," he suggested. We made no reply. He got from humor right down to solid facts. We saw he did not understand American humor.

Whatever the English may believe of our manners and customs, many of them have ennobling ideas of money-making in the States. Numbers have come here with a view to making a fortune in a few years, and to return to live in a castle with hot and cold water on every floor. When in Elston, the birthplace of Bunyan, I sought to glean some local traditions of the great preacher. But the old people with whom I talked knew nothing but Canada. Fifteen years before some one had gone to Canada from Elston, with scarcely a shilling in his pocket, and had now returned worth $65,000. These aged citizens had no special feeling against Bunyan, but they thought the time could be more profitably employed in talking about Canada. They never lived so close to Canada as I have.

Of the extent of the United States, these people are not able to grasp a proper conception. They cannot be made to realize that Canada is not concealed somewhere within the States, and one of them once asked me how far Massachusetts was from Central Park. An English friend observing an American family stopping at our hotel, said to me:

"Do you know the Fergusons?"

"No."

"Why, how's that?" he inquired in some surprise; "they come from America!"

I was obliged to confess that there were some two or three families in America, besides the Fergusons, with whom I was not personally acquainted.

They call Michigan, Mitchy-gin, and Connecticut, Connectty-cut. But the name of Chicago is their chief recreation. Even the dreadful fire-fiend was more merciful than are they. With exasperating complacency they denominate it Cthi-ka-go, Cthi-cog-o, Chick-a-go, Chee-a-go; but the favorite rendering is Shee-caggy. Several Englishmen assured me they had been as far West as Shee-caggy. [Laughter.]

Our mixed liquors and slang are never failing objects of interest to them. It is to be regretted that I was not better qualified to give them the desired information about them. [Laughter.] How they would revel in the information of an editor fresh from one of our city dailies. [Laughter.] They asked me if there were such drinks as brandy-smashes, claret-punches and gin-slings, and when I told them that I did not know for certain, but thought I had heard those things mentioned by worldly people in the States, they have said:

"Ah! how wonderful!"

I hope I have not deceived those people.

But when they pressed me to tell them why Americans called some of their drinks "coffin-makers," "soul-destroyers," "nose-painters," and "dead-shots," I felt compelled to admit that I never before heard the terms; and then they were disappointed.

England is made up of Englishmen, Americans and foreigners, and the last named are so scarce as to be immediately noticeable. [Laughter.] You do not see there an English builder with German workmen and Irish servants. The merchants, manufacturers and business men, generally, are English; their employees are English; the coachmen **are** English, the porters and laborers are English, the servant girls are English, and so are the newsboys, bootblacks, and gamins generally.   Wherever you turn, you see English, English, English!

It is an imposing spectacle.   Broad jaws, sloping shoulders, red cheeks, flaxen hair, side-whiskers, gaiters, round sack-coats, stiff hats, canes, umbrellas and eye-glasses.   All English.

More noticeable than all other Englishmen is the London boy.   I never tired while studying the London boy.   There is so much of him, not individually, but collectively.   Individually he is slim in body, with generally a white, unhealthy face, spindling legs, and rather narrow back of the head.   He wears trousers tight to his shrinking shanks, and a cap which makes him look like an orphan boarding with a maiden aunt.   He is a poor boy, without doubt, always on the street, and always in the way.   I never saw such a boy elsewhere.   He is not quarrelsome, not saucy, not addicted to smoking, and never profane, even under the most favorable circumstances.   He is a helpless youth, with a stony stare levelled into shop windows, and when not thus engaged he is rubbing up against the buildings or toppling over obstructions.   He has a dreadful tendency to be always backing up against something, and to be always missing it, to the detriment of his bones. Only they do not fall with sufficient force to break a bone.   I have seen one of them slide from a lamp post, turn a part somersault, recover himself, hit up against the post again, slip off the curb, and gradually get down on his back in the gutter—taking in all some nine seconds to do it—while an American boy would go down like a flash, stave a hole in the back of his head, and make a doctor's bill of eighteen dollars, in less than a second.   [Laughter.]

But the English are all so conservative.

There is one thing I must tell you before proceeding farther.   I dislike to deceive people.   And yet I am constantly in danger of doing it. No one to see me would doubt for an instant that I had beheld Queen Victoria.   This makes me sad, because I did not see her.   It is a humiliating confession, but I am too honest to conceal it.   I thought but little, indeed, of this disappointment when I was in England, but on returning home I was made to see the dreadful mistake I had been guilty of.   I was made to understand what a sickening failure the whole trip had been.   I have had men come to me with a glad light in their eyes to ask about the Queen, and when I have told them that I never beheld her I have seen them reel from my presence with blanched faces and quivering lips like men stricken with a sudden pestilence.

But I could not help it. These people do not seem to understand what a rare being the Queen is. I neither wish to misrepresent nor malign them, but they imagine the Queen is to be casually met with on the promenade, at the post-office, or in the ice-cream saloon. This is not so. The Queen of England is almost as secluded from public view as if she had been driven into the earth by a steam hammer. It is natural, I presume, for our people to desire to see royalty. Americans abroad have an unquenchable longing to look with their own eyes upon a member of the royal family. It is not to admire them, that we have this wish, but we want to abhor them. [Laughter.] I think this is the feeling. I made many efforts to get at the royal family to abhor them, before success crowned my efforts. I have gone a hundred miles to abhor a single member of the Queen's household.

There are but few advantages to the many drawbacks in being royal. The Queen goes nowhere really. She is the ruler of England, but there are hundreds of streets in her own city of London which she never saw. How much she has read of the gayety of the watering places, and how much sighed for just one glimpse! How frequently she has been told of the excitement of the Derby day, the exhilaration of a ride on top of a stage-coach, the fascination of a circus, the glory of the ballet, the comfort of old inns, the hilarity of a country fair, the glitter and charm of the lighted shops, the wonders of the underground railway, the delight of a soda-water fountain in full blast, and many, many other things which the commonest subject enjoys, but which she is eternally shut out from. She has her palace and her walled-in garden, and standing there she can say to the people of London,

"Here you can not come!"

But they with their miles of streets, and multitude of glories can jaw back to their queen,

"Here *you* can't come!"

This is strictly confidential. I never went by that castle wall without thinking there were just as envious eyes on one side as on the other; but I never spoke of it, as I did not wish to make trouble.

She can walk there as much as she likes, and by herself. But there is no swapping gossip and preserve recipes over the gate with the woman in the next house. [Laughter.] Nor a run out in the afternoon to see a neighbor's new shawl, and to show her own. What does she know of the exquisite pleasure of badgering a shop-keeper into lunacy? Or of the subtle excitement of hoarding up old rags to exchange for new tin-ware? [Laughter.]

There was no opportunity to get inside of Buckingham Palace—the Queen's city residence—an unpretentious four-story building, so I used

to conten... ..yself standing in front of it, admiring the coat of arms over
the gateway. It was the English coat of arms, a lion and a unicorn
standing on their hind legs squaring off at each other. It was a very
attractive object to me. I have stood before it hours at a time, lost in a
trance of delight. The lion had a smile on his face. He was the first
lion I ever saw laugh. I have seen thousands of these coats of arms, but
never saw a sedate lion among them. He is always laughing as if it
was the best joke he ever heard of, being matched against a unicorn with
a barber pole between its eyes. And it *is* absurd when you come to
think of it; for a lion could whip a unicorn around a stump, and have
its barber pole in front of a millinery shop in less than nine seconds.
You can't change the English lion. He is the one thing all the time.
But you can change an American eagle, [laughter] if you are not connected with the press.

But I like to see a lion look pleased. I think we were all intended
to be happy. A lion that won't laugh is no society for me. [Laughter.]

I had all along been anxious to revel in rural England. There was,
however, one slight drawback to the full enjoyment of the scheme.
When I told a London friend that I proposed going into the farming
region and mixing with its people, to see what they did and how they
did it, he gravely shook his head.

"The English farmer," said he, "is a fine specimen of perverse humanity. He is reticent, suspicious, jealous. Our farming country is divided
into the large estates of noblemen and gentry. These estates are sub-
divided into farms and rented to the men who form an important class
in England. They hold the possession of their lands by good behavior;
and it is the tenant's ambition to keep his place all his life, and at his
death to leave it to his oldest son. Many of the present possessors of
farms were born on them, as were their fathers. It is not only their
home, but their ancestral hall, and they guard it with jealous care
against the advances of rivals. Many a man has lost his farm through
some indiscreet remark made in the presence of a neighbor, who coveted
the place; and who lost no time in creating an unfavorable impression
of him at headquarters. Then, again, as his farm is not his own, but
always, so to speak, in the market, he is careful to keep the proceeds
from it a secret, so, if he is doing well no neighbor will strive to get his
farm by bidding higher, and thus increase the price of his rent to
retain it. There are other things, perhaps, which I do not understand,
that go to make the English farmer tight-headed; and, while I am quite
certainn one of them will treat you disrespectfully, yet I am positive you

will not have a chance to go over their farms, or mix with their households; and, as far as gaining a knowledge of them is concerned, your
mission will be fruitless."

Thus my London friend sketched the situation. When I got my letters of
introduction and started down into old Norfolk, I made about as gloomy
a procession as was ever precipitated upon that blossoming section of
England. I went direct to the ancient town of Lynn, and even if I were
to be debarred from mingling with the farmers, I had a flood of delightful sensations in the quaint, old town—a counterpart of scores of English cities.

An English town is not so cheerful appearing as an American town.
Far from it. There are no wooden buildings, airily constructed; none
painted white, with green blinds, or in neutral colors, with darker shades
for trimmings; no front yards with shrubs and turf; the residences, like
the shops, come up to the walk; are devoid of color, except the dingy
color of the brick or stone which compose them, and make no pretense
whatever to architectural display. That is reserved for the churches.
There are exceptions to this picture, in the suburbs of some of the towns,
but the general aspect is depressing to the American visitor. Where
there is not the wall of a house there is the wall of a garden, and so ma-
son-work faces every street, and the walls to the gardens are so high that
no man could look over them to see whether broken crockery or pansies
illumined the other side. There are no trees on the streets, and scarcely
a hitching post. The sidewalks are generally very narrow, and irregular
in their width, but the streets are, in all cases, finely paved. And the
people quite frequently use the roadway for walking, especially when
promenading. The High street of a country town on a Saturday evening will be filled with people, from one side to the other, with not a
team in sight.

The country towns differ from London in one very noticeable particular. The citizens are not habituated to umbrellas. Every Londoner
carries his umbrella—at least, until some American gets on familiar terms
with him. [Laughter.] He would as soon think of going away without the back of his head as without his umbrella. It is his constant companion on the promenade, in church, at the play, business, everywhere.
He doesn't carry it because he has a special fondness for it, or because he
believes there is any particular virtue in its possession. But he carries it
because it is a habit, and he could no sooner break from it than he could
from any other habit once fastened to him, unless he should carefully
diet himself, and consent to be placed under a physician's care. Which
he rarely does. He paws over shop goods with it, sticks it into pastry,

and, for all I know to the contrary, pokes it into the ribs of dead friends, to see what they died of

But the rural man seldom carries an umbrella; he is partial to a stick. From the nobleman down to what is expressively called a clod-hopper, all carry sticks. At one farmhouse I saw no less than twelve substantial sticks hung up in the hall. They were used by the farmer, and in looking over them I was very much struck by a remark he made. It was: "I must be having a new stick soon."

The English farmer is just as shrewd and sharp as his Yankee brother, but he is far more conservative. The love of home is so woven into the chords of his heart as to be inseparable from them, and the family homestead, though merely his by sufferance, becomes sacred in his eyes. To the oldest son he gives the farm, and he, in turn, gives it to his oldest son; and while shops and mills and offices are filled, still the farm is kept in the family from generation to generation. This explains why the vast estates of noblemen have remained in one family since the days of the Conqueror, and are as nearly intact to-day as when that Norman pirate awarded them to his clamorous rabble. The oldest son takes the homestead, and the brothers, if there be no surplus of property, to give them a lift in life, start themselves, or work for their brother. I am aware that much can be said against this peculiar division of property, but as I am an oldest son myself, I feel rather delicate about saying it. There is this much, however, in its favor, the place is kept in the family, and reaches that perfection which care and time invariably bring to one management. The man who has been accustomed from infancy to one arrangement of rooms and adornment, rarely cares to make a change. A repair is made here and there as needed, but the landlord is seldom petitioned to pull down the old house and erect a more modern one in its place. And if he incurs the expense without solicitation, it is an event which has no parallel.

There is a kitchen in one of those old farm houses, which I shall always remember, and which it seemed that I could never tire looking at. The floor was of red tile, worn into hollows by the feet of genera- tions of the present occupant's family. The fire-place was a marvel of width. The andirons which stood therein, contained almost enough material to have made a cookstove with ten legs. The huge mantel shelf above seemed to need all its strength to hold the shining brass candle-sticks. Dried vegetables hung in festoons from the whitewashed beams of the ceiling. The windows were as broad as they were high, with seats capacious enough to have accommodated a caucus of reformers. The chairs were of oak, straight in the legs and backs, with one quaintly carved so as to press pomegranates, angelic skulls and acorns into your spine as you leaned back in it. And when the huge deal table was set out for lunch, with a great round of roast beef in the center, supported by a full-chested pitcher of foaming ale, the advance and glory of the nineteenth century melted away from both sight and memory.

But they needed in those days the broad window benches to have courted in. There were then no mohair sofas, with spiral springs running up through, to hold you on, and if our ancestors had depended strictly upon the stiff, ungainly chairs for their wooing, this world of ours would to-day be for rent. The Norfolk parish where I spent so many pleasant days, is called West Winch, and is owned by a lord. There are only forty or fifty houses in the parish, nearly all occupied by farmers, and yet it has two public houses, and also a church which is five hundred years old. And the church has a stone coffin from the Roman age. Nearly all the parish churches have one or more of these coffins, as the churches themselves are built on the site of Roman temples or burial places. These coffins are hollowed from oblong blocks of stone, and when sealed up ready for business, one of them would weigh about half a ton. To be a pall-bearer in those days, must have been a rather gloomy and somber undertaking.

The man who goes to England and neglects to devote days to prowling about the old parish churches and church-yards, misses a genuine treat. The English are a remarkably conservative people, with the bump of reverence sorely crowding every other bump on their heads. This explains why they keep ruins, why old customs still prevail, why many of their towns are so little changed, and why they worship in temples wrinkled and scarred by age and the elements.

Many of these churches, although over five centuries old, are located in parishes numbering scarcely forty houses. The people treat them with great care and keep them together as long as possible, and, when no longer possible, they use them as ruins, and are even more tender than ever with them. It is not my purpose to speak of their composition, or architectural features, or government—that information you can find in correspondence and books. But there are some peculiar features, as compared with our churches, on which I hope to fix your attention. To tell the truth I don't cotton much, as the wordly minded say, to ancient church architecture. But you take a thorough-bred churchman, and he will spend an entire day with one church and a sandwich. [Laughter.] He will stand for one whole hour before a window, and, after he has collected his senses, will discourse fervently upon the sweep of its arch, the delicacy of its tracery and the graceful-ness of its spandrils. He will walk thirty-two times around an ancient font in a sort of ecstatic blind-staggers, and I could cut out something equally beautiful from a bath-brick with a jack-knife. But I shall not do it. Many of the churches are very, very rusty looking affairs, with plain oaken seats and blackened pillars, worried by worms and age, and both defaced by the autographic miscreant from America. Then there are, in some instances, most wonderful contrasts between the building and its furniture.

St. Paul's cathedral in London is a noble structure, but its sittings are common wooden benches without backs. It was there I first saw notices on the walls prohibiting people from walking about during the service. In an American meeting-house no such notice is seen. There, when the service is going on, no one thinks of strolling about the room, for every American meeting-house has a solemn deacon, fifty-eight years old, with steel blue eyes and a beard like a curry-comb, alongside of whom the famed Spanish inquisition tones down to a mere circus performance. [Laughter.]

Of the great number of decayed church edifices I visited, St. Bartholomew in London bears the palm. It has been hacked at by opposing religions and crumbled by the elements for the past eight hundred years. But it has its congregation and its service every Sunday. The floor is broken, the pillars which sustain the roof and separate the aisles from the nave are worn in places to a degree calculated to make one sitting near them quite nervous and thoughtful; the walls are musty, gashed and filled with doorways with no stairs leading to them, and windows nailed up, and tombs quaint, stained and mutilated. Back of the pulpit were several stone coffins, whose occupants left centuries ago in search of better ventilation, and about them a ton or so of broken stone-cornices, window frames and door facings, carefully hoarded up by the reverential wardens.

It is a novel sensation experienced by an American on visiting this dingy, broken-winded fabric. But precious few Americans visit it, however, or even know of its existence.

"Why isn't it torn down at once, and a new building put up in its place?" you ask.

Why don't you tear up the body of your great-grandfather from its burial place and put down a new body in its stead? But perhaps you never thought of it. But it can be done. So these people can pull down an old church and erect another, but they haven't thought of it.

When one of our home churches loses a couple of shingles from its roof, or a figure from its carpet, or the first tone of its paint, one church meeting follows another, former friends cease to exchange greetings or to borrow from each other a cup of sugar until Henry gets home from school, and picnics are given up, and brotherly love suspended, until the point is carried, the repair made, and a debt incurred.   [Laughter.] But here is a church which for five hundred years has been in a condition to get the whole congregation by the ears, and to send the entire parish to the devil, but the people go patiently along, raising a little money here and a little there, and using it, as they get it, to replace a stone or prop up a pillar, and the following Sunday they drop quietly in and sit for an hour on a hard bench worshiping God, and admiring the improvement. [Laughter.]

No carpet is used.   Blank stone floors are what the English delight in for their churches.   A stone floor is not so sightly or comfortable as one carpeted, but it is better adapted to burying people beneath.   They might be planted under a carpet, I suppose, but it wouldn't be so pleasant.   Some of the churches have floors of brilliantly colored tile, which are very pretty, and might answer, perhaps, the natural craving in this country for a carpet, but with snow on the heel of the incoming worshiper the result would be most disastrous to the first half-dozen pews from the door, I'm afraid.

The English combine economy with grief, and come as near to killing two birds with one stone as you ever see done.   By burying their dead within the building they secure both floor and tomb in one.   In some of the very old churches, like Westminster Abbey, for instance, the dead are rather promiscuously scattered about.   There will be fathers in the porch, mothers in the aisles, uncles and aunts in the transept, with cousins and grandmothers under the seats. [Laughter.]   I got up from listening to a service in Westminster, one morning, and found that I had been sitting on an entire family. [Laughter.]   At a very old church in Derbyshire the flagging of the walk leading from the gate to the porch is a succession of memorials to the dead resting beneath.   In Ireland are graveyards located on desolate looking islands, graveyards without the vestige of an inclosure, or with scarcely the vestige of a stone.   They are the sites of old temples, which centuries ago passed to ruin, but the places have been consecrated as places for burial, and will be used as such as long as there is a physician in practice. [Laughter.]   The British can make a graveyard go farther than we can. [Laughter.]   They have plenty of them five and six hundred years old.   But in America as soon as a graveyard becomes a little old it is dug up and a new street put down in its place. [Laughter] Several years later some one comes along, and wants his wife's uncle who had been laid there.   No one knows what has become of the old gentleman, but everybody tries to pacify the grief-stricken nephew, but he won't be comforted. He dances around and demands his uncle, and finally drags the town into a lawsuit.

There is a chapel in Norfolk which historically amounts to nothing, but which has been saved from going down to oblivion by the enterprise of its present rector. The dead in the churchyard were irregularly buried, as must necessarily follow four hundred years of interment in a one-acre lot. So the different grave stones presented a very broken front to the eye, from whichever way viewed. The rector was displeased with that. He said harmony was one of the chief objects of life, and, to produce a little of the chief object, he pulled up the grave stones and set them out in symmetrical rows. They look very pretty now, but as the signs were put up without regard to the location of the parties who had done business beneath them, the effect is not exactly picturesque upon the minds of the survivors. In fact, they don't know where to look for their dead, but have to drop the sad tear at random. This is unpleasant to the friends, and must be somewhat embarrassing to the deceased. But one of the chief objects of life is gained.

But I was speaking of farming.

My friend has two hundred acres in his farm. He had the most of it in wheat. It is a singular feature of the English climate, that, while its grain is above ground when the soil of New England has not yet escaped the fetters of frost, yet the harvest is no earlier. My friend had in his employ four men and two boys. They are the farm laborers which we hear so much about, through Mr. Arch and other agitators. I am not qualified to discuss the English farm labor question. There is, perhaps, much to be said on both sides, which is never heard. The laborers support themselves and pay their own rent, living in little stone cottages near to the farm—cottages which the owner of the estates erected for the purpose. The wages which they aspire to, and which, in some sections, is paid, is $3.75 a week. There are places where the pay is but $2.25 a week. In busy seasons the wife, and those of the children old enough, go into the field. Some of the laborers with an income of less than three dollars a week, support a family of four or five. Awful, isn't it? But before our war the wages paid to a laborer here was, at the highest, one dollar a day, and I remember one who sustained a family of five on seventy-five cents a day, and got comfortably drunk every Saturday night, too. And he paid more for his clothing than does his English brother, and it wore him a much less time. It is not unusual for a pair of English made shoes to last two years, and a pair of corduroy trousers to wear five years, and the latter can be bought for less than two dollars. I do not wish to defend the system of farm wages in England; neither is it my object to drive the poor and helpless into corduroy breeches. I think the farmers should pay their help all they can, and I hesitate to attack them for fear that they do. It is said, and I have no reason to doubt it, that many of the farm laborers do not touch a mouthful of meat from one year's end to the other. But they get along very well without it. I have seen hundreds of them and their families, and a redder-cheeked, brighter-eyed people, I never saw—even in a hotel where there is plenty of meat.

They have roses on the walls of their cottages, of course; they smoke, and are even beginning to take in the god-like sensations of chewing; and they have their beer daily. If they prefer beer to beef whose business is it? They pay less rent than does the American fellow who lives by himself. Twenty dollars a year is the highest, I believe. There are sections where the benevolent wealthy have erected model cottages at a still less rent. On the estate of the Prince of Wales, at Sandringham, there are quite a number of these cottages, of Gothic pattern, containing four or five rooms, and having a bit of garden attached. The rent is fifteen dollars per annum. This is in surly, downtrodden over-ruled England, and not in free and enlightened America. They are very pretty cottages, well-ventilated and free from lightning rods. In fact, there are precious few lightning rods in all England, which is due, perhaps, to the English people's horror of a thunder storm which they are always careful to speak of in terms of the greatest respect, calling it a tempest.

In discussing the relative wages paid the workmen of the two countries, it is well to consider the sort of equivalent they give for their pay. I contend that the American works the harder of the two. If he is on a farm he must be up and choring around at five o'clock in the morning, and he has but little relief until eight or nine o'clock in the evening. He boards with the farmer who sends him to bed when there is nothing for him to do, and drags him out again as soon as it is light-enough to see the shortest way into his clothes. And during the day he works like a steam saw-mill, spurred up, not by beer, but by an Egyptian task-master, who works like a lunatic himself, and can not be made to understand why every body about him should not do the same. I have been there myself. If he is a mechanic, and does not do a reasonable amount of work in the hours, he is discharged, and subsequently starts a saloon.

The English farm laborer gets to work at 6 A. M. and quits at 6 P. M. On one farm I visited, the men went to work at eight in the morning, and quit in the middle of the afternoon. The farmer himself does

17

but little work aside from riding about, going to market, and looking after the stock. Consequently the laborer, in the absence of a stimulating example, is inclined to establish his own pace. It is not a violently swift one. In many of the districts there is a piece of land divided up into what are called allotments, and each laborer can have an allotment (about a rood) to cultivate for himself by the payment of from $1.25 to $2.50 a year. At night, after his work, he can devote his time to this plot of ground, and the charity accomplishes two purposes—contributes to his support, and fosters a spirit of industry—thus saving him from the idleness and dissipation of the public house.

As for the mechanics, they have still less hours and a half day on Saturday. Their wages run from seventy-five cents to a dollar and a half a day.

The chief weeds with which an English farmer has to contend are thistles and poppies. Now there is nothing remarkable about a thistle unless you are barefooted, but the idea of a poppy being a weed is striking enough. You know how choice we are of them in our gardens, and what an addition to a plot are their brilliant tints. Try then to conjure up the spectacle of thousands of them in one inclosure. They are called red-weed in England, and flourish principally in the grain fields, where their deep red contrasts magnificently with the dark green of the wheat, oats and barley. I have seen fields so abounding with poppies as to look as if they were splashed with blood, and the beauty of the scene is beyond all description.

Rearing their brilliant heads among the dark green of the grain they present a picture which must touch every heart, although differently. I have seen two men at the hedge on the opposite sides of a field gaze for half an hour on the wonderful blending of color. One was speechless, with his eyes glistening with exquisite delight—he was a tourist. The other was speechless, too, but his eyes did not glisten—he was the owner of the field. [Laughter.]

There is not a corn field in all England. They use large quantities of corn, which they call maize, to feed to stock, but they import it from America. I saw but three stalks of corn in Britain. Two of them were in Shakespeare's garden at Stratford, where they equally divided with the immortal bard the admiration of American visitors. The third was making a heroic, but hopeless, fight for dear life in a flower-pot in an Edinburgh hotel. The weather is not hot enough to mature corn or tomatoes, and they have to train their fruit trees against brick walls, as we do grape vines, in order to ripen the fruit.

They don't have beans either; I mean the white cooking bean. They grow a yellowish brown bean—fields of it—which is the only bean they harvest for the winter, and that they feed to stock. When I told them of our white beans, ripened in the field, and served on the table through the winter and spring, they looked so unfriendly that I dropped the subject at once.

The absence of this article may explain, perhaps, Boston's inability to establish a successful steamship line with England.

When I made my trip, it was publicly announced by well meaning people, that I had gone to England to help put up a stove. This was a mistake. The English do not associate with stoves. I saw none there, excepting two withered looking specimens of the cooking pattern, which were on exhibition in a museum, and several mongrel affairs, half stove, half grate, which were loftily called American stoves, but which were of Scotch origin and manufacture. The English don't take to stoves, and will not use them because they like to see the fire—it is so cheerful and cozy. Once in awhile I like to feel it, but I carefully refrained from saying so. I have seen an Englishmen sit shivering for an hour in front of a fire-place, with a smile on his face. He liked to see the fire.

I have already referred to the hospitality of the English. It naturally follows that a hospitable people should be good eaters. These are, excepting at breakfast, when a very little does them, the late supper is responsible for this, I imagine. This supper comes off some three or four hours later than the tea, or about nine or ten o'clock. It is always hearty, consisting quite frequently of roast meats, salads, hot pickles, tarts, and other things calculated to make a bilious party go raving mad in the night. After a stranger has got one of these suppers concentrated in the pit of his stomach he is in a condition to commit almost any atrocity, and goes to bed very much in doubt if he will awake again and somewhat inclined to hope that he will not. Speaking to an English friend, after one of these late suppers, of the scarcity of butter and fresh bread at the English table, he explained that fresh bread and too much butter disagreed with the stomach. I made no reply; but I looked from the ruins before us up to the clock which marked 11 P. M. The English are very careful of their stomachs.

There is an accompaniment to each meal which strikes the stranger most forcibly. It is their way of saying grace. They are the most sudden people in this particular I ever saw, and have a fashion of firing off their gratitude which is most startling. The text is something like this:

"For what we are now about to receive make us truly thankful."

And this, by some families, is slid in most unexpectedly, and it has come so rapidly and with such abruptness on several occasions, that I have missed it entirely, hearing only the word "about," preceded and followed by a subdued whistling. There being no abatement in the work at the table at the time, tended to make the impression the less distinct. The giving of thanks, where it is the custom, at the end of the meal, has frequently cut off a valuable mouthful of food, so sudden and unexpected was its coming; and the conversation and happy laughter flowed along without a break, and those who were to finish did so, and every body looked contented and edified.

This is quite a contrast to our New England fashion of being grateful. I have eaten under a grace which froze the gravy [laughter], irretrievably damaged the mutton, and imbued the greater part of the guests with the gloomiest forebodings; in which the African and the South Sea Islander were looked after and secured beyond harm; and all political cabals were taken under the fifth rib, completely dumbfounded, and their evil machinations scattered to the four winds of heaven. It was a fine performance, and a good thing for humanity at large, but it made the dinner look sick. [Laughter.] I think I like the English extreme the best, but both can be bettered. And never will be.

The common use of endearing terms in the family circle makes a lively impression upon the mind of the stranger. "Love," "lovey" and "my love"; "dear," "deary" and "my dear" are the popular and soothing adjectives which are constantly floating through the domestic air. I think it is overdone when four or five "loves" or "dears" season a simple request. Yet they sound infinitely better than our "old man" or "old woman," or even "mutton-head." I never knew "mutton-head" to work well as a term of endearment; still, it is useful.

There is a popular fallacy that living in England is much cheaper than in America. It is a fallacy.

Food is more expensive in England than in America. They eat our bacon and flour, and you can not carry them across the ocean and sell them as cheaply as here at home.

It costs the English laborer less to live than our laborer, because he does not live as well. If English farmers lived as well as our farmers, they would soon be bankrupt.

The English have an exalted idea of wages in this country. As compared with their prices for help, ours must appear mountainous. And they think that saving money must be a pastime with us. And so it is, although, of course, we have other recreations. [Laughter.] Their provisions cost less, because they eat less, but their rents are less than ours. I have occasionally told them that there are females employed in the hat factories of Danbury who earn four dollars a day. I grew quite fond of imparting this bit of information, because it so amazed them. I was fond of doing it until I went to Aberdeen in Scotland, and saw women make five dollars a day in gold, cleaning herrings; then I dropped the subject. This sum is equal to ten dollars in America. There are very few concerns in this country which pay female operatives ten dollars a day, either to put linings in hats or to remove them from fish. [Laughter.]

Rents are much less, I say, there than here, startling as the statement may sound. Near Oxford street, London, are blocks upon blocks of quality residences, owned by certain earls and dukes, and rented on a hundred years' lease to aristocratic tenants at a price which makes the English stare because of its magnitude, and causes us Americans to laugh because of its insignificance. At St. John's Wood, where the west end of the city looks over its back fence upon cultivated fields, a neat three-story, brick tenement can be rented for two hundred dollars a year. Try to do the same with a similarly located property in New York City, and the owner would inveigle you up to the roof and throw you off, and no jury in the land could be found to convict him.

While on the subject of extortion I should like to take a pull at my old foe, the cabman. There is the hackney carriage running on four wheels, and the hansom cab running on two. In England they are simply known as " four-wheelers," and " two-wheelers." The latter are much the pleasanter to ride in, but the pleasure is somewhat modified by the discussion, recrimination and perspiration which invariably accompany the payment of the fare. With the four-wheelers one plucking appears to suffice, and once away from the railway station you can expect to be carried a mile in any direction at the fare established for that distance, which is one shilling.

You take a two-wheeler, are driven a half mile and throw the driver a shilling. He looks at it in a perplexed and commiserative way which is beyond all imitation and asks, " What's this for?" You patiently explain to him. He says, "eighteen pence is the fare." You protest that the distance does not warrant the charge. He is obstinate. You can force him, so the card of rates posted inside say, to drive to the nearest police station for adjudication. But you are a stranger. He may drive you to the first police station, and he may drive you over the nearest embankment. You pay him the extra sixpence, and curse the government under which he thrives. The shilling goes to his employer, and the sixpence is laid up by himself for a rainy day.

It rains a great deal in England.

When the intricacies of the 'bus lines are once mastered, traveling about London is an inexpensive and genuine pleasure. The English 'bus system is superior to ours, both in regard to the comfort of the passengers and the horses which draw them. On the box with the driver is accommodation for four persons. Running the length of the roof is a double seat, reached by a ladder on each side of the door. The 'bus has so much seating capacity and when that is occupied no more passengers are taken on. Between the 'bus driver and the cabman there is a feeling of undying hate, which is most gratifying to him who has suffered at the hands of the latter, because the wheels and motive power of the 'bus are so much greater that the utter discomfiture of the cabman is a sure thing in the event of a collision. I have sat on the box seat for an hour at a time, and have heard the driver curse the cabbies and seen him crowd them against the curb with his remorseless wheels until it did seem as if my cup of happiness would run over and drown inoffensive people. I used the word "cursing" unadvisedly, perhaps. We understand by that profanity, but the English are not given to profanity. Whether this is because there are no stoves in England, or is due to a national church, I am not able to state. But I rarely heard an oath during all my sojourn in England. [Applause.]

The English cab fares are a shilling for a mile, for one or two persons, and a sixpence for each additional mile. The law which established these prices knows more about the subject than I do. But, still, the charge appears to be a very small sum, and, especially so, when it is understood that the cabman pays from six to ten shillings a day for the use of the establishment, and must drive that number of fares before he can begin to make any thing for himself. They generally bite me, and it makes me mad enough to knock their heads off, but yet I am sorry for them. They have got to fleece somebody, I suppose, to make both ends meet; still, it would be much better if poor people did not have two ends.

But after I had been there awhile they did not scorch me so badly. I played a march on them by donning a pair of English trousers — the regular tights. In fact, they clung so tight to me that I had to take them off when I wanted to get any thing out of the pockets. [Laughter.] On engaging a cab I would bring my legs conspicuously to the front, when the driver looked into my open and ingenuous countenance he would be tempted to charge me a sixpence extra, but on glancing down at my trousers he would take another thought, and unhesitatingly compromise on a thrip-pence. [Laughter.]

PUTTING UP A STOVE PIPE.

See page 261.

The money I thus saved I gave to the South Sea Islanders, when I met them. [Applause.]

BAILEY ON PUTTING UP A STOVE PIPE.

Putting up a stove is not so difficult in itself. It is the pipe that raises four-fifths of the mischief and all the dust. You may take down a stove with all the care in the world, and yet that pipe won't come together again as it was before. You find this out when you are standing on a chair with your arms full of pipe, and your mouth full of soot. Your wife is standing on the floor in a position that enables her to see you, the pipe and the chair, and here she gives utterance to those remarks that are calculated to hasten a man into the extremes of insanity. Her dress is pinned over her waist, and her hands rest on her hips. She has got one of your hats on her head, and your linen coat on her back, and a pair of rubbers on her feet. There is about five cents' worth of pot-black on her nose and a lot of flour on her chin, and altogether she is a spectacle that would inspire a dead man with distrust. And while you are up there trying to circumvent the awful contrariness of the pipe, and telling that you know some fool has been mixing it, she stands safely on the floor, and bombards you with such domestic mottoes as, "What's the use of swearing so?" "You know no one has touched that pipe." "You ain't got any more patience than a child." "Do be careful of that chair." And then she goes off, and reappears with an armful more of pipe, and before you are aware of it she has got that pipe so horribly mixed up that it does seem no two pieces are alike.

You join the ends and work them to and fro, and to and fro again, and then you take them apart and look at them. Then you spread one out and jam the other together, and mount them once more. But it is no go. You begin to think the pieces are inspired with life, and ache to kick them through the window. But *she* doesn't lose her patience. She goes around with that awfully exasperating rigging on, with a length of pipe under each arm and a long-handled broom in her hand, and says she don't see how it is some people never have any trouble putting up a stove. Then you miss the hammer. You don't see it any where. You stare into the pipe, along the mantel, and down on the stove, and off to the floor. Your wife watches you, and is finally thoughtful enough to inquire what you are looking after, and, on learning, pulls the article from her pocket. Then you feel as if you could go outdoors, and swear a hole twelve feet square through a block of brick buildings; but she meekly observes: " Why on earth don't you speak when you want any thing, and not stare around like a dummy?" When that part of the pipe, which goes through the wall is up, she keeps it up with the broom while you are making the connection, and stares at it with an intensity that is entirely uncalled for.   All the while your position is becoming more and more interesting. The pipe don't go together, of course. The soot shakes down into your eyes and mouth, the sweat rolls down your face, and tickles your chin as it drops off, and it seems as if your arms are slowly but surely drawing out of their sockets.

Here your wife comes to the rescue by inquiring if you are going to be all day doing nothing, and if you think *her* arms are made of cast-iron; and then the broom slips off the pipe, and in her endeavor to recover her hold, she jabs you under the chin with the handle, and the pipe comes down on your head with its load of fried soot, and then the chair tilts forward enough to discharge your feet, and you come down on the wrong end of that chair, with a force that would bankrupt a pile-driver. You don't touch that stove again. You leave your wife examining the chair, and bemoaning its injuries; and go into the kitchen, and wash your skinned and bleeding hands with yellow soap. Then you go down street after a man to do the business, and your wife goes over to the neighbors with her chair, and tells them about its injuries, and drains the neighborhood dry of its sympathy long before you get home.

JOHN B. GOUGH.

BIOGRAPHY AND REMINISCENCES.

When Gough died, temperance lost her best friend. For a quarter of a century he had raised his voice against intemperance and for the purity of the home. He was born in Lancashire, England, and died in Worcester, Massachusetts, in 1888. In public lectures and in private conversations, he carried on the work of reform. Mr. Gough published several books, which were in the form of autobiography and speeches. His lectures were full of anecdotes, in the Lancashire dialect, which was rendered so exquisitely, that his wit and pathos were novel and wonderful. Mr. Gough was not a writer. He was an actor. His telling anecdotes were mostly written by others.

John B. Gough was the great war horse of the lecture platform. Beecher said of him that he lectured against intoxication, but he intoxicated his hearers with his eloquence. In his earlier lecturing days Gough was a delightful man to be with, and never grew tiresome. He did not like a small audience, and scarcely concealed his petulancy. He was a good story-teller, and seemed to live entirely for those around him.

One day a Christian gentleman, in England, came to Gough to talk about total abstinence. Said the gentleman:

"I have a conscientious objection to teetotalism, and it is this: our Savior made wine at the marriage of Cana in Galilee."

"I know He did."

"He made it because they wanted it."

"So the Bible tells us."

"He made it of water."

"Yes."

"Well, He performed a miracle to make that wine."

"Yes."

261

"Then He honored and sanctified wine by performing a miracle to make it. Therefore," said he, "I feel that, if I should give up the use of wine, I should be guilty of ingratitude, and should be reproaching my Master."

"Sir," said Gough, "I can understand how you should feel so; but is there nothing else that you put by, which our Savior has honored?"

"No, I don't know that there is."

"Do you eat barley bread?"

"No;" and then began to laugh.

"And why?"

"Because I don't like it."

"Very well, sir," said I, "our Savior sanctified barley bread just as much as He ever did wine. He fed five thousand people on barley loaves by a miracle. You put away barley bread from the low motive of not liking it. I ask you to put away wine from the higher motive of bearing the infirmity of your weaker brother, and so fulfilling the law of Christ."

One day I asked Gough to tell some of his first temperance experiences.

"Well," he said, "when I first signed the pledge, I still continued the use of tobacco. One day when I was engaged to speak at an out-door meeting, I met a friend, who said to me, 'I've some first-rate cigars; will you take a few?'

"'No thank you,' I said, 'I have nowhere to put them.'

"'You can put half a dozen in your cap,' my friend insisted. Well, I put the cigars in my cap, attended the meeting under the open sky, and ascended the platform before an audience of two thousand children. I kept my cap on to avoid taking cold, and forgot all about the cigars. Toward the close of my address, after warning the boys against all sorts of bad habits, I said:

"'Now, boys, let us give three rousing cheers for temperance. Now! Hurrah!' In my excitement I pulled off my cap, waved it vigorously, and flung the cigars right and left at the audience. The cheers changed to a roar of laughter at my expense. Nor was I relieved from my confusion when a boy stepped up on the platform, holding out 'one of those dreadful cigars,' and said, politely, 'Here is one of your cigars, Mr. Gough.'"

YOUNG MEN, AHOY!

See page 269.

GOUGH'S GREAT LECTURE.

Ladies and Gentlemen:—I read ·in the "Christian Almanack" the other day that a gentleman said: "I have drunk a bottle of wine every day for the last fifty years, and I enjoy capital health." "Yes; but what has become of your companions?" "Ah!" said he, "that is another thing; I have buried three generations of them."

On one occasion, while a British officer was urging a native to examine the claims of Christianity, two drunken English soldiers passed.

"See," said the native, "do you wish me to be like that? As a Mohammedan I could not; as a Christian I might." [Sensation.]

While I was in San Francisco, a number of young men came to me up the back stairs of the hotel after dark and revealed awful histories. One man lay on the carpet at my feet, exclaiming:

"Send me home; for the love of God, get me out of here! I will go in a freight or cattle train—any thing to get out of here!" It was the cry all around, "Drink is my curse." Everywhere we hear it, "Drink is my curse."

A poor fellow in Exeter Hall signed the temperance pledge some twenty or thirty years ago. He was a prize-fighter—a miserable, debauched, degraded, ignorant creature. A gentleman stood by his side, a builder in London, employing some hundreds of men, and he said to him—what did he say? "Stick to it?" No! "I hope you will stick to it, my friend?" No! "It will be a good thing for you if you stick to it?" No! He said this:

"Where do you sleep to-night?"

"Where I slept last night."

"And where is that?"

"In the streets."

"No, you won't; you have signed this pledge, and you belong to this society, and you are going home with me." [Applause.]

In Edinburgh they have a club-room in which reformed men spend their evenings, and young men come there to get away from temptation. One night a man came in very drunk.

"Do you know what place this is?" he was asked.

"This is a teetotalers' club."

"Yes; but you are drunk."

"I know I am; I am awfully drunk."

"What business have you here?"

"I am a teetotaler."

"But you are drunk."

"What! did you never see a drunken teetotaler? I'm drunk, and I'm a teetotaler." Some one thinking he was chaffing, said, "You had better go out."

"Gentlemen," pleaded the man, "don't put me out. I am a teetotaler. Here's my pledge. I signed it about an hour ago, and I have not touched a drop since. I have come in here for safety!"

There is a place in London where young men assemble nightly; and I tell you, young gentlemen, it was to me a fearful and appalling sight. An immense room, capable of holding some 1,500 persons, with a fine band of music at one end. I found young men there as genteel in appearance as any amongst you. The gentlemen with me knew some of them. "There," said one of them, "is a man in such-and-such a shop; there is another in another establishment." And what were they doing? In one room were the tables set with the sparkling wine, and right before that assembled crowd of 1,000 persons they had no more shame left than to be dancing in the middle of that hall with the common women of the town. I asked, "Why, I should think those young men would be ashamed of it!"

"Shame, sir! Three or four glasses of wine will destroy shame." [Applause.]

A gentleman was once lecturing in the neighborhood of London. In the course of his address he said:

"All have influence. Do not say that you have none; every one has some influence."

There was a rough man at the other end of the room with a little girl in his arms.

"Every body has influence, even that little child," said the lecturer, pointing to her.

"That's true, sir," cried the man.

Every body looked round, of course; but the man said no more, and the lecturer proceeded. At the close the man came up to the gentleman and said:

"I beg your pardon, sir, but I could not help speaking. I was a drunkard; but as I did not like to go to the public-house alone, I used to carry this child. As I came near the public-house one night, hearing a great noise inside, she said:

" 'Don't go, father.'

" 'Hold your tongue, child.'

" 'Please, father, don't go.'

" 'Hold your tongue, I say.'

"Presently I felt a big tear on my cheek. I could not go a step farther, sir. I turned round and went home, and have never been in a public-house since—thank God for it. I am now a happy man, sir, and this little girl has done it all; and when you said that even she had influence I could not help saying 'That's true, sir;' all have influence." [Applause.]

We want religion with our temperance.

I heard the Hon. Tom Marshall, of Kentucky, make a ten minutes' speech in Broadway Tabernacle, in which he said: "Were this great globe one chrysolite, and I offered the possession if I would drink one glasss of brandy, I would refuse it with scorn; and I want no religion, I want the temperance pledge." With that wonderful voice of his he thundered out: "We want no religion in this movement; let it be purely secular, and keep religion where it belongs."

Poor Tom Marshall, with all his self-confidence, fell, and died at Poughkeepsie in clothes given him by Christian charity.

A mother, on the green hills of Vermont, was holding by the right hand a boy, sixteen years old, mad with the love of the sea. And as he stood at the garden-gate one morning, she said:

"Edward, they tell me—for I never saw the ocean—that the great temptation of seamen's life is drink. Promise me, before you quit your mother's hand, that you will never drink liquor."

"I gave the promise," said he. Then he went the world over, to Calcutta, the Mediterranean, San Francisco, and the Cape of Good Hope, the North and South Poles.

"I saw them all in forty years," he said afterward, "and I never saw a glass filled with sparkling liquor that my mother's form at the gate did not rise up before my eyes; and to-day I am innocent of the taste of liquor."

Was not that sweet evidence of the power of a single word?

Yet that is not half, "for," he continued, "yesterday there came into my counting-room a man of forty years.

"'Do you know me?'

"'No.'

"'Well,' said the man, 'I was brought into your presence on shipboard; you were a passenger; they kicked me aside; you took me to your berth, and kept me there until I had slept off my intoxication. You then asked me if I had a mother. I said I never heard a word from her lips. You told me of yours at the garden-gate, and to-day I am master of one of the finest ships in New York harbor, and I have come to ask you to come and see me.'"

The drunkard is always in danger. [Applause.]

I remember riding toward the Niagara Falls, and I said to a gentleman near me, "What river is that, sir?"

"The Niagara river," he replied.

"Well," said I, "it is a beautiful stream—bright, smooth and glassy. How far off are the rapids?"

"About a mile or two."

"Is it possible that only a mile or two from us we shall find the water in such turbulence as I presume it must be near the falls?"

"You will find it so, sir."

And so I found it; and that first sight of the Niagara I shall never forget. Now launch your bark upon the Niagara river; it is bright, smooth, beautiful and glassy; there is a ripple at the bow; the silvery wake you leave behind you adds to your enjoyment; down the stream you glide; you have oars, mast, sail and rudder, prepared for every contingency, and thus you go out on your pleasure excursion. Some one cries out from the bank,

"Young men, ahoy!"

"What is it?" he asks.

"The rapids are below you.'

"Ha! ha! we have heard of the rapids below us," laughs the man, "but we are not such fools as to get into them; when we find we are going too fast to suit our convenience, then hard up the helm and steer to shore; when we find we are passing a given point too rapidly, then we will set the mast in the socket, hoist the sail, and speed to land.'

"Young men, ahoy!" comes the voice again.

"What is it?"

"The rapids are below you."

"Ha! ha! we will laugh and quaff; all things delight us; what care we for the future? No man ever saw it. 'Sufficient unto the day is the evil thereof.' We will enjoy life while we may, and catch pleasure as it flies. This is the time for enjoyment; time enough to steer out of danger when we find we are sailing too swiftly with the stream."

"Young men, ahoy!"

"What is it?"

"The rapids are below you. Now see the water foaming all around you!—see how fast you go!* Now hard up the helm!— quick! quick!— pull for your very lives!—pull till the blood starts from your nostrils and the veins stand like whipcords upon the brow! Set the mast in the socket; hoist the sail!"

---

* No pen can describe the startling eloquence of Gough in drawing this picture. His eyes flash fire, his frame shakes with righteous indignation and pity, and only those who have heard the great lecturer can appreciate the scene.

Ah! it is too late. Shrieking, cursing, howling, blaspheming, over you go; and *thousands thus go over every year by the power of evil habits,* declaring, "When I find out that it is injuring me, then I will give it up." The power of evil habit is deceptive and fascinating, and the man by coming to false conclusions argues his way down to destruction. [Applause.]

Many people begin and end their temperance talks by calling drunkards brutes. No, they are not brutes. I have labored for about eighteen years among them and I never have found a brute. I have had men swear at me; I have had a man dance around me as if possessed of a devil, and spit his foam in my face; but he is not a brute.

I think it is Charles Dickens, who says: " Away up a great many pair of stairs, in a very remote corner, easily passed by, there is a door, and on that door is written 'woman.'" And so in the heart of the vile outcast, away up a great many pair of stairs, in a very remote corner, easily passed by, there is a door, on which is written " man." Here is our business, to find that door. It may take time; but begin and knock. Don't get tired; but remember God's long suffering for us, and keep knocking a long time if need be. Don't get weary if there is no answer; remember Him whose locks were wet with dew.

Knock on—just try it—*you* try it; and just so sure as you do, just so sure, by-and-by, will the quivering lip and starting tear tell you have knocked at the heart of a man and not of a brute. It is because these poor wretches *are* men, and not brutes that we have hopes of them. They said, "he is a brute—let him alone." I took him home with me and kept the " brute " fourteen days and nights, through his delirium; and he nearly frightened Mary out of her wits, once chasing her about the house with a boot in his hand. But she recovered her wits, and he recovered his.

He said to me, " You wouldn't think I had a wife and child."

" Well, I shouldn't."

"I have, and—God bless her little heart—my little Mary is as pretty a little thing as ever stepped," said the " brute."

I asked, "Where do they live?"

"They live two miles away from here."

"When did you see them last?"

"About two years ago." Then he told me his story.

I said, " You must go back to your home again."

"I musn't go back—I won't—my wife is better without me than with me! I will not go back any more; I have knocked her, and kicked her, and abused her; do you suppose I will go back again?"

HUSH BABY, HUSH.

I went to the house with him; I knocked at the door and his wife opened it.

"Is this Mrs. Richardson?"

"Yes, sir."

"Well, that is Mr. Richardson. And Mr. Richardson, that is Mrs. Richardson. Now come into the house."

They went in. The wife sat on one side of the room and the "brute" on the other. I waited to see who would speak first; and it was the woman. But before she spoke she fidgeted a good deal.

She pulled her apron until she got hold of the hem, and then she pulled it down again. Then she folded it up closely, and jerked it out through her fingers an inch at a time, and then she spread it all down again; and then she looked all about the room and said,

"Well, William?" And the "brute" said,

"Well, Mary?"

He had a large handkerchief round his neck, and she said,

"You had better take the handkerchief off William; you'll need it when you go out." He began to fumble about.

The knot was large enough; he could have untied it if he liked; but he said, "Will you untie it, Mary?" and she worked away at it; but her fingers were clumsy, and she couldn't get it off; their eyes met, and the love light was not all quenched; she opened her arms gently and he fell into them. If you had seen those white arms clasped about his neck, and he sobbing on her breast, and the child looking in wonder first at one and then at the other, you would have said, "It is not a brute; it is a man, with a great, big, warm heart in his breast."

To show the power of love and sympathy over the human heart, I will relate a well-known incident:

"In the cabin of the steamer St. John, coming up the Hudson the other evening," writes Eli Perkins, "sat a sad, serious-looking man, who looked as if he might have been a clerk or book-keeper. The man seemed to be caring for a crying baby, and was doing every thing he could to still its sobs. As the child became restless in the berth, the gentleman took it in his arms and carried it to and fro in the cabin. The sobs of the child irritated a rich man, who was trying to read, until he blurted out, loud enough for the father to hear:

"'What does he want to disturb the whole cabin with that d—— baby for?'

"'Hush, baby, hush!' and then the man only nestled the baby closer in his arms, without saying a word. Then the baby sobbed again.

"'Where is the confounded mother, that she don't stop its noise?' continued the profane grumbler.

"At this, the grief-stricken father came up to the man, and with tears in his eyes, said: 'I am sorry to disturb you, sir, but my dear baby's mother is in her coffin down in the baggage room. I'm taking her back to her grandmother, in Albany, where we used to live. [Sensation.]

"The hard-hearted man buried his face in shame, but in a moment, wilted by the terrible rebuke, he was by the side of the grief-stricken father. They were both tending the baby." [Applause.]

Treat the drunkard kindly. Pity him, and do not scold him. Wives, speak kindly to your erring husbands. This morning I read a little story in the Pottstown Miner from the pen of "Eli Perkins."

"The morning after I lectured in Wilkesbarre," said Eli, "there was a great colliery explosion. Hundreds of Cornish miners were killed and their corpses lay at the mouth of the coal mine for recognition. Wives were wringing their hands and children were crying, and a wail of desolation filled the air.

"Sitting at the mouth by a pale corpse was a young wife. She looked at her husband, but uttered no cry; her eyes were dry. She rocked herself to and fro, her face white with anguish.

"'Oh, that I had spoke fair to him at the end!' she moaned. 'Oh that he would come to life one minute that I could say Jimmy, forgive me, but nothing can help me now. Oh, I could bear it all if I'd only spoke fair to him at the end!'

"And then at last, the story came. They had been married a year, she and Jim; and they both 'had tempers,' but, Jim, he was always the first to make up. And this very morning they had had trouble.

"It began because breakfast wasn't ready, and the fire wouldn't burn; and they had said hard words, both of them. But at the very last, though breakfast had not been fit to eat, Jim had turned round at the door and said:

"'Gi'e me a kiss, lass. You know you love me, and we won't part in ill-blood.'

"'No, Jimmy, I don't love you!' I said, petulantly.

"'Gi'e me one kiss, lass,' pleaded Jimmy.

"'No not one! and now ——' and then the tears rushed to her eyes. With awful sobs she flung her arms around the corpse. [Tears in the audience.]

"'Dear Jimmy! Darling Jimmy, speak to me now.' she moaned. 'Say you forgive me!'

"'Do not grieve so hopelessly,' I said: 'perhaps Jimmy knows what you feel now.'

" But the mourner's ears were deaf to all comfort, and the wailing cry came again and again:

" ' Oh, if I had only spoke to him fair at the last !'

* * * * * * * * * * * *

"It is not an uncommon story, this. We quarrel with those we love, and part, and meet and make up again; and death is merciful; and waits till we are at peace; yet how possible is just such an experience to any one of us, who parts with some dear one in anger, or who lets the sun go down upon our wrath!

" But it is always the noblest nature, the most loyal heart, which is the first to cry. 'I was wrong; forgive me.' " [Applause.]

BILL NYE   J. M. BAILEY
W. R. LOCKE   (DANBURRY NEWS MAN)
(PETROLEUM V. NASBY)   GEO. W. PECK

GEORGE W. PECK.

BIOGRAPHY AND REMINISCENCES.

George W. Peck was born in Henderson, Jefferson county, New York, in 1844. He gave his services to his country in the last war, and now resides in Milwaukee, in one of the most elegant mansions in that city. He has a lovely wife, whom he worships as the saints worship the angels, and sons growing up, of whom he is justly proud. Mr. Peck has published three books which have had an immense sale "Peck's Sunshine," "Peck's Fun" and "Peck's Bad Boy." Mr. Peck's writings bubble over with innocent fun.

Many of Mr. Peck's stories are true, or exaggerations from actual scenes.

The humorist tells a story about Senator Barden, of Wisconsin, which, they say, actually happened. The senator is a very plain, democratic-looking man, not above driving a dray or doing any honest work. He has a very kind, generous heart, and is always looking after the comfort of other people. At one time, as Peck tells the story, Senator Barden had a good many apples, and he thought he would do a Christian act by presenting a load of the delicious fruit to his family clergyman, a new man from the East.

When he got the dray loaded, as there was no driver at hand, the senator jumped on the load and drove up to the clergyman's house with the apples.

"Now," he said to himself, "this is a sweet Christian thing to do. How pleased the tired clergyman and his dear wife and children will be."

Then he hurriedly rolled the apples through the gate. They were big, beautiful summer pippins and red cheeked strawberries.

"Won't the parson be surprised," he said, with a laugh all over his happy face, and then he whipped up the horse and tried to get away before the minister had time to thank him.   Just as he was about to drive away, the door opened and the parson's face appeared. He didn't recognize Senator Barden in his plain clothes and with his trousers in his boots, and, being in a hurry, shouted:

"Hello you there! Drayman!"

The senator turned around.

"Who are those apples for?"

"For the parson," replied the senator, modestly.

"What are you leaving them out in the yard for then?"

The surprised senator was so struck with wonder that he made no reply.

"Look here, you fellow," screamed the parson, "if those apples are for me, you just put 'em in the cellar.   Do you hear?"

"I'm in a little of a hurry now," said the senator, "and——"

"Hurry or no hurry," interrupted the parson, "you put those apples in.   You draymen don't know your business.   You hear me?"

The senator stood still in astonishment.

"I say, man," yelled the parson, "if you don't roll those apples in the cellar, I won't accept them.   I won't be imposed on.   I——"

"All right," said the senator, recovering from his astonishment, while his hair began to rise up with indignation, "you won't have to accept them then," and he jumped off the dray, threw the two barrels of apples on, and drove off, saying to himself:

"Darn a clergyman, anyway.   He hain't got good horse sense, and, b'gosh, if he can't be polite, he can eat wormy dried apples all winter."

That night, when the clergyman found out his mistake, he was in such a hurry to apologize to the senator that he cut his sermon twenty minutes short.

"The moral of this," said Mr. Peck, "is this: Never despise an honest Wisconsin senator because he wears a ragged coat, for he may be an angel in disguise."

WON'T THE PARSON BE SURPRISED.

See page 275.

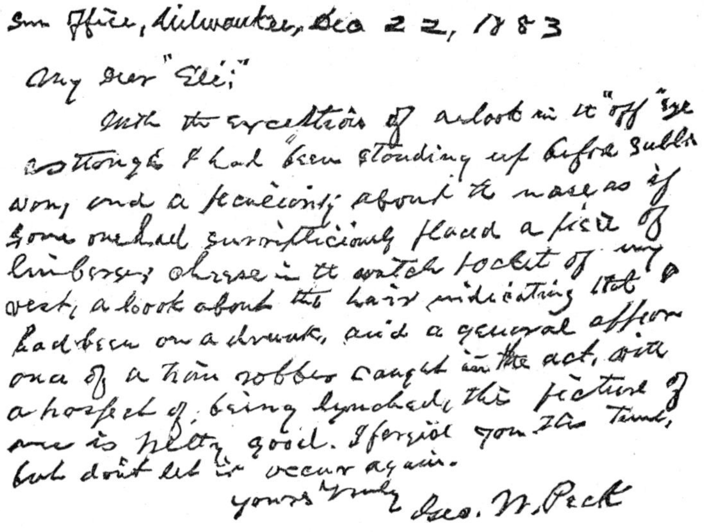

[handwritten letter]

The above is an autograph letter from George W. Peck—— a
characteristic letter.

GEORGE W. PECK'S LECTURE.

Brother Agriculturists : *—I say to the farmers of the United States
that agriculture is one of the noblest pursuits. I love the man who pursues agriculture, but I do not love the lightning-rod man, the Bohemian-oat man, and the patent-churn man who pursue the agriculturist.
[Laughter.] It is painful to see the noble farmer pursuing agriculture
and the sheriff and Bohemian-oat man pursuing the farmer.

What we farmers want, is to have our rights protected. Yes, protected ! To gain this protection we must look to the legislative power.
They must pass laws in our favor. The farmers toil early and late, and
what do they get for their recompense ? I have known a farmer to get
up at three o'clock in the morning to help up a calf that had got cast in
the barn, and the very first thing that calf did was to kick the granger's knee out of joint, when there was a hired man standing near that
the calf could have kicked. [Laughter.]

* Mr. Peck's lecture, " How I Subdued the Rebellion," a highly republican lecture, was
first "set up" for this book, but when Mr. Peck was elected by the Democrats mayor of
Milwaukee, and had one eye on the governorship, his republican lecture was suppressed and
this lecture, calculated to catch the votes of the farmers, was substituted.   M. D. L

What we want, I say, is protection against calves and railroads. [Laughter.]

I say, and without fear of contradiction, it is just such unjust discriminations by calves and railroads that is ruining our agricultural interests. This is not an isolated case. The woods are full of them. Why stand we here idle and see the bone and sinew of our land kicked around by such soulless corporations as railroads and calves.

Let us have their hides on the fence. [Laughter.]

We do not want protection against foreign wool, but we do want protection against our own rams.

Sheep raising, I believe, does not pay the average farmer.

You farmers devote a good deal of time and labor to the raising of sheep, and what do you get for it. The best sheep can not lay more than eight pounds of wool in a season, and even if you get fifty cents a pound for it, you have not got any great bonanza. Now, the State encourages the raising of wolves, by offering a bounty of ten dollars for a piece of skin off the head of each wolf. It does not cost any more to raise a wolf, than it does to raise a sheep, [laughter] and while sheep rarely raise more than two lambs a year, a pair of good wolves are liable to raise twenty young ones in the course of a year, if it is a good year for wolves. [Laughter.] In addition to the encouragement offered by the State, many counties give as much more, so that one wolf scalp will bring more money than five sheep. You will readily see that our wise legislators are offering inducements to you, that you should be thankful for. You can establish a wolf orchard on any farm, and with a pair of good wolves to start on, there is millions in it.

Farmers raise wolves! [Laughter.]

I do not favor the raising of watermelons in cold latitudes—especially the ordinary tropical melons.

What the country needs is a melon with fur on it, for cold latitudes and from which the incendiary ingredients have been removed. It seems to me that by proper care, when the melon is growing on the vines, the cholera morbus can be decreased, at least, the same as the cranberry has been improved, by cultivation. [Laughter.]

The experiment of planting homeopathic pills in the hill with the melon has been tried, but homeopathy, while perhaps good in certain cases, does not seem to reach the seat of disease in the watermelon. What I would advise, and the advice is free to all, is that a porous plaster be placed upon watermelons, just as they are beginning to ripen, with a view to draw out the cholera morbus. [Laughter.] A mustard plaster might have the same effect, but the porous plaster seems to me to be the article to fill a want long felt. If, by this means, a breed of watermelon can be raised that will not strike terror to the heart of the consumer, this agricultural address will not have been delivered in vain.

An Eastern scientist has discovered that cucumbers contain tape worms. Then all we have to say is that farmers are selling their tape worms mighty high. Twenty cents for a cucumber not bigger than a clothes-pin, that can't possibly contain tape worm enough to go around in a small family, is outrageous. But, is there anything that you raise on your farm, that does not contain something bad, except the bologna sausage? [Laughter.]

Again some of our Wisconsin agriculturists are asking:

Why not go to raising elephants?

A good elephant will sell for eight thousand dollars. A pair of elephants can be bought by a community of farmers pooling their issues and getting a start, and in a few years every farm can be a menagerie of its own, and every year we can rake in from eight to twenty-four thousand dollars from the sale of surplus elephants. It may be said that elephants are hearty feeders, and that they would go through an ordinary farmer in a short time. Well, they can be turned out into the highway to browse, and earn their own living. This elephant theory is a good one, and any man that is good on figures can sit down and figure up a profit in a year sufficient to go into bankruptcy. [Laughter.]

Would I advise the farmer to raise fish?

I say, emphatically, yes. I would suggest that you permit the subject of the artificial hatching of fish to engage your attention, and that you petition the legislature to appropriate several dollars to purchase whale's eggs, vegetable oysters and mock turtle seeds. [Laughter.] The hatching of fish is easy, and any man can soon learn it; and it is a branch of industry that many who are now out of employment, owing to circumstances beyond their control, [laughter] will be glad to avail themselves of. How, I ask you, could means better be adapted to the ends than for the retiring officers of our State to go to setting on fish eggs? [Laughter.]

When should fish be eaten?

This question has often been asked by the agricultural newspaper. This is easily answered by the scientists among our farmers. Fish should be eaten at meal time. [Laughter.]

Fish without bones are the best to raise and the easiest to eat. Many farmers eat the largest bones of the largest fish. This is a mistake. Nothing appears so much out of place as to see a farmer in business hours walking along the street picking pickerel bones out of the sides of his neck. [Laughter.]

There is but one other sadder sight than this, and that is, to see **an** old maid in a street car, her lap full of bundles, an umbrella in one hand, and a pet dog under her arm, and the lady trying to eat a juicy pear with a double set of false teeth that are loose. [Laughter.]

The subject of the artificial propagation of fish, by the farmer, has arrested the attention of many of the ablest minds of the country, and the results of experiments have been thus far so satisfactory that it is almost safe to predict that within the next ten centuries every farmer, however poor, may pick bull-heads off of his crab apple vines, and gather his winter supply of fresh shad from his sweet potato trees at less than fifty cents a pound. [Laughter.] The experiments that have been made in our own State, warrant us in going largely into the fish business. A year ago, a quantity of fish seeds were sub-soil plowed into the ice of Lake Mendota by a careful farmer, and to-day, I am informed, that the summer boarders there have all the fish to eat that any reasonable man could desire. The expense is small and the returns are enormous. It is estimated that from the six quarts of fish seeds that were planted in the lake, there are now ready for the market, at least, 11,000,000 car loads of brain-producing food, if you spit on your bait when you go fishing. [Loud laughter.]

Fish are nourishing food for the farmer. Then he knows what he is eating. The bones identify the fish. Now, a Racine farmer, who had been consuming large quantities of Chicago tenderloin, investigated his beefsteak, and found that it was a fried liver pad that a former summer boarder had pawned for his board. The farmer didn't want to lose it, so he had it cooked. A liver pad, if nicely cooked, is fine eating, with mushrooms, but, of course—well, this is an isolated case. [Laughter.]

I have been asked by several Oshkosh agriculturists if seed corn should be frozen. "Does it hurt the ears to freeze them?" This is a mooted question. I can only answer the question by telling an anecdote.

"A young Boscobel farmer and his girl went out sleighing one day, and returned with a frozen ear. [Laughter.] There is nothing very startling in the simple fact of a frozen ear, but the idea is that it was the ear next to the girl that he was foolish enough to let freeze." [Laughter.] A Wisconsin girl that will go out sleigh-riding with a young man and allow his ears to freeze is no gentleman, and ought to be arrested. Why, in Milwaukee, on the coldest days, I have seen a young man out riding with a girl, and his ears were so hot they would fairly "sis," and there was not a man driving on the avenue but would have changed places with the young man, and allowed his ears to cool.

[Laughter.] No, Wisconsin girls can not sit too close during winter weather. This climate is rigorous. [Loud laughter.]

Shall farmers spend their money for costly farm machinery?

This is a grave question. Millions of dollars, I understand, have been paid out by Wisconsin farmers to buy a new invention called a "cat teaser." This they put on fences to keep cats from sitting there and singing. It consists of a three-cornered piece of tin, nailed on the top of the fence. We hope none of our farmer friends will continue to invest in the patent, for statistics show that while cats very often sit on fences to meditate, yet, when they get it all meditated and get ready to sing a duet, they get down off the fence and get under a currant bush. [Laughter.] We challenge any cat scientist to disprove the assertion. [Loud laughter.]

The question often comes up "shall the farmer be educated?"

I have given this question much thought, and am unable to decide it. I read yesterday that a very ignorant man, unable to read or write, has lately died in Cincinnati, leaving an estate of $250,000 in steamboats and things. What a lesson this circumstance is to those farmers who will fritter away their time learning to read and write, when they might be laying up steamboats for their heirs and assigns. [Laughter.]

Knowledge is power, but steamboats are powerer. [Laughter.]

The poor farmer has many trying moments. There are times when he requires fortitude—and when he should be as bold as Peter the Hermit. There is one especial moment in the life of a young farmer, however humble or however exalted, when he feels the humiliation of his position, and blushes at what is expected of him. A moment when he feels as though he would prefer to transact the business before him through an agent. A time when his soul would fain throw off its fetters, and he feels it to be a moral impossibility for him to go through the task assigned to him, when he feels that he would almost rather die, if he were satisfied he were good enough. That time is when he has to go into a store and inquire of the gentlemanly clerk if he has got any fine-tooth combs. [Laughter.] He looks around carefully to see that no one is listening, and asks for the harrowing instrument of torture, but is careful to tell the clerk that it is dandruff that is the matter. [Laughter.]

A serious question, fraught with great interest to the farmer, is now being discussed by the Farmers' Alliance throughout our country. It is a touching subject, and I approach it with almost reverential awe. Still, in an address to the agriculturists of the whole country, I can not remain silent on the great question.

19

This question is, shall farmers employ female doctors?

I should say, in answer to this great question, that a farmer, if there was nothing the matter with him, might call in a female doctor; [laughter] but if he was sick as a horse—and when a man is sick, he is sick as a horse—the last thing he would have around would be a female doctor, and why? Because when a man wants a female fumbling around he wants to feel well. [Laughter.] He don't want to be bilous, or feverish, with his mouth tasting like cheese, and his eyes bloodshot, when a female is looking over him and taking an account of stock.

Of course these female doctors are all young and good looking, and if one of them came into a sick room where a farmer was in bed, and he had chills, and was as cold as a wedge, and she should sit up close to the side of the bed, and take hold of his hand, his pulse would run up to a hundred and fifty and she would prescribe for a fever when he had chilblains. Then if he died she could be arrested for malpractice. O, you can't fool us farmers on female doctors. [Laughter.]

A farmer who has been sick and has had male doctors, knows just how he would feel to have a female doctor come tripping in and throw her fur-lined cloak over a chair, take off her hat and gloves, and throw them on a lounge, and come up to the bed with a pair of marine blue eyes, with a twinkle in the corner, and look him in the wild changeable eyes, and ask him to run out his tongue. Suppose he knew his tongue was coated so it looked like a yellow Turkish towel, do you suppose he would want to run out five or six inches of the lower end of it, and let that female doctor put her finger on it, to see how it was furred? Not much! He would put that tongue up into his cheek, and wouldn't let her see it for twenty-five cents admission. [Laughter.]

We have all seen doctors put their hands under the bed clothes and feel a farmer's feet to see if they were cold. If a female doctor should do that, it would give a farmer cramps in the legs. [Laughter.]

A male doctor can put his hand on a farmer's stomach, and liver, and lungs, and ask him if he feels any pain there; but if a female doctor should do the same thing it would make him sick, and he would want to get up and kick himself for employing a female doctor. O, there is no use talking, it would kill a farmer—a female doctor would!

Now, suppose a farmer had heart disease, and a female doctor should want to listen to the beating of his heart. She would lay her left ear on his left breast, so her eyes and rosebud mouth would be looking right into his face, and her wavy hair would be scattered all around there, getting tangled in the buttons of his night shirt. Don't you suppose his heart would get in about twenty extra beats to the minute? You bet!

And she would smile — we will bet ten dollars she would smile — and show her pearly teeth, and her red lips would be working as though she were counting the beats, and he would think she was trying to whisper to him, and——[Laughter.]

Well, what would he be doing all this time? If he was not dead yet, which would be a wonder, his left hand would brush the hair away from her temple, and his right hand would get sort of nervous and move around to the back of her head, and when she had counted the heart beats a few minutes and was raising her head, he would draw the head up to him and kiss her once for luck, if he was as bilous as a Jersey swamp angel, and have her charge it in the bill; and then a reaction would set in, and he would be as weak as a cat, and she would have to fan him and rub his head until he got over being nervous, and then make out her prescription after he got asleep. No; all of a man's symptoms change when a female doctor is practicing on him, and she would kill him dead.

These woman colleges are doing a great wrong in preparing these female doctors for the war path, and we desire to enter a protest in behalf of twenty million farmers who could not stand the pressure. [Loud laughter.]

You farmers write and expect me to give you reliable farm information. You expect me to tell you what to raise, when to raise and how to raise it. The Farmers' Alliance asks, when should a man raise horses? In answering this I will say that I always raise horses just seven years ago. [Laughter.] That is always a great year for colts—that seven years ago. [Laughter.] Horses raised before or since may be good horses but no one wants them. Occasionally some one sells a six-year-old horse, but it does not often occur, unless the buyer insists upon that age; and then a thrifty farmer can generally accommodate him. [Laughter.]

Now us farmers who lived around here seven years ago did not have our attention called to the fact that the country was flooded with colts. There were very few twin colts, and it was seldom that a mother had half a dozen colts following her. Farmers and stock-raisers did not go round worrying about what they were going to do with so many colts. The papers, if we recollect right, were not filled with accounts of the extraordinary number of colts born. And yet you see it must have been a terrible year for colts, because there are only six horses in Milwaukee that are over seven years old. One of them was found to have been pretty well along in years when he worked for an Oshkosh farmer, in 1848, and finally the farmer who had a poor memory, owned up that he was mistaken twenty-six years. What a mortality there must have been among horses that would now be eight, nine or ten years old.   There are none of them left.   And a year from now, when our present stock of horses would naturally be eight years old they will all be dead, and a new lot of seven-year old horses will take their places.   It is singular, but it is true. That is, it is true unless farmers and horse dealers lie, and I would be slow to charge so grave a crime upon a useful and enterprising class of citizens.   No, it can not be, and yet, farmers, don't it seem peculiar that all the horses in this broad land are seven years old this spring! We leave this subject for the farmers of the land to wonder over.

In the meantime continue to hire your colts born just seven years ago. [Loud applause.]

Another want of the farmer is a farm currency. We want it fixed by the Treasury Department so we can make change easily.

What we want is a currency that every farmer can issue for himself. A law should be passed making the products of the farm a legal tender for all debts, public and private, including duties on imports, interest on the public debt, and contributions for charitable purposes. Then we shall have a new money table about as follows:

Ten ears of corn make one cent.

Ten cucumbers make one dime.

Ten watermelons make one dollar.

Ten bushels of wheat make one eagle.

Arise and sing!

CHAUNCEY M. DEPEW.

BIOGRAPHY AND REMINISCENCES.

Chauncey M. Depew was born on a farm near Poughkeepsie in 1833. He came of poor but respectable parents. When a boy he worked on the farm, and the great railroad magnate, who now makes presidents, talks politics with Gladstone and jokes with the Prince of Wales, has many a time driven the cows home in the rain. Mr. Depew graduated at Yale College, studied law, was admitted to the bar, and afterward became President of the great New York Central Railroad. His aim in life seems to be to make everybody happy. He is democratic in all his ways, takes every man by the hand, is loved at the Union League Club and is the honored guest of the St. Patrick, St. Andrews and New England Societies. Depew, Horace Porter and Ingersoll are perhaps the best after-dinner speakers of the age, and Depew is perhaps the best "all around" extemporaneous speaker in this country.

Mr. Depew has an eye like an eagle and a smile which throws sunshine all around him. He is never too busy to see a friend, even if he has to say "hail and farewell" in the same breath. I say never too busy, but I now remember calling on him once when he sent out word that he was engaged with two railroad presidents and could see no one —"not even on business."

I told the boy to tell Mr. Depew that I hadn't any business at all, only a new joke.

"All right, Eli," said Mr. Depew, laughing through the door, "come right in. But first," he said, "let me tell you my dog story.

" When I was about fourteen years old, my father lived on the old farm up at Poughkeepsie. One day, after I had finished a five-acre field of corn, my father let me go to town to see a circus. While in town I saw for the first time a spotted coach dog. It took my fancy, and I bought it and took it home. When father saw it, his good old Puritan face fell.

"'Why, Chauncey,' he said sadly, 'we don't want any spotted dog on the farm—he'll drive the cattle crazy.'

"No, he won't, father," said Chauncey, proudly ; "he's a blooded dog."

"'The next day," said Mr. Depew, "it was raining, and I took the dog out into the woods to try him on a coon, but the rain was too much for him. It washed the spots off. That night I took the dog back to the dog-dealer, with a long face. Said I : 'Look at that dog sir ; the spots have all washed off.'

"'Great guns, boy!' exclaimed the dog-dealer, 'there was an umbrella went with that dog. Didn't you get the umbrella ?'"

Mr. Depew's father was a very frugal farmer and also a very pious man. He never liked to have any time wasted in the prayer-meeting. One night, when the experiences had all been told, and the exhortations flagged, and the prayers grew feeble, Brother Depew arose and solemmly remarked :

"I don't like to see the time wasted—Brother Joslyn, can't you tell your experience?"

Brother Josyln said he'd told his experience twice already.

"Then Brother Finney can't you make a prayer or tell your experience?"

"I've told it several times to-night, brother."

"Well my brethern," said Mr. Depew, "as the regular exercises to-night seem to halt a little, and as no one seems to want to pray or tell his experience, I will improve the time by making a few observations on the tariff."

I was talking one day with Mr. Depew about demand and supply. I said the price of any commodity is always controlled by the demand and supply.

"Not always, Eli," said Mr. Depew, "demand and supply don't always govern prices. Business tact sometimes governs them."

"When," I asked, "did an instance ever occur, when the price did not depend on demand and supply?"

"Well" said Mr. Depew, "the other day I stepped up to a German butcher, and out of curiosity asked :

"What's the price of sausages?"

"Dwenty cents a bound," he said.

"You asked twenty-five this morning," I replied.

HE'S A BLOODED DOG.

See page 286.

"Ya, dot vas ven I had some. Now I ain'd got none I sells him for dwendy cends. Dot makes me a rebutation for selling cheab und I don'd lose noddings."

"You see," said Depew laughing, "I didn't want any sausage and the man didn't have any—no demand or supply, and still the price of sausage went down."

I was talking to Mr. Depew one day about his going out to dinner so much.

"Yes," he said, "I do go out a good deal."

"But how can you stand it? I should think it would give you dyspepsia. I suppose you can eat every thing?"

"No, there are two things which I always positively refuse to eat for dinner," said Mr. Depew, gravely.

"And what are they?"

"Why breakfast and supper."

"But the great crowds you have to face in heated rooms, they must wear on you?" I said.

"But the crowded dining room," said Mr. Depew, "is more healthful than a funeral. Now, I have a friend in Poughkeepsie who goes out more than I do, but he goes to funerals. He never misses one. He enjoys a good funeral better than the rest of us enjoy a dinner.

"I remember one day how I attended a funeral with my Poughkeepsie friend over in Dutchess county. The house was packed. The people came for miles around—and everybody came to mourn too. Many eyes were wet, and some good old farmers who had never seen the deceased except at a distance, groaned and shed real tears. After we had crowded our way in amongst the mourners, I turned to my friend and said:

"'George, I don't see the coffin—where is it?'

"But George couldn't answer.

"After a while I made a remark to my friend about a lovely eight-day standing clock in the hall.

"'The clock!' said George, mournfully, 'why that isn't a clock, that's the coffin. They've stood him up in the hall to make room for the mourners!'"

Mr. Depew has a well-balanced brain. There are no streaks of insanity in the Depew family. Once, while conversing with Dr. Hammond, our witty ex-surgeon-general, about insanity, I asked him how incipient insanity could be detected.

"One infallible test," said the Doctor, "is to get a good joke on a man—a real good one—and if he laughs at it, it is a sure sign that his mind is evenly balanced. An insane man never laughs at a good joke on himself. He always gets enraged. Insanity always begins in egotism. Guiteau, the crazy man who shot Garfield, laughed at his own jokes all through the trial, but when the prosecuting attorney got a joke on him, his insanity showed itself in flashing eyes and a scowl of indignation."

After my conversation with Dr. Hammond, I met Sam Cox at the Fifth Avenue hotel and told him about Hammond's theory.

"Let's go over to Madison Square," said Sam, "and try the theory on George Francis Train."

"Good," I said, and we were soon in the garden talking to the great George Francis, who sat on a bench surrounded by his usual crowd of children. Train is a vegetarian, and he was soon talking on his favorite subject.

"Yes," he said, "I am a vegetarian. Vegetables give strength. They give muscle;" and then he held up his clenched fist and gradually opened it to show the flow of red blood to the palm.

"See!" said Train, "that blood and muscle come from a vegetable diet."

"Yes," said Cox, "you are right George. Vegetables do give muscle and health. I notice that all the strong animals eat vegetables. There is the sturdy lion, he lives on vegetables—and the leopard and tiger too; that's what makes them so strong. But sheep and geese, live on meat that is what makes them so weak and —"

"I don't want to talk to a darn fool!" interrupted Train as he strode off in a huff.

Then we knew George Frances was insane.

The next morning I met Mr. Depew in the street car on his way to the Grand Central depot. Remembering Hammond's insanity test, I said, "now I will try it on Depew," so I held up the *World* and exclaimed :

"I see there's a washout on the Central!"

"A what?"

"A washout."

"A dangerous washout?"

"Not very."

" How large is it ?   I haven't seen a newspaper."

" O, ten shirts and four pair of —"

But Depew's genial laugh drowned the sentence.

" Perfectly sane," I said to myself.

One night I was lecturing to a big audience in Napoleon, Ohio. The lecture committee said they would like to have me get a joke on Judge ——, I forget his name, who sat in a front seat.   So when I was illustrating the difference between the joke and the anecdote, I said :

" The joke is the incident itself; the anecdote is a description of it.   You get a joke on a man — a description of it appears in the newspaper the next day; that is an anecdote.   Now," said I, " to illustrate the difference between the joke and the anecdote—and this is a very important illustration, and I hope the young people in the audience will remember it—suppose I were talking about a fast horse that I have; suppose I should say I have a horse that could travel from Napoleon to Toledo, a distance of — of ——

" ' Twenty-six miles," interrupted the Judge.

" Well, Judge," said I, " if you know more about this lecture than I do ———"

But I never finished the sentence.   A scream of laughter came up from the audience, and the house was a bedlam for several minutes.

When the audience had settled down, I said, " I beg the Judge's pardon for answering him so rudely, for it was very kind in him to tell me the distance, and very rude and ungentlemanly for me to answer him so bluntly, but the fact is, I had just told the young gentlemen in the audience that I would illustrate to them the difference between the joke and the anecdote, and in a way they would never forget it.   " Now this is a joke," I said.   " To-morrow it will become an anecdote—a dead cold anecdote.   It won't produce any laughter to-morrow, and, I believe, if any one should go to the Judge to-morrow and ask him in the most polite manner the distance to Toledo, I believe he would pull out his revolver and ——"   Another scream from the audience drowned the sentence.

Well it was all very well that night, and would have ended in laughter had the Judge been perfectly sane, but he had incipient insanity, egotism, and when I got onto the train the next morning, to go to Toledo, the Judge came down with a big hickory cane, to chastise me for the joke.

Five months after this the Judge went to an insane asylum. This story is absolutely true, and I appeal to every man, woman or child in Napoleon to substantiate it.

It is so different with Depew. A good story on anybody, even at the expense of himself, is his delight.

The day after his return from Europe the last time, I was in Cornelius Vanderbilt's room, in the Central Railroad office, which is next to Depew's, and told him a little story about Mr. Depew's experience on the steamer. I didn't know that the great original was listening to the story through the half open door. The story as told by the brokers in the street ran like this:

" It seems that every evening, on the ' City of Rome,' a dozen or so genial passengers clustered in the smoking saloon to tell stories and yarn about things in general. Every soul save one in the party kept his end up. The one exceptional member of the party did not laugh or indicate by even a twinkle of the eye any interest in the funniest jokes, and was as silent as a door-knob at the best stories.

" This conduct began to nettle Mr. Depew and the other spirits, and when the final seance came around they had lost all patience with the reticent and unresponsive stranger. Mr. Depew was finally selected to bring him to terms. They were all comfortably seated and in came the stranger.

" ' See here, my dear sir,' " said Mr. Depew, " ' won't you tell a story ? ' "

" ' I never told one in my life.' "

" ' Sing a song ? ' "

" ' Can't sing.' "

" ' Know any jokes ? ' " persisted Mr. Depew.

" ' No.' "

" Mr. Depew and all were prepared to give it up when the stranger stammered and hesitated and finally made it known that he knew just one conundrum.

" ' Give it to us,' " said Mr. Depew and the others in chorus.

" ' What is the difference between a turkey and me ? ' " solemnly asked the stranger.

" ' Give it up,' " said Chairman Depew.

"'The difference between a turkey and me,'" mildly said the stranger, "'is that they usually stuff the bird with chestnuts after death. I am alive.'"

Vanderbilt smiled audibly, but a merry ha! ha!! echoed from the next room.

It was the happy laugh of Depew himself, and it grew louder till I left the building. When I meet Mr. Depew now I give him the whole sidewalk, and when I ride on his railroad I walk.

HON. CHAUNCEY M. DEPEW'S LECTURE.

ENGLAND, IRELAND AND SCOTLAND.

Ladies and Gentlemen:—We started in the morning to drive to Blarney Castle, and kiss its famous stone. The road runs through a country which gives a fair idea of agricultural Ireland. We passed by the splendid farms and grand houses to study that most interesting person in Ireland, the Irish peasant. He and his family live in stone cottages about thirty feet long and one story high, with a thatched roof. The floor is of earth, and the single room is often divided so that the cow and pig may be sheltered in the other half. The Irishman's pig is a sacred thing. When I saw the proximity of the pig to-day, I said to its rosy-faced owner:

"I say, Patrick, don't you think it is unhealthful to have your pig in the house with your children?"

"An' phy shuld oi not, sor? 'It's unhealthy,' is it, ye sez. Be away wid yer nonsense! Sure the pig has never been sick a day in his life." [Laughter.]

Around the Irishman's door are always to be seen crowds of children, looking happy and light-hearted, though the driver said: "Maybe they went to bed without supper and have had no breakfast." Children swarm everywhere, for the marriage bond in Ireland is a coupon bond, and they cut one off every year.

Blarney Castle is situated half a mile from the public road, and to get to it we walked through a charming garden. The castle is a solid square stone tower 120 feet high. Round the top runs a battlement resting on piers projecting from the face of the tower. Between this battlement or coping and the face of the tower is a space of about four or six feet, and on the lower side of the coping is the famous Blarney stone, held in its place by iron bands. As you stand on the top of the wall of the castle and look at the stone, you are 120 feet from the ground on the outside, and 100 on the inside, where the different floors have fallen through, and the wall on which you are is about three feet wide. If you attempt to reach down and kiss the stone, you are inevitably pitched to the ground through the open space between the coping and the castle proper. If your friend tries to hold you, when he pulls you back, both of you fall over into the pit. It could never be touched by any human being unless he had a derrick. I knew its virtues both in politics, in law, and in love, and longed to glue my lips to its surface. I thought over Father Prout's famous lines:

> There is a stone there, that whoever kisses
>   Oh ! he never misses to grow eloquent !
> 'Tis he may clamber to a lady's chamber,
>   Or become a member of Parliament.
> A clever spouter he'll sure turn out, or
>   An out and outer to be let alone;
> Don't hope to hinder him or to bewilder him,
>   Sure he's a pilgrim to the Blarney Stone.

and then threw it a despairing kiss and climbed down. Sir Walter Scott paid the spot a memorable visit, and it never had a worthier pilgrim to its shrine. The derricks were there for him, and hence the wonderful romance and weird poetry of the Wizard of the North. Father Prout told the wondering Scott a tale about the Blarney stone surpassing the Wizard's wildest creations.

"The Blarney stone," said the witty Father Prout, "is superior to the famed stone of Memnon, the Luxor obelisk, the Sphinx's head, the Delphic oracle, the Elgin marbles, with all their sculptures, and the Philosopher's stone. It belonged to the Irish family of O'Neills, who lived in Egypt in the pre-historic period, and from the river Nile it received its name, and the twenty-first year after the sack of Troy it was brought to Ireland.

Under the castle are the dungeons for the prisoners of war or chieftain's vengeance. In these cells we realize the cruelties and nameless horrors which were inflicted on the helpless in the good old times. I crept on hands and knees through a low, narrow, winding passage, and finally emerged into the prisoner's room. No ray of light ever penetrated it, no groans or cries could be heard through the thick walls, and in a space not high enough to stand upright, in dampness and utter darkness, the poor wretches died in nameless agonies. When I came again into the light, I gave my guide his fee, and, as I bade him good-bye, he cried:

> O Blarney Castle, my darling,
>   You're nothing at all but a stone,
> And a small, little twist of ould ivy;
>   Och wisha, ullaloo, ullagone.   [Laughter.]

The rich Irish brogue and blundering bulls of the Irishman constantly amused me. Two Irishmen were crossing a field near Blarney Castle, and saw, for the first time, a jackass, which was making "daylight hideous" with his unearthly braying.

Jemmy stood a moment in astonishment, then turning to Pat, who was also enraptured with the song, he remarked:

"It's a fine ear the bird has got for music, but he's got a wonderful cowld." [Laughter.]

Again, two Irishmen were working in a quarry around the Castle, when one of them fell into a deep quarry hole. The other, alarmed, came to the margin of the hole and called out:

"Arrah, Pat, are ye killed entirely? If ye're dead, spake."

Pat reassured him from the bottom by saying, in answer:

"No, Tim, I'm not dead, but I'm spachless." [Laughter.]

But the Irish brogue is no funnier than the English brogue. One day an English farmer responded, at an agricultural fair, to the toast of "The Queen." This is the way he talked:

"Noo, gentlemen, will ye a' fill your glasses, for I'm aboot to bring forward 'The Queen.' [Applause.] Oor Queen, gentlemen, is really a wonderful woman, if I may say it; she is ane o' the guid auld sort, nae whignaleeries or falderal aboot her, but a douce daecent body. She's respectable beyond a doot. She has brocht up a grand family o' weelfaur'd lads and lasses—her auldest son bein' a credit to ony mither—and they're weel married. Gentlemen, ye'll maybe no believe it, but I ance saw the queen. [Sensation.] I did. Somebody pointed her oot tae me at Perth station, and there she was, smart and tidy-like; and says I tae myself, 'God bless that queen, my queen!' Noo, gentlemen, the whuskey's guid, the nicht is lang, the weather is wet, and the roads are saft, and will harm naebody that comes to grief. So, aff wi' yer drink tae the bottom! 'The queen!'" [Loud laughter.]

A rail ride of half a day from Blarney Castle and we are at Killarney. Whatever else may be retarded in Ireland, her railways are admirably managed; and in safety, speed, comfort, and high fare, compare favorably with any in Europe. Whoever expects to find the lakes of Killarney gems unequalled in scenic merit, will realize, if an American, that centuries of undisputed praise, the adjectives cumulating as each cycle rolls round, like the storied adulations of the old masters, produce a picture in the imagination never realized by the eye. Lake George, in our own State would smile with serene superiority upon any sheet of water in Europe, whose beauties have been celebrated in prose and poetry by the genius of every age. Nevertheless, the unquestioned charms of Killarney, the ruined abbeys and castles upon its shores, the wild legends which are connected with it, make it one of the most impressive places in the world. I never shall forget the jaunting-car ride with the wild horse and the wilder driver around to the upper end of the lake.

"See here," I shouted, as we dashed at full speed down a steep hill, "what will become of us if that horse stumbles?" "And sure yer honor," answered the driver, "why thin, I will fall out first."

At Kate Kearney's cottage the traveler takes a bit of goat's milk and potheen in memory of the famous beauty, and at the hands of her alleged granddaughter, and, leaving the jaunting-car, mounts a pony for a ride through the Gap of Dunloe. The Gap is a wild gorge in the mountain with a narrow path at the bottom, and barren and precipitous rocks at the sides.

Did you ever see those beautiful rosy cheeked Irish girls? About forty of them joined us here, and followed us through the Gap, and a brighter, merrier party never was met. They made a raid upon our pockets which cleaned out the last shilling, but it was fairly won and lost.

"Sure, sor," said a pretty girl, "an' are the winters very cold in Ameriky?"

"Yes," I said.

"Then," said this bright-eyed siren, "I have been expecting you sor, and have knitted these woolen stockings to make you comfortable at home, and keep your heart warm to ould Ireland."

"And is there nothing you will buy?" said another.

"Nothing," said I.

"Well, then," she cried, "will yer honor give me a shilling for a six-pence?"

"I am going to be married, sor," lisped a mountain beauty, "and me marriage portion is pretty near made up! and Pat's getting very weary waiting so long."

"My money is all gone," said I, when quick as a flash I heard a friend say to her:

"Mary, thry him on getting to Ameriky." [Laughter.]

Desolate as this spot is, it furnishes an opportunity for that species of landlordism which is Ireland's curse, and adds needless irritation to oppression. The man who wakes the echoes with a blast from the bugle must pay $25 a year for the privilege, the artillery-man who stirs them up with a cannon is taxed by the land-owner $50.

Oh, the poverty of Ireland!

As we emerged from the Gap and looked into the Black Valley, so called, because between the steep hills the sun only penetrates at mid-day, I noticed that it was cut up into small farms of about five acres each. Around the little stone cabins were the chickens, the goat, the pigs and the donkey. I said to one of their tenants:

"How much rent do you pay for this land?"

"For the cottage and five acres, with the privilege of pasturing sheep on the side of the mountain, we each pay $250 a year."

"In heaven's name," I said, "how can you raise enough to do that and keep body and soul together?"

"And that's all we do, sir," he answered, "and we couldn't do that except for the corn meal which comes to us from your country."

At the foot of the Black Valley we took a six-oared boat for a trip through the lakes. They are three in number—the first being eight miles wide by two in length, then a river for two miles to the middle lake, and then you shoot the rapids to the lower lake which is five miles wide by three long. The mountains rise from the water to the height of 1,700 feet, and numberless islands everywhere dot the surface. Every islet, rock and cove has its story of early and bloody strife, of love and murder, of fairy or ghostly visitant; and the boatmen religiously believe that once a year the O'Donoghue, on his snow-white horse, rises from the lake and rides to his ancient castle. All the sights to be seen are upon the land owned by Mr. Herbert, of Muckross, and the Earl of Kenmare. Every few miles you pass through a gate and pay a shilling.

"Why," I asked the driver, "is this charge made so often to ride over these roads?"

"Shame on the landlord," he said, bitterly, "with his thousands of pounds, who taxes the tourist to keep up his grounds."

Muckross Abbey is a fine old ruin, and worth the fee to visit, but when, after buying a ticket, you are mysteriously directed through a wicket gate, and climbing a steep hill are ushered into the presence of the far-famed Torc Water Fall, you involuntarily cry:

"Oh, Shade of Barnum, the Great; humbug is not a protected American product, for the wonderful Torc is surpassed in both grandeur and beauty by Buttermilk Falls, near West Point."

No greater contrast ever existed in the same country than between the cities of Belfast and Cork. While the latter is retrograding, the former has increased its population six-fold in fifty years. It is full of life and activity, and resembles an American town. Every body has something to do, and there is enough to do for all, and poverty and distress seem to be unknown. It supports four colleges and over one hundred churches. There is nothing for the sightseer in this busy hive, and so he starts for the Giant's Causeway. As you near the causeway there

20

stands out in the ocean one of the most romantic ruins in the world. The sea has cut off a projecting promontory from the land, and upon this the mediæval baron built his castle of Dunluce. The precipitous sides run down 100 feet to the water, and it is joined to the land by a causeway only eighteen inches wide. As you look at the grand old ruin and this threadlike bridge, the story of the bloody and cruel past is better told than in a thousand volumes. From its gates came the chief and his armed retainers to plunder and ravage the surrounding country, and in their train, on their return, was the father, to be tortured for his hidden treasures, then flung over the battlements, and the daughter to become the sport of the soldiers. The Bridge of Sighs never heard so many cries of suffering and despair as were borne from this lonely rock across the lonely waters. The Giant's Causeway is one of the few marvelous freaks of nature sufficiently wonderful to distinguish any country. It is only by a visit, and not by a description, that this phenomenal formation can be understood. But here, on the shores of the Atlantic, are hundreds of acres covered with stone columns more perfect than the artisan ever worked. There are millions of them. Each is about two feet in diameter. They are formed of separate blocks about a foot thick, and yet so perfectly joined that it is difficult to see where they touch, except you lift one off. The columns are from four to 100 feet in height. Some are three-sided, and from that to eight sides, but no matter how many, each side is exactly of the same dimensions as the other, and the surfaces are as smooth as if polished by machinery. In the rear they form the front of a lofty cliff, and, looking like its pipes, are called the Giant's Organ, whose music is the reverberation of the dashing waves of the ocean.

Naturalists and scientists have done their best to solve the problem of the structure of this grand temple, but after all the Irish explanation is the best. In the olden time the famous Irish giant, Fin McCoul, had a quarrel with a Scotch giant across the water. The Scotchman said he would come over and mop up the floor with Fin if it was not for getting his feet wet. Whereupon Mr. McCoul, like the fine ould Irish gentleman that he was, built this causeway for his Caledonian rival, and greeted him with the most tremendous thrashing ever given to man. What was left of the Scot, Mr. McCoul generously set up in business in a grocery, and the sea in time washed away Fin's bridge to Scotland.

Why is the Irishman poor, and why do the troubles of this people vex all the world? If you ask an Englishman the remedy, he answers, "Leave the island twenty-four hours under water." The main difficulty is that William III., at the petition of the British manufacturers, abolished all the factories in Ireland but the linen ones. In the north of

Ireland, where these still flourish, there are thrift and content. The rest of the country is necessarily purely agricultural. There are no diversified industries for the young men and women. Families are large, and the tenant farmer divides his holding among his children. If he has ten and a hundred acre farm he leaves them ten acres apiece. If they each in turn have ten, they can give their children but one acre each, and then it being impossible to either get a living off the land or pay a cent of rent, there is nothing left but to shoot the landlord. I said to a large English manufacturer:

" Why don't you solve the Irish question by establishing here new Sheffields and Birminghams, and then this island could support 10,000,-000 in comfort where 4,000,000 can not live."

" The beggars," said he, " won't work."

" But," I said, " In America they reclaim New England farms which the Yankees have abandoned, and are usefully industrious in every public and private work."

I repeated the remark of the English manufacturer to an Irish member of parliament, and asked his answer. " Well," he said, " they will not work for an Englishman."

As the Irish have no capital to start manufactories, this reply added greatly to the difficulties of the question. In her natural relations to other nations, and her own proper development, the successful and wealthy men in Ireland would be her workers in iron and steel, in cotton and wool. But alas, there are none, and so a brewer restores St. Patrick's cathedral at a cost of a million, and a distiller, Christ Church cathedral, at a cost of another million, and both are knighted here—perhaps hereafter.

A boatman on Killarney told me he supported a family of eight children on $75 a year. A bright, intelligent man, who did some work for me, said he could earn only twenty-five cents a day, and that, in the same cabin with his domestic animals, himself and ten children lived upon the food which fattened the chickens and the pigs.

An Irishman in the employ of the Central Railroad got to the bottom of the Irish question. He stepped into a meat market and asked an old lady the price of fowls.

" A dollar apiece," was the reply.

" And a dollar is it, my darlint? Why, in Ireland you might buy them for a sixpence apiece."

" Then why didn't you stay in that blessed cheap country?"

" Och, faith and there were no sixpences there, to be sure."
[Laughter.]

And yet, notwithstanding all these hard conditions, the Irish are the quickest and most cheerful of all the peasantry of Europe. While the English and continental people who are in like condition are little above the brutes, the Irish are as full of life, fire and humor as if their state was one of frolic and ease. Touch one of them anywhere and at any time, and he bubbles with fun and smart repartee. When I was in Dublin, a political orator was describing his opponent as an extinct volcano, when a voice in the audience cried:

"Oh, the poor crater."

I said to a jaunting-car driver at Queenstown, to whom I owed a shilling:

"Can you change a half-crown (two and sixpence)"?

"Change a half-crown, is it?" he cried, in mock amazement, "do you think I have robbed a bank?"

At Killarney I met a delicious bit of wit and blunder. I asked the hotel clerk to stamp a letter for me. He put on the postage stamp which bears Victoria's image, and then starting back as if horrified, said:

"Bedad, but I have stood her majesty on her head."

"Well," I said, "that is not astonishing for an Irishman, but that is a double letter, and won't go without another stamp."

"Another stamp, is it?" and slapping the second directly over the first, "Begorra," said he, "it will go now." [Laughter.]

I love the witty Irish so well, you must let me illustrate some of their characteristics. Some friends of mine, and among them a disciple of Bergh, were walking through Cork, and saw a boy of sixteen beating a donkey. Said the member of the Society for the Prevention of Cruelty to Animals:

"Boy, stop beating your brother!" and as quick as a flash the boy answered:

"I won't, father!"

I said to an Irish liveryman: "Give me a good horse for a long ride."

"All right, your honor. The best in the world."

The horse broke down in half an hour, and I said: "You rascal, why did you cheat me in this way?"

"Sure, your honor, that horse is all right, but he is a very intelligent baste, and knowing you are a stranger, he wants you to have time to see the scenery."

As I was bidding farewell to Ireland, I said to my faithful attendant: "Good-bye, Pat."

"Good-bye, yer honor," he said, pathetically. "May God bless you and may every hair in your head be a candle to light your soul to glory."

"Well, Pat," I said, showing him my bald pate, " when that time comes there won't be much of a torchlight procession." [Laughter.]

The Irish all love whisky. To be sure, there are temperance men, but even they, when the bottle comes, invariably break their best resolutions.

" Biddy," said Mulligan to his wife, who was a member of the temperance society: "I know yez are a temperance woman, but it is a bad cowld yez has, and a drop of the craythur would do yez no harrum."

"Oh, honey," replied Biddy, "I've taken the pledge; but yez can mix me a drink and force me to swally it!" [Laughter.]

A rough sail across the Irish Channel and a long ride by rail found us at midnight at Glasgow, one of the busiest workshops in the world. But we care not for the industrial and commercial activities of Scotland: the magic spell of her mountains, her lakes and wild history is upon us. In the early morning we leave behind the great town, and in a few hours are sailing over Loch Lomond, the queen of the Scottish lakes. The vast expanse of water, the beautiful islands, the mountains rising peak on peak till lost in the clouds, the beetling crags which meet the waves, make this one of the few sights which fulfil expectations. Through the passes surrounding this lake, the Highland chieftains and their clans raided the Lowland farms. The Celtic warriors of the olden time followed the golden rule of the day:

> The good old rule, the simple plan,
> That they do take who have the power,
> And they do keep who can.

The McGregors, the McFarlanes, the Colquhans, here had their lairs and fought those bloody battles which have given to literature some of ts best poetry and romance. It was over these mountains that the fire signals flashed from peak to peak, calling the clansmen to resist the invader, and it was through these glens that Rhoderick Dhu sent his fiery cross. While bold Rob Roy McGregor defied here his enemies, and far up above the beach you see the cave which was his shelter and retreat. But with all that nature has done for Scotland, and she has been very lavish, the country owes the magic charm with which her hills and vales are invested for all the world to the genius of three men—Sir Walter Scott, Robert Burns and John Knox. At every step the stranger comes upon a scene familiar to him from childhood, through those grand stories and marvelous verses of Scott and Burns. You have all read the " Lady of the Lake," but it takes a trip through the Highlands to appreciate its realistic beauty. I stood by the brawling waters of Coilantogle Ford, where Rhoderick Dhu challenged Fitz James to mortal combat, by the

Lanric Mead, Clan Alpine's gathering ground, crossed the Bridge of Turk and murmured,

> And when the brig of Turk was won,
> The headmost horseman rode alone,

rode through the Trossachs, the wild mountain gorge, at whose entrance Fitz James lost his gallant grey, and stopped at Ellen's Isle, at Loch Katrine,

> Where for retreat in dangerous hour
> Some chief had framed a rustic bower,

long enough to appreciate Scott's description:

> With promontory, creek and bay,
> And mountains that like giants stand,
> To sentinel enchanted land.

Then before me seemed to rise the kingly warrior, Fitz James, standing on the "silver strand," while from her isle came in her boat the fair Ellen.

> A chieftain's daughter seemed the maid,
> Her satin snood, her silken braid,
> Her golden brooch such birth betrayed,
> And seldom on a breast so fair
> Mantled a plaid with modest care.
> And never brooch the folds combined
> Above a heart more good and kind.

The next morning I stood upon the battlements of Stirling Castle, this famous fortress of the Scottish kings upon a rocky eminence, which overlooks a vast stretch of country. From its walls are seen the hills where Wallace bled, and the field of Bannockburn, where Bruce saved his country.

Legend and story are about every stone and stream. You stand in the room where King James stabbed the Douglass and threw his body out of the window. You sit in the chair which Queen Mary and her son each occupied when crowned. You look at the pulpit from which Knox thundered his coronation sermon to the little six-year-old king, whom he had taken from his papist mother at the cost of her imprisonment and exile, and then you begin to understand the wild tragedies of those troublous times. But the center of Scotland's strange and romantic history for a thousand years is Edinburgh, the most interesting city of Europe. On one side of the steep gorge, upon the slopes of which it is built, rises the old town with the houses, the narrow streets, the fortifications of centuries gone by, while on the other side is built one of the most beautiful of modern cities, and thus the past and the present stand sentinels over each other. Through the old town the castle is reached.

This palace and fort is built upon a rock, whose precipitous sides stand perpendicularly nearly 400 feet from the plain below. Within its walls the noblest and best of Scotland's sons have been imprisoned, executed or murdered. In a plain room, not larger than an ordinary closet, Queen Mary gave birth to James, the future king of England, and he was soon after lowered down in a basket and hurried to Stirling Castle that he might be baptized in his mother's faith, the Roman Catholic, an act which caused his mother to lose her crown at the hand of Knox, and ultimately her life at the hand of Elizabeth. My canny and frugal guide said to me: "Sir, the tower is closed which contains the crown jewels, and you can't get in."

"The doors are locked, you say?"

"Locked as tight as the Bank of England."

"Will a sovereign open them?"

"The half of it will, sir!" he fairly yelled in astonishment at the reckless prodigality of the offer. [Laughter.]

The ride of ten miles from Edinburgh to Rosslyn gave me an unusual opportunity to mark the difference in intelligence between the nationalities of the coachman class. The Irish driver is full of wit, humor and fun, but his information is limited, and he is a poor guide. The English driver is the stupidest of all mortals. He has neither imagination nor knowledge. I said to one as we drove through the ancient gates of an old walled town:

"What were those arches built for?"

"I don't know, sir."

"How long have you lived here?"

"All my life, sir."

In the square at Salisbury, stood a statue of Sidney Herbert, for many years a distinguished member of parliament. I asked the coachman: "Whose statue is that?"

"Mr. Herbert's, sir."

"Well," said I, "What did he do to deserve a statue?"

"I don't know, sir, but I think he fit somewhere." [Laughter.]

"Well, is that the reason he is dressed in a frock coat, and carries an umbrella instead of a sword?"

"Yes, sir, I think so."

I said to my driver at Torquay:

"Do many Americans come here?"

"Oh, yes, sir. H'Americans are very fond of Torquay. Only yesterday morning, sir, two h'Americans, young ladies, 'ad me out before breakfast, and they made me drive them to an h'American dentist to have a tooth plugged, and the next day I had to go there very early again, because there was some trouble with that plug. Oh, the h'Americans are very fond of Torquay, sir."

But the Scotch driver knows as much as a college professor. There is nothing in the real or legendary history of every spot we pass that he will not give you with surpassing clearness and accuracy.

I saw a dozen of the thirty-five cathedrals of England. They average eight hundred years of age. Each has its own distinctive style of architecture, and they combine all we know of that grand art. Their builders and designers are gone, forgotten and unknown, but they mark that era in the history of the race when the church of Christ saved humanity from slavery and bestiality under the heel of tyrant kings and robber nobles. Gratitude, piety, reverence and worship, having no other way of expressing devotion to the one power which, in an age when might made right, humbled the lofty and raised the lowly, could bring royalty in penance to the shrine, and save the liberty and virtue of the peasant from the feudal lord, built these vast, splendid and enduring monuments to the ever-living God. I remember, as I sat during service one Sunday in Rosslyn chapel, near Edinburgh, wondering at the skill which amidst the rude and almost savage barbarism of the twelfth century could have fashioned the graceful arches, the superb and lavish carving, the delicate handiwork everywhere visible in this most exquisite poem in stone of the middle ages. As the rector was preaching the thinnest and leanest sermon I ever heard, I became rapt in contemplation of that wondrous pillar, known as the Apprentice's Pillar, which in a forest of pillars stands alone in the curves, the spiral and serpentlike coils, which give it such remarkable beauty; and thought of the poor apprentice genius who fashioned it while his master was at Rome, studying a model, and when the master returned and saw this creation, so much finer than any he had found abroad, in a fit of jealous rage he crushed the apprentice's skull with his hammer.

After leaving Old Sarum, a drive of ten miles over unfenced plains upon which the sheep grazed in countless herds, attended as in primitive days, by the shepherd and his dog, brought me to Stonehenge. This temple was built before recorded time, and its origin is one of the mysteries of the pre-historic past.

> That there were giants in the olden time,
> These stones cry out, whether before the flood,
> (As some have dreamt) in earth's majestic prime,
> The sons of Tubal piled up here sublime
> Whatever since in mystery hath stood
> A miracle; or whether Merlin's rhyme
> Or patriarchal Druids with their brood
> Of swarming Celts upheaved them, here they stand
> In Titan strength, enormous, wonderful.

There are four rows in circles, of rough, uncut stone columns, each circle within the other. Two uprights standing about twenty-five feet high, are bound by a third, resting across them on the top, and so on all the way round. This structure is in the midst of a chalk plain, and there are no stones like it nearer than Ireland. The stones weigh about eleven tons each. Where did they come from? How did a primitive people get them there? How did they raise these vast blocks and place them upon the top of the upright supports? Have other races lived, flourished and perished with high civilization before our own? I made all these inquiries and many more of the old guide at the temple, and finally he said:

"H'I can h'always tell h'Americans by the h'odd questions they ask. Now that big stone yonder fell h'over and broke in the year 1797, and when I told this to one of your countrymen he said:

"'Well, did you see it fall?'

"'Good heavens,' said I, 'that was nearly a hundred years ago.'

"Then I was only last week pointing out to a pretty young h'American lady, how only one day in the year, and that the longest day, the first rays of the rising sun come directly over that tallest stone, and strike on that stone lying down over there with the letter 'h'A' on it, which means the altar.

"'Oh,' she said, 'I suppose you have seen it more than a thousand times.'

"'Lord bless you, miss,' said I, 'it only happens once a year.'"
[Laughter.]

Henry Irving, the actor, told me that Toole, the comedian, said to him one day: "And so you have done more in twenty years to revive and properly present the plays of Shakespeare than any man living, and were never at Stratford? Let's go at once." A few hours found them roaming over all the sacred and classic scenes by the Avon. As they were returning to the hotel in the early evening, they met an agricultural laborer coming home with his shirt outside his pantaloons, with his pipe in his mouth, stolid and content. Toole asked him:

"Does Mr. Shakespeare live here?"

"No, sor. I think he be dead."

"Well, do many people come to see his grave?"

"Oh, yes, sor."

"What did he do to make these great crowds visit his house and the church where he is buried?"

"I've lived here all my life," said Hodge, scratching his head in great perplexity, "but I don't know exactly, but I think he writ somethin'."

" Well, what did he write? "

" I think," said Hodge, solemnly, " it was the Bible." [Laughter.]

After seeing the great Gladstone and the House of Commons I went to Windsor Castle, the home of the good Queen. After viewing that superbest of chapels, with its panels of rarest stones, each bearing an appropriate text, and in the center the recumbent statue of that devotedly loved husband, to whom she erected this church as a memorial; after wandering—I had almost said for miles—through drawing rooms, reception-rooms, throne-rooms, audience chambers and banqueting halls, each wonderful in its carvings, appointments, pictures, tapestries and statuaries, we came to an apartment set apart for the trophies of England's great warriors. There are the busts of the Duke of Marlborough, with mementoes of Blenheim, and of the Duke of Wellington surrounded by relics from Waterloo, and the foremast of the flagship Victory pierced by a cannon ball, and upon the top of this most appropriate standard, the colossal statue of the famous admiral of the Victory, Lord Nelson. On either side hang the two flags which the Dukes of Marlborough and Wellington must replace before 12 o'clock on the anniversaries of the battles of Blenheim and Waterloo, or lose the vast estates voted by the nation to their ancestors for those victories. On the floor, midway between these flags and surrounded by memorials of generals, princes and kings, who have filled the world with their renown, is a plain chair made from an old oaken beam taken from the little, obscure, roofless ruin in Scotland, the "Auld Alloway's haunted kirk" of Robert Burns. Thus, in the proudest room, in the most magnificent of royal palaces, the queen of that nation upon whose dominions the sun never sets, places, amidst the most precious memorials of the glory of her empire, pays this simple and effecting tribute to the genius of the humble Ayrshire plough-boy. The American, standing there in the very shadow of the throne, buttressed as it is by an hereditary legislature and proud nobility, glories in a citizenship which confers sovereignty, and with bared head repeats the lines of Burns :

> A prince can make a belted knight,
> A marquis, duke, and a' that,
> But an honest man's aboon his might,
> The rank is but the guinea's stamp.
> The man's the gowd for a' that.
> The honest man though e'er sae poor,
> Is king o'men for a' that,
> Then let us pray that come it may,
> As come it will for a' that,
> That man to man the world o'er,
> Shall brithers be for a' that.   [Loud applause.]

JAS. G. BLAINE   WM. M. EVARTS
BENJ. F. BUTLER   DAVID B. HILL

"BILL NYE."

Edgar W. Nye, whose humor reaches as far as the English language, took his pseudonym from the Bill Nye in Bret Harte's poem, "Plain Language from Truthful James." The poem was written years before "Bill Nye" became famous, and reads:

" Ah Sin was his name;
And I shall not deny
In regard to the same
What that name might imply,
But his smile it was pensive and childlike,
As I frequent remarked to Bill Nye,"

Mr. Nye, like Artemus Ward, was born in Maine. He first saw the light near the woods of Moosehead Lake. When I asked him about his life, he said:

"We moved from Moosehead Lake when I was very young, and I lived in the West among the rattlesnakes and the Indians until I grew up. I practiced law for about a year, but," he added, without changing a muscle, "nobody knew much about it ; I kept it very quiet. I was a Justice of the Peace, in Laramie, for six years."

"Did you ever marry any one?"

"O, yes, I married my wife, and after that I used to marry others, and then try them for other offenses."

Mr. Nye is the author of several books, among which are "Baled Hay" and "Bill Nye's Chestnuts," by Belford-Clarke Co. He has also contributed to the *Century Magazine*. Every newspaper in the English language is now filled with his writings.

The attention of the public was first called to the humorist's writings, on account of his vigorous English. His language was of the wild West order. For example: Some one asked the editor of *The Boomerang* the question, "What is literature?"

"What is literature?" exclaimed Bill, half contemptuously, pointing to the columns of *The Boomerang*, "What is literature?

Cast your eye over these logic-imbued columns, you sun-dried savant from the remote precincts. Drink at the never-failing *Boomerang* springs of forgotten lore, you dropsical wart of a false and erroneous civilization. Read our 'Address to Sitting Bull,' or our 'Ode to the Busted Snoot of a Shattered Venus De Milo,' if you want to fill up your thirsty soul with high-priced literature. Don't go around hungering for literary pie while your eyes are closed and your capacious ears are filled with bales of hay."

Years after Bret Harte's poem was written, Edgar W. Nye commenced signing his articles "Bill Nye." Mr. Nye always considered the best joke ever perpetrated by an English newspaper was when *The London News* came out with a serious editorial saying that "Bill Nye" was a real character. Then Mr. Nye would get his scrapbook and read this serious editorial from *The London News*:

If ever celebrity were attained unexpectedly, most assuredly it was that thrust upon Bill Nye by Truthful James. It is just possible, however, that the innumerable readers of Mr. Bret Harte's "Heathen Chinee" may have imagined Bill Nye and Ah Sin to be purely mythical personages. So far as the former is concerned, any such conclusion now appears to have been erroneous. Bill Nye is no more a phantom than any other journalist, although the name of the organ which he "runs" savors more of fiction than of fact. But there is no doubt about the matter, for the Washington correspondent of *The New York Tribune* telegraphed on the 29th instant, that Bill Nye had accepted a post under the government. He has lately been domiciled in Laramie City, Wyoming Territory, and is editor of *The Daily Boomerang*. In reference to Acting-Postmaster-Gen. Hatton's appointment of him as postmaster at Laramie City, the opponent of Ah Sin writes an extremely humorous letter, "extending" his thanks, and advising his chief of his opinion that his "appointment is a triumph of eternal truth over error and wrong." Nye continues: "It is one of the epochs, I may say, in the nation's onward march toward political purity and perfection. I don't know when I have noticed any stride in the affairs of state which has so thoroughly impressed me with its wisdom." In this quiet strain of banter, Bill Nye continues to the end of his letter, which suggests the opinion that, whatever the official qualifications of the new postmaster may be, the inhabitants of Laramie City must have a very readable newspaper in *The Daily Boomerang*.

Below I give a specimen of Mr. Nye's handwriting:

My Dear Landon,

Why did you tender me the freedom of your happy home and then name a date when I have agreed to go elsewhere? I've not been my own master for the past six Sabbaths and the next two are beyond my control.

I cannot ask you to change your date as you have no doubt already issued the ukase so far as the other eminent men are concerned, but if you insist on the 19. or 26. I shall miss a treat which no man should miss.

Yours sincerely,
Edgar W. Nye,
"Bill."

During the preparation of this book, Mr. Nye kindly sent me the following note, which gives the true history of his family:

Dear Eli: You ask me how I came to adopt the *nom de plume* of Bill Nye, and I can truthfully reply that I did not do so at all.

My first work was done on a territorial paper in the Rocky Mountains some twelve years ago, and was not signed. The style, or rather the lack of it, provoked some comment and two or three personal encounters. Other papers began to wonder who was responsible, and various names were assigned by them as the proper one, among them Henry Nye, James Nye, Robert Nye, etc., and a general discussion arose, in which I did not take a hand. The result was a compromise, by which I was christened Bill Nye, and the name has clung to me.

I am not especially proud of the name, for it conveys the idea to strangers that I am a lawless, profane and dangerous man. People who judge me by the brief and bloody name alone, instinctively shudder and examine their firearms. It suggests daring, debauchery and defiance to the law. Little children are called in when

I am known to be at large, and a day of fasting is announced by the governor of the State. Strangers seek to entertain me by showing me the choice iniquities of their town. Eminent criminals ask me to attend their execution and assist them in accepting their respective dooms. Amateur criminals ask me to revise their work and to suggest improvements.

All this is the cruel result of an accident, for I am not that kind of a man. Had my work been the same, done over the signature of "Taxpayer" or "*Vox Populi,*" how different might have been the result! Seeking as I am, in my poor, weak way, to make folly appear foolish, and to make men better by speaking disrespectfully of their errors, I do not deserve to be regarded, even by strangers, as a tough or a terror, but rather as a plain, law-abiding American citizen, who begs leave to subscribe himself,   Yours, for the Public Weal,   EDGAR WILSON NYE.

One day I asked Mr. Nye how he kept his teeth so white.

"Oh, that's easy," he said; "all teeth will remain white if they are properly taken care of. Of course I never drink hot drinks, always brush my teeth morning and evening, avoid all acids whatever, and, although I am forty years old, my teeth are as good as ever."

"And that is all you do to preserve your teeth, is it?" I asked.

"Yes, sir; that's all—barring, perhaps, the fact that I put them in a glass of soft water nights."

Somebody asked Bill what he thought of the Democratic party.

"The Democratic party?" he repeated. "Why, a Democrat keeps our drug store over there, and when a little girl burned her arm against the cook stove, and her father went after a package of Russia salve, this genial drug store Democrat gave her a box of 'Rough on Rats.' What the Democratic party needs," said Mr. Nye, "is not so much a new platform as a car-load of assorted brains that some female seminary had left over."

An Englishman was talking with Mr. Nye about English and American humor. "In my opinion," said the Englishman, "the humor of the United States, if closely examined, will be found to depend, in a great measure, on the ascendancy which the principle of utility has gained over the imaginations of a rather imaginative people."

"Just so," replied Bill, "and, according to my best knowledge, the humor of England, if closely examined, will be found just about ready to drop over the picket fence into the arena, but never quite making connections. If we scan the English literary horizon, we will find the humorist up a tall tree, depending from a sharp knot thereof by the slack of his overalls. He is just out of sight at the time you look in that direction. He always has a man work-ing in his place, however. The man who works in his place is just paring down the half sole and newly pegging a joke that has recently been sent in by the foreman for repairs."

Speaking of mean men one day, Mr. Nye remarked:

"I've seen mean men, and Laramie used to have the meanest man I ever knew—a church member, too."

"How mean was he?" asked a by-stander.

"Why, he was so mean that he kept a Sunday handkerchief, made to order, with scarlet spots on it, which he stuck up to his nose just before the plate started round, and then left the church like a house on fire. So, after he had squeezed out the usual amount of gospel, he slipped around the corner and got home ten cents ahead, and had his self-adjusting nose-bleed handkerchief for another trip."

Mr. Nye was the guest of Lawrence Barrett and Stuart Robson, at Cohasset, Massachusetts.

When asked, how he enjoyed his visit, he said:

"O, finely. Barrett enjoyed it too. You know he was in Boston during the visit. I found Robson, however, at his house, walking under the trees and thoughtfully eating green apples, of which he is passionately fond. He raises upward of sixty barrels of apples on his estate each year, any one of which is fatal.

" 'A neighbor of mine had an odd experience with his apples the other day,' said Robson. 'He has some of this same breed. It is an apple which will turn when it is trodden upon. Nobody but a cider-press can eat one and live. This friend of mine went out one day and discovered a boy, named James, sitting up in the branches of his apple tree, eating the luscious fruit, and filling his shirt and trousers with enough to stay his stomach when he got home. 'I wish you would not do that,' said the man. 'I do not care so much for the fruit, but you are breaking the tree and disfiguring it.' 'Oh you shut up,' retorted the lad, knocking the man's glasses off, together with the bridge of his nose, with a large lignum-vitæ apple. 'If you don't go into the house and keep quiet, I will come down there and injure you.' 'Very well' said the man, "I will have to go to-morrow and tell your father about you and your insulting language.' 'All right,' said the youth. 'Go in, you old pes-simist, and get the razzle-dazzle, if you wish. I will, in the mean-time, select a few more of your mirth-provoking fruit.'

DO NOT SPEAK OF IT.

See page 311.

" The next day, full of wrath, the man went over to the boy's house, and said to the father: 'Sir, I have come to do a very disagreeable duty. I have come to tell you of your boy and the insulting language he used to me yesterday."

"Do not speak of it,' said the old man, softly. 'He told the doctor and me and his mother about it last night. He was very sorry, indeed, very sorry, indeed. Your errand is unnecessary, however, sir, the boy is dead."

A few years ago the writer passed through Laramie, and was introduced to an audience by Mr. Nye. His introduction was like this :

"*Ladies and Gentlemen :*—I am glad that it has devolved upon me to-night to announce that we are to have an interesting lecture on Lying by one of the most distinguished——[There was a long pause, for Mr. Nye's inflection indicated that he had finished and the audience roared with delight, so that it was some time before the sentence was concluded.] lecturers from the East."

Mr. Nye continued, "We have our ordinary country liars in Laramie; but Mr. Perkins comes from the metropolis. Our everyday liars have a fine record. We are proud of them, but the uncultured liars of the prairie can not be expected to cope with the gifted and more polished prevaricators from the cultured East. Ladies and gentlemen, permit me to introduce to you Eliar Perkins."

" *Ladies and Gentlemen,*" I said in reply, "I feel justly flattered by your Laramie humorist's tribute to my veracity; but truly I am not as great a liar as Mr. Nye——" and then I seemed to falter. The audience saw my dilemma and applauded, and finally I couldn't finish the sentence for some moments, but continuing I said, "I am not as big a liar as Mr. Nye——would have you think."

A day or two after this I picked up *The Boomerang* and read this paragraph:

" When Mr. Perkins was passing through Laramie, he said he was traveling for his wife's pleasure.

" 'Then your wife is with you?' suggested our reporter.

" 'O, no!' said Eli, 'she is in New York.' "

BILL NYE'S BEST SPEECHES AND LECTURES.

One of Mr. Nye's happiest hits was his talk at the recent photog raphers' convention in New York. Of course it set the photographers crazy with delight. I took notes of the speech, and afterward Mr. Nye corrected them, and the speech now appears for the first time printed from the great humorist's demi-MSS. the writer, of course putting in the applause, etc.

Said Mr. Nye, after being introduced to the photographers:

Photographers and Gentlemen:—I will say a few words about the photograph habit. [Laughter.]

No doubt the photograph habit, when once formed, is one of the most baneful and productive of the most intense suffering in after years, of any with which we are familiar. Sometimes it seems to me that my whole life has been one long, abject apology for photographs that I have shed abroad throughout a distracted country.

Man passes through seven distinct stages of being photographed, each one exceeding all previous efforts in that line.

First he is photographed as a prattling, bald-headed baby, absolutely destitute of eyes, [laughter] but making up for this deficiency by a wealth of mouth that would make a negro minstrel olive green with envy. We often wonder what has given the average photographer that wild, hunted look about the eyes and that joyless sag about the knees. The chemicals and the in-door life alone have not done all this. It is the great nerve tension and mental strain used in trying to photograph a squirming and dark red child with white eyes, in such a manner as to please its parents. [Great laughter.]

An old-fashioned dollar store album with cerebro-spinal meningitis, and filled with pictures of half-suffocated children, in heavily-starched white dresses, is the first thing we seek on entering a home, and the last thing from which we reluctantly part.

The second stage on the downward road is the photograph of the boy with fresh-cropped hair, and in which the stiff and protuberant thumb takes a leading part.

Then follows the portrait of the lad, with strongly marked freckles and a look of hopeless melancholy. With the aid of a detective agency, I have succeeded in running down and destroying several of these pictures which were attributed to me.

Next comes the young man, twenty-one years of age, with his front hair plastered smoothly down over his tender, throbbing dome of thought. He does not care so much about the expression on the mobile features, so long as his left hand, with the new ring on it, shows distinctly, and the string of jingling, jangling charms on his watch chain, including the cute little basket cut out of a peach stone, stand out well in the foreground. If the young man would stop to think for a moment that some day he may become eminent and ashamed of himself, he would hesitate about doing this.

Soon after, he has a tintype taken in which a young lady sits in the alleged grass, while he stands behind her with his hand lightly touching her shoulder as though he might be feeling of the thrilling circumference of a buzz saw. He carries this picture in his pocket for months, and looks at it whenever he may be unobserved.

Then, all at once, he discovers that the young lady's hair is not done up that way any more, and that her hat doesn't seem to fit her. He then, in a fickle moment, has another tintype made, in which another young woman [laughter] with a more recent hat and later coiffure, is discovered holding his hat in her lap.

This thing continues, till one day he comes into the studio with his wife, and tries to see how many children can be photographed on one negative [laughter] by holding one on each knee and using the older ones as a background.

The last stage in his eventful career, the old gentleman allows himself to be photographed, because he is afraid he may not live through another long, hard winter, and the boys would like a picture of him while he is able to climb the dark, narrow stairs which lead to the artist's room.

Sadly the thought comes back to you in after years, when his grave is green in the quiet valley, and the worn and weary hands that have toiled for you are forever at rest, how patiently he submitted while his daughter pinned the clean, stiff, agonizing white collar about his neck, and brushed the velvet collar of his best coat; how he toiled up the long, dark, lonesome stairs, not with the egotism of a half century ago, but with the light of anticipated rest at last in his eyes—obediently, as he would have gone to the dingy law office to have his will drawn—and meekly left the outlines of his kind old face for those he loved and for whom he had so long labored. [Applause.]

It is a picture at which the thoughtless may smile, but it is full of pathos, and eloquent for those who knew him best. His attitude is stiff and his coat hunches up in the back, but his kind old heart asserts itself through the gentle eyes, and when he has gone away at last, we do not criticise the picture any more, but beyond the old coat that hunches up in the back and that lasted so long, we read the history of a noble life. [Applause.]

Silently the old finger-marked album, lying so unostentatiously on the gouty center table shows the mile-stones from infancy to age, and back of the mistakes of a struggling photographer, are portrayed the laughter and the tears, the joys and griefs, the dimples and gray hairs of one man's lifetime. [Applause.]

THE NYE–RILEY LECTURE.

The most unique, humorous lecture of the century is being delivered by Mr. Nye and James Whitcomb Riley, the Hoosier poet. It consists of unique stories by Bill Nye and humorous or pathetic poems by Mr. Riley. At one time the audience is all in tears at Mr. Riley's pathos, and then Mr. Nye gets up and sets them screaming with laughter. It don't make much difference what Bill Nye says, for his dry way of saying it is enough to convulse an audience.

Sometimes, he tells about his dog, which he called Etymologist. "I called him thus, because I understand an etymologist spends his time collecting insects, and my dog often goes out on his researches and returns with large masses of fleas. [Laughter.] Then he eats many curious things and comes home and regrets it." [Laughter.]

The humorist tells how hard it is for a reporter to succeed now-a-days. "They have to be very enterprising. A Chicago reporter was detailed to write up a case of dissection in the medical college. He was very ambitious and went to his work early in the day—hours before the dissection took place. Before the doctors assembled, he saw the corpse lying on the table. To kill time, he commenced writing a description of the room and a description of the corpse. All at once he was startled to see the corpse move and then sit bolt upright and speak.

"'Who are you?' asked the corpse.

"'I'm a writer for *The Morning News*. Eugene Field is my name. I've been sent here to describe the dissection.'

"'What are you writing about now?'

"'I'm describing the appearance of the room and the corpse.'

"'O, pshaw, young man, you're too late for that. I sent that in to the *Tribune* yesterday.'"

Mr. Nye commences his lecture like this:

*Ladies and Gentlemen :—*The earth is that body in the solar system which most of my hearers now reside upon, and which some of you, I regret to say, modestly desire to own [laughter] and control, forgetting that "the earth is the Lord's and the fullness thereof." Some men do not care who owns the world as long as they get the fullness. [Laughter.]

The earth is 500,000,000 years of age, according to Professor Proctor, but she doesn't look so to me. The Duke of Argyll maintains that she was 10,000,000 years old last August, but what does an ordinary duke know about these things? So far as I am concerned I will put Proctor's memory against that of any low-priced duke that I have ever seen. I know there is a yearning in lecture communities for the scientific lecture. I know you love to hear the figures showing the distance of endless space and the immensity of infinity. [Laughter.] These statistics about space are very valuable. Said Professor Proctor in his lecture before the Social Science Congress:

Space is very large. [Laughter.] It is immense, very immense. A great deal of immensity exists in space. [Laughter.] Space has no top, no bottom. In fact, it is bottomless both at the bottom and at the top. Space extends as far forward as it does backward, *vice versa*. [Laughter.] There is no compass of space, nor points of the compass, and no boxing of the compass. A billion million of miles traveled in space won't bring a man any nearer to the end than one mile or one inch. Consequently, in space it's better to stay where you are, and let well enough alone. [Laughter.]

This brings me to George Washington Newton:

Newton claimed that the earth would gradually dry up and become porous, and that water would at last become a curiosity. Many believe this and are rapidly preparing their systems by a rigid course of treatment, so that they can live for years without the use of water [laughter] internally or externally.

Other scientists, who have sat up nights to monkey with the solar system, and thereby shattered their nervous systems, claim that the earth is getting top-heavy at the north pole, and that one of these days while we are thinking of something else, the great weight of accumulated ice, snow, and the vast accumulation of second-hand arctic-relief expeditions will jerk the earth out of its present position with so much spontaneity, and in such an extremely forthwith manner [laughter] that many people will be permanently strabismused and much bric-a-brac will be for sale at a great sacrifice. This may or may not be true. I have not been up in the arctic regions to investigate its truth or falsity, though there seems to be a growing sentiment throughout the country in favor of my going. [Laughter.] A great many people during the past year have written me and given me their consent. [Laughter.] I feel that we really ought to have a larger colony on ice in that region than we now have.

The earth is composed of land and water. Some of the water has large chunks of ice in it. The earth revolves around its own axle once in twenty-four hours, though it seems to revolve faster than that, and to wobble a good deal, during the holidays. Nothing tickles the earth more than to confuse a man when he is coming home late at night, and then to rise up suddenly [laughter] and hit him in the back with a town lot. [Laughter.] People who think there is no fun or relaxation among the heavenly bodies certainly have not studied their habits.

A friend of mine, who was returning late at night from a regular meeting of the Society for the Amelioration of Something-or-other, said that the earth rose up suddenly in front of him, and hit him with a right of way, and as he was about to rise up again he was stunned by a terrific blow between the shoulder blades with an old land grant that he thought had lapsed years ago. When he staggered to his feet he found that the moon, in order to add to his confusion, had gone down in front of him, and risen again behind him, with her thumb on her nose.

So I say, without fear of successful contradiction, that if you do not think that planets and orbs and one thing and another have fun on the quiet, you are grossly ignorant of their habits.

The earth is about half-way between Mercury and Saturn in the matter of density. Mercury is of about the specific gravity of iron, while that of Saturn corresponds with that of cork in the matter of density and specific gravity. [Laughter.] The earth, of course, does not compare with Mercury in the matter of solidity, yet it is amply firm for all practical purposes. A negro who fell out of the tower of a twelve-story building while trying to clean the upper window by drinking a quart of alcohol and then breathing hard on the glass, [laughter] says that he regards the earth as perfectly solid, and safe to do business on for years to come. [Laughter.] He claims that those who maintain that the earth's crust is only 2,500 miles in thickness have not thoroughly tested the matter by a system of practical experiments.

The poles of the earth are merely imaginary. [Laughter.] I hate to make this statement in public in such a way as to injure the reputation of great writers on this subject who still cling to the theory that the earth revolves upon large poles, and that the aurora borealis is but the reflection from a hot box at the north pole, but I am here to tell the truth, and if my hearers think it disagreeable to hear the truth, what must be my anguish who have to tell it. [Laughter.] The mean diameter of the earth is 7,916 English statute miles, but the actual diameter from pole to pole is a still meaner diameter, [laughter] being 7,899 miles, while the equatorial diameter is 7,925½ miles. [Applause.]

The long and patient struggle of our earnest and tireless geographers and savants in past years, in order to obtain these figures and have them exact, few can fully realize. The long and thankless job of measuring the diameter of the earth, no matter what the weather might be—away from home and friends—footsore and weary—still plodding on, fatigued but determined to know the mean diameter of the earth, even if it took a leg—measuring on for thousands of weary miles, and getting farther and farther away from home, [laughter] and then forgetting, perhaps, how many thousand miles they had gone, and being compelled to go back and measure it over again while their noses got red and their fingers were benumbed and—[Great laughter.]

These, fellow-citizens, are a few of the sacrifices that we scientists have made on your behalf, in order that you may not grow up in ignorance. [Laughter.] These are a few of the blessed privileges which, along with life, liberty, and the pursuit of happiness, are ours—ours to anticipate, ours to participate—ours to precipitate. [Applause.]

When the laughter had subsided, Mr. Riley read his exquisite poem, " Afore He Knowed who Santy Claus Wuz."

Jes' a little bit o' feller—I remember still—
'Ust to almost *cry* fer Christmas, like a youngster will.
Fourth o' July's nothin' to it !—New Year's ain't a smell ;
Easter Sunday—Circus day—jes' all dead in the shell !
Lordy, though ! at night, you know, to set around and hear
The old folks work the story off about the sledge and deer,
And "Santy" skootin' round the roof, all wrapped in fur and fuzz—
Long afore
   I knowed who
      " Santy Claus " wuz !

'Ust to wait, and set up late, a week er two ahead ;
Couldn't hardly keep awake, ner wouldn't go to bed ;
Kittle stewin' on the fire, and mother settin' here
Darnin' socks, and rockin' in the skreeky rockin'-cheer.
Pap gap, and wunder where it wuz the money went,
And quar'l with his frosted heels, and spill his liniment ;
And me a-dreamin' sleigh-bells when the clock 'ud whir and buzz,
Long afore
   I knowed who
      " Santy Claus " wuz !

Size the fire-place up, and figger how "Old Santy" could
Manage to come down the chimbly, like they said he would:
Wisht that I could hide and see him—wundered what he'd say
Ef he ketched a feller layin' fer him that way !
But I *bet* on him, and *liked* him, same as ef he had
Turned to pat me on the back and say, "Look here, my lad,
Here's my pack—jes' he'p yourse'f, like all good boys does !"
Long afore
I knowed who
"Santy Claus" wuz !

Wisht that yarn was *true* about him, as it 'peared to be—
Truth made out o' lies like that-un's good enough fer me !—
Wisht I still wuz so confidin' I could jes' go wild
Over hangin' up my stockin's, like the little child
Climbin' in my lap to-night, and beggin' me to tell
'Bout them reindeers, and "Old Santy" that she loves so well ;
I'm half sorry fer this little girl-sweetheart of his—
Long afore
She knows who
"Santy Claus" is !

[Prolonged applause.]

Mr. Nye now told his famous story about little George Oswald. It was a travesty on the old-fashioned stories in the McGuffy's school readers, and proved how true merit is always rewarded:

One day, as George Oswald was going to his tasks, and while passing through the wood, he spied a tall man approaching, in an opposite direction, along the highway.

"Ah," thought George, in a low, mellow tone of voice, "whom have we here?"

"Good morning, my fine fellow," exclaimed the stranger, pleasantly. "Do you reside in this locality?"

"Indeed I do," retorted George, cheerily, dropping his cap. "In yonder cottage, near the glen, my widowed mother and her thirteen children dwell with me."

"And how did your papa die?" asked the man, as he thoughtfully stood on the other foot awhile.

"Alas, sir," said George, as a large, hot tear stole down his pale cheek and fell with a loud report on the warty surface of his bare foot, "he was lost at sea in a bitter gale. The good ship foundered two years ago last Christmastide, and father was foundered [laughter] at the same time. No one knew of the loss of the ship and that the crew was drowned until the next spring, and it was then too late."

"And what is your age, my fine fellow?" quoth the stranger.

"If I live until next October," said the boy, in a declamatory tone of voice, suitable for a second reader, "I will be seven years of age."

"And who provides for your mother and her large family of children?" queried the man.

"Indeed, I do, sir," replied George, in a shrill tone. "I toil, oh, so hard, sir, for we are very, very poor, and since my elder sister, Ann, was married and brought her husband home to live with us [laughter] I have to toil more assiduously than heretofore."

SEE WHAT I HAVE BROUGHT YOU.

See page 319.

"And by what means do you obtain a livelihood?" exclaimed the man, in slowly measured and grammatical words.

"By digging wells, kind sir," [great laughter] replied George, picking up a tired ant as he spoke and stroking it on the back. "I have a good education, and so I am enabled to dig wells as well as a man. I do this daytimes and take in washing at night. [Laughter.] In this way I am enabled to maintain our family in a precarious manner; but, oh, sir, should my other sisters marry [laughter] I fear that some of my brothers-in-law would have to suffer." [Loud laughter.]

"You are indeed a brave lad," exclaimed the stranger, as he repressed a smile. "And do you not at times become very weary and wish for other ways of passing your time?"

"Indeed I do, sir," said the lad. "I would fain run and romp and be gay like other boys, but I must engage in constant manual exercise, or we will have no bread to eat and I have not seen a pie since papa perished in the moist and moaning sea."

"And what if I were to tell you that your papa did not perish at sea, but was saved from a watery grave?" asked the stranger in pleasing tones.

"Ah, sir," exclaimed George, in a genteel manner, again doffing his cap. "I'm too polite to tell you what I would say, and besides, sir, you are much larger than I am." [Laughter.]

"But, my brave lad," said the man, in low, musical tones, "do you not know me, Georgie? Oh, George!" [Great laughter.]

"I must say," replied George, "that you have the advantage of me. Whilst I may have met you before, I can not at this moment place you, sir."

"My son! oh, my son!" murmured the man, at the same time taking a large strawberry mark out of the valise and showing it to the lad. "Do you not recognize your parent on your father's side? When our good ship went to the bottom, all perished save me. I swam several miles through the billows, and at last, utterly exhausted, gave up all hope of life. Suddenly a bright idea came to me and I walked out of the sea and rested myself. [Laughter.]

"And now, my brave boy," exclaimed the man with great glee, "see what I have brought for you." It was but the work of a moment to unclasp from a shawl strap, which he held in his hand, and present to George's astonished gaze, a large 40 cent watermelon, which he had brought with him from the Orient." [Laughter.]

"Ah," said George, "this is indeed a glad surprise. Albeit, how can I ever repay you?" [Applause.]

Mr. Riley now read, with great pathos, his story of "Jim:"

He was jes' a plain, ever'-day, all round kind of a jour.,
    Consumpted lookin'—but la!
The jokeyest, wittiest, story-tellin', song-singin', laughin'est, jolliest
    Feller you ever saw!
Worked at jes' coarse work, but you kin bet he was fine enough in his talk,
    And his feelin's too!
Lordy! ef he was on'y back on his bench agin to-day, a carryin' on
    Like he ust to do!

Any shop-mate'll tell you they never was on top o'dirt
    A better feller'n Jim!
You want a favor, and couldn't git it anywheres else—
    You could git it o' him!
Most free-heartedest man thataway in the world, I guess!
    Give ever' nickel he's worth—
And, ef you'd a-wanted it and named it to him, and it was his,
    He'd a-give you the earth!

Allus a-reachin' out, Jim was, and a-helpin' some
    Poor feller onto his feet—
He'd a-never a-keered how hungry he was hisse'f
    So's the feller got somepin to eat!
Didn't make no difference at all to him how he was dressed,
    He ust to say to me:
" You tog out a tramp purty comfortable in winter-time,
    And he'll git along! " says he.

Jim didn't have, nor never could git ahead, so overly much
    O' this world's goods at a time—
'Fore now I've saw him, more'n onc't lend a dollar and half to
    Turn 'round and borrow a dime!
Mebby laugh and joke about hisse'f fer awhile—then jerk his coat
    And kind o' square his chin,
Tie his apern, and squat hisse'f on his old shoe bench
    And go peggin' agin.

Patientest feller, too, I reckon; at every jes' naturally
    Coughed hisse'f to death!
Long enough after his voice was lost he'd laugh and say,
    He could git ever' thing but his breath—
" You fellers," he'd sorto' twinkle his eyes and say,
    " Is a pilin' onto me
A mighty big debt for that air little weak-chested ghost o' mine to pack
    Through all eternity! "

Now there was a man 'at jes' 'peared like to me,
    'At ornt't a-never died!
" But death hain't a-showin' no favors," the old boss said,
    " On'y to Jim," and cried;
And Wigger, 'at put up the best sewed work in the shop,
    Er the whole blamed neighborhood,
He says, 'When God made Jim, I bet you He didn't do any thing else that day
    But jes' set around and feel good."

Mr. Nye now told the audience how he saw a saw-mill upon the Northern Wisconsin Railway:

Northern Wisconsin is the place where they yank a big wet log into a mill and turn it into cash as quick as a railroad man can draw his salary out of the pay-car.

The log is held on a carriage by means of iron dogs while it is being worked into lumber. These iron dogs are not like those we see on the front steps of a brown stone front occasionally. They are another breed of dogs.

The managing editor of the mill lays out the log in his mind and works it into dimension stuff, shingles, bolts, slabs, edgings, two-by-fours, two-by-eights, two-by-sixes, etc., so as to use the goods to the best advantage, just as a woman takes a dress-pattern and cuts it so she won't have to piece the front breadths and will still have enough left to make a polonaise for last summer's gown. [Laughter.]

I stood there for a long time, watching the various saws and listening to the monstrous growl and wishing that I had been born a successful timber-thief instead of a poor boy without a rag to my back.

At one of these mills, not long ago, a man backed up to get away from the carriage and thoughtlessly backed against a large saw that was revolving at the rate of about two hundred times a minute. The saw took a large chew of tobacco from the plug he had in his pistol pocket and then began on him.

But there's no use going into the details. [Laughter.] Such things are not cheerful. They gathered him up out of the saw-dust and put him in a nail keg and carried him away, but he did not speak again. Life was quite extinct. Whether it was the nervous shock that killed him, or the concussion of the cold saw against his liver that killed him, no one ever knew.

The mill shut down a couple of hours so that the head sawyer could file his saw [laughter], and then work was resumed once more.

We should learn from this never to lean on the buzz-saw when it moveth itself aright.

RILEY ON ME AND MARY.

All my feelin's in the spring,
    Gits so blame contrary
I can't think of anything
    Only me and Mary!
" Me and Mary!" all the time,
    " Me and Mary!" like a rhyme
Keeps a-dingin' on till I'm
    Sick o' " Me and Mary!"

"Me and Mary! Ef us two
    Only was together—
Playin' like we used to do
    In the Aprile weather!"
All the night and all the day
    I keep wishin' that away
Till I'm gittin' old and gray
    Jist on " Me and Mary!"

Muddy yit along the pike
    Sense the winter's freezin'
And the orchard's backard-like
    Bloomin' out this season;

> Only hcerd one bluebird yit—
>   Nary robin er tomtit;
> What's the how and why of it?
>   S'pect it's "Me and Mary!"
>
> Me and Mary liked the birds—
>   That is, Mary sorto
> Liked them first, and afterwerds
>   W'y I thought I orto.
> And them birds—ef Mary stood
> Right here with me as she should—
> They'd be singin', them birds would,
>   All fer me and Mary!
>
> Birds er not, I'm hopin' some
>   I can git to plowin':
> Ef the sun 'll only come
>   And the Lord allowin',
> Guess to-morry I'll turn in
> And git down to work agin:
> This here loaferin won't win;
>   Not fer me and Mary!
>
> Fer a man that loves like me,
>   And's afeard to name it,
> Till some other feller, he
>   Gits the girl—dad-shame-it!
> Wet er dry—er clouds er sun—
> Winter gone, er jist begun—
> Out-door work fer me er none,
>   No more "Me and Mary!"

One of Mr. Nye's best stories is about William Taylor, a good little boy in Hudson, Wisconsin.

William, the son of the present American consul at Marseilles, was a good deal like other boys while at school in his old home in Hudson, Wis. One day he called his father into the library and said:

"Pa, I don't like to tell you, but the teacher and I have had trouble."

"What's the matter now?"

"Well, I cut one of the desks a little with my knife, and the teacher says I've got to pay $1 or take a lickin'!"

"Well, why don't you take the lickin' and say nothing more about it? I can stand considerable physical pain, so long as it visits our family in that form. Of course it is not pleasant to be flogged, but you have broken a rule of the school, and I guess you'll have to stand it. I presume that the teacher will in wrath remember mercy and avoid disabling you so that you can't get your coat on any more."

"But, Pa, I feel mighty bad over it, already, and if you would pay my fine, I'd never do it again. A dollar isn't much to you, Pa, but it's a heap to a boy who hasn't a cent. If I could make a dollar as easy as you can, Pa, I'd never let my little boy get flogged that way to save a dollar. If I had a little feller that got licked bekuz I didn't put up for him, I'd hate the sight of money always. I'd feel as ef every dollar I had in my pocket had been taken out of my little child's back."

"Well, now, I'll tell you what I'll do," said his father. "I'll give you a dollar to save you from punishment this time, but if any thing of this kind ever occurs again I'll hold you while the teacher licks you, and then I'll get the teacher to hold you while I lick you. That's the way I feel about that. If you want to go around whittling up our educational institutions you can do so; but you will have to purchase them afterward yourself. [Laughter.] I don't propose to buy any more damaged furniture. You probably grasp my meaning, do you not? I send you to school to acquire an education, not to acquire liabilities, so that you can come around and make an assessment on me. [Laughter.] I feel a great interest in you, Willie, but I do not feel as though it should be an assessable interest. I want to go on, of course, and improve the property, but when I pay my dues on it, I want to know that it goes toward development work. I don't want my assessments to go toward the purchase of a school-desk with American hieroglyphics carved on it. I hope you will bear this in mind, my son, and beware. It will be greatly to your interest to beware. If I were in your place I would put in a large portion of my time in the beware business."

The boy took the dollar and went thoughtfully away to school, and no more was ever said about the matter until Mr. Taylor learned, casually, several months later, that the Spartan youth had received the walloping and filed away the \$1 for future reference. [Laughter.] The boy was afterward heard to say that he favored a much higher fine in cases of that kind. One whipping was sufficient, he said, but he favored a fine of \$5. It ought to be severe enough to make it an object. [Laughter.]

Mr. Riley now gave his experience in the late war:

I was for union—you agin it—
'Pears like, to me, each side was winner;
Lookin' at now and all 'at's in it.
        Let's go to dinner.

Le's kind o' jes' set down together
And do some pardnership fergettin'—
Talk, say, for instance, 'bout the weather.
        Er somepin fittin'.

The war, you know, 's all done and ended
And ain't changed no p'ints o' the compass,
Both North and South the health's jes' splendid
        As 'fore the rumpus.

The old farms and the old plantations
Still occupies the'r old positions—
Le's git back to old situations
        And old ambitions.

Le's let up on this blame, infernal,
Tongue-lashin' and lap-jacket vauntin'
And git home to the eternal,
        Ca'm we're a-wantin'.

Peace kind o' sort o' suits my diet—
When women does my cookin' for me—
Ther' wasn't overly much pie eat
Durin' the army. [Applause.]

Mr. Nye now told some of his famous cyclone stories :

While I was traveling out in Kansas the passengers got to talking about natural phenomena and storms. I spoke of the cyclone with some feeling and a little bitter-ness, perhaps, briefly telling my own experience, and making the storm as loud, and wet and violent as possible.

Then a gentleman from Kansas, named George L. Murdock, an old cattleman, was telling of a cyclone that came across his range two years ago last September. The sky was clear to begin with, and then all at once, as Mr. Murdock states, a little cloud, no larger than a man's hand might have been seen. It moved toward the southwest gently, with its hands in its pockets for a few moments, and then Mr. Murdock discovered that it was of a pale-green color, about sixteen hands high, with dark-blue mane and tail. [Laughter.] About a mile from where he stood the cyclone, with great force, swooped down and, with a muffled roar, swept a quarter-section of land out from under a heavy mortgage without injuring the mort-gage in the least. He says that people came for miles the following day to see the mortgage, still on file at the office of the register of deeds, and just as good as ever.

Then a gentleman named Bean, of Western Minnesota, a man who went there in an early day and homesteaded it when his nearest neighbor was fifty miles away, spoke of a cyclone that visited his county before the telegraph or railroad had pene-trated that part of the State.

Mr. Bean said it was very clear up to the moment that he noticed a cloud in the Northwest no larger than a man's hand. [Laughter.] It sauntered down in a south-westerly direction, like a cyclone that had all summer to do its chores in. Then it gave two quick snorts and a roar, wiped out of existence all the farm buildings he had, sucked the well dry, soured all the milk in the milk house, and spread desola-tion all over that quarter-section. But Mr. Bean said that the most remarkable thing he remembered was this: He had dug about a pint of angle worms that morning, intending to go over to the lake toward evening and catch a few perch. But when the cyclone came it picked up those angle worms and drove them head first through his new grindstone without injuring the worms [laughter] or impairing the grind-stone. [Laughter.] He would have had the grindstone photographed, he said, if the angle worms could have been kept still long enough. He said that they were driven just far enough through to hang on the other side like a lambrequin.

The cyclone is certainly a wonderful phenomenon, its movements are so erratic and in direct violation of all known rules.

Mr. Louis P. Barker, of northern Iowa, was also on the car, and he described a cyclone that he saw in the '70's, along in September, at the close of a hot, but clear day. The first intimation that Mr. Barker had of an approaching storm was a small cloud no larger than a man's hand [laughter], which he discovered moving slowly toward the southwest with a gyratory movement. It then appeared to be a funnel-shaped cloud, which passed along near the surface of the ground, with its apex now and then lightly touching a barn or a well, and pulling it out by the roots. It would then bound l.ghtly into the air and spit on its hands. What he noticed most carefully on the following day was the wonderful evidences of its powerful suction. It sucked a milch cow absolutely dry, pulled all the water out of his cistern, and then went around to the waste-water pipe that led from the bath-room and drew a two-year-old child, who was taking a bath at the time, clear down through the two-inch waste-pipe, a distance of 150 feet. [Laughter.] He had two inches of the pipe with him and a lock of hair from the child's head.

It is such circumstances as these, coming to us from the mouths of eye-witnesses, that lead us to exclaim: How prolific is nature, and how wonderful are all her works, including poor, weak man! Man, who comes into the world clothed in a little brief authority, perhaps, and nothing else to speak of. [Laughter.] He rises up in the morning, prevaricates, and dies. Where are our best liars to-day? Look for them where you will, and you will find that they are passing away. Go into the cemetery, and there you will find them mingling with the dust, but striving still to perpetuate their business by marking their tombs with a gentle prevarication, chiseled in enduring stone. [Laughter.]

I have heard it intimated by people who seemed to know what they were talking about, that truth is mighty and will prevail, but I do not see much show for her till the cyclone season is over. [Laughter.]

RILEY'S GOOD-BYE ER HOWDY-DO.

Say good-bye er howdy-do—
What's the odds betwixt the two?
Comin'—goin'—every day—
Best friends first to go away—
Grasp of hands you'd ruther hold
Than their weight in solid gold,
Slips their grip while greetin' you—
Say good-bye er howdy-do?

Howdy-do, and then, good-bye—
Mixes jest like laugh and cry;
Deaths and births, and worst and best
Tangled their contrariest;
Ev'ry jinglin' weddin'-bell
Skeearin' up some funeral knell.
Here's my song, and there's your sigh:
Howdy-do, and then, good-bye!

Say good-bye er howdy-do—
Jest the same to me and you;
'Tain't worth while to make no fuss,
'Cause the job's put up on us!
Some one's runnin' this concern
That's got nothin' else to learn—
If he's willin,' we'll pull through.
Say good-bye er howdy-do! [Applause.]

BILL NYE MAKES ROME HOWL!

It had been a day of triumph in Capua.   Lentulus, returning with victorious eagles, had amused the populace with the sports of the amphi-theatre to an extent hitherto unknown, even in that luxurious city.   A large number of people from the rural districts had taken advantage of half rates on the railroad, and had been in town watching the conflict in the arena, listening to the infirm, decrepit ring joke, and viewing the bogus, sacred elephant.

The shouts of revelry had died away.   The last loiterer had retired from the free-lunch counter, and the lights in the palace of the victor were extinguished.   The restless hyena in the Roman menagerie had sunk to rest, and the Numidian lion at the stock yards had taken out his false teeth for the night.   The moon, piercing the tissue of fleecy clouds, tipped the dark waters of the Tiber with a wavy, tremu-lous light.   The dark-browed Roman soldier moved on his homeward way, the sidewalk flipping up occasionally and hitting him in the small of the back.   No sound was heard save the low sob of some retiring wave as it told its story to the smooth pebbles on the beach, or the unrelenting boot-jack as it struck the high fence in the back yard, just missing the Roman tom-cat in its mad flight, and then all was still as the breast when the spirit has departed.   Anon the half-stifled Roman snore would steal in upon its deathly stillness, and then die away like a hot biscuit in the hands of the hired man.

In the green room of the amphitheatre a little band of gladiators were assembled.   The foam of conflict yet lingered on their lips, the scowl of battle yet hung upon their brows, and the large knobs on their profiles indicated that it had been a busy day with them in the arena.

There was an embarrassing silence of about five minutes, when Spartacus, gently laying his chew of tobacco on the banister, stepped forth and addressed them:

"*Mr. Chairman, Ladies and Gentlemen:* — Ye call me chief, and ye do well to call him chief who for twelve long years has met in the arena every shape of man or beast that the broad empire of Rome could furnish, and yet has never squealed.   I do not say this egotistically, but simply to show that I am the star thumper of the entire outfit.

" If there be one among you who can say that ever in public fight, or private brawl, my actions did belie my words, let him stand forth and say it, and I will spread him around over the arena, till the coroner will have to soak him out of the ground with benzine.   If there be three in all your company dare face me on the bloody sands, let them come, and I will construct upon their physiognomy such cupolas and cornices and dormer windows and Corinthian capitals, and entablatures, that their own masters would pass them by in the broad light of high noon unrecognized.

"And yet, I was not always thus—a hired butcher—the savage chief of still more savage men. My ancestors came from Sparta, Wisconsin, and settled among the vine-clad hills and citron groves of Syracuse. My early life ran as quiet as the clear brook by which I sported. Aside from the gentle patter of my angel mother's slipper on the bustle of my overalls, every thing moved along with the still and rhythmic flow of goose grease. My boyhood was one long, happy summer day. We stole the Roman muskmelon, and put split sticks on the tail of the Roman dog, and life was a picnic and a hallelujah.

"When, at noon, I led the sheep beneath the shade, and played 'Little Sally Waters' on my shepherd's flute, there was another Spartan youth, the son of a neighbor, to join me in the pastime; we led our flocks to the same pasture, and together picked the large red ants out of our doughnuts.

"One evening, after the sheep had been driven into the corral, and we were all seated beneath the 'Bammygilead' tree that shaded our cottage, my grandsire, an old man, was telling of Marathon and Leuctra, and Dr. Mary Walker, and other great men, and how a little band of Spartans at Milwaukee had stood off the police, and how they fled away into the mountains and there successfully held an annual pass over the railway. Held it for a year! I did not know then what war was, but my cheeks burned, I knew not why, and I thought what a glorious thing it would be to leave the reservation and go upon the war path. But my mother kissed my throbbing temples, and bade me go and soak my head and think no more of those old tales and savage wars. That very night the Romans landed on our coasts. They pillaged the whole country, burned the agency buildings, demolished the ranch, rode off the stock, tore down the smoke-house, and ran their war horses over the cucumber vines.

"To-day I killed a man in the arena, and when I broke his helmet clasps and looked upon him, behold! he was my friend. The same sweet smile was on his face that I had known when, in adventurous boyhood, we bathed in the glassy lake by our Spartan home, and he had tied my shirt into 1,752 dangerous and difficult knots. He knew me, smiled faintly, told me always to tell the truth, and then ascended the golden stair. I begged of the Prætor that I might be allowed to bear away the body and have it packed in ice and shipped to his relatives at Sparta, Wisconsin, but he couldn't see it. As upon my bended knees, amid the dust and blood of the arena, I begged this poor boon, and the Prætor answered: 'Let the carrion rot. There are no noblemen but Romans and Ohio men. Let the show go on. Bring forth the bobtail lion from Abyssinia.' And the assembled maids and matrons and the rabble shouted in derision, and told me to 'brace up,' and they threw peanut shells at me and told me to 'cheese it,' with other Roman flings which I do not now recall.

"And so must you, fellow gladiators, and so must I, die like dogs. To-morrow we are billed to appear at the Coliseum at Rome, and reserved seats are even now being sold at No. 162 East Third Street, St. Paul, for our moral and instructive performance, while I am speaking to you.

"Ye stand here like giants as ye are, but to-morrow some Roman dude will pat your red brawn and bet his shekels upon your blood.

"O Rome! Rome! Thou hast been a tender nurse to me. Thou hast given to that gentle, timid, shepherd lad, who never knew a harsher tone than a flute note, muscles of iron and a heart of steel. Thou hast taught him to drive his sword through plaited mail and links of rugged brass and warm it in the stomach of his foe; to gaze into the glaring eyeballs of a fierce Numidian lion even as the smooth-cheeked senator looks into the laughing eyes of the chambermaid. And he shall pay thee back till the rushing Tiber is red as frothing wine, and in its deepest ooze thy life blood lies curdled. Ye doubtless hear the gentle murmur of **my** bazoo.

"Hark! Hear ye yon lion roaring in his den? 'Tis three days since he tasted flesh, but to-morrow he will have gladiator on toast, and don't you forget it, and he will fling your vertebræ around his cage and wipe his nose on your clustering hair.

"If ye are brutes, then stand here like fat oxen waiting the butcher's knife. If ye are men, arise and follow me! Strike down the warden and the turnkey, slide our baggage out the third-story window of the amphitheatre, overpower the public and cut for the tall timber!

"O comrades! Warriors! Gladiators! If we be men, let us die like men, beneath the blue sky and by the still waters, and be buried according to Hoyle instead of having our shin-bones polished off by Numidian lions, amid the groans and hisses of the populace here in Rome, New York. Let us break loose, chaw the ear of the night watchman and go to farming in Dakota! *Then* if the fierce Roman don't like our style, he knows our postoffice address." [Applause.]

BILL WRITES HIS AUTOBIOGRAPHY.

One of the most humorous things from the pen of the great humorist is his biography, written for this book.

Editor Kings of Platform and Pulpit:—I send you my autobiography, written by myself.

Edgar Wilson Nye was born in Maine, in 1850, August 25th, but at two years of age he took his parents by the hand, and, telling them that Piscataquis county was no place for them, he boldly struck out for St. Croix county, Wisconsin, where the hardy young pioneer soon made a home for his parents. The first year he drove the Indians out of the St. Croix Valley, and suggested to the North-Western Railroad that it would be a good idea to build to St. Paul as soon as the company could get a grant which would pay them two or three times the cost of construction. The following year he adopted trousers, and made $175 from the sale of wolf scalps. He also cleared twenty-seven acres of land, and raised some watermelons. In 1854 he established and endowed a district school in Pleasant Valley. It was at this time that he began to turn his attention to the abolition of slavery in the South, and to write articles for the press, signed "Veritas," in which he advocated the war of 1860, or as soon as the government could get around to it.

In 1855 he graduated from the farm and began the study of law. He did not advance very rapidly in this profession, failing several times in his examination, and giving bonds for his appearance at the next term of court. He was, however, a close student of political economy, and studied personal economy at the same time, till he found that he could live on ten cents a day and his relatives, easily.

Mr. Nye now began to look about him for a new country to build up and foster, and, as Wisconsin had grown to be so thickly settled in the northwestern part of the State that neighbors were frequently found as near as five miles apart, he broke loose from all restraint and took emigrant rates for Cheyenne, Wyoming. Here he engaged board at the Inter-Ocean Hotel, and began to look about him for a position in a bank. Not succeeding in this, he tried the law and journalism. He did not succeed in getting a job for some time, but finally hired as associate editor and janitor of the Laramie *Sentinel.* The salary was small, but his latitude great, and he was permitted to write anything that he thought would please the people, whether it was news or not.

By and by he had won every heart by his gentle, patient poverty and his delightful parsimony with regard to facts.   With a hectic imagination and an order on a restaurant which advertised in the paper, he scarcely cared the livelong day whether school kept or not.

Thus he rose to justice of the peace, and finally to an income which is reported very large to everybody but the assessor.

He is the father of several very beautiful children by his first wife, who is still living.   She is a Chicago girl, and loves her husband far more than he deserves.   He is pleasant to the outside world, but a perfect brute in his home.   He early learned that, in order to win the love of his wife, he should be erratic, and kick the stove over on the children when he came home.   He therefore asserts himself in this way, and the family love and respect him, being awed by his greatness and gentle barbarism.

He eats plain food with both hands, conversing all the time pleasantly with any one who may be visiting at the house.   If his children do not behave, he kicks them from beneath the table till they roar with pain, as he chats on with the guests with a bright and ever-flowing stream of *bon mots*, which please and delight those who visit him to that degree that they almost forget that they have had hardly anything to eat.

In conclusion, Mr. Nye is in every respect a lovely character.   He feared that injustice might be done him, however, in this biographical sketch, and so he has written it himself.   B. N.

MY GOD WHAT A CONSTITUTION HE'S GOT.

INGERSOLL.

POET, ORATOR AND CRITIC.

BIOGRAPHY AND REMINISCENCES.

Robert Green Ingersoll was born in Dresden, New York, in 1833. His father was an austere Presbyterian clergyman. In early life Mr. Ingersoll studied law and settled in Peoria, Illinois. He made many eloquent speeches in his early life, but his magnetic speech nominating Blaine to the presidency, in 1880, brought him a national reputation. His agnostic views on religious dogmas have created discussions in two hemispheres. He has measured swords with Talmage and Judge Black, and even the great Gladstone considered Ingersoll a warrior worthy of his steel. Mr. Ingersoll has written many books, which have been read on two continents, and which have been translated into German and French. His lectures on the "Mistakes of Moses," and "Liberty for Man, Woman and Child," have been listened to from San Francisco to Halifax. The great Agnostic is beloved by his personal friends for his charities and love for his fellow-man. He now resides on Fifth avenue, New York, in a beautiful home, surrounded by countless friends, his beautiful daughters and a devoted wife.

Ingersoll is the John the Baptist of Agnosticism—an eloquent voice crying in the wilderness. In writing about the eloquence and humor of the century, you could no more leave out Ingersoll than the scientists could leave out Huxley, Darwin and Herbert Spencer. Even Gladstone, who stands on the pinnacle of England's intelligence, had to come out and measure swords with the witty Agnostic. We may all differ from Ingersoll's theology, but we must love him for being the Apostle of Freedom—"freedom for man, woman and child."

Ingersoll is one of the most charming conversers of the age, and his house is constantly filled with the brainiest people of the city. There he sits, evening after evening, in the bosom of his family, charming with his wit and wisdom his delighted guests.

The comparisons of the great orator are so mirth-provoking that you break into laughter while you are being convinced.

One night, when Ingersoll was telling what the Republican party had done—how it had freed eight million slaves and saved the republic, he was interrupted by Daniel Voorhees, who said:

"Oh, bury the past, Colonel; talk about to-day. We Democrats are not always boasting of the past."

"I will tell you," said Ingersoll, "why the Democratic party wants us to bury the past. Now why should we do so? If the Democratic party had a glorious past, it would not wish to forget it. If it were not for the Republican party, there would be no United States now on the map of the world. The Democratic party wishes to make a bargain with us to say nothing about the past and nothing about character. It reminds me of the contract that the rooster proposed to make with the horse: Let us agree not to step on each other's feet."

Colonel Ingersoll is a master of ridicule. Thousands of times he has used up a witness with ridicule and laughed him out of court.

One day, in Peoria, they were trying a patent-churn case. The opposing counsel used many scientific terms. He talked about the science of the mahcine, and how his client had always been a devotee of science.

"Sir," he said, "I do not ask this verdict for my client as an ordinary man. I ask it in the interest of science, and because he has contributed to science a valuable discovery."

"Science!" yelled the Colonel; "you want this verdict for science. The burden of your speech is for science. You are deeply and tearfully concerned about science; and I see, gentlemen of the jury [looking over at the opposing counsel's brief], I see you spell science with a 'y,' sir! C-y, cy, e-n-c-e, ence, cyence, sir."

Of course this turned the laugh on the other side, and, though the Colonel had lost his case by fair argument, he won it back again by the science of ridicule.

It is thus that Mr. Ingersoll often answers the solid argument of the theologian. If he can not deny the theologian's statement or answer his argument, he ridicules it and laughs it out of court.

Ingersoll's estimates of public men are often extremely amusing.

In response to an inquiry about Robert Collyer, he said:

"Collyer, the blacksmith? He is a great soul. He has a brain full of light, the head of a philosopher. the imagination of a poet and tne sincere heart of a child. Had such men as Robert Collyer and John Stuart Mill been present at the burning of Servetus, they would have extinguished the flames with their tears. Had Dr. Pat ton and the presbytery of Chicago been there, they would have quietly turned their backs, solemnly divided their coat tails, and warmed themselves."

"What do you think of Professor David Swing ?" was asked.

"Professor Swing," said Ingersoll, "is too good a man to have stayed in the Presbyterian church. There he was a rose amongst thistles; he was a dove amongst vultures; and they hunted him out, and I am glad he came out. I have the greatest respect for Professor Swing, but I want him to tell whether the 109th Psalm is inspired."

Being questioned about superstition, Ingersoll said:

"Superstition makes men cowards. 'Are men restrained by superstition?' you ask. Are men restrained by what you call religion? I used to think they were not; now I admit they are. No man has ever been restrained from the commission of a real crime, but from an artificial one he has.

"There was a man who committed murder. They got the evi dence, but he confessed that he did it.

"'What did you do it for?' they asked.

"'Money' said the man.

"'Did you get any money?'

"'Yes.'

"'How much?'

"'Fifteen cents.'

"'What kind of a man was he?'

"'A laboring man I killed.'

"'What did you do with the money?'

"'I bought liquor with it.'

"'Did he have any thing else?'

"'I think he had some meat and bread.'

"'What did you do with that?'

"'I ate the bread and threw away the meat; it was Friday.'

"So you see," said Ingersoll, "it will restrain in some things, but, whoever is superstitious is not quite civilized. Superstition is a souvenir of the animal world. Fear is the dungeon of the soul. Superstition is the dagger by which manhood is assassinated. And as long as anybody imagines that this world was made for him, and that there is some being who will change the order on his account, that there is some being that will send a famine because he has not prayed enough, just so long the world will be full of fear."

I have often been amazed at the Colonel's ingenious arguments. To illustrate: He is opposed to the enforcement of the old Connecticut blue laws to make people good. He believes a man made good by law is not really good at heart, but is simply made to appear good. He is a legal hypocrite.

One day a fanatical talker—a Puritanical blue-law man—who was in favor of enforcing strict Sunday laws, absolute prohibition, etc., came in on the N. Y. Central train. Mr. Ingersoll heard him talk a spell, and then asked him several questions:

"Would you like to live in a community where not one cigar could be smoked and not one drop of spirituous liquor could be sold or drunk?"

"Certainly," said the blue-law man; "that would be a social heaven."

"And you would like to live where no one could play on the Sabbath day; where no one could laugh out loud and enjoy a frolic?"

"Yes sir; that would suit me. It would be paradise to live in a community where every one was compelled to go to church every Sunday, where no one could drink a drop, where no one could swear and where the law would make every man good. There the law would make every man's deportment absolutely correct."

"Then," said Mr. Ingersoll, "I advise you to go right to the penitentiary. At Sing Sing there is a community of 1,500 men and women governed in precisely that manner. They are all good by law."

It is seldom that Ingersoll meets a man who can stand up against his eloquence and wit. The great Agnostic and Talmage met on the train the other day just after a famous Christian banker had defaulted and fled to Canada.

"That's the way with you Christians," said Ingersoll. "Here is a professed Christian who has been a class leader and a vestryman, and now the hypocrite robs a bank and away he goes to Canada."

"Did you ever hear a Christian make an uproar, Colonel, when an anti-Christian committed a crime—when he robbed a bank and fled to Canada?" asked Talmage.

"I don't remember any such case now," said Ingersoll.

"No, you are not surprised when a worldly man commits a crime. You don't notice it. It is nothing unusual. You see," continued Talmage, "you expect us Christians to be perfect. You expect us to be as pure and holy as our religion."

"Of course," said Ingersoll.

"And when you say 'of course,' you pay us a compliment, and when you show great surprise that one of us should chance to do wrong, you pay us a still finer compliment. Don't you?"

Mr. Ingersoll was silent, and commenced winding his Waterbury watch.

On another occasion Beecher got a good joke on Ingersoll. The two were always great friends, for two such great hearts could not keep apart. It seems that Mr. Beecher had a beautiful globe in his study, a present from some great manufacturer. It was a celestial globe. On it was an excellent representation of the constellations and stars which compose them. There were the rings of Saturn and satellites of Uranus. Ingersoll was delighted with the globe. He examined it closely and turned it round and round.

"It's just what I want," he said. "Who made it?"

"Who made it?" repeated Beecher, "Who made this globe? O, nobody, Colonel, it just happened!"

Ingersoll was so delighted at the good point made that he could have kissed Beecher on the spot.

Speaking of science in theology and medicine, one day Mr. Ingersoll said:

"All the advance in religion ever made was caused by the heretics Luther, John Huss, Latimer and Wycliffe and others who kicked at orthodoxy."

"What of medicine?" I asked.

"Well, all the advance that has been made in the science of medicine has been made by the recklessness of patients—medical heretics. I can recollect when they wouldn't give a man water in a fever—not a drop. Now and then some fellow would get so thirsty he would say: 'Well, I'll die anyway, so I'll drink it,' and thereupon he would drink a gallon of water, and thereupon he would burst into a generous perspiration and get well, and the next morning when the doctor would come to see him they would tell him about the man drinking the water, and he would say: 'How much?'

"'Well, he swallowed two pitchers full.'

"'Is he alive?'

"'Yes.'

"So they would go into the room and the doctor would feel his pulse and ask him:

"'Did you drink two pitchers of water?'

"'Yes.'

"'My God! what a constitution you have got.'

"I tell you," continued Ingersoll, "there is something splendid in man that will not always mind. Why, if we had done as the kings told us five hundred years ago, we would all have been slaves. If we had done as the priests told us, we would all have been idiots. If we had done as the doctors told us, we would all have been dead. We have been saved by disobedience. We have been saved by that splendid thing called independence, and I want to see more of it, day after day, and I want to see children raised so they will have it. That is my doctrine. Give the children a chance."

Mr. Ingersoll was complaining, in a humorous way, one day, on the Alton train, about the hardships the people have to endure in this world. "They have cyclones in Iowa," he said, "grasshoppers in Kansas, famines in Ireland, floods in Pennsylvania, yellow fever in Galveston, George Francis Train in New York, and small pox epidemics in Baltimore. It is very hard," said Mr. Ingersoll.

"What does all this prove?" I asked.

"It proves that the universe is not governed by a personal God, but by law—law—law. There is no personal God or devil. Such ideas are only worthy of a savage. Huxley, and Darwin, and Galileo would laugh at such ideas. If there is a personal God who drowned 20,000 people in the Johnstown flood, then He is doing very queer things. But no, it was not God, it was law. Foolish men built a weak dam. By the law of gravity the weight of water broke the dam and swept saints and sinners down to death."

"If there were a personal God, and you were in his place, could you do these things better than they are being done?" asked Fitz Hugh Lee, who happened to be on the train and sat listening, attentively.

"Why, yes. I could make some things better than they are," said Mr. Ingersoll.

"Now what is one thing that you would change and improve?" asked Governor Lee. "Tell me one thing that you would make different than it is? Do you mean to say that with our feeble intellect we could improve on anything the Almighty has made?"

"Yes, certainly I could," said Ingersoll, pushed to the wall.

"Well, tell me one single thing that you could improve on."

"My dear general," said Ingersoll, "if I had my way in this world, I would make health catching, instead of disease catching!"

INGERSOLL'S GREAT LECTURE.
LIBERTY—LOVE—PATRIOTISM.

Liberty for man, woman, child, is Ingersoll's great lecture. All of his lectures would fill a volume. So we make a selection of his best thoughts.

INTELLECTUAL LIBERTY.—I do not know what inventions are in the brain of the future; I do not know what garments of glory may be woven for the world in the loom of years to be; we are just on the edge of the great ocean of discovery. I do not know what is to be discovered; I do not know what science will do for us. I do not know that science did just take a handful of sand and make the telescope, and with it read all the starry leaves of heaven; I know that science took the thunderbolts from the hands of Jupiter, and now the electric spark, freighted with thought and love, flashes under waves of the sea; I know that science stole a tear from the cheek of unpaid labor, converted it into steam, and created a giant that turns with tireless arms the countless wheels of toil; I know that science broke the chains from human limbs and gave us, instead, the forces of nature for our slaves; I know that we have made the attraction of gravitation work for us; we have made the lightnings our messengers; we have taken advantage of fire and flames and wind and sea; these slaves have no backs to be whipped; they have no hearts to be lacerated; they have no children to be stolen, no cradles to be violated. I know that science has given us better houses; I know it has given us better pictures and better books, I know it has given us better wives and better husbands, and more beautiful children. I know it has enriched, a thousand-fold, our lives, and for that reason I am in favor of intellectual liberty.

KINDNESS.—Above all, let every man treat his wife and children with infinite kindness. Give your sons and daughters every advantage within your power. In the air of kindness they will grow about you like flowers. They will fill your homes with sunshine and all your years with joy. Do not try to rule by force.

A blow from a parent leaves a scar on the soul. [Applause.] I should feel ashamed to die surrounded by children I had whipped. Think of feeling upon your dying lips the kiss of a child you had struck.

See to it that your wife has every convenience. Make her life worth living. Never allow her to become a servant. Wives, weary and worn; mothers, wrinkled and bent before their time, fill homes with grief and shame. If you are not able to hire help for your wives, help them yourselves. See that they have the best utensils to work with. Women can not create things by magic. Have plenty of wood and coal—good cellars and plenty in them.

A STRONG GOVERNMENT.—I believe in a government with an arm long enough to reach the collar of any rascal beneath its flag. I want it with an arm long enough and a sword sharp enough to strike down tyranny wherever it may raise its snaky head. I want a nation that can hear the faintest cries of its humblest citizen. I want a nation that will protect a freedman standing in the sun by his little cabin, just as quick as it would protect Vanderbilt in a palace of marble and gold. [Applause.]

AMERICAN LABOR.—I believe in American labor, and I tell you why. The other day a man told me that we had produced in the United States of America one million tons of rails. How much are they worth? Thirty dollars a ton. In other words, the million tons are worth $30,000,000. How much is a ton of iron worth in the ground? Twenty-five cents. American labor takes 25 cents of iron in the ground and adds to it $29.-75. One million tons of rails, and the raw material not worth $20,000. We build a ship in the United States worth $500,000, and the value of the ore in the earth, of the trees in the great forest, of all that enters into the composition of that ship bringing $500,000 in gold is only $20,-000; $480,000 by American labor, American muscle, coined into gold.

AMERICA FOREVER!—I have been in countries where the laboring man had meat once a year; sometimes twice—Christmas and Easter. And I have seen women carrying upon their heads a burden that no man would like to carry, and at the same time knitting busily with both hands. And those women lived without meat; and when I thought of the American laborer, I said to myself, "After all, my country is the best in the world." And when I came back to the sea and saw the old flag flying in the air, it seemed to me as though the air from pure joy had burst into blossom.

Labor has more to eat and more to wear in the United States than in any other land of this earth. I want America to produce every thing that Americans need. I want it so if the whole world should declare war against us, so if we were surrounded by walls of cannon and bayonets and swords, we could supply all human wants in and of ourselves. I want to live to see the American woman dressed in American silk; the American man in every thing from hat to boots produced in America by the cunning hand of the American toiler.

RELIGION AND SCIENCE.—What has religion to do with science or with facts? Nothing. Is there any such thing as Methodist mathematics, Presbyterian botany, Catholic astronomy or Baptist biology? What has any form of superstition or religion to do with a fact or with any science? Nothing but hinder, delay or embarrass. I want, then, to free the schools; and I want to free the politicians, so that a man will not have to pretend he is a Methodist, or his wife a Baptist, or his grandmother a Catholic, so that he can go through a campaign, and when he gets through will find none of the dust of hypocrisy on his knees.

CHRIST.—And let me say here, once for all, that for the man Christ I have infinite respect. Let me say, once for all, that the place where man has died for man is holy ground. Let me say once for all, to that great and serene man I gladly pay—I gladly pay the tribute of my admiration and my tears. He was a reformer in His day. He was an infidel in His time. He was regarded as a blasphemer, and His life was destroyed by hypocrites who have in all ages done what they could to trample freedom out of the human mind. Had I lived at that time I would have been His friend. And should He come again He will not find a better friend than I will be. That is for the man. For the theological creation I have a different feeling. If he was in fact God, He knew there was no such thing as death; He knew that what we call death was but the eternal opening of the golden gates of everlasting joy. And it took no heroism to face a death that was simply eternal life. [Applause.]

INGERSOLL'S ELOQUENT VISION.

The following remarkably eloquent words are taken from Colonel Ingersoll's brilliant address to the veteran soldiers at Indianapolis:

The past, as it were, rises before me like a dream. Again we are in the great struggle for national life. We hear the sound of preparation—the music of the boisterous drums — the silver voices of the heraldic bugles. We see thousands of assemblages, and hear the appeals of orators ; we see the pale cheeks of women, and the flushed faces of men; and in those assemblages we see all the dead whose dust we have covered with flowers. We lose sight of them no more. We are with them when they enlist in the great army of freedom. We see them part with those they love. Some are walking for the last time in quiet woody places with the maidens they adore. We hear the whisperings and the sweet vows of eternal love as they lingeringly part forever. Others are bending over cradles kissing babies that are asleep. Some are receiving the blessings of old men. Some are parting with mothers who hold them and press them to their hearts again and again, and say nothing ; and some are talking with wives and endeavoring with brave words spoken in the old tones to drive away the awful fear. We see them part. We see the wife standing in the door with the babe in her arms—standing in the sunlight sobbing—at the turn of the road a hand waves—she answers by holding high in her loving hands the child. He is gone, and forever.

We see them all, as they march proudly away under the flaunting flags, keeping time to the wild grand music of war—marching down the streets of the great cities— through the towns and across the prairies—down to the fields of glory, to do and to die for the eternal right. [Applause.]

We go with them one and all. We are by their side on all the gory fields, in all the hospitals of pain—on all the weary marches. We stand guard with them in the wild storm and under the quiet stars. We are with them in ravines running with blood—in the furrows of old fields. We are with them between contending hosts, unable to move, wild with thirst, the life ebbing slowly away among the withered leaves. We see them pierced by balls and torn with shells in the trenches of forts, and in the whirlwind of the charge, where men become iron with nerves of steel.

We are with them in the prisons of hatred and famine, but human speech can never tell what they endured.

We are at home when the news comes that they are dead. We see the maiden in the shadow of her sorrow. We see the silvered head of the old man bowed with the last grief.

The past rises before us, and we see four millions of human beings governed by the lash—we see them bound hand and foot—we hear the strokes of cruel whips— we see hounds tracking women through tangled swamps. We see babes sold from the breasts of mothers. Cruelty unspeakable! Outrage infinite!

Four million bodies in chains—four million souls in fetters. All the sacred relations of wife, mother, father and child, trampled beneath the brutal feet of might. And all this was done under our own beautiful banner of the free.

The past rises before us. We hear the roar and shriek of the bursting shell. The broken fetters fall. There heroes died. We look. Instead of slaves we see men and women and children. The wand of progress touches the auction-block, the slave-pen and the whipping-post, and we see homes and firesides and school-houses and books, and where all was want and crime and cruelty and fear, we see the faces of the free.

These heroes are dead. They died for liberty—they died for us. They are at rest. They sleep in the land they made free, under the flag they rendered stainless, under the solemn pines, the sad hemlocks, the tearful willows, the embracing vines. They sleep beneath the shadows of the clouds, careless alike of sunshine or storm, each in the windowless palace of rest. Earth may run red with other wars—they are at peace. In the midst of battle, in the roar of conflict, they found the serenity of death. I have one sentiment for the soldiers living and dead—cheers for the living and tears for the dead. [Applause.]

INGERSOLL ON CHILDREN.

"How should you treat your children?" you ask.

"Why, be perfectly honor-bright with your children," said Ingersoll, "and they will be your friends when you are old. Don't try to teach them something they can never learn. Don't insist upon their pursuing some calling they have no sort of faculty for. Don't make that poor girl play ten years on a piano when she has no ear for music, and when she has practiced until she can play 'Bonaparte Crossing the Alps,' you can't tell after she has played it whether Bonaparte ever got across or not. Men are oaks, women are vines, children are flowers, and if there is any heaven in this world, it is in the family. It is where the wife loves the husband, and the husband loves the wife, and where the dimpled arms of children are about the necks of both."

Speaking of children, Ingersoll used these burning words that same night in his Chicago lecture:

If there is one of you here that ever expect to whip your child again, let me ask you something. Have your photograph taken at the time, and let it show your face red with vulgar anger, and the face of the little one with eyes swimming in tears, and the little chin dimpled with fear, looking like a piece of water struck by a sudden cold wind. If that little child should die, I can not think of a sweeter way to spend an autumn afternoon than to take that photograph and go to the cemetery, when the maples are clad in tender gold, and when little scarlet runners are coming, like poems of regret, from the sad heart of the earth; and sit down upon that mound, and look upon that photograph, and think of the flesh, now dust, that you beat. Just think of it. I could not bear to die in the arms of a child that I had whipped. I could not bear to feel upon my lips, when they were withered beneath the touch of death, the kiss of one that I had struck. [Applause.]

I said, and I say again, no day can be so sacred but that the laugh of a child will make the holiest day more sacred still. Strike with hand of fire, oh, weird musician, thy harp, strung with Apollo's golden hair; fill the vast cathedral aisles with symphonies sweet and dim, deft toucher of the organ keys; blow, bugler blow, until thy silver notes do touch the skies, with moonlit waves, and charm the lovers wandering on the vine-clad hills; but know, your sweetest strains are discords all, compared with childhood's happy laugh, the laugh that fills the eyes with light and every heart with joy; oh, rippling river of life, thou art the blessed boundary line between the beasts and man, and every wayward wave of thine doth drown some fiend of care; oh, laughter, divine daughter of joy, make dimples enough in the cheeks of the world to catch and hold and glorify all the tears of grief. [Loud applause.]

WHY, GRANDMA, YOU CAN'T!

See page 342.

I like to hear children at the table telling what big things they have seen during the day; I like to hear their merry voices mingling with the clatter of knives and forks. I had rather hear that than any opera that was ever put upon the stage. I hate this idea of authority. I hate dignity. I never saw a dignified man that was not, after all, an old idiot. [Laughter.] Dignity is a mask; a dignified man is afraid that you will know he does not know every thing. A man of sense and argument is always willing to admit what he don't know. Why? Because there is so much that he does know; and that is the first step towards learning any thing.

Willingness to admit what you don't know, and when you don't understand a thing—ask, no matter how small and silly it may look to other people—ask, and, after that you know. A man never is in a state of mind that he can learn until he gets that dignified nonsense out of him, and so, I say, let us treat our children with perfect kindness and tenderness.

I want to tell you that you can not get the robe of hypocrisy on you so thick that the sharp eye of childhood will not see through every veil, and if you pretend to your children that you are the best man that ever lived—the bravest man that ever lived—they will find you out every time. They will not have the same opinion of father when they grow up that they used to have. They will have to be in mighty bad luck if they ever do meaner things than you have done. When your child confesses to you that it has committed a fault, take that child in your arms, and let it feel your heart beat against its heart, and raise your children in the sunlight of love, and they will be sunbeams to you along the pathway of life. Abolish the club and the whip from the house, because, if the civilized use a whip, the ignorant and the brutal will use a club, and they will use it because you use the whip.

A good way to make a child tell the truth is to tell it yourself. Keep your word with your child the same as you would with your banker. [Applause.]

Another thing: Let the children eat what they want to. Let them commence at whichever end of the dinner they desire. That is my doctrine. They know what they want much better than you do. Nature is a great deal smarter than you ever were.

Every little while some door is thrown open in some orphan asylum, and there we see the bleeding back of a child whipped beneath the roof that was raised by love. It is infamous, and the man that can't raise a child without the whip ought not to have a child.

Don't plant your children in long, straight rows, like posts. Let them have light and air, and let them grow beautiful as palms. When I was a little boy, children went to bed when they were not sleepy, and always got up when they were.. I would like to see that changed, but they say we are too poor, some of us, to do it

Well, all right. It is as easy to wake a child with a kiss as with a blow; with kindness as with a curse.

Don't always be saying to the children, "don't." You are curbing nature. Many children hear no other word but "don't" from babyhood to twenty years.

Eli Perkins tells how a dear, old "don't" grandma came to the top of the stairs and exclaimed, "Don't, boys; don't—don't slide down those banisters. I wouldn't do it!"

"Why, Grandma, you can't," said little logical Charley, as he picked himself up from the hall floor. [Laughter.]

If the old lady could have slid down the banisters as graceful as Charley did, I'll bet banister-sliding would have taken the place of the sewing society.

I was over in Michigan the other day. There was a boy over there at Grand Rapids about five or six years old, a nice, smart boy, as you will see from the remark he made—what you might call a nineteenth century boy. His father and mother had promised to take him out riding. They had promised to take him out riding for about three weeks, and they would slip off and go without him. Well, after a while that got kind of played out with the little boy, and the day before I was there they played the trick on him again. They went out and got the carriage, and went away, and as they rode away from the front of the house, he happened to be standing there with his nurse, and he saw them. The whole thing flashed on him in a moment. He took in the situation, turned to his nurse and said, pointing to his father and mother:

"There goes the two biggest liars in the State of Michigan!" [Laughter.]

When you go home fill the house with joy, so that the light of it will stream out the windows and doors, and illuminate even the darkness. [Applause.]

INGERSOLL ON WOMAN.

"But what do you think about woman?" was asked the colonel.

"Ah, there," he exclaimed, "you touch my heart."

"I don't believe man ever came to any high station without woman. There has got to be some restraint, something to make you prudent, something to make you industrious. And in a country like Santo Domingo, where you don't need any bed-quilt but a cloud, [laughter] revolution is the normal condition of the people. You have got to have the fireside; you have got to have the home, the wife, and there by the fireside will grow and bloom the fruits of the human race. I recollect a while ago I was in Washington when they were trying to annex Santo Domingo. They said: 'We want to take in Santo Domingo.'

"'We don't want it,' said I.

"'Why,' said they, 'it is the best climate the earth can produce. There is every thing you want.'

"'Yes,' said I, 'but it won't produce men, only women. We don't want it. We have got soil good enough now.'

"'Take 5,000 ministers from New England, 5,000 presidents of colleges, and 5,000 solid business men and their families, and take them to Santo Domingo, and then you will see the effect of climate. The second generation you will see barefooted boys riding bareback on a mule, with their hair sticking out of the top of their sombreros, with a rooster under each arm going to a cock-fight on Sunday.' [Laughter.]

"You have got to have the soil; you have got to have the climate, and you have got to have another thing—you have got to have the fireside, and you have got to have woman.

"It is not necessary to be great to be happy; it is not necessary to be rich to be just and generous and to have a heart filled with divine affection. No matter whether you are rich or poor, use your wife as though she were a splendid creation, and woman will fill your life with perfume and joy. And do you know it is a splendid thing for me to think that the woman you really love will never grow old to you. Through the wrinkles of time, through the music of years, if you really love her, you will always see the face you loved and won. And a woman who really loves a man does not see that he grows older; he is not decrepit; he does not tremble; he is not old; she always sees the same gallant gentleman who won her hand and heart. I like to think of it in that way; I like to think of all passions, love is eternal, and as Shakespeare says, 'Although time with his sickle can rob ruby lips and sparkling eyes, let him reach as far as he can, he can not quite touch love, that reaches even to the end of the tomb.' And to love in that way and then go down the hill of life together, and as you go down, hear, perhaps, the laughter of grandchildren, and the birds of joy and love will sing once more in the leafless branches of age. I believe in the fireside. I believe in the democracy of home. I believe in the republicanism of the family. I believe in liberty and equality with those we love.

"I despise a stingy man. I don't see how it is possible for a man to die worth fifty millions of dollars or ten millions of dollars, in a city full of want, when he meets almost every day the withered hand of beggary and the white lips of famine. How a man can withstand all that, and hold in the clutch of his greed twenty or thirty millions of dollars, is past my comprehension. I do not see how he can do it. I should not think he could do it any more than he could keep a pile of lumber where hundreds and thousands of men were drowning in the sea. I should not think he could do it. Do you know I have known men who would trust their wives with their hearts and their honor, but not with their pocketbook; not with a dollar. When I see a man of that kind I always think he knows which of these articles is the most valuable.

"Think of making your wife a beggar! Think of her having to ask you every day for a dollar, or for two dollars, for fifty cents! 'What did you do with that dollar I gave you last week?'

"Think of having a wife that was afraid of you! What kind of children do you expect to have with a beggar and a coward for their mother? Oh! I tell you if you have but a dollar in the world and you have got to spend it, spend it like a king; spend it as though it were a dry leaf and you the owner of unbounded forests! That's the way to spend it!

"I had rather be a beggar and spend my last dollar like a king, than be a king and spend my money like a beggar. If it's got to go, let it go. Get the best you can for your family—try to look as well as you can yourself.

"When you used to go courting, how nice you looked! Ah, your eye was bright, your step was light, and you just put on the very best look you could. Do you know that it is insufferable egotism in you to suppose that a woman is going to love you always looking as bad as you can? Think of it! Any woman on earth will be true to you forever when you do your level best. Some people tell me, 'your doctrine about loving and wives and all that is splendid for the rich, but it won't do for the poor.' I tell you to-night there is on the average more love in the homes of the poor than in the palaces of the rich ; and the meanest hut with love in it is fit for the gods, and a palace without love is a den, only fit for wild beasts. That's my doctrine! You can't be so poor but that you can help somebody.

"Good nature is the cheapest commodity in the world; and love is the only thing that will pay ten per cent. to borrower and lender both. Don't tell me that you have got to be rich! We have all a false standard of greatness in the United States. We think here that a man to be great must be notorious; he must be extremely wealthy or his name must be between the lips of rumor. It is all nonsense!

"It is not necessary to be rich to be great, or to be powerful to be happy; and the happy man is the successful man. Happiness is the legal-tender of the soul. Joy and love are wealth."

SAY, TOM, LET ME WHITEWASH A LITTLE?

See page 357.

"MARK TWAIN."

BIOGRAPHY AND REMINISCENCES.

Samuel L. Clemens (Mark Twain), who has done so much to make our lives sunny, was born in Hannibal, Mo., in 1835. From his brother's printing office he went on the Mississippi river as a pilot. It was hearing the cry of the soundings "Mark one! Mark twain! Mark three!" that caused him to take his pseudonym, "Mark Twain." From the river Mr. Clemens went to Nevada, and entered journalism. He afterwards removed to San Francisco and thence to the Sandwich Islands, and, returning, gave his first lecture, "Roughing It." After traveling in Europe, he wrote "Innocents Abroad." This book made him famous, and was quickly followed by "Tom Sawyer," "The Prince and the Pauper," and other sketches. On returning from the Holy Land, he became editor of the Buffalo *Express*, but finally moved to Hartford, Conn., where he now lives in a beautiful home, surrounded by a lovely family of children. Mrs. Clemens, formerly Miss Langdon, of Elmira, N. Y., is beloved by every one in Hartford.

To show the humorist's characteristic handwriting, his preface from his "Library of Wit and Humor," is reproduced:

Compiler's Apology

Those selections in this book which are from my own works, were made by my two assistant. compilers, not by me. This is why There are not more.*

Mark Twain

Hartford   *Jan. 1 1888.*

Mr. David Welcher tells me that Mark Twain when in a good humor, told him the story of his courtship, and how he won his beautiful and wealthy wife. When Mark first met her, he was not so distinguished as now; his origin was humble, and for some years of his life he had been a pilot on the Mississippi river. The future Mrs. Clemens was a woman of position and fortune; her father was a judge, and doubtless expected "family" and social importance in his son-in-law. Clemens, however, became interested in his daughter, and after awhile proposed, but was rejected.

"Well," he said to the lady, "I didn't much believe you'd have me, but I thought I'd try."

After a while he "tried" again, with the same result, and then remarked, with his celebrated drawl, "I think a great deal more of you than if you'd said 'Yes,' but it's hard to bear." A third time he met with better fortune and then came to the most difficult part of his task—to address the old gentleman.

"Judge," he said to the dignified millionaire, "have you seen any thing going on between Miss Lizzie and me?"

"What? What?" exclaimed the judge, rather sharply, apparently not understanding the situation, yet doubtless getting a glimpse of it from the inquiry.

"Have you seen any thing going on between Miss Lizzie and me?"

"No, indeed," replied the magnate, sternly. "No, sir, I have not?"

"Well, look sharp and you will," said the author of "Innocents Abroad," and that's the way he asked the judicial luminary for his daughter's hand.

Mark has a child who inherits some of her father's brightness. She kept a diary at one time, in which she noted the occurrences in the family, and, among other things, the sayings of her parents. On one page she wrote that father sometimes used stronger words when mother wasn't by, and he thought "we" didn't hear. Mrs Clemens found the diary and showed it to her husband, probably thinking the particular page worthy his notice. After this Clemens did and said several things that were intended to attract the child's attention, and found them duly noted afterward. But one day the following entry was made:

"I don't think I'll put down any thing more about father, for I think he does things to have me notice him, and I believe he reads this diary." She was Mark's own child.

When I asked R. E. Morris, of Hannibal, who went to school with Mark when he was a boy, about the great humorist's boyhood, he said, as he stopped his painting at 520 South Fourth street:

"Know Mark? I should say I do. We were school-mates."

"Sprightly boy, you say."

"Yes, he was. He was a mischievous rascal. I was born and raised in Hannibal, and know when Mrs. Clemens moved from Florida, Monroe County, to Hannibal. Mark was a dull, stupid, slow-going boy, but he was full of pranks, and while he didn't do the meanness, he planned it and got other boys to do it. We went to school to Dr. Meredith, and Mark always sat near the foot of the class. He never took any interest in books, and I never saw him study his lessons. He left school and went to learn the printing business, and soon after that left Hannibal and went to steamboating.

"I stayed at school, got a good education, and am a painter, while Mark is a millionaire. It is a scandalous fact, that as a boy, from ten to seventeen years of age, Mark was awfully dull and stupid, and it was the wonder of the town, as to what end would be his. He was pointed out by mothers, as a boy that would never amount to nothin', if he did not actually come to some bad end. And he was the most homely boy in school, too. Pranks! I can think of a dozen of 'em, and his Huckleberry Finn is full of Hannibal episodes, worked over. I read that with as much interest as I would a diary of Hannibal, kept during my school days. Mark is three years older than myself, but he was always in a class of boys two or three years younger than himself. Still I'm painting houses and Mark is dining with kings. Don't get your trousers agin the pain't.'

Mark Twain will go down to posterity as the Dickens of America. He shows a more vivid imagination than Dickens, because his early associations were in a wilder, newer and more picturesque country. Dickens was a pure humorist. He described nature as it was. He added nothing to it. Mark Twain describes nature and character as truthfully as Dickens, and then, sometimes, peppers his truthful description with imagination. This is wit. Dickens' "Little Nell," and "Smike" and "Oliver Twist" and "Fagin" are drawn true to life—dialect and all.

Mr. Clemens' writings, like "Roughing It," will always illustrate our exaggerated early American life. His reputation as a literary man will go down in history, Boston critics to the contrary.

The quaint humor of Mr. Clemens, shows itself in his every-day life. To illustrate : At a recent dinner in Boston, there was a long religious discussion on eternal life and future punishment for the wicked ; but Mark Twain, who was present, took no part in the discussion. A lady finally applied to Mr. Twain for his opinion.

"What do you think, Mr. Twain, about the existence of a heaven or hell ?"

"I do not want to express an opinion," said Mr. Twain, gravely. "It is policy for me to remain silent. I have friends in both places."

MARK TWAIN'S LECTURES AND DINNER SPEECHES.

Mr. Clemens has a quaintness about his lectures which is indescribable. "One night," writes Eli Perkins, "I sat opposite the humorist while he made an after-dinner speech. I think it was on the occasion of the Authors' Club, dining at the Gilsey House, and, if I remember rightly, his subject or toast was 'Our children.' It matters not what the occasion was, it is the speech we want. Well, I took that speech in shorthand, and I can read it to you as Mark delivered it."

"How did he look and how did he begin," you ask?

He arose slowly and stood, half stooping over the table. Both hands were on the table, palms to the front. There was a look of intense earnestness about his eyes. It seemed that the weight of an empire was upon his shoulders. His sharp eyes looked out from under his shaggy eyebrows, moving from one guest to another, as a lawyer scans his jury in a death trial. Then he commenced, very slowly:

"Our children—yours—and—mine. They seem like little things to talk about—our children, but little things often make up the sum of human life—that's a good sentence. [Laughter.] I repeat it, little things often produce great things. Now, to illustrate, take Sir Isaac Newton—I presume some of you have heard of Mr. Newton. [Laughter.] Well, once when Sir Isaac Newton—a mere lad—got over into the man's apple orchard—I don't know what he was doing there—[laughter]—I didn't come all the way from Hartford to q–u–e–s–t–i–o–n Mr. Newton's honesty—but when he was there—in the man's orchard—he saw an apple fall and he was a–t–t–racted towards it [laughter] and that led to the discovery—not of Mr. Newton—[laughter]—but of the great law of *attraction* and gravitation. [Loud laughter.]

"And there was once another great discoverer——I've forgotten his name, and I don't remember what he discovered [laughter], but I know it was something very important, and I hope you will all tell your children about it, when you get home. Well, when the great discoverer was once loafin' around down in Virginia, and a puttin' in his time flirting with Pocahontas——O, Captain John Smith, that was the man's name!——and while he and Poka were sitting in Mr. Powhatan's garden, he accidently put his arm around her and picked something——a simple weed, which proved to be tobacco—and now we find it in every Christian family, shedding its civilizing influence, broadcast throughout the whole religious community. [Laughter.]

"Now there was another great man, I can't think of *his* name either, who used to loaf around, and watch the great chandelier in the cathedral at Pisa, which set him to thinking about the great law of gunpowder, and eventually led to the discovery of the cotton gin. [Laughter.]

"Now I don't say this, as an inducement for our young men, to loaf around like Mr. Newton, and Mr. Galileo, and Captain Smith, but they were once little babies, two days old, and they show what little things have sometimes accomplished."

In a recent dinner speech, while Mr. Twain was talking about school children, he said : "In my capacity of publisher, I recently received a manuscript from a teacher, which embodied a number of answers, given by her pupils, to questions propounded. These answers show that the children had nothing but the sound to go by ; the sense was perfectly empty. Here are some of their answers to words they were asked to define : Auriferous—pertaining to an orifice [laughter]; ammonia—the food of the gods [renewed laughter]; equestrian—one who asks questions [roars of laughter]; parasite—a kind of umbrella [shouts of laughter]; ipecac—a man who likes a good dinner. [Renewed laughter.] And here is the definition of an ancient word, honored by a great party : Republican—a sinner mentioned in the Bible. [Shouts of laughter and applause.] And here is an innocent deliverance of a zoological kind: 'There are a good many donkeys in the theological gardens.' [Great laughter.] Here also is a definition which really isn't very bad in its way : Demagogue—a vessel containing beer and other liquids. [Prolonged laughter.] Here, too, is a sample of a boy's composition on girls, which, I must say, I rather like :

"'Girls are very stuckup and dignified in their maner and behaveyour. They think more of dress than anything and like to play with dowls and rags. They cry if they see a cow in a far distance and are afraid of guns. They stay at home all the time and go to church every Sunday. They are al-ways sick. They are al-ways funy and making fun of boys hands and they say how dirty. They cant play marbles. I pity them poor things. They make fun of boys and then turn round and love them. I don't belave they ever kiled a cat or anything. They look out every nite and say, 'Oh a'nt the moon lovely!' Thir is one thing I have not told and that is they al-ways now their lessons bettern boys.''

Perhaps the best parodox in the English language, was Mr. Twain's ending to his duel story, when he told the audience how opposed he was to fighting a duel.

"Why," said he, "I'm so opposed to fighting a duel—so seriously and religiously opposed to fighting a duel, that I've made up my mind, solemnly and earnestly, that if any one ever comes to me and challenges me to fight a duel, I'll take him kindly by the hand, lead him gently out, behind the barn—take an axe—and kill him!" [Loud laughter].

I never knew Mark Twain to be embarrassed but once.

"When was that?"

Well, it was when he made a speech before the Papyrus Club, of Boston, at its annual "Ladies' Night." On that occasion Mark was struck speechless. He said so himself. He admitted it. He said:

Ladies and Gentlemen:—I am perfectly astonished—a—s—t—o—n—i—s—h—ed— ladies and gentleman——astonished at the way history repeats itself. I find myself situated at this moment exactly and precisely as I was once before, years ago to a jot, to a tittle—to a very hair. There isn't a shade of difference. It is the most astonishing coincidence that ever—but wait. I will tell you the former instance, and then you will see it for yourself. Years ago, I arrived one day at Salamanca, N. Y., eastward bound; must change cars there and take the sleeper train. There were crowds of people there, and they were swarming into the long sleeper train and packing it full, and it was a perfect purgatory of rust and confusion and gritting of teeth and soft, sweet and low profanity. I asked the young man in the ticket office if I could have a sleeping section, and he answered "No," with a snarl, that shriveled me up like burned leather. I went off, smarting under this insult to my dignity, and asked another local official, supplicatingly, if I couldn't have some poor little corner somewhere in a sleeping car, but he cut me short with a venomous "No, you can't; every corner is full. Now, don't bother me any more;" and he turned his back and walked off. My dignity was in a state now which can not be described. I was so ruffled that— well, I said to my companion, "if these people knew who I am they—" but my companion cut me short there, "Don't talk such folly," he said, "if they did know who you are, do you suppose it would help your high mightiness to a vacancy in a train which has no vacancies in it?"

This did not improve my condition any to speak of, but just then I observed that the colored porter of a sleeping car had his eye on me. I saw his dark countenance light up. He whispered to the uniformed conductor, punctuating with nods and jerks toward me, and straightway this conductor came forward, oozing politeness from every pore.

"Can I be of any service to you?" he asked. "Will you have a place in the sleeper?"

"Yes," I said, "and much obliged, too. Give me any thing, any thing will answer."

"We have nothing left but the big family state-room," he continued, " with two berths and a couple of arm-chairs in it, but it is entirely at your disposal. Here, Tom, take these satchels aboard."

Then he touched his hat and we and the colored Tom moved along. I was bursting to drop just one little remark to my companion, but I held in and waited. Tom made us comfortable in that sumptuous great apartment, and then said, with many bows and a perfect affluence of smiles:

"Now is dey anything you want, sah? case you kin have jes' any thing you wants. It don't make no difference what it is."

"Can I have some hot water and a tumbler at nine to-night, blazing hot?" I asked.

"You know about the right temperature for a hot Scotch punch."

"Yes, sah, dat you kin; you kin pen on it, I'll get it myself."

"Good! now that lamp is hung too high. Can I have a big coach candle fixed up just at the head of my bed, so that I can read comfortably?"

"Yes, sah; you kin, I'll fix her up myself, an' I'll fix her so she'll burn all night. Yes, sah; an' you can jes' call for any thing you want, and dish yer whole railroad 'll be turned wrong end up, an' inside out for to get it for you. Dat's so." And he disappeared.

Well, I tilted my head back, hooked my thumbs in my arm-holes, smiled a smile on my companion, and said, gently:

"Well, what do you say now?"

My companion was not in a humor to respond, and didn't. The next moment that smiling black face was thrust in at the crack of the door, and this speech followed:

"Laws bless you, sah, I knowed you in a minute. I told de conductah so. Laws! I knowed you de minute I sot eyes on you."

"Is that so, my boy? (Handing him a quadruple fee.) Who am I?"

"Jenuel McClellan," and he disappeared again.

My companion said, vinegarishly, " Well, well! what do you say now?" Right there comes in the marvelous coincidence I mentioned a while ago, viz., I was speechless and that is my condition now. Perceive it?

Mr. Twain was about as much astonished as old Mrs. Bagley, when Higgins announced the death of her husband out in Nevada. But we will let Mark tell it:

"Higgins was a simple creature," said Mark, with a tearful pathos in his voice and a sad look in his eye, "a very simple fellow. He used to haul coal for old Malthy. When the lamented Judge Bagley tripped and fell down the court-house stairs and broke his neck, it was a great question how to break the news to poor Mrs. Bagley. But finally the body was put into Higgins' wagon, and he was instructed to take it to Mrs. B.; but to be very guarded and discreet in his language, and not break the news to her at once, but to do so gradually and gently. When Higgins got there with his sad freight, he shouted till Mrs. Bagley came to the door.

"Then he said, 'Does the widder Bagley live here?'

"'The widow Bagley? No, sir!'

"'I'll bet she does. But have it your own way. Well, does Judge Bagley live here?'

"'Yes, judge Bagley lives here.'

"'I'll bet he don't. But never mind, it ain't for me to contradict. Is the judge in?'

"'No, not at present.'

"'I jest expected as much. Because, you know—take hold o' suthin, mum, for I'm agoing to make a little communication, and I reckon maybe it'll jar you some. There's been an accident, mum. I've got the old judge curled up out here in the wagon, and when you see him you'll acknowledge yourself that an inquest is about the only thing that could be a comfort to him!'"

It seems that social matters were conducted in a pretty rude manner out in Nevada about the time Mark Twain described "Scotty Briggs Funeral." There is no doubt but that Mr. Twain's descriptions were generally true to life. The humorist tells about another funeral out there quite as strange as the obsequies of Scotty Briggs. He says:

The church was densely crowded that lovely summer Sabbath, and all, as their eyes rested upon the small coffin, seemed impressed by the poor black boy's fate. Above the stillness the pastor's voice rose and chained the interest of every one, as he told, with many an envied compliment, how that the brave, noble, daring, little Johnny Greer, when he saw the drowned body sweeping down toward the deep part of the river whence the agonized parents never could have recovered it in this world, gallantly sprung into the stream and, at the risk of his life, towed the corpse to shore and held it fast till help came and secured it. Johnny Greer was sitting just in front of me. A ragged street boy, with eager eye, turned upon him instantly and said in a hoarse whisper:

"No—but did you though?"

"Yes."

"Towed the carkis ashore and saved it yo'self? Cracky! What did they give you?"

"Nothing,

"W-h-a-t! (with intense disgust.) D'you know what I'd a done? I'd a anchored him out in the stream and said, 'five dollars, gents, or you can't have yo' nigger.'"
[Laughter.]

"It is very amusing when Mr. Twain makes Buck Grangerford tell what a feud is. Buck had just shot at a man in the woods.

"Did you want to kill him Buck?" asked Huckleberry Finn.

"Well, I bet I did."

"What did he do to you?"

"Him? He never done nothing to me."

"Well, then, what did you want to kill him for?"

"Why, nothing—only it's on account of the feud."

"What's a feud?"

"Why, where was you raised? Don't you know what a feud is?"

"Never heard of it before—tell me about it."

"Well," says Buck, "a feud is this way: A man has a quarrel with another man, and kills him; then that other man's brother kills him; then the other brothers, on both sides, go for one another; then the cousins chip in—and by-and-by every body's killed off, and there ain't no more feud. But it's kind of slow and takes a long time." [Laughter.]

MARK TWAIN'S MASTERPIECE.

Tom Sawyer having offended his sole guardian, Aunt Polly, is by that sternly affectionate dame punished by being sent to whitewash the fence in front of the garden. The world seemed a hollow mockery to Tom, who had planned fun for that day, and he knew that he would be the laughing stock of all the boys as they came past, and saw him set to work like a "nigger." But a great inspiration burst upon him, and he went tranquilly to work. What that inspiration was will appear from what follows.

One of the boys, Ben Rogers, comes by and pauses, eating a particularly fine apple. Tom does not see him. Ben stares a moment, and then says:

"Hi-yi! you're up a stump, ain't you?"

No answer. Tom surveyed his last touch with the eye of an artist, then he gave another gentle sweep, and surveyed the result as before. Ben ranged up alongside of him. Tom's mouth watered for the apple, but he stuck to his work. Ben said:

"Hello, old chap, you got to work, hey?"

"Why, it's you, Ben; I wasn't noticing."

"Say, I'm going in a-swimming, I am. Don't you wish you could? But of course you'd ruther work, wouldn't you? Course you would!"

Tom contemplated the boy a bit, and said:

"What do you call work?"

"Why, ain't that work?"

Tom resumed his whitewashing, and answered, carelessly:

"Well, may be it is, and may be it ain't. All I know is, it suits Tom Sawyer."

"Oh, come now, you don't mean to let on that you like it?"

The brush continued to move.

"Like it? Well, I don't see why I oughtn't to like it. Does a boy get a chance to whitewash a fence every day?"

That put the thing in a new light. Ben stopped nibbling his apple. Tom swept his brush daintly back and forth—stepped back to note the effect—added a touch here and there—criticised the effect again, Ben watching every move, and getting more and more interested, more and more absorbed. Presently he said:

"Say, Tom, let me whitewash a little."

Tom considered—was about to consent—but he altered his mind. "No, no; I reckon it wouldn't hardly do, Ben. You see, Aunt Polly's awful particular about this fence—right here on the street, you know—but if it was the back fence I wouldn't mind, and she wouldn't. Yes, she's awful particular about this fence; it's got to be done very careful; I reckon there ain't one boy in a thousand, may be two thousand, that can do it in the way it's got to be done."

"No—is that so? Oh, come now; lemme just try, only just a little. I'd let you, if you was me, Tom."

"Ben, I'd like to, honest Injun; but Aunt Polly—well, Jim wanted to do it, but she wouldn't let him. Sid wanted to do it, but she wouldn't let Sid. Now don't you see how I'm fixed? If you was to tackle this fence, and anything was to happen to it——"

"Oh, shucks! I'll be just as careful. Now lemme try. Say—I'll give you the core of my apple."

"Well, here. No, Ben; now don't; I'm afeard——"

"I'll give you all of it!"

Tom gave up the brush with reluctance in his face, but alacrity in his heart. And while Ben worked and sweated in the sun, the retired artist sat on a barrel in the shade close by, dangling his legs, munched his apple, and planned the slaughter of more innocents. There was no lack of material; boys happened along every little while; they came to jeer, but remained to whitewash. By the time Ben was fagged out, Tom had traded the next chance to Billy Fisher for a kite in good repair; and when he played out, Johnny Miller bought it for a dead rat and a string to swing it with; and so on, and so on, hour after hour. And when the middle of the afternoon came, from being a poor, poverty-stricken boy in the morning, Tom was literally rolling in wealth. He had, besides the things I have mentioned, twelve marbles, part of a jew's harp, a piece of blue bottle-glass to look through, a spool cannon, a key that wouldn't unlock anything, a fragment of chalk, a glass stopper of a decanter, a tin soldier, a couple of tadpoles, six fire-crackers, a kitten with only one eye, a brass door-knob, a dog-collar—but no dog—the handle of a knife, four pieces of orange-peel, and a dilapidated old window sash. He had had a nice, good, idle time all the while—plenty of company—and the fence had three coats of whitewash on it! If he hadn't run out of whitewash, he would have bankrupted every boy in the village.

Tom said to himself that it was not such a hollow world after all. He had discovered a great law of human action without knowing it, namely, that in order to make a man or a boy covet a thing, it is only necessary to make it difficult to attain.

A dinner speech that the Scotch newspapers could never understand was Mark's at the anniversary festival of the Scottish Corporation of London. In response to the toast of "The Ladies," Mark Twain replied. The following is the speech as reported in the *London Observer :*

I am proud, indeed, of the distinction of being chosen to respond to this especial toast, to " The Ladies," or to women if you please, for that is the preferable term, perhaps; it is certainly the older, and therefore the more entitled to reverence. [Laughter.] I have noticed that the Bible, with that plain, blunt honesty which is such a conspicuous characteristic of the Scriptures, is always particular to never refer to even the illustrious mother of all mankind herself as a "lady," but speaks of her as a woman. [Laughter] It is odd, but you will find it is so. I am peculiarly proud of this honor, because I think that the toast to women is one which, by right and by every rule of gallantry, should take precedence of all others—of the army, of the navy, of even royalty itself—perhaps, though the latter is not necessary in this day and in this land, for the reason that, tacitly, you do drink a broad general health to all good women when you drink the health of the Queen of England and the Princess of Wales. [Loud cheers.] I have in mind a poem just now which is familiar to you all, familiar to every body. And what an inspiration that was (and how instantly the present toast recalls the verses to all our minds) when the most noble, the most gracious, the purest, and sweetest of all poets says:

> "Woman! O woman!—er—
> Wom——"

[Laughter.] However, you remember the lines; and you remember how feelingly, how daintily, how almost imperceptibly, the verses rise up before you, and as you contemplate the finished marvel, your homage grows into worship of the intellect that could create so fair a thing out of mere breath, mere words. And you call to mind now, as I speak, how the poet, with stern fidelity to the history of all humanity, delivers this beautiful child of his heart and his brain over to the trials and the sorrows that must come to all, sooner or later, that abide in the earth, and how the pathetic story culminates in that apostrophe—so wild, so regretful, so full of mournful retrospection. The lines run thus:

> " Alas!—alas!—a—alas.
> ———Alas!———alas!"

—and so on. [Laughter.] I do not remember the rest; but, taken altogether, it seems to me that poem is the noblest tribute to woman that human genius has ever brought forth—[laughter]—and I feel that if I were to talk hours I could not do my great theme completer or more graceful justice than I have done now in simply quoting that poet's matchless words. [Renewed laughter.] The phases of the womanly nature are infinite in their variety. Take any type of woman, and you shall find in it something to respect, something to admire, something to love. And you shall find the whole joining you heart and hand. Who was more patriotic than Joan of Arc? Who was braver? Who has given us a grander instance of self-sacrificing devotion? Ah! you remember, you remember well, what a throb of pain, what a great tidal wave of grief swept over us all when Joan of Arc fell at Waterloo. [Much laughter.] Who does not sorrow for the loss of Sappho, the sweet singer of Israel? [Laughter.] Who among us does not miss the gentle ministrations, the softening influences, the humble piety, of Lucretia Borgia? [Laughter] Who can join in the heartless libel that says woman is extravagant in dress when he can look back and call to mind our simple and lowly mother Eve arrayed in her modification of the Highland costume. [Roars of laughter.] Sir, women have been soldiers, women have been painters, women have been poets. As long as language lives the name of Cleopatra will live. And not because she conquered George III.—[laughter] —but because she wrote those divine lines:

> " Let dogs delight to bark and bite,
> For God hath made them so."

[More laughter.] The story of the world is adorned with the names of illustrious ones of our own sex—some of them sons of St. Andrew too—Scott, Bruce, Burns, the warrior Wallace, Ben Nevis—[laughter]—the gifted Ben Lomond, and the great new Scotchman, Ben Disraeli.* [Great laughter.] Out of the great plains of history tcwer whole mountain ranges of sublime women—the Queen of Sheba, Josephine, Semiramis, Sairey Gamp; the list is endless—[laughter]—but I will not call the mighty roll, the names rise up in your own memories at the mere suggestion, luminous with the glory of deeds that can not die, hallowed by the loving worship of the good and the true of all epochs and all climes. [Cheers.] Suffice it for our pride and our honor that we in our day have added to it such names as those of Grace Darling and Florence Nightingale. [Cheers.] Woman is all that she should be—gentle, patient, long-suffering, trustful, unselfish, full of generous impulses. It is her blessed mission to comfort the sorrowing, plead for the erring, encourage the faint of purpose, succor the distressed, uplift the fallen, befriend the friendless—in a word, afford the healing of her sympathies and a home in her heart for all the bruised and persecuted children of misfortune that knock at its hospitable door. [Cheers.] And when I say, God bless her, there is none among us who has known the ennobling affection of a wife, or the steadfast devotion of a mother but in his heart will say, Amen! [Loud and prolonged cheering.]

---

* Mr. Benjamin Disraeli, at that time Prime Minister of England, had just been elected Lord Rector of Glasgow University, and had made a speech which gave rise to a world of discussion.

DWIGHT L. MOODY.

THE GREAT REVIVALIST.

BIOGRAPHY AND REMINISCENCES.

Dwight L. Moody, the evangelist of the nineteenth century, was born at North-field, Mass., February 5, 1837. His father lived in an old-fashioned frame house, and, by farming a few acres and working at his trade (which was that of a stone mason) earned a comfortable living for his family. This comprised seven children, of which Dwight was the youngest. When Dwight was but four years old, his father died suddenly. Mrs. Moody bore with a brave heart the weight of the family cares and steadfastly refused to part from any of her children.

Through poverty and self denial Dwight grew up — a sturdy, healthy, self-reliant boy. He was full of animal spirits, and liked fun and anecdotes so much more than study that his record in school was poor; but he was observant, watchful and susceptible to lessons learned from real life or nature.

At the age of seventeen, he left Northfield for Boston. After long search for employment, his uncle, Samuel S. Holton, a shoe merchant, agreed to hire him at a small salary. He soon became an attendant at the Congregational church. Through the direct personal effort of his teacher in the Sunday-school, he was converted, and gave himself to the service of God. At the age of twenty Mr. Moody left Boston for Chicago, in order that he might have a more extended field. He found it. As teacher in Sunday-school, as street solicitor for scholars, as mission worker among sailors, visitor to prisons and hospitals, his work was constant and self-denying. A little later he hired a vacant room in a degraded portion of Chicago, and, gathering around him crowds of abandoned men and women and unfortunate children, he preached the gospel to them and saved many souls. A larger room became necessary, and within a year the average attendance at his Sunday-school was 650.

In 1860 he was made city missionary of the Young Men's Christian Association, made longer tours over the city, assisting destitute families and praying with them.

In 1861 he became active in the organization of a system of visitation and prayer meetings among the troops gathered at Camp Douglas, near the city of Chicago. After the fall of Donelson, in February, 1862, he was sent to bear consolation to wounded and dying volunteers. Many of his most vivid and impressive anecdotes and illustrations are drawn from incidents in his battle-field experience.

In 1862 he was married to Miss Emma C. Revell. His wife was an active worker in missions, and in harmony with his self-denying life. To them have been born two children—Emma and Willie—whose names are often mentioned in his anecdotes.

In 1863 a large building was erected in Chicago for his Sunday-school and congregation. This was burned in the great fire of 1871. Mr. Moody then went East, holding revivals in Brooklyn, Philadelphia and elsewhere, receiving contributions to rebuild his church. He was thus enabled to build a mammoth wooden tabernacle on the old site. One thousand children were present on the Sunday after it was finished. Finding the demand for evangelical labor in other fields urgent, he began to visit other cities and churches and hold special religious services. In nearly all the large cities of the Union he has labored successfully. In 1871 he met Mr. Ira D. Sankey, the sweet singer, and soon associated him as a co-worker in the ripened harvest field. Together they labored in America, England, Ireland, Scotland, and both at home and abroad created such a revival of religious interest as this century had not seen before.

A devout student of the Bible, uneducated, except in the art of saving souls, intensely earnest, untiring in activity, Dwight L. Moody is the foremost evangelist of the century.

His weapon to convert men's souls has been the typical story— the modern parable. His best anecdotes and stories are contributed to this book, and no parables except those of our Saviour are better or more powerful for good.

In speaking of the necessity of a new birth, one day, Mr. Moody said : "The sinner must have a new heart. A man has bought a farm, and he finds on that farm an old pump. He goes to the pump and begins to pump. And a person comes to him and says:

"'Look here, my friend, you do not want to use that water. The man that lived here before, he used that water, and it poisoned him and his wife and his children—the water did.'

"'Is that so?' says the man. 'Well, I will soon make that right. I will find a remedy.' And he goes and gets some paint, and he paints up the pump, putties up all the holes, and fills up the cracks in it, and has got a fine-looking pump. And he says: 'Now I am sure it is all right.'

"You would say, 'What a fool to go and paint the pump when the water is bad!' But that is what sinners are up to. They are trying to paint up the old pump when the water is bad. It was a new well he wanted. When he dug a new well it was all right. *Make the fountain good, and the stream will be good.* Instead of painting the pump and making new resolutions, my friend, stop it, and ask God to give you a new heart."

Mr. Moody is now president of the Congregational Theological Seminary, but still gives much time to revival work.

MOODY'S THEOLOGY.

STORIES, ANECDOTES, PATHOS, RELIGION.

The sunny side of life will be in heaven; still there is sunlight here. Love is sunlight, the kiss of love is a ray of sunlight and it will melt a human soul. Christianity is all sunlight. It is a kiss for a blow. A soul can be warmed with love and love will save it.

One day a Christian gentleman came to me, all in tears. He said: "I have just gotten my brother out of the penitentiary. Will you not take an interest in him? Let me bring him to you. Will you be introduced to a convict?"

"Bring him to me," I said. "Let me take him by the hand. Let us see what kindness and love will do."

The gentleman brought him in and introduced him, and I took him by the hand and told him I was glad to see him. I invited him up to my house, and when I took him into my family I introduced him as a friend. When my little daughter came into the room, I said:

"Emma, this is papa's friend." And she went up and kissed him, and the man sobbed aloud. After the child left the room, I said,

"What is the matter?"

"O, sir," he said, "I have not had a kiss for years. The last kiss I had was from my mother, and she was dying. I thought I would never have another one again."

His heart was broken.

A lady came into the office of the New York City Mission, and said that, although she did not think she could do very much of active work for the Lord, yet she should like to distribute a few tracts. One day she saw a policeman taking a poor drunken woman to jail—a miserable object, ragged, dirty, with hair disordered; but the lady's heart went out in sympathy toward her. She found the woman after she came out of jail, and just went and folded her arms around her and kissed her. The woman exclaimed, "My God ! *what did you do that for?*" and she replied:

"I don't know, but I think Jesus sent me to do it."

"Oh, don't kiss me any more," said the woman, "you'll break my heart. Why, nobody hasn't kissed me since my mother died."

But that kiss brought the woman to the feet of the Saviour, and for the last three years she has been living a godly, Christian life, won to God by a kiss.

A KISS IS BETTER THAN A BLOW.

One morning my dear little daughter Emma got up cross and spoke in a cross way, and finally I said to her:

" Emma, if you speak in that way again, I shall have to punish you."

Now it was not because I didn't love her ; it was because I did love her, and if I had to correct her it was for the good of the little child. One morning she got up cross again. I said nothing, but when she was getting ready to go to school she came up to me and said:

" Papa kiss me."

I said, " Emma, I can not kiss you this morning."

" Why, father ?"

" Because you have been cross again this morning. I can not kiss you."

" Why, papa, " said Emma, " you never refused to kiss me before."

" Well, you have been naughty this morning."

" Why don't you kiss me? " she said again.

" Because you have been naughty. You will have to go to school without your kiss."

She went into the other room where her mother was and said, " Mamma, papa don't love me. He won't kiss me. I wish you would go and get him to kiss me."

" You know, Emma," said her mother, " that your father loves you, but you have been naughty."

So she couldn't be kissed and she went down stairs crying as if her heart would break, and I loved her so well that the tears came into my eyes. I could not help crying, and when I heard her going down stairs I could not keep down my tears. I think I loved her then better than I ever did, and when I heard the door close I went to the window and saw her going down the street weeping. I didn't feel good all that day. I believe I felt a good deal worse than the child did, and I was anxious for her to come home. How long that day seemed to me. And when she came home at night and came to me and asked me to forgive her, and told me how sorry she felt, how gladly I took her up and kissed her, and how happy she went up stairs to her bed. It is just so with God. He loves you, and when He chastises you, it is for your own good. If you will only come to Him and tell Him how sorry you are, how gladly He will receive you and how happy you will make Him, and oh, how happy you will be yourself.

THE MOTHER RULES BY LOVE.—The other night I was talking in the inquiry-room to a noble-looking young man, who was in great agony of soul. I asked him what had made him anxious. Was it the address or any of the hymns? He looked up in my face, and said, "It was my mother's letter." She had written him, asking him to attend that meeting, and had said she would be praying for him when he was at the meeting. The thought of his mother's prayers and agony had gone home to his heart, and that night he found the Savior.

THE CHURCH WINS BY LOVE.—In Chicago, a few years ago, there was a little boy who went to one of the mission Sunday-schools. His father moved to another part of the city, about five miles away, and every Sunday that boy came past thirty or forty Sunday-schools to the one he attended. And one Sunday a lady, who was out collecting scholars for a Sunday-school, met him and asked why he went so far, past so many schools.

"There are plenty of others," said she, "just as good."

"They may be as good," said the boy, "but they are not so good for me."

"Why not?" she asked.

"Because they love a fellow over there," he answered.

Ah! love won him. "Because they love a fellow over there!" How easy it is to reach people through love! Sunday-school teachers should win the affections of their scholars if they wish to lead them to Christ.

LOVE HAS SAVED A MOTHER.—I remember when on the North Side I tried to reach a family time and again and failed. One night in the meeting I noticed one of the little boys of that family. He hadn't come for any good, however; he was sticking pins in the backs of the other boys. I thought if I could get hold of him it would do good. I used always to go to the door and shake hands with the boys, and when I got to the door and saw this little boy coming out, I shook hands with him, and patted him on the head, and said I was glad to see him, and hoped he would come again. He hung his head and went away. The next night, however, he came back, and he behaved better than he did the previous night. He came two or three times after, and then asked us to pray for him that he might become a Christian. That was a happy night for me. He became a Christian and a good one. One night I saw him weeping. I wondered if his old temper had got hold of him again, and when he got up I wondered what he was going to say.

"I wish you would pray for my mother," he said. When the meeting was over I went to him and asked, "Have you ever spoken to your mother or tried to pray with her?"

"Well, you know, Mr. Moody," he replied, "I never had an opportunity; she don't believe, and won't hear me."

"Now," I said, "I want you to talk to your mother to-night." For years I had been trying to reach her and couldn't do it.

So I urged him to talk to her that night, and I said, "I will pray for you both." When he got to the sitting-room he found some people there, and he sat waiting for an opportunity, when his mother said it was time for him to go to bed. He went to the door undecided. He took a step, stopped, and turned around, and hesitated for a minute, then ran to his mother and threw his arms around her neck, and buried his face in her bosom. "What is the matter?" she asked—she thought he was sick. Between his sobs he told his mother how for five weeks he had wanted to be a Christian; how he had stopped swearing; how he was trying to be obedient to her and how happy he would be if she would be a Christian, and then went off to bed. She sat for a few minutes, but couldn't stand it, and went up to his room. When she got to the door she heard him weeping and praying, "Oh, God, convert my dear mother." She came down again, but couldn't sleep that night. Next day she told the boy to go and ask Mr. Moody to come over and see her. He called at my place of business—I was in business then—and I went over as quiet as I could. I found her sitting in a rocking-chair weeping. "Mr. Moody," she said, "I want to become a Christian." "What has brought that change over you, I thought you didn't believe in it?" Then she told me how her boy had come to her, and how she hadn't slept any all night, and how her sin rose up before her like a dark mountain. The next Sunday that boy came and led that mother into the Sabbath-school and she became a Christian worker.

Oh, little children, if you find Christ tell it to your fathers and mothers. Throw your arms around their necks and lead them to Jesus!

LOVE WON A COAL MINER.—When I was holding meetings a little time ago at Wharnecliff, in England, a coal district, a great burly collier came up to me and said, in his Yorkshire dialect:

"Dost know wha was at meetin' t'night, Mr. Moody?"

"No," I answered.

"Why," said he, "Sandy Sykes was there."

The name was a familiar one. Sandy was a very bad man, one of the wildest, wickedest men in Yorkshire, according to his own confession, and according to the confession of every body who knew him.

"Well," said the man, "he cam' into meetin' an' said you didn't preach right; he said thou didn't preach nothin' but the love o' Christ, an' that won't do for drunken colliers; ye wan't shake 'em over a pit, and he says he'll ne'er come again."

Sandy thought I didn't preach about hell.   Mark you, my friends, I believe in the pit that burns, in the fire that's never quenched, in the worm that never dies; but I believe that the magnet that goes down to the bottom of the pit is the love of Jesus.   I didn't expect to see Sandy again, but he came the next night, without washing his face, right from the pit, with all his working clothes upon him.   This drunken collier sat down on one of the seats that were used for the children, and got as near to me as possible.   The sermon was love from first to last.   He listened at first attentively, but by-and-by I saw him with the sleeve of his rough coat, wiping his eyes.   Soon after we had an inquiry meeting, when some of those praying colliers got around him, and it wasn't long before he was crying:

"O, Lord, save me; I am lost; Jesus have mercy upon me;" and he left that meeting a new creature.   His wife told me herself what occurred when he came home.   His little children heard him coming along—they knew the step of his heavy clogs—and ran to their mother in terror, clinging to her skirts.   He opened the door as gently as could be.   He had had a habit of banging the doors.   When he came into the house and saw the children clinging to their mother, frightened, he just stooped down and picked up the youngest girl in his arms, and looked at her, the tears rolling down his cheeks.

"Mary, God has sent thy father home to thee," and kissed her.

He picked up another, "God has sent thy father home," and from one to another he went, and kissed them all; and then came to his wife and put his arms around her neck,

"Don't cry, lass," he sobbed, "don't cry.   God has sent thy husband home at last; don't cry," and all she could do was to put her arms around his neck and sob.   And then he said: "Have you got a Bible in the house, lass?"   They hadn't such a thing.   "Well, lass, if we haven't we must pray."   They got down on their knees, and all he could say was:

> "Gentle Jesus, meek and mild,
> Look upon a little child;
> Pity my simplicity—

for Jesus Christ's sake, amen."   It was a simple prayer, but God answered it.   While I was at Barnet, some time after that, a friend came to me and said: "I've got good news for you; Sandy Sykes is preaching the gospel everywhere he goes—in the pit, and out of the pit, and is winning every body to the Lord Jesus Christ."

JESUS SAVES BY LOVE.—An aged man, over ninety years of age, was asked by his pastor this question:

"My dear aged friend, do you love Jesus?"

His deeply-furrowed face was lit up with a smile that sixty-seven years of discipleship had imparted, and grasping my hand with both of his, said:

" Oh! I can tell you something better than that."

" What is that ? " I asked.

" Oh, sir ! " he said. " He loves me."

LOVE SAVES THE CHILDREN.—My little boy had some trouble with his sister one Saturday and he did not want to forgive her. And at night he was going to say his prayers and I wanted to see how he would say his prayers, and he knelt down by his mother and said his prayers, and then I went up to him and I said:

" Willie, did you pray?"

" Yes, papa, I said my prayers."

" Yes, but did you pray?"

" I said my prayers."

" I know you said them, but did you pray? "

He hung his head.

" You are angry with your sister?"

" Well, she had no business to do thus and so."

" That has nothing to do with it, Willie; you have the wrong idea, my boy, if you think that you have prayed to-night."

You see he was trying to get over it by saying, " I said my prayers to-night." I find that people say their prayers every night, just to ease their conscience.

" Willie," I said, " if you don't forgive your sister, you will not sleep to-night. Ask her to forgive you."

He didn't want to do that. He loves the country, and he has been talking a great deal about the time when he can go into the country and play out-doors. So he said:

" Oh, yes, I will sleep well enough; I am going to think about being out there in the country."

That is the way that we are trying to do; we are trying to think of something else to get rid of the thought of these sins, but we can not. I said nothing more to him. I went on studying, and his mother came down stairs. But soon he called his mother and said:

" Mother, won't you please go up and ask Emma if she won't forgive me?"

Then I afterward heard him murmuring in bed, and he was saying his prayers. And he said to me:

" Papa, you were right, I could not sleep, and I can not tell you how happy I am now."

Don't think, my friends, that there is any peace until your sins are put away. My dear friends, the gospel of the Lord Jesus Christ is the gospel of peace.

LOVE CONQUERS ALL THINGS.—In Brooklyn, one day, I met a young man passing down the streets. At the time the war broke out the young man was engaged to be married to a young lady in New England, but the marriage was postponed. He was very fortunate in battle after battle, until the Battle of the Wilderness took place, just before the war was over. The young lady was counting the days at the end of which he would return. She waited for letters, but no letters came. At last she received one addressed in a strange handwriting, and it read something like this :

"There has been another terrible battle. I have been unfortunate this time ; *I have lost both my arms.* I can not write myself, but a comrade is writing this letter for me. I write to tell you that you are as dear to me as ever ; but I shall now be dependent upon other people for the rest of my days, and I have this letter written to release you from your engagement."

This letter was never answered. By the next train she went clear down to the scene of the late conflict, and sent word to the captain what her errand was, and got the number of the soldier's cot. She went along the line, and the moment her eyes fell upon that number she went to that cot and threw her arms round that young man's neck and kissed him.

"I will never give you up," she said. "These hands will never give you up ; I am able to support you ; I will take care of you."

My friends, you are not able to take care of yourselves. The law says you are ruined, but Christ says, "I will take care of you."

MOTHER'S LOVE.—I knew a mother who, like Christ, gave her life for love.

When the Californian gold fever broke out, a man went there, leaving his wife in New England with his boy. As soon as he got on and was successful he was to send for them. It was a long time before he succeded, but at last he got money enough to send for them. The wife's heart leaped for joy. She took her boy to New York, got on board a Pacific steamer, and sailed away to San Francisco. They had not been long at sea before the cry of " Fire ! fire !" rang through the ship, and rapidly it gained on them. There was a powder magazine on board, and the captain knew the moment the fire reached the powder every man, woman and child must perish. They got out the life boats, but they were too small ! In a minute they were overcrowded. The last one was just pushing away, when the mother pleaded with them to take her and her boy.

"No," they said, "we have got as many as we can hold."

She entreated them so earnestly, that at last they said they would take one more. Do you think she leaped into that boat and left her boy to die ? No ! She seized her boy, gave him one last hug, kissed him, and dropped him over into the boat.

"My boy, " she said, "if you live to see your father, tell him *that I died in your place.*" That is a faint type of what Christ has done for us.

RELIGION IS LOVE AND SYMPATHY—I want to tell you a lesson taught me in Chicago a few years ago. In the months of July and August a great many deaths occurred among children, you all know. I remember I attended a great many funerals; sometimes I would go to two or three funerals a day. I got so used to it that it did not trouble me to see a mother take the last kiss and the last look at her child, and see the coffin-lid closed. I got accustomed to it, as in the war we got accustomed to the great battles, and to see the wounded and the dead never troubled us. When I got home one night I heard that one of my Sunday-school pupils was dead, and her mother wanted me to come to the house. I went to the poor home and saw the father drunk. Adelaide had been brought from the river. The mother told me she washed for a living, the father earned no money, and poor Adelaide's work was to get wood for the fire. She had gone to the river that day and seen a piece floating on the water, had stretched out for it, had lost her balance, and fallen in. The poor woman was very much distressed.

"I would like you to help me, Mr. Moody," she said, "to bury my child. I have no lot, I have no money."

Well, I took the measure for the coffin and came away. I had my little girl with me and she said:

"Papa, suppose we were very, very poor, and mamma had to work for a living, and I had to get sticks for the fire, and was to fall into the river, would you be very sorry?"

This question reached my heart.

"Why, my child, it would break my heart to lose you," I said, and I drew her to my bosom.

"Papa, do you feel bad for that mother?" she asked.

This word woke my sympathy for the woman, and I started and went back to the house, and prayed that the Lord might bind up that wounded heart. When the day came for the funeral, I went to Graceland. I had always thought my time too precious to go out there, but

I went. The drunken father was there and the poor mother. I bought a lot, the grave was dug and the child laid among strangers. There was another funeral coming up, and the corpse was laid near the grave of little Adelaide. And I thought how I would feel if it had been my little girl that I had been laying there among strangers. I went to my Sabbath-school thinking this; and suggested that the children should contribute and buy a lot in which we might bury a hundred poor little children. We soon got it, and the papers had scarcely been made out when a lady came and said:

"Mr. Moody, my little girl died this morning; let me bury her in the lot you have got for the Sunday-school children."

The request was granted, and she asked me to go to the lot and say prayers over her child. I went to the grave—it was a beautiful day in June—and I remember asking her what the name of her child was. She said Emma. That was the name of my little girl, and I thought "what if it had been my own child!" We should put ourselves in the laces of others. I could not help shedding a tear. Another woman came shortly after and wanted to put another one into the grave. I asked his name. It was Willie, and it happened to be the name of my little boy. The first two laid there were called by the same names as my two children, and I felt sympathy and compassion for those two women.

If you want to get into sympathy, put yourself into a man's place. We need Christians whose hearts are full of love and sympathy. If we haven't got it, pray that we may have it, so that we may be able to reach those men and women that need kindly words and kindly actions far more than sermons. The mistake is that we have been preaching too much and sympathizing and loving too little. The gospel of Jesus Christ is a gospel of love and deeds and not of words.

CHRIST WANTS THE SINNER TO COME JUST AS HE IS.—I have read of an artist, who wanted to paint a picture of the Prodigal Son. He searched through the madhouses, and the poorhouses, and the prisons, to find a man wretched enough to represent the prodigal, but he could not find one. One day he was walking down the streets and met a man whom he thought would do. He told the poor beggar he would pay him well, if he came to his room and sit for his portrait. The beggar agreed and the day was appointed for him to come. The day came, and a man put in his appearance at the artist's room.

"You made an appointment with me," he said, when he was shown into the studio.

The artist looked at him.

"I never saw you before," he said. "You can not have an appointment with me."

"Yes," said the man, "I agreed to meet you to-day, at ten o'clock."

"You must be mistaken; it must have been some other artist; I was to see a *beggar* here at this hour."

"Well," says the beggar, "I am he."

"You?"

"Yes."

"Why, what have you been doing?"

"Well, I thought I would dress myself up a bit, before I got painted."

"Then," said the artist, "I do not want you; I wanted you as you were; now, you are of no use to me." That is the way Christ wants every poor sinner—just as he is.

CHRIST WILL BEAR OUR BURDENS.—I like to think of Christ as a burden-bearer. A minister was one day moving his library up stairs. As the minister was going up-stairs with his load of books, his little boy came in and was very anxious to help his father. So his father just told him to go and get an armful and take them up stairs. When the father came back, he met the little fellow about half way up the stairs, tugging away with the biggest in the library. He couldn't manage to carry it up. The book was too big. So he sat down and cried. His father found him, and just took him in his arms, book and all, and carried him up stairs. So Christ will carry you and all your burdens.

LET YOUR LIGHT SHINE.— One dark night a friend of mine was walking along one of the streets of Chicago. It was very dark. Pretty soon he met a man with a lantern. The man was blind.

"My friend," he said, "are you really blind?"

"Yes."

"Then, why are you so foolish as to carry a lantern?"

"To keep people from stumbling over me!"

Christians, let us learn a lesson from this. Let us hold up our Christian lights—hold up Christ. Let us not hide our lights under the bushel and let the world stumble over us.

Sinners, don't be afraid to change your life. Christians be zealous. Don't rust out.

I knew a professed Christian, whose little boy was converted, and he was full of praise. When God converts boy or man, his heart is full of joy—can't help praising. His father was a professed Christian, I say. The boy wondered why he didn't talk about Christ, and didn't go down to the special meetings.   One day, as the father was reading the papers, the boy came to him and put his hand on his shoulder, and said :

"Father, why don't you praise God?   Why don't you sing about Christ? Why don't you go down to these meetings that are being held?"

The father opened his eyes, and looked at him, and said, gruffly:

"I am not carried away, with any of these doctrines.   I am established."

A few days after they were getting out a load of wood.   They put it on the cart.   The father and the boy got on top of the load, and tried to get the horse to go.   They used the whip, but the horse wouldn't move—he was established.

THE LITTLE ORPHAN'S PRAYER.—A little child, whose father and mother had died, was taken into another family.   The first night she asked if she could pray, as she used to.

"Oh, yes," said the new mother.

"So she knelt down, and prayed as her first mother taught her; and when that was ended she added a little prayer of her own: "Oh God, make these people as kind to me as father and mother were."   Then she paused and looked up, as if expecting the answer, and added:

"Of course God will."

How sweetly simple was that little one's faith; she expected God to "do," and, of course she got her request.

FAITH WILL SAVE YOU.—Suppose I should meet a person to-night when I go away from here—a person that I had met in rags every day, and should see him all dressed up, and should say to him, "Halloa, beggar!"

"Why, Mr. Moody, I ain't no beggar; I ain't."

"Well, you were last night. I know you. You asked me for money."

"True, but I was standing here, and a man came along and put ten thousand dollars in my hand, real money, and I've got it in the bank now."

"How do you know you stretched out the right hand to take it?"

"Right hand!   What do I care which hand!   I've got the money, I have."

And so people talk about the right kind of faith.   Any kind of faith will do that will get the good.   There would be no trouble about peace and happiness if men had faith in Christ.

BELIEF.—Not long ago a man said to me, "I can not believe."

"Whom?" I asked.

He stammered, and said again, "I cannot believe."

I said, "Whom?"

"Well," he said, "I can't believe."

"Whom?" I asked again.

At last he said, "I can not believe myself."

"Well, you don't need to. You do not need to put any confidence in yourself. The less you believe in yourself the better. But if you tell me you can't believe God, that is another thing; and I would like to ask you why?"

WAITING FOR THE SAVIOR.—A family in a southern city were stricken down with yellow fever. It was raging there, and there were very stringent sanitary rules. The moment any body died, a cart went around and took the coffin away. The father was taken sick and died and was buried, and the mother was at last stricken down. The neighbors were afraid of the plague, and none dared to go into the house. The mother had a little son and was anxious about her boy, and afraid he would be neglected when she was called away, so she called the little fellow to her bedside, and said:

"My boy, I am going to leave you, but Jesus will come to you when I am gone."

The mother died, the cart came along and she was laid in the grave. The neighbors would have liked to take the boy, but were afraid of the pestilence. He wandered about, and finally started up to the place where they had laid his mother and sat down on the grave and wept himself to sleep. Next morning he awoke and realized his position— alone and hungry. A stranger came along and seeing the little fellow ritting on the ground, asked him what he was waiting for.

The boy remembered what his mother had told him and answered, "I am waiting for Jesus," and told him the whole story.

The man's heart was touched, tears trickled down his cheeks, and he said:

"Jesus has sent me."

"You have been a good while coming sir," said the boy.

He was provided for. So it is with us. To wait for results we must have courage and patience and God will help us.

SHORT OF VIRTUE.—In Chicago, when our constitution was young, a bill was passed that no man should be a policeman that was not a certain height—five feet six. The commissioners advertised for men to come sound and be examined, and they must bring good letters of recommendation with them. Now, as they are passing from one man to another, examining their letters and trying their height, suppose there are two of us want to get in, and I say to my friend, "There is no man has a better chance than I have; I have got letters from the supreme judge, from the mayor and leading citizens of Chicago; no man can have better letters." He says, "Ah, my friend, my letters are as good as yours." Well, the chief commissioner says, "Look here, Moody, these letters are all right, but you must be up to the standard;" so he measures me, and I am only five feet, and he says, "You are half a foot too short." My friend looks down on me and says, "I have got a better chance than you." Well, he stands up and is measured, and is only one-tenth of an inch short, but he goes with me. He has "come short." I admit some men have come shorter than others, but that is the verdict God has brought in—all are guilty.

IF I ONLY HAD.—A man who had charge of a swing-bridge opened it just to oblige a friend, who said there was plenty of time for his boat to go through before the train of cars came along. But a moment after the lightning-like express came thundering on and dashed into the dark waters below. The bridge-keeper, whose neglect had caused the disaster, lost his reason, and his life since has been spent in a mad-house. The first and only words he uttered when the train leaped into the open chasm were, "If I only had," and he has gone on constantly repeating the vain regret. Ah! that will be the cry of the lost in another world—"If I only had."

LITTLE THINGS.—It is amazing what little things sometimes keep men from God. One man came to me and told me that his business was that of selling a kind of soap which was advertised to do remarkable work in taking out grease spots.

"The soap will do all that is claimed for it," said he; "but the truth is, it rots the clothes; and if I become a Christian I must give up my business; and I can't afford to do it."

And so in his case it was soap which kept him out of the kingdom of God.

SCEPTICS ILLUSTRATED.—A couple of commercial travelers went to hear a minister preach. He explained that men don't find out God; that it is God who has to reveal His nature to man; that it is all a matter of revelation; that God reveals Christ to man. When they went back to the hotel they began to talk the matter over, and both maintained that they could not believe any thing except they could reason it out. An old man there heard the conversation, and remarked:

"I heard you say you could not believe any thing except you could reason it out. Now, when I was coming down in the train I noticed in the field some geese and sheep and swine and cattle eating grass. Can you tell me by what process that grass is turned into hair, and bristles, and feathers, and wool?"

They could not.

"Well, do you believe it is a fact?"

"Oh yes, we can't help but believe that."

"Well, then, I can't help but believe in the **revelation of Jesus Christ.** I have seen men who have been reclaimed and reformed through it, and who are now living happy, when before they were outcasts from society." The two commercial men were silenced by that old man's outspoken faith.

How Rich and How Poor.—A couple of friends of mine in the war called upon one of our great Illinois farmers, to get him to give some money for the soldiers, and during their stay he took them up to the cupola of his house and told them to look over yonder, just as far as their eyes could reach, over that beautiful rolling prairie, and they said, "That is very nice." Yes, and it was all his. Then he took them up to another cupola, and said, "Look at that farm, and that, and that;" these were farms stocked, improved, fenced, and they said, "Those are very nice;" and then he showed them horses, cattle, and sheep-yards, and said, "They are all mine." He showed them the town where he lived, which had been named after him, a great hall, and building lots, and those were all his, and he said:

"I came out West a poor boy, without a farthing, and I am worth all this;" but when he got through my friend said:

"How much have you got up yonder?" and the old man's countenance fell, for he knew very well what that meant. "What have you got up there—in the other world?"

"Well," he said, "I have not got any thing there."

"Why," said my friend, "what a mistake! A man of your intelligence and forethought and judgment to amass all this wealth; and now, that you are drawing near to your grave, you will have to leave it all. You can not take a farthing with you, but you must die a beggar and a pauper;" and the tears rolled down his cheeks as he said,

"It does look foolish."

Only a few months after, he died, as he had lived, and his property passed to others.

"Hold the Fort, for I Am Coming."—When General Sherman went through Atlanta toward the sea—through the Southern States—he left in the fort in the Kenesaw Mountains a little handful of men to guard some rations that he brought there. And General Hood got into the outer rear and attacked the fort, drove the men in from the outer works into the inner works, and for a long time the battle raged fearfully. Half of the men were either killed or wounded; the general who was in command was wounded seven different times; and when they were about ready to run up the white flag and surrender the fort, Sherman got within fifteen miles, and through the signal corps on the mountain he sent the message:

"*Hold the fort; I am coming.* W. T. Sherman.*"*

That message fired up their hearts, and they held the fort till reinforcements came, and the fort did not go into the hands of their enemies. Our friend, Mr. Bliss, has written a hymn entitled 'Hold the Fort, for I Am Coming," and I'm going to ask Mr. Sankey to sing that hymn. I hope there will be a thousand young converts coming into our ranks to help hold the fort. Our Savior is in command, and He is coming. Let us take up the chorus.

> Ho! my comrades, see the signal
> Waving in the sky!
> Reinforcements now appearing,
> Victory is nigh!
>
> *Chorus—*" Hold the fort, for I am coming,"
> Jesus signals still,
> Wave the answer back to heaven,
> " By Thy grace we will."
>
> See the mighty hosts advancing,
> Satan leading on;
> Mighty men around us falling,
> Courage almost gone.—*Chorus.*
>
> See the glorious banner waving,
> Hear the bugle blow,
> In our Leader's name we'll triumph
> Over every foe.—*Chorus.*
>
> Fierce and long the battle rages,
> But our Help is near;
> Onward comes our Great Commander,
> Cheer, my comrades, cheer!—*Chorus.*

PARTING WORDS.—"Another story," said Mr. Moody, "and I have done to-day.

"It was Ralph Wallace who told me of this one: A certain gentleman used to be a member of the Presbyterian church. He is a good man, but his heart has grown old. One day his sweet, little boy was taken sick. When he went home, his wife was weeping, and she said:

"'Our boy is dying; he has had a change for the worse. I wish you would go in and see him, John.'

"The father went into the room and placed his hand upon the brow of his dying boy, and could feel the cold, damp sweat was gathering there; that the cold, icy hand of death was feeling for the chords of life.

HOLD THE FORT.

See page 376.

"'Do you know, my boy, that you are dying?' asked the weeping father.

"'Am I, father? Is this death? Do you really think I am dying?'

"'Yes, my son, your end on earth is near.'

"'And will I be with Jesus to-night, father?'

"'Yes, you will be with the Savior.'

"'Father, don't you weep, for when I get there I will go straight to Jesus, and tell Him that you have been trying all my life to lead me to Him.'

"God has given me two little children," said Mr. Moody, "and ever since I can remember I have directed them to Christ, and I would rather they carried this message to Jesus—that I had tried all my life to lead them to Him—than have all the crowns of the earth; and I would rather lead them to Jesus than give them the wealth of the world. I challenge any man to speak of heaven without speaking of children. 'For of such is the kingdom of heaven.'"

T. DeWITT TALMAGE.

THE GREAT PREACHER, A SECOND CALVIN.

BIOGRAPHY AND REMINISCENCES.

T. DeWitt Talmage, D. D., was born in New Jersey in 1832, the youngest of a family of twelve children. His parents were Christians, and their good training caused the conversion of DeWitt when eighteen years of age. He received his literary training in the University of New York, and afterward graduated from the theological school at New Brunswick, N. J. The first three years of his ministerial career were spent in Belleville, N. J., from whence he was called to Syracuse, N. Y. After laboring there three years, he went to Philadelphia, where he remained seven years, during which time he earned a high place among the preachers of that city. His congregations were large, and his church rapidly increased in membership, until it became widely known as the popular church of the city. Many large and important congregations were now extending calls to him. He accepted a call from the Central Presbyterian Church of Brooklyn, then in a state of decline, in preference to others, because he saw in Brooklyn an opportunity to build up a free church.

At the end of a year and a half the old edifice could no longer accommodate the congregations, and a tabernacle was built, and dedicated in September, 1870. This building, which originally was designed to seat 3,000 persons, was enlarged a few months later. Just before the hour of service, December 22, 1872, the tabernacle was burned. In a few minutes several churches were offered to the congregation for occupancy until their own house could be restored. The Academy of Music was engaged until a still larger structure was built to take the place of the old. The building was enlarged until it accommodated nearly 6,000 persons. The tabernacle was crowded at every service. On the 14th of October, 1889, the second tabernacle was burned to the ground, but it will soon be rebuilt.

When I said to the great preacher that the Lord seemed to deal hardly with his church, he said: "No, the Lord has blessed us all the time."

"But what a loss," I said. "Three hundred thousand (?) dollars!"

"Oh, no! the Lord is chastising the insurance companies. We were fully insured."

Besides the regular congregation, Dr. Talmage preaches to several millions through the press of the United States, Europe and Australia, which publishes his sermons regularly.

Dr. Talmage is in great demand as a lecturer, but makes all other things subordinate to his ministerial work. Personally, he is one of the most modest and unassuming of men. His appearance is not at all clerical, but more resembles a prosperous business man. He is of pleasant address and sociable disposition. He is not only a preacher among preachers, but a man among men.

In doctrine, Talmage is absolutely orthodox. He has never changed his belief like Beecher, nor leaned toward the Agnostics like Heber Newton. His sermons abound in ancedotes like Moody's, Collyer's and Patton's. Sometimes his stories provoke laughter but they always convince. He always looks on the bright side of life and his greatest lecture is called "The Bright Side of Life." His illustrations are startling.

One day, to illustrate the cost of salvation, he used this parable:

"Mamma," said a little child to her mother, when she was being put to bed at night, "Mamma, what makes your hand so scarred and twisted, and unlike other people's hands?" "Well," said the mother, "my child, when you were younger than you are now, years ago, one night, after I had put you to bed, I heard a cry, a shriek, upstairs. I came up, and found the bed was on fire and you were on fire; and I took hold of you and I tore off the burning garments, and while I was tearing them off and trying to get you away I burned my hand, and it has been scarred and twisted ever since, and hardly looks any more like a hand; but *I got that, my child, in trying to save you.*"

I wish I could show you the burned hand of Christ—burned in plucking you out of the fire; burned in snatching you away from the flame. Ay, also the burned foot, and the burned brow, and the burned heart—burned for you. By His stripes we are healed.

In religion we have said that Mr. Talmage is orthodox. Beecher often called him an old Hunker. He never strays from Calvinism. He takes no stock in Darwin's theories, and has no sympathy with Beecher's theory (?) that everlasting burning does not overtake the ᵥicked. He maintains, with Moody, that the miracles did occur as ᵥpresented, and has no patience with Heber Newton, who accounts for them through natural causes. Still, Mr. Talmage never quarrels with the theologians. He begs them all to work for Christianity. When asked about opposing some new theological ideas one day, he said:

"No, I haven't time. I will keep on the main track. There is nothing gained to Christianity by wrangling. You remember the story of the two brothers," he said, "who went out to take an evening walk, and one of them looked up to the sky and said:

"'I wish I had a pasture-field as large as the night heavens. And the other brother looked up into the sky, and said:

"'I wish I had as many oxen as there are stars in the sky.'

"'Well,' said the first, 'how would you feed so many oxen?'

"'I would turn them into your pasture,' replied the second.

"'What! whether I would or not?'

"'Yes, whether you would or not.'

"And there arose a quarrel; and when the quarrel ended, one had slain the other."

One day, speaking of joining the church, Mr. Talmage said: "Every Christian should anchor to a church. If he gets into trouble, the church will take care of him. A pious captain of a Cunarder was riding over to Philadelphia on the cars. A young man came and sat down by him, when the captain said:

"'Going over to Philadelphia?'

"'Yes, I'm going there to live,' replied the young man.

"'Have you letters of introduction?' asked the old captain.

"'Yes,' said the young man, and he pulled some of them out.

"'Well,' continued the old sea-captain, 'haven't you a church certificate?'

"'Oh, yes,' replied the young man, 'I didn't suppose you would want to look at that.'

"'Yes,' said the sea-captain, 'I want to see that. As soon as you get to Philadelphia, present that to some Christian church. I am an old sailor, and I have been up and down in the world, and it's my rule, as soon as I get into port, to fasten my ship, fore and aft, to the wharf, although it may cost a little wharfage, rather than have my ship out in the stream, floating hither and thither with the tide.'"

Mr. Talmage is always talking about heaven. One day he said:

"Well, my friends, heaven comes very near to-day. It is only a stream that divides us—the narrow stream of death; and the voices there and the voices here seem to commingle, and we join trumpets and hosannahs and hallelujahs, and the chorus of the united song of earth and heaven is, 'Home, Sweet Home.'

"And this," he continued, "reminds me of a war story: In our last dreadful war, the Union and rebel troops were encamped on opposite banks of the Rappahannock, and one morning the brass band of the Northern army played the 'Star-Spangled Banner,' and

I NEVER DID LIKE CODFISH.

See page 381.

all the North cheered: Then, on the opposite side of the Rappa-hannock, the brass band of the Confederates played 'My Mary-land' and 'Dixie,' and then all the Southern troops cheered and cheered. Put after a while one of the bands struck up 'Home, Sweet Home,' and the band on the opposite side of the river took up the strain, and when the tune was done the Confederates and the Federals all together united, as the tears rolled down their cheeks, in one great 'Huzza! huzza!'

"So will all Christians unite in heaven—the 'Home, Sweet Home.'

"Going to heaven! what a sweet saying!" exclaimed Talmage.

"A Christian man," he continued, "was dying in Canada. His daughter Nellie sat by the bedside. It was Sunday evening, and the bell of the old church was ringing, calling the people to church. The good old man, in his dying dream, thought that he was on the way to church, as he used to be when he went in the sleigh across the river; and as the evening bell struck up, in his dying dream he thought it was the call to church. He said:

"'Hark, children, the bells are ringing; we shall be late; we must make the mare step out quick!' He shivered, and then said: 'Pull the buffalo-robe up closer, my lass! It is cold crossing the river; but we will soon be there, Nellie, we will soon be there!' And he smiled and said, 'Just there now.'

"No wonder he smiled. The good old man had got to church. Not the old Canadian church, but the temple in the skies. Just across the river."

TALMAGE'S LECTURES.
ELOQUENT, LOGICAL, ORTHODOX.

Ladies and Gentlemen:—Before talking about agreeable or pleasant people, I will say something about disagreeable people:

Of all the ills that flesh is heir to, a cross, crabbed, ill-contented man is the most unendurable, because the most inexcusable. No occasion, no matter how trifling, is permitted to pass without eliciting his dissent, his sneer, or his growl. His good and patient wife never yet prepared a dinner that he liked. One day she prepares a dish that she thinks will particularly please him. He comes in the front door, and says.

"Whew! whew! what have you got in the house? Now, my dear, you know that I never did like codfish." [Laughter.]

Some evening, resolving to be especially gracious, he starts with his family to a place of amusement. He scolds the most of the way. He can not afford the time or the money, and he does not believe the entertainment will be much, after all. The music begins. The audience is thrilled. The orchestra, with polished instruments, warble and weep, and thunder and pray, all the sweet sounds of the world flowering upon the strings of the bass viol, and wreathing the flageolets, and breathing from the lips of the cornet, and shaking their flower-bells upon the tinkling tambourine.

He sits motionless and disgusted. He goes home, saying: "Did you see that fat musician that got so red blowing that French horn? He looked like a stuffed toad. Did you ever hear such a voice as that lady has? Why, it was a perfect squawk! The evening was wasted."

And his companion says, "Why, my dear!"

"There you needn't tell me—you are pleased with every thing. But never ask me to go again!"

He goes to church. Perhaps the sermon is didactic and argumentative. He yawns. He gapes. He twists himself in his pew, and pretends he is asleep and says, "I could not keep awake. Did you ever hear any thing so dead? Can these dry bones live?"

Next Sabbath he enters a church where the minister is much given to illustration. He is still more displeased. He says, "How dare that man bring such every-day things into his pulpit? He ought to have brought his illustrations from the cedar of Lebanon and the fir-tree, instead of the hickory and sassafras. He ought to have spoken of the Euphrates and the Jordan, and not of the Kennebec and Schuylkill. He ought to have mentioned Mount Gerizim instead of the Catskills. Why, he ought to be disciplined. Why, it is ridiculous!"

Perhaps, afterward, he joins the church. Then the church will have its hands full. He growls, and groans, and whines all the way up toward the gate of heaven. He wishes that the choir would sing differently, that the minister would preach differently, that the elders would pray differently. In the morning, he said, "The church was as cold as Greenland;" in the evening, "it was hot as blazes." They painted the church; he didn't like the color. They carpeted the aisles; he didn't like the figure. They put in a new furnace; he didn't like the patent. He wriggles and squirms, and frets, and stews, and worries himself. He is like a horse that, prancing and uneasy to the bit, worries himself into a lather of foam, while the horse hitched beside him just pulls straight ahead, makes no fuss and comes to his oats in peace. Like a hedge-hog, he is all quills. [Laughter.] Like a crab, that you know always goes the other way, and moves backward in order to go forward, and turns in four directions all at once, and the first you know of his where-abouts you have missed him, and when he is completely lost he has gone by the heel—so that the first thing you know you don't know any thing —and while you expected to catch the crab, the crab catches you. [Laughter.]

So some men are crabbed—all hard-shell, and obstinancy and oppo-sition. I do not see how he is to get into heaven, unless he goes in back-ward, and then there will be danger that at the gate he will try to pick a quarrel with St. Peter. [Laughter.] Once in, I fear he will not like the music, and the services will be too long, and that he will spend the first two or three years in trying to find out whether the wall of heaven is exactly plumb. Let us stand off from such tendencies. Listen for sweet notes rather than for discords, picking up marigolds and harebells in preference to thistles and coloquintida, culturing thyme and anemones rather than nightshade. And in a world where God hath put exquisite tinge upon the shells washed in the surf, and planted a paradise of bloom in the child's cheek, and adorned the pillars of the rock by hang-ing a tapestry of morning mist, the lark saying, "I will sing soprano," and the cascade replying, "I will carry the bass," let us leave it to the owl to hoot, and the frog to croak, and the beast to growl, and the grumbler to find fault. [Applause.]

Now we will talk about agreeable people:

Strange that, in such a very agreeable world, there should be so many disagreeable people! So many everywhere but—here! [Laughter.] I see by your looks, my friends, that none of you belong to this class. These good-humored husbands before me are all what they ought to be, good-natured as a May morning; and when the wife asks for a little spending-money, the good man of the purse says, "All right; here's my pocket-book. My dear, take as much as you want, and come soon again." [Laughter.] These wives at eveningtide always greet their companions home with a smile, and say, "My dear, your slippers are ready and the muffins warm. Put you feet up on this ottoman. Bless the dear man!" [Laughter.] These brothers always prefer the com-panionship of their own sisters to that of any one else's sister, and take them out almost every evening to lectures and concerts. And I suppose that in no public building to-night in this city, or in any other city, is there a more mild, affable, congenial and agreeable collection of people than ourselves.

The world has a great many delightful people who are easily pleased. They have a faculty of finding out that which is attractive. They are like a bee that no sooner gets out of the hive than it pitches for a clover-top. They never yet walked into a picture-gallery but they were refreshed and thankful. They saw some exquisite gem that kindled their admiration. There was some pleasant face in a picture that for hours kept looking over their shoulder.

They will never forget how in one of them a vine in filial affection, with its tender arm hugged up an old grandfather of a tree that was about to feel the stiff breeze.

They never came from a concert, but there was at least one voice that they admired, and wondered how in one throat God could have placed such exhaustless fountains of harmony.

They like the spring, for it is so full of bird and bloom, and, like a priestess, stands swinging her censer of perfume before God's altar; and the summer is just the thing for them, for they love to hear the sound of mowing-machines, and battalions of thunderbolts grounding arms among the mountains; and autumn is their exultation, for its orchards are golden with fruit, and the forests march with banners dipped in sunsets and blood-red with the conflicts of frost and storm. [Applause.]

And they praise God for winter, that brings the shout of children, playing blind-man's buff, with handkerchief they can see through, around a blazing fire, and the snow shower that makes Parthenons and St. Mark's Cathedrals out of a pigeon-coop, and puts brighter coronets than the Georges ever wore on the brow of the bramble, and turns the wood-shed into a "royal tower" filled with crown jewels; and that sends the sleigh-riding party, in buffalo robes, behind smoking steeds, with two straps of bells, and fire in the eye, and snort of the nostril, and flaunt of the mane, impatient of the sawing of the twisted bit and the reins wound around the hands of the driver, till, coming up to the other gay parties, we slacken the rein and crack the whip, and shout, "Go 'long, Charley!" and dart past every thing on the road, and you can only take in the excited roan span by putting your foot against the dash-board, and lying back with all you strength, and sawing the bit, while the jolly hearts in the back seats mingle the ha, ha, ha, ha! with the jingle, jingle, jingle of the sleigh-bells, and the hostler of the hotel grabs the bridle of your horses, while you go in to warm and take a glass of—very weak lemonade! [Laughter.]

Now, there are many people thus pleased with all seasons, and complain not in any circumstances. If you are a merchant, they are the men whom you want for customers; if you are a lawyer, they are the men you want for clients and jurors; if you are a physician, they are the men you want for patients; but you don't often get them, for they cure themselves by a bottle of laughter, taken three or four times a day, well shaken up. Three cheers for the good-natured man; three groans for the gouty and sour-tempered! [Applause.]

One more description of disagreeable people and I have done:

Scene — A crisp morning. Carriage with spinning wheels, whose spokes glisten like splinters of the sun. Roan horse, flecked with foam, bending into the bit, his polished feet drumming the pavement in challenge of any horse that thinks he can go as fast. Two boys running to get on the back of the carriage. One of them, with quick spring, succeeds. The other leaps, but fails and falls. No sooner has he struck the ground than he shouts to the driver of the carriage, "Cut behind!"

Human nature the same in boy as man. All running to gain the vehicle of success. Some are spry and gain that for which they strive. Others are slow and tumble down; they who fall crying out against those who mount, "Cut behind!"

A political office rolls past. A multitude spring to their feet, and the race is on. Only one of all the number reaches that for which he runs. No sooner does he gain the prize, and begin to wipe the sweat from his brow, and think how grand a thing it is to ride in popular preferment, than the disappointed candidates cry out, "Incompetency! Stupidity! Fraud!" Now let the newspapers and platforms of the country "Cut behind!"

There is a golden chariot of wealth rolling down the street. A thousand people are trying to catch it. They run. They jostle. They tread on each other. Push, and pull, and tug! Those talk most against riches who can not get them. Clear the track for the racers! One of the thousand reaches the golden prize and mounts. Forthwith the air is full of cries: "Got it by fraud! Shoddy! Petroleum aristocracy! His father was a rag-picker! His mother was a washerwoman! I knew him when he blackened his own shoes! Pitch him off the back part of the golden chariot! Cut behind! Cut behind!" [Laughter.]

It is strange that there should be any rivalries among ministers of religion, when there is so much room for all to work. But in some things they are much like other people. Like all other classes of men, they have one liver apiece, and here and there one of them a spleen. In all cases the epigastric region is higher up than the hypogastric, save in the act of turning a somersault. Like others, they eat three times a day when they can get any thing to eat. Besides this, it sometimes happens that we find them racing for some professional chair or pulpit. They run well—neck and neck—while churches look on and wonder whether it will be "Dexter" or the "American Girl." Rowels plunge deep, and fierce is the cry, "Go 'long! Go 'long!" The privilege of preaching the gospel to the poor on five thousand dollars a year is enough to make a tight race anywhere. But only one mounts the coveted place; and forthwith the cry goes up in conventions and synods: "Unfit for the place! Can't preach! Unsound in the faith! Now is your chance, oh, conferences and presbyteries, to *cut behind!*" [Laughter.]

A fair women passes. We all admire beauty. He that says he don't, *lies.* A canting man, who told me he had no admiration for any thing earthly, used, instead of listening to the sermon, to keep squinting over toward the pew where sat Squire Brown's daughter. Whether God plants a rose in parterre or human cheek, we must admire it, whether we will or not. While we are deciding whether we had better take that dahlia, the dahlia takes us. A star does not ask the astronomer to admire it, but just winks at him, and he surrenders, with all his telescopes. This fair woman in society has many satellites. The boys all run for this prize. One of them, not having read enough novels to learn that ugliness is more desirable than beauty, wins her. The cry is up: "She paints! Looks well; but she knows it. Good shape; but I wonder what is the price of cotton! Won't she make him stand around! Practicality worth more than black eyes! Fool to marry a virago!"

In many eyes success is a crime. "I do not like you," said the snowflake to the snowbird. "Why?" said the snow-bird. "Because," said the snowflake, "You are going up and I going down!" [Applause.]

We have to state that the man in the carriage on the crisp morning, though he had a long lash-whip, with which he could have made the climbing boy yell most lustily, did not "cut behind." He was an old man; in the corner of his mouth a smile, which was always as ready to play as a kitten that watches for some one with a string to offer the slightest inducement. He heard the shout in the rear, and said: "Good-morning, my son. That is right; climb over and sit by me. Here are the reins; take hold and drive."

Thank God there are so many in the world that never "cut behind," but are ready to give a fellow a ride whenever he wants it. Here is a young man, clerk in a store. He has small wages, and a mother to take care of. For ten years he struggles to get into a higher place. The first of January comes, and the head of the commercial house looks round and says: "Trying to get up, are you?" And by the time three more years have passed the boy sits right beside the old man, who hands over the reins, and says, "Drive!" Jonathan Goodhue was a boy behind the counter; but his employer gave him a ride, and London, Canton and Calcutta heard the scratch of his pen. Lenox, Grinnell, and the Aspinwalls carried many young men a mile on the high road of prosperity.

There are hundreds of people whose chief joy is to help others on. Now it is a smile, now a good word, now ten dollars. May such a kind man always have a carriage to ride in and a horse not too skittish! As he goes down the hill of life, may the breeching-strap be strong enough to hold back the load!

When he has ridden to the end of the earthly road, he will have plenty of friends to help him unhitch and assist him out of the carriage. On that cool night it will be pleasant to hang up the whip with which he drove the enterprises of a lifetime, and feel that with it he never "cut behind" at those who were struggling. [Applause.]

TALMAGE'S GREAT TEMPERANCE LECTURE.

Joseph's brethren dipped their brother's coat in goat's blood, and then brought the dabbled garment to their father, cheating him with the idea that a ferocious animal had slain him, and thus hiding their infamous behavior.

But there is no deception about that which we hold up to your observation to-night (or to-day). A monster such as never ranged African thicket or Hindostan jungle hath tracked this land, and with bloody maw hath strewn the continent with the mangled carcasses of whole generations; and there are tens of thousands of fathers and mothers who could hold up the garment of their slain boy, truthfully exclaiming: "It is my son's coat; an evil beast hath devoured him."

There has, in all ages and climes, been a tendency to the improper use of stimulants. Noah, as if disgusted with the prevalence of water in his time, [laughter] took to strong drink. By this vice, Alexander the Conqueror was conquered. The Romans at their feasts fell off their seats with intoxication. Four hundred millions of our race are opium eaters. India, Turkey and China have groaned with the desolation; and by it have been quenched such lights as Halley and De Quincey. One hundred millions are the victims of the betel-nut, which has specially blasted the East Indies. Three hundred millions chew hashish, and Persia, Brazil and Africa suffer the delirium. The Tartars employ murowa; the Mexicans, the agave; the people at Guarapo, an intoxicating quality taken from sugar-cane; while a great multitude, that no man can number, are disciples of alcohol. To it they bow. Under it they are trampled. In its trenches they fall. On its ghastly holocaust they burn.

Could the muster-roll of this great army be called, and they could come up from the dead, what eye could endure the reeking, festering putrefaction and beastliness? What heart could endure the groan of agony?

Drunkenness: does it not jingle the burglar's key? Does it not whet the assassin's knife? Does it not cock the highwayman's pistol? Does it not wave the incendiary's torch? Has it not sent the physician reeling into the sick-room; and the minister with his tongue thick into the pulpit? Did not an exquisite poet, from the very top of his fame, fall a gibbering sot, into the gutter, on his way to be married to one of the fairest daughters of New England, and at the very hour the bride was decking herself for the altar; and did he not die of delirium tremens, almost unattended, in a hospital?

Tamerlane asked for one hundred and sixty thousand skulls with which to build a pyramind to his own honor. He got the skulls, and built the pyramid. But if the bones of all those who have fallen as a prey to dissipation could be piled up, it would make a vaster pyramid.

Who will gird himself for the journey, and try with me to scale this mountain of the dead—going up miles high on human carcasses, to find still other peaks far above, mountain above mountain, white with the bleached bones of drunkards?

We have too much law.

The Sabbath has been sacrificed to the rum traffic. To many of our people, the best day of the week is the worst. Bakers must keep their shops closed on the Sabbath. It is dangerous to have loaves of bread going out on Sunday. The shoe store is closed; severe penalty will attack the man who sells boots on the Sabbath. But down with the window-shutters of the grog-shops! Our laws shall confer particular honor upon the rum-traffickers. All other trades must stand aside for these. Let our citizens who have disgraced themselves by trading in clothing and hosiery and hardware and lumber and coal, take off their hats to the rum-seller, elected to particular honor. It is unsafe for any other class of men to be allowed license for Sunday work. But swing out your signs, on ye traffickers in the peace of families, and in the souls of immortal men! Let the corks fly and the beer foam and the rum go tearing down the half-consumed throat of the inebriate. God does not see! Does He? Judgment will never come! Will it? [Voices "Yes! yes!"]

People say, "Let us have more law to correct this evil." We have more law now than we can execute. In what city is there a mayoralty that dare do it? The fact is, that there is no advantage in having the law higher than public opinion. What would be the use of the Maine law in New York? Neal Dow, the mayor of Portland, came out with a posse and threw the rum of the city into the street. But I do not believe that there are three mayors in the United States with his courage or nobility of spirit.

I do not know but that God is determined to let drunkenness triumph, and the husbands and sons of thousands of our best families be destroyed by this vice, in order that our people, amazed and indignant, may rise up and demand the extermination of this municipal crime. There is a way of driving down the hoops of a barrel so tight that they break.

We can't regulate intemperance.

We are in this country, at this time, trying to regulate this evil by a tax on whisky. You might as well try to regulate the Asiatic cholera, or the smallpox, by taxation. The men who distil liquors are, for the most part, unscrupulous; and the higher the tax, the more inducement to illicit distillation. New York produces forty thousand gallons of whisky every twenty-four hours; and the most of it escapes the tax. The most vigilant officials fail to discover the cellars and vaults and sheds where this work is done.

Oh, the folly of trying to restrain an evil by government tariffs! If every gallon of whisky made, if every flask of wine produced, should be taxed a thousand dollars, it would not be enough to pay for the tears it has wrung out of the eyes of widows and orphans, nor for the blood it has dashed on the altars of the Christian church, nor for the catastrophe of the millions it has destroyed forever.

Oh! we are a Christian people! From Boston a ship sailed for Africa, with three missionaries and twenty-two thousand gallons of New England rum on board. Which will have the most effect; the missionaries, or the rum?

Shall we try the power of the pledge? There are thousands of men who have been saved by putting their names to such a document. I know it is laughed at; but there are men who, having once promised a thing, do it. "Some have broken the pledge." Yes; they were liars. But all men are not liars. I do not say that it is the duty of all persons to make such signature; but I do say that it will be the salvation of many of you.

The glorious work of Theobald Matthew can never be estimated. At his hand four millions of people took the pledge, including eight prelates and seven hundred of the Roman Catholic clergy. A multitude of them were faithful.

Dr. Justin Edwards said that ten thousand drunkards had been permanently reformed in five years.

Through the great Washingtonian movement in Ohio, sixty thousand took the pledge; in Pennsylvania, twenty-nine thousand; in Kentucky, thirty thousand, and multitudes in all parts of the land. Many of these had been habitual drunkards. One hundred and fifty thousand of them, it is estimated, were permanently reclaimed. Two of these men became foreign ministers, one a governor of a State several were sent to Congress. Hartford reported six hundred reformed drunkards; Norwich, seventy-two; Fairfield, fifty; Sheffield, seventy-five. All over the land reformed men were received back into the churches that they had before disgraced; and households were re-established. All up and down the land there were gratulations and praise to God.

The pledge signed, to thousands has been the proclamation of emancipation. [Applause.]

There is no cure but prohibition.

I think that we are coming at last to treat inebriation as it ought to be treated, namely, as an awful disease, self-inflicted, to be sure, but nevertheless a disease. Once fastened upon a man, sermons will not cure him; temperance lectures will not eradicate the taste; religious tracts will not arrest it; the gospel of Christ will not arrest it. Once under the power of this awful thirst, the man is bound to go on; and if the foaming glass were on the other side of perdition, he would wade through the fires of hell to get it. A young man in prison had such a strong thirst for intoxicating liquors, that he cut off his hand at the wrist, called for a bowl of brandy in order to stop the bleeding, thrust his wrist into the bowl and then drank the contents.

Stand not, when the thirst is on him, between a man and his cups! Clear the track for him! Away with the children; he would tread their life out! Away with the wife; he would dash her to death! Away with the Cross; he would run it down! Away with the Bible; he would tear it up for the winds! Away with heaven; he considers it worthless as a straw! "Give me the drink! Give it to me! Though hands of blood pass up the bowl, and the soul trembles over the pit,—the drink! give it to me! Though it be pale with tears; though the froth of everlasting anguish float in the foam; give it to me! I drink to my wife's woe; to my children's rags; to my eternal banishment from God and hope and heaven! Give it to me! the drink!"

The rum fiend is coming into your homes.

Oh, how this rum fiend would like to go and hang up a skeleton in your beautiful house, so that when you opened the front door to go in you would see it in the hall; and when you sit at your table you would see it hanging from the wall; and when you open your bedroom you would find it stretched upon your pillow; and waking at night you would feel its cold hand passing over your face and pinching at your heart!

There is no home so beautiful but it may be devastated by the awful curse. It throws its jargon into the sweetest harmony. What was it that silenced Sheridan's voice and shattered the golden scepter with which he swayed parliaments and courts? What foul sprite turned the sweet rhythm of Robert Burns into a tuneless ballad? What brought down the majestic form of one who awed the American senate with his eloquence, and after a while carried him home dead drunk from the office of secretary of state? What was it that crippled the noble spirit of one of the heroes of the late war, until the other night, in a drunken fit, he reeled from the deck of a Western steamer and was drowned! There was one whose voice we all loved to hear. He was one of the most classic orators of the century. People wondered why a man of so pure a heart and so excellent a life should have such a sad countenance always. They knew not that his wife was a sot.

"Woe to him that giveth his neighbor drink!" If this curse was proclaimed about the comparatively harmless drinks of olden times, what condemnation must rest upon those who tempt their neighbors when intoxicating liquor means copperas, nux vomica, logwood, opium, sulphuric acid, vitriol, turpentine and strychnine! "Pure liquors;" pure destruction! Nearly all the genuine champagne made is taken by the courts of Europe. What we get is horrible swill!

Women! we call upon you to help us!

I call upon woman for her influence in the matter. Many a man who had reformed and resolved on a life of sobriety, has been pitched off into old habits by the delicate hand of her whom he was anxious to please.

Bishop Potter says that a young man, who had been reformed, sat at a table, and when the wine was passed to him refused to take it. A lady sitting at his side said, "Certainly you will not refuse to take a glass with me?" Again he refused. But when she had derided him for lack of manliness he took the glass and drank it. He took another and another; and putting his fist hard down on the table, said, "Now I drink until I die." In a few months his ruin was consummated.

I call upon those who are guilty of these indulgences to quit the path of death. Oh, what a change it would make in your home! Do you see how everything there is being desolated! Would you not like to bring back joy to your wife's heart, and have your children come out to meet you with as much confidence as once they showed? Would you not like to rekindle the home lights that long ago were extinguished? It is not too late to change. It may not entirely obliterate from your soul the memory of wasted years and a ruined reputation, nor smooth out from anxious brows the wrinkles which trouble has plowed. It may not call back unkind words uttered or rough deeds done—for, perhaps, in those awful moments you struck her! It may not take from your memory the bitter thoughts connected with some little grave; but it is not too late to save yourself and secure for God and your family the remainder of your fast-going life.

But perhaps you have not utterly gone astray. I may address one who may not have quite made up his mind. Let your better nature speak out. You take one side or the other in the war against drunkenness. Have you the courage to put your foot down right, and say to your companions and friends: "I will never drink intoxicating liquor in all my life, nor will I countenance the habit in others?" Have nothing to do with strong drink. It has turned the earth into a place of skulls, and has stood opening the gate to a lost world to let in its victims, until now the door swings no more upon its hinges, but day and night stands wide open to let in the agonized procession of doomed men.

Do I address one whose regular work in life is to administer to this appetite? I beg you get out of the business. If a woe be pronounced upon the man who gives his neighbor drink, how many woes must be hanging over the man who does this every day, and every hour of the day!

A philanthropist going up to the counter of a grogshop, as the proprietor was mixing a drink for a toper standing at the counter, said to the proprietor, "Can you tell me what your business is good for?" The proprietor, with an infernal laugh, said, "It fattens graveyards!"

God knows better than you do yourself the number of drinks you have poured out. You keep a list; but a more accurate list has been kept than yours. You may call it Burgundy, Bourbon, Cognac, Heidseck, Hock; God calls it strong drink. Whether you sell it in low oyster cellar or behind the polished counter of first-class hotel, the divine curse is upon you. I tell you plainly that you will meet your customers one day when there will be no counter between you. When your work is done on earth, and you enter the reward of your business, all the souls of the men whom you have destroyed will crowd around you and pour their bitterness into your cup. They will show you their wounds and say, "You made them;" and point to their unquenchable thirst, and say, "You kindled it;" and rattle their chain, and say, "You forged it." Then their united groans will smite your ears, and with the hands, out of which you once picked the sixpences and the dimes, they will push you off the verge of great precipices; while, rolling up from beneath, and breaking among the crags of death, will thunder:

"Woe to him that giveth his neighbor drink!"

TALMAGE'S INTERESTING THOUGHTS.

PROTESTANTISM.— The term Protestantism reminds us of the prompt answer which was given by Wilkes, who was asked by a Romanist, "Where was your church before Luther?" "Where was your face before you washed it this morning?" replied Wilkes.

INCONSISTENCY.— A poor boy slyly takes from the basket of a market woman a choke pear — saving some one else from the cholera — and you smother him in the horrible atmosphere of Raymond street jail, or New York Tombs, while his cousin, who has been skilful enough to steal $50,000 from the city, you will make a candidate for the New York Legislature.

SIN.— The Egyptian queen was a fool when she dissolved a priceless pearl in a single cup of pleasure! The Indian chief was a fool when he, underrating the momentum of the current, and thinking he could stem the mighty flood, launched his canoe in the rapids and went over Niagara! He is a fool who sports with a deadly serpent! A man is a fool who, unarmed and alone, springs to combat with a lion! But sin is stronger than a lion, and more venomous than a serpent! The momentum of its destroying flood is mightier than Niagara's, and, more precious than all queenly regalia, it dissolves in one cup of evil gladness "the Pearl of Great Price!"

THE BIBLE.— After the battle before Richmond had been over several days, a man was found dead, with his hand on the open Bible. The summer insects had taken the flesh from the hand, and there was nothing but the skeleton left; but the skeleton fingers lay on the open page, and on this passage: "Yea, though I walk through the valley of the shadow of death, I will fear no evil; Thy rod and Thy staff they comfort me. Well, the time will come when all the fine novels we have on our bedroom shelf will not interest us, and all the good histories and all the exquisite essays will do us no good. There will be one Book, perhaps its cover worn out and its leaf yellow with age, under whose flash we shall behold the opening gates of heaven

REMORSE.—For every sin, great or small, conscience, which is the voice of God, has a reproof more or less emphatic. Charles IX., responsible for the St. Bartholomew massacre, was chased by the bitter memories of his deeds, and in his dying moments said to his doctor, Ambrose Parry :

"Doctor, I don't know what's the matter with me ; I am in a fever of body and mind, and have been for a long while. Oh, if I had only spared the innocent and the imbecile and the crippled!" Rousseau declared in old age that a sin he committed in his youth still gave him sleepless nights. Charles II., of Spain, could not sleep unless he had in the room a confessor or two friars. Cataline had such bitter memories he was startled at the least sound. Cardinal Beaufort, having slain the Duke of Gloucester, often in the night would say:

"Away! away! Why do you look at me?"

Richard III., having slain his two nephews, would sometimes in the night leap from his couch and clutch his sword, fighting apparitions.

RICHES.—Among the Sierra Nevada mountains I was walking with some of the passengers to relieve the overladen stage, and one of them gave me his history. He said : "With my wife I came to California twenty years ago. We suffered every hardship. I went to the mines, but had no luck. I afterward worked at a trade, but had no luck. Then I went to farming, but had no luck. We suffered almost starvation. Every thing seemed to go against us. While we were in complete poverty my wife died. After her death I went again to the mines. I struck a vein of gold which yielded me forty thousand dollars. I am now on my way to San Francisco to transfer the mine, for which I am to receive one hundred thousand dollars."

"Then," said I, "you are worth one hundred and forty thousand dollars."

"Yes," he said, "but it comes too late. My wife is gone. The money is nothing to me now."

LIFE.—I once stood on a platform with a clergyman, who told this marvelous story: "Thirty years ago two young men started out to attend Park Theater, New York, to see a play which made religion ridiculous and hypocritical. They had been brought up in Christian families. They started for the theater to see that vile play, and their early convictions came back upon them. They felt it was not right to go, but still they went. They came to the door of the theater. One of the young men stopped and started for home, but returned and came up to the door, but had not the courage to go in. He again started for home, and went home. The other young man went in. He went from one degree of temptation to another. Caught in the whirl of frivolity and sin, he sank lower and lower. He lost his business position. He lost his morals. He lost his soul. He died a dreadful death, not one star of mercy shining on it. I stand before you to-day," said that minister, "to thank God that for twenty years I have been permitted to preach the gospel. I am the other young man."

FORGIVENESS.—An old Christian black woman was going along the streets of New York with a basket of apples that she had for sale. A rough sailor ran against her and upset the basket, and stood back, expecting to hear her scold frightfully; but she stooped down and picked up the apples and said: "God forgive you, my son, as I do." The sailor saw the meanness of what he had done, felt in his pocket for his money, and insisted that she should take it all. Though she was black, he called her mother, and said: "Forgive me, mother, I will never do any thing so mean again." Ah! there is a power in a forgiving spirit to overcome all hardness. There is no way of conquering men like that of bestowing upon them your pardon, whether they will accept it or not.

DESTINY.—In the State of Ohio there is a court-house that stands in such a way that the rain-drops that fall on the north side go into Lake Ontario and the Gulf of St. Lawrence, while those that fall on the south side go into the Mississippi and the Gulf of Mexico. Just a little puff of wind determines the destiny of a rain-drop for two thousand miles. What a suggestive thought, that you and I may be setting in motion influences that shall determine a man's destiny for eternity!

MERCIES.—There was a man who came over from New York some years ago, and threw himself down on the lounge in his house, and said, "Well, every thing's gone." They said, "What do you mean?" "Oh," he replied, "we have had to suspend payment; our house has gone to pieces—nothing left." His little child bounded from the other side of the room, and said:

"Papa, you have me left." And the wife, who had been very sympathetic and helpful, came up and said:

"Well, my dear, you have me left." And the old grandmother, seated in a corner of the room, put up her spectacles on her wrinkled forehead and said:

"My son, you have all the promises of God left." Then the merchant burst into tears and said:

"What an ingrate I am! I find I have a great many things left. God forgive me."

SALVATION.—I was reading of a ship that was coming from California during the time of the gold excitement. The cry of " Fire! fire!" was heard on shipboard, and the captain headed the vessel for the shore, but it was found that the ship would be consumed before it reached the beach. There was a man on deck fastening his gold around him in a belt, just ready to spring overboard, when a little girl came up to him and said:

" Sir, can you swim ?" He saw it was a question whether he should save his gold or save that little child, and he said:

" Yes, my darling, I can swim," and he dashed his gold on the deck. "Now," he says, "put your arms around my neck; hold on very hard; put your arms around my neck."

And then the man plunged into the sea and put out for the beach, and a great wave lifted him high upon the shore, and when the man was being brought to consciousness he looked up; the little child, with anxious face, was bending over him. He had saved her.

SELF.—General Fisk says that he once stood at a slave-block where an old Christian minister was being sold. The auctioneer said of him, " What bid do I hear for this man? He is a very good kind of a man; he is a minister." Somebody said:

"Twenty dollars." (He was very old, and not worth much.)

"Twenty-five," said a second.

"Thirty," "Thirty-five," "Forty."

The aged Christian minister began to tremble; he had expected to be able to buy his own freedom, and he had just seventy dollars, and expected with the seventy dollars to get free. As the bids ran up the old man trembled more and more.

"Forty," "Forty-five," "Fifty," "Fifty-five," "Sixty," "Sixty-five."

The old man cried out, *"Seventy for my soul. Not a cent for the body!"* The men around were transfixed. Nobody dared bid; and the auctioneer struck him down to himself.

"Done—done! Soul and body for seventy dollars!"

The wicked value the body more than the soul.

MAN.—I never saw the honors of this world in their hollowness and hypocrisy so much as I have seen them within the last few days, as I have been looking over the life and death of that wonderful man, Charles Sumner. Now that he is dead the whole nation takes off the hat. The flags are at half-mast and the minute-guns on Boston Common throb, now that his heart has ceased to beat. Was it always so? While he lived, how censured of legislative resolutions, how caricatured of the pictorials, how *charged with every motive mean and ridiculous;* how, when struck down in the senate-chamber, there were hundreds of thousands of people who said, "Good for him, served him right!" Oh Commonwealth of Massachusetts! who is that man that sleeps to-night in your public hall, covered with garlands and wrapped in the Stars and Stripes? Is that the man who, only a few months ago, you denounced as the foe of Republican and Democratic institutions? Is that the same man? You were either wrong then or you are wrong now—a thing most certain, Oh Commonwealth of Massachusetts! When I see a man like that pursued by all the hounds of the political kennel so long as he lives, and then buried under garlands almost mountain high, and amid the lamentations of a whole nation, I say to myself, " What an unutterably hypocritical thing is all human applause and all human favor!" You took twenty-five years in trying to pull down his fame, and now you will take twenty-five years in trying to build his monument. You were either wrong then or you are wrong now. My friends, was there ever a better commentary on the hollowness of all earthly favor?

BAPTISM.—When I was in San Francisco a few summers ago, at the close of the preaching service, a young man came up on the steps of the pulpit and said:

" You don't know me, do you?"

" No," I replied, " I do not remember you."

Said he, " I am James Parrish. Don't you know James Parrish?"

" Oh, yes," I said, " I do know you; I remember." Then the scene all flashed back upon me of a small room in Syracuse, New York, and a dying mother who sent for me and an elder of the church to come and baptize her children; and again I saw her lying there as she turned to me and said, " Mr. Talmage, I sent for you; I am going to die, but I can't die until my children are in the church of God. Will you please to baptize them?" And " in the name of the Father, and of the Son, and of the Holy Ghost," I baptized them. Then she folded her hands and said, " It is enough. Lord Jesus, come quickly."

What was the use of having her children in the church?

I said to the young man standing on the pulpit stairs in San Francisco, " Oh, yes, I suppose you yourself have become a Christian, haven't you?"

" Oh, yes," he said, " I have."

" I knew you would," I said. " Any young man who had a mother like yours could not help but be a Christian."

A father said to his son, " You are too young to connect yourself with the church of God;" and the next day, while they were out in the fields, there was a lamb that had strayed away, and it was bleating for its mother, and the father said to the son:

"Take that lamb over to the fold to its mother."

" Father," said the boy, " I guess not; you had better let it stay out here six months, and see whether it lives or not; and if it lives then we can take it in."

The father felt the truth at his heart, and said:

" My son, take that lamb in, and you go yourself the next time the Lord's fold opens."

"Suffer the little children to come unto Me, and forbid them not, for of such is the kingdom of heaven."

ROBERT COLLYER.

THE BLACKSMITH PREACHER.

BIOGRAPHY AND REMINISCENCES.

The Rev. Dr. Robert Collyer was born in Yorkshire, England, in 1822. His parents were poor. He came to America as a blacksmith and settled in a little hamlet in Pennsylvania. George Alfred Townsend gives many reminiscences about Mr. Collyer when he was a village blacksmith like Elihu Burritt. The great preacher studied hard, and his wisdom and glowing eloquence soon raised him above the shop into scholastic and theological circles, until he now presides over one of the most beautiful Unitarian churches in New York. Dr. Collyer and Dr. John Hall are said to be two of the handsomest, and, at the same time, two of the most modest clergymen in public life. Dr. Collyer has written several books, and his lectures have been widely popular, especially his favorite lecture " Grit."

Dr. Collyer is always looking on the sunny side of life. " A dear good old lady taught me to look for the silver lining," said the doctor.

" How did she teach you ? " I asked.

" By example," said the doctor, smiling benignly. " She was a very poor woman and was overwhelmed with trouble. She had a drunken husband and a sick baby. Still she was always cheerful.

" One day I said : ' Mary you must have some very dark days ; they must overcome you with clouds sometimes.'

" ' Yes,' she replied ; ' but then I often find there's comfort in a cloud.'

" ' Comfort in a cloud, Mary ? '

" ' Yes,' she said ; ' when I am very low and dark I go to the window ; and if I see a heavy cloud I think of those precious words, " A cloud received Him out of their sight," and I look up and see the cloud sure enough, and then I think—well, that may be the cloud that hides Him ; and so you see there is comfort in a cloud.' "

Dr. Collyer is a strictly temperate man, but still likes a good dinner. English roast beef and plum pudding are his favorite dishes.

The doctor told me that one of his best dinners was almost spoiled by a joke.

" But a joke ought to spice a dinner," I said.

" It did spice this dinner a little too much," said the doctor.

" I was dining one evening at Delmonico's, and had arrived at the cheese stage of my repast. A delightful piece of Roquefort was set before me, ripe, vivacious, self-mobilizing. There is nothing I like better than a lively cheese, and I had just transferred a spoonful of the delicacy in question to my plate, when Henry Bergh, sitting at a neighboring table, sprang to his feet with a cry of horror, clutched my wrist with an iron grasp, and exclaimed:

" 'Hold, monster! Never shall you swallow a mouthful of that cheese in my presence!'

" 'And why not?' I inquired in perplexed amazement.

" 'Because, cruel man, I am a member of the Society for the Prevention of Cruelty to Animals, and I will not sit by calmly and see those innocent insects tortured.'"

Dr. Collyer tells a good many anecdotes at his own expense, but they are all as pure as our Savior's parables. One day Mr. Collyer was talking to a good old colored man down in Kentucky. Mr. Collyer always wears his white clerical tie, so the conversation was naturally about preachers.

"So, Uncle Jack," said Dr. Collyer, "you don't much believe in the idea that men are called to preach."

"Wall sah, de Lawd mout call some niggers ter preach, but it sorter 'peers ter me dat whar de Lawd calls one old man, Laziness calls er dozen. Nine nigger preachers outen ten is de laziest pussens in de worl' sah."

"How do you know Uncle Jack?"

"Case I'se a preacher merse'f, sah."

This caused a scream from all the clergyman in the car.

Dr. Thomas, of Chicago, who believes a good deal like Collyer, said afterward that he had some experience about being called to preach once that reminded him of the old colored man's call.

"How was it?" asked Collyer.

"Well," said the doctor, "I had a call at an advance salary to go to Richmond, after considering it a good while I finally concluded

"HOW DO YOU KNOW, UNCLE JACK?"

See page 400.

to remain in Chicago. About a week afterward some one sent my wife the Richmond *Telegram* in which was this poem :

"Beloved flock," the parson said, then paused and wiped his eyes,
" As pastor and as people we must sever tender ties;
I've a call to go to Richmond to be their chosen pastor;
A call so loud to disobey, I fear, would grieve the Master."

Replied the spokesman of the flock: "Though loud the call may be,
We'll call you louder to remain, an X for every V.
Whatever Richmond offers you we'll give to keep you here,
We trust you'll hear a voice divine, our call's so loud and clear."

With sobbing voice the parson said: "My duty's clearer now;
I'll stay with you, beloved ones; to heaven's will I bow,
So let us sing 'Blest Be the Tie,' and sing it clear and strong;
To leave you when you call so loud would be exceeding wrong!"

Then in his study he sat down, a letter to indite
Unto the church at Richmond. Thus did the parson write:
"I've wrestled o'er your call with prayer; the Lord bids me to stay,
And, consecrated to His work, I dare not disobey."

Dr. Collyer tells me that he got the following story from Dr. E. H. Chapin, the great Universalist divine :

A pious old Kentucky deacon—Deacon Shelby—was famous as a shrewd horse dealer. One day farmer Jones went over to Bourbon county, taking his black boy, Jim, with him, to trade horses with brother Shelby. After a good deal of dickering, they finally made the trade, and Jim rode the new horse home.

"Whose horse is that, Jim ?" asked some of the horse-trading deacon's neighbors, as Jim rode past.

"Massa Jones', sah."

"What! did Jones trade horses with Deacon Shelby ?"

"Yes, Massa Jones dun traded wid de deakin."

"Goodness, Jim! wasn't your master afraid the deacon would get the best of him in the trade?"

"Oh no!" replied Jim, as his eyes glistened with a new intelligence, "Massa knowed how Deakin Shelby has dun got kinder pious lately, and he was on his guard !"

One day Dr. Collyer was talking about repentance before his Sabbath-school class. "Of course," he said, "you can not expect forgiveness without repentance. It is not a one-sided act."

A little while afterward the Doctor called up a little girl and questioned her about the lesson.

"Now, Mary, tell us all what you must first do to have your sins forgiven."

"Well," said little Mary, with a lisp, "I des I must first do out and do the sin."

Dr. Collyer has a big, loving heart, and was never known to resent an indignity. The soft answer was always in his mouth. One day the blacksmith preacher bought a horse of a Pennsylvania farmer. The next day the horse strayed into the road and a mean neighbor caught him and put him in the pound. When Mr. Collyer called on him the next morning, the man said, very savagely:

"Yes, I did catch your horse in the road and I put him in the pound, and I'll do it again!"

"Neighbor," replied Dr. Collyer with a polite smile, "not long since I looked out of my window in the night and saw your cattle in my meadow, and I drove them out and shut them in your yard; and I'll do it again."

Struck with the doctor's reply, the man liberated the horse from the pound, and paid the charges himself.

"A soft answer turneth away wrath."

"Speaking of politeness," said the doctor, "I learned my first lesson in that accomplishment from a young lady."

"How was it?" I asked.

"Well, one evening a sweet, young lady, came round the corner of our church in great haste. I think she was hastening to catch a car. As she abruptly turned the corner she ran against a boy who was small and ragged and freckled. Stopping as soon as she could, she turned to him and said.

"'I beg your pardon; indeed, I am very sorry.'

"The small ragged and freckled boy looked up in blank amazement for an instant; then, taking off about three-fourths of a cap, he bowed very low, smiled until his face became lost in the smile, and answered.

"'You can hev my parding, and welcome, Miss; and yer may run agin me and knock me clean down, an' I won't say a word.'

"After the young lady passed," said the doctor, "the boy turned to a comrade and said, half apologetically, 'I never had any one ask my parding, and it kind o' took me off my feet.'"

"One day," said the doctor, "a good, old Scotchman, unconsciously paid me a great compliment. I had preached a strong, plain sermon—just such a sermon as a blacksmith would preach. When I got through, the old gentleman came up to me and I asked him how he liked the sermon.

" 'Well, sir,' was the unequivocal reply, 'I can't say that I liked it very well. It was a little too pline for me. I likes a preacher as joombles the r'ason and confoonds the joodgment; and of all the born preachers I've heerd, you cooms the furthest from that.' "

The doctor, who speaks the Scotch and Yorkshire dialects as well as English, delights to tell this story.

Dr. Collyer, like Chapin and Beecher and Dr. Storrs, always makes every text simple and plain. There was nothing like the vagueness of Emerson about their reasoning.

Dr. Chapin used to tell about a little experience he had with a dear, good, old colored preacher down in Kentucky. After Chapin had talked with Uncle Jacob a little while, the old colored clergy-man turned to him and said: " Yes, Brudder Chapin, we preachers must wuck with energy, ef we wucker tall. Scriptah says, 'Wotsomever you hastest fer to do you oughter dust it wid all yo' hawt an' mine an' stren'th.' An' above all things, doan pronasticrate."

" Don't whichtycrate, Uncle Jacob? What do you mean?" asked Chapin.

" I mean doan pronasticrate, Brudder Chapin. Doan put off tell nex' week whatchah orter done lass year. Time, Brudder Chapin, is a mighty hahd hoss to head. Tharfo' it behoofs you, as Scriptah says, to ketch him by the fetlock ef you wantah come undah de wiah 'fo' he does."

DR. COLLYER'S LECTURE TO YOUNG MEN
ON TWO EMIGRANTS.
GENESIS IX. 31, 32.

If you take a map of the region in which the man lived, whose story I want to touch for you as it touches my own heart, I think you will be able to form some idea of what he did in contrast with what he set out to do. Haran is about a day's march from the old homestead he left, while Canaan is ten or twelve; and it is easy going to Haran, one would think, but very hard to Canaan, because after you leave the place at which he halted, and push on toward that he aimed at, you have to cross a river over which there is or was no bridge, a desert of seven days' journey, and the rugged passes of the mountains. So that to reach Haran from Ur would be a sort of picnic, but to reach Canaan after that would be a painful pilgrimage, which would demand about all the pluck and courage there was in you.

Then, if we could see this Edessa, as it came to be called at a later day, we might guess how Terah caught the idea of going to Canaan. Edessa is a pretty little place, travelers say, as you shall find anywhere in old Chaldæa. It stands in a sort of desert, beside a deep, clear spring, in the midst of shade-trees and fruit-trees, and, above this, there rises a great rock on which there has stood a fortress, time out of mind, to which they could retreat when the enemy came, and defend themselves when there was no hope that they could do this on the plain. This was about the sum and substance then of Edessa, a small place standing by itself in a desert, very pleasant and good to live in if you are content to live in a small way, and nourish no ambition for a wider and larger life.

Now, Terah, if we may trust the old traditions, was a brass-founder in this pent-up place, and his special line of business was the making of molten gods. But such an industry as that must have been rather limited, for good reasons. Only so many would be wanted, at the most, and they would not wear out as wagons do, and plows, but the older they grew, the better the people would like them. Nor would there be any great improvement possible, except by permission of the priests, who are usually the last men in the world to admit that such things can be improved; so the poor man could not strike a new idea in this matter of the molten gods, and push the old incumbents from their stools, or melt them over and bring them out in a finer fashion, allowing buyers so much for the old metal.

We may guess, therefore, in what a strait Terah found himself at last, and why he may have begun to look with longing eyes westward. This Canaan away over the river, the desert, and the mountains, seems to have been a sort of Pacific Slope in those times; a splendid land of promise, in which you could live to your heart's content, when once you got there; widen the whole horizon of your life; find untold outlets for your powers; plant the stocks anew which had no room to grow in the pent-up garden-plat of Edessa, and then die when your time came, happy in the thought that you had made your stroke, and opened the way toward a larger and fairer life.

So Terah, as I have come to think of him, it may be because I am an emigrant myself, began to look with longing eyes toward the land of Canaan. He was ready, as he thought, to give up comfort for freedom; and a home and workshop in a pent-up place, in which he was bound to follow time-honored traditions and usages, for a tent, if it must be so, on the breezy slopes away beyond the mountains, with the ocean for his boundary on the one side and the desert on the other; and to exchange the safe citadel on the rock for the nobler fastness of a manhood that would hold its own against the world, and win.

It was a tremendous thing, as things stood then, to do. I think I can see him through the mists of time, sitting there in his workshop with his gods about him, trying to count the cost, and all the time, as he thinks of it, the plan grows more and more feasible. Then he consults the young men about it, his son and nephew; and of all things in the world, of course, this is what they would like to do, especially his son, who has already begun to dream of a wider and higher life for himself. So there would be a notice, we may presume, sent through the town, of a house and shop for sale, and the molten gods withal, at the buyer's own price, because Terah must be rid of them, he is going far away. Then the roots of his life would be torn out of the soil in which they had flourished, from father to son, ever since the time of the Tower of Babel. And there would be weeping among them, I think, and visits made to the graves of those they had loved, and the homes of their kinsfolk all about; and then, on a morning, you would see them set out on their day's march to Haran, where they would halt, and start on the morrow toward the river and the promised land. That morrow never came to Terah. How it was, we do not know—we know only this, that forward to Canaan he does not take another step. Haran itself is a pleasant place, I hear, with plenty of good land about it; and there would be a better chance for life and a living, it may be, there, than any he had left behind him in Edessa. Be this as it may, reason or none, there he stayed a great while, and there he died. One day's march from the place he had left, ten or twelve from that he dreamed of, far away yet from the promised land. And so, never now will he see the white glories of Lebanon, never the summer splendors of Hermon and Sharon, and never the blue sea turning to gold as he watches it at sunset from the crests at Carmel. He started on a journey; it ended, one might almost say, in a jaunt. He dreamed of the mountains, and settled on a flat. His ideal was freedom, to be bought with a great price; he struck this one stroke for it, and accepted comfort again on good securities. He went back no more; but then, he went forward no farther —got his chance just this once at a singular, separate, generous, free life, which held in its heart unknown treasures of greatness and worth, if he had only gone forth that morning, and made them his own. The morning came, and Terah was not ready. He was not to be one of the units in our life, after all, but only one of the vulgar fractions; not one of the men who stand out in clear and bold relief against the darkness of the ages, but one of the masses of men—Terah, the father of Abraham, who set out for the promised land, and then halted at the end of the one day's march.

But now, as I watch him sitting there, I am moved to make some plea for a kindlier judgment than this I have rendered touching his failure. It is clear, for one thing, that he is far on in years when he feels this impulse to strike out toward a wider and finer life, and so his years would tell against him. Old men soon tire of new adventures. They are "afraid of that which is high." Then this was not only change which was waiting in his outward life, but a wrench to his inward life also. This son of his, who grows to be one of the supreme men, you know, of the world, has set his face already against the old gods, and is no doubt looking forward to the new home as a place where he will not only be free to go where he will and do what he will earthward, but heavenward too; and I think Terah guesses this is just what will befall them. So we may imagine where the main trouble lies. Here is a man setting out on a great new enterprise, at a time of life when nature opposes instead of helping him; looking forward with his eyes, while his heart is looking backward; a man with Canaan on his lips and Edessa in his marrow; giving up the old paths which are as familiar to him as his own dooryard, to wander away over hills and dales all new to him, and all strange. I do not wonder the old man's heart failed him. He needed more than an impulse to lift him out of his old life. Only an inspiration could do that, and I am not sure even this could have mastered him when so much of life lay behind him. And so he must have said, sadly enough, "It is no use. I will not go back, but I can not go forward. I will settle down here, and wait for the angel of death. I can still do a very good day's work in Haran. They have no such gods here as I used to turn out in the old place. Their ideals are low. I will go to work and improve them." Something like this he must have said to the young men, while they talked with him of the better land, its freedom and beauty, and its rich reward. They spoke of freedom, he preferred safety; of the mountains, he was wedded to the flat; of the sea, he liked the little river better, purling along in the sunshine; of great rides across the greensward, he liked his arm-chair better, on the porch in summer, and in winter by the fire. "So Terah took Abram his son, and Lot his brother's son, and Sarah his daughter-in-law, and went forth with them from Ur of the Chaldees to go to Canaan; and they came to Haran and dwelt there, and Terah died in Haran."

But we have to notice, again, that this is by no means the end of the one day's march, for now we see what we have come to call " evolution " at work. Terah brings the young men so far toward this larger and better life he would fain have found, and then the impulse in him to go forward is mastered by the longing to sit still. But the time comes when that which was only an impulse in the father changes in the son to an inspiration, through which he not only carries out the whole intention of Terah, but does more than he ever dreamed of doing, because that which was only a desire in the first man to better himself, becomes in the second, a blessing to the race, and the whisper of ambition in the one man changes in the other to the voice of God.

I need not dwell long on this point in the story. I need only say that there is no evidence, or hint even, of a Divine light and leading in what these men are doing, until Terah is dead. But then God speaks to his son, bids him get out of Haran, and pass over to the promised land; and once there he becomes the spring-head of the floods of blessing to which the prophets belong and the psalmists, the seed of a mighty and matchless harvest the world is reaping still for the everlasting life. So, while the old man never saw the promised land, the young man saw it, and pre-empted it, as we say, for the home of the race which lay in his loins when he did cross the river and the mountains, and saw the land he had been dreaming of so long, while the old father's arm was about his neck, holding him back from his great desire. And so it seems but the simple truth to say that some touch of this glory rests on the old man's grave, after all, because we have no sure reason to think that the son would have gone to Canaan if the father had not set out to go, even if he did break down at the end of the first day's march. The impulse came first, the inspiration followed; but who shall be sure we could have had the one without the other? There are those, I suppose, in Edessa to-day, who have come straight down from some man who was quite content to stay there when Terah tore out the roots of his life; called him an old fool, perhaps, for not letting well enough alone; bought his molten gods, it may be—a dead bargain—made money on them ; and never once in all his life, looked beyond the palm-trees and the spring; but in all the world you would hardly find a poorer story of what men may do for the world's help and blessing than such a line of men would have to tell you. It is the first step which costs; and taking this first step, I love to believe, did something very noble for the genius and inspiration which has made our Bible the supreme book of the world, and this Hebrew line the greatest touching the religious life the world has ever known. Terah's dream never came true; but then, he had the dream, and did something to make it come true to his son, and so to the race. They say the way to hell is paved with good intentions. Well, here is one of the good intentions, then, that pave the way to heaven. He did see the promised land, after all, through the eyes of the man he had gotten from the Lord; and there was a strain of the sturdy striving which had paid the price of leaving the old place, in him who would never stop until he came to the new. So his feet also are beautiful upon the mountains, though he never saw them. I said he started on a journey, and it ended in a jaunt; but this must not blind us to what that jaunt must have cost him—the great sorrow of parting—the heart-ache of the man who seems to have stopped for the bone-ache. He did not do all he set out to do, let us allow this; but he did more than any other man of his clan in Edessa; and dying in Haran, he was not only one day's march on the road to this larger and finer life, but he had made it so much easier for the young men to go right on to the end.

And so this man's life touches yours and mine, and opens out toward some truths we may well lay to our hearts, and this is the first: That, if I want to do a great and good thing in this world, of any sort, while the best of my life lies still before me, the sooner I set about it the better. For, while there is always a separate and special worth in a good old age, this power is very seldom in it, I would try to verify; and it is not your old Philip, but your young Alexander, who conquers the world. I can remember no grand invention, no peerless reform in life or religion, no noble enterprise, no superb stroke of any sort, that was not started from a spark in our youth and early manhood. Once well past that line, and you can dream of Canaan; but the chances are, you will stop at Haran, so this putting off any great and good adventure from your earlier to your later age is like waiting for low water before you launch your ship. If we want to make our dream of a nobler and wider life of any sort come true, we must push on while the fresh strong powers are in us, which are more than half the battle. The whole wealth of real enterprise belongs to our youth and earlier manhood. It is then that we get our chance of rising from a collective mediocrity into some sort of distinct nobility. We may be ever so sincere after this, as far as we can go; but we shall only go to Haran. Yes, and we may have a splendid vision, as when this man saw Hermon and Sharon and the sea in his mind's eye, as he sat in his chair; and a noble and good intention, as when he started for the mountains, and halted on the plain; but just this is what will befall us also, if we are not true to this holy law of our life.

This is my first thought; and my second must take the form of a plea with those who do strike out to do grand and good things in this world, and do not halt, but march right on, and then nourish a certain contempt for those who still lag behind. The chances are, it is because these begin too late, that they end too soon; and it is no small matter that they begin at all. For myself, I can only blame them, when, with the visions of a nobler life haunting the heart, they tell me that Haran is good enough for anybody, and we need none of us look for anything better. If they know all the while, as this man knew, that the land of promise still lies beyond the line at which they have halted, and will say so frankly, though they may go only the one day's march, I can still bare my head in reverence before such men. I know what it is to leave these Edessas of our life, and what it costs; how the old homes and altars still have the pull on you, and the shadows of the palm-trees, and the well at which you have drunk so long, and what loving arms twine about you to hold you back from even the one day's march. So, when I hear those blamed who stop short still of where I think they ought to be, I want to say, have you any idea of what it has cost them to go so far as that, and whether it was possible for them to go any farther? And then, is it not a good thing anyhow to take those who belong to them the one day's march, and, setting their faces toward the great fair land of promise, leave God to see to it, that this which may be no more than an impulse in the man who has to halt, may grow again to a great inspiration in the son of his spirit and life who goes right on?

And this, I think, is what we may count on in every honest endeavor after a wider and better life. So I like the suggestion that the way the eagle got his wings, and went soaring up towards the sun, grew out of the impulse to soar. That the wings did not precede the desire to fly, but the desire to fly preceded the wings. Something within the creature whispered: "Get up there into the blue heavens; don't be content to crawl down in the marsh. Out with you!" And so, somehow, through what would seem to us to be an eternity of trying—so long it was between the first of the kind that felt the impulse, and the one that really did the thing, done—it was at last, in despite of the very law of gravitation, as well as by it; and there he was, as I have seen him, soaring over the blue summits, screaming out his delight, and spreading his pinions twelve feet, they said, from tip to tip.

I like the suggestion, because it is so true to the life we also have to live—trying and failing; setting out for Canaan, and stopping at Haran; intending great things, and doing little things, many of us, after all. I tell you again, the good intention goes to pave the way to heaven, if it be an honest and true intention. There is a pin-feather of the eagle's wing started somewhere in our starting—a soaring which goes far beyond our stopping. We may only get to the edge of the slough, but those who come after us will soar far up toward the sun.

So let me end with a word of cheer. The Moslem says: "God loved Abdallah so well that He would not let him attain to that he most deeply desired." And Coleridge says: "I am like the ostrich: I can not fly, yet I have wings that give me the feeling of flight. I am only a bird of the earth but still a bird." And Robertson, of Brighton, says: "Man's true destiny is to be not dissatisfied, but forever unsatisfied."

And you may set out even in your youth, therefore, with this high purpose in you I have tried to touch. You will make your way to a good place, a wider and more gracious life, do a great day's work, rise above all mediocrity into a distinct nobility, find some day that, though you have done your best, you have fallen far below your dream, and the Canaan of your heart's desire lies still in the far distance. All great and grand things lie in the heart of our strivings.

Dr. Collyer has the poetic instinct. All his prose is but another form of poetry.

The following poem is from the Doctor's fruitful pen.

A PSALM OF THANKSGIVING AFTER THE GREAT FIRE OF 1871.

O Lord our God, when storm and flame
    Hurled homes and temples into dust,
We gathered here to bless Thy name,
    And on our ruin wrote our trust.

Thy tender pity met our pain,
    Swift through the earth Thine angels ran,
And then Thy Christ appeared again,
    Incarnate, in the heart of man.

Thy lightning lent its haughty wing
    To bear the tear-blent sympathy,
And fiery chariots rushed to bring
    The offerings of humanity.

Thy tender pity met our pain,
    Thy love has raised us from the dust,
We meet to bless thee, Lord, again,
    And in our temples sing our trust.

SAM JONES.

PREACHER, TALKER, REFORMER AND WIT.

BIOGRAPHY AND REMINISCENCES.

Samuel Jones was born in Chambers county, Alabama, October 16, 1847. While a child his parents removed to Cartersville, Barlow county, Georgia, where he now resides, near Bill Arp. He comes from a church family and from a family of preachers, four of his uncles having been clergymen. His father was a brilliant lawyer, and his mother a most religious woman. The seeds of religious conviction were planted in the bosom of the great revivalist by his mother, and Mr. Jones' veneration for that sainted mother crops out in all his sermons. Mr. Jones studied law with his father, and began his law practice with brilliant prospects, but dissipation drew him away from his work and well nigh eclipsed his talents.

A solemn exhortation from Mr. Jones' father on his death bed caused him to reform, and he soon afterward married Miss Laura McElwain, of Eminence, Ky., a lovely character, who still cheers his life in his good work.

From a lawyer Mr. Jones became a traveling Methodist preacher in 1872. As a revivalist he met with extraordinary success, until he attracted the attention of Rev. T. DeWitt Talmage, who employed him in a grand revival at the Brooklyn Tabernacle.

Mr. Jones' first great revival was in St. Louis. Here J. B. McCullough, the editor of the *Globe*, really brought the great preacher out. Mr. McCullough had his sermons reported verbatim, sometimes filling six columns of the *Globe*. Mr. McCullough is a good Catholic, and his generous support of a Protestant clergyman should be appreciated by the whole Protestant church in America.

Mr. Jones uses plain language. He uses the every-day language of the street. Clergymen who bore their audiences call it slang, but Mr. Jones wins souls with this every-day language. Our orthodox clergy, seeing his works, have been compelled to endorse him.

Mr. Jones is sensational and so was Paul, and Peter the Hermit and Gough and Beecher and Wendell Phillips and Spurgeon, and his meetings produce intense interest and he always reaps an immense harvest of converts whom he turns over to any church in the fold of Christ.

Sam Jones (he prefers to be called plain Sam Jones) preaches without notes, depending upon the inspiration of the moment.

One day, while in conversation with the great revivalist, I asked him how he could preach such long sermons, night after night, without notes when such great men as John Hall, Prof. Swing, Storrs and Cuyler always read their sermons.

"It's easy enough," said Sam, "easy enough if you go to work in the right way. Now," he continued, "if I was to tell my serv-ant girl to go to the shop and get some sugar and bluing, some coffee and starch, some cakes, some soap and some almonds, some candles and spice, some nuts and some tea, some potash and butter, she would say:

"'Oh dear, sir, I never can think of all that.'

" But suppose I should say, 'look here, Betty, you know to-mor-row your mistress is going to have a large wash, and she will want some bluing and soap, candles and potash; the next day she will have company, and will want some tea and coffee, sugar, spice, nuts, cakes, butter and almonds.'

" 'Thank you, sir,' says Betty, 'now I can think of them all.'

"So it is in preaching. You want a logical, but simple arrange-ment."

Sam Jones makes a great deal of money out of his lectures, but not so much out of his preaching; still he has very little love for money.

"Are you saving your money?" I asked the revivalist, one day on the train.

"Saving my money!" he exclaimed, " What for ? Why a man who saves money is a miser. Christ didn't have a bank account. Josh Billings says the old miser that has accumulated his millions and then sits down with his millions at last, without any capacity for enjoying it, reminds him of a fly that has fallen into a half-barrel of molasses. There you've got the picture just as complete as Josh Billings ever drew a picture.

"No sir," continued Sam, "I never had much money—never will I reckon. I saw in the papers some time ago where a man had died in North Carolina and left Sam Jones a wonderful legacy—and all that sort of thing. I was at home at the time. Several of my friends ran up with the paper, and said:

"'Sam, did you see this?'

"'Yes.'

" ' What are you going to do about it?'

" ' I ain't going to do anything.'

" ' Well, I'd write on and tell them where you are.'

" ' No sir,' said I, ' I am getting on right well without a legacy, and God knows what I'd do if I had one. I am getting on so well without one that I don't want to fool with one.'

"Don't you see? I want you all to have legacies and live in fine houses, and I will go around and take dinner with you, and let you pay the taxes and servants, and I will enjoy the thing. Don't you see? That is a good idea, ain't it?"

"If I get wealth without religion," continued Sam, thoughtfully, "why, I'll be poor in the next world. Cornelius Vanderbilt was the richest man that ever bade America good-bye, and stepped into eternity. He turned to his oldest boy and passed $75,000,000 into his hands; $25,000,000 additional he turned over to the rest of his heirs, and, then in his last moments, turned to his Christian wife and asked her: ' Wife, please sing,

"Come, ye sinners, poor and needy;
Weak and wounded, sick and sore.' "

" The richest man that America ever produced asking his wife to sing the song of a beggar!"

I do not think there is a man living who can use as strong English as Sam Jones, or rather, as strong Saxon. The great but pedantic Dr. Johnson once said, speaking of one of Addison's essays: "There is not virtue enough in it to preserve it from putrefaction." Sam Jones would have said in his bold Saxon: "There ain't wit enough in it to keep it sweet." One day, when the reporters had been criticising the revivalist's Saxon language, he became indignant, and said:

" Do you want my opinion of these reporters, who abuse our meetings?"

"Yes."

" Well, in my humble opinion, I will be in heaven when these stinking miserable little reporters who malign me are sitting on one ear in hell, trying to keep cool by fanning themselves with the other."

" Do they ever answer back to you from the audience when you talk so savagely?" I asked.

"Yes, often. Every now and then a burnt sinner will squeal. Sometimes they get a good joke on me, too. One day, in St. Louis," continued the preacher, laughing, "an awful funny thing happened. I had been attacking the gamblers and drunkards for an hour, and I said a drunkard is lower than a dog. 'Why,' said I, 'I've seen a man and a dog go into a saloon, and, in an hour, the man would get beastly drunk, and stagger out like a hog, while the dog would come out and walk away like a gentleman.'

"Just then a shabby, blear-eyed man arose tremblingly, and started to leave the church.

"'Stop! young man,' I said. 'Stop!'

"The young man stood still, with a thousand eyes on him.

"'If you'd rather go to hell than hear me preach, just go on!'

"'Well,' replied the man, after a pause, 'I believe I'd rather.' And out he went.

"Ha! ha! ha!" chuckled Sam, "it was a good one, wa'nt it?

"The very next night," continued the preacher, "I saw the same man in the audience. By and by I saw him standing up.

"'Well,' said I, kindly, 'what do you want, my man?'

"'I want to know, Elder, if you think you can get the devil out of me?'

"'O, yes,' I said, 'but I don't think it would improve you any. The little left would be worse than the devil.'

"I suppose you learn a good deal from your audiences?" I suggested.

"Oh, yes. A good old Christian lady rose one night and said she had got repentance.

"'Do you know what true repentance is, mother?' I asked.

"'Yes. It is being sorry for your meanness and feeling that you ain't going to do it any more.'

"'That's the best definition of repentance I ever heard in my life mother,' I said. 'That *is* repentance. Good Lord, I am so sorry for my meanness that I don't intend to do it any more. And now mother,' said I, 'Do you know what true religion is?'

"'Yes.'

"'What?'

"'It's this,' said the old lady: 'If the Lord will just forgive me for it, I won't *want* to do it any more.'

"'Right mother!' said I. 'There is repentance and religion in a nutshell, so every man in the world can get hold of it.'"

SAM JONES'S GREATEST SERMON.

THUNDER AND LIGHTNING ON SINNERS' HEADS.

Brothers and Sisters :—I don't care so much about my text as I do about my sermon, but did you ever see such a string of pearls as this text—such a monosyllabic utterance ?

Let—your—light—so—shine—before—men—that—they—may—see—your—good—works—and—glorify—your—Father—which—is—in—Heaven.

I have frequently gone into a community, and while there, I have kicked the bushel off a great many men's lights, and they would fall out with me and say I put their light out. And I didn't. Their light had gone out over ten years before, when they went and turned that bushel down over it. It went out the minute they turned that bushel over it. Sometimes it is the bushel of neglect. Sometimes it is the bushel of willful transgression. Sometimes it is the bushel of avarice. And there are a thousand bushels that will be furnished you at any time you want one to turn down over your light. And at any moment, if you put a bushel over your light—if your light was burning and you have taken and turned a bushel and put over it—you will find your light is out. And don't be foolish enough to think that the man that removed the bushel put your light out. It was the bushel turned down over it that put the light out.

Never mind about other people's lights. Look after your own light. Some clergymen, instead of shedding their own light by preaching Christ, are looking after Tom Paine and Ingersoll—looking after false lights. [Applause.]

Who cares about Bob Ingersoll's infidelity, or who cares about any body else's infidelity? The difference between Ingersoll and the church-man is that the man in church believes every thing, and won't do any-thing, while Bob Ingersoll is a sort of theoretical infidel, who gets $1,500 a night for being one, and you dead Christians here, like fools, are one for nothing and board yourselves. That's all there is about it. [Laughter.]

Church members should let their lights shine by their actions. Win the sinner by love. A worldly man recently entered one of the churches in Indianapolis, and was allowed to stand fifteen minutes in the aisle. Then he walked around to another aisle. No Christian offered him a seat. By and by, after he got tired out standing, he leaned over to a brother who had his light under a bushel, and ventured to inquire:

"What church is this?"

"Christ's church, sir — Christ's," said the church member, impatiently.

"Is he in?" asked the man, meekly.   [Laughter.]

The churchman left his light under the bushel, and went and got the stranger a seat.   He was so mad about it that when he got back to his bushel, the light was out.   [Laughter.]

How many Christians here to-night have put out their light?

Many clergymen, instead of making Christ shine, are trying to shine themselves.   Their sermons are not to save sinners, but they are made to win the praise of men.   They read well, but they don't save souls.

The good, old colored sexton in Memphis jumped up one day, and said:

" Brethren, I've been hearing this book preaching for years.   Our pastors don't put the fodder down low enough.   I went to see our preacher in his study, this morning, and he had six books open before him.   I said to him:

"' Brother, if you get one sermon out of six books, you are going to put that fodder up where I can't reach it, and where a great many others can't reach it, and we will all go in, Sunday morning, hungry, and come out starving — starving for Christ's plain, simple food.'"   [Applause.]

And that's a fact.   Every one can reach a thing when it is on the ground, and as far as I am concerned, I believe it is the Christly way to find a common level and stand on that level to preach to the masses. And if you see me drop down at all while I am here, you may know that I am seeking a level and that's all the meaning there is in it at all.   If you see my style don't exactly suit you, and the grammar, and rhetoric and logic are a little butchered, I am just endeavoring to adapt my style to my crowd; don't forget that, and I'll find your level before I leave you.   [Laughter.]

I want a man to do every thing in earnest.

If I see a young lawyer, instead of pouring over Blackstone, spending his evenings in saloons or flirting with girls along the street it don't need the tongue of a prophet to say that fellow will never get but one case and the sheriff will get his client.   [Laughter.]

I see a young fellow starting out to be a doctor.   I see him loitering away his time and spending his evenings in parties, and paying no attention to physiology and anatomy and hygiene, and so forth.   I turn around and I can see what you will be.   You will have but one patient, and the undertaker will get him next day, and that will wind up your practice.   [Laughter.]

I see a preacher starting out. He never looks in a book, never thinks, never studies; he is going to open his mouth and let the Lord fill it. Well, the Lord does fill a fellow's mouth as soon as he opens it, but He fills it with air. [Laughter.] And there's many an old air-gun going through this country professing to be a preacher. [Laughter.] I thave listened to some men preaching an hour, and they didn't say one hing in the hour; and I got perfectly interested seeing how the fellow could dodge every idea in the universe and talk an hour. [Laughter.] I just watched him. That kind of preaching is worse than book preaching.

I see a farmer the first three months of the year, instead of cleaning out his fence corners and repairing his fences and turning his land and being just as energetic and active in January as he is in May—instead of that he is loitering around doing nothing. I don't need any tongue of the prophet to tell how he will come out farming. I have seen him down South. I have watched him, and I have told him before he started in how he would come out, too. Said I: " I'll tell you what will happen to you. You'll buy you corn from the West; you put in forty acres to the old mule;" and said I, "before the year is out the grass will have your cotton, and the birds will have your wheat, and the buzzards will have your mule, and the sheriff will have you [laughter]; and that's about where you'll wind up." Didn't mean any thing—that's the trouble. [Laughter.]

But, on the other hand, when I see a young lawyer pouring over his books day after day, and night after night he burns the midnight oil, and I see the blood fading from his cheek, and his eyes growing brighter every day, I don't need the tongue of the prophet to tell you there will be one day a judge of the supreme court; that there will be one day one of the finest lawyers that America ever produced.

You let me watch a fellow the first three months after he joins the church, I can tell you whether he means business or not. I see him begin to stay out of his prayer meetings, and begin to neglect his duty, and begin to think that he has got more religion than he wants, and he'll run the rule of subtraction or division through it, instead of the rule of addition, and I know just about where he'll land at. You are there now. [Laughter.] When I see a man come into the church of God Almighty, and he feels like " I'm going to take every chance for the good world, I'm going to get all the good out of every thing that comes my way, or comes within a mile of me, or ten miles of me," and I see him do his best, and at his place, and he is drawing in from all sources in heaven and earth, and I see that man as he begins to move forward in his church, and begins to be one of the pillars in church — I don't mean p-i-l-l-o-w-s— you've got a great many of this sort of pillars in your churches in this town, good old cases for others to crawl in, and lay their heads on, and go to sleep; that sort of pillows! downy fellows! [Laughter.]

If I had children who would not read a book, and would not be interested in any thing that ought to be interesting to intelligent beings, I would learn them all to play cards. [Laughter.] The little simpletons, I would run them on that line. [Laughter.] If I had a daughter who was such a simpleton that she had only just sense enough to behave herself, I would send her to a hook-nosed French dancing-master [laughter], and I would tell him to make her graceful, and "if her head is a failure, I want you to make it up on the feet." [Renewed laughter.] The law of compensation, of checks and balances, ought to work here, ought it not? I would say to the hook-nosed Frenchman: "Bring her feet up right. She is a failure in her head." I would learn her to dance gracefully, and marry her off to some ball-room dude, and buy them a place away off in the country, and tell them never to come and see me. When I got anxious to see them, I would take her mother, and go, and see them. [Laughter.]

Of course, this is irony, for I should never have such children, and you all know that I am opposed to dancing.

I was sitting in a train some time ago, and the train rolled up to the station, and just up on the platform, near by, were three ladies. One of the ladies said to the other:

"Are you going to the ball to-night?"

"No, I'm not going," was the reply.

"Oh, I forgot. You Methodists don't go to such places. Pshaw! I wouldn't be a Methodist; I want to enjoy myself."

"Well," said her friend, "I am a Methodist—thank God— and I don't want to go to such places."

"No Methodism for me!" and then the train rolled off, and I felt like jumping on the top of that train myself and hollering, "Hurrah for Methodism!" [Laughter.] And whenever she goes into co-partnership with ball-rooms and with all of the worldly amusements that embarrass the Christian and paralyze his power—whenever the Methodist Church goes into co-partnership with these things, I will sever my connection with her forever. And I love her and honor her to-day because she has stood like a bulwark against these things, and denounced them from first to last.

"Oh," but you say, "I don't believe in Puritanism. I don't believe in that. I believe the Lord means us to enjoy ourselves a little."

Yes, that is the way I used to talk.

"Why don't the Lord want us to dance? There ain't no harm in that," you say.

I tell you, I can go to houses—houses morally dark and morally degrading as perdition itself—and I can look at that poor, lost woman and ask her, "Where did you take your first downward step to death and hell?"

"At a ball room," she says.

There is not a family—I speak it because I believe it—there is not a family in the city of St. Louis where the father who trains his children for ball rooms and germans can lay his hands upon the head of his daughter and say: "This daughter will die as pure as an angel." You can not say it. Other men's daughters as pure, as lovely as yours, have been down with the devil's feet on them—and a woman never gets up when the devil puts his feet on her once! Submission to Christ—there is the test.

Imagine Christ dancing.

I never saw a spiritual man in my life who would stand up and ask me, "Do you think there is any harm in the dance?" Why don't you ask me if I think there is any harm in a prayer meeting, or I think there is any harm in family prayer? You know there ain't. And whenever you hear a fellow asking if there is any harm in the dance, you can reply, "You lying old rascal, you know there is." [Laughter and applause.]

Mr. Jones, turning to the ministers seated behind him, asked, "Why don't you say Amen?" [Renewed laughter and applause.]

That young man says, "I would join the church, but I love to dance." That young lady says, "I would join the church but I love to dance." Well, young lady, go on. We will say that you go to two hundred balls—that is a big allowance, ain't it?—and that you dance hundreds of sets. By and by you die without God and without hope, and down into the flames of despair you go forever; and as you walk the sulphurous streets of damnation you can tell them: "I am in hell forever, it is true, but I danced four hundred times, I did." [Laughter.] Now, won't that be a consolation?

What do you want to dance for, young lady; what use is it to you? If I had to marry a dozen times—and I am like the Irishman who said he hoped he would not live long enough to see his wife married again, [laughter] if I had to marry a dozen times, I would never go to a ball-room to get my wife. I used to dance with the girls, but when I wanted to marry I did not go to the ball-room to get my wife. A fellow might possibly get a good one in the ball-room, but many a fellow hasn't.

[Laughter.] God gives a man a good wife but he gets a bad one from the devil, and he has to go where that devil is to get her. [Renewed laughter.]

What good does it do you to be able to dance? Take the best girl in this town after her family is reduced to a fearful crisis by her father's business reverses. Now they are poor and that girl must earn a living. I will introduce her to a dozen of the leading citizens of the town, and give her a worthy recommendation in every respect. She is just what every body would want as a music teacher, as a clerk or in any other capacity, but I will add as a postscript to the recommendation, "she is a first-class dancer," [laughter] and that will knock her out of every job she applies for in this world. And so with every sin. And I declare to you to-night that the thing that keeps us away from God and out of the church, that is the price we put on our soul.

Then there is the man who wants to drink.

He says: "I would be religious if it were not for so and so," and I never think of this without thinking of an incident in which a husband sat by his wife at a revival meeting. When the penitents were asked to come to the altar, he was asked by his wife: "Come, won't you give yourself to God?" He shook his head and went home.

That night she said to her husband, "I saw you were affected. I wish you had given your heart to God!"

He said: "Wife, I can not be a Christian in the business I am in."

She said: "I know that."

He was a liquor dealer.

And she added: "Husband, I want you to give up your business and give your heart to God."

"Oh, wife, I can't," he said, "I can't afford it."

"Well, husband," she said, "how much do we clear every year on whisky?"

"We clear $2,000 a year, my darling."

"But how long, husband, shall we live to run this business?"

"Twenty years, and then we'll have $40,000."

"Forty thousand dollars! Now, my darling husband, if we could get $40,000 all in a lump, would you sell your soul to hell for that sum? Would you?"

"No, wife," he said. "No, no! no!! I'll close out my business in the morning and I'll give my heart to God, right now. I would not sell my soul for four million dollars!" [Applause.]

Christ will save us if we follow Him; God will shield us if we trust in Him.

I learned a great lesson in my relations toward God in a little incident that happened at my own home. We had in our employ a colored servant girl nursing for us. She was rather a careless, indifferent servant. I was sitting in the room one morning, just after breakfast, and this girl walked in and my wife said:

"Sally, you can go to your home this morning, and tell your mother to come over after awhile and I will pay your wages to her. I don't want you any longer, Sally, you may go."

I looked up from my book and the girl stood there, full face toward my wife, and the tears commenced running down her cheek, and directly she turned to my wife and she says:

"Mrs. Jones, please ma'am, don't turn me off. I know I'm the poorest servant you ever had, but I don't want to be turned off. Please ma'am keep me."

I commenced to beg for the poor girl, and said: "Wife, bear with her a little while longer." And then I thought to myself: "If the Lord Jesus were to come down this morning and discharge me and tell me, 'I don't want you any longer,' I would fall down at His feet and say: Blessed Savior, don't turn me off. I know I'm the poorest servant you ever had, but, blessed Christ, keep me in Thy life employ.'"

Oh, blessed Christ! So good to us! So merciful to us! But we must stand by God if we expect Him to stand by us. We must stand as firm as old Daniel did. They got after Daniel, you know, and said:

"If you don't stop prayin' to God and go to prayin' to the king, he'll put you down in the lions' den."

"Let them do what they please," said Daniel, and down he went on his knees and the next minute he went. He knew that if he did wrong he would go to hell; if he did right he'd go to heaven. God went down with him into the den, and the first thing Daniel knew a big lion went to sleep and Daniel stretched himself by his side, and, pillowing his head on the shaggy mane of the brute, said: "This beats hell." I choose to serve God, forever, and I stand in no fear of kings. [Laughter.]

Now, don't criticise me; I'm doing the best I can. Don't find fault because there is an occasional laugh. I don't care what a man does while I'm skinning him; if he laughs, it is all right. But if you will hold while I skin the price of hides will go down, I assure you of that.

I was getting on a railroad train some months ago in my State, and a gentleman boarded the train at one of the stations, and, after shaking hands and talking a moment, I asked him the news.

"Well," he said, "nothing special, I believe, except I came very near being killed last night."

"How was that?" I asked.

Said he: "The agent at the depot in our town was lying on the platform of the depot, drunk. He had been drunk several days. I went up to him to help him into the depot, and when I did so, he jerked out his pistol and shot at me twice, and came very near hitting me."

"Well," said I, "do you mean to say that the agent at the depot in your town had been drunk for several days? Why," said I, "the officers of this road are very strict with their employes. How is it this man maintains his position if he drinks that way?"

"I can't tell you, sir," said the gentleman, "only this man, this agent, is brother-in-law to the president of the road."

Well, when he said that, I saw it all in a moment, and then I said to myself: "How is it God puts up with me as He does? How is it God has borne with me as He has?" And I found the answer is this: Not because God was my brother-in-law, but because God was my father; and isn't it astonishing how God will bear with His children?

Let your light so shine—but bridle your tongues? O, how much damage our idle tongues have done!

Husband, how often have you wronged your wife with your tongue? Wife, how often have you stabbed your husband by a hasty word! Mother, how often has your child winced and shrunk away from you under the merciless power of your tongue?

The prettiest, whitest tombstone I ever saw, and the prettiest epitaph I ever read was when I visited an old friend in Georgia. He said he had lost the best wife a man ever had, and he led me out to the little white tombstone. There were only a few words on it—the date of her birth and her death—and then, underneath, this one line:

"She made home pleasant."

Of all the places in the world, home should be the most pleasant; but this can never be without bridled tongues. The wife, as she bends over that pale, waxen face, cries out in the agony of her heart, "Husband, precious, forgive those unkind words." The husband, as he stands by the coffin and looks upon the last remains of his wife, cries out, "Good Father, forgive every unkind word I uttered." My innocent little child runs into my study, where I sit, worn out with writing. It is little five-year-old Bob, or perhaps four-year-old Laura, and he gathers my arm and scatters the ink. Then I turn around and say:

"Oh, you little brat!" or "You mischievous little wretch, get out of here!"

He straightens up with a look of surprise, turns around and walks out of the room. I try to go ahead with my work, but I don't write

SHE MADE HOME HAPPY.

See page 422.

five lines. I say, "He didn't think. I will hunt him up and beg his pardon." I go out on the back porch and there I find little Bob crying as if his heart would break. I take him up in my arms and say, "Forgive me, my little pet ; I didn't think." And the little one sobs out :

"Mamma told me not to bother you, but I forgot. I ask you to forgive me."

O, if you want to be received into the inner kingdom, you must have a converted tongue.

Oh, these tongues of ours! These tongues of ours! We Methodists pour the water on, and the Presbyterians sprinkle it on, and the Baptists put us clean under, but I don't care whether you sprinkle, or pour, or immerse, the tongue comes out as dry as powder. Did you ever see a baptised tongue? [Laughter.] Say, did you? [Laughter.] Did you ever see a tongue that belongs to the church? You will generally find the tongue among man's reserved rights. [Laughter.] There come in some reservations, and always where there is a reservation the tongue is retained. The tongue! The tongue! The tongue! Pambus, one of the middle-age saints, went to his neighbor with a Bible in his hand and told him, "I want you to read me a verse of Scripture every day. I can't read, and I want you to read to me." So the neighbor opened the Bible and read these words:

I will take heed to my ways that I sin not with my tongue.

Pambus took the book out of his hand and walked back home, and about a week after that the neighbor met him, and he said :

" Pambus, I thought you were to come back and let me read you a passage of Scripture every day ?" and Pambus said :

"Do you recollect that verse you read to me the other day ?"

"No," said the neighbor.

"Well," said Pambus, "I will quote it :

I will take heed to my ways than I sin not with my tongue.

"And," he said, "I never intend to learn another passage of Scripture until I learn to live that one."

Oh, me! If every man, woman and child in this house to-night would go away from here determined to live that passage of Scripture."

Once in Jerusalem a great crowd—it was 1,800 years and more ago, as the legend goes, or the allegory—a great crowd was gathered in Jerusalem, and they were gathered around a dead dog, and they stood and looked, and one of them said:

" That is the ugliest dog I ever saw." Another said: "Oh, he is not only the ugliest dog I ever saw, but I don't believe his old hide is worth taking off him." Another said: "Just look how crooked his legs are." And so they criticised the poor dog. And directly one spoke up and said, "Ain't those the prettiest, pearly white teeth you ever looked at?" And they walked off and said, "That must have been Jesus of Nazareth that could have found something good to say about a dead dog." Oh, me! I like those people that always like to see something kind in people in their ways and walks of life. As bad as we are maybe, Jesus will see some thing good in us.

Down South before the war we used to put a nigger on the block and sell him to the highest bidder. Sometimes he would run away and we could not get him on the block, but we would sell him on the run.

"How much for him running away."

Well, brother, when God Almighty turned this world over to Jesus Christ he turned it over on the run, running away from God, running away to hell and death, and the Lord Jesus Christ came as swift as the morning light and overtook this old world in her wayward flight, threw His arms around her and said:

"Stop, stop, let us go back to God. Let us go back."

Oh, Jesus Christ, help every man here to say: "I will go back. I have strayed long enough. I will go back now." Will you, brother? God help every man to say, "This night I have taken my last step in the wrong direction, and have turned round." That is just what God wants sinners to do—to turn round—to turn round. Will you to-night say, "God being my helper, I will stop. I will turn my attention to Heavenly things and eternal things. I will look after my soul, if I starve to death." Will you do that?

Now we are going to dismiss this congregation, and those who wish to retire can do so, but I hope those who are not Christians will remain, and if you are a Christian and want to help us, remain with us. Let us make this Friday night a night of preparation for a higher and a better life. Let one hundred of us say: "I want to prepare to enter the church on Sunday morning." If there is any man interested in his soul let him stay and talk and pray with us to-night.

"MRS. PARTINGTON."

THE AMERICAN MRS. MALAPROP.

BIOGRAPHY AND REMINISCENCES.

Benjamin P. Shillaber, born in New Hampshire, 1814, was a printer at Dover, New Hampshire, in 1830, and in 1835 went to Demerara, Guiana, as a compositor, and remained there three years. From 1840 to 1847 he was in the printing office of the Boston *Post*, and after that time for three years was connected with the same paper editorially. It was at this period that he wrote under the name of "Mrs. Parting-ton," and gained a reputation as a humorist by the quaintness of his style and matter. Between 1850 and 1852 he tried his hand at newspaper proprietorship in the *Pathfinder and Carpet-Bag*, but returned to the *Post* 1853 56. From 1856 he was for ten years one of the editors of the Boston *Saturday Evening Gazette*. He has published "Rhymes with Reason and Without;" "Poems;" "Life and Sayings of Mrs. Partington;" "Knitting Work," and other volumes.

No American has caused more delight to his countrymen than Benjamin P. Shillaber. He is the American "Yellow Plush," but Thackeray's Yellow Plush papers never began to cause the laughter —innocent laughter, that Mrs. Partington's sayings have.

During the preparation of this book, Mr. Shillaber wrote the following letter to Mr. Bok, which will go down as the most authentic history of his *nom de plume*:

My Dear Mr. Bok:—The beginning of the Partington paragraphs was something like the loss of Silas Wegg's leg, "in an accident." There was no intention or pre-meditation in the matter, and the result was a great surprise to me. It was at a time when steamers twice a month brought news from Europe, and one arrival brought the intelligence that breadstuffs had advanced in price. This was the occasion for a three-line paragraph, which, I think, I "set up" without writing, stating that "Mrs. Partington said that it made no difference to her whether the price of flour increased or not, as she always had to pay just so much for half a dollar's worth." The name was not chosen, but it came with a sudden memory of Sydney Smith's dame who mopped back the Atlantic when it overflowed into her cottage at Sidmouth. I had no intention of aught beyond the moment. Flattered by the success of this virgin effort, which was copied everywhere, I tried it again, with like success, and what was begun in a sportive moment became a sort of *point d'appui* for many things latent in my inkstand, until the little one became a thousand. I was surprised to find that Mrs. Partington was a *bona fide* name, and I regretted that, under the circumstances, I had not taken another, but it had grown into public favor, and could not be changed without being abandoned altogether, and therefore was continued until the offense became mountainous. I justified it to myself by laying the original blame on Sydney Smith, to whose assumption I had merely given "a local habitation and name" on this side of the water. His character, however, said nothing; mine was garrulous, and that is all the story.

B. P. SHILLABER.

THE PARTINGTON LECTURE.

Ladies and Gentlemen:—It was with strong emotion of wonder that Mrs. Partington read in the papers that a new wing was to be added to the Cambridge Observatory.

"What upon airth can that be for, I wonder? I dare say they are putting the new wing on to take more flights arter comics and such things; or to look at the new ring of the planet Satan—another link added to his chain, perhaps, and, gracious knows, he seems to go father than ever he did before."

She stopped to listen as the sounds of revelry and drunkenness arose upon the night air; and she glanced from her chamber, over the way, where a red illuminated lantern denoted "Clam Chowder." Why should she look there just at that moment of her allusion to Satan? What connection could there be, in her mind, between Satan and clam-chowder? Nobody was present but Ike, and Isaac slumbered.

Mrs. Partington was in the country one August; and for a whole month not one drop of rain had fallen. One day she was slowly walking along the road, with her umbrella over her head, when an old man, who was mending up a little gap of wall, accosted her, at the same time depositing a large stone upon the top of the pile.

"Mrs. Partington, what do you think can help this 're drought?"

The old lady looked at him through her spectacles, at the same time smelling a fern leaf.

"I think," said she in a tone of oracular wisdom, "I think a little rain would help it as much as anything." It was a great thought. The old gentleman took off his straw hat and wiped his head with his cotton handkerchief, at the same time saying that he thought so too.

"Does Isaac manifest any taste for poetry, Mrs. Partington?" asked the schoolmaster's wife, while conversing on the merits of the youthful Partington.

The old lady at the time was basting a chicken which her friends had sent her from the country.

"Oh, yes!" she said, smiling; "he is very partially fond of poultry, and it always seems as if he can't get enough of it."

The old spit turned by the fire-place in response to her answer, while the basting was going on.

"I mean," said the lady, "does he show any of the divine afflatus."

The old lady thought a moment.

"As for the divine flatness, I don't know about it. He's had all the complaints of children; [laughter] and, when he was a baby, he fell and broke the cartridge of his nose; but I hardly think he's had this that you speak of." [Laughter.]

The roasting chicken hissed and spluttered, and Mrs. Partington basted it again.

"What is the matter with Mrs. Jinks, doctor?" asked Mrs. Partington as Dr. Bohn passed her house. She had been watching him for half an hour through a crack in the door, and people who saw the end of a nose thrust through the crack stopped a moment to look at it.

"She is troubled with varicose veins, madam," replied the doctor, blandly.

"Do tell!" cried the old lady. "Well, that accounts for her very corse behavior. If one has very corse veins what can you expect? Ah, we are none of us better than we ought to be and ——"

"Good morning, mem," broke in Dr. Bohn, as he turned away and the old lady closed the door.

"No better than we ought to be!"

What an original remark on the part of the old lady, and how candid the admission! The little front entry heard it, and the broad stair that led to the chamber heard it, and Ike heard it, as he sat in the kitchen daubing up the old lady's Pembroke table with flour and paste, in an attempt to make a kite out of a choicely-saved copy of the *Puritan Recorder*. "We are no better than we ought to be"—generally.

"If there is any place where I like to ransact business in," said Mrs. Partington, "it is in a bank. There is no beatin' down there. All you have to do is to put your bill on the counter and they exonerate it at once."

"Speaking of intemperance," said the old lady, solemnly, with a rich emotion in her tone, at the same time bringing her hand, containing the snuff she had just brought from the box, down upon her knee, while Lion, with a violent sneeze, walked away to another part of the room, "intemperance is a monster with a good many heads, and creeps into the bosoms of families like any conda or an alligator, and destroys its peace and happiness, forever."

"But, thank Heaven," she continued, a "new Erie has dawned upon the world, and soon the hydrant-headed monster will be overturned! Isn't it strange that men will put enemies into their mouths to steal away their heads?"

"Don't you regard taking snuff as a vice?" we asked, innocently.

"If it is," she replied, with the same old argument, "it's so small a one that Providence won't take no notice of it; and, besides, my oil factories would miss it so!"

Ah, kind old heart, it was a drunkard's argument! [Applause.]

When they were talking about Vesuvius, the old lady said, "La me! Why don't they give it sarsaparilla to cure its eruptions?" [Laughter.]

The old lady says that she "intended the concert of the Female Cemetery last evening, and some songs were extracted with touching pythagoras." She declares "the whole thing went off like a Pakenham shot, the young angels sung like syrups," and, during the showers of applause, she remembered she had forgot her parasol.

When a friend spoke of suffering the agonies of death, the old lady interrupted her: "La me!" she said, "here I have been suffering the bigamies of death for three mortal weeks. First I was seized with a bleeding phrenology in the left hampshire of the brain, which was exceeded by a stoppage of the left ventilator of the heart. This gave me an inflammation in the borax, and now I'm sick with the chloroform morbus. There's no blessing like that of health, particularly when you're sick!" [Laughter.]

Speaking of statues, the old lady says she prefers the Venus de Medicine to any other statute she knows of.

"Here's **Dr. Johnson's Dictionary,**" said Mrs. Partington, one day, as she handed it to Ike; "study it contentively, and you will gain a great deal of inflammation." [Laughter.]

"Overland roots from India!" said the old lady, on hearing the Indian news read. "Bless me!" she exclaimed, "those must be the roots they make the Indian meal of!"

They were talking about the right of suffrage, when Mrs. Partington overheard them, and remarked:

"How these men talk about exercising their right of suffering! As if nobody in the world suffered but themselves! They don't know of our sufferings. We poor creturs must suffer and say nothing about it, and drink cheap tea, and be troubled with the children and the cows, and scrub our souls out; and we never say a thing about it. But a man comes on regularly once a year, like a Farmer's Almanac, and grumbles about his sufferings; and it's only then jest to choose a governor, after all. These men are hard creturs to find out."

This was intended as a lesson to Margaret, who was working Charlotte and Werter, on a blue ground, at her side; but Margaret had her own idea of the matter and remained silent, while Ike yelled and sang:

> I wish you a merry Christmas
> And a happy New Year,
> With your stomach full of money
> And your pocket full of beer,

as he skipped into Mrs. Partington's kitchen, where the old dame was busily engaged in cooking breakfast on Christmas morning.

"Don't make such a noise, dear," said the kind old lady, holding up her hand: "You give me a scrutinizing pain in my head, and your young voice goes through my brain like a scalpel-knife. But what did the good Santa Cruz put into your stocking, Isaac?" And she looked at him with such an arch and pleased expression, as he took out of his pocket a jack-knife and a hum-top painted with gaudy colors! Ike held them up, joyously; and it was a sight to see the two standing there—she smiling serenely upon the boy's happiness, and he, grateful in the possession of his treasures.

"Ah!" said she, with a sigh, "there's many a house to-day, Isaac, that Santa Cruz won't visit; and many a poor child will find nothing in his stocking but his own little foot!"

It might have been a grain of the snuff she took, it might have been a fleeting mote of the atmosphere; Mrs. Partington's eyes looked humid, though she smiled upon the boy before her, who stood trying to pull the cord out of her reticule to spin his new top with.

"People may say what they will about country air being so good for 'em," said the old lady, "and how they fat upon it; for my part I shall always think it is owing to the vittles. Air may do for cammamiler and other reptiles that live on it, but I know that men must have something substantialer."

The old lady was resolute in this opinion, conflict as it might with general notions. She is set in her opinions, very, and, in their expression, nowise backward.

"It may be as Solomon says," said she, "but I have lived at the pasturage in a country town all one summer, and I never heard a turtle singing in the branches. I say I never heerd it, but may be so too; for I have seen 'em in brooks under the tree, where they, perhaps, dropped off. I wish some of our great naturalists would look into it." With this wish for light, the old lady lighted her candle and went to bed.

"I can't believe in spiritous knockings," said Mrs. Partington, solemnly, as a friend related something he had seen which appeared very mysterious. "I can't believe about it; for I know, if Paul could come back, he would envelop himself to me here, and wouldn't make me run a mile, only to get a few dry knocks. Strange that the world should be so superstitious as to believe such a rapsody, or think a sperrit can go knocking about like a boy in vacation! I don't believe it, and I don't know's I could if that teapot there should jump off the table right afore my eyes." She paused; and, through the gloom of approaching darkness, the determined expression of her countenance was apparent. A slight movement was heard upon the table; and the little black teapot moved from its position, crawled slowly up the wall and then hung passively by the side of the profile of the ancient corporal. The old lady could not speak, but held up her hands in wild amazement, while her snuff-box fell from her nervless grasp, and rolled along on the sanded floor. She left the room to procure a light; and, as soon as she had gone, the teapot was lowered by the invisible hand to its original station; and Ike stepped out from beneath the table, stowing a large string away in his pocket and grinning prodigiously.

"What a label it is upon the character of Boston!" said Mrs. Partington, as she read a speech on the liquor bill, that reflected on Boston. "There is no place where benevolence is so aperient as here. For my part, I don't know where so much is done for the suffering; and any body can see it that can read; for how often we see 'Free Lunch' in the windows of our humane institutions! [Laughter.] You never see such things in the country, as much better as they think themselves.

"I think," said Mrs. Partington, getting up from the breakfast table, "I will take a tower, or go upon a discursion. The bill says, if I collect rightly, that a party is to go to a very plural spot, and to mistake of cold collection. I hope it won't be so cold as ours was, for the poor last Sunday; why, there wasn't money efficient to buy a foot of wood for a restitute widder.

"But there is no knowing how all these things will turn out, till they take place." [Laughter.]

Poor old lady! she wasn't thinking of this lecture, when she said: "We shall all come to an end some day, though we may never live to see it." [Laughter.]

WHAT IS THE MATTER WITH YOU, MY FRIEND?

See page 431.

THE "FAT CONTRIBUTOR."

BIOGRAPHY AND REMINISCENCES.

A. Miner Griswold, the "Fat Contributor," was born in Pennsylvania in 1837. He is now associated with Alexander Sweet in the editorship of *Texas Siftings*. Mr. Sweet has made humorous reputations on three newspapers, and is one of our most prolific humorous writers. Mr. Griswold is a great favorite with the D. K. E. college fraternity, and the thousands of "Delta Kaps" throughout the country never have a convention without the "Fat Contributor" to make them happy. There is no man more universally loved by the journalistic fraternity than Griswold. His genial face is lighted up by a perpetual smile. He is married to a beautiful, golden-haired wife, who presides gracefully over their beautiful home in New York.

Mr. Griswold often tells about a tramp he saw on a New York door-step.

He was tenderly holding his head in his hands when the Fat Contributor came along and thus accosted him:

"What's the matter with you my friend?"

"I'm in doubt, sir; I'm in a state of doubt."

"In doubt? What about?" asked Griswold, tenderly.

"Well, sir, I went into that alley gate up there to get suth'in to eat; I might a-knowed suth'in 'd happened, for there was a dead book agent layin' on the flower bed and a liniment man with the side of his head all caved in, leanin' up again the peach tree."

"Well?"

"You see, I allus was venturesome; so I very politely stepped up and, taking off my hat asked a woman standin' there, would she be kind enough to give me a berry pie and some breast of chicken?"

"Well, what happened then?"

"Now, Mr. Griswold, that's what I'm in doubt about. I'm thinking it over now. I don't seem to make out whether I got the pie, or the back porch fell down on me, or perhaps I fell asleep under a pile driver. I don't know any thing about it, but, to give

431

myself the benefit of the doubt, I believe I'd sooner work half an hour than go into that yard again. I would!"

A Cincinnatian, who was about to fail in business, went to Griswold and asked his advice.

"I'll tell you how it is" said the Fat Contributor, "you can make a fortune by going into bankruptcy, if your debts are only big enough. The more you owe, you know, the more you make. Do you see?"

"No; I don't really see how I shall make money by losing it," said the unfortunate friend. "I owe enough, the Lord knows, if that's all you want, but how I'm ever to pay even fifty cents on the dollar and have any thing left to commence over again, is one of the things I can't see into."

"But you don't want to pay your debts, man. Well, but you are a green 'un—that is too good. Pay! Ha! ha! What are you going to fail for?"

"Because I can't help it. Now, what are you laughing about?"

"I'm laughing because you don't seem to understand that you can't afford to fail in these hard times unless you can make a snug thing out of it. You mustn't plunge headlong into ruin, you know, with your eyes shut," said brother Griswold, adjusting his diamond pin.

"Mustn't I?"

"No! Never do in the world. Have your wits about you, and keep your head clear. Don't let the trouble worry you into fogging your brain with too much drink. Wouldn't do it at all. Keep you eye peeled and watch for the main chance."

"Yes—yes; I see. But how, Mr. Griswold—how?"

"Well, first, you must appoint your own receiver, and be sure to select the stupidest man you can find. Get a man who don't know enough to drive a cow, and too lazy to add up a column of figures, even if he knows how. If you can find an ignoramus that can't read, so much the better. Make him believe there ain't hardly any thing to divide, and you can buy him off cheap."

"So, ho, that's the way, is it? Go on, I'm learning fast."

"If the man you get is green enough and not too blamed awkward to stumble onto the true state of things acidentally, you won't have a bit of trouble. Divide with him right on the start, and—"

"But the creditors—what are they to do?"

"Them? The creditors! Oh! never mind them. You just take care of yourself. You can't take care of everybody when you fail; but take care of yourself, my boy, and if you fail often enough you'll die a millionaire. I've tried it myself, you know. Look at me! Failed eight times, and now I'm president of two savings banks, and to-morrow I'm going to endow a theological seminary."

And Brother Griswold consulted his magnificent stem-winder, and said it was about time to go in and join Elder Mines and Deacon Skinner to arrange about the $4,000 which the church had lent him for safe-keeping.

THE FAT CONTRIBUTOR'S LECTURE.

HIS PHILOSOPHICAL DISQUISITION ON INJUN MEAL.

Ladies and Gentlemen :—My subject is Injun Meal. My lecture is a scientific treatise on the American Indian. I shall treat the Indian fairly. I shall not treat him so often as he would like, but I will treat him honestly and scientifically, with no humor or levity.

It is comparatively but a few years ago that this vast continent, now resonant with the hum of commerce and manufactures, and radiant in the garb of civilization, was one vast forest in which the Indian ruled supreme. But the Indian has been compelled to retire. I put it as mildly as possible, out of consideration for the feelings of any sensitive savage who may be in this assembly to-night [laughter]—to retire before the onward march of civilization. "He has been compelled," in the language of an eloquent Indian orator, "to land on other lands, and to climb—other climes"—and I might add, to live—on other liver! Once he wore the white man's scalp at his belt, but now the white man 'belts him over the scalp.' He has followed upon the scent of the red man, until the red man hasn't a red cent.

In the language of the psalmist:

> Once here the lone Indian took his delights
> Fished, fit and bled;
> Now most of the inhabitants is whites
> With nary red.

The decline of the American Indian, so sudden as to presage his early and final extinction, was due to a combination of causes which I will not stop to enumerate. They are too well known. There was one, however, to which I must allude, more potent than all the rest. The white man introduced it, at the same time that he introduced gunpowder, but it has proved a more potent destroyer than the white man's bullet. This dreadful scourge, this fearful destroyer of the Indians, whose victims outnumber those destroyed by pestilence and war combined, was——[here Mr. Griswold would pause in a perplexed way, striving to recall the name, then he would draw a piece of paper from his pocket, adjust his eyeglasses and scan it carefully to make sure of no mistake] whisky! [Laughter.] That was it. Whisky destroyed the Indians. I put it down so that I would remember it. [Laughter.] And any man will remember it if he puts enough of it down. [Laughter.]

The Indians took to whisky with a readiness that can hardly be accounted for when we consider how many years they had been without it. In an incredibly brief period of time after the discovery of America by Columbus, every savage—of any pretentions whatsoever—had whisky on his sideboard and in his wine cellar. [Laughter.]

"Who?" said Logan, in that eloquent and touching speech of his, delivered before one of the early Washingtonian societies, at Washington, "who ever entered Logan's cabin hungry—and didn't get a drink!"

The Indians were not given to poetry. The most of the poetry written by the Indians has been found, upon careful examination, to have been composed by white people. [Laughter.] I have written some very beautiful Indian poetry myself. There was a period in my life when I didn't seem to think any thing of throwing off a poem—and the public didn't seem to think any thing of it, either! [Laughter.]

Some years ago, while editing a paper in the far West, I received some verses written by the widow of a celebrated Indian killer, eulogizing her deceased husband, with a request to copy. The first verse, I remember, ran like this—the other verses walked. [Laughter]:

> My husband he was galliant,
>   My husband he was gay,
> And when he took a warlike stand
>   The Injuns run'd away.
> He laugh'd a laugh of scornful wrath
>   To see the cowards flee
> With their high, their low, their—
>   Pum-a-diddle, rip-a-tog-a—
> Rally-goggle, jum-bo-ree! [Laughter.]

There were ninety-five verses in all, and each verse had a like satisfactory termination.

The Indian ladies were not of a literary turn of mind. They didn't care to vote. Not being literary there were no blue stockings among them. In fact very few stockings—of any color whatsoever. They were not passionately fond of dress. There is no instance on record where a business Injun—a thorough business Injun—has been compelled to make an assignment, on account of his wife's extravagance in dress. [Laughter.]

The diversions of the Indians were of the most innocent and cheerful description. They consisted principally in running the gauntlet and burning gentlemen at the stake. I think, in the latter case, I should prefer to have my steak done as rare as possible.

Running the gauntlet is an ingenious combination of the gymnastic, calisthenic and acrobatic exercises, intensified by the exciting phases of the chase, which run quite through it. The Indians form two lines, between which the culprit is to run, and jocosely brandish sled stakes, cleavers, plow-handles, bedstead wrenches, cistern poles—and other stuffed clubs, the judicious exercise of which is calculated to produce the highest muscular development, while their application on the gentleman under treatment has the most exhilarating effect.

The Indians had many interesting traditions; one in particular I recall. There was once an adventurous young Indian—a sort of copper-colored Christopher Columbus—who, before the discovery of America, wanted to get up an expedition to discover Europe. [Laughter.] He told the Indians that way across that great body of salt water was an old world, and assured them that if they didn't discover it pretty soon, some one would come over from there and discover them. And if he had succeeded in his plan, the whole current of emigration would have turned from America to Europe. [Laughter.] Indians would have gone over there, planted colonies and driven out the white men. [Applause.]

He claimed, this Indian did, that by taking a Cunard steamer and sailing many days—in those times ocean steamers only sailed days; they tied up nights—he would reach the old world, to the perpetual confusion of Columbus.

He asked, in case they did not open communication with Europe, how they could expect to have the luxuries of the East here—such as the cholera—and the rinderpest? He advised, among other things, that a ship-load of Indian missionaries accompany the expedition, for the purpose of introducing the principles of Indian morality in sections of the old world corrupted by Eastern civilization.

In the midst of this harangue, news was telegraphed to the Indians that Columbus had come [laughter] and the red man's expedition to discover Europe came to an untimely end. [Applause.]

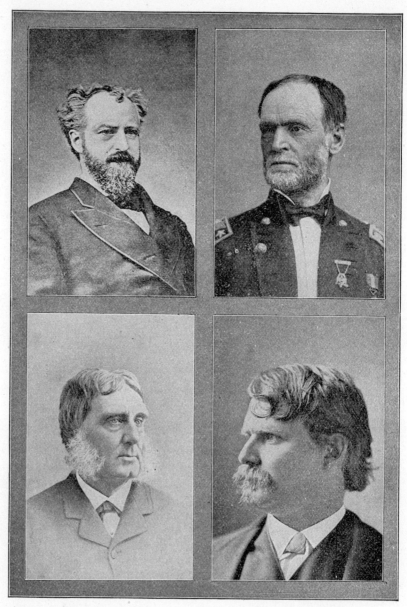

ROSCOE CONKLING   GEN. W. T. SHERMAN
GEO. WM. CURTIS   HENRY WATTERSON

"BILL ARP."

BIOGRAPHY AND REMINISCENCES.

The name of Major Chas. H. Smith, the great Southern humorist, whose *nom de plume* is "Bill Arp," is familiar in every Southern household. He was born in Gwinnett county, Georgia, in 1826. His father came to Savannah from Massachusetts and his mother was a South Carolinian. Major Smith graduated at Athens university, Georgia; was admitted to the bar in 1860, and then gave his services to the State in the late war. During the war the humorist wrote his first letter from the camp in Virginia, afterwards published by G. W. Carleton. They were charming bits of humor, and Watterson's *Courier-Journal* said of his letter to Artemus Ward in 1865 : " It is the first chirp of any bird after the surrender, and gives relief and hope to thousands of drooping hearts."

Major Smith fought bravely on the Southern side, and wrote as he shot, but when the surrender came he ran up the old flag from the gable of his Cartersville palm house, dropped his sword, seized the plantation hoe and led a battalion of negroes in the field. He is reconstructed now, and no man loves the republic more than he.

The whole life of "Bill Arp" has been humorous, and no man will stop hard work quicker and more cheerfully than he to hear a good joke.

When I asked him one day if he really ever killed many Yankees, he said:

" Well, I don't want to boast about myself, but I killed as many of them as they did of me."

Speaking of pensions one day, Mr. Arp said:

" Every Yankee soldier ought to have a pension."

" But they were not all injured in the army, were they?" I asked.

"Yes, they all did so much hard lying about us poor rebels that they strained their consciences."

Bill Arp tells a good story of an occurrence in New York when he came here to lecture in Chickering Hall. He said he was standing on the steps of the Astor House, one afternoon, with a friend, when a man with a decidedly military bearing hobbled up.

He greeted my friend as he passed.

"That's a fine soldierly lookin g chap," I said.

"Yes; he's a veteran—Colonel Jones, of the G. A. R."

"Did he lose his leg on the battlefield?"

"Yes; at Gettysburg."

"Ah! Repelling Pickett's charge, I suppose."

"No; a monument fell on it."

They tell this story in Rome, Georgia, about the Major. They say that in the summer of 1863, "Bill Arp" was in the Richmond hospital. The hospital was crowded with sick and dying soldiers and the Richmond ladies visited it daily, carrying with them delicacies of every kind, and did all they could to cheer and comfort the suffering. On one occasion a pretty miss of sixteen was distributing flowers and speaking gentle words of encouragement to those around her, when she overheard a soldier exclaim: "Oh, my Lord!"

It was "Bill Arp."

Stepping to his bedside to rebuke him for his profanity, she remarked: "Didn't I hear you call upon the name of the Lord? I am one of His daughters. Is there any thing I can ask Him for you?"

Looking up into her bright, sweet face, Bill replied: "I don't know but you could do something for me if I wasn't married."

"Well," said she, "what is it?"

Raising his eyes to hers and extending his hand, he said: "As you are a daughter of the Lord, if I wasn't married, I'd get you to ask Him if He wouldn't make me His son-in-law."

Major Andrews, a Yankee captain, was telling some jolly Rebs in Georgia about his experience at Bull Run.

"The only time that I ever really felt ashamed in my life was in that Bull Run battle," said the major. "My horse fell under me, and I was obliged to ride an army mule during the rest of the engagement, and he finally carried me clear into the rebel lines."

"Yes, I remember the incident well," said "Bill Arp," who was standing by, "I found that mule with a U. S. brand on him the next day after the battle."

FLOWERS AND WORDS OF ENCOURAGEMENT.

See page 438.

" You did, really?" said the major, hardly expecting to be corroborated so promptly. "Where did you find him?" asked the major.

Bill saw that there was a door wide open as he replied, "Stone dead behind a rail fence."

" Shot?"

" No ; mortification."

Bill Arp is such a good citizen now, and so loyal to the republic, that you would hardly believe how zealous he was for the Confederacy, in '62.

A friend of mine, Major Munson, had charge of the Dalton district, in Georgia, when the humorist surrendered. It was a hard thing for him to do it, and it took a week or two to come down to it, but he finally laid down his sword. As Bill delights to tell good stories on the Yankees, I can not resist telling the story of his final surrender, as Major Munson gave it to me. Of course the major puts in the Southern dialect a little stronger than Bill uses it now, but the reader must remember that when the incident occurred, Bill was still unreconstructed :

"Most of the 'Confeds' came in very quietly," said the major, " and seemed glad to have the thing settled, but once in a while I struck a man who hated to come under. One day a big, handsome man with tangled hair, and with Virginia red mud on his boots, came in to talk about surrendering. It was Bill Arp.

" 'Dog on it, sir,' he began in the Georgia dialect, 'I have come in, sir, to see what terms can be secured in case I surrender.'

" 'Haven't you surrendered yet?' I inquired.

" 'No, sir! Not by a dog-on sight! I said I'd die in the last ditch, and I've kept my word.'

" 'Whose company did you belong to?'

" 'Belong! Belong! Thunderation! I didn't belong to any one's company! Why, sir, I fought on my own hook.'

" 'Where was it?'

" 'No matter, sir; no matter. I can't be crushed. I can be insulted, but not crushed. Good day, sir. I'll see the United States weep tears of blood before I'll surrender. Haven't a card, but my name is Arp—Colonel Bill Arp.'

" He went off, but in about a week he returned and began :

" ' As the impression seems to be general that the Southern Confederacy has been crushed, I called to see what terms would be granted me in case I concluded to lay down my sword.'

"'Unconditional surrender,' I briefly replied.

"'Then, dog on it, sir, I'll never lay it down while life is left. The cause is lost, but principle remains. You can inform General Sheridan that Bill Arp refuses to surrender.'

"Colonel Arp returned two weeks later. He seemed to have had a hard time of it, as his uniform was in rags and his pockets empty.

"'Look a-here, Captain,' he said as he came in, 'I don't want to prolong this bloody strife, but am fo'ced to do so by honor. If accorded reasonable terms I might surrender. What do you say?'

"'The same as before.'

"'Then you are determined to grind us to powder, eh? Sooner than submit I'll shed the rest of my blood! Send on your armies, Captain—I am ready for 'em!'

"Just a week from that day, Colonel Arp came in again, said he'd like to surrender, drew his rations with the rest, and went off in great good humor to his Cartersville farm."

BILL ARP'S LECTURE!

Ladies and Gentlemen:—Bill Arp, from whom I got my *nom de plume* and Big John were samples of the rough, uncultured men, in the newly settled country of North Georgia and North Alabama. Every community had such men. They constituted a large class among the backwoodsmen of the South, from thirty to forty years ago. They were generally poor and uneducated, and they enjoyed life more than they enjoyed money. They were sociable and they were kind. When one was sick they nursed him; when he died, they dug his grave and buried him, and that was the end of the chapter. As the Scriptures say of the old patriarchs, "And Jared lived to be 800 years old and he died." There is no other epitaph or obituary.

A little farther north are the simple mountaineers of East Tennessee, and their kindness and generosity is only exceeded by their poverty. One day Eli Perkins says he was riding up along the foot of the Cumberland mountains in East Tennessee, when he met the typical East Tennessean and the following dialogue ensued:

"Which way is the county seat?" asked Eli:

"I didn't know," she said, with a look of wonderment, "that the county had any seat." [Laughter.]

"What is the population of your county?"

"I dun no," said the old lady, chewing her snuff stick, "I reckon it's up in Kentucky." [Laughter.]

A mile farther on, the same writer met one of those smoke-colored Tennesseans and his wife. Their sole possessions seemed to be a brindle dog and a snuff stick.

"Got any whisky about yer?" asked the old clay-eater.

"Whisky is a deceitful, dangerous and unhealthful drink," said Eli, "I'm sorry to hear you ask for it."

"Whisky!!" said the old Tennessean, "why, whisky stranger, it's the best drink in the world. That's what saved Bill Fellers' life."

"But Bill Fellers is dead—died five years ago," said a by-stander.

"That's what killed him—didn't drink any whisky. Poor Bill, he never knew what killed him. How he must have suffered." [Laughter.]

Then there was a middle class, who owned and worked their own farms and built churches and jails like civilized people, and filled them with their best citizens. They were good Methodists and Baptists, and obeyed the law—as Webster used to say, re-spec-ta-ble cit-i-z-e-n-s!

But there was still another class that more signally marked the people and the history of the South—a class of more ambition and higher culture. The aristocracy of the South was, before the war, mainly an aristocracy of dominion. The control of servants or employés is naturally elevating and ennobling, much more so than the mere possession of other property. The Scriptures always mention the number of servants, when speaking of a patriarch's consequence in the land. This kind of aristocracy brought with it culture and dignity of bearing. Dominion dignifies a man just as it did in the days of the centurion who said, "I say unto this man go, and he goeth, and to another come, and he cometh." Dominion is the pride of a man—dominion over something. A negro is proud if he owns a possum dog, and can make him come and go at his pleasure. A poor man is proud if he owns a horse and a cow and some razor-back hogs. The thrifty farmer is proud if he owns some bottom land and a good horse and top buggy, and can take the lead in his country church and country politics. But the old Anglo-Saxon stock aspires to a higher degree of mastery. They glory in owning men, and it makes but little difference whether the men are their dependents or their slaves. The glory is all the same if they have them in their power. Wealthy corporations and railroad kings and princely planters have dominion over their employés, and regulate them at their pleasure. It is not a dominion in law, but is almost absolute in fact, and there is nothing wrong or oppressive about it when it is humanely exercised. In fact, it is generally an agreeable relation between the poor laborer and the rich employer. An humble, poor man, with a lot of little children coming on, loves to lean upon a generous landlord, and the landlord is proud of the poor man's homage.

The genuine Bill Arp used to say he had rather belong to Col. Johnson than be free, for he had lived on the Colonel's land for twenty years, and his wife and children have never suffered, crop or no crop; for the Colonel's wife threw away enough to support them, and they were always nigh enough to pick it up.

He was asked one day how he was going to vote, and replied : "I don't know until I ax Colonel Johnson, and I don't reckon he can tell me, till he sees Judge Underwood, and maybe Underwood won't know till he hears from Alek Stephens but who in the dickens tells little Alek how to vote I'll be dogged if I know."

Those simple people had their courtings and matings. They had their coon hunts and country parties, that the aristocracy farther South knew nothing about. They used to have a unique kissing game up there in the mountains that they still keep up over in East Tennessee. This is the way they practiced it:

A lot of big-limbed, powerful young men and apple-cheeked, buxom girls, gather and select one of their number as master of ceremonies. He takes his station in the center of the room, while the rest pair off and parade around him. Suddenly one young woman will throw up her hands and say :

"I'm a-pinin." [Laughter.]

The master of ceremonies takes it up and the following dialogue and interlocution takes place :

"Miss Arabella Jane Apthorp says she's a-pinin. What is Miss Arabella Jane Apthorp a-pining fur?"

"I'm a-pinin' fur a sweet kiss."

"Miss Arabella Jane Apthorp says she's a-pinin' fur a sweet kiss. Who is Miss Arabella Jane Apthorp a-pinin' fur a sweet kiss frum."

"I'm a-pinin' fur a sweet kiss frum Mr. William Arp." (Blushes, convulsive giggles and confusion on the part of Miss Arabella Jane Apthorp at this forced confession.) Mr. William Arp now walks up manfully and relieves the fair Arabella's pinin' by a smack which sounds like a three-year old steer drawing his hoof out of the mud. [Laughter.]

Then a young man will be taken with a sudden and unaccountable pinin', which after the usual exchange of questions and volunteered information, reveals the name of the maiden who causes the gnawin' and pinin'. She coyly retreats out doors, only to be chased, overtaken, captured and forcibly compelled to relieve her captor's distress.

At one of these entertainments which it was the narrator's fortune to attend, there was a remarkably beautiful young woman, who had been married about a month. Her husband was present, a huge, beetle-browed, black-eyed young mountaineer, with a fist like a ham. The boys fought shy of the bride for fear of incurring the anger of her hulking spouse. The game went on for some time, when symptoms of irritation developed in the giant. Striding into the middle of the room, he said :

" My wife is ez pooty, 'n' ez nice, 'n' sweet ez any gyurl hyah. You uns has known her all her life. This game hez been a-goin' on half an hour, an' nobody has pined fur her onct. Ef some one doesn't pine fur her pooty soon, thar will be trouble." [Laughter.]

She was the belle of the ball after that. Every body pined for her. [Laughter.]

The dominion of the old aristocracy of the South was not over their own race, as it was at the North, but over another, and it was absolute both in law and fact ;

Hence it naturally grew into an oligarchy of slave-owners, and the poorer whites were kept under the ban. There was a line of social caste between them, and it was widening into a gulf, for the poor white man could not compete with slave labor, any more than the farmer or mechanic can now compete with convict labor, in the hands of lessees. There are but a thousand or so of convicts in the State of Georgia, and this does not amount to an oppression; but there were two hundred thousand slaves, and the poor white had but little chance to rise with such formidable foes. This kind of slave aristocracy gave dignity and leisure to the rich ; and Solomon says, that in leisure there is wisdom ; and so these men became our statesmen and jurists and law-makers, and they were shining lights in the councils of the nation ; but it was an aristocracy that was exclusive, and it shut out and overshadowed the masses of the common people, like a broad spreading oak overshadows and withers the undergrowth beneath it.

But now a change has come! There are only two general classes of people at the South—those who have seen better days and those who haven't. The first class used to ride and drive, but most of them now take it a-foot or stay at home. Seventy-five per cent of them are the families of old Henry Clay Whigs. Thirty-five years ago they were the patrons of high-schools and colleges, and stocked the learned professions with an annual crop of high-strung graduates, who swore by Henry Clay and Fillmore and Stephens and Toombs and John Bell and the Code of Honor. They were proud of their birth and lineage, their wealth and culture, and when party spirit ran high and fierce they banded together against the pretensions of the struggling democracy.

When I was a young man, a Whig girl deemed it an act of amiable condescension to go to a party with a Democratic boy. But the wear and tear of the war, the loss of their slaves, and a mortgage or two to lift, broke most of these old families up, though it didn't break down their family pride. They couldn't stand it like the Democrats, who lived in log cabins, and wore wool hats and copperas breeches.

I speak with freedom of the old Georgia democracy, for I was one of them. The wealth and the refinement of the State was in the main centered in that party known as the old-line Whigs. Out of 160 students in our State university, thirty-five years ago, 130 of them were the sons of Whigs. I felt politically lonesome in their society, and was just going over to the Whig party, when I fell in love with a little Whig angel who was flying around. [Laughter.] This hurried me up, and I was just about to go over to that party, when suddenly the party came over to me. I don't know yet whether that political somersault lifted me up or pulled the little angel down—but I do know she wouldn't have me, and at last I mated with a Democratic seraph who had either more pity or less discrimination. She took me, and she's got me yet; she surrendered, but I am the prisoner. [Laughter.]

These grand old gentlemen of the olden time were the pioneers in all the great enterprises of their day. They sowed the seed and we are reaping the harvest. They planted the trees and we are reaping the fruit. They laid the foundations of the proud structure of our Commonwealth, and we have built upon it. My good old father took $5,000 of stock in the Georgia railroad before it was built. He kept it for twelve years without a dividend, and when financial embarrassment overtook him, the stock was down at its lowest point, and he sold it to Judge Hutchins at $27 a share. There was a gloom over the family that night, but I tried to disperse it, for I told them that I had just made a matrimonial arrangement with the judge's daughter, [laughter] and maybe the stock matter would come out all right; and it did. I got it all back for nothing, and the judge's lovely daughter to boot, and it was the best trade I ever made in my life.

Most of these old families are poor, but they are proud. They are highly respected for their manners and their culture. They are looked upon as good stock, and thoroughbred, but withdrawn from the turf. Their daughters carry a high head and a flashing eye, stand up square on their pastern joints, and chafe under the bit. They come just as nigh living as they used to as they possibly can. They dress neatly in plain clothes, wear starched collars and corsets, and a perfumed handkerchief. They do up their hair in the fashion, take Godey's Lady's Book or somebody's bazar. If they are able to hire a domestic, the darky finds out in two minutes that free niggers don't rank any higher in that family than slaves used to.

The negroes who know their antecedents have the highest respect for them, and will say Mas' William or Miss Julia with the same deference as in former days. One would hardly learn from their general deportment that they cleaned up the house, made up the beds, washed the dishes, did their own sewing and gave music lessons—in fact, did most everything but wash the family clothes. They won't do that. I've known them to milk and churn, and sweep the back yard, and scour the brass, but I've never seen one of them bent over the wash-tub yet, and I hope I never will. I don't like to see any one reduced below their position, especially if they were born and raised to it. In the good old times their rich and patriarchal fathers lived like Abraham, Jacob and Job. They felt like they were running an unlimited monarchy on a limited scale. When a white child was born, it was ten dollars out of pocket, but a little nigger was a hundred dollars in, and got fifty dollars a year better for twenty years to come.

The economy of the old plantation was the economy of waste. Two servants to one white person in slave times was considered moderate and reasonable. In a family of eight or ten—with numerous visitors and some poor kin—there were generally a head cook and her assistant, a chambermaid, a seamstress, a maid or nurse for every daughter and a little nig for every son, whose business it was to trot around after him and hunt up mischief. Then there was the stableman and carriage driver and the gardener and the dairy woman, and two little darkies to drive up the cows and keep the calves off while the milking was going on. Besides these there were generally half a dozen little chaps crawling around or picking up chips, and you could hear them bawling and squalling all the day long, as their mothers mauled them and spanked them for something or for nothing with equal ferocity. This was the paradise of Dixie. The masters were happy, and so were the slaves.

But the good old plantation times are gone—the times when these old family servants felt an affectionate abiding interest in the family, when our good mothers nursed their sick and old helpless ones, and their good mothers waited so kindly upon their "mistis," as they called her, and took care of the little children by day and by night.

Our old black mammy was mighty dear to us children, and we loved her, for she was always doing something to please us, and she screened us from many a whipping. It would seem an unnatural wonder, but nevertheless it is true, that these faithful old domestics loved their master's children better than their own, and they showed it in numberless ways without any hypocrisy. Our children frolicked with theirs, and all played together by day and hunted together by night, and it beat the Arabian Nights to go to the old darky's cabin of a winter night and hear him tell of ghosts and witches and jack-o'-lanterns and wild cats and graveyards, and we would listen with faith and admiration until we didn't dare look around, and wouldn't have gone back to the big house alone for a world full of gold.

Bonaparte said that all men were cowards at night, but I reckon it was these old niggers that made us so, and we have hardly recovered from it yet.

When I used to go a-courting I had to pass a graveyard in the suburbs of the little village, and it was a test of my devotion that I braved its terrors on the darkest night and set at defiance the wandering spirits that haunted my path. Mrs. Arp appreciated it then, for she would follow me to the door when I left, and anxiously listen to my retiring footsteps. But now she declares she could hear me running up that hill by the graveyard like a fast-trotting pony on a shell-road.

It was a blessed privilege to the boys of that day to go along with the cotton wagons to Augusta, or to Macon or Columbus, and camp out at night and hear the trusty old wagoners tell their wonderful adventures, and it was a glorious time when they got back home again, and brought sugar and coffee and molasses and had shoes all round for both white and black, and the little wooden measures in them, with the names written upon every one.

They had genuine corn shuckings in those days, and corn songs that were honest, and sung with a will that beat a camp-meeting chorus—and they had Christmas, too, for white folks and black folks. Little red shawls and bandanas and jackknives and jews-harps and tobacco and old-fashioned pipes were laid up for the family servants, who always managed to slip up about break of day with a whisper of "Christmasgif" before the family were fairly awake.

Then how I remember how we all used to scream at the quarrels the darkies had. They were always so fierce—their eyes would snap fire so, and then it would all die out in smoke.

There had been some hard words between Julius and Moses on several occasions, but one day the collision came; Julius went round to the kitchen and spied Moses talking to his girl. An awful jealousy filled his whole being and he began:

"Look heah, boy; I'ze dun got my eyeball on you, an' de fust thing you know I'll pound ye to squash!" [Laughter.]

"Shoo! Does you know who you is conversin' wid?" demanded Moses. Doan' you talk to me dat way, black man."

"Who's black man?"

"You is."

"You was a liah, sah!"

"So was you!"

"Look out, boy! A feller dun called me liah one time, an' de county had to bury him."

"An' you look out fur me, black man. I'ze mighty hard to wake up, but when I gits aroused I was pizen all de way frew." [Laughter.]

"Shoo! I jist want to say to you dat de las' fight I was in it took eight men to hold me. Doan' you git me mad, boy; doan' you do it."

"Bum! I dass put my hand right on yo' shoulder."

"An' I dass put my hand on yours."

"Now what yo' gwine ter do?"

"Now what yo' gwine ter do?"

"Shoo!"

"Shoo!" [Laughter.]

And after standing in defiance for a moment, each backed slowly away, and went about his business, to renew the "defi" at the first opportunity, and always with the same result.

But it's all over now—and slaves and masters are gone, and the new South has come! Like Job of old, these proud old masters have all been put upon trial. They lost their noble sons in the army, and their property soon after. The extent of their afflictions no one will ever know, for the heart knoweth its own bitterness, but they have long since learned how to suffer and be strong.

I have now in mind a proud old family, living in quiet obscurity—the children of one of Georgia's noblest governors, a statesman of national reputation. They are poor, but they are not subdued. Their children work in the field and milk the cows and chop the firewood, but they have never forgotten or dishonored their grand old ancestor, from whom they sprung. I recall another one who, forty-five years ago, represented us in the National Congress—who was for many years almost a monarch in his rule over hundreds of employés, and whose draft was honored for thousands of dollars. With tottering gait and trembling fingers he now bargains for a nickel's worth of soda, but still is grand and noble in his poverty. Always cheerful, he welcomes those who visit him with the same kindness and dignity which characterized him in his better days.

I believe the day of prosperity is coming back, and the children of the present generation will yet reap an inestimable blessing from the great calamity.

" Hard indeed was the contest for freedom and the struggle for independence," but harder still has been the struggle of these old families to live up to the good old style with nothing hardly to live upon. Society is exacting, and then there were the long-indulged habits of elegance and ease which are hard to be broken. The young can soon learn to serve themselves, but the middle-aged and old found it no labor of love to begin life anew on an humbler scale.

What a change it was to the refined and dignified housewife when the chambermaid withdrew and set up for herself, and the good old cook, who had grown fat and greasy with service, departed from the old homestead in search of freedom, and the good lady, who was well versed in the theory of cooking, had to take her first lesson in its practice. The times have wonderfully changed since then—some things for better, some for worse.

The grand old aristocracy is passing away. Some of them escaped the general wreck that followed the war, and have illustrated by their energy and liberality the doctrine of the survival of the fittest—but their name is not legion.

A new and hardier stock has come to the front—that class, which, prior to the war, was under a cloud, and are now seeing their better days.

The pendulum has swung to the other side. The results of the war made a new South, and made an opening for them and developed their energies. With no high degree of culture, they have nevertheless proved equal to the struggle up the rough hill of life, and now play an important part in running the financial machine. Their practical energy has been followed by thrift and a general recuperation of wasted fields and fenceless farms and decayed houses. They have proved to be our best farmers and most prosperous merchants and mechanics. They now constitute the solid men of the State, and have contributed largely to the building up of our schools and churches, our factories and railroads, and the development of our mineral resources. They are shrewd and practical and not afraid of work.

The two little ragged brothers who sold peanuts in Rome in 1860 are now her leading and most wealthy merchants. Two young men who then clerked for a meager salary are now among the merchant princes of Atlanta. These are but types of the modern self-made Southerner— a class who form the most striking contrast to the stately dignity and aristocratic repose of the grand old patriarchs and statesmen, whose beautiful homes and long lines of negro houses, adorned the hills and groves of the South some thirty years ago.

But business is business now, and we must keep up with it or get run over and be crushed and forgotten. The only apprehension about this modern class, is the disposition of some of them in our cities to place their children as far above a safe and substantial social footing as they themselves used to be below it—a disposition to assume an aristocracy that will not stand the test of time, much less of misfortune. They have seen what a power gold exerts over the human family, and are too much inclined to use it for selfish purposes. They will spoil their children with money and luxury, and then in another generation the pendulum will swing back again. Even the religion of some of them is gilded with a golden gloss and made a matter of business calculation. Their practical views in this regard remind me of a venerable and learned Frenchman, who said to a lady not long ago, "Madam, a man must join ze church in zis countree to have ze privilege of good society vile he lives, and insure a Christian burial ven he die. I vas a Roman Catholic at home, but I tinks I vill join ze Episcopal Church very soon ; I like him ze pest." Before she met him again he had joined the Baptist church.

"I thought you liked the Episcopal the best ?" said she.

"I does, madam, but ven I ask ze cashier how much he charge me by ze year, he say he reckon about a hundred dollars. Then I ask the Presbyterian cashier, and he tink about fifty dollars, and ze Methodist cashier say about twenty-five—but ze Baptist cashier look at my old coat, and say ten dolla· is enough for me, so I make ze contract and join heem."

A few days after, the venerable doctor was found to be in a great hurry. He said he was looking for the cashier of his church. "What for ?" he was asked. "Why, mine freend, zat cashier forgot mine contract, and he keep sending me his leetle notes, wanting five dollars for zis ting and five dollars for zat ting, and so I get ze life insurance tables, which say I shust have six years to live, and zat makes sixty dollar, and for cash in advance it comes down to forty-eight dollars, and I pay heem all up in fool to-day and take von clear receipt, and then zey buries me when I die, and I go straight up to heaven, vere zey troubles me no more."

But there is one feature in the new order of things which has surprised and bewildered the most philosophic minds, that is the disposition which the present generation have to educate their daughters. In the good old times the sons were the special objects of the parents' care.

The better classes gave to both sons and daughters a first-class education if they could, but if either had to be neglected it was the daughters. The female colleges were few, while the male colleges abounded all over the land, and were thronged with the sons of wealthy and aristocratic Southerners. Now the rule is reversed. The pendulum is swinging. The boys are sacrificed and the girls are sent to college.

This is all very well, I reckon, and if it is not, I don't see how we are going to help it. The trouble is to find out who these college girls are going to marry. I don't suppose they will marry any body until somebody asks them, but it's natural and very proper for man and wife to be pretty much alike, mentally and socially. They should, as it were, class together, like the cotton buyer classes his cotton, or the merchant his sugar, or the farmer his cattle, or the geologist his strata of rocks. I don't allude to property at all, for that is about the last consideration that secures real happiness in wedded life, though I wouldn't advise any poor man to marry a poor girl just because she is poor, and I hope none of these girls will ever refuse a rich man because he is rich.

Money is a right good thing in a family, and no sensible girl will turn up her nose at it. Money is a social apology for lack of brains or education or graceful manners, but it's no apology for lack of honesty or good principles. Money enables a man to step up higher in the social circle than he could do without it. Hence we see a rich man without culture ranks pretty well with a poor man with culture. Hence it is that lawyers and doctors and teachers and preachers and editors, however poor, move in the same strata with bankers and merchants, however rich. The difference is that money may be lost, but education and culture can not be; and when an uneducated man loses his money, he loses caste, and must step down and out.

The value of a man's money depends, however, upon the manner in which he obtained it. Shoddy fortunes don't amount to anything. They may shine for a while in gilded coaches and splendid halls, but they will not last. If the possessor does not lose it, his children will spend it, and leave the world as poor as their father came into it. A fortune gained in a year rarely sticks to anybody. Five years is not secure. But one gained by the pursuit of an honorable calling for ten, twenty or thirty years brings with it that high social position which justly entitles a man to be called one of the aristocracy. It is a great mistake for any body to desire a fortune to come suddenly. It would embarrass him. A big pile of surplus money will make a fool of most any body on short acquaintance. It takes a man several years to learn its best uses, and to handle it with becoming dignity. If a man never rode in a phaeton behind a spanking team, it takes him a good while to get used to that. He doesn't know exactly what to do with his hands or his feet, whether to lean complacently back or cautiously forward. If the vehicle crosses a sudden rise, he dosen't rise with it in graceful undulations, but humps himself awkwardly and imagines that every body is observing his conscious embarrassment.

Money-making sense is very good sense, but I know a wealthy young man, without culture, who was made to believe that an ostrich egg which he saw in a museum was laid by a giraffe. I know a nabob in Atlanta, who subscribed for Appleton's Cyclopedia, and when they came said that he didn't know there was but one volume, and refused to pay for any more. And there is another one there whom I have known since his boyhood when he plowed barefooted in a rocky field over threadsafts and dewberry vines at ten dollars a month. He now swims in shoddy luxury and lucky wealth. He took me through his new and elegant mansion. He talked gushingly about his liberry room. He showed me a beautiful piece of furniture in the dining room, and when I said it was *unique*, he said no, it was a sideboard. [Laughter.] When I inquired after the health of his wife, he said she had a powerful bad pain in her face and the doctor said it was newralogy, but he believed she had an ulster in her nose.

But what troubles me is that these girls are climbing up where there are no boys, or very few at most. Mental culture begets mental superiority, and that raises one socially and puts him or her in a higher strata. There are, I suppose, not less than ten or fifteen educated girls in the South to every educated young man; but where are the boys? They are in the stores or the workshops or on the farms. It did not use to be so, but the bottom rail is now on the top. I don't know that it can be helped for the war left our people so poor they can't send all their children off to college, and so they send the girls and put the boys to work to pay for it. The consequence will be that these girls when they go home can't find any body good enough for them. A nice, clever, country girl graduated last year, and when she came home and asked her farmer brother to name his fine colt Bucephalus, after Alexander's famous horse:

"Why, Mary," he said, "I didn't know that Tom Alexander had any horse." [Laughter.]

Well, now, you see a college girl is not going to marry a man like that —that is, not right away quick, on the first asking. She will wait a year or so at least for some chevalier Bayard or some first-honor man to come along, but by and by she will get tired waiting, for he won't come, and then, in a kind of desperation, she will mate with some good, honest, hard-working youth, and educate him afterwards. Maybe this will all work out very well in the long run; for it's the mother who makes the man, and if she is smart, so will her children be. Of course it will delay and put off these early marriages, which our wives and mothers say are all wrong.

I have been very intimate with a lady for thirty-five years, who was married at sweet sixteen, but she thinks it would be awful for her daughters to do likewise unless the offer was a very splendid one in all respects. I reckon that was the reason why she went off so soon. [Laughter.]

I did not marry my first love, but Mrs. Arp did—[laughter]—bless her heart—and she now declares I took advantage of her innocent youth and gave her no chance to make a choice among lovers. That is so, I reckon, for I was in a powerful hurry to secure the prize and pressed my suit with all diligence for fear of accidents.

Once before I had loved and lost, and I thought it would have killed me, but it didn't, for I never sprung from the suicide stock. I had loved a pretty little school-girl amazingly. I would have climbed the Chimborazo mountains and fought a tiger for her—a small tiger. And she loved me, I know, for the evening before she left for her distant home, I told her of my love and my devotion, my adoration and aspiration and admiration and all other "ations," and the palpitating lace on her bosom told me how fast her heart was beating, and I gently took her soft hand in mine and drew her head upon my manly shoulder and kissed her. Delicious feast—delightful memory. It lasted me a year, I know, and has not entirely faded yet, for it was the first time I had ever tasted the nectar on a school-girl's lips. I never mention it at home, and I never quote this passage when my wife comes to my lecture—no, never—but I think of it sometimes on the sly—yes, on the sly. I never saw her any more, for she never came back. In a year or so she married another feller and was happy, and, in course of time I married Mrs. Arp, and was happy, too. So it is all right and no loss on our side.

The old Southern girl was thus described by the poet:

Her dimpled cheeks are pale;
She's a lily of the vale,
    Not a rose.
In a muslin or a lawn
She is fairer than the dawn
    To her beaux.

'Tis a matter of regret
She's a bit of a coquette of
   Whom I sing.
On her cruel path she goes
With half a dozen beaux
   On her string.

I still love to dwell and linger upon those heavenly days. I love to look back over my checkered life, and in sweet memories live over the past and treasure up the good of it and lament the bad of it. Memory was given to us for some good purpose, and I have no respect for a man who wants to blot out every thing behind him and keep rushing ahead in a wild hunt for fame or fortune.

"Stop, poor sinner, stop and think," was one of the first hymns I ever learned, and it fits me now as well as it did then.

I thought of all this the other day as the cars swept along the base of Stone mountain, and as I looked upon its barren and majestic summit, memory carried me back to the days of my gushing youth when there was a lofty tower up there, and Mrs. Arp, who was then my loving sweetheart, and I mounted its spiral stairs and sat together at the top in sweet communion with nature and ourselves, and as I looked into her soft, hazel eyes, it seemed to me we were a little nearer heaven than I had ever been before. It was a glorious hour, but it could not last, for there was a storm impending and the lightning flashed and the thunder pealed, and we hurried down to a safe retreat. Not long afterwards the storm came, and the winds blew and beat upon that tower and it fell. Just so it is with our life and our ambition. The mountain's top is grand and charming for a little while—but it is bleak and cold and dangerous. Our safest refuge and happiest retreat is down among the humble flowers that blossom at its base.

But what are the college girls going to do when they graduate and settle down in the old homestead? It will be right hard to descend from the beautiful heights of astronomy, the enchanting fields of chemistry and botany, the entertaining grottos of history and geology, and the charming chambers of music and social pleasures down to the drudgery of washing dishes, scouring brass kettles, making little breeches, and doing all sorts of household and domestic work. It will take a good, strong resolution and common sense and filial respect to do it, and do it gracefully and cheerfully, and be always ready to brighten up the family hearth with her educated smile. Such girls are not only happy in themselves, but they make others happy, and that is the highest, purest and noblest of all ambitions.

Be content, then, with your lot, however humble, and enjoy what you have got; and if you haven't got any thing, then enjoy what you haven't got, and be contented still.

I know every true man wishes from his heart it was so that the dear creatures did not have to work, only when they felt like it. I never see ladies of culture and refinement doing the household drudgery but what it shocks my humanity, and I feel like Mr. Bergh ought to establish a society for the prevention of cruelty to angels. The burden of bearing children and raising them is trial enough, and involves more of the wear and tear of the sinews of life than all the men have to endure. Mothers are entitled to all the rest and indulgence that is possible, and those who have brought up eight or ten children ought to be retired on a comfortable pension from the government.

There is an old gander at my house, who, for four weeks, stood guard by his mate as she set on her nest. She plucked the down from his breast and covered her eggs, and when she left them for food he escorted her to the grass and escorted her back with a pride and a devotion that was impressive. My respect for geese has been greatly enlarged since I made their more intimate acquaintance.

Woman loves money, but she loves it for its uses. You never knew one to be a miser. She wants it to spend, and there is no goodlier sight than to see her enter a fashionable dry goods store with a well-filled purse. What a comfort it must be to a loyal husband to surprise his wife with a liberal sum and say:

"Now, my dear, just spend it to suit yourself." What a harmonizing effect it has upon domestic affairs! Woman is a philosopher by instinct. Solomon considered his long experience and said, "It is good for a man to enjoy the fruits of all his labor, and to live joyfully with his wife whom he loveth, for this is his portion." But this was no new or surprising thing to woman. She knew it before. She understands the secret of human happiness, and it is astonishing how readily she can accommodate herself to surrounding circumstances. During the war, when the husbands were away, the wives lived cheaper and managed better than ever before. They patched and pieced and turned old garments wrong side out; they made coffee out of potatoes and rye and ground peas, and stewed salt out of smoke-house dirt. Mothers who used to call in the family doctor if a child had a sore toe, or the green-apple colic, soon learned to do their own practice, for the doctors all went off to the army.

Many men get discouraged if they can't do some big thing, or the crop fails, and they mope around and do nothing, but a woman never gives up. The more oppressed, the more she is aroused, and many a good, easy, good-for-nothing sort of a husband is kept up and sustained by his diligent and managing wife. Woman loves dress and jewelry, for it is her nature to be fond of the beautiful, and why shouldn't she?

Our Heavenly Father dresses the birds with plumage and the fields with flowers and the heavens with stars. We all love to see the ladies arrayed in garments as rich and as lovely as they can afford. It was this that made Ahasuerus hold out the golden sceptre to his queen, and saved a nation from destruction. Isaac understood this when he sent Rebecca the ear-rings and bracelets. Moses says the ear-rings weighed half a shekel apiece, which, according to the Hebrew tables, made the pair cost exactly sixty-two and a half cents. Couldn't catch Rebecca now with such jewelry as that. But they had a curious way of courting in those primitive days, for whenever a bashful lover ventured to kiss his girl, the Scriptures tell us he lifted up his voice and wept. They had fool boys then. [Laughter.]

But after all, there need be no serious or gloomy apprehension concerning the future of the sons and daughters of the South. If the boys can not go to college they will gather culture by absorption and association, and acquire property by diligence and industry. Our young men have learned that it is best to remain in the land of their birth, and few emigrate to another clime; and, indeed, the attachments of the Southern people to their neighbors and kindred and country are stronger than those of our Northern brethren. Our society is not made up of a mixture of all races. We have a common ancestry, and have assimilated in thought and habits and customs and languages and principles. Added to this, we have the influence of a genial climate, mild winters, fertility of soil, lovely sunsets, variegated scenery, with fruits and flowers abounding everywhere to sweeten and make glad the rosy days of our childhood. We have more latitude and longitude. Our homes are more spacious, and our manhood is comforted with the memories of our youth, when we roamed over the fields and forests, and hunted the deer and turkey by day and the 'coon and 'possum by night. It is a hard struggle for our young men to emigrate from the homes of their childhood, and when they do, a resolution to return at some future day lingers with them like a sweet perfume, and comforts them on their weary way.

Not so with the sons of New England, or the remote, inclement North. Their earliest training is to go—go West—go anywhere for business. They snap the cord that binds them to home and State and kindred as they would snap a thread. I do not know a people upon earth who have less emotional love or veneration for home and the local memories of childhood than the universal, cosmopolitan Yankee.

I use the term respectfully—for there is no other that designates the descendants of the Puritans. I use it advisedly, for I have mingled with them, and know them, and have many relatives in the old Bay State. I had three male cousins in one family, and they were off almost as soon as they began to wear breeches—one to Australia, one to California, and the other to Jeddo, in Japan. They are at home in every land but ours. They venture boldly among the bears and panthers and the wild Indians of the West, but the Kuklux and the barbarians of the South have been a combination of terrors too terrible and appalling.

We have been calling them kindly ever since the war We have tendered the olive branch, and gave cordial welcome to those few who did venture among us. We have sold them cotton and sugar and rice and tobacco, and bought their patent medicines and fly-traps and picture papers and Yankee notions and gimcracks and all their tom-fooleries, and go to all their circuses and monkey shows; but still they seem to be afraid of us. I know we whipped them pretty bad during the late war—that is, at first and all along the middle, but at last they got the best of it, and it looks like they ought to be satisfied, and make friends. We used to think slavery was the cause of all this alienation, but slavery has been abolished twenty-five years, and their dislike of us remains about the same.

Now, the Yankee is an Anglo-Saxon, and has many admirable traits of character, some of which we have not, but need, and we have been living in the hope that he would come down and live with us, and teach us economy and contrivance, and mix up and marry with us, and give us a cross that would harmonize the sections, but he will not. The last census shows that there are 180,000 more females than males in the New England States.

Before the war their educated young ladies used to venture South and teach school, and our young men and widowers married them, and they made good wives and good mothers; but they don't come now, and their young men keep going off, and the poor girls up there are in a bad fix. I have been trying to persuade some of our poor and proud young men who seem so hard to please at home, to go up there and take the pick of the lot, and bring them down here, and they say they would if the girls would send them the money to travel on. [Laughter.]

My good father was born in Massachusetts. He came South just seventy years ago, with a cargo of brick, and never returned. Well, he couldn't return, for he was shipwrecked. and lost his cargo, and had nothing to return on. My good mother was born in Charleston, and was hurried away from there to Savannah during the yellow fever panic of 1814. She went to school to my father, and he married her. When I was old enough to understand my peculiar lineage, I wondered that I could get along with myself as well as I did. When a small chap, I used to bite myself and bump my head against the door; but my good mother always said:

"You can't help it Bill; it is South Carolina fighting Massachusetts." A storm lost my father's cargo, and caused him to settle down in Savannah. It was a fearful pestilence that hurried my mother away from Charleston when she was an orphan child. · So I was the child of storm and pestilence and two belligerent States—how could I behave? But for these remarkable combinations, I reckon my father would have lived and died in the old Bay State, and my mother in Charleston; but what would have become of me? [Laughter.] But fifty years' residence made my father a good Southern man, and the Palmetto Cross made me a high-strung rebel, and on the eve of secession I loaded my pen with paper bullets and shot them right and left. We soon found out it would take some other sort to whip them in fight, and I joined the army. But we have all made friends again after a fashion, and now love one another's money with a devotion that is unaffected and supreme.

The hatred of many of the Northern people to those of the South arose, in part, from their jealousy of our power and influence in the councils of the nation; for it is a historic fact that the statesmen of the South controlled the government for fifty years. Nearly all the presidents and their cabinets were Southern men. Another cause of their enmity was our condemnation of their immoral practices in trade and the pursuit of money. Our people set themselves up as a kind of blooded aristocracy, and had negroes to wait upon them, and do the menial service these people had to do themselves. Hence they began a fanatical crusade against slavery—notwithstanding they had sold us the slaves and the sin with them more than a century ago, and warranted the title to us and our heirs forever. But, I repeat, slavery has been abolished for twenty-five years, and they seem to dislike us as much as before. This can not be accounted for, unless it is like a feller who killed a dog for biting him, and after the dog was dead he kicked him and mauled him and cursed him until a friend who stood by remonstrated, and said:

"Don't you see the brute is dead—what are you beating him now for?"

"Dog on him," said he, "I want to teach him that there is a little hell and punishment after death." [Laughter.]

The Yankee moralist reminds me of a man who became convinced of the evils of the liquor traffic. He sold out his stock of whiskey and joined the Good Templars, and then lectured the man he sold to for pursuing such an ungodly calling. [Laughter.]

Now, while we all admit that the abolition of Southern slavery will eventually prove a blessing, yet we have no apologies to make for the institution as it was, and we have no sympathy with the manner of the change. Judge Tourgee says, in his "Fool's Errand," that nobody but fools would have forced freedom in such a summary way. We believe that slavery was established in the providence of God; it was the same providence that caused its overthrow, and I don't question Providence.

In an address on education in the South, delivered some months ago before the American Institute of Instruction, by Rev. A. D. Mayo, we find the first acknowledgment we have ever seen from a Northern source of the real part that Southern slavery has played in the history of the negro race. The whole address breathes a spirit and purpose at once noble, refined and appreciative. Dr. Mayo says: "The colored people must be told that no six millions of people in any land was ever, on the whole, so marvelously led by Providence as they for the past two hundred and fifty years. Indeed, all the good there ever was in slavery was for them. It was that severe school of regular work and drill in some of the primal virtues which every race must get at the start; and American slavery was a charity school contrasted with the awful desolation of the centuries of war and tyranny by which every European people has come up to its present station of civilized life."

The Southern negro is away in advance of the Congo negro. He is Christianized. The Congoite is still a savage, eating snakes and snails. The negro is religious, but he warps his religion to fit his every-day life. Eli Perkins says he asked a good, old colored clergyman in Tennessee:

"Uncle Josh, don't you believe in the efficacy of special prayer?"

"What you mean by special prayer?" asked Uncle Josh, picking a turkey feather off his trousers.

"By special prayer I mean where you pray for a special thing."

"Wal, now, Mister Perkins, dat depends. It depends a good deal on what yo' pray for."

"How is that, Uncle Josh?"

"Wal, I allays notice dat when I pray de Lord to send one of Massa Shelby's turkeys to de ole man it don't come, but when I prays dat He'll send de ole man after de turkey, my prayer is allays answered. [Laughter.]

The negro is a distinct nation—one of the original creations of the Almighty, and has original traits and habits and instincts as all the unmixed nations have. He loves the present good and has no morbid desire for the accumulation of riches; unlike the white man, he rarely cheats or swindles anybody, and unlike the white man, never steals on a large scale. He would not rob a bank. If he finds $1,000 in the road he takes it to his employer, but he will take a chicken from the roost or a breast pin from the bureau, or a dollar from the drawer with perfect satisfaction and a peaceful conscience. Small pilfering is the extent of his capacity and the extent of his inclination. When my stable boy finds a hen's nest, I feel like thanking him for bringing me half the eggs. When our cook hides away a little flour, Mrs. Arp shuts her eyes and says nothing, for it hurts their feelings so bad to be accused when they are guilty.

But for hard work, contented work, humble work, who could take their places on the drays and the steamboats and the railroads, who would do the white man's bidding with so little murmuring and so much cheerfulness. The negro is still an important factor in our Southern homes and Southern industries, and with all his faults, we like him and are willing for him to remain. We must study him and apologize for him like we do other nations. The Indian outranks him in his emotional nature, for the Indian has gratitude and has revenge largely developed. He will traverse swamps and a wilderness to reward a friend, and he will do the same thing to avenge an enemy, but the negro will do neither. He never pines away in the chain gang. When his term is out, he is the same unconcerned creature, and frequently repeats his crime and goes back to convict work. When he is under the gallows he uniformly denies the justice of his sentence and says he is going to Jesus, and so dies in the faith of an ignorant superstition. A special Providence has thrown him among us, and our faith is that the same Providence will take care of him and of us. He is grafted on to the Southern tree. Other nations have been similarly transplanted and still live and prosper. The Jews, like the mistletoe that fastens and feeds upon every tree, still find a home in every land and yet have preserved their habits and religion and nationality, and so we think that the white and the black races can live together in peace.

In recurring to the grand old days that are past, I sometimes feel sad because our children know so little of what the South was in the good times, say from twenty-five to thirty years ago—nothing of the old patriarchal system—nothing of slavery as it was—nothing of those magnificent leaders and exemplars of the people, such as Clay and Calhoun and Berrien and Crawford and the Lamars and Styles.

They and their illustrious compeers molded manners and sentiment and chivalry and patriotism, and stood up above the masses like the higher heads overtop the rest in a field of golden grain. But the diffusion of knowledge is now bringing the masses up to the standard of education which these noblemen created. The field of grain is coming up to a uniform and unbroken level. The chances of men for fortune and for fame are more generally diffused, and more nearly equal than they have ever been, and the rise of a man from the humblest walks of life is no longer considered a miracle.

The Joe Brown type is in the ascendant — the pendulum is always swinging. Generations play at see-saw — up to-day, down to-morrow — but still the pivot on which they play is rising higher and higher at the South. Then let us not complain about that which we can not help, for whether we are up or down, we have a goodly heritage. Let us all stand fast — stand fast by our land and our people, and by the blessed memories of the past.

Arise and sing! [Laughter.]

BILL ARP TO ARTEMUS WARD.

ROME, GA., September 1, 1865.

Mr. Artemus Ward, Showman. SIR: The reason I write to you in perticler, is because you are about the only man I know in all " God's country " so-called. For some several weeks I have been wantin to say sumthin. For some several years we rebs, so-called, but now late of said country deceased, have been tryin mighty hard to do somethin. We didn't quite do it, and now it's very painful, I assure you, to dry up all of a sudden, and make out like we wasn't there.

My friend, I want to say somethin. I suppose there is no law agin thinkin, but thinkin don't help me. It don't let down my thermometer. I must explode myself generally so as to feel better. You see, I'm tryin to harmonize, I'm tryin to soften down my feelins. I'm endeavoring to subjugate myself to the level of surroundin circumstances, so-called. But I can't do it until I am allowed to say somethin. I want to quarrel with somebody and then make friends. I ain't no giant killer. I ain't no Norwegian bar. I ain't no boar-constrikter, but I'll be hornswaggled if the talkin and writin and slanderin has got to be all done on one side any longer. Sum of your folks have got to dry up or turn our folks loose. It's a blamed outrage, so-called. Ain't you editors got nothin else to do but peck at us, and squib at us, and crow over us? Is every man what can write a paragraph to consider us bars in a cage, and be always a-jobbin at us to hear us growl? Now you see, my friend, that's what's disharmonious, and do you jest tell 'em, one and all e pluribus unum, so-called, that if they don't stop it at once or turn us loose to say what we please, why we rebs, so-called, have unanimously and jointly and severally resolved to—to—to—think very hard of it—if not harder.

That's the way to talk it. I ain't agoin to commit myself. I know when to put on the breaks. I ain't goin to say all I think, like Mr. Etheridge, or Mr. Adderrig, so-called. Nary time. No, sir. But I'll jest tell you, Artemus, and you may tell it to your show. If we ain't allowed to express our sentiments, we can take it out in hatin; and hatin runs heavy in my family, sure. I hated a man once so bad that all the hair cum off my head, and the man drowned himself in a hog-waller that night. I could do it agin, but you see, I'm tryin to harmonize, to acquiess, to becum calm and sereen.

Now, I suppose that, poetically speakin,

In Dixie's fall,
We sinned all.

But talkin the way I see it, a big feller and a little feller, so-called, got into a fite, and they fout and fout a long time, and everybody all round kept hollerin, "hands off," but helpin the big feller, until finally the little feller caved in and hollered enuf. He made a bully fite, I tell you, Selah. Well, what did the big feller lo? Take him by the hand and help him up, and brush the dirt off his clothes? Nary time! No sur! But he kicked him arter he was down, and throwed mud on him, and drugged him about and rubbed sand in his eyes, and now he's gwine about huntin up his poor little property. Wants to confiscate it, so-called. Blame my jacket if it ain't enuf to make your head swim.

But I'm a good Union man, so-called. I ain't agwine to fight no more. I shan't vote for the next war. I ain't no gurrilla. I've done tuk the oath, and I'm gwine to keep it, but as for my bein subjugated and humilyated and amalgamated and enervated as Mr. Chase says, it ain't so—nary time. I ain't ashamed of nuthin neither—ain't repentin—ain't axin for no one-horse, short-winded pardon. Nobody needn't be playin priest around me. I ain't got no twenty thousand dollars. Wish I had; I'd give it to these poor widders and orfins. I'd fatten my own numerous and interestin offspring in about two minutes and a half. They shouldn't eat roots and drink branch-water no longer. Poor unfortunate things! to cum into this subloonary world at sich a time. There's four or five of them that never saw a sirkis or a monky-show—never had a pocket-knife nor a piece of chees nor a reesin. There's Bull Run Arp and Harper's Ferry Arp and Chicahominy Arp that never saw the pikters in a spellin book. I tell you, my friend, we are the poorest people on the face of the earth—but we are poor and proud. We made a bully fite, Selah, and the whole American nation ought to feel proud of it. It shows what Americans can do when they think they are imposed upon—"so-called." Didn't our four fathers fight, bleed and die about a little tax on tea, when not one in a thousand drunk it? Bekaus they succeeded, wasn't it glory? But if they hadn't, I suppose it would have been treason, and they would have been bowin and scrapin round King George for pardon. So it goes, Artemus, and to my mind, if the whole thing was stewed down it would make about half pint of humbug. We had good men, great men, Christian men who thought we was right, and many of 'em have gone to the undiscovered country, and have got a pardon as is a pardon. When I die I am mighty willing to risk myself under the shadow of their wings, whether the climate be hot or cold. So mote it be. Selah!

Well, maybe I've said enough. But I don't feel easy yet. I'm a good Union man, certain and sure. I've had my breeches died blue, and I've bot a blue bucket, and I very often feel blue, and about twice in a while I go to the doggery and git blue, and then I look up at the blue serulean heavens and sing the melancholy chorus of the Bluetailed Fly. I'm doin my durndest to harmonize, and think I could succeed if it wasn't for sum things. When I see a blackguard goin around the streets with a gun on his shoulder, why right then, for a few minutes, I hate the whole Yankee nation. Jerusalem! how my blood biles! The institution what was handed down to us by the heavenly kingdom of Massachusetts, now put over us with powder and ball! Harmonize the devil! Ain't we human beings? Ain't we got eyes and ears and feelin and thinkin? Why, the whole of Africa has cum to town, women and children and babies and baboons and all. A man can tell how fur it is to the city by the smell better than the milepost. They won't work for us, and they won't work for themselves, and they'll perish to death this winter as sure as the devil is a hog, so-called. They are now basking in the summer's sun, livin on rosting ears and freedom, with nary idee that the winter will come again, or that castor oil and salts cost money. Sum of 'em over a hundred years old are whining around about going to kawlidge. The truth is, my friend, sombody's badly fooled about this bizness. Sombody has drawd the elefant in the lottery, and don't know what to do with him. He's just throwing his snout loose, and by and by he'll hurt sombody. These niggers will have to go back to the plantations and work. I ain't agoin to support nary one of 'em, and when you heer any one say so you tell him "it's a lie," so-called. I, golly! I ain't got nuthin to support myself on. We fought ourselves out of every thing excepin children and land, and I suppose the land is to be turned over to the niggers for graveyards.

Well, my friend, I don't want much. I ain't ambitious, as I used to was. You all have got your shows and monkeys and sircusses and brass bands and organs, and can play on the patrolyum and the harp of a thousand strings, and so on, but I've only got one favor to ax you. I want enough powder to kill a big yaller stump-tail dog that prowls around my premises at night. Pon my honor, I won't shoot at anything blue or black or mulatter. Will you send it? Are you and your folks so skeered of me and my folks that you won't let us have any ammunition? Are the squirrels and crows and black racoons to eat up our poor little corn-patches? Are the wild turkeys to gobble all around us with impunity? If a mad dog takes the hiderphoby, is the whole community to run itself to death to get out of the way? I golly! it looks like your people had all took the rebelfoby for good, and was never gwine to get over it. See here, my friend, you must send me a little powder and a ticket to your show, and me and you will harmonize sertin.

With these few remarks I think I feel better, and I hope I hain't made nobody fitin mad, for I'm not on that line at this time.

I am truly your friend, all present or accounted for.

P. S.—Old man Harris wanted to buy my fiddle the other day with Confederit money. He sed it would be good agin. He says that Jim Funderbuk told him that Warren's Jack seen a man who had jest come from Virginny, and he said a man had told his cousin Mandy that Lee had whipped 'em agin. Old Harris says that a feller by the name of Mack C. Million is coming over with a million of men. But nevertheless, notwithstandin, somehow or somehow else, I'm dubus about the money. If you was me, Artemus, would you make the fiddle trade?

Yours truly,

BILL ARP.

WENDELL PHILLIPS.

Oliver Wendell Holmes tells this story about Wendell Phillips. It occurred when slavery was the bone of contention between the North and the South and every body took one side or the other.

"One day," said Mr. Holmes, "I was riding in the cars near Philadelphia, when several Southern clergymen got into the car. When one of them heard that Wendell Phillips the great anti-slavery agitator was on board, he asked the conductor to point him out. The conductor did so, and the Southern clergyman came up to the orator, and bowing, said:

"'I beg pardon, but you are Mr. Phillips—Mr. Wendell Phillips, of Boston?'

"'Yes, sir.'

"'I should like to speak to you about something, and I trust, sir, you will not be offended,' said the Southern clergyman, politely.

"'There is no fear of it,' was the sturdy answer, and then the minister began to ask Mr. Phillips, earnestly, why he persisted in stirring up such an unfriendly agitation in the North, about the evil of slavery, when it existed in the South.

"'Why,' said the clergyman, 'do you not go South and kick up this fuss and leave the North in peace?'

"Mr. Phillips was not the least ruffled, and answered, smilingly:

"'You, sir, I presume, are a minister of the gospel?'

"'I am sir,' said the clergyman.

"'And your calling is to save souls from hell?'

"'Exactly, sir.'

"'Then why do you stay here in Pennsylvania, agitating the question of salvation? why don't you go right down to hell, where the sinners are and save 'em?'"

One day I met Mr. Phillips on the streets of Boston. He was going along faster than usual, and said he was on his way to Faneuil

ABRAHAM LINCOLN   HORACE GREELEY
JEFFERSON DAVIS   WENDELL PHILLIPS

Hall, where there would probably be a very exciting meeting. President Grant had called out the troops in New Orleans to suppress riots. There was a great Democratic crowd in the old historic hall, and it appeared dangerous for a Republican to attempt to speak. I entered in front, and just as I cast my eyes on the platform, I saw Mr. Phillips begin to ascend it from the speaker's entrance. A Democratic orator was speaking, but no sooner had Mr. Phillips' head appeared above the platform than the people began to shout, "Phillips, Phillips!" Very soon he was addressing the audience, and endeavored to conciliate and pacify his hearers.

"In all cases where great peril existed to citizens," he said, "it was the duty of the government to protect them. No sooner had he finished the sentence than a number of men began to hiss.

The great orator paused a moment, and then an inspired wrath took hold of him, his great eyes gleamed, and in a blast of irony he exclaimed:

"Truth thrown into the cauldron of hell would make a noise like that."

BEECHER'S ESTIMATE OF WENDELL PHILLIPS.

The power to discern right amid all the wrappings of interest and all the seductions of ambition was singularly his. To choose the lowly for their sake: to abandon all favor, all power, all comfort, all ambition, all greatness—that was his genius and glory. He confronted the spirit of the nation and of the age. I had almost said, he set himself against nature, as if he had been a decree of God overriding all these other insuperable obstacles. That was his function. Mr. Phillips was not called to be a universal orator, any more than he was a universal thinker. In literature and in history he was widely read; in person most elegant; in manners most accomplished; gentle as a babe; sweet as a new-blown rose; in voice, clear and silvery. He was not a man of tempests; he was not an orchestra of a hundred instruments; he was not an organ, mighty and complex. The nation slept, and God wanted a trumpet, sharp, far-sounding, narrow and intense; and that was Mr. Phillips. The long roll is not particularly agreeable in music or in times of peace, but it is better than flutes or harps when men are in a great battle, or are on the point of it. His eloquence was penetrating and alarming. He did not flow as a mighty gulf stream; he did not dash upon the continent as the ocean does; he was not a mighty rushing river. His eloquence was a flight of arrows, sentence after sentence, polished, and most of them burning. He shot them one after the other, and where they struck they slew; always elegant, always awful. I think scorn in him was as fine as I ever knew it in any human being. He had that sublime sanctuary in his pride that made him almost insensitive to what would by other men be considered obloquy. It was as if he said every day, in himself, "I am not what they are firing at; I am not there, and I am not that. It is not against me. I am infinitely superior to what they think me to be. They do not know me." It was quiet and unpretentious, but it was there. Conscience and pride were the two concurrent elements of his nature.

He lived to see the slave emancipated, but not by moral means. He lived to see the sword cut the fetter. After this had taken place he was too young to retire, though too old to gather laurels of literature or to seek professional honors. The impulse of humanity was not at all abated. His soul still flowed on for the great under masses of mankind, though like the Nile it split up into diverse mouths, and not all of them were navigable.

After a long and stormy life his sun went down in glory. All the English-speaking people on the globe have written among the names that shall never die, the name of that scoffed, detested, mob-beaten Wendell Phillips. Boston, that persecuted and would have slain him, is now exceedingly busy in building his tomb and rearing his statue. The men that would not defile their lips with his name are to-day thanking God that he lived.

He has taught a lesson that the young will do well to take heed to— the lesson that the most splendid gifts and opportunities and ambitions may be best used for the dumb and the lowly. His whole life is a rebuke to the idea that we are to climb to greatness by climbing up on the backs of great men; that we are to gain strength by running with the currents of life; that we can from without add anything to the great within that constitutes man. He poured out the precious ointment of his soul upon the feet of that diffusive Jesus who suffers here in His poor and despised ones. He has taught the young ambitions too—that the way to glory is the way, oftentimes, of adhesion simply to principle; and that popularity and unpopularity are not things to be known or considered. Do right and rejoice. If to do right will bring you into trouble, rejoice that you are counted worthy to suffer with God and the providences of God in this world.

He belongs to the race of giants, not simply because he was in and of himself a great soul, but because he bathed in the providence of

God, and came forth scarcely less than a god; because he gave himself to the work of God upon earth, and inherited thereby, or had reflected upon him, some of the majesty of his master. When pigmies are all dead, the noble countenance of Wendell Phillips will still look forth, radiant as a rising sun—a sun that will never set. He has become to us a lesson, his death an example, his whole history an encouragement to manhood—to heroic manhood.

ARCHDEACON FARRAR.

The Right Rev. F. W. Farrar, D. D., F. R. S., Archdeacon of Westminster, is the foremost preacher of the Church of England. He occupies the position in church circles so long adorned by the late Dean Stanley. His scholarship is wide and deep. His " Life of Christ" and "Seekers after God," have had a wonderful influence amongst the disciples of liberal Christian thought. Dr. Farrar visited America in 1884, and preached in the chief cities of the Union and gave his famous lecture on Dante.

ARCHDEACON FARRAR'S ARGUMENT.

Rev. Archdeacon F. W. Farrar, examines the philosophy and morality of Seneca, the wisest of the pagan philosophers, Marcus Aurelius the loftiest and most moral pagan ruler, and Epictetus, the most moral and just of pagan stoics, and finds that pagan morality failed to bring happiness to humanity, and that *Christ is a necessity.*

With all the learning and morality of Socrates and Plato, who preceeded Seneca, says the Archdeacon, and with Seneca still living, Rome was barbarous and beastly, and brutal Caius Cæsar flourished. Nero, who was Seneca's pupil, was as miserable and wicked as his people. Seneca was contemporary with Christ, and his own pupil, Nero, not only slew the Christians, but finally slew Seneca himself.

Archdeacon Farrar thus describes the barbarism of Rome: Caius Cæsar ruled Rome when the highest pagan morality flourished. The wicked reigns of Paul of Russia, and Christian VII. of Denmark, were angelic compared to those of Caius Cæsar and Nero. The madness of Caligula, another name for Caius, showed itself sometimes in gluttonous extravagance, as when he ordered a supper which cost more than forty-thousand dollars; sometimes in a *bizarre* and disgraceful mode of dress, as when he appeared in public in women's stockings, embroidered with gold and pearls ; sometimes in a personality and insolence of demeanor towards every rank and class in Rome, which made him ask a senator to supper, and ply him with drunken toasts, on the very evening on which he had condemned his son to death; sometimes in sheer raving blasphemy, as when he expressed his furious indignation against Jupiter for presuming to thunder while he was supping, or looking at the pantomimes ; but most of all in a ferocity which makes Seneca apply to him the name of " Bellua," or " wild monster," and say that he seems to have been produced " for the disgrace and destruction of the human race."

It was an age of the most enormous wealth, existing side by side with the most abject poverty. Around the splendid palaces wandered hundreds of mendicants, who made of their mendicity a horrible trade, and even went so far as to steal or mutilate infants in order to move compassion by their hideous maladies. This class was increased by the exposure of children, and by that overgrown accumulation of landed property which drove the poor from their native fields. It was increased also by the ambitious attempt of people whose means were moderate to imitate the enormous display of the numerous millionaires. The great Roman conquests in the East, the plunder of the ancient kingdoms of Antiochus, of Attalus, of Mithridates, had caused a turbid stream of wealth to flow into the sober current of Roman life. One reads with silent astonishment of the sums expended by wealthy Romans on their magnificence or their pleasures. And as commerce was considered derogatory to rank and position, and was, therefore, pursued by men who had no character to lose, these overgrown fortunes were often acquired by wretches of the meanest stamp—by slaves brought from over the sea, who had to conceal the holes bored in their ears or even by malefactors who had to obliterate by artificial means the three letters which had been branded by the executioner on their foreheads. But many of the richest men in Rome, who had not sprung from this convict origin, were fully as well deserving of the same disgraceful stigma. Their houses were built, their coffers were replenished, from the drained resources of exhausted provincials. Every young man of active ambition or noble birth, whose resources had been impoverished by debauchery and extravagance, had but to borrow fresh sums in order to give magnificent gladiatorial shows, and then, if he could once obtain an aedileship, and mount to the higher offices of the State, he would in time become the procurator or proconsul of a province, which he might pillage almost at his will. Enter the house of a Felix or a Verres. Those splendid pillars of mottled green marble were dug by the forced labor of Phrygians from the quarries of Synnada; that embossed silver, those murrhine vases, those jeweled cups.

those masterpieces of antique sculpture, have all been torn from the homes or the temples of Sicily or Greece. Countries were pillaged and nations crushed that an Apicius might dissolve pearls in the wine he drank, or that Lollia Paulina might gleam in a second-best dress of emeralds and pearls which had cost 40,000,000 sesterces, or more than $160,000.

Each of these " gorgeous criminals " lived in the midst of an humble crowd of flatterers, parasites, clients, dependents and slaves. Among the throng that at early morning jostled each other in the marble atrium were to be found a motley and heterogeneous set of men. Slaves of every age and nation—Germans; Egyptians; Gauls; Goths; Syrians; Britons; Moors; pampered and consequential freedmen; impudent, confidential servants; greedy buffoons, who lived by making bad jokes at other people's tables; Dacian gladiators, with whom fighting was a trade; philosophers, whose chief claim to reputation was the length of their beards; supple Greeklings of the Tartuffe species, ready to flatter and lie with consummate skill, and spreading their vile character like a pollution wherever they went; and among all these a number of poor but honest clients, forced quietly to put up with a thousand forms of contumely and insult, and living in discontented idleness on the sportula or daily largesse which was administered by the grudging liberality of their haughty patrons. The stout old Roman burgher had well-nigh disappeared; the sturdy independence, the manly self-reliance of an industrial population were all but unknown. The insolent loungers who bawled in the forum were often mere stepsons of Italy, who had been dragged thither in chains—the dregs of all nations, which had flowed into Rome as into a common sewer, bringing with them no heritage except the specialty of their national vices. Their two wants were bread and the shows of the circus; so long as the sportula of their patron, the occasional donative of an emperor, and the ambition of political candidates supplied these wants, they lived in contented abasement, anxious neither for liberty nor for power.

It was an age at once of atheism and superstition. Strange to say, the two things usually go together. Just as Philippe Egalité, Duke of Orleans, disbelieved in God, and yet tried to conjecture his fate from the inspection of coffee-grounds at the bottom of a cup—just as Louis XI. shrank from no perjury and no crime, and yet retained a profound reverence for a little leaden image which he carried in his cap—so the Romans under the empire sneered at all the whole crowd of gods and goddesses whom their fathers had worshiped, but gave an implicit credence to sorcerers, astrologers, spirit-rappers, exorcists and every species of impostor and quack. The ceremonies of religion were performed with ritualistic splendor, but all belief in religion was dead and gone. " That there are such things as ghosts and subterranean realms, not even boys believe," says Juvenal, " except those who are still too young to pay a farthing for a bath." Nothing can exceed the cool impertinence with which the poet Martial prefers the favor of Domitian to that of the great Jupiter of the Capitol. Seneca, in his lost book " Against Superstitions," openly sneered at the old mythological legends of gods married and gods unmarried, and at the gods Panic and Paleness, and at Cloacina, the goddess of sewers, and at other deities whose cruelty and license would have been infamous even in mankind. And yet the priests and Salii and Flamens and Augurs continued to fulfill their solemn functions, and the highest title of the Emperor himself was that of Pontifex Maximus, or Chief Priest, which he claimed as the recognized head of the national religion. " The common worship was regarded," says Gibbon, " by the people as equally true, by the philosophers as equally false, and by the magistrates as equally useful." And this famous remark is little more than a translation from Seneca, who, after exposing the futility of the popular beliefs, adds: " And yet the wise man will observe them all, not as pleasing to the gods, but as commanded by the laws. We shall so adore all that ignoble crowd of gods which long superstition has heaped together in a long period of years, as to remember that their worship has more to do with custom than with reality." " Because he was an illustrious senator of the Roman people," observes St. Augustine, who has preserved for us this fragment, " he worshiped what he blamed, he did what he refuted, he adored that with which he found fault." Could any thing be more hollow or heartless than this? Is there any thing which is more certain to sap the very foundations of morality than the public maintenance of a creed which has long ceased to command the assent, and even the respect of its recognized defenders? Seneca, indeed, and a few enlightened philosophers, might have taken refuge from the superstitions which they abandoned in a truer and purer form of faith. "Accordingly," says Lactantius, one of the Christian Fathers, " he has said many things like ourselves concerning God." He utters what Tertullian finely calls " the testimony of A MIND NATURALLY CHRISTIAN." But, meanwhile, what became of the common multitude? They too, like their superiors, learnt to disbelieve or to question the power of the ancient deities; but, as the mind absolutely requires some religion on which to rest, they gave their real devotion to all kinds of strange and foreign deities, to Isis and Osiris, and the dog Anubus, to Chaldæan magicians, to Jewish exorcisers, to Greek quacks, and to the wretched vagabond priests of Cybele, who infested all the streets with their Oriental dances and tinkling tambourines. The visitor to the ruins of Pompeii may still see in her temple the statue of Isis, through whose open lips the gaping worshipers heard the murmured answers they came to seek. No doubt they believed as firmly that the image spoke, as our forefathers believed that their miraculous Madonnas nodded and winked. But time has exposed the cheat. By the ruined shrine the worshiper may now see the secret steps by which the priest got to the back of the statue, and the pipe entering the back of its head through which he whispered the answers of the oracle.

It was an age of boundless luxury—an age in which women recklessly vied with one another in the race of splendor and extravagance, and in which men plunged headlong, without a single scruple of conscience, and with every possible resource at their command, into the pursuit of pleasure. There was no form of luxury, there was no refinement of vice invented by any foreign nation, which had not been eagerly adopted by the Roman patricians. "The softness of Sybaris, the manners of Rhodes and Antioch, and of perfumed, drunken, flower-crowned Miletus," were all to be found at Rome. There was no more of the ancient Roman severity and dignity and self-respect. The descendants of Æmilius and Gracchus—even generals and consuls and prætors—mixed familiarly with the lowest *canaille* of Rome, in their vilest and most squalid purlieus of shameless vice. They fought as amateur gladiators in the arena. They drove as competing charioteers on the race-course. They even condescended to appear as actors on the stage. They devoted themselves with such frantic eagerness to the excitement of gambling, that we read of their staking hundreds of pounds on a single throw of the dice, when they could not even restore the pawned tunics to their shivering slaves. Under the cold marble statues, or amid the waxen likenesses of their famous stately ancestors, they turned night into day with long and foolish orgies, and exhausted land and sea with the demands of their gluttony. "Woe to that city," says an ancient proverb, "in which a fish costs more than an ox;" and this exactly describes the state of Rome. A banquet would sometimes cost the price of an estate; shell-fish were brought from remote and unknown shores, birds from Parthia and the banks of the Phasis; single dishes were made of the brains of the peacocks and the tongues of nightingales and flamingoes. Apicius, after squandering nearly a million of money in the pleasures of the table, committed suicide, Seneca tells us, because he found that he had only $400,000 left.   Cowley speaks of

> "Vitellius' table, which did hold
> As many creatures as the ark of old."

"They eat," said Seneca, "and then they vomit; they vomit, and then they eat."   But even in this matter we can not tell any thing like the worst facts about

> "Their sumptuous gluttonies and gorgeous feasts
> On citron tables and Altantic stone,
> Their wines of Setia, Cales, and Falerne,
> Chios, and Crete, and how they quaff in gold,
> Crystal and myrrhine cups, embossed with gems
> And studs of pearl."

Still less can we pretend to describe the unblushing and unutterable degradation of this period as it is revealed to us by the poets and the satirists.   "All things," says Seneca, "are full of iniquity and vice; more crime is committed than can be remedied by restraint.   We struggle in a huge contest of criminality; daily the passion for sin is greater, the shame in committing it is less. . . . Wickedness is no longer committed in secret; it flaunts before our eyes, and

> "The citron board, the bowl embossed with gems,
> .   .   .   .   whate'er is known
> Of rarest acquisition; Tyrian garbs,
> Neptunlan Albion's high testaceous food,
> And flavored Chian wines, with incense fumed,
> To slake patrician thirst: for these their rights
> In the vile streets they prostitute for sale,
> Their ancient rights, their dignities, their laws,
> Their native glorious freedom,

has been sent forth so openly into public sight, and has prevailed so completely in the breast of all, that innocence is not rare, but non-existent."

And it was an age of deep sadness.   That it should have been so is an instructive and solemn lesson.   In proportion to the luxury of the age were its misery and its exhaustion.   The mad pursuit of pleasure was the death and degradation of all true happiness.   Suicide—suicide out of pure *ennui* and discontent at a life overflowing with every possible means of indulgence—was extraordinarily prevalent.   The stoic philosophy, especially as we see it represented in the tragedies attributed to Seneca, rang with the glorification of it.   Men ran to death because their mode of life had left them no other refuge.   They died because it seemed so tedious and so superfluous to be seeing and doing and saying the same things over and over again; and because they had exhausted the very possibility of the only pleasures of which they had left themselves capable. The satirical epigram of Destouches,

> "Ci-gît Jean Rosbif, écuyer,
> Qui se pendit pour se désennuyer,"

was literally and strictly true of many Romans during this epoch. Marcellinus, a young and wealthy noble, starved himself, and then had himself suffocated in a warm bath, merely because he was attacked with a perfectly curable illness. The philosophy which alone professed itself able to heal men's sorrows applauded the supposed courage of a voluntary death, and it was of too abstract, too fantastic, and too purely theoretical a character to furnish them with any real or lasting consolations. No sentiment caused more surprise to the Roman world than the famous one preserved in the fragment of Mæcenas, which may be paraphrased

> "Numb my hands with palsy,
> Rack my feet with gout,
> Hunch my back and shoulder,
> Let my teeth fall out;
> Still, if Life be granted,
> I prefer the loss;
> Save my life and give me
> Anguish on the cross."

Seneca, in his 101st letter, calls this "a most disgraceful and most contemptible wish;" but it may be paralleled out of Euripides, and still more closely out of Homer. "Talk not," says the shade of Achilles to Ulysses in the Odyssey

> "'Talk not of reigning in this dolorous gloom,
> Nor think vain lies,' he cried, 'can ease my doom.
> Better by far laboriously to bear
> A weight of woes, and breathe the vital air,
> Slave to the meanest hind that begs his bread,
> Than reign the sceptered monarch of the dead.'"

But this falsehood of extremes was one of the sad outcomes of the popular paganism. Either, like the natural savage, they dreaded death with an intensity of terror; or, when their crimes and sorrows had made life unsupportable, they slank to it as a refuge, with a cowardice which vaunted itself as courage.

And it was an age of cruelty. The shows of gladiators, the sanguinary combats of wild beasts, the not unfrequent spectacle of savage tortures and capital punishments, the occasional sight of innocent martyrs burning to death in their shirts of pitchy fire, must have hardened and imbruted the public sensibility. The immense prevalence of slavery tended still more inevitably to the general corruption. "Lust," as usual, was "hard by hate." One hears with perfect amazement of the number of slaves in the wealthy houses. A thousand slaves was no extravagant number, and the vast majority of them were idle, uneducated and corrupt. Treated as little better than animals, they lost much of the dignity of men. Their masters possessed over them the power of life and death, and it is shocking to read of the cruelty with which they were often treated. An accidental murmur, a cough, a sneeze, was punished with rods. Mute, motionless, fasting, the slaves had to stand by while their masters supped. A brutal and stupid barbarity often turned a house into the shambles of an executioner, sounding with scourges, chains and yells. One evening the Emperor Augustus was supping at the house of Vedius Pollio, when one of the slaves, who was carrying a crystal goblet, slipped down and broke it. Transported with rage, Vedius at once ordered the slave to be seized, and plunged into the fish-pond as food to the lampreys. The boy escaped from the hands of his fellow-slaves, and fled to Cæsar's feet to implore, not that his life should be spared — a pardon which he neither expected nor hoped — but that he might die by a mode of death less horrible than being devoured by fishes. Common as it was to torment slaves, and to put them to death, Augustus, to his honor be it spoken, was horrified by the cruelty of Vedius, and commanded both that the slave should be set free, that every crystal vase in the house of Vedius should be broken in his presence, and that the fish-pond should be filled up. Even women inflicted upon their female slaves punishments of the most cruel atrocity, for faults of the most venial character. A brooch wrongly placed, a tress of hair ill-arranged, and the enraged matron orders her slave to be lashed and crucified. If her milder husband interferes, she not only justifies the cruelty, but asks in amazement: "What! is a slave so much of a human being?" No wonder that there was a proverb, "As many slaves, so many foes." No wonder that many masters lived in perpetual fear, and that "the tyrant's devilish plea, necessity," might be urged in favor of that odious law which enacted that, if a master was murdered by an unknown hand, the whole body of his slaves should suffer death — a law which more than once was carried into effect under the reigns of the emperors. Slavery, as we see in the case of Sparta and many other nations, always involves its own retribution. The class of free peasant proprietors gradually disappears. Long before this time Tib. Gracchus, in coming home from Sardinia, had observed that there was scarcely a single freeman to be seen in the fields. The slaves were infinitely more numerous than their owners. Hence arose the constant dread of servile insurrections; the constant hatred of a slave population to which any conspirator revolutionist might successfully appeal; and the constant insecurity of life, which must have struck terror into many hearts.

Such is but a faint and broad outline of some of the features of Seneca's age; and we shall be unjust if we do not admit that much, at least, of the life he lived, and nearly all the sentiments he uttered, gain much in grandeur and purity from the contrast they offer to the common life of

"That people victor once, now vile and base."

* 　 * 　 * 　 * 　 * 　 * 　 * 　 * 　 * 　 *

After Caligula and Nero (A. D. 121) came Marcus Aurelius, the purest pagan the world has ever seen. He was almost a Christian. Aurelius was emperor of Rome and master of the world. His philosophy was ennobling and his teachings pure and sweet. But still, he saw no future immortality and happiness. Christianity includes all of the good in Aurelian stoicism and then adds a crown of immortality. All Aurelius could say was, "Since it is possible that thou mayest depart from life this very moment, regulate every act and thought accordingly." . . . Death certainly and life, honor and dishonor, pain and pleasure, all these things happen equally to good men and bad, being things which make us neither better nor worse, therefore they are neither good nor evil."

"Hippocrates cured diseases and died; and the Chaldæans foretold the future and died; and Alexander and Pompey and Cæsar killed thousands, and then died; and lice destroyed Democritus, and other lice killed Socrates; and Augustus and his wife and daughter and all his descendants and all his ancestors are dead; and Vespasian and all his court, and all who in his day feasted and married and were sick and chaffered and fought and flattered and plotted and grumbled and wished other people to die and pined to become kings or consuls are dead; and all the idle people who are doing the same things now are doomed to die; and all human things are smoke and nothing at all; and it is not for us, but for the gods, to settle whether we play the play out, or only a part of it. *'There are many grains of frankincese on the same altar; one falls before, another falls after; but it makes no difference.'* And the moral of all these thoughts is, 'Death hangs over thee while thou livest: while it is in thy power be good. 'Thou hast embarked, thou hast made the voyage, thou hast come to shore; get out.

If, indeed, to another life there is no want of gods, not even there. But if to a state without sensation, thou wilt cease to be held by pains and pleasures.'"

Nor was Marcus at all comforted under present annoyances by the thought of posthumous fame. "How ephermal and worthless human things are," he says, "and what was yesterday a little mucus, to-morrow will be a mummy or ashes." "Many who are now praising thee, will very soon blame thee, and neither a posthumous name is of any value, nor reputation, nor anything else." What has become of all great and famous men, and all they desired, and all they loved? They are "smoke and ash and a tale, or not even a tale." After all their rages and envyings, men are stretched out quiet and dead at last. Soon thou wilt have forgotten all, and all will have forgotten thee. But here, again, after such thoughts, the same moral is always introduced again: "Pass then through the little space of time conformably to nature, and end the journey in content. Just as an olive falls off when it is ripe, blessing nature who produced it and thanking the tree on which it grew."

The morality of paganism was, on its own confession, *insufficient.* It was tentative, where Christianity is authoritative; it was dim and partial, where Christianity is bright and complete; it was inadequate to rouse the sluggish carelessness of mankind, where Christianity came in with an imperial and awakening power; it gives only a *rule,* where Christianity supplies a *principle.* And even where its teachings were absolutely coinncident with those of Scripture, it failed to ratify them with a sufficient sanction; it failed to announce them with the same powerful and contagious ardor; it failed to furnish an absolutely fault-less and vivid example of their practice; it failed to inspire them with an irresistable motive; it failed to support them with comfort, hope and happy immortality *after a consistent and moral life.*

Seneca, Epictetus, Aurelius, are among the truest and loftiest of pagan moralists, yet Seneca ignored the Christians, Epictetus despised, and Aurelius persecuted them. All three, so far as they knew any thing about the Christians at all, had unhappily been taught to look upon them as the most detestable sect of what they had long regarded as the most degraded and the most detestable of religions.

There is something very touching in this fact; but, if there be some-thing very touching, there is also something very encouraging. God was their God as well as ours—their Creator, their Preserver, who left not Himself without witness among them; who, as they blindly felt after Him, suffered their groping hands to grasp the hem of His robe; who sent them rain from heaven, and fruitful seasons, filling their hearts with joy and gladness. And His Spirit was with them, dwelling in them, though unseen and unknown, purifying and sanctifying the temple of their hearts, sending gleams of illuminating light through the gross darkness which encompassed them, comforting their uncertainties, making intercession for them with groaning which can not be uttered. And more than all, *our* Savior was *their* Savior, too ; He, whom they regarded as a crucified malefactor, was their true, invisible King; through His righteousness their poor merits were accepted, their inward sicknesses were healed ; He whose worship they denounced as an "execrable superstition," stood supplicating for them at the right hand of the Majesty on high.

Stoical philosophy had no influence over the heart and character; " it was sectarian, not universal; the religion of the few, not of the many. It exercised no creative power over political or social life; it stood in no such relation to the past as the New Testament to the Old. Its best thoughts were but views and aspects of the truth; there was no center around which they moved, no divine life by which they were impelled; they seemed to vanish and flit in uncertain succession of light."

But Christianity, on the other hand has glowed with a steady and unwavering brightness; it not only sways the hearts of individuals by stirring them to their utmost depths, but it molds the laws of nations, and regenerates the whole condition of society. It gives to mankind a fresh sanction in the word of Christ, a perfect example in His life, a powerful motive in His love, an all-sufficient comfort in the life of immortality made sure and certain to us by His resurrection and ascension. But if without this sanction and example and motive and comfort, the pagans could learn to almost do His will; if, amid the gross darkness through which glitters the degraded civilization of imperial Rome, an Epictetus and an Aurelius could live blameless lives in a cell and on a throne, and a Seneca could practice simplicity and self-denial in the midst of luxury and pride, how much loftier should be both the zeal and the attainments of us to whom God has spoken by his Son? What manner of men ought we to be?

PROFESSOR DAVID SWING.

BIOGRAPHY.

Professor David Swing was born in Cincinnati, on the 18th of August, 1831. He pursued his early studies at Oxford, Ohio, but subsequently went to Miami University, where he graduated in 1852. Professor Swing and President Harrison were classmates at Miami. After a brief pastorate, Professor Swing was appointed classical tutor in Miami University; a position which he filled with great honor for more than twelve years. He then removed to Chicago, and became pastor of a Presbyterian church, on the North Side. He soon became famous. But his teaching was of too broad a character to please the conservative element of Presbyterians. At the instance of Dr. Patton he was tried for heresy, but the verdict was in his favor. Desiring, however, to live in perfect peace, Dr. Swing left the Presbyterian body, and became pastor of the Central Church, which now worships in the Central Music Hall, Chicago. Professor Swing is almost universally recognized as the greatest preacher of the West. He preaches only once on the Sabbath, and usually takes the months of July, August and part of September for vacation.

PROFESSOR SWING'S SCHOLASTIC THOUGHTS.

Education does not imply stores of knowledge or information; it means the expansion of the brain. The mind is created full of tendencies or aptitudes, and, expanded by education and training, these tendencies develop into great forces. The soul of the Indian girl contains a tendency toward a love of the beautiful. She will prefer a wild flower to a stone or a stick, and will enjoy a local love song to quite a high degree. This aptitude in the natural wild girl can, by education, be enlarged in successive generations until we have, instead of this Indian maid, a De Stael, or a Charlotte Bronté, or a Mrs. Browning. By this process of enlarging by use, a muttering red man becomes a Cicero or Tacitus, or a flowing writer or an exquisite artist. In pursuing, for thousands of years, this work of evoking mental forces, two inquiries have attended the advancing race—what studies do most strengthen the mind ? and what kind of information is of most absolute value ? It is perfectly safe to say that no answer has yet come to these questions. It is perhaps equally safe to say that none ever will come, it being probably true that there are many studies of equal merit, just as there are thousands of landscapes of equal sweetness, and thousands of faces and forms of equal beauty.

For many centuries it has been assumed that the study of the dead languages, that is, the dead great languages—Latin and Greek—and of the higher mathematics, is the labor which gives best results, the exercise which turns a plowboy into an orator or a statesman or a philosopher. College courses have been run amid these three shapes of toil and information, and it came to pass long ago, that a mind not reared upon this strong food was deemed still an infant, having known only the weakness that comes from a diet of diluted milk. That power of prejudice, the power of what has long been, over the frail form of what might be, which we see in old medicine, or old religion, or old politics, reappears in old education, and a scholar or a thinker without the help of Latin and Greek was as impossible as a state without a king, or a salvation without a clergyman. The feeling in favor of the classic course has not been all a prejudice, for that was and is a noble course of mental progress, but it was a prejudice so far as it denied the value of all other forms of mental industry, and failed to perceive that what the human mind needs is exercise, and not necessarily Greek exercise or Latin exercise. A special must not thus dethrone a universal. A king may be a good governor, but his courtiers and sons and daughters must not overrate the crowned man and predict the utter failure of any nation that may ever dare attempt to live without the help of a throne and royal children. Evidently, the greatest, widest truth is, that the mind is made more powerful by exercise, and it will always be a secondary consideration whether this exercise shall come by loading the memory with the words and forms found in several languages, by compelling the judgment to work continually amid the many possibilities of syntax and translation, or shall come by a direct study of facts and causes and laws, as found in science and history and literature.

It favors the classic course amazingly that no other course of mental development has ever been attempted in what is called the great era— the Christian era; but it might well shake our opinion, the thought that the Greeks and Latins became great without being fed exclusively upon a diet of grammars and dictionaries and mathematics. Richter asks, "Whither do those sunflowers turn which grow upon the sun?" So may we ask, what made mighty those children that were born into the classic tongues? What made the man Pericles and the man Plato? and the women Sappho and Aspasia? What seven-years course had they in dead languages? There can be but one answer, and that must be that the mind is made powerful and great by all far-reaching after the truths and fancies around it—by a constant and loving effort to enlarge its powers and accumulations. Pericles and Plato and Cicero and Humboldt and Mill and Webster and Clay were educated by intellectual toil and hope and zeal in their adjacent worlds, whatever those worlds may have been. The class-rooms of Oxford and Cambridge are, indeed, good worlds for the forming mind to master, but not many of the eagles of genius have, comparatively speaking, taken, in such linguistic schools, their first lessons in lofty flight. All the ages are school-houses, and the great men have been those who never played truant nor shirked, but who loved the school-house, whether it was by the Nile, under Rameses, or at Athens, under Pericles, or at Oxford, under Elizabeth or Victoria.

The Latin and Greek tongues once possessed an inestimable worth, because there was little of broad and powerful thought outside of those two literatures, and within them there were a power and beauty not yet, perhaps, surpassed. Soon after the opening of the Christian drama, the human mind became enslaved by a politico-religious government, which discouraged all thought, except that which tended to establish a throne and mark out an expensive way to a strange heaven, or a still more strange hell. Mind grew narrower and weaker as the centuries passed by. Scholars were content to write the life of some ascetic monk, and to fill up with miracles a life that had been empty of both usefulness and food. Far along in the clouded periods, when some of the monks happened upon Latin and Greek books, it was as though the deaf had begun to hear, the blind to see and the dumb to speak. Compared with a biography of some whining zealot, whose glory lay in the scarcity of his food and in the abundance of his personal dirt, the poems of Homer and Virgil, and the orations of Cicero and the meditations of Plato were full of almost divine beauty, and thus exalted by a value both intrinsic and relative, Latin and Greek ascended the throne in the great kingdom of mind and sentiment. No broader or freer literature than the old classic thought has ever existed. From Homer to Tacitus there was freedom of the mind. No church or state told the thinkers what to think or express. Indeed each ruler was himself a scholar of his period, and, republic or empire, the state was always literary in its tastes and works. The rulers and statesmen were all poets or orators and philosophers, with full permission to select any theme, and to say upon it whatever pleased the hand that held the pen. Through the Latin and Greek gates there rushed out upon the dark Christian ages a stream of intellectual liberty and power. Out of stones so noble, the colleges and universities, which now reckon their ages by centuries, built up their greatness of merit and fame, and our age will never be able to express too much gratitude toward those old states which furnished the new epoch with such foundations of mental and spiritual development.

We come now to a universal phenomenon—that of the pupil excelling the master. Moses was surpassed by Daniel and Isaiah. Watts' engine is superseded. The man who taught music to Beethoven is forgotten in the splendor of his humble student. Modern Europe has moved far beyond old Greece, and in the modern languages and literature and sciences, all said and thought of on the coast of the old Mediterranean finds its amazing equivalent. Once the roll of human greatness read thus: Homer, Hesiod, Æschylus, Euripides, Pericles, Plato, Virgil, Cicero, Cæsar, Tacitus, and the splendor of the catalogue none will have the rashness to deny; but in the later centuries the book so long sealed has been opened, and there have been added Dante and Milton and Shakspeare and Goethe and Schiller, and such thinkers as Bacon and Newton, and such students as Cuvier and Humboldt and Muller and Darwin and Huxley and Agassiz. By these enormous additions the equilibrium of the old earth has been disturbed, and a side, which once lay in perpetual shadow, enjoys now a long summer time. The buried palms and ferns of the Arctic latitude tell us that what is now the North Pole, and the region of almost lifeless frost, was once a land upon which the warm sun shone, and over which hot thunder-storms passed. Some external force came to make the planet revolve upon some new inclination of its axis, and to remand to night and ice a continent which had once enjoyed the seasons, which now bless America or France. Into the intellectual world came a wonderful company of modern princes—a Newton, equaling a Plato, and a Shakspeare balancing all antiquity; and, under the heavy footsteps of all these moderns, the earth has been whirled about, and a longer and deeper shadow falls upon the land, where Demosthenes once thundered and Sappho once sang. With this tipping over of the earth, the Greek and Roman lands lost their exclusiveness of empire, and were invited to become only brotherly states in a world-wide republic. The reasons for the long, patient study of those old tongues have, in part, thus passed away, since they are no longer the languages which contain the most or the best of human learning and thought. As acquisitions and as mental exercises, those languages will always be valuable, but this will take place henceforth, in a world where other studies, equally valuable in all respects, will present their claims to the student, old or young, abounding in wealth or pinched by poverty. As language is made up of embalmed ideas, the modern tongues must be confessed to be powerful rivals of Greek and Latin, for the world having grown larger since Homer and Virgil, the modern tongues contain more ideas than were held by all the ancient kingdoms and republics.

Not only is it questionable whether the dead languages should any longer outrank, as studies, the great modern dialects, but it is also a matter of grave doubt whether an argument can be framed in support of the educational theory which devotes years, early and late, to the study of any of the forms of speech, ancient or modern. It may seem a form of mortal sin — a sin beyond the reach of masses and holy water — to confess that there exists, under Heaven, any such doubt, and yet something must be said on this linguistic mania, even though the utterance should prove most amazing and unwelcome. Language in essence is a catalogue of names. Words are the names of things and of actions. If Æschylus spoke of *kumaton anarithmaton gelasma*, he saw and embalmed in sound the beautiful truth of nature, and the merit lies not in the sounds of the vowels and consonants, but in the genius that saw, in the morning ripple of the sea, "the numberless smiles of the waves." What the human soul needed was some one able to lay upon the broad ocean that sweetness of expression which had been sought for and found only upon the lips and face of woman. If a smile is a sudden flash of light and kindness, then what an interpreter of the ocean is he who first tells us to look out upon its widespread and delicate smilings! But it is not the language that is so great; it is the sudden spiritualizing of the ocean. Language is only a name for the strange beauty of the water, and, hence, it is of no consequence whether the name be "*kumaton anarithmaton gelasma*," or the "sea's innumerable smile," or the "many twinkling smile of the waves," or whether the Frenchman or German or Spaniard bedecks the simile with his raiment of words and syntax. The expression uttered by the Greek poet becomes the world's single fact and property, and the possession of a hundred languages by any one individual will not add anything whatever to that morning and evening radiance of the Atlantic or Pacific. When we who had spent seven years over Greek, first stood upon the sea-shore, our hearts asked the old dead tongue to help us estimate that infinite scintillation of the flood, and did we not, all of us, bless God that He had permitted us to study Greek? Did we not feel that all who had not read the "Prometheus" in the original were cut off from nature, as though born blind? What a mistake of a name for a substance! for now, when all we ex-denizens, far away at last from college walls, happen upon the beach, and look out upon the blue, we ask for no more blessed expression of the scene than our own tongue can bring us in its powerful sounds, "the numberless smiles of the waves." Gœthe expressed the same thought in the German, Lamartine in the French, and thus let the speech change a thousand times, there is only the one thought hidden away in the varied accents.

In any one of the great modern tongues there is now stored away all the facts of the earth up to this date. If Virgil asked us to note the beauty of the moon at midnight, when it passes in and out amid fleecy clouds, we so do, and our heart is happy or sad, as was his, it being of no importance that he called the planet "luna," while we call it "moon," and that he called "nubila" those masses which we call "clouds." Compared with the grandeur of the scene, all these varia- tions of the vowels and intonations are things of childish importance. It might, therefore, easily come to pass that the student, young or old, may, in the study of many tongues, be giving years of time to accidental matters, instead of to those facts of being and action which are the per- manent and valuable estate of man. A certain Roman orator we call Cicero. In his own day he may have been called Tullius. Intimate friends may have called him Marcus. We do not now know how his family pronounced the "c" or the "u." But let it be true that this lawyer had three names, and that there are many possible ways of utter- ing those names, the one fact only remains valuable—the man himself. As such he has entered into the world's intellectual and moral riches, and we have him, be we German or French or English, in our lip and tongue service. Compared with this gold of possession, all else is dust. To compare the thoughts of this lofty Roman with the thoughts of Burke and Pitt and Sumner, in the arena of political study; to pass over to morals, and compare him with Puffendorf and Spencer; to pass to religion, and compare him with Wesley or Stuart Mill or Jefferson; to pass to rhetoric, and compare his mode of argument with that of Fox or Webster or Clay—would be to be engaged in pursuits greater than a mastery of these tongues, in which all these widely separated minds may have done their sincere thinking in the sight of man and God. Their words, like their clothing or their food, were local and incidental. Indeed, of less importance than the food these chieftains ate, for that food might be good for us to imitate or avoid, whereas it is of little value to us that Cicero called that being *Deus* whom we call God, and that quality "pietas" which we call "piety." It is the unchanging contents of the earth man must chiefly seek, and so brief is life that its lamp burns out before we have read the great volume of events and experiences, and no time is left for the study of those strange marks and sounds in which Egyptian or Persian or Athenian or Roman may have made record of his life or wisdom or sentiment. A hundred languages have passed away, in all of which the golden rule was putting forth its slow leaves, and men care not with what gutturals or labials or aspirates the first moralists began to express the worth to society of brotherly love. As man himself has come along over lands which have become deserts, passing in and out of temples and homes which have become dust, and falling into tombs which have no stone and by which no flower blooms, and yet he is here to-day in divine splendor; so truths, like the law of love, have come along, stepping from language to language, and then leaving to decay or neglect the stairway of their long ascent. So subordinate is language to idea that the Christian world, which rests its hope upon the beatitudes of Jesus, does not know in what speech He first said, "Blessed are the pure in heart." As the sea changes its shore line, and leaves far inland temples which once stood where the solemnity of the waves joined in the worship, and yet it is the same sea, flowing and re-flowing in tide and storm, so humanity leaves as dead and abandoned its old shores of speech, and along some new coast of forms and sounds flows and re-flows with a tide of wisdom and emotion rising higher as the ages pass. Each great language, English, French, German, is the present shore of the living sea, and if borne into one of these tongues, that tongue is for you or me a measureless main. It is the aggregate of the past six thousand years.

Do I speak French?

Not yet have I learned the universe hidden away in the language of my birth and soul. When you have caught up with the world's facts, then, if time remains, you might ask what the Frenchman would call those facts. After having studied the life, the tendencies, the loves of the sunworshipers and the Egyptians; after having seen the Queen of Sheba journeying to behold the greatness of Solomon; after having committed to memory the sublime chants of Job; after an inquiry into old liberty and old bondage, and into old science and art, it might be of interest to know what letters and sounds a Frenchman would use in expressing the world's history, but to know all about the wanderings of Ulysses and his son is the thing to be desired more than the information that the French called the father Ulysse and the son Telemaque.

Let it be conceded that persons who are to devote all their life to intellectual pursuits have time for mastering several of the great dialects, ancient and existing; it yet remains a fair inquiry, what quantity of this linguistic work may enter into those courses of study over which the multitude must pass. Must young persons who have only one idea learn ten ways of expressing it? Or must this person, often a beautiful girl, find ten ideas in the grand language of her native land? What made a Rubenstein was not a score of pianos, but it was genius and labor, practicing upon one adequate instrument. It is well known that, when some years ago certain thousands of families, men and women, were flying before a great conflagration, one citizen was seen to remove from his library nine violins of all ages and pedigrees—a scene made laughable, even at such a gloomy time, by the equally well-known fact that this lover of the fiddle could not, from any or all of the strings, elicit more than the one-ninth part of a tune. As the cart-load of instruments moved onward toward a place of safety, even the best friends of the amateur could not help wishing that the noble gentleman had less of fiddle and more of music. In the department of fashionable education a similar event may be detected in the fact that many young persons are learning more ways of expressing thought than they have thoughts to express, and instead of having ten ideas of value, they give promise of reaching, at last, ten methods of stating one idea, and perhaps a small one at that. For suppose your beautiful daughter of seventeen years has, by much toil and expense, learned to say in five tongues, "He has the pretty yellow dog;" in Greek: *Ehei kalon chloon kuna;* in Latin: *Habet bellum canem gilvum;* in French: *Il a un joli chien de jaune;* in German: *Er hat den schönen gelben Hund;* and could she by industry find the Chinese and Zulu vowel sounds, used by those remote people, to convey that idea of property in an animal, it would be well for the girl and parent to remember that, amid all this variety of speech, there is only the same yellow dog all the time. Under some other theory of education, the mind might have mastered the whole science of Cuvier, and have moved away from the yellow dog to study the whole animal kingdom, from the elephants of India to the garden-making birds of the tropics, and the bank-swallow of America. The poor man, in the cold of mid-winter, does not need ten shovels with which to put one ton of coal into the scuttle, but what he craves is ten tons of coal and one good shovel. It might be of interest to him to know the shape of a Russian or Hindoo scoop, to gaze at the kind of instrument by which the Hebrews put wheat into a sack, or apples into an ox-cart, but the highest happiness of the multitude will always come more from the coal they may possess in December, than from any collection they might covet of old and modern utensils of lifting and moving fuel from vault to grate. If the remark will not give any offense, it may be let fall here, that there are thousands of boys and girls, older and younger, whose ability to express thought has quite outgrown the thought they have on hand awaiting expression, and, having mastered a great many styles of saying things, they are finding themselves in the position of having nothing to say. When the lovely young lady, who had mastered her French and Italian and Spanish, was led by some machine-loving gentleman to gaze for a moment at the great engines in the hydraulic works of Chicago, asked him, in her delight, whether the big wheel was turned by men or by a horse, it gave him no peace that she could have put the inquiry into any one of the modern tongues. The questions placed him, for a time, beyond the consolation of philosophy and religion.

The prevailing idea among the upper American classes that even their little children must learn French, and to that end must speak it at the table, is highly blamable, for reasons more than one. It is based upon entire ignorance of the fact that it will require the life-time of each mortal to master the language of his birth and country. All the young years given by Americans to the study of French are years turned away from the greatest language yet known to man. All the acquisitions of the human race, all the sciences, and arts, and histories, and sentiments of humanity have passed into the English tongue. Each word stands for an idea, and in each great modern dialect all ideas reappear. He that has perfectly mastered his own language has a store of information immense in bulk and rich in value. To excavate many channels for a river is to lessen the unity and power of the stream otherwise majestic. It will always be proof of some blunder of judgment, or of some stubborn vanity, when Americans will be found using a little French and German and Italian, who have not mastered the English of William Wirt, or of Tennyson, or of the eloquent Ruskin. It is not languages man needs, but language. It is not a room full of violins, but the power to make music. It is therefore simply painful to hear a fashionable girl or woman or man combining several languages in conversation, when the listener knows well that this bright talker could not by any possibility compose an essay in the English of Washington Irving, or Charles Sumner, or the poet Whittier. While they have trifled with grammars and lexicons, or have said elegantly this or that compliment of the season, their own grand English has moved away from their mind and heart just as husband and home at last disappear from the world of the artful beauty, leaving in her possession the old faded bouquets and the old yellow cards of invitation to dinner or to dance—invitations sent and accepted long ago, when the forehead was smooth and the lips red.

A modern language is a prodigious affair. All will admit that, as a system of sounds for expressing truths, the Greek language has no equal.

but it comes short in just this particular—that the Greeks had not as much to express as the Germans and French and English now have in their keeping. An island has become a continent, a river has widened into a sea. Each of these three modern tongues holds in its embrace a universe, while Greek held only a star. To master one of these new forms of speech, is the task of a life, and happy the American who shall ever reach in his own tongue the ease and skill reached in their own tongue by Chateaubriand and Lamartine, and by Castelar in his dialect, or by Schiller in the rich German. Such a result can not be reached by attempts to study the words of Lamartine and Gœthe, but by studying the same universe as that which enveloped them, and by compelling our own English harp to play for us all our sincere and passionate music. It must be that the popularity of French comes from a forgetfulness of the absolute immensity of the English language—an immenseness which asks for many years of early and late study, and which should so capti- vate each one born into its confines, that, like the contented soul, one should never care to wander away from home.

The chase after French must come from the want of thought as to the greatness of our own speech, and hence must be one of the popular delusions of the age, but there lies against this worship of French a sep- arate objection. In our generation that nation is not coming to us as Greece came, laden with deep and inspiring thoughts. Greek speech was once the speech of the world's greatest minds. We recall Plato and Aristotle and Thucydides, and that type of manhood. These were the men who projected Greek into the old courses of study. But that old type of manhood is now standing in England and Germany and America, and the French verbs and nouns and adjectives are coming to us only in the name of fashion and Paris. *"Parlez-vous Francais?"* simply means, "Have you seen Paris?" Have you some of her dresses, her dramas, her wall paper, her furniture, her luxury? A language which sets us all wild for elegant clothing, and for handsomer furniture, and for new shapes of wedding cards, and which so delights us at the drama, can never come in the dignity of those old classic verbs which never men- tioned any thing except the great emotions and exploits of the soul. The Greek showed man human life in its wars and travels and rhetoric and logic and liberty and æsthetic yearnings, but the French of our boarding-schools does little for the average student, except enable him or her to read the bill of fare at a fashionable hotel, and to call by the charming name of *buffet* what once was a sideboard, and to buy and enjoy as an *escritoire* what had once been known as a writing-desk, and to feel wise over that progress which removes from a lady her work-table, and places before her a *chiffoniere.* So far as the study of this modern dialect inflames the young heart in the direction of bills of fare and novelties for the parlor or dining-room, it can hardly compare favorably with the study of those classic forms which ignored the hotel-keeper and the cook, and introduced the student to Homer and Cicero.

The world's facts and experiences being gathered up in language, there must needs be men skilled in different languages, that the goods of one land may be transported to another country. Thus Champollion became a transfer boat to ship Egyptian history and learning from hieroglyph to French. Others came to forward the goods from French to English. Immense is this carrying trade—Carlyle carried Gœthe across the channel; Longfellow has brought Dante across the sea. But not all the educated need embark in this form of importation, for what we all need is not the key to the hieroglyphics on the old rocks, but the English of the things thus recorded. The Sermon on the Mount is jour-neying around the world in two hundred tongues, but it is not an acquaintance with these forms the young or old soul needs, but the Sermon on the Mount in the native tongue of Him who must live and die among its sublime lessons. Diamonds may be re-set, and having passed a gen-eration upon a queen's hand, they may be seen on the neck of her daughter, and at last be transferred to a coronet; but the essential value is in the glittering stones themselves, be they on forehead or finger. It is not otherwise with the truths which man has evolved from his obser-vation and experience. They are all one, whether they are whispered to his ear by English, or Greek, or Arabian lips, and blessed is he to whom some one of these great voices has come with its infinite utterances about time and the world called timeless. When, therefore, a distin-guished clergyman declared that when a minister of the Gospel was not keeping well up in Greek, he was losing the use of the right arm, he simply blundered along, for the right arm of an orator or statesman or thinker or preacher can never be in any manner the power to read a foreign text, but it must always be the power to examine or establish a theme which does not depend in the least upon the vowels and con-sonants of a time or place. Not a single great idea in the Bible is await-ing any new light from the linguist. The Greek and Hebrew lexicons can do nothing toward answering a single one of the problems of man-kind; can shed no light upon the existence of a God, or a life beyond, or upon the path of duty, and hence a long dwelling over those old forms can not be the right arm of a clergyman. His inspiration must come from ideas mighty as the human race, and not from any wonder-ment what some particle may have implied when Moses was a lad, or when John was baptizing in the wilderness.

Even when a whole life is given to one's native English or native French, so inadequate still is that language to express the soul, that it seems a form of wickedness to divide the heart between many masters, and to have n_ supreme friend. Chateaubriand, the greatest master of the French tongue, when he stood near the Niagara Falls almost a hundred years ago, and saw evening coming down from the sky upon all the sublime scene; saw the woods growing gloomy in the deep shadows, and heard the sound of the waters increasing its solemnity as the little voices died away in the night's repose, said: "It is not within the power of human words to express this grandeur of nature." Skilled as he was in a most rich and sensitive form of speech, that speech, all of whose resources he knew so well, now failed him, and his spirit had to remain imprisoned, there being no gateway by which its sentiments could escape to the heart of his countrymen. What are you and I to do, then, if we have not loved early, and late, and deeply, our own English —that English which is now the leader in literature and all learning; if we have not mastered its words, its elegancies, its power of logic, and humor, and pathos, and rhythm, and have not permitted our minds to become rich in its associations; if we have for years gone along with a heart divided in its love, or with a mind that has studied words more than has thought and prayed, and laughed, and wept, amid the sublime scenes of nature, or the more impressive mysteries of mankind? *"Parlez vous Francais?"* Not well; not at all; would to Heaven we could even learn to speak English!

SPURGEON.

THE ELOQUENT, THE EARNEST AND THE BELOVED.

The Rev. Charles Haddon Spurgeon is the Beecher of **England.**
He has always taught a religion of love and happiness. He has
won the people to him by love, and won them to Christianity, by
Christ's love. Beecher and Cuyler and Dr. Hall, after hearing the
famous Baptist in his Tabernacle, always come back to America
enraptured with the great preacher. Spurgeon's Tabernacle is analo-
gous to Plymouth Church when Beecher was at his zenith.

C. H. Spurgeon is the son of a Congregational minister. He
was born at Kelvedon, Essex, in 1834. He became a Baptist com-
municant while he was yet a very young man, and assumed the pastorate of a Baptist church at Waterbeach. He had already made
local fame as a "boy preacher." From Waterbeach he went to New
Park Chapel, Southwark, London, and here he rose to immediate
popularity. This was in 1853. From the New Park Chapel he
moved twice to larger halls, but they in turn proving inadequate, the
Metropolitan Tabernacle was projected by him, and was opened in
1861. The Tabernacle was dedicated free from debt. It is a monster building, seating between 6,000 and 7,000 people, and is located
in Newington Butts. This building, with some modifications, is
the present house of worship. The Tabernacle has been filled on
nearly every occasion when Mr. Spurgeon occupied the pulpit. On
several occasions, when he has preached in a larger hall, the congregation has been still greater. At the Crystal Palace and Agricultural
Hall, Islington, 20,000 people came to hear him. Notwithstanding his extraordinary power of drawing and holding hearers,
Mr. Spurgeon is not an orator in the usual sense of the term.
Neither has he a commanding figure, nor an impassioned or florid
delivery. People go and listen to him and are pleased without

knowing why. They go again and have the same experience and
then try again and again with like results. The speaker is earnest, and ready, and is fascinating because of the ever present
touch of human kindness in his tone and manner. His voice is clear
and sweet, and that is the extent of his qualifications for pleasing
platform effects.

Mr. Spurgeon's teachings have been strictly orthodox, perhaps
nearer to Calvin's than to that of any teacher of later times.
A couple of years ago it was announced that Spurgeon had
renounced the doctrines of the Baptists, but while his action led to a
permanent separation from the Baptist Union of Great Britain and
Ireland, the Tabernacle society and its pastor have remained Baptists in all the essentials of doctrine and practice. Mr. Spurgeon
withdrew from the Union because he believed it too liberal and following the lead of the Broad Churchists in the cardinal doctrines of
atonement, justification by faith, incarnation, total depravity and
eternal punishment. After several conferences the difference was
narrowed down to the single point of eternal punishment, and the
union declined to make belief in that a test of fellowship.

On the question of communion, Mr. Spurgeon occupies middle
ground between open and close. Those in his congregation who
are Christians, but have never been baptized by immersion, may
receive communion twice, but on presenting themselves a third
time, if they belong in the neighborhood, they are requested to
become members by the usual methods or retire from the communion service.

Spurgeon's salary has been his only source of personal income.
He has never spoken as preacher or lecturer for pay outside of his
pulpit. In his pastoral and general church labors he has been aided
by his wife, whom he married when a young man.

When I asked Mr. Moody what he thought of Spurgeon, he said:
"He is a perpetual stream of Christian sunlight. One Sunday
morning in London," continued Mr. Moody, "Spurgeon said to me,
just before he commenced his sermon: 'Moody, I want you to
notice that family there in one of the front seats, and when we go
home I want to tell you their story.'

"When we got home," said Moody, "I asked him for the story,
and he said:

"'All that family were won by a smile.'

"'Why,' said I, 'how's that?'

MR. SPURGEON, WOULD YOU ALLOW ME TO SPEAK TO YOU?

See page 493.

" ' Well,' said he, ' as I was walking down a street one day, I saw a child at a window ; it smiled, and I smiled, and we bowed. It was the same the second time ; I bowed, she bowed. It was not long before there was another child, and I had got in a habit of looking and bowing, and pretty soon the group grew, and at last, as I went by, a lady was with them. I didn't know what to do. I didn't want to bow to her, but I knew the children expected it, and so I bowed to them all. And the mother saw I was a minister, because I carried a Bible every Sunday morning. So the children followed me the next Sunday and found I was a minister. And they thought I was the greatest preacher, and their parents must hear me. A minister who is kind to a child and gives him a pat on the head, why, the children will think he is the greatest preacher in the world. Kindness goes a great way. And, finally, the father and mother and five children were converted, and they are going to join our church next Sunday.'

"Won to Christ by a smile!" said Moody. "We must get the wrinkles out of our brows, and we must have smiling faces, if we want to succeed in our work of love."

Speaking of love one day, Mr. Spurgeon said :

"In the French Revolution, a young man was condemned to the guillotine, and shut up in one of the prisons. He was greatly loved by many, but there was one who loved him more than all put together. How know we this? It was his best earthly friend, his own father, and the love he bore the son was proven in this way : When the lists were called, the father, whose name was exactly the same as the son's, answered to the name, and the father rode in the gloomy tumbril out to the place of execution, and his head rolled beneath the axe instead of his son's, a victim to mighty love. See here an image of the love of Christ for sinners. 'Greater love hath no man than this; that he laid down his life for his friends.' But Jesus died for the ungodly ! He is the friend of sinners. There is no friendship like Christ's."

One day a poor little orphan boy in London came up to Mr. Spurgeon and said: "Mr. Spurgeon, would you allow me to speak to you?"

"Certainly," he said, "get upon my knee."

The little fellow got up and said: "Mr. Spurgeon, supposing that your mother was dead, and that your father was dead, and that you were put into this institution, and that there were other little boys that had no father or mother, but that they had cousins and uncles and aunts, and that they brought them fruit and candy and a lot of things. Don't you think that you would feel bad? 'Cause that's me?"

The tears came to his eyes and he put his arms around him and kissed him and gave him a handful of money. The little fellow had pleaded his cause well. "When men come to God and tell their story," says Mr. Spurgeon, "I don't care how vile you are, I don't care how far down you have got, I don't care how far off you have wandered—if you will tell it all into His ear, the relief will soon come."

When asked which was the best sermon he ever preached, the eloquent divine said: "My best sermon was the one which had the most love and the most Christ in it. One day," continued Spurgeon, "a young man preached a showy sermon before the great Jonathan Edwards, and when he had finished he asked Mr. Edwards what he thought of it.

"'It was a very poor sermon indeed,' said Edwards.

"'A poor sermon!' said the young man, 'It took me a long time to study it.'

"'Ay, no doubt of it.'

"'Why, then, do you say it was poor? Did you not think my explanation of the text to be accurate?'

"'Oh, yes,' said the old preacher, 'very correct indeed.'

"'Well, then, why do you say it is a poor sermon? Didn't you think the metaphors were appropriate, and the arguments conclusive?'

"'Yes, they were very good, as far as that goes, but still it was a very poor sermon.'

"'Will you tell me why you think it a poor sermon?'

"'Because,' said the old minister, 'there was no Christ in it.'

"'Well,' said the young man, 'Christ was not in the text; we are not to be preaching Christ always, we must preach what is in the text.'

"'Then don't take a text without Christ in it. But you will find Christ in every text if you examine it. Don't you know, young man, that from every town, and every village, and every little hamlet in England, wherever it may be, there is a road to London?'

"'Yes,' said the young man.

" ' Ah! ' said the old divine, ' and so from every text in Scripture there is a road to the metropolis of the Scriptures, that is Christ. And, my dear brother, your business is, when you get to a text, to say, " Now, what is the road to Christ? " and then preach a sermon, running along the road towards the great metropolis—Christ.

" ' No,' the old clergyman continued, ' I have never yet found a text that had not a plain and direct road to Christ in it; and if ever I should find one that has no such road, I will make a road. I would go over hedge and ditch but I would get at my Master, for a sermon is neither fit for the lord nor yet for the peasant unless there is a savor of Christ in it.' "

" You must continue to call upon Christ," said Spurgeon, " as the Turkish lady who fell in love with Thomas à Becket's father called upon him. Becket's father, Gilbert, went to the Crusades, and was taken prisoner by the Saracens. While a prisoner this Turkish lady loved him, and when he was set free and returned to England, she took an opportunity of escaping from her father's house — took ship, and came to England. But she knew not where to find him she loved. And all that she knew about him was that his name was Gilbert. She determined to go through all the streets of England, crying out the name of Gilbert, till she had found him. She came to London first, and passing every street, persons were surprised to see an Eastern maiden, attired in an Eastern costume, crying, ' Gilbert! Gilbert! Gilbert! ' And so she passed from town to town, till one day, as she pronounced the name, the ear for which it was intended finally caught the sound, and they became happy and blessed.

" And so the sinner to-day knows little, perhaps, of religion, but he knows the name of Jesus.

" Take up the cry, sinner, and to-day, as thou goest along the streets, say in thine heart, ' Jesus! Jesus! Jesus! ' and when thou art in thy chamber, say it still, ' Jesus! Jesus! Jesus! ' Continue the cry, and it shall reach the ear for which it is meant."

A sorrowful Christian, half converted, was talking with Spurgeon about Christians enjoying themselves. " I don't think they should try to enjoy themselves in this world," he said, " I think there must be something in the Roman Catholic religion, from the extremely starved and pinched appearance of a certain ecclesiastic.

Look," said he, "how the man is worn to a skeleton by his daily fastings and nightly vigils! How he must mortify his flesh!

"There is no call for the Christian to mortify the flesh," said Spurgeon. "Let savages do that, not Christians. The probabilities are that your emaciated priest is laboring under some internal disease, which he would be heartily glad to be rid of, and it is not conquest of appetite, but failure in digestion, which so reduces him; or, possibly, a troubled conscience, which makes him fret himself down to the light weights. Certainly I have never met with a text which mentions prominence of bone as an evidence of grace. If so, 'the living skeleton' should have been exhibited, not merely as a natural curiosity, but as the standard of virtue. Some of the biggest rogues in the world have been as mortified in appearance as if they had lived on locusts and wild honey. It is a very vulgar error to suppose that a melancholy countenance is the index of a Christian heart. Do not cut yourself with stones, and weep, but look up to Christ, with a smile of joy and hope in your eye!"

REV. JOSEPH PARKER

THE GREAT ENGLISH PREACHER.

The Rev. Joseph Parker and the Rev. Mr. Spurgeon are the great preachers of England. They are the Talmage and Beecher of Great Britain.

During his American tour, some one asked Mr. Parker what he thought of Bible theology.

"We must have some system of theology," said Mr. Parker. "If every man was left to get up his own system of astronomy, geology, medicine and architecture, things would go on but slowly. The Bible is, at all events, something to begin with."

Speaking of the fighting doctors, one day Mr. Parker said: "One doctor says bolus, and another says globule. Globule calls Bolus a butcher, and Bolus calls Globule a quack, and the hydropathist says, 'Beware of pick-pockets.' And Bolus will not speak to Globule, though Globule says, 'Let us make it up and begin again;' and Bolus says, 'Never, as long as I live. I will leech and blister and cup and bleed and do things with scientific vigor.'"

Speaking of paying ministers Mr. Parker said: "Why people think they do us a great favor by coming to hear us preach. A Scotchman asked a minister for five shillings, and in return for the favor said, 'I'll give you a day's hearing some time.'

"It is undoubtedly understood by many that in listening to a minister they are conferring a favor upon him. A person once asked me to lend him a sovereign, and in support of his request informed me that he had long attended my ministry. Possibly," continued Mr. Parker, smiling, "the man richly deserved a sovereign for having done so; at the same time it is a popular mistake to suppose that the minister is the party receiving the favor. He gives his hearers his best thinking, his best power of all kinds, and it is, therefore, a pity to show him thankfulness by borrowing money of him."

One of Mr. Parker's finest bits of word painting was his description of the great W. E. Gladstone, who was his personal friend:

"If you ask me to describe, personally, the Rt. Hon. W. E. Gladstone," said Mr. Parker, "I could not do so beyond describing the two or three dominant lines in his face. Every time I looked at him he took on a new aspect. Every thing depended on the intellectual action of the moment. I could not begin to tell you of the grandeur of that rough, strong face when the spirit of the man is aroused.

"When he is amused his face lights up, and even that Cæsar-like nose is almost agreeable as a patch of sunshine on a great crag. Is he stern? Then let his antagonist seek some other man. Is he listening? He is an eagle on a mountain crag as if intent on seeking his prey. Then that voice; was there ever one like it? Not boisterous, not loud, but round, rolling and rich; monotonous indeed, but so dignified that the monotony is forgotten in the intellectual action that the voice reveals. It rises gradually and you are not aware that the thunder is going to roar until you find yourself in the center of the storm."

After speaking of Gladstone's versatility of knowledge, Dr. Parker continued: "Now let me speak of Gladstone's progressiveness. Strange as it may appear, Gladstone began life as a Tory. You should hear him pronounce the word Tory now. You think it consists of two syllables, but when he says it, it seems to be a polysyllable.

" He is ending his career as a leader of philosophical liberalism. When the struggle for home rule in Ireland was first begun, when a small party in Parliament made it the question of the day to the exclusion of all other business, then, in Gladstone's judgment, it was the demand of a faction and not of a people. But when the general election in Ireland sent 80 out of 103 Home Rule members to Parliament, then Gladstone recognized the claim, in a substantial sense, of a nation. Then he acted with the belief that Parliament exists for the people and not the people for Parliament.

" He aims to convince the country. The bill which I believe will form the text of any bill that will be introduced in Parliament in favor of home rule must be modeled on Gladstone's bill. It has gone so far that the nation can not recede from that position. We must allow something for words spoken in panic such as followed his bill. Men now, day by day, are drawing nearer to his position. Day by day, men are studying Irish history and character and historical precedents, and the end is not far off. When Chamberlain and others left him and he stood alone, it was without a sign of withdrawing or budging from his position. His belief is that righteousness will prevail in the long run.

" The Liberal Unionists are a curious kind of inexpressible middle quantity. Are they repenting? I will answer by an anecdote. An American lady, in retrenching expenses in the household, conceived the notion of beginning the operation by making that part of her little boy's garments which is known in some parts of America by the euphonious and pleasant name of pants. She made them alike before and behind, and some relative of the lady asked how she succeeded. The lady said: 'Very nicely; but they are so made that at a short distance off I can't tell whether Johnnie is coming home or going away.' Some relative of the lady must have made the political pants of the Liberal Unionists.

"If the leaders withdraw, then the people will lead the way. That is an American idea. No aristocracy can really understand the people. I don't blame the aristocrats; they were born so. They are reared to believe that the land is theirs, whereas it is given to all mankind. Gladstone lives among the people, and he stands for the people, and is hailed everywhere in England as 'The People's Willie.' He can not fawn on royalty.

"It has been asked whether any tenderness was in the Spartan granite of Gladstone's character. If tears of imbecility, shed over the drivel of hypocrisy, is what is meant by tenderness, then Gladstone is not tender. But I have seen him after dinner, while going back to the days of the union of England with Ireland, take down from the shelves a history and read aloud, until the sorrows and atrocities in connection with that event caused his voice to break, and finally he would have to lay down the book in tears. The question of home rule in Ireland is always with him in conversation. He is approaching 80 years of age. When last I saw him he looked as vigorous and ready for battle, his port as erect, his eye as bright, his voice as resonant as ever."

The Rev. Joseph Parker was called by Plymouth Church to succeed Mr. Beecher, and would have filled the place, if he had been left untrammeled. As it is, Dr. Lyman Abbott preaches in Beecher's pulpit, but no human being will ever fill Beecher's place. God made one Beecher and destroyed the die.

A HUNDRED ANECDOTES OF A HUNDRED MEN.

REMINISCENCES, JOKES, ANECDOTES AND ELOQUENCE.

(BY ELI PERKINS.)

STORIES ABOUT MR. WANNAMAKER.

Postmaster John Wannamaker has been for years superintendent of probably one of the largest Sunday-schools in the world. Mr. Wannamaker has a theory that he will never put a boy out of his school for bad conduct. He argues if a boy misbehaves himself, it must be through bad training at home, and that if we put him out of the school, no one will take care of him.

Well, this theory was put to the test one day.

A teacher came to him, and said, "I've got a boy in my class, that must be taken out; he breaks the rules continually, he swears and uses obscene language, and I can not do any thing with him."

Mr. Wannamaker did not care about putting the boy out, so he sent the teacher back to his class. But he came again, and said, that unless the boy was taken from his class, he must leave it. Well, he left, and a second teacher was appointed. The second teacher came with the same story, and met with the same reply from Mr. Wannamaker. And he resigned. A third teacher was appointed, and he came with the same story as the others. Mr. Wannamaker then thought he would be compelled to turn the boy out at last.

One day, when a few teachers were present, and Mr. Wannamaker said: "I will bring this boy up, and read his name out in the school, and publicly excommunicate him."

Then a sweet young lady came up, and said to him: "I am not doing what I might for Christ; let me have the boy; I will try and save him." But Mr. Wannamaker said: "If these young men can not do it, you will not." But she begged to have him, and Mr. Wannamaker consented.

"She was a wealthy young lady," said Mr. Wannamaker, "surrounded with all the luxuries of life. The boy went to her class, and for several Sundays he behaved himself, and broke no rule. But one Sunday he broke one, and, in reply to something she said, spit in her face. She took out her pocket-handkerchief, and wiped her face, but she said nothing. Well, she thought upon a plan, and she said to him: 'Johnnie, please come home with me.'

"'No,' says John, 'I won't; I won't be seen on the streets with you.'

"She was fearful of losing him altogether if he went out of the school that day, and she said to him: 'Will you let me walk home with you?'

"'No, I won't,' said he; 'I won't be seen on the street with you.'

"Then the young lady thought of another plan. She thought on the 'Old Curiosity Shop,' and she said:

"'I won't be at home to-morrow, Johnnie, but if you will come round to the front door on Wednesday morning, there will be a little bundle for you.'

"'I don't want it,' said John, savagely, "you may keep your old bundle.'

"The young lady went home, but made the bundle up. She thought that curiosity might make him come.

"Wednesday morning arrived, and he had got over his mad fit, and thought he would just like to see what was in that bundle. The little fellow knocked at the door, which was opened, and he told his story.

"She said: 'Yes, here is the bundle, Johnnie.'

"The boy opened it, and found a vest and a coat, and other clothing, and a little note, written by the young lady, which read something like this:

"DEAR JOHNNIE:—Ever since you have been in my class I have prayed for you every morning and evening, that you might be a good boy, and I want you to stop in my class. Do not leave me.

"The next morning, before she was up, the servant came to her and said there was a little boy below, who wished to see her. She dressed hastily, and went down-stairs, and found Johnnie on the sofa, weeping. She put her arms around his neck, and he said to her:

" ' My dear teacher, I have not had any happiness since I got this note from you. I want you to forgive me.'

" 'Won't you let me pray for you to come to Jesus?' said the teacher; and she went down on her knees and prayed. And now," says Mr. Wannamaker, "that boy is the best boy in his Sunday-school. And so it was love that won that boy's heart."

The best story this year was told at Saratoga, at the memorable meeting of Mr. Wannamaker and Jay Gould, who were introduced by myself.

"The details of the office of the Postmaster-general," said Mr. Wannamaker, "are often very disagreeable. Changing officers who have families is often painful. So I let Mr. Clarkson attend to this, telling him to do every thing business-like and conscientiously."

"Your turning this work over to Clarkson," said Eli, smiling, "is like the case of a young woman, years ago, in our church. She was a good young lady, but would always wear very showy toilets, attracting the attention of the whole church. One day some good sisters expostulated with her about her worldly ways.

" ' The love of these bright bonnets,' they said, ' will draw your soul down to perdition.'

"Still the somewhat worldly sister continued to wear a bright bonnet. But finally, one night," said Eli, "came repentance. The young lady came to prayer meeting in a plain hat. She arose and said:

" 'I feel, brothers and sisters, that I have done wrong. I know that my love for bright bonnets was ruining my future life. I knew it was endangering my soul, and that it would draw me down to perdition. But I will never wear that hat again. Never! It shall not destroy my soul. I'm through with it. I've given it to my sister.' "

LOWELL'S GREATEST POEM.

When a deed is done for Freedom, through the broad earth's aching breast
Runs a thrill of joy prophetic, trembling on from east to west;
And the slave, where'er he cowers, feels the soul within him climb
To the awful verge of manhood, as the energy sublime
Of a century bursts full-blossomed on the thorny stem of Time.

Through the walls of hut and palace shoots the instantaneous throe,
When the travail of the Ages wrings earth's systems to and fro;
At the birth of each new Era, with a recognizing start,
Nation wildly looks on nation, standing with mute lips apart,
And glad Truth's yet mightier man-child leaps beneath the Future's heart.

For mankind are one in spirit, and an instinct bears along,
Round the earth's electric circle, the swift flash of right or wrong;
Whether conscious or unconscious, yet Humanity's vast frame,
Through its ocean-sundered fibers, feels the gush of joy or shame;
In the gain or loss of one race, all the rest have equal claim.

Once, to every man and nation, comes the moment to decide,
In the strife of Truth with Falsehood, for the good or evil side;
Some great cause, God's new Messiah, offering each the bloom or blight,
Parts the goats upon the left hand, and the sheep upon the right,
And the choice goes by forever 'twixt that darkness and that light.

Hast thou chosen, O my people, on whose party thou shalt stand,
Ere the Doom from its worn sandals shakes the dust against our land?
Though the cause of Evil prosper, yet 'tis Truth alone is strong;
And albeit she wander outcast now, I see around her throng
Troops of beautiful, tall angels, to enshield her from all wrong.

We see dimly, in the Present, what is small and what is great;
Slow of faith how weak an arm may turn the iron helm of Fate;
But the soul is still oracular—amid the market's din,
List the ominous stern whisper from the Delphic cave within!
"They enslave their children's children, who make compromise with Sin!"

Slavery, the earth-born Cyclops, fellest of the giant brood,
Sons of brutish Force and Darkness, who have drenched the earth with blood,
Famished in his self-made desert, blinded by our purer day,
Gropes in yet unblasted regions for his miserable prey;
Shall we guide his gory fingers where our helpless children play?

'Tis as easy to be heroes as to sit the idle slaves
Of a legendary virtue carved upon our Father's graves;
Worshipers of light ancestral make the present light a crime.
Was the Mayflower launched by cowards? steered by men behind their time?
Turn those tracks toward Past, or Future, that make Plymouth Rock sublime?

They were men of present valor—stalwart old inconoclasts;
Unconvinced by ax or gibbet that all virtue was the Past's,
But we make their truth our falsehood, thinking that has made us free,
Hoarding it in moldy parchments, while our tender spirits flee
The rude grasp of that great impulse which drove them across the sea.

New occasions teach new duties! Time makes ancient good uncouth;
They must upward still, and onward, who would keep abreast of Truth;
Lo, before us gleam her camp-fires! we ourselves must Pilgrims be,
Launch our Mayflower and steer boldly through the desperate winter sea,
Nor attempt the Future's portal with the Past's blood-rusted key.

THURLOW WEED ON INGERSOLL.

Thurlow Weed, at the age of eighty-two, delivered this little speech before the Nineteenth Century Club:

Mr. President:—In speaking of Colonel Robert G. Ingersoll's agnosticism, I will say, in all kindness, that the Colonel is a gentleman of education, with a well-stored mind and attractive personal manners, who speaks fluently and eloquently. Colonel Ingersoll is not a believer in a religion which has been making the world wiser, better and happier for almost nineteen centuries. Without questioning Colonel Ingersoll's sincerity or impugning his motives, I am persuaded that if half the time and labor expended in fortifying himself with arguments against religion had been devoted to an intelligent and impartial consideration of the evidences establishing its truths, the country would have had a gifted follower of Him whose mission, labors and character, viewed merely from a worldly standpoint, inspire admiration, affection and gratitude.

No act of the Savior's life and no word He ever uttered has been, or can be, construed or tortured into hostility to the welfare and happiness of every member of the human family. Human laws are founded upon the divine law. All that concerns our happiness here and our hopes of happiness hereafter is derived from the Scriptures.

On the other hand, what has infidelity done for us? Who profits by its teachings? After depriving its followers of their belief in a future, how does it compensate them? What does it offer in exchange for a life of immortality? If, for example, Colonel Ingersoll should be summoned to the bedside of a dying friend or relative, what words of comfort or of hope could he offer? Of what service could he be to that stricken friend? Would he aggravate the sufferings of one whose last hours needed soothing by telling him there was nothing but the cold, dark grave awaiting him? This cruel theory is repelled, not only by revelation, but by the laws of nature. Nature is instinct with evidences and confirmations of the truths of revelation. The vegetable and floral world only die to live again. The products of the earth live and die annually. The buried acorn reproduces the living oak. And yet infidelity insists that man, the image of his Creator, wonderfully endowed and gifted, under whose auspices the world has been enlightened, elevated and adorned, is, after a brief existence, to be as though he had never been.

Contrast the labors of Voltaire and Paine with those of John Wesley. Can it be said with truth that the two former made any one better or happier? Hundreds of thousands of the followers of John Wesley have lived and died, and other hundreds of thousands survive, rejoicing in their conversion from a sinful to a Christian life. The memory of Wesley is everywhere cherished by the good and the pure, while Voltaire and Paine are only remembered for the evil, rather than for the good, they did.

If it be urged that the promises of the Savior have not all been realized, that sin still abounds, and that the world is as bad as ever, it may be answered that religion is working out its mission : that its benign influences are constantly extending, and that light is irradiating the darkest recesses of heathenism and idolatry. It requires no argument to demonstrate the fact that our race is improved by civilization, or that civilization owes its origin and progress to religion. To religious influences we are indebted for all the reforms which benefit society. Our Sunday-schools were instituted in obedience to a divine command. In these schools children are taught, " without money and without price," all that concerns their present welfare and their future happiness. These intellectual nurseries have enriched and fertilized, and continue to enrich and fertilize, every city, village, hamlet and household throughout the Christian world. If religion had done nothing more than to bless our race with the consecrating influences of Sunday-schools, scoffers should be shamed into silence.

Infidels of all ages found their strongest arguments against revealed religion upon what they regard as improbable. And yet we are not called on to believe anything more incomprehensible than our own existence. We might, with about the same degree of reason, deny this fact, as to refuse to believe in a future existence. We know that we live in this world. Is it unreasonable to believe that we may live in another world? If we are to believe nothing but what we understand, we should go through life incredulous and aimless. We are ready enough to believe on information the things that relate to this world. But we are slow to believe in prophecy and revelation, though both are corroborated by observation, experience and events. Infidelity, claiming superiority in " reason " and common sense, asks us to believe that all of grandeur and sublimity, all of vastness and power in the beautiful heavens and upon the bountiful earth, comes by chance; that every thing is self-created and self-existing, and that law, order and harmony are accidents. Those who accept this theory would find its application to their business affairs anything but advantageous. Infidelity and communism are kindred in character, and aim, by different methods, to undermine the sanctions and securities upon which the world's welfare and happiness rest. Infidelity strikes at religion, communism at property. One seeks to weaken our faith, and the other demands for the idle and worthless an equal share in the savings of the industrious and frugal. Agrarianism (communism of a milder type) came to us some forty years ago from England, with Fanny Wright and Robert Dale Owen as its apostles. This bad element has been reinforced by communism from France and Germany. All three are working out their destructive mission in a city where, unhappily, they find co-operation and sympathy. To these birds of ill omen comes infidelity, equally aggressive, with Robert G. Ingersoll as its teacher. If it be said that, unlike the communistic leaders, Mr. Ingersoll is a "gentleman and a scholar," the danger is thereby intensified.

The strongest argument urged against Christianity, from the days of Voltaire and Paine, is that bad men made a profession of it; that hypocrites are found in all our churches. This is true. But is it not equally true that every thing intrinsically valuable gets debased? Frauds are practiced in business. The richest fabrics have their imitations. Gold and silver coins are debased or counterfeited. The evils, however, resulting from impositions of this nature are not serious. The intelligence of our people and the penalties to which offenders are subjected afford adequate protection, and for one hypocrite who makes a false profession there are at least nine conscientious, devoted Christians.

Another argument against religion is that our Savior was an impostor, and as a corollary that His teachings exert a baneful influence. And yet both of the accusations are disproved by the experience of 2,000 years. If Jesus of Nazareth had been an impostor, His name and every thing connected with it would hardly have survived a second generation. There would then have been no occasion for the labors of Voltaire, Paine or Ingersoll. Other and numerous false teachers have appeared and disappeared. But time and truth have been attesting the divinity of our Savior. His apostles and their successors, obeying His instructions, have carried and are carrying the glad tidings to the uttermost ends of the earth. As far and as fast as this gospel travels, the world is civilized and its inhabitants benefited.

Civilization and its beneficent institutions abound by the religion which our Savior instructed His apostles to preach to the heathen. Geographical lines are not more distinctly established than those which mark the progress of missionaries; and while religious light brightens the Christian world, its rays dawn upon the darkest portions of the earth. What have the doctrines of Confucius, Mohammed and other false teachers done for their followers but to hold them for centuries in ignorance and barbarism? [Applause.]

DON PIATT'S FUNNY SPEECH.

Don Piatt, the great satirest and humorist was called upon for a speech before the Hatchet Club, on the 22d of February, Washington's birthday. He arose and said.

Ladies and Gentlemen:—Mark Twain and Petroleum V. Nasby, dined with Eli Perkins at the latter's residence in New York, on Washington's birthday, last year. The conversation at that dinner I shall never forget. The stories told and the truthful reminiscences brought out at that dinner would fill a small book.

After the last course, and after the ladies had withdrawn, the conversation turned upon horses. Finally Mr. Twain laid down his cigar and asked Perkins and Nasby if they had ever heard of a fast horse he (Mark) used to own in Nevada.

" I think not," said Nasby.

" Well, gentlemen," continued Mr. Twain, as he blew a smoke ring and watched it, " that was a fast horse. He was a very fast horse. But he was so tough-bitted that I couldn't guide him with a bit at all."

" How did you guide him?" asked Eli.

" Well, gentlemen, I had to guide him with electricity. I had to have wire lines and had to keep a battery in the wagon all the time in order to stop him."

" Why didn't you stop him by hollering who-a?" asked Eli.

"Stop him by hollering who–a!" exclaimed Mr. Twain. "Why I could not holler loud enough to make that horse hear me. He traveled so fast that no sound ever reached him from behind. [Laughter.] He went faster than the sound, sir. Holler who–a and he'd be in the next town before the sound of your voice could reach the dash board. [Laughter.] 'Travel fast?' I should say he could. Why I once started from Virginia City for Meadow Creek right in front of one of the most dreadful rain-storms we ever had on the Pacific coast. Wind and rain? Why the wind blew eighty miles an hour and the rain fell in sheets. I drove right before that storm for three hours—just on the edge of that hurricane and rain for forty miles."

"Didn't you get drenched?" asked Perkins.

"Drenched? No, sir. Why, I tell you, I drove right in front of that rainstorm. I could lean forward and let the sun shine on me, or lean backward and feel rain and catch hailstones. When the hurricane slacked up the horse slacked up, too, and when it blew faster I just said 'g—lk!' to the horse and touched the battery, and away we went. Now I don't like to lie about my horse, Mr. Perkins, and I don't ask you to believe what I say, but I tell you truthfully that when I got to Meadow Creek my linen duster was as dry as powder. Not a drop of rain on the wagon seat either, while the wagon box was level full of hailstones and water, or I'm a ——, a ——" [Great laughter.]

"Look here gentlemen," interrupted Mr. Nasby, "speaking of the truth, did you ever hear about my striking that man in Toledo?"

Mark said he had never heard about it.

"Well, sir, it was this way: There was a man there—one of those worldly, skeptical fellows, who questioned my veracity one day. He said he had doubts about the truthfulness of one of my cross-roads inci-dents. He didn't say it publicly, but privately. I'm sorry, for the sake of his wife and family, now, that he said it at all—and sorry for the man, too, because he wasn't prepared to go. If he'd been a Christian it would have been different. I say I didn't want to strike this man, because it's a bad habit to get into—this making a human chaos out of a fellow man. But he questioned my veracity and the earthquake came. I struck him once—just once. I remember he was putting down a carpet at the time and had his mouth full of carpet-tacks. But a man can't stop to discount carpet-tacks in a man's mouth, when he questions your veracity, can he? I never do. I simply struck the blow."

"Did it hurt the man much?" asked Eli.

"I don't think it did. It was too sudden. The bystanders said if I **was** going to strike a second blow they wanted to move out of the

State. Now, I don't want you to believe me and I don't expect you will, but to tell you the honest truth, Mr. Perkins, I squashed that man right down into a door-mat, and his own wife, who was tacking down one edge of the carpet at the time, came right along and took him for a gutta-percha rug, and actually tacked him down in front of the door. Poor woman; she never knew she was tacking down her own husband! What became of the tacks in his mouth? you ask. Well, the next day the boys pulled them out of the bottoms of his overshoes, and——"
[Loud laughter drowned the speaker's voice.]

"Gentlemen!" interrupted Eli, "it does me good to hear such truths. I believe every word you say, and I feel that I ought to exchange truths with you. Now, did you ever hear how I went to prayer-meeting at New London, Conn., in a rain storm?"

They said they had not.

"Well, gentlemen," said Eli, "one day I started for the New London prayer-meeting on horseback. When I got about half-way there, there came up a fearful storm. The wind blew a hurricane, the rain fell in torrents, the lightning gleamed through the sky, and I went and crouched down behind a large barn. But pretty soon the lightning struck the barn, knocked it into a thousand splinters, and sent my horse whirling over into a neighboring corn patch."

"Did it kill you, Mr. Perkins?" asked Mr. Twain, the tears rolling down his cheeks.

"No, it didn't kill me," I said, "but I was a good deal discouraged."

"Well, what did you do, Mr. Perkins."

"What did I do? Well, gentlemen, to tell the honest Connecticut truth, I went right out into the pasture, took off my coat, humped up my bare back, and took eleven clips of lightning right on my bare backbone, drew the electricity all out of the sky, and then got on to my horse and rode into New London in time to lead at the evening prayer-meeting.

"Arise and sing!" [Loud laughter.]

JOSEPH COOK.

When Joseph Cook was asked if any thing came by chance, he said:

"No, no, no; God and his law are behind everything."

"How will you prove it?"

"By this illustration," said Mr. Cook: "The Scotch philosopher, Beattie, once went into his garden and drew in the soft earth the letters C. W. B. He sowed these furrows with garden cresses, smoothed the earth and went away. These were the initials of his little boy, who had never been taught any thing concerning God, although he had learned to read. 'Ten days later,' says Beattie, 'the child came running to me in amazement, and said: "My name has grown in the garden."

"'Well, what if it has?' said the philosopher: 'that is nothing,' and turned away.

"But the child took his father by the hand, led him to the garden plat, and said: 'What made those letters?'

"'I see very well,' the father replied, 'that the initials of your name have grown up here in the garden. That is an accident,' and he turned away again.

"The child followed him, took him by the hand, brought him back to the spot, and said, very earnestly: 'Some one must have planted the seeds to make the letters.'

"'Then you believe those letters can not have been produced by chance,' said the father.

"'I believe somebody planted them,' said the son, who probably did not know what chance meant.

"'Very well,' said the father, 'look at your hands and your feet; consider your eyes and all your members. Are they not skillfully arranged? How did your hand get its shape?'

"'Somebody must have made my hands,' said the boy.

"'Who is this some one?' asked the father.

"'I do not know,' said the child.

"'Do you feel certain that somebody planted those seeds, and sure that some one made your hands?'

"'Yes,' said the boy, with great earnestness.

"And then the father communicated to the child the name of the great Being by whom all things are made, and the boy never forgot the lesson nor the circumstances which led to it."

DR. PENTECOST ON GOD'S APPROVAL.

"One winter's day," said Dr. Pentecost, "I was at a railway station at New York. There was a large crowd of persons desiring to go from New York to Boston, and we all had to pass through a narrow way by the gatekeeper. Everybody had to show his ticket, and, as usual, there were many who could not conveniently find them. They said they had them, but the gatekeeper was inexorable.

"'You must show your ticket,' he said, 'if you please.'

"There was both grumbling and swearing on the part of the passengers. After most of them had passed through, a gentleman said to the ticket-collector:

"'You don't seem to be very popular with this crowd.'

"The ticket-collector just cast his eyes upwards to the ceiling on the floor above, where the superintendent's office was, and said:

"'I don't care anything about being popular with this crowd; all I care for is to be popular with the man up there.'"

EDMUND CLARENCE STEDMAN.

BIOGRAPHY.

Edmund Clarence Stedman was born in Hartford, October 8, 1833. He is now a member of the N. Y. Stock Exchange, where he is called the banker-poet. Mr. Stedman has made himself famous as a poet, critic and journalist. His most ambitious critical work has been the publication of his "History of American Literature" in nine octavo volumes, completed during the present year.

Mr Stedman has written volumes, but we select only the sketch:

KEARNY AT SEVEN PINES.

So that soldiery legend is still on its journey—
    That story of Kearny who knew not to yield?
'Twas the day when, with Jameson, fierce Berry and Birney,
    Against twenty thousand he rallied the field.
Where the red volleys poured, where the clamor rose highest,
    Where the dead lay in clumps through the dwarf-oak and pine:
Where the aim from the thicket was surest and nighest
    No charge like Phil Kearny's along the whole line.

When the battle went ill, and the bravest were solemn,
    Near the dark Seven Pines, where we still held our ground,
He rode down the length of the withering column,
    And his heart at our war-cry leaped up with a bound;
He snuffed, like his charger, the wind of the powder,
    His sword waved us on, and we answered the sign;
Loud our cheers as we rushed, but his laugh rang the louder,—
    "There's the devil's own fun, boys, along the whole line!"

How he strode his brown steed! How we saw his blade brighten
In the one hand still left—and the reins in his teeth!
He laughed like a boy when the holidays heighten,
But a soldier's glance shot from his visor beneath.
Up came the reserves to the medley infernal,
Asking where to go in—through the clearing or pine?
" Oh, anywhere! Forward! 'Tis all the same, Colonel;
You'll find lovely fighting along the whole line! "

O, evil the black shroud of night at Chantilly,
That hid him from sight of his brave men and tried!
Foul, foul sped the bullet that clipped the white lily,
The flower of our knighthood, the whole army's pride!
Yet we dream that he still, in that shadowy region,
Where the dead form their ranks at the wan drummer's sign,
Rides on, as of old, down the length of his legion,
And the word still is—" Forward! " along the whole line.

ANECDOTES ABOUT TRAVERS, STEWART, CLEWS AND JEROME.

Mr. Wm. R. Travers was a unique character. He was not a literary man. He did not write anecdotes but he perpetrated jokes, and he perpetrated so many that he kept the literary men of New York busy for years recording them. Mr. Travers married a daughter of the Hon. Reverdy Johnson, of Baltimore, and ex-minister to England, after which he moved to New York and formed a partnership with Leonard Jerome, whose daughter married Lord Randolph Churchill. He died in Bermuda, March 19, 1887.

Travers was a stammerer. He never spoke three consecutive words without stammering. This stammer added to the effectiveness of his wit, as Charles Lamb's stammer added to his wit. His fame got to be so great as a stammerer that he was made the hero of a thousand stammering stories, which he never heard of until they were read to him from the newspapers. But his shoulders were broad enough and his heart was big enough to father them all.

One day Mr. Travers went into a bird-fancier's in Centre street.

" H–h–have you got a–a–all kinds of b–b–birds ?" he asked.

" Yes, sir, all kinds," said the bird-fancier, politely.

" I w–w–want to b–buy a p–p–parrot," hesitated Mr. T.

" Well, here is a beauty. See its golden plumage ! "

"B–b–beautiful," stammered Travers. "C–c–can he t–t–talk?"

"Talk!" exclaimed the bird-fancier. "If he can't talk better than you can I'll give him to you!"

"Mr. Travers," says Jay Gould, "once went down to a dog-fancier's in Water street to buy a rat-terrier.

"'Is she a g–g–good ratter?' asked Travers as he poked a little, shivering pup with his cane.

"'Yes, sir; splendid! I'll show you how he'll go for a rat,' said the dog-fancier—and then he put him in a box with a big rat."

"How did it turn out?" I asked Mr. Gould.

"Why, the rat made one dive and laid out the frightened terrier in a second, but Travers turned around, and sez he—'I say, Johnny, w–w–what'll ye t–t–take for the r–r–rat?'"

Henry Clews, the well-known bald-headed banker, who always prides himself on being a self-made man, during a recent talk with Mr. Travers had occasion to remark that he was the architect of his own destiny—that he was a self-made man.

"W–w–what d–did you s–ay, Mr. Clews?" asked Mr. Travers.

"I say with pride, Mr. Travers, that I am a self-made man—that I made myself—"

"Hold, H–henry," interrupted Mr. Travers, as he dropped his cigar, "w–while you were m–m–making yourself, why the devil, d–did–didn't you p–put some more hair on the top of y–your h–head?"

One day Colonel Fisk was showing Mr. Travers over the "Plymouth Rock," the famous Long Branch boat. After showing the rest of the vessel, he pointed to two large portraits of himself and Mr. Gould, hanging, a little distance apart, at the head of the stairway.

"There," says the Colonel, "what do you think of them?"

"They're good, Colonel—you hanging on one side and Gould on the other; f–i–r–s–t rate. But Colonel," continued the wicked Mr. Travers, buried in thought, "w–w–where's our Savior?"

Mr. Travers, who is a vestryman in Grace church, says he knows it was wicked, but he couldn't have helped it if he'd been on his dying bed.

"One day," says Henry Clews in his "Thirty Years in Wall Street," "after Mr. Travers had moved to New York, an old friend from Baltimore met him in Wall Street. As it had been a long time since they saw each other, they had a considerable number of topics to talk over. They had been familiar friends in the Monumental City, and were not, therefore, restrained by the usual social formalities.

"'I notice, Travers,' said the Baltimorean, 'that you stutter a great deal more than when you were in Baltimore.'

"'W-h-y, y-e-s,' replied Mr. Travers, darting a look of surprise at his friend; 'of course I do. This is a d-d-damned sight b-b-bigger city.'"

Travers saw Jay Gould one afternoon standing in front of the Stock Exchange buried in deep thought.

"'Clews,' he said, turning to the banker, 'that's a queer attitude for G-G-Gould.'

"'How so?' asked Clews.

"'Why he's got his hands in his p-p-pockets—his own p-p-pockets.'"

Travers belonged to McAlister's "400," was a good deal of an aristocrat and was always saying spiteful things about tradesmen like Astor, Lorillard and A. T. Stewart. Stewart was elected on one occasion to preside at a meeting of citizens during the war. Travers was present in the audience. When Mr. Stewart took his gold pencil case from his pocket and rapped with its head on the table for the meeting to come to order, Travers called out, in an audible tone, "C-cash!" which brought down the house, and no one laughed more heartily than Mr. Stewart, although it was a severe thrust at himself.

One of Travers' best *bon mots* was inspired by the sight of the Siamese twins. After carefully examining the mysterious ligature that had bound them together from birth, he looked up blankly at them and said, "B-b-br-brothers, I presume."

Mr. Clews says that the last time he saw Travers, the genial broker called at his office. Looking at the tape, Clews remarked:

"The market is pretty stiff to-day, Travers."

"Y-y-yes, but it is the st-st-stiffness of d-d-death."

One day, many years ago, Mr. Travers was standing on the curb of New street, opposite the Exchange, buying some stock from a gentleman whose aspect was unmistakably of the Hebrew stamp.

"Wh-wh-what is your name!" asked Travers.

"Jacobs," responded the seller.

"B–b–but wh–what is your Christian name?" reiterated Travers.

The Hebrew was nonplussed, and the crowd was convulsed with laughter.

The first time Mr. Travers attempted to find Montague street, in Brooklyn, he lost his way, although he was near the place. Meeting a man, he said:

"I desire to r–reach M–Montague st–street. W–will you b–be kik–kind enough to pup–point the way?"

"You–you are go–going the wrong w–way," was the stammering answer. "That **is** M–Montague st–street there."

"Are y–you mimick–mimicking me, making fun of me–me?" asked Mr. Travers, sharply.

"Nun–no, I assure you, sir," the other replied. "I–I am ba–badly af–flict–flicted with an imp–impediment in my speech."

"Why do–don't y–you g–get cured?" asked Travers, solemnly. "G–go to Doctor Janvrin, and y–you'll get c–cured. D–don't y–you see how well I talk? H–he cu–cured m–m–me."

An obtuse Englishman, a friend of Lord Randolph Churchill, was dining with Larry Jerome and Mr. Travers. An Englishman was always the natural prey of Jerome and Travers. They pumped him full of the most astonishing stories of Travers' career as warrior, editor, hunter, fisherman, yachtsman, statesman, guide, philosopher and friend.

"I came f–from a large f–f–family," stammered Mr. Travers. "There were t–t–ten of us b–b–boys, and each of us had a s–s–sister."

"Ah, indeed!" remarked the obtuse Englishman, "twenty of you."

"No," said Travers, scornfully, "l–l–leven."

K. Q. PHILANDER DOESTICKS.

Below is the first article Mortimer M. Thompson—"Doesticks" —wrote. It was first published in Rochester, but Chas. A. Dana, ever a great lover of wit, saw its merits, and one day, in the absence of Horace Greeley, republished it in the *Tribune*. The article was extensively copied, and made Doesticks famous. Mr. Thompson was a brother of " Fanny Fern," whose husband was James Parton. We give the article as recited by Doesticks in a lecture :

Ladies and Gentlemen :—I have been to Niagara—you know Niagara Falls—big rocks, water, foam, table rock, Indian curiosities, squaws, moccasins, stuffed snakes, rapids, wolves, Clifton House, suspension bridge, place where the water runs swift, the ladies faint, scream and get the paint washed off their faces ; where the aristocratic Indian ladies sit on the dirt and make little bags ; where all the inhabitants swindle strangers ; where the cars go in a hurry, the waiters are impudent and all the small boys swear.

When I came in sight of the suspension bridge, I was vividly impressed with the idea that it was "some" bridge ; in fact a considerable curiosity, and a " considerable " bridge. Took a glass of beer and walked up to the Falls ; another glass of beer and walked under the Falls ; wanted another glass of beer, but couldn't get it ; walked away from the Falls, wet through, mad, triumphant, victorious ; humbug ! humbug ! Sir, all humbug ! except the dampness of every thing, which is a moist certainty, and the cupidity of every body, which is a diabolical fact, and the Indians and niggers every where, which is a satanic truth.

Another glass of beer — 'twas forthcoming — immediately — also another, all of which I drank. I then proceeded to drink a glass of beer; [laughter] went over to the States, where I procured a glass of beer—went up-stairs, for which I paid a sixpence; over to Goat Island, for which I disbursed twenty-five cents; hired a guide, to whom I paid half a dollar—sneezed four times, at nine cents a sneeze—[laughter] went up on the tower for a quarter of a dollar, and looked at the Falls—didn't feel sublime any; tried to, but couldn't; took some beer, and tried again, but failed—drank a glass of beer and began to feel better—thought the waters were sent for and were on a journey to the——[pointing downward amid great laughter] thought the place below was one sea of beer —was going to jump down and get some; guide held me; sent him over to the hotel to get a glass of beer, while I tried to write some poetry— result as follows:

Oh, thou (spray in one eye) awful, (small lobster in one shoe,) sublime (both feet wet) master-piece of (what a lie) the Almighty! terrible and majestic art thou in thy tremendous might—awful (orful) to behold, (cramp in my right shoulder,) gigantic, huge and nice! Oh, thou that tumblest down and riseth up again in misty majesty to heaven—thou glorious parent of a thousand rainbows—what a huge, grand, awful, terrible, tremendous, infinite, old swindling humbug you are; what are you doing there, you rapids, you—you know you've tumbled over there, and can't get up again to save your puny existence; you make a great fuss, don't you?

Man came back with the beer, drank it to the last drop, and wished there had been a gallon more—walked out on a rock to the edge of the fall, woman on the shore very much frightened—I told her not to get excited if I fell over, as I would step right up again—it would not be much of a fall anyhow—got a glass of beer of a man, another of a woman, and another of two small boys with a pail—fifteen minutes elapsed, when I purchased some more of an Indian woman and imbibed it through a straw; it wasn't good—had to get a glass of beer to take the taste out of my mouth; legs began to tangle up, effects of the spray in my eyes, got hungry and wanted something to eat—went into an eating-house, called for a plate of beans, when the plate brought the waiter in his hand. I took it, hung up my beef and beans on a nail, eat my hat, [laughter] paid the dollar a nigger, and sided out on the step-walk, bought a boy of a glass of dog [laughter] with a small beer and a neck on his tail, with a collar with a spot on the end—felt funny, sick—got some soda-water in tin cup, drank the cup and placed the soda on the counter, and paid for the money full of pocket—[laughter] very bad headache; rubbed it against the lamp-post and then stumped along; station-house came along and said if I did not go straight he'd take me to the watchman—[laughter] tried to oblige the station-house, very civil station-house, very—met a baby with an Irish woman and a wheelbarrow in it, [loud laughter] couldn't get out of the way; she wouldn't walk on the sidewalk, but insited on going on both sides of the street at once; tried to walk between her; [laughter] consequence collision, awful, knocked out the wheel-barrow's nose, broke the Irish woman all to pieces, baby loose, court-house handy, took me to the constable, [laughter] jury sat on me, and the jail said the magistrate must take me to the constable; objected; the dungeon put me into the darkest constable in the city; got out and here I am prepared to stick to my original opinion.

Niagara non est excelsus (ego fui) humbugest! Indignus admirationi! [Loud laughter.]

EUGENE FIELD'S LECTURE.
BIOGRAPHY.

Eugene Field was born in Boston, Mass., in 1850. He received a classical education, and has since become famous as a journalist and wit. He published "Culture's Garland" in 1887.

Mr. Field is quite famous as a lecturer in the vicinity of St. Joseph, Mo., where he has delighted thousands of audiences. His last great lecture was delivered in Kalamazoo, Mich., before the Kalamazoo College. Mr. Field says he thought it was the morgue when he accepted the engagement. It was a charming medley of poetry and prose, however, and is published in this book for the first time.

Ladies and Gentlemen:

A little peach in the orchard grew,
A little peach of emerald hue:
Warmed by the sun and wet by the dew,
          It grew.

One day, walking the orchard through,
That little peach dawned on the view
Of Johnny Jones and his sister Sue—
          Those two. [Laughter.]

Up at the peach a club they threw:
Down from the limb on which it grew,
Fell the little peach of emerald hue—
          Too true. [Laughter.]

John took a bite, and Sue took a chew,
And then the trouble began to brew,—
Trouble the doctor couldn't subdue,—
          Paregoric too. [Laughter.]

Under the turf where the daisies grew,
They planted John and his sister Sue;
And their little souls to the angels flew—
          Boo-hoo! [Sensation.]

But what of the peach of emerald hue,
Warmed by the sun, and wet by the dew?
Ah, well! its mission on earth is through—
          Adieu! [Applause.]

At the panorama of the Battle of Shiloh in Chicago a few days ago, a small, shriveled-up man made himself conspicuous by going around the place sniveling dolorously. He did not appear to be more than five feet high. He was dressed all in black, and his attenuated form and gray whiskers gave him a peculiarly grotesque appearance. He seemed to be greatly interested in the panorama; and, as he moved from one point of view to another, he groaned and wept copiously. A tall, raw-boned man approached him; he wore gray clothes and a military slouch hat, and he had the general appearance of a Missourian away from home on a holiday.

"Reckon you were at Shiloh, eh, stranger?" asked the tall, raw-boned man.

"Yes," replied the small, shriveled-up man, "and I shall never forget it; it was the toughest battle of the war."

"I was thar," said the tall, raw-boned man; "and my regiment was drawn up right over yonder where you see that clump of trees."

"You were a rebel, then?"

"I was a Confederate," replied the tall, raw-boned man; "and I did some right smart fighting among that clump of trees that day."

"I remember it well," said the small, shriveled-up man, "for I was a Federal soldier; and the toughest scrimmage in all that battle was fought amongst that clump of trees."

"Prentiss was the Yankee general," remarked the tall, raw-boned man; "and I'd have given a good deal to have seen him that day. But, dog-on me! the little cuss kept out of sight, and we uns came to the conclusion he was hidin' back in the rear somewhar."

"Our boys were after Marmaduke," said the small, shriveled-up man; "for he was the rebel general, and had bothered us a great deal. But we could get no glimpse of him; he was too sharp to come to the front, and it was lucky for him too."

"Oh, but what a scrimmage it was!" said the tall, raw-boned man.

"How the sabres clashed, and how the minies whistled!" cried the small, shriveled-up man.

The panorama brought back the old time with all the vividness of a yesterday's occurrence. The two men were filled with a strange yet beautiful enthusiasm.

"Stranger," cried the tall, raw-boned man, "we fought each other like devils that day, and we fought to kill. But the war's over now, and we ain't soldiers any longer—gimme your hand!"

"With pleasure," said the small, shriveled-up man; and the two clasped hands.

"What might be your name?" inquired the tall, raw-boned man.

"I am Gen. B. M. Prentiss," said the small, shriveled-up man.

"Gosh, you say!" exclaimed the tall, raw-boned man.

"Yes," re-affirmed the small, shriveled-up man; "and who are you?"

"I," replied the tall, raw-boned man, "I am Gen. John S. Marmaduke." [Loud laughter.]

> I wished I lived away down East, where codfish salt the sea,
> And where the folks have pumpkin-pie and apple-sass for tea.
> Us boys who's livin' here out West, don't get more'n half a show:
> We don't have nothin' else to do but jest to sort o' grow.

Oh ! if I wuz a bird I'd fly a million miles away
To where they feed their boys on pork and beans three times a day ;
To where the place they call the Hub, gives out its shiny spokes,
And where the folks—so father says—is mostly women-folks. [Laughter.]

The members of the Boston Commercial Club are charming gentle-men. They are now the guests of the Chicago Commercial Club, and are being shown every attention that our market affords. They are a fine-looking lot, well-dressed and well-mannered, with just enough whiskers to be impressive without being imposing.

"This is a darned likely village," said Seth Adams, of the Boston Commercial Club, after being in Chicago a day or two. "Every body is rushin' 'round an' doin' business as if his life depended on it. Should think they'd git all tuckered out 'fore night, but I'll be darned if there ain't just as many folks on the street after night-fall as afore. We're stoppin' at the Palmer tavern ; an' my chamber is up so all-fired high, that I can count all your meetin'-house steeples from the winder."

Last night five or six of these Boston merchants sat around the office of the hotel, and discussed matters and things. Pretty soon they got to talking about beans ; this was the subject which they dwelt on with evident pleasure.

"Waal, sir," said Ephraim Taft, a wholesale dealer in maple-sugar and flavored lozenges, "you kin talk 'bout your new-fashioned dishes an' high-falutin' vittles; but, when you come right down to it, there ain't no better eatin' than a dish o' baked pork 'n' beans."

"That's so, b' gosh!" chorussed the others.

"The truth o' the matter is," continued Mr. Taft, "that beans is good for everybody—'t don't make no difference whether he's well or sick. Why, I've known a thousand folks—waal, mebbe not quite a thousand; but—waal, now, jest to show, take the case of Bill Holbrook: you remember Bill, don't ye?"

"Bill Holbrook?" said Mr. Ezra Eastman; "why, of course I do! Used to live down to Brimfield, next to the Moses Howard farm."

"That's the man," resumed Mr. Taft. "Waal, Bill fell sick—kinder moped round, tired like, for a week or two, an' then tuck to his bed. His folks sent for Dock Smith—ol' Dock Smith that used to carry round a pair o' leather saddlebags—gosh, they don't have no sech doc-tors nowadays! Waal, the dock, he come, an' he looked at Bill's tongue, an' felt uv his pulse, an' said that Bill had typhus fever. Ol' Dock Smith was a very careful conserv'tive man, an' he never said nothin' unless he knowd he was right.

"Bill began to git wuss, an' he kep' a-gittin' wuss every day.   One mornin' ol' Dock Smith sez, 'Look a-here, Bill, I guess you're a goner; as I figger it, you can't hol' out till nightfall."

"Bill's mother insisted on a con-sul-tation bein' held; so ol' Dock Smith sent over for young Dock Brainerd.   I calc-late, that, next to ol' Dock Smith, young Dock Brainerd was the smartest doctor that ever lived.

"Waal, pretty soon along come Dock Brainerd; an' he an' Dock Smith went all over Bill, an' looked at his tongue, an' felt uv his pulse, an' told him it was a gone case, an' that he had got to die.   Then they went off into the spare chamber to hold their con-sul-tation.

"Waal, Bill he lay there in the front room a-pantin' an' a-gaspin', an' a wond'rin' whether it wuz true.   As he wuz thinkin', up comes the girl to git a clean tablecloth out of the clothes-press, an' she left the door ajar as she come in.   Bill he gave a sniff, an' his eyes grew more natural like; he gathered together all the strength he had, an' he raised himself upon one elbow, an' sniffed again.

"'Sary,' says he, 'wot's that a cookin'?'

"'Beans,' says she, 'beans for dinner.'

"'Sary,' says the dyin' man, 'I must hev a plate uv them beans!' [Laughter.]

"'Sakes alive, Mr. Holbrook!' says she, 'if you wuz to eat any o' them beans, it'd kill ye!'

"'If I've got to die,' says he, 'I'm goin' to die happy; fetch me a plate uv them beans.'

"Waal, Sary, she pikes off to the doctors.

"'Look a-here,' says she, 'Mr. Holbrook smelt the beans cookin', an' he says he's got to have a plate uv 'em.   Now, what shall I do about it?'

"'Waal, doctor,' says Dock Smith, 'what do you think 'bout it?'

"'He's got to die anyhow,' says Dock Brainerd; 'an' I don't sup-pose the beans'll make any diff'rence.'   [Laughter.]

"'That's the way I figger it,' says Dock Smith; 'in all my practice I never knew of beans hurtin' any body.'

"So Sary went down to the kitchen, an' brought up a plateful of hot baked beans.   Dock Smith raised Bill up in bed, an' Dock Brain-erd put a piller under the small of Bill's back.   Then Sary sat down by the bed, an' fed them beans into Bill until Bill couldn't hold any more.

"'How air you feelin' now?' asked Dock Smith.

"Bill didn't say nuthin'; he jest smiled sort uv peaceful like, an' closed his eyes.

"'The end hez come,' said Dock Brainerd, sof'ly; 'Bill is dyin'.'

"Then Bill murmured kind o' far away like (as if he was dreamin'), 'I ain't dyin'; I'm dead an' in heaven.' [Loud laughter.]

"Next mornin' Bill got out uv bed, an' done a big day's work on the farm, an' he hain't hed a sick spell since. When they asked him about it he said : 'They may talk about beans bein' onhealthy, but I'd a bin ded to-day, by ginger, if I hadn't eaten 'em.'" [Laughter.]

GEORGE W. CABLE'S READINGS.

Mr. George W. Cable has usually read his sketches to audiences of late years. One of his favorite sketches, full of dramatic art, is "Mary Richling's Ride," from "Dr. Sevier." It is given here as read by Mr. Cable:

Ladies and Gentlemen:—Mary Richling, the heroine of the story I read to-night, was the wife of John Richling, a resident of New Orleans. At the breaking out of the Civil War, she went to visit her parents in Milwaukee. About the time of the bombardment of New Orleans, she received news of the dangerous illness of her husband, and she decided at once to reach his bedside, if possible. Taking with her her baby daughter, a child of three years, she proceeded southward, where, after several unsuccessful attempts to secure a pass, she finally determined to break through the lines.

About the middle of the night, Mary Richling was sitting very still and upright on a large, dark horse that stood champing his Mexican bit in the black shadow of a great oak. Alice rested before her, fast asleep against her bosom. Mary held by the bridle another horse, whose naked saddle-tree was empty. A few steps in front of her the light of the full moon shone almost straight down upon a narrow road that just there emerged from the shadow of woods on either side, and divided into a main right fork and a much smaller one that curved around to Mary's left. Off in the direction of the main fork the sky was all aglow with camp-fires. Only just here on the left there was a cool and grateful darkness.

She lifted her head alertly. A twig crackled under a tread, and the next moment a man came out of the bushes at the left, and without a word, took the bridle of the led horse from her fingers, and vaulted into the saddle. The hand that rested a moment on the cantle as he arose, grasped a "navy six." He was dressed in dull homespun, but he was the same who had been dressed in blue. He turned his horse and led the way down the lesser road.

"If we'd of gone three hundred yards further," he whispered, falling back and smiling broadly, "we'd 'a' run into the pickets. I went nigh enough to see the videttes settin' on their hosses in the main road. This here ain't no road; it just goes up to a nigger quarters. I've got one o' the niggers to show us the way."

"Where is he?" whispered Mary; but before her companion could answer, a tattered form moved from behind a bush a little in advance, and started ahead in the path, walking and beckoning. Presently they turned into a clear, open forest, and followed the long, rapid, swinging stride of the negro for nearly an hour. Then they halted on the bank of a deep, narrow stream. The negro made a motion for them to keep well to the right when they should enter the water. The white man softly lifted Alice to his arms, directed and assisted Mary to kneel in her saddle, with her skirts gathered carefully under her, and so they went down into the cold stream, the negro first, with arms outstretched above the flood; then Mary, and then the white man — or, let us say plainly, the spy — with the unawakened child on his breast. And so they rose out of it on the farther side, without a shoe or garment wet, save the rags of their dark guide.

Again they followed him, along a line of stake-and-rider fence, with the woods on one side and the bright moonlight flooding a field of young cotton on the other. Now they heard the distant baying of house-dogs, now the doleful call of the chuck-will's-widow, and once Mary's blood turned, for an instant, to ice, at the unearthly shriek of the hoot-owl just above her head. At length they found themselves in a dim, narrow road, and the negro stopped.

"Dess keep dish yeh road fo' 'bout half mile, an' you strak 'pon de broad, main road. Tek de right, an' you go whah yo' fancy tek you."

"Good-bye," whispered Mary.

"Good-bye, Miss," said the negro, in the same low voice; "good-bye, boss; don't you fo'git you promise tek me thoo to de Yankee, when you come back. I'se 'feered you gwine fo'git it, boss."

The spy said he would not, and they left him. The half-mile was soon passed, though it turned out to be a mile and a half, and at length Mary's companion looked back as they rode single file, with Mary in the rear, and said, softly:

"There's the road," pointing at its broad, pale line with his six-shooter.

As they entered it and turned to the right, Mary, with Alice again in her arms, moved somewhat ahead of her companion, her indifferent horsemanship having compelled him to drop back to avoid a prickly bush. His horse was just quickening his pace to regain the lost position, when a man sprang up from the ground on the farther side of the highway, snatched a carbine from the earth and cried: "Halt!"

The dark, recumbent forms of six or eight others could be seen, enveloped in their blankets, lying about a few red coals. Mary turned a frightened look backward and met the eyes of her companion.

"Move a little faster," said he, in a low, clear voice. As she promptly did so she heard him answer the challenge, as his horse trotted softly after hers.

"Don't stop us, my friend; we're taking a sick child to the doctor."

"Halt, you hound!" the cry rang out; and as Mary glanced back, three or four men were just leaping into the road. But she saw also her companion, his face suffused with an earnestness that was almost an agony, rise in his stirrups with the stoop of his shoulders all gone, and wildly cry:

"Go!"

She smote the horse and flew. Alice awoke and screamed.

"Hush, my darling," said the mother, laying on the withe; "mamma's here. Hush, darling, mamma's here. Don't be frightened darling baby. O, God, spare my child!" and away she sped.

The report of a carbine rang out and went rolling away in a thousand echoes through the wood. Two others followed in sharp succession, and there went close by Mary's ear the waspish whine of a minie-ball. At the same moment she recognized, once—twice—thrice—just at her back where the hoofs of her companion's horse were clattering—the tart rejoinders of his navy six.

"Go!" he cried again. "Lay low! lay low! cover the child!"

But his words were needless. With head bowed forward and form crouched over the crying, clinging child, with slackened rein and fluttering dress, and sun-bonnet and loosened hair blown back upon her shoulders, with lips compressed and silent prayers, Mary was riding for life and liberty and her husband's bedside.

"O, mamma, mamma," wailed the terrified little one.

"Go on! Go on!" cried the voice behind: "they're saddling up! Go! go! We're goin' to make it! We're going to make it! Go-o-o!"

And they made it! [Applause.]

MAX O'RELL.

BIOGRAPHY.

We will let Max Blouet (Max O'Rell) tell his own story:

Dear Eli:—My grandfather was an officer in the French army, and was called Max Blouet. During the Napoleon war, he was taken prisoner by the English and sent to England, where he met an Irish girl, Miss O'Rell, whom he loved, courted, married, and brought back to France. Such is the origin of my *nom de plume.* I first used it on the title-page of "John Bull and His Island."

PAUL BLOUET.

MAX O'RELL'S LECTURE ON THE SCOTCHMAN.

Ladies and Gentlemen:—The Scotchman possesses a genius for business, as the following dialogue would indicate. One of his favorite proverbs is, "He will soon be a beggar who does not know how to say no." A laird of Lanarkshire was one day accosted by one of his neighbors as follows:

"Laird, I need £20 sterling. If you will be kind enough to accept my note, you will be repaid in three months."

"No; it is impossible, Donald."

"But why, Laird? You have often rendered a like service to your friends."

"Impossible, Donald, I repeat,"

"Then you mean to refuse me?"

"Listen, Donald, and follow my reasoning: As soon as I accepted your note you would go and draw the £20?"

"Yes."

"When the maturity of the note arrived, I know you, and that you would not be ready. Then we should quarrel. Very well! but, Donald, I should rather that we should quarrel at once, while the £20 is in my pocket." [Laughter.]

Scotchmen themselves enjoy telling this anecdote.

Donald—Have you heard, Duncan, that Sawney McNab has been condemned to six months in prison for having stolen a cow?

Duncan—What a fool that McNab is! As if he could not have bought the cow—and never paid for it! [Laughter.]

This may, perhaps, explain why the prisons in Scotland are comparatively empty. Donald often appears before the justice of the peace, but rarely in the police courts. Every day Donald addresses the following prayer to God:

O, Lord! grant that this day I take no advantage of any one, and that no one takes advantage of me. But, if, O, Lord! Thou canst accord but one of these favors, let no one take advantage of me.

To illustrate Scotch thrift, I tell a little anecdote that was told me in Scotland:

A worthy father, feeling death at hand, sends for his son to hear his last counsels. "Sandy," he says to him, "listen to the last words of your old father. If you want to get on in the world, be honest. Never forget that, in all business, honesty is the best policy. You may take my word for it, my son—I hae tried baith." [Laughter.]

The Jews never got a footing in Scotland; they would have starved there. They came, but they saw—and gave it up. You may find one or two in Glasgow, but they are in partnership with Scotchmen, and do not form a band apart. They do not do much local business; they are exporters and importers. The Aberdonians tell of a Jew who came once to their city and set up in business; but it was not long before he packed up his traps and decamped from the center of Scotch cuteness.

"Why are you going?" they asked him. "Is it because there are no Jews in Aberdeen?"

"Oh, no," he replied; "I am going because you are all Jews here." [Laughter.]

The Scotchman believes in two trinities; the Father, Son and the Holy Ghost, and pounds, shillings and pence. Sandy is still more religious, that is to say, still more church-going than the Englishman. He treats his Creator, however, as a next-door neighbor. If he comes across a big word, a dictionary word, he explains it to the Lord. At evening prayers once, I heard the master among a thousand other supplications, make the following:

"O, Lord, give us receptivity; *that is to say*, O, Lord, the power of receiving impressions."

The entire Scotch character is there. What forethought! What cleverness! What a business-like talent!

Another prayer was: "O, Lord, have mercy on all fools, idiots and the members of the town council!"

The rigidness of the Scotch Sabbath is beyond my powers of description; it is still sterner in Scotland than in England. When excursion trains were first put on between Edinburgh and Glasgow, a minister expostulated with a lady passenger who was going on Sunday to visit a sick relative.

"Where are you going?" said he.

"To Glasgow," answered she.

"No, you are going to hell!"

"Oh!" returned the undaunted lass. "Then, I'm all right for I bought a return ticket!" [Laughter.]

BRET HARTE.

NOVELIST, LECTURER AND WIT.

One of Bret Harte's funniest lecture stories was his account of the first jury trial in California. Up to August, 1850, all criminals had been tried by lynch law, and, if pronounced guilty by the boys, they were hung to a tree. But times began to mellow down a little, and certain solid citizens began to sigh for good old Eastern law. They wanted the jury trial of the father, and as provided for by the constitution. So at Big Gulch, in 1849, when a man had been accused of stealing horses, they decided for the first time in California to give the culprit a fair jury trial—the first jury trial, I say, in California.

Twelve good men were chosen on the jury, and the witnesses were brought before them. Some swore to the good character of the accused and some swore that he was a horse-stealer from way back. When the last witness got through, the jury retired to give a verdict. They hadn't been in the jury-room over ten mintes, when a crowd of outsiders came pounding at the door.

"What do you fellers want?" asked the foreman.

"Want to know if you jurymen havn't got most through?"

"Not quite," said the foreman.

"Well, hurry up—we can't wait much longer—we've got to have this room to *lay out the corpse in !* "

WHY BRET HARTE MURDERED A MAN.

The following account of how Bret Harte became a murderer, has never before been printed. It is now printed from Mr. Harte's manuscripts:

*   *   *   *   *   *   *   *   *   *   *

"Dead! Dead as Wilkes Booth! Stone cold! I tell you."

"Fudge and nonsense," said my friend, the rector, offering me a cheap cigar. "I don't believe it."

"You must believe it — I swear it!" I said, trying to light my cigar.

"Tell me how it happened, then. It's strange," he replied.

"Well, you see, I had sold Jacob Einstein my old clothes for a great many years. He was always hard and close at his bargains.

I once tried, I remember, to get him to buy a standing crop, as it were — to make him advance something on a contract to deliver a suit I had on a month later — but he said, 'Deshe schtoc brokers' ways is against de conscience.' That got me mad, for I knew it was a pretense.

"Well, year after year Jacob kept getting richer through me. By and by he bought a big house; he had thirteen children; he became a vestryman; he joined the Union League Club, and went into politics and all that sort of thing; but he always kept the old stand with the gold balls just the same, and was on hand whenever I wanted to raise a little money on a coat.

"The richer he grew, the closer bargains he used to drive. He got it down so fine at last that a man was hardly sure of making a meal off a coat. He kept growing richer, and I kept growing poorer.

"But the thing that riled me was the airs the fellow put on. One day I met him on Fifth avenue, walking with the governor. He was dressed very fine, and wore a large diamond ring and breastpin. I looked at the fellow, and he cut me dead. I said to myself, 'That man is doomed.' I went to my room and thought for an hour how to revenge myself. At length I hit on a plan."

"What was it?" inquired the rector.

"Well, I went back to my room, took off my vest, buttoned my coat round my neck, and walked to my friend the pawnbroker. I found Jacob in an ill humor.

"'Dere is too many holes in dish blanket,' he was saying to a poor customer, who was trying to negotiate a loan.

"'Jacob,' I cried, interrupting him. 'I'm in a hurry. I've brought you a vest made for the Prince of Wales; it has never been worn.'

"Jacob looked curiously at the vest from a corner of his eye.

"'De monish is very scarch,' he said.

"'You are lying, Jacob,' I replied. 'The papers all say it's a drug.'

"'It's a drug for de well folks, not for de poor and sick, like me,' said Jacob.

"'What'll you give for this new vest?' said I.

"'Dat vesht,' said he, thrusting the nail of his forefinger, which he had let grow long for that purpose, through one of its seams, 'dat

PROF. DAVID SWING   EUGENE FIELD
GEO. W. CABLE   BRET HARTE

vesht ish out of schtyle. It ish old ash de coat of Joseph. I don't want de ting at all. What will you take for it as a favor?'

" 'Five dollars,' I said.

" 'Shut de safe, shut de safe, Shadrach,' cried Jacob to his son. 'Deshe men have come to rob me. Twenty-five cents ish a fortune to give for such a vesht.'

" 'Five dollars, Jacob,' I said, firmly.

" 'Thirty cents, for de shake of an old friend; not one penny more.'

" 'Jacob Einstein, what have you to say why you should not give five dollars for that vest?' I asked, solemnly.

"He said nothing. I took the vest slowly from him.

" 'It is a very rich cloth,' I said, taking a pinch of it between my thumb and finger, and snapping it like an expert. 'Hello! what is this? It feels thick here,' and thrusting my hand through a hole in the pocket to a remote corner of the vest, I slowly drew forth and unfolded to the light my ten-dollar bill.

"I looked at Jacob; he was white as a lily.

" 'De God of Abraham,' he cried, and fell to the ground.

"We tried to shake him into consciousness. It was no use, Jacob was more than dead.

"I tell you that I am tired of starving. I am going to be even with my friends. I have begun with the pawnbroker."

ANECDOTES OF GOULD, FISK AND DREW.

Mr. Jay Gould, is a lay figure for hundreds of the best jokes on "the street." The great financier was born at Stratton Falls, Delaware county, N. Y., in 1836. His father was John B. Gould, who cultivated a small farm and ran a grocery store. At the age of twenty, Gould surveyed Delaware county, mapped it, and peddled the books himself. After this, Mr. Gould bought an interest in a tannery, then married Miss Miller, whose father was connected with railroads and who gave him his first start in that line. Mr. Gould's experience in his partnership with Jim Fisk, who was killed by Edwin S. Stokes, is well known. Fisk was a big, generous, whole-souled boy, while Gould was a shrewd, calculating man. Gould is a moral and temperate man, but he is not a church member. His favorite daughter was baptized by Dr. Paxton, whose pathetic remarks caused Gould to shed his first tears in public.

One day last summer the Rev. Doctor Cuyler, of Brooklyn, was making some inquiries as to the religious status of the guests in Saratoga. Meeting Mr. Morrosini, Gould's old Italian partner, he asked him about Gould's religious status.

" Gould, I suppose is a moral man, isn't he," said the Doctor.

" Gould whatee ?" asked Morrosini, with his Italian accent.

" I say, I suppose Gould is a moral man—he keeps the Sabbath, doesn't he ?"

" Gould keepee the Sab-bath!" repeated Morrosini. " Gould keepee the Sab-bath! Why, Gould keepee any thing he get his hands on—you try heem!"

" Colonel Fisk was full of fun, and Gould was dry and thoughtful, still he always enjoys a dry joke.

Once I had occasion to spend an hour with Fisk, Daniel Drew and Gould in their palatial Erie office, and a record of that hour I then wrote out. Fisk was being shaved as I entered, and his face was half covered with foaming lather. Just then some one came in and told him that the gentlemen in the office had made up a purse of $34 to be presented to little Peter, Fisk's favorite little office boy.

"All right," said the Colonel, smiling and wiping the lather from his face. " Call in Peter."

In a moment little Peter entered with a shy look and seemingly half frightened.

" Well, Peter," said the Colonel, as he held the envelope with the money in one hand and the towel in the other, " what did you mean, sir, by absenting yourself from the Erie office, the other day, when both Mr. Gould and I were away, and had left the whole mass of business on your shoulders ?"

Then he frowned fearfully, while Peter trembled from head to foot.

" But, my boy," continued Fisk, "I will not blame you; there may be extenuating circumstances. Evil associates may have tempted you away. Here, Peter, take this (handing him the $34) and henceforth let your life be one of rectitude—quiet rectitude, Peter. Behold me, Peter, and remember that evil communications are not always the best policy, but that honesty is worth two in the bush."

As Peter went back to his place beside the outside door, every body laughed, and Fisk sat down again to have the other side of his face shaved.

Pretty quick in came a little, dried-up old gentleman, with keen gray eyes surmounted by an overpowering Panama hat. The Erie Railway office was then the old gentleman's almost daily rendez- vous. Here he would sit for hours at a time, and peer out from under his broad brim at the wonderful movements of Colonel Fisk. Cautious, because he could move but slowly, this venerable gentle- man, who has made Wall Street tremble, hitched up to the stock indicator, all the time keeping one eye on the quotations and the other on the Colonel. As a feeler, he ventured to ask:

"How is Lake Shore, this morning, Colonel?"

" Peter," said Fisk, with awful gravity, "communicate with the Great American Speculator and show him how they are dealing on the street!"

The old man chuckled, Gould hid a smile while smoothing his jetty whiskers, and little Peter took hold of the running tape with Daniel Drew. It was the beginning and the ending—youth and experience—simplicity and shrewdness—Peter and Daniel!

Little Peter was about ten years old, and small at that. Fre- quently large men would come into the Erie office and " bore " the Colonel. Then he would say:

" Here, Peter, take this man into custody, and hold him under arrest until we send for him!"

"You seem very busy to-day?" I remarked to the Colonel one morning.

" Yes, Eli," said Fisk, smiling. "I'm trying to find out from all these papers where Gould gets money enough to pay his income tax. He never has any money—fact, sir! He even wanted to borrow of me to pay his income tax last summer, and I lent him four hundred dollars, and that's gone, too! This income business will be the ruination of Gould." Here the venerable Daniel Drew concealed a laugh, and Gould turned clear around, so that Fisk could only see the back of his head, while his eyes twinkled in enjoy- ment of the Colonel's fun.

When Montaland, the great opera singer, arrived from Paris, Fisk had just said farewell to " Josie," and so he took extra pains to make a good impression on his beautiful prima donna.

On the first sunshiny afternoon after Montaland had seen the Wonderful Opera House, Fisk took her out to Central Park behind his magnificent six-in-hand.   Passing up Fifth avenue, Montaland's eyes rested on A. T. Stewart's marble house.

" Vat ees zat ? " she asked, in broken French.

" Why, that is my city residence," said Fisk, with an air of profound composure.

" *C'est magnifique—c'est grande!* " repeated Montaland, in admiration.

Soon they came to Central Park.

" Vat ees zees place ? " asked Montaland.

" O, this is my country seat; these are my grounds—my cattle and buffalos, and those sheep over there compose my pet sheepfold," said Fisk, twirling the end of his moustache *à la* Napoleon.

" *C'est tres magnifique!* " exclaimed Montaland in bewilderment. " Mr. Feesk is one grand Américain ! "

By and by they rode back and down Broadway, by A. T. Stewart's mammoth store.

" And is zees your grand *maison*, too ? " asked Montaland, as she pointed up to the iron palace.

" No, Miss Montaland ; to be frank with you, that building does not belong to me," said Fisk, as he settled back with his hand in his bosom—" that belongs to Mr. Gould ! "

One day I called at the Erie office.   Col. Fisk's old chair was vacant and his desk was draped in mourning.   Fisk's remains lay cold and stiff, just as he fell at the Grand Central Hotel, pierced by the fatal bullet from Stokes' pistol.   His old associates were silent, or gathered in groups to tell over reminiscences of the dead Colonel, whose memory was beloved and revered by his companions.

Mr. Gould never tires telling about Fisk's good qualities.   Even while he is telling the quaintest anecdotes about his dead partner, his eyes glisten with tears.

"One day," said Mr. Gould, "Fisk came to me and told me confidentially about his first mistake in life."

"What was it ?" I asked.

HE CRIED AND FELL TO THE GROUND.

See page 526.

"Well," said Gould, as he laughed and wiped his eyes alter-nately, "Fisk said that when he was an innocent little boy, living on his father's farm up at Brattleboro, Vermont, his father took him into the stable one day, where a row of cows stood in their uncleaned stalls.

"Said he, 'James, the stable window is pretty high for a boy, but do you think you could take this shovel and clean out the stable?'

"' I don't know, Father,' said Fisk, 'I never have done it."

"'Well, my boy, you are a very smart boy, and if you will do it this morning, I'll give you this bright silver dollar,' and Fisk's father patted him on his head, while he held the silver dollar before his eyes.

"'Good,' says Fisk, 'I'll try,' and then he went to work. He tugged and pulled and lifted and puffed, and finally it was done, and his father gave him the bright silver dollar, saying:

"'That's right, James, you did it splendidly, and now I find you can do it so nicely, I shall have you do it every morning all winter.'"

One day a poor, plain, blunt man stumbled into Fisk's room. Said he:

"Colonel, I've heard you are a generous man, and I've come to ask a great favor."

"Well, what is it, my good man?" asked Fisk.

"I want to go to Lowell, sir, to my wife, and I haven't a cent of money in the world," said the man, in a firm, manly voice.

"Where have you been?" asked the Colonel, dropping his pen.

"I don't want to tell you," replied the man, dropping his head.

"Out with it, my man, where have you been?" said Fisk.

"Well, sir, I've been to Sing Sing State Prison."

"What for?"

"Grand larceny, sir. I was put in for five years, but was par-doned out yesterday, after staying four years and one half. I am here, hungry and without money."

"All right, my man," said Fisk, kindly, "you shall have a pass, and here—here is five dollars. Go and get a meal of victuals, and then ride down to the boat in an Erie coach, like a gentleman. Commence life again, and if you are honest and want a lift, come to me."

Perfectly bewildered, the poor convict took the money, and six months afterward Fisk got a letter from him. He was doing a thriving, mercantile business, and said Fisk's kindness and cheering words gave him the first hope—his first strong resolve to become a man.

Ten minutes after the poor convict left, a poor young negro preacher called.

"What do you want? Are you from Sing Sing, too?" asked Fisk.

"No, sir; I'm a Baptist preacher from Hoboken. I want to go to the Howard Seminary in Washington," said the negro.

"All right, brother Johnson," said Fisk. "Here, Comer," he said, addressing his secretary, "give brother Johnson $20, and charge it to charity," and the Colonel went on writing without listening to the stream of thanks from the delighted negro.

One day the Colonel was walking up Twenty-third street to dine with Mr. Gould, when a poor beggar came along. The beggar followed after them, saying, in a plaintive tone, "Please give me a dime, gentlemen?"

Mr. Gould, who was walking by Fisk, took out a roll of bills and commenced to unroll them, thinking to find a half or a quarter.

"Here, man!" said Fisk, seizing the whole roll and throwing it on the sidewalk, "take the pile."

Then looking into the blank face of Mr. Gould, he said, "Thunderation, Gould, you never count charity, do you?"

Somebody in Brattleboro came down to New York to ask Fisk for a donation to help them build a new fence around the graveyard where he is now buried.

"What in thunder do you want a new fence for?" exclaimed the Colonel. "Why, that old fence will keep the dead people in, and live people will keep out as long as they can, any way!"

What a miserable reprobate the preachers all make Fisk out to be! And they are right. Why, the scoundrel actually stopped his coupe one cold, dreary night on Seventh avenue, and got out, inquired where she lived and gave a poor old beggar woman a dollar. He seemed to have no shame about him, for the next day the debauched wretch sent her around a barrel of flour and a load of coal. One day the black-hearted scoundrel sent ten dollars and a bag of flour around to a widow woman with three starving children; and, not content with this, the remorseless wretch told the police captain to look after all the poor widows and orphans in his ward and send them to him when they deserved charity. What a shameless performance it was to give that poor negro preacher twenty dollars and send him to Howard University! And how the black-hearted villain practiced his meanness on the poor, penniless old woman who wanted to go to Boston, by paying her passage and actually escorting her to a free state-room, while the old woman's tears of gratitude were streaming down her cheeks! Oh, insatiate monster! thus to give money to penniless negro preachers and starving women and children!

JOHN J. CRITTENDEN'S ELOQUENCE.

John J. Crittenden, the eloquent Kentucky lawyer, was once defending a murderer. Every one knew the man was guilty, but the eloquence of Crittenden saved him.

"Gentlemen," said Crittenden, at the end of his great plea, "'to err is human, to forgive divine.' When God conceived the thought of man's creation, he called to him three ministering virtues, who wait constantly upon the throne—Justice, Truth and Mercy—and thus addressed them:

"'Shall we make this man?'

"'O, God, make him not,' said Justice, sternly, 'for he will surely trample upon Thy laws.'

"'And Truth, what sayest thou?'

"'O, God, make him not, for none but God is perfect, and he will surely sin against Thee.'

"'And Mercy, what sayest thou?'

"Then Mercy, dropping upon her knees, and looking up through her tears, exclaimed:

"'O, God, make him; I will watch over him with my care through all the dark paths he may have to tread.'

"Then, brothers, God made man and said to him: 'O, man, thou art the child of mercy; go and deal mercifully with all thy brothers.'"

ROSCOE CONKLING AND CHARLES O'CONNOR.

Roscoe Conkling came into Charles O'Connor's office one day, when he was a young lawyer, in quite a nervous state.

"You seem to be very much exicted, Mr. Conkling," said Mr. O'Connor, as Roscoe walked up and down the room.

"Yes, I'm provoked—I am provoked," said Mr. Conkling. "I never had a client dissatisfied about my fee before."

"Well, what's the matter?" asked O'Connor.

"Why, I defended Gibbons for arson, you know. He was convicted, but I did hard work for him. I took him to the supreme court and back again, to the supreme court again, and the supreme court confirmed the judgment and gave him ten years. I charged him $3,000, and now Gibbons is grumbling about it—says it's too much. Now, Mr. O'Connor, I ask you, was that too much?"

"Well," said O'Connor, very deliberately, "of course, you did a good deal of work, and $3,000 is not such a very big fee, but to be frank with you, Mr. Conkling, my deliberate opinion is that he might have been convicted for less money!"

WILLIAM M. EVARTS AND CHAUNCEY M. DEPEW.

Hon. William M. Evarts is the only man, except Chauncey Depew, who can be witty and not lose his dignity. Mr. Evarts sat at our table at the States yesterday.

Among other things I asked the great lawyer about some of the witticisms which have been attributed to him.

"The best thing the newspapers said I perpetrated," replied Mr. Evarts, "I wasn't guilty of at all."

"What was that?" I asked.

"It happened when I was Secretary of State. Every morning the State Department elevator came up full of applicants for foreign missions. One morning, when the applicants for missions was extremely large, Catlin, the *Commercial Advertiser* humorist, remarked: 'That is the largest collection for foreign missions you've had yet.' The newspapers attributed the saying to me, but Catlin was the real criminal."

"After that you sent poor Catlin out of the country, didn't you?"

"O, no, I rewarded him by making him consul at Glasgow—and afterwards promoted him."

Speaking of Mr. Evarts' farm up at Windsor, I told him I understood that he raised a large quantity of pigs for the express purpose of sending barrels of pork to his friends.

"Yes, I am guilty of that," said Mr. Evarts. "I've been sending Bancroft pork for years, and if his 'History of America' is successful it will be largely due to my pen."

A few years ago Mr. Evarts sent his usual barrel of pickled pork to Bancroft with this letter:

DEAR BANCROFT:—I am very glad to send you two products of my pen to-day—a barrel of pickled pork and my Eulogy on Chief Justice Chase. Yours, EVARTS.

Chauncey Depew says: "Evarts once sent a donkey up to his Windsor farm in Vermont. About a week afterwards Mr. Evarts received the following letter from his little grandchild:

DEAR GRANDPA—The little donkey is very gentle, but he makes a big noise nights. He is very lonesome. I guess he misses you. I hope you will come up soon and then he won't be so lonesome. MINNIE.

Evarts says when the Baptists came to Rhode Island they praised God and fell on their knees, then they fell on the aborigi—nese.

When I asked the Ex-Secretary about the early settlement of Rhode Island, he said:

"Yes, the Dutch settled Rhode Island and then the Yankees settled the Dutch."

JEFFERSON ON FRANKLIN.

Thomas Jefferson, when minister to France, being presented at court, some eminent functionary remarked:

"You replace Dr. Franklin, sir."

"I succeed Dr. Franklin," was Mr. Jefferson's prompt reply; "no man can replace him."

LINCOLN'S ILLUSTRATION.

When the telegram from Cumberland Gap informed Mr. Lincoln that "firing was heard in the direction of Knoxville," he remarked that he was glad of it.

Governor Sprague had the perils of Burnside's position upper-most in his mind, who was present and who could not see why Mr. Lincoln should be "glad of it," and so expressed himself.

"Why, you, see, Governor," responded the President, "it reminds me of Mistress Sallie Ward, a neighbor of mine, who had a very large family. Occasionally one of her numerous progeny would be heard crying in some out-of-the-way place, upon which Mistress Sallie would exclaim, 'There's one of my children that isn't dead yet.'"

EDWARD EVERETT ON JUDGE STORY.

Everett was entertained at a public dinner, before leaving Boston for England to assume the duties of a minister at the English court. The celebrated Judge Story, who was present on the occasion, gave as a sentiment.

"Genius is sure to be recognized where Ever-ett goes."

Everett gratefully responded with another sentiment. "Law, Equity and Jurisprudence; no efforts can raise them above one Story."

GENERAL SHERMAN ON "PAP" THOMAS.

General Sherman is fond of telling thrilling incidents of the great war. I was talking with the General one day about General Thomas, when he put his hand to his head as if in deep thought and exclaimed:

"Here's something about Thomas: You see General Thomas was junior to me in rank but senior in service. 'Pap,' as the boys called him, was a severe disciplinarian. Well, in the Atlanta campaign he had received many complaints about the pilfering and plundering committed by one of his brigades, and, being resolved to put this offense down, he issued some strict orders, menacing with death any who should transgress. The brigade in question wore for its badge an acorn, in silver or gold, and the men were inordinately proud of this distinctive sign. Several cases of disobedience had been reported to the General, but the evidence was never strong enough for decisive action, until one day, riding with an orderly down a by-lane outside the posts, Thomas came full upon an Irishman who, having laid aside his rifle, with which he had killed a hog, was busily engaged in skinning the animal with his sword-bayonet, so as to make easy work with the bristles, etc., before cooking pork chops. 'Ah,' cried the General, 'you rascal, at last I have caught you in the act. There is no mistake about it this time, and I will make an example of you, sir!'

"'Bedad! General, honey!' said the Irishman, straightening himself up and coming to the salute, 'it's not shootin' me that you ought to be at, but rewardin' me.'

"'What do you mean, sir?' exclaimed General Thomas.

"'Why, your Honor!' the soldier replied, 'this bad baste here had just been disicratin' the rigimental badge; and so I was forced to dispatch him. It's 'atin' the acorns that I found him at!' Even General Thomas was obliged to laugh at this, and the soldier saved his life by his wit."

GARFIELD'S WIT.

At one of Proctor's lectures, a lady wished for a seat, when General Garfield brought one and seated her.

"Oh, you're a jewel," said she.

"Oh, no," replied Garfield, "I'm a jeweler; I've just set the jewel."

McCOSH'S IMPRESSION.

"Ah, I have an impression!" exclaimed Dr. McCosh, the president of Princeton College, to the mental philosophy class. "Now, young gentlemen," continued the doctor, as he touched his head with his forefinger, "can you tell me what an impression is?"

No answer.

"What; no one knows? No one can tell me what an impression is? exclaimed the doctor, looking up and down the class.

"I know," said Mr. Arthur. "An impression is a dent in a soft place."

"Young gentleman," said the doctor, removing his hand from his forehead and growing red in the face, "you are excused for the day."

WEBSTER ON SELF-EVIDENCE.

"What do you mean by 'self-evident?'" asked President Web-'ster of Union College of his mental philosophy class.

"I don't know, sir," replied the student.

"Well, I will try and illustrate," said the president. "Speaking about mythology—suppose I should ask you if there ever was such a person as the 'fool killer?'"

"I should say I don't know—I never met him."

"That is 'self-evident,'" said the Doctor.

DAVID B. HILL ON GROVER CLEVELAND.

"Uncle Billy, a venerable servant on President Cleveland's private car," said Governor Hill, "was very proud of having once gone fishing with President Cleveland."

"'How did you come out, Billy?'" I asked.

"'Well, when we war up in Wes Firginny las' spring, the President he says Dan Lamont and I, us free, we's "go in Cahoot," Well we gets eighteen fish.'

"'How did the President divide?'

"'Well Marse President, he takes eighteen fish and Lamont he takes de rest.'

"'And what did you get, Uncle Billy?'

"'Well, I'do know,' scratching his head; then brightening up he said: 'I reckons I got the "Cahoot."'"

PRESIDENT HARRISON ON GENERAL SCOTT.

President Benj. Harrison belonged to the Volunteers in the late war, while General Scott was a West Pointer of the deepest dye. When Scott got old and foolish, all the Volunteer officers used to make fun of him.

"One day," said General Harrison, "General Scott went into a hospital in Washington to express sympathy with the patients.

" " 'What is the matter with you, my man?' asked the General as he gazed at a poor man with a sore leg.

" ' Oh, I've got gangrene, General.'

" 'Gangrene! why, that's a very dangerous disease, my man— v-e-r-y d-a-n-g-e-r-o-u-s,' said General Scott. 'I never knew a man to have gangrene and recover. It always kills the patient or leaves him demented. I've had it myself.' "

FITZ HUGH LEE AND GENERAL KILPATRICK.

On the evening before the last unsuccessful attempt to storm the defenses of Fredericksburg, some of the skirmishers were endeavoring, under cover of darkness, to draw closer to the rebel works. One of Fitz Hugh Lee's men discovered Kilpatrick's cavalry and shouted:

"Hello, Yanks! Howdy?"

"We're all right. Were bound to come and see you!"

"Come on!" shouted Fitz Hugh's men. "We've got room enough to bury you!"

SEWARD JOKED BY DOUGLAS.

When the Kansas-Nebraska bill was being debated, Senator Seward tapped Douglas on the shoulder and whispered in his ear that he had some "Bourbon" in the Senator's room which was twenty years old, and upon which he desired to get Douglas' judgment. The orator declined, saying that he meant to speak in a few minutes, and wished his brain unclouded by the fumes of liquor. At the conclusion of his speech, Douglas sank down, in his chair, exhausted, hardly conscious of the congratulations of those who flocked around him. At this juncture, Seward seized the orator's arm, and bore him off to the senatorial sanctum.

"Here's the Bourbon, Douglas," said Seward, "try some—its sixty years old."

"Seward," remarked Douglas, "I have made to-day the longest speech ever delivered; history has no parallel for it."

"How is that?" rejoined Seward, "you spoke for two hours only."

"Why," said Douglas, "a moment before I rose to speak you invited me to partake of some Bourbon twenty years old, and now you offer me some of the same liquor, with the assertion that it is sixty years old!—a forty years' speech was never delivered before."

VOORHEES, TANNER AND SECRETARY NOBLE.

The day that Corporal Tanner arrived at the Interior Department to receive his commission as commissioner of pensions, Henry Watterson and Daniel Voorhees happened to be present. Tanner, every one knows, was as brave as a lion and lost both feet in the war. He was a private without much education and a very ordinary, loose-jointed but picturesque-looking man, and he has grown more picturesque with age.

As the Corporal hobbled into Secretary Noble's room in the Interior Department, he saluted the Secretary and said:

"Hello, Gen'ral—come down to qualify—to be sworn in!"

"Ah, Corporal Tanner?" said the Chesterfieldian Noble.

"Yes, Tanner—come to qualify."

"Let me introduce you to Senator Voorhees and Editor Watterson, Corporal," said the Secretary, suiting the action to the word.

"Glad to see you, Senator," said Tanner. "Glad to see an honest enemy. While Jeff Davis was shooting off my feet, you and Watterson and Thurman were shooting us in the rear. Glad to see you!"

"And you've come to Washington to get your commission and be qualified as commissioner of pensions?" remarked the Wabash Senator.

"You're right I have," said the Corporal, his eyes twinkling with excitement.

"Well, I'll be dog-on!" was the only reply, as Voorhees took a quid of tobacco and looked out of the window.

"Yes, going to be qualified to-day," continued Tanner.

"Well, my friend," said Voorhees, surveying the Corporal from head to foot, this government is not inspired—it is not Providence. Noble, its representative, can swear you in, but the Department of Education and all hell couldn't qualify you!"

"WHAT DO YOU MEAN, SIR?"

See page 543.

M. QUAD (CHAS. B. LEWIS).

He smiled blandly as he halted for a moment in front of the City Hall. He looked like a man who could palm off almost anything on the public at 100 per cent. profit and yet leave each customer in a grateful mood. He had a tin trunk in his hand, and as he sailed down LaFayette avenue, the boys wondered whether the trunk contained bug juice or horse liniment. The stranger stopped in front of a handsome residence, his smile deepened, and he mounted the steps and pulled the bell.

"Is the lady at home?" he inquired of the girl who answered the bell.

The girl thought he was the census taker, and she seated him in the parlor and called the lady of the house. When the lady entered, the stranger rose, bowed and said:

"Madam, I have just arrived in this town after a tour extending clear down to Florida, and wherever I went I was received with glad welcome."

"Did you wish to see my husband?" she asked, as he opened the tin trunk.

"No, madam, I deal directly with the lady of the house in all cases. A woman will appreciate the virtues of my exterminator and purchase a bottle, where a man will order me off the steps without glancing at it."

"Your—your what?" she asked.

"Madam," he replied, as he placed a four-ounce phial of dark liquid on the palm of his left hand; "madam, I desire to call your attention to my Sunset Bedbug Exterminator. It has been tried at home and abroad, and in no case has it failed to—"

"What do you mean, sir?" she demanded, getting very red in the face. "Leave this house, instantly."

"Madam, I do not wish you to infer from my—"

"I want you to leave this house!" she shrieked.

"Madam, allow me to explain my—"

"I will call the police!" she screamed, making for the door, and he hastily locked his trunk and hurried out.

Going down the street about two blocks he saw the lady of the house at the parlor window, and instead of climbing the steps he stood under the window and politely said:

"Madam, I don't wish to even hint that any of the bedsteads in your house are inhabited by bedbugs, but—"

"What! What's that?" she exclaimed.

"I said that I hadn't the remotest idea that any of the bedsteads in your house were infested by bedbugs," he replied.

"Take yourself out of this yard!" she shouted, snatching a tidy off the back of a chair and brandishing it at him.

"Beg pardon, madam, but I should like to call your—"

"Get out!" she screamed; "get out, or I'll call the gardener!"

"I will get out, madam, but I wish you understood—"

"J-a-w-n! J-a-w-n!" she shouted out of a side window, but the exterminator agent was out of the yard before John could get around the house.

He seemed discouraged as he walked down the street, but he had traveled less than a block when he saw a stout woman sitting on the front steps of a fine residence, fanning herself.

"Stout women are always good-natured," he soliloquized as he opened the gate.

"Haven't got any thing for the grasshopper sufferers!" she called out as he entered.

There was an angelic smile on his face as he approached the steps, set his trunk down, and said:

"My mission, madam, is even nobler than acting as agent for a distressed community. The grasshopper sufferers do not comprise a one-hundredth part of the world's population, while my mission is to relieve the whole world."

"I don't want any peppermint essence," she continued, as he started to unlock the trunk.

"Great heavens, madam, do I resemble a peddler of cheap essences?" he exclaimed. "I am not one. I am here in Detroit to enhance the comforts of the night—to produce pleasant dreams. Let me call your attention to my Sunset Bedbug Exterminator, a liquid warranted to—"

"Bed what?" she screamed, ceasing to fan her fat cheeks.

"My Sunset Bedbug Exterminator. It is to-day in use in the humble negro cabins on the banks of the Arkansaw, as well as in the royal palace of her Majesty Q—"

"You r-r-rascal! you villyun!" she wheezed; "how dare you insult me, m—"

"No insult, madam, it is a pure matter of—"

"Leave! Git o-w-t!" she screamed, clutching at his hair, and he had to go out in such a hurry that he couldn't lock the trunk until he reached the walk.

He traveled several blocks and turned several corners before he halted again, and his smile faded away to a melancholy grin. He saw two or three ragged children at a gate, noticed that the house was old, and he braced up and entered.

"I vhants no zoap," said the woman of the house, as she stood in the door.

"Soap, madam, soap? I have no soap. I noticed that you lived in an old house, and as old houses are pretty apt to be infested—"

"I vhants no bins or needles to-day!" she shouted.

"Madam, I am not a peddler of Yankee notions," he replied. "I am selling a liquid, prepared only by myself, which is warranted to—"

"I vhants no baper gollers!" she exclaimed, motioning for him to leave.

"Paper collars! I have often been mistaken for Shakespeare, madam, but never before for a paper collar peddler. Let me unlock my trunk and show—"

"I vhants no matches—no dobacco—no zigars!" she interrupted; and her husband came round the corner and, after eying the agent for a moment, remarked:

"If you don't be quick out of here I shall not have any shoking about it!"

At dusk last night the agent was sitting on a salt barrel in front of a commission house, and the shadows of evening were slowly deepening the melancholy look on his face.

THAD. STEVENS AND ALECK STEPHENS.

Thad. Stevens, the great Northern radical, and Alex. Stephens, of Georgia, the great Southern radical, met after Appomattox and talked about the war.

"Well, Mr. Stephens," said old Thad., "how do you rebels feel after being licked by the Yankees?"

"We feel, I suppose a good deal as Lazarus did," said the Georgia fire eater.

"How is that?"

"Why Thad., poor Lazarus was licked by the dogs, wasn't he?"

ZACK CHANDLER ON DEMOCRACY.

Zack Chandler had three men working in a saw-mill in the woods below Saginaw. During Lincoln's last campaign, Zack went up to the saw-mill to see how the men were going to vote. He found that each had a different political faith. One was a Democrat, one a Republican and one a Greenbacker. A farm-boy had just killed a fine woodchuck, and Zack offered to give it to the man who would give the best reason for his political faith.

"I'm a Republican," said the first man, "because my party freed the slave, put down the rebellion and never fired on the old flag."

"Good!" said old Zack.

"And I am a Greenbacker," said the second man, "because if my party should get into power every man would have a pocket full of money."

"First-rate!" said Uncle Zack. "And now you," addressing the third: "Why are you a Democrat?"

"Because, sir," said the man trying to think of a good democratic answer—"because—because I want that woodchuck!"

BLAINE'S KIL–MA–ROO STORY.

In the Blaine Presidential campaign, the Democrats were continually saying that Blaine would be a radical President.

"He'll get up a war with Germany about Samoa," they said, "or get us into an embroglio with France on account of the Suez Canal."

But at heart Blaine is a conservative man. To illustrate, Blaine used this illustration:

"Yes," he said, "the Democrats always have some trouble ahead, but it is always imaginary. The Republicans are going to wreck the republic by high tariff, one day, and bankrupt the nation through the pension office the next. But all this trouble is imaginary. When we get to it it is gone.

"The Democrats remind me of the story of the man who was carrying something across Fulton ferry in a close box. Every now and then he would open the box curiously, peep in and then close the lid mysteriously. His actions soon excited the curiosity of a naturalist who sat on the seat by him. Unable to conceal his curiosity further, the naturalist touched him on the shoulder and said:

"'I beg pardon, sir, but I'm curious to know what you have in that box. What is it?'

"'Oh, I don't want to tell. It will get all over the boat.'

"'Is it a savage animal?'

"'Yes—kills every thing.' Then the man peeped in again.

"Still growing more curious, the naturalist begged him to tell its name.

"'It's a Kil-ma-roo from the center of Africa—a very savage beast—eats men and—'

"'And what do you feed it on?' interrupted the naturalist.

"'Snakes, sir—plain snakes.'

"'And where do you get snakes enough to feed such a monster?' asked the eager but trembling naturalist.

"'Well, sir, my brother in Brooklyn drinks a good deal, has delirium tremens, and when he sees snakes we just catch 'em and—'

"'But these are imaginary snakes,' argued the naturalist. 'How can you feed a savage beast on imaginary snakes?'

"'Why, the fact is,' said the man, opening the box and blowing in it, 'Don't say a word about it, but this is an imaginary Kil-ma-roo.'"

DR. HAMMOND, DR. BLISS AND GEN. SHERIDAN.

One day when they were criticising Dr. Bliss, General Sheridan came to the Doctor's defense.

"Dr. Bliss was a good physician," said General Sheridan, "he saved my life once."

"How? How did Bliss save your life?" asked Dr. Hammond.

"Well," said Sheridan, "I was very sick in the hospital after the battle of Winchester. One day they sent for Dr. Agnew of Philadelphia, and he gave me some medicine, but I kept getting worse. Then they sent for Dr. Frank Hamilton and he gave me some more medicine, but I grew worse and worse. Then they sent for Dr. Bliss, and—"

" And you still grew worse ? "

" No, Dr. Bliss didn't come ; he saved my life ! "

CHIEF JUSTICE FULLER.

Chief Justice Fuller, when a boy, belonged to a debating club in Oldtown, Me. One evening capital punishment was debated. The deacon of the church was for hanging. Young Fuller was opposed.

Said the deacon, quoting from the Mosaic law : " Whoso sheddeth man's blood, by man his blood shall be shed." Thinking this to be a bombshell to his opponents he dwelt upon it till his time had expired, when the boy sprang to his feet and said :

" Supposing we take the law which the gentleman has quoted and see what the logical deduction would come to. For example, one man kills another ; another man kills him, and so on until we come to the last man on earth. Who's going to kill him ? He dare not commit suicide, for that same law forbids it. Now, deacon," continued the boy, " what are you going to do with that last man ? "

The boy's logic called out rounds of applause and vanquished the deacon.

JUDGE OLDS.

Judge Olds, of Richmond, was examining a man who had pleaded guilty of bank robbery.

" Did you have any confederates ? " asked the judge.

" No, jedge," said the prisoner, " the fellers that helped me was democrats, o' course, but they wasn't rebs."

GEN. SICKLES ON HOWARD'S DRUMMER.

" Speaking of war stories," said General Sickles, " the best thing happened over in Howard's Eleventh Corps. It seems that they had a drummer boy over there who always lived well. He was in Col. Arrowsmith's regiment, the 26th N. Y. This drummer, while the regiment was on the move, had a penchant for foraging on his own account, and the chickens had to roost high to escape his far-reaching hands. Whenever night overtook them, this drummer had a good supper provided for himself. On one occasion he had raked in a couple of turkeys and had put them into his drum for convenience in carrying. When the regiment was halted for the night, Colonel Arrowsmith immediately ordered dress parade, and the drummers were expected to beat up. The forager made his drumsticks go, but the quick-eyed Colonel noticed that he was not drumming.

" 'Adjutant,' said the Colonel, 'that man isn't drumming. Why ain't he drumming?'

"The Adjutant stepped up to him, saying, 'Why ain't you drumming?'

" 'Because,' said the quick-witted drummer, 'I have got two turkeys in my drum, and one of 'em is for the Colonel.'

"The Adjutant went back and the Colonel asked, 'What is it?'

" 'Why, he says he has got two turkeys in his drum, and one of 'em is for the Colonel.'

"Up to this point the conversation had been carried on *sotto voce*, but when the Adjutant reported, Colonel Arrowsmith raised his voice so that all could hear.

" 'What! Sick is he? Why didn't he say so before? Send him to his tent at once.' "

GREELEY TAKEN FOR A CLERGYMAN.

Stephen Girard's will prohibited clergymen from ever entering the doors of Girard College. One day Horace Greeley, who usually wore a white tie, and otherwise looked like a Methodist clergyman, was passing in when the janitor shouted:

"Here, you can't pass in here, sir; the rule forbids it."

"The —— I can't," replied the excited editor.

"All right, sir," rejoined the janitor; "pass right in."

SHERMAN AND PRESIDENT TAYLOR.

Gen. W. T. Sherman, has been the subject of a thousand good stories. One of the best occurred when President Taylor, after the war with Mexico, sent the young captain out to Arizona and Southern California, to investigate the value of our new possessions gained from Mexico, by the war. Sherman was gone a year. He penetrated the sandy deserts of Arizona and New Mexico, and looked over the cactus country of southern California · and then returned to Washington, and called on the President.

"Well, Captain," said President Taylor," what do you think of our new possessions, will they pay for the blood and treasure spent in the war?"

"Do you want my honest opinion?" replied Sherman.

"Yes, tell us privately just what you think."

"Well, General," said Sherman, "it cost us one hundred millions of dollars, and ten thousand men, to carry on the war with Mexico."

"Yes fully that, but we got Arizona, New Mexico and Southern California."

"Well, General," continued Sherman, "I've been out there and looked them over—all that country, and between you and me, I feel that we'll have to go to war again. Yes, we've got to have another war."

"What for?" asked Taylor.

"Why to make 'em take the d—d country back!"

SENATOR EVARTS AND GOVERNOR HILL.

Mr. Evarts, with all his learning, often had to listen to long bursts of empty oratory, from young and inexperienced lawyers. Many years ago, when Gov. David B. Hill was practicing law, he had a case where Evarts was his opponent. Hill was delivering his maiden speech. Like most young lawyers, he was florid, rhetorical, scattering and weary. For four weary hours he talked at the court and the jury, until every body felt like lynching him. When he got through, Mr. Evarts deliberately arose. looked sweetly at the Judge, and said:

" Your Honor, I will follow the example of my young friend who has just finished, and submit the case without argument."

Then he sat down, and the silence was large and oppressive.

SHERMAN AND JOSEPH JEFFERSON.

When I asked General Sherman what was the bravest thing he ever did, he said:

" Well, I saved a man's life once."

" Who was it ? "

"Joe Jefferson."

" Why, how did you save his life ? "

" But I did, though," continued Sherman, "and I look back to it with unalloyed pride and pleasure. It is something to be proud of —saving such a life as belonged to Joe Jefferson."

" How did it happen ? Please tell me."

"Well," said Sherman, solemnly. "It occurred last summer. We were both in the parlor up-stairs, talking to some ladies. Joe had to leave early, and excused himself. After he went out I noticed a bundle of manuscript on the floor. I thought at first it belonged to me, but finding mine safe, I hurried out to the elevator after Joe, but he had gone by way of the stairs. I halloed 'Joe, Joe,' but he didn't hear me. I ran down after him two steps at a time. I finally caught up with him, and handing him the manuscript, said :

" 'Here, Joe, you've forgotten something.'

"A serious expression spread over his face, as he took it, and said, in a tremulously solemn and impressive voice :

" 'My God, you've saved my life !'

"It was his autobiography, which he was engaged upon at the time."

ROBERT TOOMBS AND JOHN B. FLOYD.

Robt. Toombs and John B. Floyd, both members of Jeff Davis' cabinet, were talking of where they would like to be buried. It was after the war, and notwithstanding defeat, each loved Democracy and the Confederacy. They had been reading letters from

R. Barnwell Rhett, John Slidell and Henry A. Wise, brother cabinet officers.

"When I die," said Floyd, very seriously, "I wish I could be buried right under that Confederate monument in Richmond."

"What for?" asked Toombs.

"Because I want my last sweet rest to be where a Yankee will never come."

"I would be buried there, too," said Toombs, "but I hate the Devil worse than I hate a Yankee, and I almost wish I could be buried in the colored cemetery."

"Wha—what for?" asked Floyd, deeply surprised.

"Because," said Toombs, "the devil will never trouble me there. He'd never think of looking for an old rebel democrat in a colored graveyard!"

JOE BROWN, TOOMBS AND ALEX STEPHENS.

Senator Joe Brown once came near fighting a duel with Bob Toombs. Toombs and he had a quarrel as to reconstruction measures, and the story is that they both expected to fight. Toombs made no preparation for the duel. Joe Brown went about his arrangements in the same practical business way for which he is so noted, and which has made him a success as a fortune maker, and a great statesman. He drew up his will, put his estate in order, and clipped all the trees of his orchard in practicing with his pistol. I think it was in this affair that Brown called Toombs an unscrupulous liar, and that Toombs, in talking to one of his friends about it, characterized Brown as a hypocritical old deacon, saying:

"What can I do with him? If I challenge him he will dodge behind the door of the Baptist Church," and he then referred to the statement of Ben Hill, in reply to Alexander H. Stephens, wherein Hill refused to fight, saying to Stephens: "Sir, I have a family to support, and a God to serve, but you have neither."

This remark of Toombs was reported to Brown, and Brown went to his church, and got a certificate, stating that he had left it. He sent the certificate to Toombs, and told him that he would be glad to accommodate him, and that he would accept any challenge he might make. It was while Toombs was waiting to make the challenge that he practiced with his pistol. Toombs knew that he was a good shot, and he saved his life by not saying any thing more about it.

FORAKER ON DANIEL VOORHEES.

" The best story about Senator Daniel Voorhees," said Ex-Governor Foraker, of Ohio, " is laid years ago in Terre Haute. The distinguished Senator was once a hard-working lawyer. On one occasion he defended a gambler for killing a man. There were some doubts about the case—whether it was murder or manslaughter. Voorhees made a superb plea, but still the gambler's friends were afraid he would be convicted. They had plenty of money and had raised $5,000 to influence a juryman, as those were old times when justice was not as pure as now. Well, they picked out a weak juryman and agreed to give him $5,000 if he would ' hang the jury.'

" The man earned his money," said Foraker, " for, sure enough, the jury disagreed. The next day there was a meeting of Voorhees and the friends to pay the faithful juryman.

"' You earned the money,' said the friends of Voorhees, ' and here it is with our thanks.'

"' Earned it,' said the juryman. ' I guess I did. I kept that jury out two days. I wouldn't give them a wink of sleep till they agreed with me in a verdict of manslaughter.'

"' How did they stand when they first went out ? ' asked Voorhees.

"' Well, there were eleven of them for acquittal—but I brought 'em round ! '"

BLAINE, CONKLING, HAMLIN.

James G. Blaine, our Secretary of State, used to have a fund oi anecdotes before he became a conspicuous presidential candidate, but of late years he professes to sit still and let other people tell the funny stories.

It seems that Blaine, and Lincoln's old vice-president, Hamlin, didn't agree very well in the last years of Hamlin's life. I presume it was political jealousy. Still Blaine never criticised Hamlin. He said he liked him, and I believe he did.

"Why Hamlin," he continued, "saved the life of a dear friend once. Yes, he saved my poor friend Brooks from sure death."

"How was it?" asked a bystander.

"Brooks says Hamlin saved his life three distinct times in the Mexican War, and that he could never repay him the debt of gratitude he owed him. It was this way: Brooks says he always kept his eye on Hamlin during an engagement. Whenever Hamlin ran, he ran, too, and three times Hamlin saved his precious life."

Blaine and Conkling said savage things about each other for years, but their friendship never fully ceased till Blaine said, "Conkling struts into the Senate like a turkey gobbler." This the Senator never forgave, and, after it, he never missed a chance to ridicule the Maine statesman.

When Blaine was up for the presidency in 1884, a friend went to Conkling and asked him if he would take the stump for the Maine Senator.

"I can't," said Conkling, spitefully, "I have retired from criminal practice."

Mr. Blaine got even with Conkling for this by telling a story about Conkling's vanity. "One day," said Mr. Blaine, "when Conkling and I were friends, the proud New York Senator asked Sam Cox whom he thought were the two greatest characters America ever produced?"

"I should say," said Cox, solemnly, "I should say the two most distinguished men in America have been General Washington and yourself."

"Very true," said Conkling, "but I don't see why you should drag in the name of Washington." [Laughter.]

HENRY W. LONGFELLOW'S FUNNIEST POEM.

The poet Longfellow wrote this funny poem for Blanche Roosevelt:

> There was a little girl, and she had a little curl
> Right in the middle of her forehead;
> And when she was good, she was very, very good,
> And when she was bad, she was horrid.

SWING, COLLYER, JONES, FITZ HUGH LEE.

There is no one so easily shocked by an oath, or even an irreligious story, as Dr. Collyer. Still he used to delight in telling how near Professor Swing came to swearing.

"It is true," said Dr. Collyer, "that the Rev. David Swing and I are very dear friends, and that I really am very fond of him. But Mr. Beecher told me a story about Brother Swing's profanity that quite upset me."

"How was it?"

"Well," said the Doctor, with mock gravity, "I don't say it myself, but Beecher says that one day while Dr. Swing was a guest of Stuart Robson and Mr. Crane at Cohasset, his conversation bordered on profanity."

"Impossible," I exclaimed. "What were the circumstances?"

"Well," said Dr. Collyer, still very solemn, "it happened this way: Robson, Crane and Swing were at anchor, with their lines out for blue fish. After a long and patient waiting, something caught Robson's line and he exclaimed, excitedly:

"'I just had a d—n good bite!'

"'So did I?' said Dr. Swing."

When some one told the story to Sam Jones, he said: "Well, Swing came about as near swearing as the Richmond editors did to lying, when I held my revival there."

"How was that?" I asked.

"You see we had been accusing the Richmond editors of lying about our meetings, and the term, 'lying editors,' got into common use. Even children used it. One day a little son of Governor Fitz Hugh Lee, who had been off at school with some worldly boys, who made him forget his father's Christian teachings, came home with this conundrum:

"'Father,' he said, 'what is the difference between a man who dyes wool on lambs and a Richmond editor?'

"'Well, now, really my son,' said the Governor, beaming benignly on his offspring. 'I am not prepared to state. What is the difference?'

"'Why, pa, one is a lamb dyer and the other a ——'

"'What! what! my son!' interrupted the Governor.

"'—— a Richmond editor, I was going to say, before you interrupted me.'"

MOSEBY, ELLSWORTH, KILPATRICK AND
FITZ HUGH LEE.

"Talk about my war record," said Colonel Moseby at a political meeting in Alexandria, Va. "My war record is a part of the State's history. Why, gentlemen, I carried the last Confederate flag through this town."

"Yes," replied Fitz Hugh Lee, "for I was there at the time."

"Thank you for your fortunate recollection," gratefully exclaimed Moseby. "It is pleasant to know that there still lives some men who move aside envy and testify to the courage of their fellow beings. As I say, gentlemen, my war record is a part of the State's history, for the gentleman here will tell you that I carried the last Confederate flag through this town."

"That's a fact," said Fitz Hugh Lee. "He carried the last Confederate flag through this town, but Kilpatrick and Ellsworth were after him, and he carried it so blamed fast you couldn't have told whether it was the Confederate flag or a small-pox warning."

THADDEUS STEVENS.

One day Thad. Stevens was practicing in the Carlisle courts, and he didn't like the ruling of the Presiding Judge. A second time the Judge ruled against "old Thad." when the old man got up with scarlet face and quivering lips and commenced tying up his papers as if to quit the court room.

"Do I understand, Mr. Stevens," asked the Judge, eying "old Thad." indignantly, "that you wish to show your contempt for this court ?"

"No, sir; no, sir," replied "old Thad." "I don't wan't to show my contempt, sir; I'm trying to conceal it!"

GENERAL LOGAN'S PLAIN TALK.

Daniel Voorhees, who knew John A. Logan in southern Illinois before the war, tells us that on a certain occasion young Logan found it necessary to doubt the word of a man, and told him so without any circumlocution.

"Don't you call me a liar, sir," said the man, excitedly, "I have a reputation to maintain, and I mean to maintain it, sir."

"I know it," said Logan, "and you are maintaining it every time you tell a lie."

LONGSTREET ON FAST MARCHING.

"Jabe Mathis," said General Longstreet, "of the 13th Georgia, was a good soldier, but one day, when the Confederates were retreating from the gory field of Gettysburg, Jabe threw his musket on the ground, seated himself by the roadside and exclaimed with much vehemence:

"'I'll be doggon if I walk another step! I'm broke down! I can't do it!' And Jabe was the picture of despair.

"'Git up, man,' exclaimed the Captain, 'don't you know the Yankees are following us? They'll get you sure.'

"'Can't help it,' said Jabe, 'I'm done for; I'll not march another step!'

"The Confederates passed along over the crest of a hill and lost sight of poor, dejected Jabe.

"In a moment there was a fresh rattle of musketry and a renewed crash of shells. Suddenly Jabe appeared on the crest of the hill, moving like a hurricane and followed by a cloud of dust. As he dashed past his captain, that officer said:

"'Hello, Jabe! thought you wasn't going to march any more.'

"'Thunder!' replied Jabe, as he hit the dust with renewed vigor; 'you don't call this marching, do you?'"

GENERAL EWELL ON THE IRISHMAN.

"During the war," said General Ewell, "several Confederate regiments were ordered to march, although none of the privates knew their destination. When they set out, the road was narrow, and the captain in command of one regiment gave the order:

"'By doubling! Right face! Forward, march!'

"'To Dublin!' shouted an Irishman in the ranks. 'Arrah, good luck, me boys! We're going to Dublin! Sure, the gineral has found out the right place to go to at last!'

"'Where do you say we're going?' called two or three voices.

"'To Dublin, don't ye hear?'

"'Keep still, you foreign bog-trotter!'

"'Ah ha, me boys!' continued Tim. 'When yez gets to Dublin, It'll be you will be the foreigners there, and it'll be me that'll be the native American.'"

HENRY WATTERSON ON SUMNER AND GREELEY.

Mr. Watterson, who always maintained that the anti-slavery republicans like Sumner, Greeley and old Ben Wade only loved the colored man just to get his vote and use, delights to quote this speech which Watterson says was delivered by old Abram Jasper at the colored picnic at Louisville during the last presidential campaign:

"Feller freemen," says he, "you all know me. I am Abram Jasper, a republican from way back. When there has been any work to do, I has done it. When there has been any votin' to do, I has voted early and often. When there has been any fightin' to do, I have been in the thick of it. I are 'bove proof, old line and tax paid. And I has seed many changes, too. I has seed the Republicans up. I has seed the Democrats up. But I is yit to see a nigger up. T'other night I had a dream. I dreampt that I died and went to heaven. When I got to de pearly gates ole Salt Peter he says:

"'Who's dar?' sez he.

"'Abram Jasper,' sez I.

"'Is you mounted or is you afoot?' says he.

"'I is afoot,' says I.

"'Well, you can't get in here,' says he. 'Nobody 'lowed in here 'cept them as come mounted,' says he.

"'Dat's hard on me,' says I, 'arter comin' all dat distance.' But he never says nothin' mo', and so I starts back an' about half way down de hill who does I meet but dat good ol' Horace Greeley. 'Whar's you gwine, Mr. Greeley?' says I.

"'I is gwine to heaven wid Mr. Sumner,' says he.

" 'Why, Horace,' says I, 'tain't no use. I's just been up dar an nobody's 'lowed to get in 'cept dey comes mounted, an' you's afoot."

" 'Is dat so ?' says he.

"Mr. Greeley sorter scratched his head, an' arter awhile he says, says he: 'Abram, I tell what let's do. You is a likely lad. Suppose you git down on all fours and Sumner and I'll mount an' ride you in, an' dat way we kin all git in.'

" 'Gen'lemen,' says I, 'do you think you could work it ?'

" 'I know I kin,' says bof of 'em.

" So down I gits on all fours, and Greeley and Sumner gets astraddle, an' we ambles up de hill agin, an' prances up to de gate, an' old Salt Peter says:

" 'Who's dar ?'

" 'We is, Charles Sumner and Horace Greeley,' shouted Horace.

" 'Is you both mounted or is you afoot ?' says Peter.

" 'We is bof mounted,' says Mr. Greeley.

" 'All right,' says Peter, 'all right,' says he ; 'jest hitch your hoss outside, gen'lemen, and come right in.' "

WADE HAMPTON, SUMNER AND BEN WADE.

Gen. Wade Hampton, of South Carolina, and Charles Sumner were talking in the rotunda of the Senate Chamber, after the war, about the reconstructed South. General Hampton was praising the people and the States of Virginia and South Carolina.

"They are great States — and a brave people live in Virginia and South Carolina," said the General.

Just then Ben Wade came up and joined in.

" Yes," said Ben Wade, "I have known a good many people who went down there myself, and splendid people they were, too, as brave and high-toned as the Huguenots."

" You did, sir?" said Wade Hampton, proudly.

" Oh, yes, sir. I knew some of the greatest men Virginia and South Carolina ever saw, sir — knew 'em intimately, sir," continued old Ben, confidentially drawing his chair closer to General Hampton.

"Who did you know down thar, sir — in the old Palmetto State?" asked General Hampton.

"Well, sir, I knew General Sherman, General Grant and General Kilpatrick, who went—"

"Great guns!" interrupted Hampton; and then he threw down his cigar and rushed straight into the bar-room to drown his troubles.

SITTING BULL AND GENERAL MILES.

Sitting Bull, when at the Red Cloud agency, was interviewed by the Quaker Indian Commissioners. They asked him if he had any grave grievance.

Sitting Bull was silent.

By and by he clutched his tomahawk and said: "Indian very sensitive. Indian no like being lied about. If Indian ever get back to the white man again, he'll scalp the white-livered son of a gun who's been telling around that Sitting Bull graduated at West Point."

HOW BISHOP POTTER WAS INTRODUCED TO MAYOR GRANT.

The dignified Bishop Potter and our worldly Mayor Grant did not know each other the other day. They are acquainted now. It seems that Mayor Grant went into Knox's, the hatter, to get his silk hat ironed after being caught in the centennial rain-storm parade. After handing his hat to the attendant to be ironed, the Mayor stood bare-headed waiting.

Just then in came the dignified Bishop Potter, who mistook Mayor Grant for one of the shop walkers. Walking up to the Mayor, the Bishop held out his hat to him and asked:

"Have you a hat like this?"

Mayor Grant, in the coolest manner took the hat, turned it over, examined it closely, looked at the inside, then at the outside and then remarked in slow and measured tones:

"No sir, I haven't a hat like that, and if I had sir, I am d——d if I would wear it!"

Just then Mr. Knox came along, and seeing the dilemma, introduced the Bishop to the Mayor, when they both screamed with laughter.

PHILIP D. ARMOUR.

Henry Villard asked Philip D. Armour to define a mugwump.

" I am not a politician," said Mr. Armour, the king of pork pack-
ers. " I don't think I can tell in plain language what a mugwump
is, still I think I saw one once."

" Where ? " asked Mr. Villard.

" We raised one in Stockbridge, N. Y., where I was born. We
had a very wicked farmer there—very wicked—John Whitney was
his name, but one day he surprised every one by leaving the world
and his wicked associates and joining the Baptist church. He
remained an exemplary church member three days, but coming into
town one day he got drunk and the church turned him out."

" What then ? "

" Well, Whitney came back into the world again, but the boys
wouldn't speak to him. They even went so far as to hold a meeting in the Bellow's bar-room and resolved not to receive him back.
" Whitney is too mean for us," they said.

" What became of poor Whitney when both the church and the
devil refused to receive him ? " asked Villard.

" When I left Stockbridge to go to Chicago," said Armour, " I
left poor Whitney there, dangling between the church and the
world. I never heard of him for years, till he turned up in Kansas.
He was a mugwump and was making speeches in favor of civil
service."

SUSAN B. ANTHONY.

Susan B. Anthony always speaks extemporaneously. One day,
after hearing Prof. Swing, Theodore L. Cuyler asked her if she
remembered Swing's sermon.

" Remember it ! " said Susan, "why, good gracious, Brother
Cuyler, Prof. Swing, like all you clergymen, couldn't remember it
himself ! He had to have it written down."

THE SHARP RETORT.

"Eli Perkins," says Alex. Sweet, "was wounded at Gettysburg
by a minie-ball through his right leg. The other day Eli made a
nice retort when an editor maliciously referred to his game leg.

"It's not fair," said Eli, "for you to attack my weakest part. Did I ever attack your brains?"

BELMONT AND BUFFALO BILL.

One day Belmont, the agent of the Rothschilds, asked Buffalo Bill if he ever saw a pack of live wolves.

"Been chased by 'um hundreds of times, sir. Once I 'lowed it was all up with us. The bronchos was runnin' so fast that they almost spun the wheels offen the buckboard; but the wolves gained on us at every jump. Then, as a last desperate resort, jest as the ravenin' animals was surroundin' us, I took the stranger who was ridin' with us by the neck an' pitched him out. Jest as he lit, I heered him holler: 'I'm a real estate agent.'"

"Of course they tore him to pieces before your eyes," said Belmont.

"Nope! They all shook hands with him, called him brother, an' asked him how business was up in Kansas."

BAYARD TAYLOR'S JOKE.

Bayard Taylor and a party of American students were on the railroad platform at Heidelberg. One of the American students happened to crowd a Heidelberg student, when he drew himself up scowled pompously, and said:

"Sir, you are crowding; keep back, sir."

"Don't you like it, sonny?" asked the American.

"Sir!" scowled the pompous German student, pushing a card into the face of Bayard Taylor, "allow me to tell you, sir, that I am at your service at any time and place."

"Oh, you are at my service, are you?" said Taylor. "Then just carry this satchel to the hotel for me!"

COX, BUTLER, GREELEY.

In 1865 there seemed to be no end of trouble between Sam Cox and Ben Butler. They had a wrangle in the House every day. One day Cox was particularly loaded for Ben. He had a speech full of sarcasm and cutting rebuke. He ridiculed Butler's Dutch Gap Canal and his spoons experience in New Orleans. To give emphasis to his speech, Sam would reach his right hand high above his head and shake his open fingers as they radiated like the spokes of a wagon wheel.

Well, old Ben sat through the speech with his one good eye half shut, not moving a muscle. When Cox had finished and taken his seat, Ben rose—calm, dignified and impressive—and stood in the aisle. For a half minute he said nothing. Then he began:

"Mr. Speaker."

Another pause, long and ponderous. Every body waited, with hushed breath, for him to continue. Raising his arm, Ben reproduced exactly the awful shaky gesture of Cox. Then he permitted his arms to fall again and for another half minute stood still and silent.

"That is all, Mr. Speaker," said the shrewd and sarcastic son of Massachusetts. "I just wanted to answer the gentleman from Ohio."

Judging from the wild laughter and applause which followed, old Ben's speech was at once the shortest and the best ever delivered in the Lower House.

But Cox got even with Butler.

Not long after this, Butler had been making a long speech on the tariff. Every body was tired, but Ben would suffer no one to interrupt him. In fact, by the courtesy of the House, no one can interrupt a speaker unless to ask a question, and that with the consent of the speaker. So Butler continued his tariff harangue. After about an hour had passed, Mr. Cox arose and said in a loud tone:

"Mr. Speaker!"

"The gentleman from Ohio," said the Speaker.

"I arise," said Mr. Cox, "on a question of privilege. I wish to ask the gentleman from Massachusetts a question."

"The gentleman from Ohio," said the Speaker, turning to Butler, "wishes to ask the gentleman from Massachusetts a question."

"Very well, go on!" said Butler.

"The gentleman from Ohio has the floor," said the Speaker.

Mr. Cox then arose solemnly and said:

"Mr. Speaker: I wish to ask the gentleman from Massachusetts a question. I wish to ask him if he hasn't——hasn't——got m–o–s–t t–h–r–o–u–g–h ?"

This was followed by such a scream of laughter that Butler never finished his speech, and Sam had his revenge.

This is the way Ben Butler and Horace Greeley met:

Butler saw Greeley standing in a crowd one day, in front of the Astor House, and wishing to have a little innocent fun with him, walked up to the group and, taking the *Tribune* philosopher by the hand, said :

"Mr. Greeley and I, gentlemen, are old friends. We have drank a good deal of brandy and water together."

"Yes," said Mr. Greeley, "that is true enough, General, you drank the brandy and I drank the water."

Sam Cox was a great political favorite. He was famous for moving into new congressional districts and starting a canvass. The following good story is told in regard to this peculiarity. One day Mr. Frank Carpenter, the correspondent who has written such wonderful and interesting letters from China and India, called on Mr. Cox. It was just after his election in a new district. Mr. Carpenter was not recognized by Mr. Cox during this solemn interview :

"Your name," said Mr. Carpenter, in an assumed bass voice, " is Cox ?"

" I have the honor."

"S. S. Cox?"

" The same."

"Sometimes called Sunset Cox ?"

"That is a sobriquet by which I am known among my more familiar friends."

"You formerly resided in Columbus, Ohio ?"

"That happiness was once mine."

" Represented that district in Congress ? "

"I enjoyed that distinguished honor, and, I may add, at a somewhat early age."

"After a while they gerrymandered the district so as to make it quite warm for an aspiring democrat? "

" You have evidently read the history of your country to good purpose, my friend."

"Then you moved to New York, where you stood a better show ?"

" Well, my friend, your premise is correct. I did move to New York. But your conclusion is hardly admissible in the form of a necessary sequence. My reasons for moving to New York were not wholly political."

" We won't discuss that. After unsuccessfully trying the State-at-large you availed yourself of the opportunity afforded by the death of the Hon. James Brooks to move into his district ? "

" I moved into the district formerly represented by the honorable gentleman you name, but again I must dissent from your conclusions."

" Let that pass. You were elected to Congress from Mr. Brooks' former district ? "

" I was. But let me remark, my friend, that at this moment my time is very much occupied. Your *resumé* of my biography, faulty as some of your deductions are in point of logic, is deeply interesting to me, and at a time of greater freedom from pressing engagements I would be glad to canvass the subject with you at length. But just now, being unusually busy, even for me, I must request you to state the precise object of your visit, and let me add that I shall be glad to serve you."

" I have no favor to ask," said Mr. Carpenter, gravely. "I am an admirer of yours. I always vote for you, and always want to do so if I can. I called this morning merely to inquire if you had selected your next district."

Mr. Cox simply looked astounded.

" Yes, Mr. Cox," continued Carpenter, "I'm your friend. I'm glad to see you. I want to shake your hand. My brother and I have watched you these last thirty-five years, and I must say I have a great admiration for you. Why, I believe you're the luckiest man I ever saw ; indeed, I do. I was in the gallery the day you were sworn in as a new member, back in 1857. My brother lived in Ohio, and he had written to me all about you, and so I watched you as soon as I could pick you out on the floor. Then I remember, when the Democrats went to pieces in Ohio under Vallandigham's leadership, you jumped over to New York. I thought it was a mighty reckless thing to do, but bless my soul if you weren't back here again in 1869. Then you took it into your head to spread yourself over all New York State in 1872, and you ran for congressman-at-large. I was awful sorry when Lyman Tremain beat you, but I declare, if old Brooks, of the *Express*, didn't go off and die on account of the Credit Mobilier censure, and when Congress met in 1873 you rushed in, got the nomination to his vacant seat, and blamed if you weren't sworn in, shoulder to shoulder, with Lyman Tremain, the man who beat you for congressman-at-large. Yes, sir, there you two stood, side by side, and then you went out when Cleveland appointed you to Turkey, but you got tired over there, came back home, found that Mr. Pulitzer, of the *World*, wanted to resign his seat and you went right in and were elected to fill the vacancy. I never saw the like! Why you've got the greatest luck I ever saw, I swear."

" But, my friend ——"

" Hear me, Mr. Cox. I admire you. I believe you could float clear around Cape Horn on a shingle without wetting your coat-tail."

The last sentence so delighted Cox that he put his arms right around Carpenter and exclaimed:

" Admire me ? — why I love you, Carp ! "

CLARA MORRIS' JOKE ON MARY ANDERSON.

Clara Morris says Mary Anderson stepped up to a type-writer of the Fifth Avenue Hotel and asked her to write a letter for her to Narragansett Pier.

" How do you spell it, Miss Anderson ? " asked the type-writer.

" O, any one can spell it—N-a-r-r-o—— O, you spell it your self ! "

" But I can't ! " said the type-writer.

" Can't you write the letter if I don't spell it ? "

" No."

" Then I'll go to Newport ! "

LINCOLN AND STANTON.

When they were selecting the Quaker Indian commissioners, Lincoln called in Chase and Stanton and explained what kind of men he wanted to appoint.

" Gentlemen, for an Indian commissioner," said the President, " I want a pure-minded, moral, Christian man—frugal and self-sacrificing."

" I think," interrupted Stanton, " that you won't find him."

" Why not ? "

" Because, Mr. President, he was crucified about 1,800 years ago."

JEFF DAVIS SEES HUMOR.

" The most humorous thing I ever heard of," said Jefferson Davis, " was the surprising humor of one of Joe Johnson's soldiers from Georgia."

" How was it ? " asked General Beauregard.

" Well they bucked and gagged this Georgia soldier for stealing chickens, but he screamed with laughter as soon as they took the gag out. Then they tied him up by the thumbs but all the time he laughed louder and louder."

" ' What are you laughing at ? ' asked the officer.

" Breaking into louder and more hilarious laughter, he screamed, ' Why I'm the wrong man ! ' "

PRESIDENT ARTHUR HEARS AN ELOQUENT REPLY.

When President Arthur was practicing law in New York, before he became President, he defended a poor Irish woman, who was to be " sent up " for vagrancy. She was a good woman, but could get no work. Judge Brady was very severe on the woman, and cross-examined her somewhat rudely, Arthur thought.

" Have you any means of support, madam ? " asked Judge Brady, severely.

" Well, yer honor," she replied, quietly " I have three, to tell the truth."

" Three ! "

" Yis sor."

" What are they ? "

" Me two hands, yer honor," answered the poor creature, " me good health and me God ! "

" Tears came into Brady's eyes," said Arthur, " as he waived the woman away."

HENRY WATTERSON ON OSCAR WILDE.

One night Oscar Wilde was in Washington, and there were many senators and congressmen present. The long-haired æsthetic was delivering himself of an eloquent tirade against the invasion of the sacred domain of art by the meaner herd of trades-people and miscellaneous nobodies, and finally, rising to an Alpine height of scorn, exclaimed :

"Ay, all of you here are Philistines—mere Philistines!"

"What does Oscar call us?" asked Henry Watterson of John Sherman, who sat in front.

"He calls us Philistines," said Sherman, softly.

"I see," said Watterson, "we are Philistines, and that, I reckon, is why we are being assaulted with the jawbone of an ass."

GENERAL SHERIDAN ON GENERAL SCOTT.

General Scott was, perhaps, the proudest man in the Union army. He never appeared except in a full-dress uniform, covered with gilt spangles and buttons. Sheridan, Sherman and Grant were just the opposite. Horace Porter, who was present, says : "Grant received General Lee's sword at Appomattox while dressed in a common soldier's blouse."

"One day," said Sheridan, who had been talking about General Scott's vanity, "one day General Scott called on a lady away out in the suburbs of Washington. Her little boy had never seen a soldier, especially such a resplendent soldier as General Scott. When the General rang the bell, the boy answered it. As he pulled open the door, there stood the General in gilded epaulets, yellow sash and a waving plume on his hat.

"Tell your mother, little man," said the General, "to please come to the door a moment; I want to speak to her."

Charlie went up-stairs and appeared before his mother, with the most awe-struck face.

"Mamma, some one at the door wants to see you," he said, tremblingly.

"Who is it, my son?"

"O, I don't know, mamma, but I dess it's Dod."

GENERAL BRAGG ON GENERAL PRICE.

General Bragg says General Price's army was about worn out at Pea Ridge. His soldiers straggled all over the field. Price rode up in the midst of all the disorder and shouted :

"Close up, boys! d—n you, close up! If the Yankees were to fire on you when you're straggling along that way they couldn't hit a d—n one of you! Close up!"

GENERAL LEE AND JEFFERSON DAVIS.

"We made a great mistake," said General Lee to Jeff Davis, "in the beginning of our struggle, and I fear, in spite of all we can do, it will prove to be a fatal mistake."

"What mistake is that, General?" asked Mr. Davis.

"Why, sir, in the beginning we appointed all our worst generals to command the armies and all our best generals to edit newspapers. As you know, I have planned some campaigns and quite a number of battles. I have given the work all the care and thought I could, and sometimes, when my plans were completed, as far as I could see, they seemed to be perfect. But when I have fought them through, I have discovered defects in advance. When it was all over, I found, by reading a newspaper, that these best editor-generals saw all the defects plainly from the start. Unfortunately, they did not communicate their knowledge to me until it was too late." Then, after a pause, he added: "I have no ambition but to serve the Confederacy; I do all I can to win our independence. I am willing to serve in any capacity to which the authorities may assign me. I have done the best I could in the field, but I am willing to yield my place to these best generals, and I will do my best for the cause editing a newspaper."

LINCOLN'S COLORED VISITOR.

"One day an old negro, clad in rags and carrying a burden on his head, ambled into the Executive Mansion and dropped his load on the floor. Stepping toward President Lincoln, he said :

"' Am you de President, sah?'

" Being answered in the affirmative, he said :

" ' If dat am a fac', I'se glad ter meet yer.   Yer see, I libs way up dar in de back ob Fergenna, an' I'se a poor man, sah.   I hear dar is some pervishuns in de Con'stution fer de cullud man, and I am 'ere to get some ob 'em, sah.' "

SHERMAN IN EARNEST.

" What would you do if you were I and I were you ? " tenderly inquired a young swell of grizzled old General Sherman.

" Well," said the General, putting on his glasses and taking a long look at it, as it stood there sucking the head of its cane, " I'll tell you what I'd do.   If I were you I would throw away that vile cig-aret, cut up my cane for firewood, wear my watch-chain underneath my coat, and stay at home nights and pray for brains."

i.. D.